ONE AMERICAN'S
OPINION

FOR PATRIOTS WHO LOVE THEIR COUNTRY

R. LYNN WILSON

ONE AMERICAN'S OPINION
FOR PATRIOTS WHO LOVE THEIR COUNTRY

iUniverse books may be ordered through booksellers or by contacting:

iUniverse
1663 Liberty Drive
Bloomington, IN 47403
www.iuniverse.com
1-800-Authors (1-800-288-4677)

ISBN: 978-1-5320-0321-9 (sc)
ISBN: 978-1-5320-0323-3 (hc)
ISBN: 978-1-5320-0322-6 (e)

Library of Congress Control Number: 2016912386

Print information available on the last page.

iUniverse rev. date: 11/30/2016

ONE AMERICAN'S
OPINION

CONTENTS

PREFACE

This book is written from the acquired knowledge in my head, copious ardent research, and the intrinsic values in my heart to reflect my dyed-in-the-wool conservative soul and my enormous love for my country. It is that soul and love that provide the motivation for me to commit the time and energy to author another book. This book was intended to be a one-year project to offer my observations and opinion on the 2014 midterm national election. One year turned into three years as I discovered through my research the true intent of the progressive movement in America. That true intent is to replace our traditional American values that have made our country the greatest society in history with Marxist ideology. I was also taken aback by how invasive this progressive ideology has become in the functioning of local, state, and federal government and its current and potential impact on our American society. Based upon what I learned, the book's focus changed from an election to an in-depth look at our country's future.

One of the biggest problems I experienced was keeping the content I used to support my opinions current over the three-year period. Many of the actual events I use are ongoing and it was difficult to avoid outdated material. I constantly updated information until the book went to press. The whole book was in perpetual motion as I wrote. I am sure by the time you read the book, you will find outdated information but that in no way changes the facts at hand, my opinions, or the book's final premise.

I felt considerable dismay on many occasions as I observed Americans, who love their country, stand up for traditional American values and our Constitution only to be viciously attacked by progressives with opposing beliefs. These attackers include our own federal government. I thought Washington represented all citizens regardless of political ideology and was compelled by the Constitution to protect free speech? Not so, in a progressive world. On many occasions, I have wondered if I might wind up being one of the people who are attacked after this book is published. My five o'clock Glenlivet scotch-on-the-rocks brought out considerable courage and I was motivated to continue writing. Actually, I didn't need the Glenlivet. When I searched my conservative American sole, I only needed my love for my country and concern for my family's and my fellow Americans' future to find the courage and determination I needed to finish and publish this book.

I don't know why I feel so patriotic but I do and I am proud of it. I suppose it is because we are so extraordinarily lucky to live in the most wonderful and successful country in the history of the Earth in terms of economic opportunity, standard of living, personal freedom, and personal safety. I'll be damned if I can sit back and not do something to counter the people who want to take that away from us for their own demented and nefarious purposes. This book, my guest editorials in the local newspaper, monetary contributions to conservative organizations, ranting with my conservative family and friends, and my well-informed vote in every election are my contributions to that end.

ACKNOWLEDGEMENTS

This book would not be possible without the following great American hcrocs: Samuel Huntington, Roger Sherman, William Williams, and Oliver Wolcott from Connecticut; Thomas McKean, George Reed, and Caesar Rodney from Delaware; Button Gwinnett, Lyman Hall, and George Walton from Georgia; Charles Carroll of Carrollton, Samuel Chase, William Paca, and Thomas Stone from Maryland; John Adams, Samuel Adams, Elbridge Gerry, JOHN HANCOCK, and Robert Treat Payne from Massachusetts; Josiah Bartlett, Mathew Thornton, and William Whipple from New Hampshire; Abraham Clark, John Hart, Francis Hopkinson, Richard Stockton, and John Witherspoon from New Jersey; William Floyd, Francis Lewis, Philip Livingston, and Lewis Morris from New York; Joseph Hewes, William Hooper, and John Penn from North Carolina; George Clymer, Benjamin Franklin, Robert Morris, John Morton, George Ross, Benjamin Rush, James Smith, George Taylor, and James Wilson from Pennsylvania; William Ellery and Stephen Hopkins from Rhode Island; Thomas Heyward, Jr., Thomas Lynch, Jr., Arthur Middleton, and Edward Rutledge from South Carolina; Carter Braxton, Benjamin Harrison, Thomas Jefferson, Francis Lightfoot Lee, Richard Henry Lee, Thomas Nelson, Jr., and George Wythe from Virginia.

If you did not recognize who these people are, they are the signers of the Declaration of Independence. They are the founders of our great country. As I wrote their names, I felt a strong sense of pride but I also felt a sense of sadness as I wondered how they would feel if they were alive today and observed what is happening to the country they fought for and risked their lives for.

I want to recognize and express my unmitigated appreciation to all the men and women who have served or are currently serving in our armed forces and who have so gallantly and proudly preserved our safety and freedom—especially those who have given their lives in the line of duty and their families.

I want to recognize and applaud the elected officials and government employees who have served in local, state, and federal government and have stood up and made decisions in the best interest of the American people they work for and not for their own personal or their political party's best interest. Unfortunately, this is an increasingly limited group but a group we should hold in very high regards and support to the fullest. Henry Kissinger is quoted as saying, "Corrupt politicians make the other 10 percent look bad."

I want to also recognize my wonderful wife, Robyn. Just like my last book, this book would not be possible without her. Her incredible encouragement and support kept me writing and her honest critiques and editing were invaluable.

I want to recognize conservative organizations like The Heritage Foundation, Judicial Watch, and The James Madison Institute in Florida for their work in supporting conservatism in America. These organizations are vital in uncovering unscrupulous and anti-American activity by progressives and their Marxist movement and then educating the public. To help further those efforts, I will donate a portion of the revenue obtained from this book to these three organizations. As a supporting member of The Heritage Foundation and Judicial Watch, the information I obtained from them in doing my research for the book was invaluable.

Finally, I want to extend my great appreciation and strong support to all the conservatives and classic liberals who stand up to the progressives who are taking our America away from us. I especially want to thank those who have paid a significant personal price in doing so.

CHAPTER 1

Why the Book?

_____

When I wrote my book on leadership titled *Exploring Great Leadership: A Practical Look From the Inside*, I had no intent or desire to write another. So, why in the "Sam Hill" am I compelled to do it? Sam Hill is an old euphemism coined in the 1830s for the "Devil" or "Hell". On second thought, Sam Hill is not expressive enough. How about this? Television news anchor Howard Beale (played by Peter Finch) said in the 1976 satirical move *Network*, "I'm mad as hell and I'm not going to take this any more!" That's better. I am mad as hell that America is under massive attack by devious self-serving people who want to change the America I love. That is why I am writing this book.

I am not alone in my feelings. Every time I mention I'm writing a book; I am asked, "What's it about?" I tell them it's about what is politically happening to our country and its effect on our future. I almost always get the same reaction. People routinely convey far more than casual interest in their comments and with their facial expressions. Many have asked when the book is coming out and where they can buy it. We are talking about good friends, new acquaintances, and people I do not know such as employees at check out counters. I did not get close to the same intensity of reaction for my first book. Americans who believe in the Declaration of Independence, the Constitution, and traditional American values are feeling more and more like Howard Beale. This book is my challenge to you patriotic Americans, who feel as I do, to stick your head out the window and shout with me "I'm mad as hell and I'm not going to take this any more!"

I want to begin by asking an important question. What makes us right and the other side wrong? The answer can be found through an understanding of what makes America America and what makes us Americans. I am going begin by examining my own childhood and adolescence and how that has made me the American I am. I would encourage you to do the same as you are reading.

Before we start, I want to share with you what I heard in a PragerU video. PragerU is a project that produces conservative educational videos that are five minutes in length and can be found on the Internet. This particular video is titled "Sticks and Stones" and features comedian Tom Shillue, host of *Red Eye* on Fox News. He said, "I grew up in a rougher and meaner, less sensitive, world. Did this rough and meaner world better prepare me to be a well-adjusted, happy adult? I would say yes." He used a saying by his mother that we all remember from our own childhood. That saying is, "Sticks and stones can break my bones but words can never hurt me." Shillue concluded that saying is not utilized enough today. He commented, "The result is hyper-sensitive teenagers and college students." This is a very real and concerning issue that has serious implications for the future of our society and will be discussed later. This is certainly not reflective of my childhood and who I became. I am sure it is not reflective of your childhood or who you are either. Otherwise, you would not be reading this book. With that thought in mind let's begin.

I grew up in a small town in the mountains of Eastern Kentucky. I am a genuine hillbilly. My little hometown of Harlan is actually quite famous. In the 1930s, it was referred to as "Bloody Harlan" and was in the national news quite often. It got its name from the bloody and deadly war between the coal mining companies, union organizers, and coal miners who were union sympathizers. My dad, who was a state policeman at the time, told me stories of how they set up road blocks to stop Chicago gangsters from coming into town and using machine guns and explosives to shoot up and blow up cars and buildings and create bloody scenes that caused fear and havoc. What he described was straight out of an Elliott Ness movie. Thankfully, that was before my time.

There have been several movies, documentaries, televisions shows, and books about Harlan. One of my favorites and one of the most famous is *Thunder Road* starring Robert Mitchum. The National Geographic Channel had a series of five television shows between December 2015 and March 2016 titled *Kentucky Justice* that was filmed in Harlan County and spotlighted the Harlan County Sheriff Department's fight against a growing drug problem. The longest televised show featuring Harlan was the award winning television series *Justified* on the FX network that ended in 2015 after a five-year run. It was filmed elsewhere as was *Thunder Road*. The only thing in that television series that resembles what I remember of Harlan is the picture of the Harlan skyline at the beginning of the show.

I use the term Harlan skyline rather loosely since the population of Harlan is now only 2,000. The total county is only 28,000. Those population numbers are down from 6,000 and 55,000 respectively when I grew up there. That is what happens when a community is nestled in the foothills of the Appalachian Mountains and the only significant industry is the dying coal industry.

The only shows actually filmed in Harlan are the documentaries that depict the area as a poster child for Appalachia, hillbillies, growing marijuana, and making moonshine. Believe it or not, "good" moonshine is pretty good. Just before the 2014 mid-term elections Bret Baier did a Fox News special about the impact the Environmental Protection Agency (EPA) regulations has had on slashing employment and how that would influence Senate elections in Kentucky and Louisiana. One half of the hour-long show was about the devastation of jobs in the coal industry in Harlan and Harlan County.

OK, enough about my hometown but why are hometowns important? They are important because they are instrumental in defining who we are and what we become. We develop what I call our mental being (our core psychological makeup) from our hereditary genes and during the first four to five years of our lives from the continuous interaction with our parents or substitute caregivers and our environment. In all but rare cases, the culture of our hometown is a very powerful part of that environment. It plays a major role during those formative years and during our adolescence in determining who we are and how we think.

I'll share an interesting study with you that supports this point. One morning my wife and I were having breakfast with friends. I was discussing my mental being theory from my leadership book with them. The husband told us about a book he was reading that gave reasons why certain people achieve more academically and athletically than others who are in the same grade in school and who have similar mental and athletic ability. I became interested because of my theory regarding the psychology of why we are the way we are.

After breakfast, my wife and I went straight to Barnes & Noble. The book is titled *Outliers* and was written by the best-selling author Malcolm Gladwell. As I thumbed through the book, I found a big surprise. Chapter six was titled *Harlan, Kentucky*. The chapter was about my hometown and discussed how cultural legacies play such an important role in directing attitudes and behavior that persists generation after generation. For example, people in Harlan and the greater southern Appalachian geographic area were prone to feuding in the 1800s and early 1900s. The Hatfield-McCoy feud is the most famous but family feuding was prevalent throughout a large geographic region in Appalachia where immigrants from the Scottish Lowlands, Northern England, and Northern Ireland settled.

These immigrants were herders rather than farmers due to the rugged landscape in which they lived before they came to America. They adhered strongly to what sociologists call a "culture of honor". Farmers tended to be cooperative and help each other. Herders were more isolated in a territory prone to lawlessness and felt they needed to be aggressive to gain a reputation of being strong, defensive, and willing to fight or even kill to prevent their herds from being stolen. They placed loyalty to family above all else. When these immigrants moved to America and settled in this Appalachian region, they brought this culture of honor with them and feuds between families were common.

In the 1990s two psychologists at the University of Michigan decided to do a study on the culture of honor. They used students from southern states whose heritage originated from these immigrants that settled in Appalachia over 200 years ago and students from northern states that did not have this heritage. During several situations where the students were subjected to some type of confrontation, even mild confrontation, the southern students became insulted and pushed back. In some instances they were willing to fight.

4

The students from the north who did not have this heritage took each of these encounters in stride and brushed them off. Even though the family feuding ended roughly 100 years ago, the culture of honor is generational and still prevails today. It is astounding how culture and subculture prevail over such a long period of time, have significant impact on who we are, and we are usually clueless about it. I was very glad to read Gladwell's chapter on Harlan because I have always been just like those students from the southern states when I felt infringed upon and never understood why. Now I know. It was a revelation for me. The concept of cultural heritage is very important in understanding ourselves.

Oh, by the way, Gladwell's answer as to why some kids excel over others with the same mental and athletic ability is because kids who start in school when they are older excel against those who start to school younger because of the age difference. This phenomenon took place even though the kids were only a few months apart.

I moved to Frankfort, Kentucky my sophomore year in high school but it was my hometown and the friends I grew up with in Harlan who influenced my early development and the personal values that are the beliefs I adhere to today. When I was a kid, I played outside with my friends at every opportunity. On non-school days, I didn't come home until the appointed time given to me by my parents, which was usually 9 P.M. or 10 P.M. I did come home for dinner or let them know if I was going to eat at someone else's house. Most of the time they only had a general idea where I was or who I was with. As long as I followed the rules, demonstrated responsibility, and stayed out of trouble, I developed trust with my parents and was allowed considerable freedom. These many experiences taught me to be independent and responsible.

If I engaged in occasional mischief or did not do what I was supposed to do, being caught was not much fun. My dad spanked with a belt as did most of my friend's dads. We used to brag to each other that our dad had a bigger belt than their dad and ours spanked harder. It was a badge of courage to get a spanking. I have to admit; however, that during the spanking I would just as soon not be getting one. Sometimes, I would get a lecture rather than a spanking. The lectures hurt worse than the spankings. I never wanted my parents to be disappointed in me.

One of the dumbest things my parents did was to make me eat all the food on my plate. Some evenings, I spent a long time at the dinner table. It was a game of wits between my parents and me. It depended upon the evening who finally won. I still have a problem today leaving food on my plate and my parents have been dead for decades. This is a great example of the lingering effects from our childhood discipline. My parents made me clean my plate because they grew up during the Great Depression and I can't leave food on my plate today because their experience was handed down. I have found that being forced to clean our plate at dinnertime happened to a lot of us who grew up during the same time period.

When I played with my friends at a very young age, we had fun and significant personal interaction. There were no electronic devises to interfere with our socialization. For example, we played Mother May I, You're It, Dodge Ball, Army with our toy shoulders and toy guns, and Fox and Hound. The foxes used chalk on the sidewalk to lead and mislead the hounds and our game covered many city blocks. It was always challenging to see which team of foxes could find the cleverest spot to hide at the end of the game. For example, we hid in places like empty railroad coal cars and on top of single story buildings. Great fun! I still don't know how we didn't get injured? We did have to dodge a few security guards. The police stopped us a few times and asked what we were doing. After explaining to them we were playing a game of hide and seek (Fox and Hound), they usually told us to be careful and left us alone. Once or twice, they told us to leave the area. Our playtime was creative, interactive, and gave us a lot of "outdoor" exercise. It is amazing how much fun my friends and I could have by putting large empty cardboard boxes together and making playhouses or forts.

When we got older we played basketball, football, baseball (at which I was never very good), and still kept some of our more challenging games like Fox and Hound. We shot BB guns without putting our eyes out. We occasionally sneaked off into the mountains when my parents were not at home to target practice with my 22-caliber rifle and my dad's old German Mauser pistol. In retrospect, that wasn't the smartest thing we ever did even though we were very careful. As I look back,

I surprise myself at how daring we were. I guess I did learn to have confidence in myself and not be risk-adverse.

I was pretty self-sufficient and creative in my personal enjoyment. Once, I built a pretty darn good basketball goal on my driveway. I used heavy plywood for the backboard and a big wooden square pole to bolt the backboard onto. I got a couple of my friends to help me concrete it in the ground. There were an uncountable number of pick-up basketball games and games of h-o-r-s-e played on that basketball goal. I recently went into a large national sporting goods store and was very surprised at what I saw. They had several adjustable-height basketball goals on fancy heavy metal square poles that ranged from $600 to $1,800. They were much, much nicer than the one I built. I bet the kids who play basketball on those have no more, if not as much, fun than my friends and I did playing on ours that was homemade.

Even if these basketball goals were available in stores when I was a kid, none of my friends nor I could afford the $600 model, let alone the one for $1,800. Times have changed considerably regarding the money my friends and I had to spend growing up and the money kids have today to spend and I am talking about families with the same socio-economic status. We were lucky to buy an RC Cola and a Moon Pie at the corner grocery for a grand total of 10 cents. I remember when they went up to 10 cents each.

Once, I made a wooden motorless go-cart. It wasn't very fancy but a lot of fun. Especially, since I designed and made it myself. The multitude of electronic games we see today did not exist. We didn't even have the electronic game of *Pong*. Remember *Pong*? I had to rely on interaction with my friends, family, and my own imagination to have fun.

When we got hurt, our parents applied witch-hazel or hydrogen peroxide, put on a Band-Aid with a kiss, and sent us back outside. If someone broke a bone, it was neat to be the first or one of the first to sign the cast and the person with the broken bone loved the attention. We didn't ever go to the doctor or the emergency room unless the injury was obviously serious. We were pretty tough kids and had no expectation of being coddled. We needed just enough TLC to feel loved and secure.

When we were older, we played some games that in retrospect do not feel as cool as an adult as they did as a young person. Those games included "hubcap" (rolling a found hubcap in the street toward a car and yelling "hubcap") and throwing snowballs or water balloons at cars as they went by. We also occasionally bought cigars and chewing tobacco at a neighborhood market. We would take the cigars down to the river bank and smoke them while we fished and used the chewing tobacco as bait. The cigars made us sick and the chewing tobacco was gross but we did it anyway. The grocery owner always looked at us somewhat funny when he sold them to us. I guess making a sale was more important to him than following his conscience. We were certainly mischievous. As I write this, I somewhat cringe that we did these less-than-stellar things. I can thankfully say that neither my friends nor I ever damaged property, bullied anyone, or did anything illegal.

Acceptable mischievous behavior (whatever that means) as an adolescent gives us personal emotional references as to what is right or wrong and teaches us to be more understanding, ethical, and honest as we mature into adults for those of us who do mature into adults. It also takes some of the mystery out of doing things we shouldn't. I will give you an example. When my kids saw me drinking wine, beer, or some other alcoholic beverage when they were young, they would ask me for a drink. Instead of saying, "No, you are not old enough," I would give them a taste. They always thought the tastes were "yucky" and none of my three kids are big drinkers today. They still remind me of those experiences. Allowing them to have the tastes took the mystery out of drinking alcoholic beverages. If they had asked for more, we would have had a long talk.

While I was growing up, I had constant interpersonal interactions with friends, acquaintances, and people I did not know. I developed strong social skills as a result of those interactions—sometimes as a result of adverse interactions with each other. For example, one of my best friends started running around with another crowd and began to pick on me. His aggression became worse and I became somewhat afraid of him. He had become a bully. One day I was walking down the street with an older neighborhood friend. Coincidently, my bully-friend was walking on the sidewalk across the street. I said to my neighborhood friend, "Do you think he can beat me up?" My neighborhood friend said, "No, he's just got your goat." So, I decided to find out. I yelled across the street, "Do you want to fight?" He would not answer me and just kept on walking. In light of my newfound courage, I did not let it go until I threw a couple of more barbs his way. It is easier to be brave when you have an older neighbor by your side. My old bully-friend never bothered me again. Bullying cannot be legislated. It only gets worse. The person being bullied has to stick up for herself or himself. Sometimes, a person needs a little help like I did.

Do you know where the phrase "got your goat" came from? Being from Kentucky, I need to know these things. Racehorses are very hyper. In order to calm them down the night before a race, sometimes a goat was put in the stall with them. An unscrupulous competitor would steal the goat during the night. Now you know!

I got a call one evening from one of my best friends to tell me that one of our mutual friends was killed in a car wreck along with his mother and sister. His dad was driving and the only one to survive. It was very tragic and I felt very sad even though he and I were rivals. I played first-chair trumpet in our high school band and he was working very hard and making progress to take it away from me. I still feel sad about his death as I write this. Tragedy is a part of life and we should never be sheltered from experiencing the reality of it—even at a young age. To do so, inhibits well-grounded psychological development during our formative years.

I could tell you many stories like these where my interactions with others did not always meet my expectations, my wishes, or result in a positive situation. My parents were always supportive but never sheltered me from real life experiences even when they were not so positive. I said in my last book that some of the best learning experiences in life are from the school of hard and soft knocks. Adversity is a fact of life and we need to learn mature and effective ways to deal with that adversity rather than be sheltered from it or become victimized by it.

My mother did not have a college degree but her career in retail management was very successful. I learned my determination and grit to succeed from her. My father died when I was in the eighth grade. That was very difficult for me. When he was alive he pushed me very hard in school. If I did not make straight A's, he grounded me after school until my report card showed straight A's. Yes, he grounded me after school for the entire next grading period. I think that behavior was because of my dad's history in school. He was very intelligent but dropped out of college and had a career of mixed success. I assume he was determined that I not make the same mistake. His approach caused a mild rebellion on my part. I knew when he would get home and I would sneak off after school with my friends and play when I was supposed to be grounded. I always got away with it—I think?

One of the things that I remember about school was the "chair of honor" in seventh grade math class. About once per month, we all competed at the blackboard doing math problems. The last one standing got to sit at a desk in the front of the room. Our class was very competitive and I fortunately got to sit at that desk most of the time. That was a special honor that the class respected because we had respect for each other. Our teacher loved the competition in her class and felt it made us better students.

My dad gave me multiple chores to do around the house and yard on a regular basis. He was a self-made handyman and loved to repair and build things. I was his boy Friday. Once, we built a pretty good-sized fishing boat together. That sounds nice but I didn't always appreciate the time I had to spend on chores and projects when I would rather be playing with my friends or going to bed earlier. In retrospect, he did teach me to be independent, industrious, self-sufficient, and most importantly taught me responsibility.

After my father died, my grades went to hell. My academic success progressively waned during high school and during my first year of college my grades were awful. It was a significant struggle after my freshman year but I graduated from undergraduate school with decent grades and I was first or second in my class academically in graduate school. Even though my dad was deceased, I believe my academic behavior in high school and my freshman year in college directly resulted from rebellion against his heavy handedness regarding my grades when I was younger. We are weird creatures aren't we? This story is another good example of how parental influence during childhood and adolescence continues through our adulthood.

Even though I rebelled against my dad's tough hand regarding education, chores, and projects after he died, I thank both my mother and father for what they gave me. I inherited genes from them that provided me with good intellect. Their parenting gave me the motivation, desire, and ability to develop the skills and personal goals for a successful career as a healthcare system CEO. Their parenting also gave me what I needed to be willing to pay the price of achieving that successful career through sacrifice and hard work.

Life in communities has changed considerably since I grew up, especially in smaller communities. When I was in grade school, junior high, and high school; we had several rituals and celebrations at school. Every morning we said allegiance to the American flag and a short prayer to God. We honored and celebrated national holidays like New Years, Valentine's Day, Easter, July 4th, Memorial Day, Labor Day, Halloween, Thanksgiving, and Christmas. We even celebrated Columbus Day and holidays honoring presidents like Washington and Lincoln. In grade school, we hand-made symbols, had discussions, and performed skits to learn and honor the meaning of these holidays. Rituals and celebrations happened all over town on major holidays and everyone participated who wanted to participate—which was practically everyone. It was great fun and provided wonderful feelings of pride and joy as we celebrated these events as a community and what they meant to our American and Judeo-Christian religious heritage. If you didn't want to participate, that was your choice.

Church was a big deal. We had all the protestant denominations and a Catholic church. I went to a Baptist church. Some weeks, I would be at church five times. I went to Boy Scouts once a month, Royal Ambassadors (a Baptist religious boys group with levels of achievement like the Boy Scouts) once per month, prayer meeting on Wednesday nights (occasionally), choir practice every Saturday, and church every Sunday. Before I was old enough to be a Royal Ambassador I belonged to a religious based group at church for very young boys and girls. We were called Sunbeams. Yeah—we were called Sunbeams. My non-Baptist friends had fun with that one. A lot of church but that is the way it was. If you didn't go to church, that was considered…? Actually, as I think about it, I don't remember knowing anyone who did not go to church somewhere at least on occasion.

The events in my childhood and adolescence have shaped my personal beliefs and values, my personal political ideology, and my passion to preserve that ideology. I respect, listen to, and learn from others' opinions and my wife and I have a very healthy, positive, and sharing relationship. However, that said, I am a fiercely independent person. I have a reputation for standing up for what I believe, even in the face of adversity. I am very proud of what I accomplished during my career both for my employer and for my community. When I retired, I received the Chamber of Commerce's annual award given to the business leader recognized for their contribution to business and the community. That was one of the highlights of my career.

I don't need some outside entity telling me what I need or don't need and how to run my life, especially the government or some misguided radical group. I believe in accountability. I am personally accountable for my actions and success and all individuals should be accountable for their own actions and success or lack thereof. I am very pragmatic and look at the total picture and the long-term results in relation to specific actions. Common sense and the written law should be the rule in taking these actions or judging the actions of others.

I believe in individual rights, freedom, and success but not at the expense of others. In that same vein, individuals do not owe their fellow man materialistic equality but that does not mean that individuals shouldn't be charitable to those truly in need. The Declaration of Independence says, "We hold these truths to be self-evident, that all men are created equal, that they are endowed by their Creator with certain unalienable Rights, that among these are Life, Liberty and the pursuit of Happiness." Nowhere in the Declaration of Independence does it say society should be for the collective good. It says that our society is based upon individual achievement and that every member of our society has the equal right to achieve what he or she desires in life.

I believe in strong family values where parental rights trump government dictates regarding children unless there is child abuse that is defined by reality and common sense and not the government. Parents are responsible for the values, well-being, and discipline of their children. It is not the responsibility of government, some do-gooder organization, or some politically motivated organization to usurp that responsibility.

I learned how to successfully interact with others even in difficult and adversarial situations while being honest, respectful, and tolerant regarding their opinions, feelings, and individual rights. Even though I am very competitive and opinionated, I put issues in their proper perspective and do not easily overreact but I stand up for what I believe, even in the face of adversity.

I developed great pride in what America stands for, its principals of government, its heritage, and its position in the world. The Constitution says, "WE THE PEOPLE of the United States, in Order to form a more perfect Union, establish Justice, insure domestic Tranquility, provide for the common defense, promote the general Welfare, and secure the Blessings of Liberty to ourselves and our Posterity, do ordain and establish this Constitution for the United States of America." The American civilization is the greatest civilization the world has ever known. No civilization can match us when it comes to individual freedom, personal security, economic achievement, ingenuity, gritty resolve, generosity, and world leadership. I have thought many times how extremely lucky I am to be born in America and not anywhere else. America has given me the chance to start with nothing financially and achieve success— twice. The first time was after my first college degree and the second time was after graduate school. I enjoyed a very successful career and was very successful economically. I will also add that I paid my own way through college both times. I used student loans without government subsidy. I paid a fair interest rate and it took a long time to pay the loans back but I did it.

It is obvious that I am a dyed-in-the-wool conservative and I am becoming more devout day by day when I see what is happening with our local, state, and federal governments. America is under siege by people who don't respect what America stands for, its principals, its heritage, or its position in the world. Can America, as we know it, survive? That is what this book is about. I couldn't stand by idly and see our incredible American way of life be destroyed without standing up and pushing back to defend what I believe.

I love my country dearly. I am so proud and so lucky to be an American. We have the most successful country in the history of the world. So why would anyone in America want to change that? We are going to talk about who these people are, what their motives are, and how they are doing it. We will discuss the only way to stop these devious and self-serving people and whether or not we can. Do you have the desire, will, and determination to stand up and be counted in the face of this anti-America movement? If you are unsure, I think you will know by the end of the book. If you are sure, this book will only embolden you.

What makes us right and the other side wrong? Our traditional American beliefs and values reflect the beliefs and values of the majority of American society and have provided us with unparalleled success in the world and in our personal lives. These beliefs and values were inherited from the original colonists and other ancestral immigrants who built this great nation to achieve a better life for themselves and their families. Our founding fathers articulated those beliefs and values in the Declaration of Independence and the Constitution. If the minority in our country who want to change America do not like the beliefs and values that our country was founded upon, they can do what the original colonists did who had a similar problem. They can go exploring and relocate to an existing country that reflects "their" beliefs and values or search for unoccupied land and start their own colony.

CHAPTER 2

What's a Liberal?

We hear the terms democrat, republican, liberal, conservative, independent, libertarian, and progressive to identify individuals by their political ideology. Liberal and democrat are commonly used interchangeably and that is accurate. Conservative and republican are commonly used interchangeably and I agree with one caveat that I will discuss in chapter 3. Progressive is used interchangeably with liberal and democrat but that is not accurate. Although progressives share basic ideology and behavioral characteristics with liberals, they have distinguishing characteristics that are significantly different from liberals I refer to as classic liberals. Because of those differences, I have devoted an entire chapter to progressives. I also want to clarify that when I use the terms democrat or republican, I am referring to political ideology and not to the Democratic or Republican Parties.

Independents and libertarians are autonomous from major political party association but not autonomous from the political ideology of liberals and conservatives. Independents ideologically revolve around the political center, have no loyalty to the Democratic or Republican Parties, and don't want to be identified with either. Independents do; however, tend to be more conservative than liberal as a group. Libertarians are often said to be radical conservatives. That is not true in terms of being radical. Webster's Dictionary defines radical as relating to or constituting a political group associated with views, practices, and policies of extreme change. Libertarians have stronger anti-big government and pro-individual freedom beliefs than typical conservatives but they do not differ in basic ideology. I am not going to include independents and libertarians in the book as political classifications. To do so would add unnecessary complexity. Just think of independents as borderline conservatives or borderline liberals and libertarians as strong conservatives.

In a perfect world, which political ideology is best for America—liberal or conservative? First of all, the world is not perfect, never has been, and never will be. This is a very important thought to keep that in mind as you read the book. Secondly, conservatives would say conservative politics is best and liberals would say liberal politics is best. The truth is that a balance of liberalism and conservatism is best. Each political ideology should be balanced with the other to obtain the best outcome possible for our society as long as that political ideology is in keeping with the principals and laws as spelled out in the Declaration of Independence and the Constitution. The exception is progressive liberal politics. With these thoughts in mind, let's begin to define and understand liberals, conservatives, and progressives.

So, what's a liberal? A classic liberal is a person who genuinely interprets and supports the Declaration of Independence and the United States Constitution through liberal ideology based upon her or his personal beliefs and values. Although classic liberals and progressive liberals share basic liberal ideology, progressive liberals differ from classic liberals in that they interpret and support liberal ideology in a radical way and with total disregard to the Declaration of Independence or the Constitution. We will analyze this difference between progressive liberals and classic liberals in chapter 4.

In chapter 1, I referred to a person's core psychological makeup as their mental being. It is that mental being that is the basis of one's beliefs and values that determine his or her behavior. That is what makes a liberal a liberal, a conservative a conservative, and a progressive a progressive. Mental being is the product of the core personality traits we genetically inherit and learn during childhood. By the time an individual reaches adulthood, these traits are established and only subject to a certain degree of tweaking and maturing but not changing. Examples of those traits are the degree to which we are secure versus insecure, trusting versus distrusting, confidant versus unconfident, narcissistic vs. altruistic, caring vs. uncaring, insightful versus naive, idealistic versus pragmatic, controlling versus empowering, tolerant versus intolerant, etc. This chapter will focus on core personality traits, liberal beliefs and values, and resultant liberal behaviors. For writing simplicity, I am going to utilize the following terminology for the remainder of the book. Since beliefs and values are so closely related, I am going to use beliefs to designate both. In addition, beliefs and ideology are basically one and the same and I will use those terms interchangeably according to which term best fits the narrative.

It is important to remember that when you have seen one individual liberal you have seen one individual liberal. I said in my leadership book that people are like snowflakes—no two alike. You will not find all of the liberal beliefs and behaviors presented in this chapter present in every individual. You will find; however, that all of the beliefs and behaviors taken collectively do define a liberal when liberals are taken as a group. That same scenario applies to conservatives and progressives.

I have tried many times to understand what makes liberals politically think and act the way they do. Being of a strong conservative mindset, I can't get into a liberal's political head. I am sure they feel the same about me. I'm not aware of any formal studies regarding the psychological analysis of what makes a liberal think and act like a liberal, a conservative think and act like a conservative, or a progressive think and act like a progressive but I sure would love to see one.

Although not based upon a formal psychological study, I did find some interesting and insightful analysis on the PragerU site I mentioned in chapter1. The founder is Dennis Prager who is a syndicated talk show host, columnist, author, and public speaker. Here is a summary of what is on their website under Mission, Vision, and About Us. Their mission is to present the ideas that led to the creation and development of the United States as the freest and most prosperous nation in history. Their vision is to use the Internet to give millions of people the ability to understand the fundamental values that shaped America and the "intellectual ammunition" people need to defend those values. About us says they want to make the most persuasive and entertaining case possible for the values that have made Western civilization in general and America specifically the source of so much freedom and wealth. It went on to say that those values are Judeo-Christian at their core and include the concepts of freedom of speech, freedom of the press, free markets, and a strong military to protect those values.

There are two five-minute video courses on the website that offer great insight into the differences between liberals and conservatives. The first video is about how the left and right see the country. It is titled, "How do you judge America?" It says conservatives believe America is the best society ever created and does good things for people in other countries. Liberals believe America is a flawed country and morally no better, if not inferior, to many other countries. The video said that the intensity of that belief for liberals increases proportionately to where that liberal is on the continuum from left to far left or from classic liberal to progressive liberal.

The second video is about how the liberals and conservatives see individuals. It is titled, "How do you make society better?" This video says liberals believe the way to a better society is "doing battle" with society's moral failings and concentrate efforts on sexism, racism, intolerance, xenophobia, Islamophobia, and homophobia. Politics becomes the vehicle for the improvement of society and the focus is always on "social revolution"; i.e., fix society versus fixing the individual. Conservatives believe the way to be a better society is almost always through the moral improvement of the individual with each person doing battle with her or his weaknesses and flaws. The video concluded that the liberal approach only makes society worse and conservatives are opposed to the liberal approach since society is not fundamentally bad. Change happens gradually with conservatism because it is focused upon the individual.

If you have young children or adolescents still under your wing, I would highly recommend that you check out the PragerU website. The website says that students are no longer learning that America is a land of opportunity, a defender of freedom around the world, and a source of pride. Instead, they are taught that America is a land of inequity, racism, imperialism, and, ultimately, shame that can only be redeemed through the adoption of radical progressive ideas. They said, "At PragerU, we believe that every student deserves the opportunity to learn the founding principles that have made the United States the freest, most prosperous, and most generous society in human history." Their videos are educational, thought provoking, and well worth anyone's time. You might want to check out PragerU for yourself.

Although there is no professional research regarding what makes a liberal think and act like a liberal, a conservative think and act like a conservative, or a progressive think and act like a progressive; I can identify obvious basic core personality traits that compose the mental being of liberals, conservatives, and progressives and their resulting beliefs and behaviors. There are many of the same core personality traits present in all three classifications. What we are talking about in this chapter as well as the next two chapters is dominate core personality traits that "politically differentiate" liberals, conservatives, and progressives from each other.

When I discussed the psychology of leadership in my other book, I expressed that I am not a practicing psychologist or a research psychologist. Obviously, the same applies here. Any psychological competence I possess is based upon any minuscule expertise left over from college psychology 101, my experience in leadership positions, and my 71 years of experience as a practicing human being in our complex society. My psychological analysis of liberals, conservatives, and progressives is based upon those factors, my personal observations, and my personal experiences.

I learned a long time ago to never discuss politics or religion with anyone unless you share the same philosophy. It is amazing how these two subjects are extraordinarily personal and elicit such a strong response when there is disagreement. I assume we are so emotionally invested in those two topics that any disagreement is like a personal attack on our intimate mental being that results in a visceral response. Even our favorite sports teams do not generate the level of emotion as politics. Religion seems to be the only equal. When I do discuss politics with my liberal friends, we keep it on a superficial and friendly level. Usually, it is kept to just friendly teasing. It astonishes me that except for politics, my liberal friends and I are almost always philosophically in lock-sync. How can we be so philosophically opposed in politics and so philosophically the same in most everything else? I don't have a clue.

Not surprisingly, I don't have a problem discussing politics with my conservative friends and we regularly have vigorous discussions on the topic. Many times our discussions are basically self-therapy sessions in an effort to make our conservative souls feel better because we are so upset about the current political situation in our country.

I am a Fox News junkie. It is the only television network news programing that has any semblance of non-biased political news and Fox is not perfect. Sometimes, I think CNN is objective and then I observe differently. My liberal friends take strong issue with me regarding Fox. They routinely tell me that you can't trust Fox News because it is so biased in supporting conservatism. I explain to them that Fox does have opinion-based programs that are purely conservative and they promote and endorse the conservative side of the story. Those programs do not pretend to be otherwise but I still don't catch them twisting the facts. I will admit some news anchors show their conservative bias upon occasion but that is the exception rather than the rule. Fox has one news anchor who has his own news show and I believe is "liberal biased" based upon his demeanor as he is reporting the news. I do not ever catch any Fox programs spinning the news or omitting news to distort the truth.

Fox News has many liberal news commentators and liberal guest contributors that express their liberal views on a regular basis. Fox also exposes liberal reports and "edited" news clips taken from liberal oriented news and opinion television programs that distort the truth against conservatives and conservatism. Fox additionally exposes the mainstream news media for ignoring meaningful and important news stories that are not favorable to the liberal cause but are important for the public to know.

The opinions I express in this chapter regarding liberal core personality traits and beliefs and behaviors come from a multitude of sources other than Fox News. I occasionally watch news shows, news commentary shows, and 60 Minutes on mainstream television. Those news shows as well as 60 Minutes are usually liberally oriented. I have also obtained significant material from the articles and editorials in my local newspaper, The Wall Street Journal, other national newspapers, The Daily Caller from The Heritage Foundation, Judicial Watch publications, and the Internet. I have been known to watch CNN and MSNBC. I have to admit the extent to which I can tolerate these two liberal biased networks is limited, especially very progressive MSNBC.

My liberal friends tell me I can't critique the liberals I observe on Fox News as being representative of liberal thinking and liberal political ideology because they are not true liberals. Some of my liberal friends even call them liberal wackos. I explain to these friends that the liberals I am listening to on Fox include Democratic Representatives and Senators (both national and state), liberal political strategists and pollsters, liberal opinion writers and news reporters, current and potential liberal political candidates, the chairwoman of the Democratic Party, current and past democratic White House Cabinet members, democratic campaign leaders (including those who worked in President Obama's two campaigns), the top people in the Obama administration and president Obama himself.

Who else is there to critique? ? I will admit an abundance of these individuals are progressive liberals but aren't these the very people who develop and implement liberal strategy and expound about liberalism for the public to read, hear, and emulate? Aren't these the liberals calling the shots and making governmental decisions that affect all of us? Progressives are still liberals, albeit at the far left end, practicing liberal ideology.

I said people are like snowflakes—no two alike. This characteristic is much stronger within the liberal ranks than with conservatives. Liberals have a much wider range of ideological intensity. There are moderate liberals who are so close to the political center they share many core personality traits and ideology with conservatives. I have a friend who fits into that category. We have meaningful, enjoyable, and academic political conversation without quarreling. It seems that the preponderance of liberals; however, fall in varying degrees from left of the political center to the far left.

As a liberal individual moves toward the far left, the liberal core personality traits that make up their mental being are significantly more pronounced and their liberal beliefs that determine their liberal ideology are much more intense. Their behavior reflects this intensity. That is why progressive liberals are in a league of their own. Conservatives do not exhibit this same variable range of intensity. They seem to simply fall into one of two categories. They are either right of the political center or fundamentally right of the political center. I will explain that distinction in the next chapter.

We will begin our psychological analysis of liberals by discussing their core personality traits. The most interesting and dominant liberal core personality trait is idealism versus pragmatism. Idealism is the trait that provides the unwavering dedication and serious effort by liberals to achieve their political ideology. I find the basic beliefs of liberals to be very honorable. These basic beliefs include such things as raising the standard of living for those less fortunate, equal rights for everyone, helping those in need, and environmental preservation. Who can argue with that? A liberal's intentions to achieve his or her beliefs routinely have merit.

A major difference between liberals and conservatives is that liberals routinely do not put their actions to achieve their beliefs into perspective with the total picture and do not pragmatically balance those actions with any undesirable consequences that might result. The focus is unequivocally on achieving the ideological goal. Many times this results in unintended consequences and, ironically, often creates a result that is oxymoronic to the intent.

I believe this liberal intensity and commitment results from her or his impassioned devotion to his or her liberal beliefs. Any obvious adverse outcomes are completely overshadowed and obliterated and any hidden adverse outcomes are not investigated. Reality is based upon emotion rather than fact and this results in inadvertent naivety on the part of those involved. I find it very interesting that this naivety seems to only apply to one's liberal political views and not to the person as a whole. It is complicated and something I can't explain.

A great example of this trait would be the continuing support and growth of existing and new government entitlement programs. Supporting and helping those in need is admirable and desirable but without pragmatic and common sense restrictions, these programs are unaffordable and unsustainable resulting in a disastrous economic burden on our country. Even if the so-called rich were taxed at 100 percent of income, these programs are unsustainable. Where is the money going to come from? What is the end game? There isn't any, except to keep supporting these programs and to increasingly tax the rich, private corporations, and even the non-rich to pay for it. This is unworkable in the long run and left unchecked, our government would eventually collapse.

The European Union is a good example. Their economic disaster has been temporarily avoided more than once by kicking the problem down the road until it rises again because the basic issues were never addressed and resolved. Greece is the most obvious example but they certainly are not alone. This is the same direction our country is headed because of the actions of our liberal politicians. In addition to significantly increasing our national debt, government entitlement programs are thrusting recipients deeper and deeper into poverty rather than providing a way out of poverty toward a positive future. This issue of poverty is an example of the oxymoronic outcomes I referred to above and will be discussed later in the book.

There is a theory by Cloward and Piven (a husband and wife team who are ultra liberal Columbia University sociology professors) that promotes unchecked entitlement programs by the government as a means to bring about sudden radical change in society. They expound the overload of the welfare system to the point of collapse, which they say will result in a guaranteed income for everyone and end poverty. Cloward and Piven are in the progressive category—the really progressive category. Actually, I would call it the wacko progressive category. I want to share with you that I saw them on a stage with president Obama and other progressive democrats during an announcement by the president. It was a long time ago and I have forgotten what the announcement was. The important point is that they were there together. We will examine such relationships among progressives as the book unfolds.

Here is another real life example of this core personality trait from a different perspective. This example involves the release of the Senate Intelligence Committee report on the Central Intelligence Agency's (CIA) interrogation of al Qaeda operatives after 9/11. The report was actually a Senate "democratic" report in that it was a document review performed 100% by democratic staff. For that reason, all republicans on the committee refused to participate. No one involved with the interrogations or the legal opinion to justify them was interviewed for the report nor was there any effort to verify the information contained in the report. The report was 6,000 pages long and cost $40 million. Unbelievable! Our government at work—with your and my money! The report concluded that the interrogations were torture, illegal, and did not result in any useful information. The CIA staff and the Bush administration officials who were involved say the interrogations were appropriately approved, resulted in significant useful information (including how to locate Bin Laden), and top-level Senate democrats (including the chairman of the Senate committee who released the report, Diane Feinstein) were thoroughly informed at the time. I heard a 19-year veteran CIA senior analyst say, "The report was pre-cooked and void of any inconvenient facts."

I watched on television one of the psychologists who designed and administered the interrogations. He was incensed this report was so politically biased and incorrect. He said when he personally water boarded Khalid Sheikh Mohammed, the chief mastermind behind 9/11, Mohammed said "your country will turn on you" and specifically mentioned the liberal media and our society in general. I routinely enjoy judge Jeanine Pirro's hard hitting and most always on-target opening statements on her Fox News television show. Judge Jeanine said Senator Feinstein turned our enemies into victims. How true! A 2011 Fox News poll asked if Americans supported interrogations such as waterboarding to gain information from terrorist suspects and 63% said yes. Only 30% were opposed and 7% didn't know. A Rasmussen poll in December 2014 indicated that the 63% has dropped to 47% and 33% were unsure. The 16% drop in those who supported the interrogations appeared to move into the "not sure" category. We humans have short memories. Terrorists like Mohammed know us very well and use our weaknesses to bolster their confidence in fighting us.

Democratic congressional leaders, the White House, and other liberals supported the release of the report with some saying it exposes our human rights atrocities to the world. I guess that somehow cleanses our country of our "dastardly deeds". There was at least some dissension in the Obama administration. Secretary of State, John Kerry, asked that the report be postponed and he was ignored. I am sure he heard an earful from other countries that were implicated in the report. The current CIA Director and assistant CIA Director during the interrogations, John Brennan, defended the CIA and said important information was obtained although he was very measured in his news conference.

I watched Ms. Feinstein, speak regarding why she wanted the report released. She said, "It is really about American values and morals. History will judge us by our commitment to a just society governed by law and willingness to face the ugly truth and say never again." I challenge Ms. Feinstein and these other people supporting the report's release to name one country in the world that has a better human rights record than us. What would these democratic politicians say if we had experienced another major attack like 9/11 on our country and the CIA had not done everything they could to prevent it? What would that Senate Intelligence Committee report say then?

Even if the Senate democrats were correct in their report, which they were not, why would they do such a foolish thing? Even the White House acknowledged there was significant concern about the safety of our embassies and military around the world and put them on high alert. Several other countries that are (were?) allies asked us not to do this because it implicates them. What did that do to the future safety of our CIA agents and those throughout the world working with them? How about the future ability of our CIA to effectively operate anywhere around the world? How about our credibility with any other government or intelligence organizations? How about the future safety of our country when the world cuts us off from intelligence information? How weak does this make us look in the eyes of the world including our most ardent enemies? I could go on and on but this is enough to make the point. This is a great example of well-intentioned liberal idealism gone amok without any regard for the truth or the pragmatic consequences.

Some said the report was released so Ms. Feinstein could get back at the CIA for monitoring her efforts regarding the report. Some say it was the democrats getting back at the republicans for the mid-term elections. I don't believe any of that. I believe it was Ms. Feinstein and her colleagues doing what they believe was the right thing to do based upon their liberal ideology. Since Ms. Feinstein had to give up her committee chairmanship, it was her last opportunity to leave her liberal legacy before the republicans took over the Senate.

Another liberal core personality trait is rationalization. Liberals are very passionate in supporting and defending their ideology and have a strong adherence to the adage that the end justifies the means. It is commonplace for liberals to take actions or verbally assert whatever is necessary to support and defend a point even if it is contradictory to reason or fact. I see this all the time on television and the frequency and intensity depends upon the specific individual involved and where they are on the scale from just left of center to far left. The most glaring example I can think of is the unwavering support for Obama's assertions regarding his accomplishments as president. I read these testaments to Obama often in op-eds and letters to the editor and I sit there dumbfounded as I read them.

One of my absolute favorites is an op-ed syndicated by the Tribune Content Agency in July 2015 written by a liberal pundit named Dick Meyer. He is the Chief Washington Correspondent for the Scripts Washington Bureau. His op-eds are the epitome of naive rationalization. I have no doubt that Mr. Meyer is as "pure as the morning snow" in his thinking but his op-eds are always contradictory to reason or fact. This particular op-ed was headlined "Mr. Obama, on behalf of ungrateful nation, I thank you". He commented on the Iran Deal, Obamacare, our economy, Obama being the first black president, and the Obama administration demonstrating dignity and honesty while being free of corruption. Yes, he actually said that. Mr. Meyer stated, "President Obama will go down in history as an extraordinary president, probably a great one." I will not comment and just let you digest that one.

He wrote one in January of this year that was equally as naive in rationalizing reality. After praising Obama for the economy, Obamacare, and Cuba, Meyer said, "If not dazzling and charismatic, the president has been steady and honest in trying times. That will look big in history's mirror." There are other sincere liberal pundits such as Ann McFeatters whose op-eds are just as naive in consistently rationalizing liberal actions.

Like the trait of idealism, I believe this trait of rationalization is a result of the strength of conviction for her or his liberal beliefs even though it can result in inaccurate and even destructive behavior. When it involves classic liberals, it is a result of visceral emotion and dishonesty is unintended. Unfortunately, progressive liberals are dishonest and use this trait to achieve an intended outcome through duplicitous behavior.

Here are a few examples of that duplicitous behavior. During the last presidential election, there were significant personal attacks on Mitt Romney that had no basis of fact; i.e., Harry Reid's assertion on the Senate floor that he heard from a reliable source that Romney paid no taxes. Reid basically admitted last year during a CNN television interview he lied and with a smirk on his face, acted proud of the fact he did lie and Romany did not win. How disgusting for a political leader in a position of responsibility like Reid. It was so bad that even The Huffington Post was critical of him.

One of Obama's top election officials, Stephanie Cutter, asserted that Romney had committed felonious actions and Debbie Wasserman Schultz, Democratic National Committee Chair, made the same assertions. They knew their assertions were not true but put out these misstatements of truth in an effort to get their candidate elected. How about when Susan Rice stated repeatedly the attack on Benghazi was a spontaneous action brought about by a video that was then reaffirmed over and over by Obama and Hillary Clinton?

When I watch progressive liberals speaking or being interviewed on television regarding politics, I see this duplicitous behavior on a consistent basis. Although these actions by Reid, the election official, Schultz, and Rice were by progressive liberals, the liberal base supported the mantra. It is unusual The Huffington Post stood up to Reid. In today's environment, progressives are taking over the leadership positions in liberal politics and classic liberals are following them even if the progressives are being dishonest. This is a very disturbing trend.

A book was recently published on the topic of progressive liberals taking over liberalism in America and classic liberals following this progressive movement. The book is titled *The Closing of the Liberal Mind* and is written by Kim R. Holmes who is a Distinguished Fellow at The Heritage Foundation and a former U.S. Assistant Secretary of State. I was glad to see Holmes's book because it strongly supports my position. The following is from his book and an article he wrote in The Daily Signal, a daily publication of The Heritage Foundation. Liberalism is no longer "mainly about ideas". It is about "power". It is about "who has it and who does not". Liberal research has become "proving a point rather than discovering the truth" and "science is treated as the private preserve" of liberal ideology. Holmes commented, "Mistaking as they do their ideology for morality, they see no reason to shun the most cynical of political tactics to get their way. For them, the end justifies the means."

Holmes remarked today's liberalism has forsaken its American roots and is becoming more like the European Left. The European Left is a European political party founded in 2004 that operates an association of democratic socialist and communist political parties. He gave Franklin D. Roosevelt, John F. Kennedy, and even Bill Clinton as examples of the liberalism of old. He said classic liberals have "surrendered" to the progressive liberals and "liberals profess to be the party of the open mind and have become anything but". Liberal intellectuals used to "love open debate" but now "stifle debate" because they do not need debate when all the big questions have been answered by their ideology.

Holmes used the old adage that "he who controls knowledge controls power" and said the liberals of today are using their "own truth" as a "will to power to be imposed by law and government fiat". He also commented that they have "become masters" at controlling not only knowledge but also popular culture. He concluded "intolerance is championed in the name of tolerance, closed-mindedness in the name of open-mindedness, and hatred in the name of compassion". He said this "deception" was dangerous because Americans don't expect liberals to be "authoritarian wolves in sheep's clothing" because liberals are supposed to be the "good guys" and the guardians of American values like free speech. He stated it was no longer "liberalism". It now should be called "illiberalism". I call it "progressivism".

Here is a different version of the rationalization trait. I see this frequently on television. This version is when liberal actions or inactions are justified to a fault. Liberals will stick to their position even in the face of overwhelming evidence to the contrary. The net outcome is to defend their position without any adherence to pragmatic or factual reasoning. I never know if the person is being dishonest on purpose to justify their position or is just being reckless with the truth. This is another liberal trait in which I see significant variation in intensity depending upon the individual. It is amazing to me how these liberals stick to their point with the same argument even in the face of specific indisputable contrary information by those in opposition. Sometimes the liberal will change the original justification for their position when the opposing position becomes too overwhelming. I have even seen the liberal's new justification actually contradict their old one and then deny it is a contradiction. I just sit there in amazement.

The next trait is inordinate ideological bias. It is related to the trait of idealism versus pragmatism and involves focusing on selected facts or information to express and support a liberal ideological position when a pragmatic focus would tell a different story and be contrary to the position taken. This trait is not one of dishonesty or ill intent but reflects the unwavering commitment to his or her ideology and resulting blindness to pragmatic reality. It is the ultimate case of "don't confuse me with the facts".

I observe this trait on a constant basis. My wife and I observed numerous examples as we watched the George Zimmerman trial on television. It is amazing how one can get hooked on something as monotonous as a trial. While much of the formality and witness testimony can get tedious and boring, there is an element of strategy and cleverness between the prosecution and defense in presenting their cases that can be fascinating. Recording and fast-forwarding through the trial can take care of most of the boring. As you know the Zimmerman trial was a major event in the news media and was covered live on television in it's entirely by CNN/ Headline News and covered regularly during the day by Fox News. Each television news service had lawyers and experts give their opinions throughout the day and evening. My wife and I sat in astonishment on a consistent basis wondering if we were watching the same trial as many of the lawyers and experts. We were always in lockstep with our opinions.

I understand it is not uncommon for individuals to mentally see the same situation differently but the differences in opinions we heard on television were startling. It was obvious that some lawyers and experts, both liberal and conservative, were pontificating regarding the trial without doing their homework. It was also obvious the liberal lawyers and experts were expressing inordinate liberal bias whether they had done their homework or not. Those watching would have never known about this bias unless they actually watched the trial unfold as we did.

We saw sloppy interview preparation on the part of some conservative lawyers but not political bias. Unfortunately, this liberal bias occurs in mainstream news on a regular basis.

I observed two examples of this trait on the same day in the editorial section of my local newspaper. A national columnist wrote an editorial regarding the mistreatment of Native Americans and the lasting affect this mistreatment has had upon them. I agreed with many things he said until I read where he blamed their poverty and alcoholism on "our long history of brutalizing" them. I don't disagree that our government has done things in the past that have caused problems for Native Americans but what the columnist described was not the reason for their current plight. The true reasons were nowhere to be found in his editorial because it did not fit his liberal ideology.

I happen to have first-hand knowledge regarding this issue and have researched pertinent information as well. Before I retired, my organization obtained a preferred contract with the Rosebud Indian Reservation in South Dakota to provide cardiac surgery to their tribal members. I met and became friends with some wonderful Native Americans who were very devoted to their people and to solving their tribe's problems. As our organization's CEO, I even attended an honest to goodness powwow. I have to admit that we sat around a large conference table at a remote resort rather than sitting around a fire in a remote camp smoking a pipe. The later would have been a lot more exotic but even sitting at this conference table was a great experience and one that I will never forget. This powwow was a business meeting consisting of tribal leaders from several states and representatives from the Indian Health Services, which administered the contract. After a couple of years, we cancelled the contract because the government regulations involved with it were so onerous. The cost and hassle of the record keeping and audit requirements were not worth it. We did continue to provide cardiac surgery and other medical services without a contract.

During this experience with Rosebud, I visited the reservation two or three times and personally observed the problems of alcoholism and abject poverty mentioned in the editorial. These two problems are a reality even though the government provides them with a great deal of money. I am also aware of a Native American tribe in North Carolina called the Lumbee tribe that has never received any government money. Congress never recognized the Lumbees as a sovereign nation; therefore, they never had a treaty with the U.S. government. That tribe is self-sufficient and does not have the social and economic issues I saw at Rosebud. Why? The absence of receiving government handouts and government oversight creates a culture of self-reliance and responsibility that prevents the problems that are prevalent at Rosebud. This concept does not only apply to Native Americans, as we will discuss later.

The information I just articulated is nowhere in the columnist's editorial. If he had taken the time and effort to do his homework, he would have discovered the same information I presented regarding the Lumbees. It isn't hard to do. The columnist apparently didn't research tribes like the Seminole tribe in Florida either. My local newspaper reported they made $2.4 billion last year through their business ventures. I do not want to diminish problems experienced by Native Americans but the editorial was obviously written to intentionally express and promote a liberal biased opinion regardless of the facts.

The other example in the editorial section was a political cartoon by a national cartoonist that is actually worse. One has to do some digging to discover the story of the Lumbee tribe and the Seminole story was probably only reported in Florida. This political cartoon was a criticism of Supreme Court Justice Antonin Scalia before he died regarding the decision by the Supreme Court on the Voting Rights Act of 1965 that was widely reported in the news. No digging is necessary to get a full and accurate story on this one.

The cartoon shows Justice Scalia tearing up the act indicating that the act was totally abolished which is not true. What the Supreme Court did was to get rid of the section of the act that required nine states to get permission from the Department of Justice (DOJ) in order to change their voting laws because of past discrimination practices. These discrimination practices took place almost 50 years ago. The Supreme Court made their decision after reviewing historical voting statistics in the effected states, which showed that section was no longer needed. If you looked at the cartoon as well as liberal news stories on the topic, one would think the entire law was abolished and this was a huge step backwards in equal rights. The cartoon as well as many mainstream news stories pushed the points that reflected liberal ideology at the expense of the real and accurate story.

Are liberals in these situations being dishonest? A good case study to answer that question would be the Senate Intelligence Committee report on the CIA interrogations. Does that report reflect honest or dishonest inordinate ideological bias? It is probably both, depending upon the individual involved. I believe this trait for the vast majority of liberals is not one of dishonesty or ill intent but reflects the intense commitment to his or her ideology and the resulting lack of objectively by not taking into account contrary information. Progressive liberals are a different matter. They routinely deal in dishonesty. You will read about their dishonest behavior throughout the book. I hear on a regular basis this trait is also a common conservative core personality trait. One can find examples on an isolated basis but that is not true on a universal basis. This trait is actually a very important distinction between liberals and conservatives and the impact of that distinction on American politics is significant. We will look at the conservative side of this behavior in the next chapter.

Inordinate ideological bias is continually seen during election campaigning, congressional hearings, daily news interviews, and television Sunday talk shows. The Democratic Party must routinely distribute talking points. I am amazed and impressed by how all liberals are in lockstep with the Democratic Party on political issues and routinely talk the "party line". It is quite remarkable. Obama's falling popularity created an easing of inordinate ideological bias during the last mid-term elections but it has now returned in full force. I always comment, "Well, they got the memo!" Considering the liberals' past political success with this behavior, I often think republicans should learn from it and copy it. Every time, though, I recant on that thought. I will explain why in the next chapter.

Have you also noticed what happens when a liberal strays from "the memo"? I have seen liberals, especially liberal politicians, routinely get back in line rather quickly. I assume they were taken to the preverbal woodshed. You can ask New Jersey Senator Robert Menendez about that woodshed. He came under investigation in 2013 by the Justice Department for illegal transactions between himself and a Florida ophthalmologist. He was the top Democrat on the Senate's Foreign Relation's Committee and has been an outspoken critic of the Obama administration's approach to Iran's nuclear program and the normalization of relations with Cuba.

The Justice Department indicted Menendez in April of last year after their investigation. It appears the charges against him could have merit but there have been several congressmen in the past who were probably guilty of similar or worse charges and nothing happened to them. The charges are shoved under the rug for "loyal soldiers". It is interesting that Menendez was charged before Attorney General Eric Holder left the Justice Department and after he opposed Obama's Cuban and Iranian policies. A coincidence? It appears politically suspicious to me.

An editorial by the editorial board of The Wall Street Journal and other pundits have indicated they think so as well. Joe Scarborough, of MSNBC's *Morning Joe*, asked why other politicians like Bill and Hillary Clinton were not held to the same standard. He referred to the book *Clinton Cash* and the $150 million reportedly received by their foundation over the last decade from contacts they made during public service. More about that later.

One of the core personality traits I routinely observe when liberals are interviewed about politics is denial. Denial results in divert and switch tactics involving situations where liberals are asked a legitimate question and an accurate direct answer would be unfavorable to liberal political leaders, the position of the Democratic Party, or liberal ideology. Instead of answering the question directly, they divert any negativity away from the issue in question by giving an answer that has no bearing on the question asked.

Here is an example I witnessed on television. A liberal was asked if Egyptian Prime Minister Hosni Mubarak's ouster during the Arab Spring uprising could result in potential implications for Israel and the Middle East and should the United States government have supported Mubarak to preserve stability in the region? The liberal answered by saying Mubarak's ouster was a great example of democracy in action to end dictatorial suppression. Obviously, the answer had no relation to the question. When asked the same question again with stronger emphasis on what the United States should have done, the liberal gave give the exact same answer. The answer given is usually in relation to the question but not a direct answer to the question.

Speaking of the Arab Spring, there was a political cartoon in my local newspaper that depicted it well. There were two pictures. The first picture was titled "The Arab Spring" and depicted a bird's nest on a tree limb with three eggs. One egg was labeled FREEDOM. The second egg was labeled EQUALITY. The third egg was labeled FRATERNITY. The second picture was titled "Years Later" and depicted three vultures on a tree limb. The first vulture was labeled TERROR. The second vulture was labeled WAR. The third vulture was labeled DESPOTISM. That doesn't sound much different from transitioning our traditional American culture to a progressive dominated culture. More about that in chapter 4.

I observed this next example while I was watching one of Megyn Kelly's shows on Fox News. Actually, this story portrays multiple traits we have covered in this chapter. The story concerns an interview she did with a conservative and a liberal who was considerably left of the political center and most likely was a progressive. The conservative heads up an organization that supports military veterans. The liberal owns a consulting firm and has worked with Bill and Hillary Clinton. The interview was about Obama's commencement address at West Point when he defended his position on foreign policy. There was significant negative response regarding Obama's commencement speech by both conservative and liberal news media and political pundits on both sides of politics. The liberal news media included The New York Times and The Washington Post, which was a pleasant surprise.

Videotapes were shown of the polite reception Obama got from the West Point Cadets versus the strong standing ovation that George W. Bush got in 2008 when he gave his address. Megyn asked the two guests about the criticism Obama got from the pundits and the news media. Not surprisingly, there was robust debate between the conservative and the liberal. The liberal said anyone who thinks this criticism from liberals is shocking is listening to Rush Limbaugh. In response, the show played a video of Limbaugh's criticism of the speech that showed otherwise.

The liberal said liberal newspapers like the Times and the Post have always been against many of Obama's approaches to foreign policy (really?) and gave drone strikes as an example. He went on to say that our current foreign policy problems, including al Qaeda's rise in the world, go back to the Bush era. The liberal would have to be living on a different planet to provide the responses he did unless he was using the tactic of divert and switch. He never did answer the question regarding Obama's speech. I guess he felt that after his other comments he had avoided that issue.

The conservative pushed back hard in countering the liberal's statements and the liberal's rebuttal to the conservative rudely accused the conservative of showing political bias. The liberal's rebuttal also contained comments that appeared to be critical of the conservative's experience as a military veteran. Megyn took a strong stance with the liberal saying the conservative was a decorated war veteran and the liberal should respect him as such.

The liberal said he respected the conservative as a veteran but again pushed hard saying he does not respect his partisan rhetoric. The liberal forcefully went on and on about how bad foreign policy was under Bush and how great it is under Obama. It was one of, if not the most, egregious cases of hypocrisy I have ever seen. I wish I were able to portray in writing the degree of intensity, resolve, and absolute falsehood that I witnessed in the liberal's divert and switch practices. He was totally clueless he was being so intensely hypocritical. Or, was he? It was classic.

Here is an example of denial and divert and switch by the liberal news media. When liberal newscaster Brian Williams was caught lying about some of his experiences as a reporter, he was suspended for six months. He was basically fired as the NBC nightly news anchor. The liberal news media defended Williams by divert and switch. They suddenly accused Fox's Bill O'Reilly of several instances of exaggerated and incorrect news reporting as far back as the early eighties. What Williams did in the past has absolutely nothing to do with Bill O'Reilly. I assume they chose O'Reilly as their divert and switch target because O'Reilly hosts the number one conservative talk show on television and Williams' news show was number one in mainstream news—tit-for-tat. O'Reilly denied the accusations against him. Williams did not.

Even if O'Reilly did lie, it has no bearing on Williams lying. Any lies by O'Reilly do not excuse Williams behavior or promote that "everyone does it" so it's OK. Classic divert and switch. It was announced that Williams is now a "breaking news" anchor in an effort to help MSNBC improve its ratings. He has got a tough job ahead.

Here is an example of liberal denial using divert and switch that exposes an assault by your president on your pocketbook as a taxpaying American. It involves "so-and-so did it too" as with Williams and O'Reilly. I heard a liberal on television respond to criticism of Obama spending too much time vacationing versus spending time in Washington running the country. The liberal defended Obama by saying that he took only 131 vacation days in his first term and Bush took 1,060 vacation days in his first two terms. It is amazing that Obama had been in office for over six years when that comment was made and liberals were still using divert and switch toward Bush for a multitude of "stuff".

Let's take a hard look at Obama versus Bush regarding official travels and vacation time. Obama travels all over the country on a regular basis campaigning and raising money for democrats and the Democratic Party. He does this far more than Bush did. These days might as well be vacation days since he is not doing presidential work. He usually tacks on a public speech regarding some current issue at the fundraising location to cover for the trip but make no mistake that the purpose of the trip is political fund raising. I heard all presidents campaigned for their party while in office. Did they to the extent Obama has? The answer is no. It appears that speaking and receiving adulation in front of handpicked friendly groups is something Obama loves to do.

Most of Bush's so called vacation time was spent at his ranch in Texas and the majority of the time he was working with his cabinet members and White House staff. His time was not spent flying to elaborate vacation spots at taxpayer's expense. Let me elaborate. Bush did not spend Christmas in Hawaii every year with his family, a weekend of golf in Florida playing with campaign contributors and Tiger Woods, or summer vacations in Martha's Vineyard paid for with your tax money. Judicial Watch reported the 2014 transportation expenses for the Obamas' Hawaiian Christmas was $7.8 million and their vacation trip to Martha's Vineyard was $2.8 million. That does not include lodging, food and other expenses, which are significant. Judicial Watch recently obtained information that showed accommodation expenses for Secret Service personnel for Obama's Christmas in Honolulu and his vacation in Martha's Vineyard totaled $1, 243, 057. Judicial Watch also reported the Secret Service earned an "Animal House reputation at Martha's Vineyard for wild parties, fights, and late-night carousing".

In December of 2014, Judicial Watch finally obtained all the expenses for the 17 day 2013 Christmas trip to Hawaii through their Freedom of Information Act (FOIA) requests. The total cost was $8,098,060. The 2015 Christmas flight expenses were $3,590,313 according to what Judicial Watch obtained from the Air Force. Obama went on Air Force One and the First Lady went on another very nicely appointed government plane that is the equivalent of a Boeing 757 routinely used by First Ladies, members of the cabinet, and Congress. Did you ever get a "thank you note" from the Obamas for the Christmas gifts you have given them? I didn't either. They took a second plane in addition to Air Force One to Argentina in March of this year so they could use the second plane for sightseeing. I wonder how much that cost us? The Washington Free Beacon said the two-day trip to Argentina cost $1.4 million. Did that include the second plane?

It was reported that Obama paid his own green fees when he played golf with Tiger Woods in Florida; therefore, the golf trip only cost us about $1 million for transportation and security. That's a pretty good deal for the president. That trip was about two weeks before sequestration began and he is out of Washington playing golf on taxpayer's money (except for green fees). How many million-dollar weekends of golf have you played?

In 2013 it was announced that Obama and his family were going on a trip to Africa, including a safari, at a cost estimated to be between $60 million and $100 million. It was touted that the "investment in the trip" would provide a significant return to the United States economy. If anyone believes that, I have a very nice bridge to sell at a bargain price. Could it be that Obama wanted to return to his roots where his father and his father's family are from and bask in the glory of visiting as President of the United States? Obama and his family did not do the safari so they didn't make it to Kenya. I guess public outrage regarding the safari got to his or someone's better judgment. I think the $60 million to $100 million-expense figure still stands.

He finally made it to Kenya in July of last year for his homecoming trip. The flight time alone was reported at 29 hours for a total cost of $6 million. That does not include the cost for personal expenses and security expenses. I read in multiple sources that security for this trip was the most difficult thus far in Obama's presidency because of the presence of the terrorist group al-Shabab, which pretty much has its way in that country. How much more did that cost for security versus normal security costs? How about the significant implications regarding the President of the United States being in an unusually risky situation when it was not necessary?

A report by Judicial Watch said in 2013, when the Obamas were in Belfast for the G8 Summit, Michelle took a side trip to Dublin. She and her entourage booked 30 rooms at the five-star Shelbourne Hotel. Michelle stayed in the 1,500 square foot Princess Grace suite at a cost of $3,500 per night. The total cost to taxpayers for the entire trip to Ireland was reported to be $8 million. This report did not specify if that number included all expenses incurred or was just only transportation expenses. The Obamas don't always get to travel together. Another Judicial Watch report said that while Obama had to go to California last February to play golf, speak at a cyber-security summit, and headline a Democratic Party fundraiser; Michelle and the kids spent Valentine's Day weekend skiing in Aspen, Colorado. That Aspen trip cost you $57,100 for flight expenses on a Gulfstream jet. That does not include the costs of Secret Service personnel, accommodations, meals, rental cars, lift tickets for skiing at Buttermilk, and other related expenses.

That isn't the only time Obama and his family could not travel together. That last Judicial Watch report I quoted also included information on Michelle's trip to China in March of 2014, which included their children and her mother. That trip costs taxpayers $362,500 in transportation costs. Judicial Watch was still waiting for their FOIA request to be answered for the total costs. I hope they are not holding their breath for that information. The Daily Caller revealed that Michelle and her family stayed in an $8,350 per night presidential suite at a Beijing hotel. I guess the suite in Dublin was too small when Michelle stayed there and she needed something a little bigger this time. Although Michelle was supposedly in China to promote her educational agenda, she and her family found ample time to visit many of China's famous sites. Nice!

This is not the only trip taken by Michelle, her daughters, and her mother at your expense. In June of last year, they traveled to London, England and Milan, Vicenza, and Venice in Italy. Judicial Watch reported flight expenses on this trip to be $240,500. As before, the government has not responded to their FOIA request for all the additional expenses that were incurred. Michelle was on official business to talk about her educational and food programs and again they fortunately found time to visit popular tourist sites. How lucky! Venice is one of my wife's and my favorite places to visit. Michelle was even fortunate enough to have afternoon tea with Prince Harry at Kingston Palace while she was in London.

A recent 2015 Obama travel report by Judicial Watch showed a golf outing in Palm Springs in June, a trip with his children in July to New York, and his family vacation to Martha's Vineyard in August totaled $3,115,688 for transportation only. They have not been able to find out all the other expenses. The trip to New York for one day to "hang out" with his daughters and their friends and go to a Broadway play cost you $309,505 for travel.

Here is a Judicial Watch report on one of Obama's latest trips. The White House touted Obama's visit to Eugene, Oregon in October 2015 to spend a couple of hours with the families of those killed at Umpqua Community College. Obama was frugal on this trip. He was also able to spend time with "his family" in the Rancho Santa Fe resort community in San Diego and go to not one but two fundraisers for the Democratic Party in Los Angeles. They must have been real glad to see him at those fundraisers. At least one of them cost $33,400 per person. With all this activity, he was reportedly still able to play several rounds of golf at Rancho Santa Fe. Whew! What a president has to go through. All of this on one trip for only $2,001,468 in known flight costs. We do not know the other expenses because they are a mystery. How crass for the White House to tout Obama's trip to Oregon as a trip to visit the victims' families when Oregon was basically a "side trip"!

Judicial Watch said, as of May 2016, the "known" travel expenses for all Obama travel was $74,124,562. I wonder what the total cost would be counting all expenses including personal expenses, non-security and security staff cost, flying the presidential state car, etc.? I am sure that $74 million number is only the proverbial tip of the iceberg. I enjoyed and agreed totally with a quote I read by Judicial Watch President Tom Fitton. He said, "Taxpayers are being gouged by President Obama for unnecessary travel for political fundraising and vacations. Mr. Obama seems to confuse Air Force One with Uber."

How do you feel about Obama's lavish expenditures on himself and his family while so many Americans are struggling through tough economic times? Robert Grey gave us an interesting thought in his book titled *Presidential Perks Gone Royal* written in 2012. He wrote the British taxpayers paid $57.8 million in 2011 to maintain its royal family but in the same year it cost American taxpayers $1.4 billion to house and serve the Obamas, their friends, and visiting campaign contributors in the White House.

A report released by the conservative based National Taxpayers Union showed the number of trips and time spent out of the country by Obama are comparable to Bush and Clinton and about double that of Reagan during the same time period during their presidencies. I read they are going to do a similar study for First Ladies. The number of foreign trips by Obama and Bush might be comparable but the presidential lifestyle of Obama and his family is not the presidential lifestyle of Bush and his family as it was purported to be by liberal pundits making the comparison that "Bush did it too". Most importantly, what others might have done or might not have done does not excuse one's own behavior.

I elaborated considerably here to make a simple point but I also want to use this elaboration to begin making a much bigger and much more important point that will continually unfold as you read. I believe Obama does not carry out his presidential responsibilities in a manner that is in the best interest of the country but rather in a manner that actualizes his personal dreams and aspirations. That is a very strong statement but I believe after you read this book you will agree, if you don't agree already.

Here is one last story on Obama's lifestyle as president. In researching the cost to tax payers for Obama's family vacations to Martha's Vineyard for the past several years, I found a website that detailed the cost for 2014. The White House rented 12 houses on the island for a cost of $3 million per day. Cirque du Soleil gave a $125 million private performance and the Disney Corporation constructed a $4 billion miniature Disneyland for the children. Michelle hired a team of artists to paint portraits of the family and paid each of them a retainer of $500,000 per week. Most of the costs for the vacation were for security measures to protect the president. For example, 78,000 Secret Service agents protected the president at a cost of $1.2 billion per day. One aircraft carrier and 28 other ships were stationed of the coast to guard the island. Forty-three new jets were ordered for the mission at a cost of $145 million each. After Obama's vacation was over, the jets were dumped into the ocean. The total cost of Obama's vacation to American taxpayers was $37 billion. After intense grueling by reporters regarding the costs, the White House Press Secretary said, "We understand that some of these expenses may seem unnecessary but can we really put a price on Barack Obama's comfort and piece of mind?" My source for this information is The Daily Caller. OK, This is political satire and not really true. It just feels like it when I see what the president and Congress spends using our hard-earned tax money so easily and irresponsibly.

That concludes my review of liberal core personality traits that compose liberal mental being. This review was not exhaustive but will give us a background with which to proceed in identifying liberal beliefs (ideology) and resulting behaviors. As we proceed, remember that a liberal's intensity of conviction in ideology and their resulting behavior is proportionate to where they reside on the liberal scale from just left of center to far left.

One of, if not the most, compelling liberal ideologies is social justice, also known as collectivism. This ideology supports everyone in society having a certain minimum standard of living regarding such things as income, living conditions, material goods, education, and healthcare. If individuals don't obtain that standard on their own, then liberal ideology supports providing that standard through various forms of income redistribution. Government is the most dominate agent in implementing social justice to achieve social and economic reform by imposing significant taxes on the so-called rich and heavy taxes on business. I find it interesting that the minimum categorization of "rich" changes to a lower income level, as more taxes are needed to support income redistribution practices. That's done in lieu of controlling or curtailing those practices. I refer you back to my previous comments regarding liberal intensity to achieve liberal beliefs even in light of the negative pragmatic consequences.

In addition to income taxes, there are sales taxes and many hidden taxes and fees as a result of government regulations and laws that go into the government coffers to support income redistribution programs. These taxes are referred to as regressive taxes and collectively take income from everyone no matter what her or his socioeconomic position including the people they are financially helping. These taxes are a liberal oxymoron. Income redistribution is one of the most intrusive and failed liberal ideologies in our society and will be addressed extensively in later chapters.

A different aspect of social justice that is becoming more dominant in our society is political correctness. When the beliefs and behaviors of minority groups conflict with the majority, minority beliefs and behaviors are increasingly recognized and honored by the liberal community regardless of the outcome or infringement on the majority. This is a great hypocrisy! Instead of being income redistribution, it is beliefs and behaviors redistribution. A friend sent me a cartoon called Libtards with Linus and Lucy that is a "take off" on Charlie Brown. Lucy says, "Republicans are racist, sexist, homophobic, gun-toting religious fanatics." Linus says, "But you support Muslims, who are racist, sexist, homophobic, gun-toting religious fanatics." Lucy gets mad and responds, "That's their culture. You have no right to judge them." Enough said!

The far left progressives are the biggest culprits in driving this hypocrisy but it is increasingly becoming more pervasive throughout the entire liberal community. A great example is the onslaught against religious freedom in our schools and public places. It used to include Santa Claus, Christmas trees, nativity scenes, and prayer. Now, they are going after the Easter Bunny. Look out Tooth Fairy! They just might find something against you too. Recently, prayer at government meetings and college graduations has been attacked. The American flag will probably be next. Actually, there are already rumblings. This is such a growing and serious issue for our American society; I have devoted an entire chapter to it.

We can never ignore liberal ideology regarding environmentalism better known as climate change. This ideology takes the well-being of the environment to the extreme resulting in the onslaught of traditional energy sources, family income, economic growth, and personal freedom. It has created a significant liberal political movement to support non-traditional energy sources such as wind power, solar power, and battery power over the use of traditional fuels like coal, natural gas, and gasoline. There is also a push against nuclear power. Although great strides have been made, these alternative technologies are not yet cost effective or practical to significantly replace traditional energy sources. I agree with funding research to develop these and other alternative energy sources to replace traditional energy but they should not be "shoved down our throats" in a way that is not practical or cost effective. This is putting the cart before the horse. Or maybe I should say, "It's putting the battery before the dinosaur." You might have to think about that one for a second.

Federal laws and regulations to curtail the use of traditional energy add great expense to our family energy costs and the products we buy and stifles economic growth. In some cases, it appears to be more of an act of tax and control rather than an act of curtailment. For instance, in chapter 8 we will look at the enormous negative impact of cap and trade legislation and the financial windfall that would be obtained by the federal government and certain private individuals. Regulations like cap and trade not only add significant costs to our lives, they are extremely restrictive toward our personal freedom.

Liberal environmentalism champions the theory moralized by liberal scientists that environmental pollution caused by man is the major contributor to global warming and climate change. Scientists, in all honesty, have no idea regarding the true impact environmental pollution has on the environment. There are many liberal scientists who have claimed they have proof of global warming but were found to be lying and fabricating their data. Didn't these scientists study the ice age in school or the constant periods of change the Earth and its atmosphere have gone through over millions and billions of years? Do you know how old the Earth is? It is estimated to be 4.54 +/- 0.05 billion years old. How can scientists be that precise? Supposedly, they can date fossils. It is certainly over my head.

Here is something else over my head. Do you know what the Paleocene-Eocene Thermal Maximum (PETM) is? I didn't, until I looked it up. And, in all honesty, I'm still not sure but here is the explanation I read in Wikipedia. The PETM refers to a climate event at the temporal boundary between the Paleocene and Eocene epochs. Are you following me? Hang on! The absolute age and duration of the event remain uncertain but are thought to be close to 55.8 million years ago and lasted for 170,000 years. The PETM has become a focal point of considerable geoscience research because it provides our best past analog to understand the impacts of global warming and massive carbon input into the ocean and atmosphere, including ocean acidification. It is estimated that there was a temperature rise of 41 degrees Fahrenheit and extreme changes in the Earth's carbon cycle during this period. Here comes the best part of what I read and it is something I do understand. It is now widely accepted that the PETM represents a case study for global warming and massive carbon input to the Earth's surface but the cause, details, and overall significance of the event "remain perplexing".

I saw a reference to the PETM on a website called livescience.com. They acknowledged the PETM as the most significant period of global warming in history but then said our current global warming event that started during the Quaternary Period of the Cenozoic Era (65.5 million years ago until now) is caused by human activity. How is that possible when is it accepted science that humans only began on Earth between 2.5 and 3.2 million years ago? These scientists sure use a lot of big words for a simple hillbilly like me. I often wonder if they even understand themselves what they are saying when I see all the gobbledygook and contradictions they report.

Never confuse these climate scientists with facts. I think facts frustrate them. At least some of the newspapers I read, present this stuff in a much simpler way. Here are some of the local headlines I have read: NASA, NOAA: 2014 warmest year ever measured (How about PETM or the Cenozoic Era?); Climate change could threaten half of North American bird species (That's concerning because the birds in Florida are beautiful.); Study blames global warming for 75 percent of very hot days (It does get very hot and humid in Florida.); Carbon dioxide at "disturbing," "daunting" high level (Does that scare you?); and Atomic scientists: Warming puts Earth closer to doom (If the last headline didn't scare you, I am sure this one did.).

Here are some simple unscientific and interesting stories that contradict the climate change "silliness" expounded by these liberal progressive so called climate experts. Do you ever read *Ask Marilyn* in Parade magazine in the Sunday newspaper? She said a team of researchers reported that the increase in the human population and the resulting demands for drinking water, irrigation of crops, etc. could account for as much as 42% of the rise in the oceans as water is pumped from our underground aquifers. She said much of this water evaporates or runs off into our rivers and winds up in the oceans; therefore, only about half of the oceans' rise results from warmer water. That might be a stretch but is certainly interesting.

This second story appeared in my Naples, Florida newspaper. The newspaper said, during the Cenozoic Era (See how knowledgeable you are now, after reading the above.), Florida was nothing but a limestone outcropping of the mainland that was almost completely submerged by water. The article said this shallow water sanctuary was perfect habitat for marine life of all kinds including 50-foot megalodon sharks. We get our share of shark bites in Florida but a megalodon bite would be a "gulp". The climate scientists of today say Florida is going to be under water again. I wonder if that includes the return of magalodons. I certainly hope not.

The last one I want to share with you is an op-ed by Matt Ridley in The Wall Street Journal. The headline said, "Whatever Happened to Global Warming?" His op-ed was in response to the 2014 United Nations (U.N.) meeting of world leaders in New York City to pledge urgent action against climate change. Many leaders did not show up but our leader, Obama, did. The last sentence in the op-ed addressed Ridley's skepticism about global warming. He said, "Let's hope that the

U.N. admits to as much on day one of its coming jamboree and asks the delegates to pack up, go home, and work on more pressing global problems like war, terror, disease, poverty, habitat loss, and the 1.3 billion people with no electricity." I have to add that he is a member of the British House of Lords and the author of the book titled *The Rational Optimist*. Rational he is! Obama was not so rational in his speech at the conference.

I guess these genius climate scientists with all of their big words and fancy statistics believe the Earth's evolution has now ceased and man has the knowledge and power to make the Earth what we want it to be. Move over God and Mother Nature. Oh, we mustn't forget where these scientists get the majority of their funds that pay for their research and their salaries—liberal progressive government grants. These scientists recently released an interim report from a climate change study mandated by Congress. Since it is getting harder to prove "global warming", we are now experiencing "climate change".

This report began in 2012 and has involved more than 250 scientists and federal government officials. The following is a synopsis of what the interim report says. The nation's average temperature has risen as much as 1.9 degrees since record keeping began in 1895. Wow! This is a time period of one hundred and twenty years out of millions and billions of years of Earth climate history. It gets better. The report also says that extreme weather such as droughts, storms, and heat waves can be "seen with our own eyes". I wonder if cave men and women could see them too?

The report got even better. It says winter storms have increased in frequency and intensity and shifted northward since the 1950s, heavy downpours are increasing by over 70 percent in the Northeast, heat waves are going to intensify, and droughts are going to get stronger in the Southwest. Sounds like these scientists could get a job on television as weather forecasters, if their day jobs don't work out. The report concludes that these events will result in "assorted harms" across the country throughout this century and beyond. It actually said, "Global warming is rapidly turning America the beautiful into America the stormy, sneezy, and dangerous."

Are you shaking in your boots yet? Well, just hold on, there's more. We will experience smoke filled air from wildfires, smoggy air from pollution, a longer pollen season, and more diseases from tainted food, water, mosquitoes, and ticks. Those vicious ticks! We are practically all going to die before our time just like the dinosaurs. I wonder what they will call our extinct civilization? Maybe they will call us the "climatesaurs". Wait! We can be OK, if we act now, says the 840-page report. White House Science Czar, John Holdren, commented that we have many opportunities to take cost-effective actions to reduce the damage. Is that statement an oxymoron! If you want to learn about wacko progressivism, just read some of the things Holdren has said and written. Actually, you will in chapter 5.

The climate report indicates the sea level has risen eight inches since 1880 and is projected to rise between one foot and four feet by the year 2100. Let's get out our calculators. The sea level has risen eight inches in one hundred and thirty-four years and these scientists project it to rise one to four feet in eighty-six years. I'll let you figure that one out. I can't, even if I were to believe in global warming. Maybe they should ask Marilyn. If their projections are accurate, it is a wonderful opportunity for me. I live four miles from the ocean on a golf course. My house is four and one-half feet above sea level. See what that means? I will have beachfront property on a golf course. Can you imagine what my property will be worth then! Shucks, I got so excited that I forgot my age. I am now 71 years old. Add 86 years to my age and that makes me 157 years old. No way my wife or I can live that long. Wait! We have Obamacare for our health and longevity. Darn, on second thought, not even Obamacare can give us that kind of longevity.

Here is bit of information to share with you in relation to this ridiculous report. About the time the report came out there was a fascinating anthropological discovery by a team of 16 anthropologist, geneticists, and cave divers that has significant bearing on the report's assertions. Scientists discovered the human skeleton of a female believed to be 12,000 years old in a cave that was more than 140 feet under water. Why is that important? The scientists said this person was a hunter-gatherer who was crossing the bearing strait from Russia to America 12,000 years ago before the rise in sea level when the glaciers melted. I wonder what man-made pollutants they had 12,000 years ago polluting the atmosphere that would cause climate change and the rise in the oceans due to melting glaciers? They certainly didn't have automobiles, coal fired electrical plants, or pollutant spewing manufacturing plants. Maybe if they keep searching that cave, they will find an interim climate change report inscribed on the wall that will enlighten us to the answer.

Maybe that is not necessary. After I wrote the above, I received a climate change report from a friend that was reported by the Associated Press (AP) and published in The Washington Post. The article said the Arctic Ocean is warming up, icebergs are growing scarcer and in some places the seals are finding the water too hot, according to a report to the Commerce Department yesterday from the American Consulate, at Bergan, Norway. Reports from fisherman, seal hunters and explorers all point to radical change in climate conditions and hitherto unheard-of temperatures in the Arctic Zone. Exploration expeditions report that scarcely any ice has been met as far as 81 degrees 29 minutes.

Soundings to a depth of 3,100 meters showed the Gulf Stream still very warm. Great masses of ice have been replaced by moraines of earth and stones, the report continued, while at many points well known glaciers have entirely disappeared. Very few seals and no white fish are found in the eastern Arctic, while vast shoals of herring and smelts which have never before ventured so far north, are being encountered in the old seal fishing grounds. Within a few years, it is predicted that due to the ice melt the sea will rise and make most coastal cities inhabitable. This report was published on November 2, 1922. That is 93 years ago. I don't know why these people go to so much trouble to develop new reports. Why don't they just combine them all into one and change the date as time moves on.

A December 2014 syndicated news article by The Washington Post cited a study based upon 24 ocean expeditions between 2007 and 2013 that said, "Thanks to humans, there are now over 5 trillion pieces of plastic, weighing more than 250,000 tons, floating in water around the world." I wonder how the expeditions counted all that plastic. Can you imagine how much time it took and how far and wide they had to travel to ensure the accuracy of their report? I will say this. The people who do these studies and write these reports are certainly dedicated to their liberal environmental ideology to a "fault"—so to speak.

No one loves the environment more than I do and I strongly believe that we should make every "reasonable" (emphasis on reasonable) effort to curb pollution, even if no other country is willing to do so. It is our moral responsibility to the Earth and our fellow man. I retired to one of the most environmentally rich places on Earth and it is absolutely beautiful. Our place of retirement was chosen for that reason and for the wonderful people who live here. I currently serve on a committee that develops policy for an environmental organization. The organization's purpose is environmental education and to take actions including legal action to balance economic growth and the environment. Our organization takes a very practical and responsible approach and our efforts have been very successful.

A balanced approach is in contrast with and is more effective than a situation in the community from which I moved. Land values were highly inflated because the only land available for development without the city building significant infrastructure to accommodate new growth could not be developed because of a beetle. Yes, a beetle. These little beetles were supposedly, but not proven to be, the only species of their kind in the world. How many species of beetles are there in the world? Who knows but I doubt these beetles would ever be missed or create a worldwide beetle crisis if they became extinct. I understand and support drawing the line to prevent extinction of a species but come on!

Here is a pollution issue that is never talked about but is a serious problem that is real, immediate, and not some obscure theory. My wife and I toured some of the most beautiful land on Earth. We visited nine islands in the South Pacific. I was surprised and disappointed when I saw landfills on some of these gorgeous islands. But, what are they to do? I also saw a lot of households burning trash in their yards. Which is worse? I think landfills are worse but that gets back to the issue of polluting the atmosphere. Every time I empty the garbage, I wonder how much longer we can keep infusing all this trash in our earth and covering it up. I'm proud to say that my recycling can is bigger and much much more full than my trash can that has contents headed to the landfill. That makes me feel somewhat better—but! Trash disposal is something we in the United States can successfully work toward improving even if no other country does. Why don't scientists and government officials who are so concerned about the Earth's environment spend time studying and resolving this real and immediate issue instead of wasting time and our money chasing a "wild goose"? We will catch that "wild goose" and see what the progressives are really up to in chapter 8.

No one can argue that reasonable efforts should be made in our country to curtail atmospheric pollution, even if it is not the cause of global warming or global climate change. But, how about the other industrialized countries that pollute the atmosphere and give only false rhetoric regarding their efforts to address the problem? Obama and China made a joint announcement in 2014 that the United States would reduce carbon emissions between 26% and 28% from 2005 levels by the year 2025 and that China would peak its emissions by 2030 and get 20% of its power from non-fossil fuel by then as well. Let's take a quick look at those numbers. China emits roughly 23% of the world's carbon emissions, the United States 15%, India 6%, Russia 5%, Brazil 4%, and Japan 4%. All other countries emit the rest, which is roughly 1% to 2% each or 43%. I estimate that carbon admissions in the United States have decreased 10% to 12% since 2005 based upon what I found on the Internet. That would require us to decrease admissions by another 16% to 18% to meet Obama's goal.

Let's say China actually reduced their fossil fuel emissions by 20% and, for simplicity, let's ignore the fact the time periods for the U.S. and China goals are 5 years apart and assume China will continue increasing its pollution between now and 2030. Simple math would produce the following results. Actually, if someone believes that China will even follow through on their commitment, I have some more incredible bridges for sale—cheap! OK, here are the results. This agreement between Obama and China will reduce the world's carbon emissions at best by a total of 7% and that is assuming no other countries increase their emissions. The agreement is nothing more than political hype and potential smoke and mirrors for Obama and his political cohorts to push more regulations on us including cap and trade.

An economist with The Heritage Foundation named Stephen Moore, who I like very much, said it simply and succinctly. In November 2014, he wrote an article in The Daily Signal. He commented, "That sound you are hearing from across the Pacific is the Chinese rulers and

Beijing laughing at us. This is not a planet-saving climate-change pact. Rather, this plan represents unilateral economic disarmament by the United States as Beijing continues its quest to replace America as the globe's economic superpower." He also said the economic costs and loss of jobs would be extraordinary if we abide by the agreement.

Decreasing pollution in the Earth's atmosphere can only happen when all the world polluters honestly and effectively address the problem. This is not going to happen. A December 2015 article in The Wall Street Journal reported in response to future energy needs that the Philippines is going to double their number of coal-fired plants as is Vietnam. Manila will become the world's most dependent country on coal. Indonesia wants to expand their number of coal-fired plants. Japan is building dozens of new coal-fired plants to replace their nuclear power plants. And, our friend China recently "added" enough coal-fired capacity to power millions of homes.

Here is an excerpt I found on the White House website taken from Obama's speech at the December 2015 Paris climate conference that was a total waste of world leaders time. The conference accomplished nothing but spewing a lot of "hot political air", wasting taxpayers' dollars, and oxymoronically adding pollution to the atmosphere from jet planes flying to the conference. Obama said:

> This summer, I saw the effects of climate change firsthand in our northernmost state, Alaska, where the sea is already swallowing villages and eroding shorelines; where permafrost thaws and the tundra burns; where glaciers are melting at a pace unprecedented in modern times. And it was a preview of one possible future—a glimpse of our children's fate if the climate keeps changing faster than our efforts to address it. Submerged countries. Abandoned cities. Fields that no longer grow. Political disruptions that trigger new conflict, and even more floods of desperate peoples seeking the sanctuary of nations not their own.

What planet was Obama on? Certainly not Earth, even though he referenced Alaska. Other world leaders backed him up, especially on the comment about the impact of climate change on world peace. How embarrassing for people who are supposed to be leading the world to make such asinine comments. Here is what the world non-leaders think. According to The Daily Signal that I received in November 2015, the U.N. did a survey called "My World" to determine the issue that matters most to people around the world. Almost 9 million people responded and climate change came in "dead last". The Daily Signal also referenced a Pew Research study that reported climate change ranked 22nd out of 23 public policy priorities listed as levels of concern in the United States.

It doesn't make sense that Americans should be subjected to significant restrictions and significant costs in a hopeless and senseless effort. Liberal ideology says, "We must prevent man made climate change to save the Earth!" I will let you conjure up your own response to that one. I'm out of "whopper" bridges. This is one of my personal greatest liberal ideological pet peeves that has enormous negative implications for America. You will read more about this subject later as it relates to specific chapters. Why would liberals burden our society with massive costs and restrictions based upon fabricated theory? Liberals are honestly pursuing their beliefs. Progressive liberals are pursuing nefarious reasons that we will discuss as the book progresses.

Liberal ideology strongly supports abortion and gay rights. There are differences as to what should constitute legal abortion among liberals but no dissension against the act itself. Those much further to the left have turned a blind eye to the killing by unscrupulous physicians and medical personnel of fetuses that were born alive. Liberals support gay rights including marriage, child rearing, and any other right that is extended to heterosexual individuals. Conservatives are ideologically split on both of these issues and we will discuss those differences in the next chapter.

Liberals are purported to be more ideologically supportive of legal and illegal immigrants, minorities, and women than conservatives. This is a political ruse concocted by progressive liberals to gain votes and power and it has been a very successful strategy. These issues will be discussed extensively in later chapters.

Liberal ideology also supports significant government regulation of business to protect the people from the capitalist claws of greed and economic suppression. This is a significant issue for all Americans. It harks back to the ideological concept of collectivism. Liberal politicians support and are strongly supported by labor unions and this has noteworthy impact on liberal behavior. Ironically, there are many on Wall Street and in corporate America who vote for and contribute large sums of money to liberal candidates who oppose the free enterprise system when it is the free enterprise system that provides them with their wealth and success. I have never figured that one out. This topic will also be discussed in later chapters.

A very significant liberal ideology is our country should not practice exceptionalism. Exceptionalism is a term used to denote that our country strives for and succeeds in being wealthier, having military advantage, and more world influence than any other country on the planet. Liberals, especially progressive liberals, believe America should not strive for or experience this influence and should support globalism. Globalism is the concept that all countries should be relatively equal in wealth, military might, and worldly influence. Some far to the left believe there should be a "one world order" which means there would be one central government that would rule all countries on Earth. Exceptionalism is arguably the most important issue of the day for America as well as for the entire world. It will be discussed extensively in chapter 9 and in other chapters.

Gun control—gun control—gun control. Do you think we will ever hear the end of it? It always seems to have a life of its own and becomes a hot topic anytime a situation arises involving gun violence. Liberal ideology supports significant gun control legislation. A Rasmussen poll found that 77% of likely voters believe most politicians raise gun control issues just to get elected rather than to address real problems. The Daily Signal published a November 2014 report that supports that point. It said, according to the Federal Bureau of Investigation (FBI), murders in the United States dropped from 23,326 in 1994 to 14,196 in 2013—a decrease of 39%. The DOJ said gun-related homicides declined from 18, 253 in 1993 to 11,101 in 2012, which ironically is also a decrease of 39%. The DOJ said non-fatal gun-related crimes dropped 69% from 1993 to 2011.

The Daily Signal report raised the following question, "Where does this idea of an epidemic of rising gun violence come from?" The answer given was, "The most significant factor may be the large-scale media coverage of and public interest in mass shootings." The report said the combination of these two factors creates the illusion that an "uncommon event is happening all the time" and that violent crime is rampant. The report quoted a Pew Research poll that indicated 56% of Americans believe that violent crime or gun-related crime was up during the last 20 years. I want to clarify that gun violence has been up in some major cities as a result of the actions by progressive politicians and we will discuss the specifics in later chapters.

The report concluded that terms like "gun violence" could be deliberately manipulated to serve political agendas. It said gun control advocates frequently cite that 33,000 Americans are victims of gun violence every year when in reality two-thirds of those victims are suicides. Suicides are a very serious matter but are being used to distort the truth. The report said, "Their goal is simple: scare citizens into supporting policies that curb the sale and possession of fire arms. Some in the media are willing accomplices, exploiting their position to advance the cause of gun control." Chapter 6 looks extensively at liberal media bias.

There is strong liberal support for a ban of assault rifles and multiple-round clips. There is also liberal support for extensive universal background checks on people purchasing guns. I think most liberals would support a total ban of guns. The Second Amendment is there for a reason and I don't need to explain that reason to those that support it. There are some who say the loss of citizen gun power gives citizen control to the government. At the risk of sounding melodramatic, that is good food for thought and should be kept in mind as you read what is happening in America today and how we became America in the beginning.

This issue is not going to go away even though none of the gun control measures that have been proposed would have prevented the terrible tragedies that have been used in support of gun control legislation. There was an assault rifle ban by the federal government from 1994 to 2004 that was abandoned because it did not work. Some of the states and cities having the most comprehensive background checks have some of the worst records on gun deaths. Liberal politicians govern all of those places but mainstream news never makes that connection. Albert Einstein said, "The definition of insanity is doing the same thing over and over again and expecting different results."

All extreme gun control will do is give crooks another avenue to make money by selling guns through the black market and drive "gun-less" perpetrators to find other means to do their horrific deeds like homemade bombs or knives. The recent murder of a British lawmaker is a good example. She was shot and stabbed and gun ownership is all but forbidden in England. Bloomberg reported a study by the DOJ that said almost 40% of the prison inmates said they obtained the firearms used in their crimes from family or friends and 39% said they got their weapon from an illegal street source.

Both bombs and knives have recently been substituted for guns to kill others. For example, my local newspaper reported a fatal attack in Sweden that makes the point. A masked man, dressed in black, stabbed people with a sword at a public school. Several students were wounded and a teacher and one student died before the police killed the attacker. Until he began to stab people, the attacker was thought to be playing a Halloween prank because of the way he was dressed. How about all the murders in Israel by the Palestinians using knives? Last year, a college student stabbed four people on a California college campus. Are we going to push anti-knife legislation too? Where there's a will to kill, there's a way with these troubled people.

We should be spending our money and effort in addressing mental illness and socio-economic issues which are the real culprits of violent murders and mass shootings instead of growing government bigger to enforce gun control laws that do not work and are restrictive of our rights as citizens. It is not surprising but extremely disappointing that there hasn't been any meaningful discussion in addressing mental illness from a detection or treatment perspective in an effort to curtail violence. We now have the new issue developing involving homegrown radical

Muslim terrorism that inters into the discussion of citizens owning guns for self-protection.

It is amazing to me that the overwhelming majority of homicides in our country take place in ghetto areas of large, medium, and even small cities and absolutely nothing is being done or even discussed to curb this problem. This is a tragic circumstance and is a topic that has no traction in liberal discussion or action. I will give you my theory as to why this serious issue is not addressed by liberals or even conservatives for that matter. It is an extremely difficult problem to address and will take perseverance over decades and generations. It will take the establishment of a culture where children are cared for and loved in a non-dysfunctional home by their parents. Notice the "s" in parents that denotes a mom and a dad. It will also take the development of economic opportunity in ghetto areas for young people to overcome their seduction to crime. Most of all, it will take a significant curtailment of government entitlements to get the ball rolling. Politicians can't come to grips with this approach because of the fear of backlash and more importantly for them—votes. This applies equally to democratic and republican politicians. This is an enormous issue for our country and you will find additional discussion on minority crime and minority poverty later in the book.

Here is an interesting article I read in my local newspaper regarding homicides I thought you might find interesting. It is a story about anthropologists trying to solve a "whodunit" that dates back 430,000 years. I have to say that I trust these forensic scientists more than I trust the climate scientists. The anthropologists theorized they had discovered the first known evidence of a human murder. They found evidence of two sharp blows to the head of a Neanderthal hominid they concluded were inflicted by another human. The murdered human was found in a cave in Spain and is believed to be a male who was approximately 20 years old when he was murdered. Either a wooden spear or stone hand axe are suspected as the murder weapon.

Danielle Kurin, a forensic anthropologist at U.C. Santa Barbara was quoted as saying, "Anthropologists are always asking what makes us human and are humans inherently violent. This study contributes to that debate by suggesting intentional assault between two people has deep roots in our hominid human history." Rolf Quam, a paleoanthropologist at Binghamton University said, "One implication of the study is that murder is a very ancient human behavior."

The anthropologists commented in their study's report there was evidence of cannibalism among early humans dating back 900,000 years ago but this was the first real evidence of murder. They also said the murdered human had been buried by throwing him in a large pit with other humans. The article ended with a quote from Ignacio Martinez Mendizabal of the University of Alcala in Madrid. He said, "We believe that the intentional interpersonal violence is a behavior that accompanies humans since at least 430,000 years ago, but so does the care of sick or even the care of the dead. We have not changed much in the last half million years."

This story reminds me of a very important point that needs to be emphasized. I always find it interesting to read about life on Earth from the beginning of man through today, especially as it has existed during the last 3,000 years. The reference to "life on Earth" in an average American's mind is but a few decades, if that long. That gives him or her a very skewed perspective of the evolution of our American society in comparison to the evolution of other societies around the world or societies now extinct. The average American does not appreciate or understand how man and society have evolved and how lucky we are to be Americans. She or he do not have reference, either currently or historically, to appreciate and be thankful for our freedoms, personal safety, economic opportunity, or standard of living.

No country in the world has close to what we have in America and we did not attain any of our attributes at their expense. Yet, as we have discussed and will discuss in depth as the book unfolds, we hear loud rhetoric regarding how terrible our country is. These people do not put their rhetoric in perspective with the total accurate picture and mostly their rhetoric is just plain false. These people are self-destructing through their own behavior and don't have a clue. Unfortunately, they are taking the rest of us with them.

An op-ed by one of my favorite conservative pundits, Cal Thomas, regarding Obama's recent rhetoric on gun control sums up this issue a little more profoundly than I did. He said, "It is also another display of what is at the heart of liberalism and that is that intent trumps results. Liberals are never held accountable for their failed policies, but are praised for having the right attitude, or worthy goals. As the saying goes, the road to hell is paved with good intentions. For the left, they have built a multilane highway and the rest of us have to pay the tolls."

That concludes my personal observations and opinions on liberal core personality traits, liberal ideology and beliefs, and resulting liberal behavior. If any liberals are reading this chapter and disagree with it because it doesn't fit you, please remember what I said, "When you have seen one liberal you have seen one liberal." However, when you look at liberalism in its totality, this chapter get's it right.

CHAPTER 3

What's a Conservative?

I said in the last chapter the terms republican and conservative are commonly used interchangeably except for one significant caveat. Here is that caveat. Many republican politicians have fallen into the political trap of making decisions based upon their political future rather than their best conservative judgment. For that reason, I want to emphasize that my analysis of conservatives in this chapter relates to credible conservative politicians rather than the republican politicians who choose to protect their political rear-ends rather than support and vote for conservative values as they were elected to do. This phenomenon of selling out conservative beliefs and values to protect the politician's own interest has become more and more prevalent in the Republican Party.

Before we define who conservatives are, let's take a quick look at the origin of the Republican Party (also known as the Grand Old Party or GOP) and its founding principals. The Republican Party became the second major political party in our country as a result of the Whig Party self-destructing in 1854 and the recruitment of some members from the short-lived Free Soil Democrats. Before the Whig Party imploded, it produced four presidents and was the major party in the country in opposition to the rival Democratic Party. The Whig Party appealed to entrepreneurs and commercial farmers. It did not appeal to subsistence farmers or unskilled workers. It was founded upon the principals of congressional supremacy over the office of the president and favored modernization, banking, and economic protectionism to stimulate manufacturing.

Researching this information was a reminder to me that our economy until recent times was based upon manufacturing, whereas today, we are fast becoming an economy based on the digital age. There are politicians today in both parties who still pretend, either honestly or dishonestly, to support middle class manufacturing jobs being brought back to the United States from other countries. That's never going to happen in a serious manner unless our workers in manufacturing take a significant cut in pay and benefits. We need to slow down the outsourcing of manufacturing to other counties as much as possible and retrain workers who are willing to be retrained for non-manufacturing jobs. It is time our country embraces a digital age economy and supports it like the old Republican Party supported manufacturing in the mid 1800s. If not, we are subject to being left behind in the fast changing world economy because we cannot compete with the cheap labor cost of other countries nor can we be a country based on isolationism.

The name, Whig Party, was chosen to be synonymous with the Whigs of 1776 who fought for U.S. independence. Whig meant "opposing tyranny". The Democratic Party stood for "sovereignty of the people" and majority rule. The Whigs advocated the rule of law, an enduring unwavering written constitution, and protections for minority interest against majority tyranny.

When the Whig Party self-destructed in 1854, most of its supporters morphed into the Republican Party, which was made up of northern white Protestants, businessmen, small business owners, professionals, factory workers, farmers, and blacks—yes blacks. The Republican Party was pro-business and pro-banking. It also supported the gold standard, railroads, high tariffs to protect factory workers, and pro-industrial growth. The Republican Party dominated politics until1932 when the party lost its support during the Great Depression that lasted from 1929 until 1940. The New Deal coalition under progressive democratic president Franklin D. Roosevelt (FDR) became dominant from 1932 until 1964. How? Just like today, they bought votes with handouts to the voters in their "New Deal". Today it's called entitlements. I read the republicans were split on the New Deal. Not much has changed, has it?

Do you know why the Whig Party self-destructed? It self-destructed because of the internal tension over slavery. Those who did not support slavery went to the Democratic Party—right? Wrong! The main reason the Republican Party emerged from the Whig Party was to combat the Kansas-Nebraska Act of 1854 that created the territories of Kansas and Nebraska. The Act also effectively repealed the Compromise of 1820, which had prohibited slavery in those territories. The new Act allowed white settlers in those two territories to determine through popular sovereignty whether or not to allow slavery. Who designed this new law? Democratic Senator Stephen Douglass of Illinois of the Lincoln Douglass Debate fame designed it. Yes, a democrat designed it, not a republican.

Those who opposed slavery and supported racial equality formed the Republican Party. This is one of the biggest ruses perpetrated by democrats today. They want you to believe they have historically been the supporters of racial equality and opposed slavery. It is just the opposite. Democrats do not support the black race any more than republicans. Based upon what I observe today, I feel they support blacks less than republicans by using them for their own political purposes.

So, what's a conservative? A conservative is a person who literally interprets and supports the principles and laws of the Declaration of Independence and the United States Constitution through classic conservative ideology based upon his or her personal beliefs. You may notice that I said "literally" in referring to conservatives instead of "genuinely" when I referred to liberals. This is a subtle but important distinction in that liberals interpret the Constitution more "liberally" than do conservatives. Pun intended.

Before we start, I want to reiterate what I have previously said about categorizing people. When you see one conservative you have seen one conservative; however, conservative individuals are not as diverse in the intensity of her or his core personality traits or beliefs and behaviors as liberals. Even taking the progressive liberals out of the equation, this is still true. The intensity of core personality traits for liberals and their conviction toward liberal beliefs and behaviors is all along the political spectrum from left of center to far left of center. It is like a radio volume dial. The more you turn the dial to the left, the more the liberal intensity. The more you turn the dial to the right, the less liberal intensity and the more moderate a liberal becomes.

In contrast to liberals, I put conservatives either at the "moderate right" of the political center or what I call the "fundamental right" of the political center. The only major difference in the two is the strength of the conservative's religious ideology and how that affects their beliefs and behaviors on issues like abortion and homosexuality. There is no sliding intensity variable along a political spectrum. It's more like flipping a switch up and down rather than turning a dial. A conservative is basically either moderate or fundamental. There is a degree of variation involved with individuals but any effect on their conservative thinking is minimal. There are those republican politicians that portray to be conservative and I honestly do not know what their political beliefs are because they go with the political wind. They certainly do not fall into the ideological category of being a conservative. We will get to that later.

This analysis regarding the variation in intensity between liberals and the lack of variation among conservatives is another one of those things I have thought about and for which I have no answer. I sometimes hear white supremacy groups referred to as radical conservative groups. Totally not true. These groups no more fit the conservative mantra than the Black Panthers fit the liberal label. These are just radical groups with their own agenda and are neither conservative nor liberal. No. Tea Partiers are not conservative radicals either. I know, because I am one.

It has been refreshing to see some of the more recently elected republican politicians stand by their conservative heritage and fight liberals and the republican establishment to implement classic conservative values no matter how intense the pushback. These politicians were supported and elected by the Tea Party movement during the 2012 and 2014 mid-term elections and are referred to as radical Tea Partiers, even by other republicans. Radical? Really? Standing up for classic conservative values in the face of adversity is radical?

I can see liberals like Nancy Pelosi trashing the Tea Party, but fellow republicans doing the same? Pelosi said the Tea Party was "Astroturf". Then, when the Tea Partiers showed their might in 2012, she called them "radicals". It is shocking to me there were republicans who joined Pelosi in criticizing the Tea Party politicians as radicals because they strongly supported conservative principals. It is because of this type of republican behavior that I included a caveat in using the terms conservative and republican interchangeably. I am a proud Tea Partier. I strongly endorse conservative values and I am by no means radical. The 2014 mid-term elections produced several new republicans in Congress but the Tea Party movement was not as strong as it was in 2012.

My comments do not mean I'm opposed to political diversity and everyone should think the same. I strongly believe in diverse political ideas between conservatives and conservatives, liberals and liberals, and even conservatives and liberals. Diversity in ideas is tantamount to strong effective outcomes. I am against the compromising of core conservative beliefs by certain republican politicians resulting in self-serving actions in an attempt to "keep" their jobs versus "doing" their jobs. In the past, I have always been against term limits because I felt valuable experience would be lost in the process. Now, I am supportive of term limits. They have potential to lessen the incentive for politicians to do whatever is necessary to keep their jobs in perpetuity and provide themselves with the outrageous lifetime personal benefits they lavish on themselves. The advantage of getting rid of numerous incompetent politicians through term limits outweighs the unfortunate result of losing good ones

I mentioned in the last chapter I thought it was quite remarkable that liberals were in such lock-step with the Democratic Party regarding the "party line" on issues and it always appeared they all "got the memo". Well, I honestly believe they literally do get a memo and except in unusual political circumstances follow that memo to a T. I said I have thought that conservatives should learn from the democrats' success in practicing that behavior but always recanted the thought. Here's why. Do we want a bunch of programed politicians representing us and voting for us? I don't! What I want is diversity of thought and ideas in making the best decisions possible. I want to see politicians truly representing their constituents by making hard decisions while at the same time willing to debate and compromise their positions to facilitate the best outcomes for our country. That can't happen when you have an authority like the Democratic Party or Republican Party telling you what to say and do.

We will start our discussion on "what's a conservative" by examining conservative core personality traits. The overriding difference in core personality traits between conservatives and liberals is idealism versus pragmatism. Conservatives are dedicated to their political ideology but not to the intense degree as liberals are to their ideology. Conservative actions to achieve conservative ideology do take into account any pragmatic adverse consequences in accomplishing the end game. It is unusual to observe naivety in the thought processes and actions of conservatives. I recently read a quote by William F. Buckley that supported that thought. He said, "Conservatism, except when it is expressed in pure idealism, takes into account reality." As I said, I am a dyed-in-the-wool conservative. I described myself in my leadership book as a leader who is pragmatic, uses common sense, is intuitive, relies upon empirical data, learns from others, uses realistic dreaming, and makes decisions based upon ethical standards and an organization's values. If I substituted "the Declaration of Independence and the United States Constitution" for "organization", the description for my own leadership traits wouldn't be a bad description for conservative core personality traits.

If I use pragmatism, common sense, intuition, reliance upon empirical data, learning from others, realistic dreaming, decision making based upon ethical standards, and beliefs and values based upon the literal interpretation of the Declaration of Independence and the United States Constitution to describe conservative core personality traits, then the core personality traits described in the last chapter for liberals do not apply to conservatives. Conservatives do not exhibit the core personality traits of idealism, rationalization, actions or inactions justified to a fault, inordinate ideological bias, denial, and divert and switch.

A liberal may say that I am excessively conservatively biased, cannot see reality, and my analysis of conservatives and liberals regarding core personality traits is grossly flawed. This is something I have thought about on many occasions when I have analyzed liberal and conservative behavior—especially in writing this book. This book is written through the eyes of a conservative and I make no excuses or apologies for doing so; however, there is one thing you should know about me and that is I hate like hell to be wrong. Not that I have to always to be right but I diligently do my homework to the best of my ability in order to be as accurate as I can possibly be. I strive for and expound the truth even when the truth is found to be different from what I had hoped to find.

It is a badge of courage for me to be the ultimate pragmatist. I always tease my wife that I am Bond—James Bond. I use that analogy because I am very proud of my ability to cut through the proverbial smoke and mirrors and focus on the heart of an issue or problem. I'm not saying I'm infallible to bias or mistakes. No one is but, at the risk of sounding arrogant, I'm pretty damn good and I don't get it wrong very often.

On that rather profound proclamation of personal extolment, we are now going to switch to conservatives' beliefs and behaviors and compare them to the liberal beliefs and behaviors discussed in the last chapter. The most distinct difference between the two is individualism versus collectivism. Conservatives believe strongly in individualism. It goes to the very core of the Declaration of Independence and the United States Constitution, which are the prime foundations of our country. The Declaration of Independence says that all men are created equal. It does not say all men are to forever be equal. It then says that all men have the right to life, liberty, and the pursuit of happiness. That means everyone has the opportunity to achieve her or his individual dreams (individualism); not be compromised, minimized, deprived, restricted, or coerced into sharing what you have or could have with others to achieve equality in society (collectivism). Rather than go into a lot of philosophical litany and give examples on this issue here, you will see this profound philosophical difference ubiquitously throughout the book.

Conservatives are the ones who literally believe in majority rule; not today's democrats as was proposed by the Democratic Party in the 1800s. I don't mean conservatives want the majority to walk all over or beat down the minority. I mean that the majority should have their beliefs and ideology be the dominant rule in society while at the same time respect the beliefs and ideology of the minority. It should not be the other way around as is happening today through political correctness. I am amazed at how the tail (progressive liberals) is wagging (and whipping) the dog (conservatives) on this issue. No puns intended this time. The problem is that the far left liberal progressive tail is more aggressive and persistent than the conservative dog and wags and wags until the conservative dog gives in or doesn't know the tail is even wagging it until it is too late.

I want to go on record as stating unequivocally that conservatives care as much about the environment as liberals. I have already given you my personal diatribe on the environment and my opinion is not unique among conservatives. Global Warming! Climate change! What a travesty. Like it or not, Mother Nature does what she wants to do. I won't deny that we humans "probably" contribute to climate change to some degree but the real question is how much? Is the amount dangerous to our environment? No one on this Earth really knows. Conservatives believe in a reasonable, practical, and common sense approach toward balancing environmental preservation with society's needs, regulation, and monetary costs.

There is significant diversity in beliefs and behaviors regarding abortion among conservatives depending upon one's religious beliefs. Fundamental conservatives do not believe in abortion. Other conservatives do. The diversity in beliefs and behaviors on this issue regardless of one's political ideology should be respected because there is in reality no right or wrong position unless it breaks the law. I can hear pushback now on my comments but no one has the right to push their beliefs and behaviors on others just because they see things differently. Either side in this controversy should recognize and respect the other's opinions and move on. This is one of those things in life that will never be settled by debate. The intensity of feelings only becomes worse between those debating because of the subject's emotional divisiveness. It detracts from the bigger political picture and sucks energy from other political issues.

No matter what a conservative's ideology is on abortion, conservatives do not hate women as portrayed and promoted by progressive liberals. How ridiculous! Many conservatives are women and they don't hate themselves. Do conservative males hate their wives, mothers, sisters, and female friends because they are women? Of course not! Progressive liberals recite fabricated rhetoric to make their political points on this issue and these fabrications are a distortion of reality (the end justifies the means).

Conservatives do not hate homosexuals or those who identify as transgender. There is; however, great variation in beliefs among conservatives regarding homosexuality and transgender identity that leads to very different conservative opinions. Many fundamental conservatives believe homosexuality and transgender identity are not normal behavior and oppose providing them with the same rights and privileges afforded heterosexuals. Some fundamental conservatives believe homosexuals and transgender people can be changed to heterosexuals with proper help and counseling. Moderate conservatives support gay and transgender rights but many do not support their marriages because of religious beliefs. This is perhaps the most controversial issue among conservatives as a group

Here is my opinion. To get very basic—maybe too basic for some—the major purpose in nature for the male gender and female gender is to procreate and preserve the species. However, nature has biological and psychological variation among all the species on Earth—human and non-human. We humans, just like other animals on Earth, do not all fit into neat little traditional homogeneous opposite sex packages of male and female. Homosexuality and true transgender issues are not psychological but rather biological. I will give you a non-human example. My wife once had a male dog that was homosexual. He gave off an odor to other male dogs that attracted them to him as if he were a female dog in heat. Other male dogs actually physically engaged with him in a sexual way. The veterinarian had to give him hormones, which prevented this homosexual interaction from happening. This situation was not psychological. It was physiological.

Homosexuality and transgender identity are in the minority and subject to discriminatory judgment by some people in the majority. Those who do not believe homosexuality and transgender identity to be a normal course of nature have the right to be entitled to their beliefs but they do not have the right to deny these minorities their rights with one exception. There has been significant controversy regarding the religious rights of business owners and civil servants who do not want to support gay and transgender weddings because of their religious beliefs. They should not be forced to do so. In every situation I have studied, the motive of those who were denied the service was to make a "political statement" and not to obtain a just end result. In 100% of the cases, there were equal alternatives available. We need to respect people's religious beliefs and use common sense.

I have always been curious as to what percent of the population falls into a sexual orientation category other than heterosexual. A syndicated news story published last year by The Washington Post addressed this question. A survey was done by an Internet based research firm called YouGov. From what I could find out about YouGov, they are a legitimate research firm with reasonable accuracy. Thirty-one percent of the Millennials who participated in a survey said they were less than 100% heterosexual and 4% were not sure. Eighty-six percent of baby boomers and seniors said they were 100% heterosexual. The survey indicated that 25% of democrats identified as something else other than "completely straight" while only 9% of republicans did. The article concluded the YouGov numbers indicated that defined categories of sexual orientation matter less now than ever. Only 25% of the seniors in the survey agreed that human sexuality is a continuous scale between 0% and 100% and not black-and-white but more than 50% of the Millennials agreed. I don't know what these numbers mean, if anything, but they sure are interesting. I am one of those Americans who cannot relate to "degrees" of sexuality. I guess it depends upon one's interpretation.

The Washington Post also quoted a Gallup survey that said Americans believe roughly 25% of the population was non-heterosexual when in reality only about 4% call themselves lesbian, gay, bisexual, or transgender. I don't know if these two surveys contradict each other or not. YouGov measures degrees of being heterosexual versus the Gallup survey, which is black or white; you either are or you're not.

The Washington Post published an article in 2014 that reviewed a study by the Centers for Disease Control (CDC) on the topic. The CDC said they polled 34,557 people and 96.6% identified as straight, 1.6% identified as gay or lesbian, and 0.7% identified as bisexual. The remaining 1.1% identified as: something else (0.2%); did not know (0.4%); or refused to answer (0.6%).

These statistics point out that no one really knows the true percentage of the population that is heterosexual, homosexual or transgender but, without question, the percent of homosexuals is a very small percent of the population and the number of people who are transgender is extremely small. Keep this in mind when you read chapter 10 and the absurd impact being forced through political correctness upon our society regarding this issue.

Contrary to what liberals say, conservatives are not opposed to new immigration laws, including amnesty. Conservatives are opposed to new immigration laws that do nothing to improve the situation and would probably make things worse. For example, the immigration law passed in the democratic dominated Senate before the 2014 midterms allowed current illegal aliens to become citizens. The law contained a clause that would have also allowed their extended family members who are not currently living in the United States to become citizens. These changes in our laws were estimated to push the number of illegal aliens that could obtain citizenship from eleven million to thirty million. And, the Senate bill did not improve our weak border security. Why not? Harry Reid pronounced that border security is strong. We were lucky that the House could stop such nonsense when the Senate couldn't. The major differences in what republicans and democrats want is that democrats want more Hispanic votes and republicans want effective border security along with reasonable versus wholesale transition for illegals to citizenship.

We must always remember that more legal Hispanic workers also mean increased opportunity for union membership. This is a huge plus for democrats by creating more union dues resulting in increased political contributions. Time will tell who wins this battle. It will be very interesting since Obama is pursuing executive action on immigration before he leaves office and republicans control both the House and the Senate.

Here is one interesting tidbit on the Hispanic population. My cardiologist is from the Dominican Republic and very conservative. He and I got into a lengthy conversation one day regarding Hispanic voting practices. He was very passionate about the fact that the Hispanic population is very diverse in many ways including political ideology. He reminded me of how many countries of origin and cultures are represented in the United States and said it was a big mistake to lump every Hispanic together in one group and label them as "Hispanic". He makes a good point and we see it done all the time. Hispanics are not by themselves. How about women, blacks, and other population categories that the progressive liberal politicians like to use in their propaganda to solicit votes? One other thing my cardiologist said hit home in a very disturbing way. He said he came to America for opportunity and the progressive government is turning America into what he left.

I support common sense immigration reform that includes tight border security. I heard someone say once, "What are we going to do? Load all of the illegal aliens on buses and send them home." Sending all illegals home is not realistic and will never happen. Let's use our common sense and do the right thing—amnesty and legalized citizenship for current illegal aliens who do not have a criminal record or some other legitimate reason to be deported. That does not include legal citizenship for their close relatives back home. The process should be similar to the current process in place that allows immigrants to achieve legal citizenship but due to the number of illegal aliens involved, some reasonable accommodations will have to be made.

The government currently delves out billions of dollars in tax money to support these immigrants. The Daily Signal reported that at least 51 % of immigrant households receive welfare such as Medicaid, food stamps, and housing subsidy. Seventy-six percent of immigrant households with children receive government welfare. I do not have any idea of what percent receiving welfare are legal versus illegal. I doubt the government does either. We need to clean up this illegal abuse of taxpayer money.

Here are three typical real life stories to support legalized citizenship and strong border security. First, there is the issue of fairness for the immigrants who have made the effort to obtain legal citizenship. I know a person from Jamaica who became a United States citizen through the proper channels. I might add that I am very proud of him as he is of himself. I asked him how he felt about those who are here illegally. He felt it was wrong and everyone should follow the law like he did. He is not the only person who got their citizenship legally who has told me that. Good immigration law isn't rocket science. It is unfortunately being used today as democratic political posturing at its worst.

Before I retired, a patient in one of our ICUs was an illegal alien who had been severely injured in an automobile accident. He was in ICU for almost a year. His bill was over $1million and he had no money or insurance to pay for it. His mother wanted him home in Mexico. His brother wanted to keep him in our hospital at our expense and threatened us if we didn't. We decided to transfer him to a hospital in Mexico by medical air transport at a cost to us of about $25,000. That was expensive but cheaper than what it was costing us to keep him in ICU. Unfortunately, the patient died in a Mexico hospital after about three months, which is another story in itself. The state paid us approximately $20,000 in Medicaid money funded through taxes and we had no choice but to pass the remainder of the cost of his care along to our other patients. This is not an isolated case. There are enormous costs involved in medical services and entitlement benefits afforded to non-tax paying illegal aliens?

I live in Southwest Florida and I routinely see the value of tightening the borders. I read a guest commentary in our local newspaper that is an eye opener on this topic. It was written by a local county judge. He said 30% to 50% of all the offenders he sees in his court for driving without a valid driver's license are in the country illegally. He went on to say that frequently the people who leave the scene of an accident are here illegally and have no insurance. That drives up the cost of insurance for the rest of us.

The judge concluded his guest commentary by saying there are very inconsistent deportation practices by Immigration and Customs Enforcement (ICE). To back up his assertion, he told a story about a defendant in his court who had been deported four times and every time the defendant came back he used new documents with a different name. The judge said when we have laws that are not uniformity enforced or not enforced at all there is a diminished respect for the rule of law. I couldn't agree with him more. His last comment applies not only to illegal aliens but to legal citizens as well.

I want to also share a January 2016 report from The Daily Signal that brings up an aspect of immigration we never hear about. The report said almost 500,000 foreigners traveled to the United States legally last year for business and leisure and are nowhere to be found after their visas expired. How many of those illegal immigrants do we have in the country? Who knows?

Here is a story about legal illegal immigration. Do you know what an "anchor baby" is? It is a child born to a wealthy Chinese woman who pays an organization to bring her to the U.S. (usually on a tourist visa) to have her baby so the child will be a U.S. citizen. I saw an estimate that said between 40,000 and 300,000 anchor babies are born in the U.S. each year. Not a very accurate estimate but it makes the point. The vast majority is born in Southern California. ICE is trying to crack down on the practice but it appears their efforts are not stopping it.

We will talk much more in-depth on different aspects of immigration in chapters 6 and 7. Before we leave immigration in this chapter, I want to clarify the number routinely given as the illegal immigrant population in the U.S. I read an interesting article in The Daily Signal on the topic. The standard number given is 11 million. The source of that number is The Pew Research Center, the Center for Immigration Studies, and the Department of Homeland Security (DHS). That 11 million number has been used for more than a decade and one source for the data was the U.S. Census Bureau that "asked immigrants" if they were here illegally. Duh! The individual who runs ICE testified before congress the number of illegals could be as high as 15 million. A 2005 Bear Sterns study estimated the number to be 20 million. The bottom line is we really have no idea how many illegal immigrants are in the United States. The Heritage Foundation suggested it would cost taxpayers $6 trillion over the lifetime of these immigrants, if only 11 million illegal immigrants were given amnesty. How about 15 million, 20 million, or more? We desperately need to close our border as tight as possible as soon as possible for more reasons than one.

I understand immigration is a very tough issue to control but we have made a mess of it for ideological and political reasons. When one looks at a single year, the number of illegals coming into the U.S. is very significant. Multiply that annual number by multiple years and decades. The number is astounding and what is the true impact on our country? What else is out there with immigration that we don't know about? In later chapters, we will talk about what we do know and it is an ugly and scary picture.

I could write an entire book on why labor unions are contrary to conservative ideology and the best interest of the country. Labor unions are strongly supported by liberals because labor union practices are in theory analogous to liberal ideology. In actual practice; however, my experience is that labor unions do not support employees as they preach. I have had considerable experience in opposing union activity. I was involved in one union decertification and successfully defeated two union attempts. During my first year out of college, I was forced to join a union against my will and experienced first hand the lies and negativity that a union can dish out. Labor unions create political corruption by reciprocating liberal support with enormous political donations to liberal candidates. Without question unions significantly harm the American economy as well as the employees they portray to support.

I said the starkest difference between conservative beliefs and behaviors and liberal beliefs and behaviors is individualism versus collectivism. The number two difference between conservative beliefs and behaviors and liberal beliefs and behaviors is exceptionalism versus globalism. I defined these concepts in the last chapter. This difference in philosophy is creating enormous national security and foreign policy issues for our country. Because of this topic's complex nature and importance, I will defer further discussion until chapters 8 and 9 when we discuss the actions or more appropriately the lack of actions on the part of the current progressives in power in Washington.

Here is a curious difference between conservatives and liberals I read about in The Daily Signal that will be controversial at best. A prominent sociologist and his associate released a report that proclaimed republicans are happier and more stable in their marriages than democrats. If I haven't stirred up any liberals yet who are reading my book, that oughta do it. The report discussed many factors leading up to its conclusion. The factors included demographics, culture, religious affiliation, race, education, and attitude toward the institution of marriage as it relates to relationships and family. I am not touching this one with "any length" pole and my bridges are all sold out. The report did conclude when demographic and cultural differences are controlled, the difference shrank to 3%. If my memory serves me correctly from my college class in statistical analysis, a 3% difference is almost always within the margin of error. I'm going to call that one even and get outa here.

I do want to leave you with a serious thought as we close this chapter. There are many similarities between conservatives and classic liberals. These last two chapters were devoted to pointing out differences between the two for the purpose of identifying political ideologies and resulting behaviors, which will enhance discussion throughout the book. The diversity of beliefs and behaviors between conservatives and classic liberals creates a healthy ideological political balance for our society. In a true and successful America, the things that make us different will make us stronger and the things that make us similar will bring us together as One Nation Under God, Indivisible, with Liberty and Justice for All. The same cannot be said for progressive liberals, as you will see in the next chapter.

CHAPTER 4

What's a Progressive?

Are progressives liberals, socialists, communists, or Marxists? No, Yes, Yes, and Yes! A progressive is a very aggressive wolf in liberal clothing and we are going to unclothe that wolf in this chapter. Progressives are so far left that they deserve their own classification. It has been my observation they possess many of the same core personality traits and liberal beliefs and behaviors as classic liberals but there are three distinct differences.

The first difference is that progressive liberal core personality traits and beliefs and behaviors are on steroids as compared to liberals in general. For example, the progressive current White House Czar on science and technology, John Holdren, once promoted adding birth control to the public water supply to control population. He has also been credited with supporting the concept that emphasizes the young over the old in health and life decisions on the premise that older people would not be discriminated against since they were once young themselves. A former progressive White House Czar, Cass Sunstein, said in one of his books that animals might be thought of as humans and be given legal status to sue in order to stem animal abuse. Look out for those dogs, cats, and hamsters. Better be nice to your goldfish and parakeets. There's always a lawyer lurking around the corner. Actually, Sunstein is back teaching law at Harvard University.

The second difference is that progressives believe they know what is best for society and push their ideas on others. Sunstein co-authored a book titled *The Nudge* which said, "People in general need public and private organizations to help them make decisions since they are prone to make poor choices and look back in bafflement." It does not surprise anyone that progressives do not see their pronouncements applying to themselves when those pronouncements do not suit them personally. Abraham Lincoln said in his Gettysburg Address, "Government of the people, by the people, for the people." Progressives probably would agree with Lincoln regarding "of the people" and for the people but "by the people" is not in their vocabulary. We miss you Abe.

A glaring example of progressive hypocrisy is when president Obama advised all Americans to be prudent and patient when he first entered office because of the bad economic conditions and the spiraling out of control national debt. What did he do? Shortly after his election he took his wife, Michelle, to dinner in New York City on Air Force One. What did that cost when you include the cost of the jet and the security entourage? From what I read, the cost to fly Air Force One is roughly $228,000 per hour. That cost is reported to be 27% higher since Obama took office. The round-trip flight time is about 1hour and 15 minutes between Washington and New York City. Quick math shows the travel cost for Air Force One to be approximately $285,000. I have no clue regarding the cost for transporting the presidential state car to New York City and the costs for security. I understand that the car is transported in a cargo plane. Have you ever spent that much on dinner for two? Actually you have. It was just for someone else.

I didn't think I could top that one but I can. Obama and Michelle flew to Los Angeles in March of last year to appear on separate talk shows. Obama was on Jimmy Kimmel Live and Michelle was on the Ellen DeGeneres' show. Additionally, Obama attended a fundraiser. What else is new! Michelle flew in a different airplane and I understand it was not a Piper Cub or even a Learjet. Think B-I-G. The White House Deputy Press Secretary said, "The president's and First Lady's schedules were not in sync in order to travel together." This is an absurd extravagant waste of taxpayer money when our economy continues to struggle.

Obama went to Denver for a fund raising event in July 2014. This was during the time when the border-crossing debacle involving the illegal alien children was unfolding and he chose not to take a side trip to the Texas border to personally observe the tragedy? Judicial Watch reported the cost for Air Force One was $695,894. They also uncovered some of the security costs for the trip, which included $17,124 for local transportation and $183,259 for lodging for a total of $200,383. How about meals and other expenses for security that were not in the Judicial Watch report? The total known cost for the trip was $896,277 and does not include the personal costs for Obama and his entourage or meals and all transportation costs for his security. How much of this cost was paid by the Democratic Party, since this was a fundraiser for them? The White House keeps that formula secret according to Judicial Watch. I can assure you we taxpayers paid a major portion, if not all of the costs. Obama always finds something to do that appears to be presidential on these trips to justify cost-shifting those expenses to us. I assume other presidents have done the same thing. The question is how many times compared to Obama and how much of the costs were shifted to their respective political parties versus taxpayers?

My memory tells me that no sitting president has made even close to as many fund raising trips as Obama. As I said in chapter 2, I believe they are significant ego trips to allow him to present himself to friendly crowds and receive adulation. In addition to the fundraising event in Denver, Obama gave a talk at a local park in which he criticized republicans and touted a strong economy. I guess he has to rationalize his lavish lifestyle somehow. Oh, he did go to a local bar rather than some fancy place. He played pool and drank a beer with "the guys". He was too busy to travel 242 miles to the Texas border and see first hand the terrible illegal immigration problem he caused that is costing us untold billions of dollars. I guess he felt it was more important to be seen at the bar to show what a regular guy he is. Had he gone to the border, he might have learned something about the horrors many of those children and adults are enduring because of the mess he created. Then the cost of his trip might legitimately be justified. You will read a multitude of examples of progressive hypocrisy as the book progresses.

The third difference between classic liberals and progressives is the most concerning. Classic liberals are sincere in their behavior to implement liberal ideas in our society because they believe society would be better living their ideology. Progressives have a sinister goal. That goal is power and control. They do not see themselves as equals but rather above society in accomplishing their objectives. The dictates and laws imposed by progressive politicians do not apply to them. Progressives are socialists, communists, and Marxists working together in a common cause to achieve the overthrow of traditional America and the American Dream.

I found a great definition of the American Dream on Wikipedia. It said, "The American Dream is a national ethos of the United States, a set of ideals in which freedom includes the opportunity for prosperity and success, and an upward social mobility for the family and children, achieved through hard work in a society with few barriers." American writer and historian, James Truslow Adams (no relation to John), said in 1931, "Life should be better and richer and fuller for everyone, with opportunity for each according to ability or achievement regardless of social class or circumstances of birth." The American Dream is derived from the principals engrained in the Declaration of Independence and the Constitution, which are the foundation of our country. I have often said that if the progressives were to ever accomplish their goal of destroying the American Dream they would self-destruct in their quest for power to implement their divergent ideologies. Currently they have a common enemy. If they win, the enemy becomes each other.

Remember the House Committee on Un-American Activities (HUAC) in the 40s, 50s, 60s, and 70s? That committee would have a field day today in Washington and elsewhere in our country searching out and stopping disloyal and subversive progressive activities against America. There would be a lot of empty seats in the White House, Congress, and in federal, state, and local governments if the HUAC was alive and doing its job. Senator Joseph McCarthy said during a speech in 1950 that he had a list of more than 200 known communists serving in the State Department. McCarthy was actually censored by the Senate for his repeated unsubstantiated comments about Communists inside the federal Government and elsewhere. I wonder what McCarthy would say today about Congress and the Obama administration?

It seems so unfathomable that these progressives could infiltrate American political culture the way they have and get away with it but it is a stark reality. They did it through "deceit" by telling people what they wanted to hear whether it was true or not and giving away "freebees" through multiple entitlements. How can our society be so gullible? I wish I knew! When I think of this phenomenon, I am always reminded of the story of Moses going to the mountain to speak to God and obtain the Ten Commandments. While he was gone, the Israelites he led out of Egypt turned to sin and gluttony. They lost sight of the hardships and atrocities they endured when the Egyptians enslaved them and the beliefs and behaviors that brought the good life to them after they escaped. If Moses had not returned and stopped them, their new society would have totally self-destructed.

This is a good lesson for America to draw from. It is inherent for society to forget the principals and struggles that made it successful and then resort to personal gluttony and indulgent societal norms rather than appreciating and continuing the principals and struggles it took to obtain that success and to sustain it. Ask the Romans what happens when society abandons those principles and struggles. The Roman Empire, one of the greatest societies in the history of the world, was brought to its knees and destroyed because of this phenomenon. The progressives are aggressively manipulating our society through deception and gifts to support their progressive goals, especially their goal of power and control in perpetuity.

Now, let's look at progressive personal core traits in comparison with the personal core traits identified for liberals. We will start with idealism. Progressives are idealistic to the point of absurdity. For example, suggesting that animals might sue people to promote animal rights or the mayor of New York City, Michael Bloomberg, telling New Yorkers they can't buy 32 oz. sodas in restaurants and theaters in his attempt to save them from obesity. How about two 16 oz. sodas at a higher cost and two paper or plastic cups instead of one cup to dispose of in the environment or recycle? No pragmatism here! And, what's a movie without those super-sized cups of soda and bags of popcorn? Would the theaters start having intermissions during the movies and encourage moviegoers to get soda refills since most of their profits come from the refreshment counter? Theaters did that when I was a kid during epic movies like Cecil B. DeMille's *Ten Commandments* and *The Greatest Show on Earth*. No reason why we can't do it again.

How about the 32 oz. sodas people take home from the grocery store? Are they going to put soda surveillance cameras in our homes? At least the court got it right in stopping the ban. I guess New York City is so easy to run that the mayor and his staff are looking for something to do to make them relevant and earn their salaries. Well, I can't say that about the mayor because he is one of the richest men in the world and only took a salary of $1 per year. Could we say you get what you pay for? Sounds like he is a progressive who ran as a republican. Actually, he was a democrat before then and left office as an independent. Never judge a politician, conservative or liberal, by what they say. Judge them by what they do.

Here is a more recent update on taxing sodas that took place in June of this year. Philadelphia did pass a soda tax of 1.5 cents per ounce on sugary and diet drinks. The only other city in the U.S. that has a tax on soda is Berkley, California. No surprise there. I found it interesting that most of the estimated additional $90 million in revenue will go to the general fund and not to pre-kindergarten, community schools, and recreation centers as thought by many of those who campaigned for it. The American Beverage Association has promised the issue will wind up in court. I wish them the best of luck. This is a regressive tax that will hit the poor and middle class the hardest. I thought it was the middle class and the poor the progressives wanted to help? Never confuse the progressives with the facts when they have a hidden agenda. In this case, the agenda is generating more revenue for their progressive programs disguised as doing something good for individual citizens and for the community at large.

It has taken almost three years to research and write this book. The current events, like the one above, that I use to explain and support my opinions are the products of a very dynamic environment. I often wondered if the book could be completed with all the information contained in it being current. Over time, I became convinced that was not going to happen no matter how hard I tried. I would be sitting here writing updates in perpetuity. However, you will find many updates throughout the book as new information occurs before publication. None of these updates or the lack of more current information change any premise I have made.

Having said what I just said, here is an update on New York City's progressive governance. New Yorkers elected a new mayor in 2014 named Bill de Blasio. It was reported in The Wall Street Journal the new mayor is an unabashed liberal activist and political strategist who was sympathetic to the Occupy Wall Street movement. Judicial Watch reported he was an active supporter of the communist Sandinista regime in Nicaragua in the 1980s. His association with the Sandinistas was also mentioned in The Wall Street Journal article. He is a great example of a resolute progressive.

Those 16 oz. sodas might be a whole lot easier to swallow in the future for New Yorkers after this guy gets through as mayor. He has already created significant controversy. Not only did he try to get rid of the time-honored tradition of horse-drawn carriage rides in Central Park to protect the horses from animal abuse (Sunstein's kind of guy), he has offended every policeman and policewomen in New York City. It was reported de Blasio told his son to be cautious around the police because he was a "young man of color". The mayor's wife is black. A major campaign promise was to cease the "stop and frisk" tactic used by police. Shootings have gone up significantly in high-risk areas of the city since the stop and frisk practice has been curtailed.

The mayor has been severely criticized and deservedly so for comments he made supporting demonstrations on racial discrimination and his personal response to the shooting death of two New York City policemen while they were sitting in their car. The gunman was apparently inspired by these demonstrations and said on the Internet two police should be killed for every black killed. He indicated he was going to do just that and did. The police saw the mayor's verbal comments and actions regarding the situation as not "having their backs". In response, you probably saw on television the police "give him theirs" at the hospital and at one of the funerals.

The disruptive political controversies by this progressive mayor are far from over. In fact, after I wrote the last update, the mayor announced the city would ban polystyrene foam take-out food containers, doggy bag containers, and drink containers for all food establishments that have a gross income of $500,000 and over. I saw a rebuttal that said the substitutes are less environmental friendly than the polystyrene foam. Like I said, never confuse these progressives with the facts.

Oh, and the mayor declared he has moved past the rift with the police and has gained the footing to move on to other matters. I wonder if the police feel the same way? What is it called when the leader of the land "declares to the people" (and the police) that something is to be? I call it a progressive decree as in "king and kingdom". Crime statistics in New York City indicate the police have not "moved on". We will look at that in chapter 10 when we review crime statistics in some of our major cities.

In June of this year, crime statistics went up in New York City government. The FBI is conducting an investigation of criminal corruption and has arrested three top New York Police officials and a political fundraiser close to mayor de Blasio. The mayor is under investigation himself. I am always amazed that progressives who resolutely profess to do what is in the best interest of their fellow man appear to be involved in corruption much more often than the conservatives who progressives claim take advantage of everyone in society to support the so-called corrupted rich.

It was announced after the 32 oz. soda debacle in New York City that the Food and Drug Administration (FDA) was going to ban trans-fats in foods for our well-being. Another progressive decree! In response to the ban, Neil Cavuto commented during his show on Fox News that we have finally put the Pillsbury Dough Boy's picture on the wall at the post office. Well said, Neil! I am all for healthy eating habits but we must never lose sight of progressives and their quest for power and control over us. I wonder if the progressives making that decision on trans-fat even remotely analyzed and considered the business and individual freedom implications of that decision. Even if they did, they really don't care. Remember the progressives always know what is best for us and the end always justifies the means. As I write this, a question comes to mind. Who made progressives "Kings and Queens of our Mountain"? Society did! Those who voted for them and those who didn't vote at all! A non-vote is, in effect, a vote and a non-vote is worse than a vote one regrets.

Unfortunately, the issue of progressives controlling what we eat never goes away. The Washington Times reported the following. A

2014 Government Accounting Office (GAO) study said 1,086,000 kids stopped buying school lunches because of the new nutrition standards imposed upon them by the Hunger-Free Kids Act of 2010 that was promoted by Michelle Obama. That Act sets policy and standards for the national school lunch program. It cost taxpayers $11.6 billion in 2012. The kids were throwing out their fruits and vegetables and boycotting the lunchrooms. This program led to higher food costs and odd food parings such as a "cheese stick with shrimp" in order for the schools to comply with the complicated standards. The new standards were said to be exhaustive including calorie ranges, sodium limits, zero tolerance for trans fats, and specific ounce amounts for meats and grains. The food was unappetizing and led to enormous waste. The compliance issues and the rebellion by the kids created a morale problem with school cafeteria workers.

In spite of this GAO study, the United States Department of Agriculture (USDA) claimed the standards were "proving popular" and the GAO in spite of its own study said participation will probably improve over time as the students get used to it. This is another classic example of never confusing progressives with facts if those facts are not consistent with their world. They truly believe if you nudge people long enough they will be compliant. This school lunch program sounds more like a "shove" rather than a nudge. It will be interesting to see who wins the battle in the end—the kids or Michelle and the government.

A few months ago I learned of another program under the Hunger-Free Kids Act that exemplifies progressive behavior out of control or maybe I should say progressive behavior in control. Kids are encouraged to eat a free breakfast at school. The kid's family income is irrelevant. The program's rational is that kids who eat a good breakfast tend to perform better in school, have better attendance, and exhibit fewer behavioral problems. I think they have their cause and effect backwards but let's move on with their rationale. The Act's website said children who eat a good breakfast develop healthy eating habits, visit the school nurse less, and are less likely to be obese.

I'm not sure that's true but let's give them the benefit of the doubt and look at what I learned in my own community. Our school system actually makes money off this program because of the reimbursement they get from the federal government. It gets better. A friend of mine told me about a kid who loves their breakfast at school after they eat breakfast at home because she can get brownies. I did not make that up. I saw a school sponsored video promoting the program in our school system and the kids were eating frosted cookies for breakfast. OK, lets summarize. In order to encourage healthy eating habits for school children, the federal government entices school systems with federal funds. In order to get the federal funds, the school systems entice the school children with brownies and frosted cookies. Only in Progressiveland! I have a really big gingerbread icing-covered bridge to sell to anyone who isn't "frosted" by that hypocrisy.

A quick look at a USDA website shows this program cost $3 billion in 2011, which was up substantially from previous years. I could not find current costs. Wonder why? I also learned that our local school system gave away an iPad2 to the student who had the most entries. How did they get entries? The more free breakfasts they ate, the more entries they got. Let's put this in perspective. The school system incentivizes the kids with sugar disguised as breakfast and an iPad2 to eat more school breakfasts so the school system can make money off the federal government. The federal government incentivizes local school systems with more money under the pretense of better nutrition to gain more control over them. Like I said, only in Progressiveland!

I could not find the current costs of the USDA breakfast program but, according to The Washington Free Beacon, the Office of Inspector General reported the USDA made $6.2 billion in improper payments in 2013. The school breakfast program had the highest rate for improper payments with over 25% of all disbursements being incorrect. Those improper payments amounted to $831 million with $716 million of the payments being overpayments. It can get worse. The USDA made $2.6 billion in improper payments in the food stamp program of which $2 billion was overpayments. According to Judicial Watch, total improper payments by the USDA rose to $6.9 billion in 2014. A record $80.4 billion were given to people for free groceries. Many of those people did not qualify. No wonder people love welfare.

Here is something even worse than worse. There is a law titled the Improper Payments Elimination and Recovery Act, which requires the

USDA to conduct annual risk assessments to identify programs that make significant improper payments of $10 million or more. Significant is $10 million or more? Only for the government! Judicial Watch said the USDA has violated the law for the past four years and refuses to implement a more efficient verification process before handing out benefits because it would create barriers for families that need help. We are still in Progressiveland.

These USDA programs are great examples of what I mean by progressives being on steroids to obtain votes for power and control. Think about what happens if they gain as much control of our schools as they have with our government. They keep finding ways to throw more money at our schools, which equates to more control. How about the Common Core Standards Initiative? Common Core combined with these funding programs could seal the deal to allow progressives to control our kids by totally controlling the schools funding. If schools don't comply with what the "government" wants our kids to be taught and "how" to be taught, than the government can cut off their funding and the schools are so dependent on that funding they will have to capitulate or close down.

There was an article in my local newspaper about a Harvard University medical expert who is recommending abolishing sodium and an analyst with the Natural Resources Defense Council (whatever the heck that is) said sugar might become a target as well. The political cartoon in the same paper that day got it right. It showed a picture of a fast food counter with a McGovernment logo sign over it that said: no saturated fat; no trans-fat; no fries; no meat; no pop; and no ice cream. The employee at the counter "told" the customer, "You'll have a tofu burger and large broccoli."

This ideological assault on our personal liberty is a startling reality and the longer progressives control government the more we become a model for George Orwell's *1984*. As I wrote this, I started to think of all the laws, policies, and regulations the Obama administration and Obama's progressive politician friends have imposed upon Americans to obtain power and control and benefit themselves during the last 7 years. In most cases, the end result was exactly the opposite of what they said was their goal. We also discovered what they said to gain public support was routinely untruthful. Think Obamacare, immigration, the war on terror, the Guantanamo Bay prisoner swap, relations with Cuba, the Iran nuclear deal, etc. We will dissect these and other progressive political scams later.

Progressives are idealistic to the point of ridiculousness but are they naive? Absolutely not! Not in the slightest! They are the most calculating, aggressive, uncompromising, and focused ideological group on the planet. A classic liberal does not feel or think this way. Classic liberals support their beliefs and values to a fault but they also acknowledge the right of non-liberals to disagree. For that reason, classic liberals are open to compromise. Not progressives. It is their way or the highway. There is no compromise. Anyone or any group who gets in their way is subject to ridicule or some overt or covert action to remove them from relevance. Think about the routine behavior in Congress by progressives Harry Reid and Nancy Pelosi. How about Obama and his administration?

The model used by progressives to achieve their ideological goals is contained in Saul Alinsky's book published in 1971 titled *Rules for Radicals: A Pragmatic Primer for Realistic Radicals.* This is a very diabolical book unless you are a radical looking for information on how to "manipulate" others to your cause. Alinsky wrote his book to unite low-income communities ("Have-Nots") in order to empower them to achieve political, social, and economic equality with the rich ("Haves") and the middle class ("Have-little, Want-mores"). Those descriptive titles in parenthesis are not mine; they are his. He said he wrote the book to educate people on how to change the world from what it is to what they believe it should be.

Alinsky outlined several tactics to accomplish change. Here are a few of them. He said if the end justifies the means, then it is permissible to utilize unorthodox tactics to achieve your goal. Communication is considered the most important aspect of organizing; therefore, caution should be exercised as to what words are used. The organizer needs to establish his or her identity as a leader and a positive force so followers will have faith in them. Look for ways to increase insecurity, anxiety, and uncertainty. A threat is usually more terrifying than the "thing" itself. Make the enemy live up to their own book of rules because no one can live up to all their own rules. Ridicule is man's most potent weapon. Power is achieved from not only what the organizer has but from what the enemy thinks the organizer has. A good tactic is utilizing what people enjoy so they are "doing their thing". Keep the pressure on; never let up. If one pushes a negative hard enough, it will push through and become a positive because the public sympathizes with the underdog. Pick the target, freeze it, personalize it, and polarize it by cutting off the support network and any sympathy. Go outside the expertise of the enemy and blind-side them with irrelevant arguments that they are forced to address.

I can't remember if the following came directly from Alinsky's book but it is a standard progressive tactic. Don't push too hard and/or too fast for radical change or a backlash will occur and the effort would most likely be thwarted. Organizers push their change agenda slowly and methodically so those subject to change won't know what hit them until it is too late and overt opposition is avoided. Then, any reversal of that change would be unrealistic or worse than the change itself. In effect, this is brainwashing and creating a new paradigm for the people who were manipulated. National, state, and local progressive politicians consistently use Alinsky's tactics and progressives other than politicians are increasingly using his tactics to push the progressive movement.

I said idealism overshadows pragmatism with well-meaning liberals and they excessively rationalize away any unwanted consequences in their unwavering intensity and commitment to achieve liberal ideology. This is true for progressives in a different way. Progressives are working toward achieving an unstated nefarious ideological agenda. The end justifies the means is the epitome of progressive liberal traits. Whatever it takes and damn any unwanted consequences in the process. A great example is the so-called Affordable Care Act. Affordable care sounds good doesn't it? Healthcare has long had a reputation in the United States for being expensive and unaffordable for many. So Obama, Pelosi, and Reid pushed this new law by saying it will make healthcare available and affordable for all Americans. Pelosi even said, "We need to pass the bill so we can see what is in it away from the fog." This is a perfect example of progressive mentality! Progressives like Pelosi know what is best for us. Trust them, let them do their thing, and don't ask any questions.

When the healthcare bill is fully implemented, if it ever is, the bill will: be much more expensive for everyone; not provide care to everyone; restrict care to everyone; and destroy the best healthcare system in the world. Obama, Pelosi, and Reid knew that from the beginning. As time passes and the bill continues to unfold, that fact becomes more and more evident. So why did they say what they did? The bill was designed to not work so it will ultimately push the United States into national healthcare.

A national healthcare bill would have never passed. The Affordable Care Act is a Trojan horse. They knew it would be extremely difficult if not impossible to repeal the Act and go back to our old system when Americans found out the real agenda. Alinsky again! Why would they do such a thing to us? Power and control! Healthcare is over one-fifth of our economy and affects every single citizen. Socialized medicine is the single most effective means to transform our government into another government model. Think a progressive Marxist model. If you think I am "loony tunes" that America could ever become a Marxist based nation, let's see what you believe after you read the remainder of the book.

Once the government has power and control over its citizens through socialized medicine the *horse* is out of the barn. The progressive politicians in the *cat-bird* seat would be in *hog* heaven. They would *milk* it for everything they could until the *cows* come home. America's only chance is for non-progressives to get their *ducks* in a row, wake up the *lambs* on their way to slaughter, kick the progressive *donkey's* ass by *beet*-ing and *squash*-ing him, and make the progressive's *chickens* come home to roost. A bit *corny* I suppose but fun to write. Food-for-thought so to speak.

In chapter 2, we talked about the following liberal core personality traits: idealism; rationalization; the end justifies the means; justification of actions or inactions to a fault; inordinate ideological bias; denial; and divert and switch. Progressives possess all of these traits on steroids but none are as problematic to Americans as "the end justifies the means" trait because of its disastrous and controlling impact on people's lives. No matter what progressives proclaim about improving the lives of their fellow man, their fellow man is a pawn toward their end game.

I want to revisit and emphasize three very important progressive characteristics: 1) they want power and control; 2) they believe they know what is best for society; and 3) they do not see themselves subject to the same rules they impose on society. They see themselves in a league of their own and superior to everyone else. Sound like some famous leaders of old? Stalin, Lenin, Hitler, and Mao. How about more contemporary leaders like Pol Pot, Chávez, or Castro? How about our own leader today?

Two liberal beliefs that are distinctive for progressives are collectivism and globalism. Progressives promote collectivism for different reasons than classic liberals who only want social justice. Progressives diabolically support income redistribution to further their power and control. The more American citizens fall into the bottomless trap of becoming dependent upon government entitlements, the more they vote in perpetuity for those who "hand out the bacon". It gives a new meaning to "government pork". It's a heck of a deal if you're a progressive. Especially, when we taxpayers pay for it literally and figuratively for the rest of our and our succeeding generation's lives with no way out and our country becomes deeper and deeper in debt. Progressives stay in power forever and are not subject to the same laws, restrictions, and economy because they make the rules and find ways around the negatives for themselves.

Globalism is a narcissistic behavioral characteristic of progressives. They act as if they believe any negative action in the world toward the United States is a result of past American exceptionalism. Progressives in Washington believe they can influence the world by "sucking up" to world leaders who are not friendly to the United States and win them over. They do this by giving these world leaders undue trust and respect and unwavering compromise. Members of the Obama administration and Obama himself believe they are that influential. This is a very flawed and very dangerous approach to world affairs for our country's success and safety. It results from their narcissistic naivety. We will delve much deeper into this issue when we discuss Washington's current approach to foreign affairs.

Another concept of globalism supported by some progressives is the concept of one world order, which means one government for the entire world. It is not surprising that there are individuals who believe they could run the world better than anyone else. It is somewhat incomprehensible that a human being could be that narcissistic but we know they are out there. One name that comes to mind is George Soros and we will look at some of his actions in that regard in the next chapter.

We have explored the psychology and motivations of progressive behavior. The rest of this chapter and the remaining chapters in the book examine what progressive behavior has done, is doing, and will do to this great country of ours. Hold on to your seats. It isn't pretty!

The following is a progressive behavior that is perhaps their most distinctive and is exceptionally troubling. Progressives love to bash America. They use all the liberal core personality traits to do this but the two that stand out most to me are inordinate ideological bias and the end justifies the means. They use facts and information, sometimes true and sometimes false, in a very selective and distorted manner to make false points to achieve their agenda of destroying America's ideological foundation. Why would they do that when that ideological foundation has made the United States the greatest country the world has ever seen? They do it because that ideological foundation does not allow them to achieve their nefarious goals of power and control. They are so fervent and unrelenting they drag classic liberals and, even on occasion, conservatives along with them. Let's take a look at some of their contrived bashing versus reality.

Progressives extol the United States stole the land from the American Indians, embraced slavery, discriminates against women and minorities, promotes the rich at the expense of the middle class and the poor, and is responsible for other distortions progressives create to accomplish their agenda. Let's debunk some of their distortions with reality regarding the evolution of our country. The American Indians are most commonly believed to have migrated to what is now the United States about 13,000 years ago across the Bering Strait. Another theory is that American Indians migrated from the South American west coast. No one knows the Indians' actual origin. The point is that American Indians migrated here just like Europeans. Could both migration theories be true and the two Indian factions were the first to fight each other for land on

U.S. soil? Interesting thought. We do know many American Indian tribes were fighting each other before and after our European ancestors migrated here. Here is another interesting thought. Were the American Indians the first humans on what is now U.S. soil or did "they" take the land from other humans?

Progressives blame Columbus for "non-indigenous people" taking over this land and they want Indigenous Appreciation Day in lieu of Columbus Day. Columbus was actually Genoan (Italy was not a country until 1861) versus Spanish as popularly thought and, as you know, he has been historically recognized as the first explorer to come to the Americas. His purpose was to find trade routes to Asia for Spain. Whoops! He sure got lost! He gets a lot of blame for being this cruel Spaniard who "conquered America" and employed "unbridled violence" toward indigenous cultures to obtain natural resources and take ownership of their land. Columbus landed in the Bahamas. He never set foot on what is now the United States and was no crueler than any other world explorer at that time. Think about what kind of person one would have to be to get on a very small ship, go out to sea for months, and have no idea where you are going or what awaits you.

It is now believed the Vikings were the first people to discover the United States about 500 years before Columbus landed in the Caribbean in 1492. Jamestown was founded in 1607 by the English and is considered the first permanent colony although there were some attempts by Europeans to settle before then. These settlers had to endure brutal winters, scarce food, primitive conditions, and high mortality. Jamestown lasted about 100 years. The Pilgrims came in 1620 and by 1770 there were about 2 million people in the 13 British Colonies.

During the evolution of the United States, we were caught in the middle of a fight between the British and the French called the French Indian War that lasted from about 1756 to 1763. The Boston Tea Party on December 16, 1773 was the beginning of the end for British rule of our original colonies. The American Revolution officially began in April of 1775 and did not end until September 1783. We declared our independence from Great Britain on July 4, 1776. The Hessian Germans fought with the British and France and Spain fought with us during the Revolutionary War? Although some American Indians living in the East fought with us, most fought with the British as did American slaves who were promised their freedom by the British.

The expansion of our country south and west was difficult. We fought battles with and purchased land from other countries. The United States acquired Florida and land west of the Mississippi River in the continental U. S. from France, Spain, the British, and Mexico? I found it interesting that we bought Alaska from the Russians in 1867. This issue is much more complicated and not the same as the progressives would like you to believe. We did not just simply come to America and "steal the land" from the Indians.

Our relationship with the American Indians was arduous at best. In the beginning, George Washington and Secretary of War Henry Knox wanted to educate the American Indians and assimilate them into the larger society. For various reasons, both sides resisted that approach. We then signed treaties with several American Indian tribes that were broken by both sides resulting in many conflicts. Western American Indian tribes resisted any association with the United States government. Obviously the U.S. government won out in the end. It is extremely unfortunate that the issue between American Indians and European settlers could not have resulted in a much better outcome than we have today. Neither side was innocent in this less than desirable outcome. That was especially true during the War of 1812 when the British gave the American Indians considerable weaponry to encourage them to attack settlers in the Northwest Territory, which they did.

I would like to hear the progressives who routinely bash the evolution of the United States describe what they believe should have happened. Should there be no America except for the Indians? Do the progressives really believe that is realistic considering the evolutionary history of the world? Do the progressives believe "they" should have colonized here first, screened those that followed, and sent those who did not agree with them back home? What would their colonies have been like? One big utopian family? What would their Constitution say? Actually, they probably wouldn't have one. Written laws are cumbersome and get in the way of progressive governance. What would they have done when reality showed up on their shores from other geographical lands reflecting the world's historically cruel migratory evolution, forced its way in, and developed America in its fashion rather than the America we have today? They don't have a clue! All they can do is spew out their fallacious criticisms of the greatest country to ever exist.

I have studied the geographic development of the United States. I am astounded and astonished at what people went through to colonize the United States in order to obtain freedom of religion, freedom from oppression, and opportunity in life. Every tiny corner of the world, from the beginning of civilized man, has been one of exploration and conquest. Historically, those conquests have ranged from plain old ugly to extreme brutality and no part of the world has been immune since civilization began. Conquests continue in many parts of the world even today. If our country had not been colonized by the people who did and for the reasons they did, others would have. What would have happened to the American Indians then? Whatever that country would have been like, it would not have the freedom and opportunity that is afforded to those of us who live in America today including the American Indians. Bashing America is the ultimate case of progressive-do-not-confuse-me-with-the-facts.

Here is another one. Slavery has been going on for thousands of years and is still rampant across the world. A PBS story estimated that approximately 12 million slaves were bought from Africa to North America, South America, Central America, and the Caribbean between 1500 and the 1860s. I read only 4% to 5% of those slaves wound up in the United States. I verified these numbers on several websites. Slavery ended in the U.S. in 1867 with the 13th Amendment of the Constitution. Do you know how those slaves were captured and put into slavery in the first place? They were captured by other African tribes and traded for such things as rum, guns, and gunpowder. We will look at slavery in America and debunk progressive falsehoods regarding women and minorities in chapter 10. The world has never been nor ever will be utopian, as progressives would like you to believe. The world is a wonderful place but it also is a cruel place. I cannot express my feelings strong enough to thank God I was born and raised in America.

The progressives never seem to stop their don't-confuse-me-with-the-facts political propaganda. Do you ever think the progressives will shut up about the "middle class"? Because it is the largest voting block, progressives will not shut up talking about how the middle class is so mistreated and in financial need. The progressives always tout how they are going to give the middle class a utopian life once they are in office. I find it interesting that the progressives don't say much about the needs of the poor. They just shower them with entitlements for their votes. They can't do that as lavishly with the middle class so they make promises to help them become richer.

Well, they had their chance from 2009 until 2011 when they controlled the House, the Senate, and the White House. Did they do it? No! They had a decent chance from 2011 to 2015 when they still controlled the Senate and the White House. They didn't do it then, either. When are they going to do it? The progressive ranting to help the middle class is a falsehood in an effort to get votes and no financial class of Americans is better off after Obama took office. That includes the so-called wealthy who progressives claim prey on the middle class and the poor. We will address that issue later in much more depth.

The United States was the first country in the history of the world that allowed "rule by the people" as stipulated in our Constitution? The Constitution was printed in German for Philadelphia and Dutch for New York because of the number of citizens who could not speak English in those cities? We are a nation founded by immigrants looking for a better life for themselves and their families. Even the American Indians are immigrants. As far as we know, no human species was on this land we call America when man first appeared on Earth.

The progressives claim our country is rife with discrimination. Name me one society in the world in which the citizenry practices less discrimination than ours. Just one! There aren't any. That is another progressive utopian fallacy. It is progressive hypocrisy. Humans are human and less than perfect. I would think the progressives would be sympathetic about our imperfections since they profess to know more than the rest of us and therefore have to nudge us in the right direction as we look back in bafflement.

America bashing is one of the progressives' best weapons to take our country down and replace it with their self-serving evil ideology. The next chapter is a paper I wrote in September 2009 for my family and friends regarding the progressive movement in our country. I call it my 2009 Epistle. It is presented exactly as I wrote it with only a few minor grammatical and punctuation changes for clarity. I did provide a few noted updates. The first few paragraphs are a generalized repeat of what you have read so far, so bare with me on that. I added my epistle to the book because of its content regarding the complexity of progressive organizations in the U.S. and the interrelationships between them. I used the term radical versus progressive in the epistle, as they are one in the same.

Even though the material is seven years old, the content is still accurate today and is a mini-version of this book even though the Epistle and this book were written totally independent of each other. That point in itself is very alarming, because it demonstrates how radical progressivism has gotten progressively worse. Another pun intended!

The genesis of the information contained in the paper is based upon my many hours of intense listening, note taking, and fascination with Glen Beck's shows when he was on Fox News. He provided extensive coverage of what was happening in Washington with the Obama administration and with other progressives like George Soros. Glen was trashed by the liberal establishment as being nothing more than a fabricator of untrue conspiracy theories. I said I hate like hell to be wrong? For that reason, I did hours and hours of my own research on the Internet and with the news media regarding what I heard on Glen's shows and did not find any of his information to be false.

It is more than interesting that the websites of the progressive organizations I researched have since been cleansed and much of the website information I used to verify Glen's assertions is no longer available. This cleansing is also validation that Glen was correct in what he said. He certainly hit more than a few nerves. The organizations I discuss are by no means all the organized progressive groups. There are many more out there. The general population would be shocked and alarmed if they understood how prevalent, intertwined, and anti-America these groups are.

CHAPTER 5

My 2009 Epistle!

Well, here is my epistle I've been promising for weeks. It seems each day there is something else to investigate, so today I'm cutting it off. I had no idea what I was getting into when I started. I used the knowledge I gained from watching Fox News and what I read in the print media to begin. But, as I began to verify on the Internet what I saw and read, I was amazed at what else I found. Not only did I confirm Fox News coverage, I found much more. So much more that it is not reasonable to cover it all without writing a book so I'm only going to cover enough to present a picture of what is going on. My biggest disappointment, besides what is happening to our country, is the total lack of investigative reporting by the mainstream media. I truly don't understand it. In the past, whether it would be Democratic or Republican news, what I have found and written about here would be daily headline news. If it were not for Fox News and conservative radio, I shudder to think how uninformed Americans, including me, would be about what is going on. I now know there is a lot on the Internet, but it does not have the impact of mainstream media on the total society yet. Very-very scary!

I want to start by talking about why I love America. We have the greatest country in the world. We have the highest standard of living, we have the most freedom, we are the safest internally and externally and we have great mores and values. No, we are not perfect. We certainly have our areas where improvement is needed and should continually strive to solve our issues, although realistically there is no such thing as a perfect society. I guess life would be pretty boring if there were. One can pick and choose aspects of other societies and tout they are better, but no other country is even close when you put it all together. Our country was founded by people who were tired of government tyranny and taxation. They wanted freedom and opportunity and created a constitution that would support that dream after a long and hard-fought battle. They took great risks and made great sacrifices so we could have and enjoy what we have today. Our country was built on dreams of a better life, opportunity, self-reliance, and hard work. That is the American Dream.

That "Dream" has brought millions of immigrants to the United States over centuries. It has made our country what it is—the most diverse and powerful country in the world economically and militarily with a heart of gold toward each other and others around the world. Contrary to what some say, no other country gives or has ever given more economically to people in need around the world, protected them from harm, and supported their freedom than the United States. On the other hand, no one should ever mistake our country standing up for itself for anything else but standing up for itself. I understand and support globalization and its implications, but this world is full of bullies, thugs, and people who are jealous of everything we have and stand for and would like to see nothing more than to take advantage of us and see us fail. The reason I am sending you this epistle is that I am 100% convinced—not 99.9%—but 100% convinced that there are people in power in this country who because of their ideology and their quest for power are trying to change the way we live and the things we stand for. I have never felt this in my entire life no matter which party has been in office and it is scary and disturbing. I am, however; heartened and proud of the way Americans are standing up to this "push" by them. I think they have grossly underestimated the American people and what we stand for. The rest of my epistle is to explain why this is happening, what is happening, and why it is wrong.

First of all, this is not a Republican vs. Democrat issue. It is not even a left (liberal) vs. right (conservative) issue. Some degree of balance is always good. Although I am basically a conservative, I support several liberal views; i.e., abortion, stem cell research, reasonable environmental regulation, and gay rights for example. I guess I could be called a centrist, a moderate, or even a libertarian. This issue is about far left liberal radicalism. Let me explain the differences in personality and ideology. There are semi-conservatives in the Democratic Party and semi-liberals in the Republican Party. I think that is good. Any politician, regardless of his or her party affiliation, demonstrates political behaviors and expresses political rhetoric that is common to all politicians. Let's talk about political differences beyond those common behaviors and rhetoric for politicians and for society in general in terms of left, right, far left, and far right ideology.

Interestingly, I don't see much or hear much from the far right, although they do pop-up from time to time, especially during elections. I don't think they differ a lot from the right in their beliefs and behaviors. They certainly do not display the radicalism as does the far left. They are much more rigid and intense in some of their beliefs than are other conservatives, i.e.; religion, abortion, and gay rights, but I am going to lump them with the right on my analysis as apparently the far left does as well. On 9/11 of this year, the Democratic National Committee on its web site MyBarackObama.com called for its readers to combat the "Right Wing Terrorist" who are against healthcare reform. I guess that includes me, since I demonstrated at a Tea Party event.

The right are generally pragmatic and factual, endorse traditional values, support the inclusion of religion in society, oppose big government and taxation, support the Constitution and believe as those who wrote it, support capitalism, and adhere to the American Dream as I described above. Even though there may be some variation in ideology for the right (i.e., abortion and gay rights issues), the right and far right are not as diverse in personality traits as the left and far left. I guess when you're right-you're right. Pun intended.

I don't know if my own conservative biases create my observation about the right or not. Interesting. The left do not have the same personality traits as those far left and tend to be idealistic and naïve about society; are usually very passionate in making or defending their point and say what is needed to do so even if contradictory to reason or fact; support minority ideas and rights in deference to the majority; tend to support mass society over individualism; support government as the change agent for social improvement through government tax funded programs, policy, and law; support the redistribution of wealth; and support significant government control and oversight of business.

There is no right or wrong between right and left ideology. It depends upon your personality and what you believe. I think the great majority of people identify with one ideology or the other, but not 100% with only one. As I said before, I agree with the right with a little left thrown in. I will say; however, that I personally feel very passionate that the ideology of the left is not best for the success of our country and our society. I believe the left are well-meaning and good people who have a utopian psychology.

As much as many would like otherwise, utopia or anything close does not or ever will exist. The human nature of people does not allow that. When I was in college, I studied B. F. Skinner who is recognized in some circles as the most influential psychologist in the 20th Century. His story has always been one of my favorites about societal behavior. He unfortunately died an unhappy man because two utopian communities founded upon his utopian ideas eventually were abandoned. The fiction book, *Animal Farm*, written in 1945 by George Orwell is another good example of human nature and behavior in utopian communities. (Update: I will review Orwell's book in chapter 13.)

I have always said that it is people who believe similarly to Skinner who would unknowingly self-destruct and never know what hit them. We don't need these people making decisions for the majority of us and we sure as heck don't need them being led down the proverbial primrose path by far left radicals making decisions that will destroy our country and our lives as we know it. I hope these comparisons and analyses are clear the way I intended and not offensive to anyone. They are difficult to make in such an abbreviated manner without writing a book and I'm certainly not a research psychologist. (Update: Well, I did write this book but I am still not a research psychologist.)

Now let's talk about far left radicalism which is a whole different animal than the left or right and is dangerous and destructive. It is vicious and mean spirited against those who disagree. Deception is a common practice. Since radicalism is based upon accomplishing its ideology at all costs, it is reckless and irresponsible. Ideology is supposed to represent the people not visa-versa. Radicalism has always been out there, but in my life time it has never had any real opportunity to be in the mainstream until now. The only other time it came into the White House was in the early to mid 1900s with FDR and Woodrow Wilson. Obviously it did not sustain itself in a big way, although it took about forty-five years to rid government of some of the radical things FDR instituted.

Let me explain why I feel this is so dangerous and destructive. The current radical movement has been developing over the past 40 to 50-years and finally hit the perfect storm: radicals prevalent in Congress and in the White House; a significant web of radical organizations and influential people in the United States to support and push radicalism; a huge financial political war chest; the unrest in the country due to the economy and the Iraq war; and no significant push back from the mainstream media. Do the radicals want socialism, Marxism, communism, fascism, anarchy, collectivism, or progressivism? Take your pick. It depends upon the individual or the group as to what politics they are supporting. The common element they all share is that they have professed their commitment to effect radical change in our government. In its simplest form they are aggressively taking a totalitarian approach to change America to their ideology versus allowing freedom of the people to decide their own governance. It is about power, control and corruption under the guise of pursuing left ideology for the benefit of society. Radicals claim to be the liberators of the poor, minorities, those with needs, etc. when in reality they are their suppressor because it gives them power.

The more crises and disasters in our country, the more opportunity there is for radical ideology to flourish because of confusion, uncertainty, and fear. Rahm Emanuel said you never waste a good crisis. The radicals have motivation to create and sustain problems versus improve or solve them. We really don't know how far they would go in radicalizing our government if they had the power. Power can be an enormous motivator. At minimum, it would mean a more powerful government with more powerful politicians and more control over business, our environment, our health, our social freedoms, our religious freedoms, our ability to make individual decisions, and our ability to individually succeed in life. It means redistribution of wealth and heavy taxation on everyone to pay for it all. Ideology would become more important than the people it is supposed to serve, but would serve those in power well. Hypocrisy by those in power would be worse than now. You would not see them living under the same rules and economic conditions as those that they govern.

Just look around the world today. If this radical transition were to ever happen in our country, it is highly unlikely it could ever change back. No country ever has. Unwinding socialist based programs, government controls and power, etc. would be next to impossible if not impossible. The majority of people would soon start to depend upon the government to take care of them and would acquiesce to and support government control and policies. No matter what your ideology, you would have no choice economically but to acquiesce. The American Dream that our country was built upon and has thrived on becomes very elusive. It is a form of brainwashing society. When people gradually and continually lose over time what they have that is important to them economically and emotionally and can't do anything about it, people tend to accept the positives they are given afterward as better than the bad they experienced in the process. We become more average as a country and lose our position as the most powerful country in the world. Can you imagine the United States having the same stature in the world as the European socialist based countries like England, France, Italy, Greece and Germany which would leave the communist countries of Russia and upstart China to be the most powerful in the world? Maybe we would become a powerful communist country like them. Shudder to think! Next I want to discuss how the far left radicals are gaining significant power and why our Democracy as we know it is in danger.

First of all, this is a very complicated subject that is very difficult if not impossible to present in this short dissertation without oversimplifying the complexities. Bear with me as I continue to try to present this as simply as possible without writing a book. One very important thing to keep in mind as you read this is the web of entanglements between people and organizations and think in terms of a conspiracy. There is much more out there than what is exposed here which reinforces my findings and enlarges the web. Let's start with Saul Alinsky and his writings on radicalism, particularly his last book written in 1971 titled *Rules for Radicals* which is the primer for radical organizing. He says revolutionaries do not flaunt their radicalism. They infiltrate from within-gradually. He also says you do or say whatever it takes to gain power. He also recognizes Lucifer as the first true radical recognized in the world. Nice thought!

It is worth noting that supposedly Hillary Clinton did her senior college thesis on Saul Alinsky's teachings. While she and Bill were in the White House they had Wellesley College suppress her thesis from access by anyone. Interesting! More importantly, Obama used Alinsky's book to teach organizing workshops in the late 1980s. There is no doubt, as you will see, that these principles, whether by design or not, are used extensively by the radicals in Washington in driving toward their goals. Let's start with Obama himself. Obama and his family spent approximately 20 years in Reverend Jeremiah Wright's church, contributed significant money and expressed a close relationship with him. Wright is without question a radical who is anti-white and anti-American and repeatedly expounded this philosophy in his sermons.

Obama's kickoff event for his run for the Senate was at the home of Bill Ayers, a founding member of radical and violent Weather Underground. In 2005 Obama defended the New Deal policies of FDR, which included radical ideas. Obama is also quoted in his book, *Dreams from My Father: A Story of Race and Inheritance*, as choosing his friends carefully which included Marxist professors. Michelle Obama said during the campaign that for the first time in her adult life she was proud of America. Obama said during his campaign there would be a civilian force highly trained and as well funded as the military for domestic purposes (think Acorn, Apollo, AmeriCorps, Tides and unions—especially SEIU). Obama also said in a campaign speech, "We are five days away from fundamentally transforming America". Each of these events by themselves might be explained away but there is a definite pattern here that will have more meaning as we continue.

Let's now talk about Obama's closest advisors. We have Rahm Emanuel, David Axelrod, and Valerie Jarrett who are all products of the Chicago political machine. Emanuel had the nickname of "Rahm-bo" because of his take no prisoners' attitude. It is also interesting that there is a tie between Jarrett's mother and Ayers' father in that Ayers' father, a very successful Chicago businessman, chaired The Erickson Institute her mother founded; however, I did not find any significance to that. Just interesting.

In the past few days Obama changed his mind about going to Copenhagen to support Chicago's bid for the Olympics. It was reported that Jarrett and Michelle changed his mind. Jarrett has said Obama is like a brother. She apparently has helped Michelle obtain her jobs in Chicago and some have called her the Carl Rove for Obama. She reportedly is a significant slumlord in Chicago with ties to a convicted felon slumlord as well as major Chicago politicians. If Chicago obtains the Olympics they will in all likelihood lose millions if not billions of dollars as have other Olympic venues when they are already in a deficit situation. The citizens are split 50/50. Who stands to gain most from Chicago getting the Olympics? My guess is the politicians including Jarrett and her buddies from the sale of ghetto property for the Olympic facilities. It is worthy of note that Michelle and Jarrett took a government 727 to Copenhagen while Obama took Air Force One the next day, which cost US taxpayers millions of dollars in White House travel costs. ??? Stay tuned.

Then we have the Czars and others who are not officially called Czars but are called advisors. Although all presidents have had them since FDR started the concept, no president has had even close to as many as Obama. At last count, he has a total in excess of 40. These Czars are not confirmed by Congress and are directly accountable to the president. Although, not a lot is known about many of them, we do know the radical nature of several. The most famous is Van Jones, the ex-Green Jobs Czar. I saw Valarie Jarrett in a video say that they had been watching him for a long time and were lucky to capture his energy and ideas. He is very smart and is a forceful speaker. I could write several paragraphs about all the video clips where I saw him and what I read about him, but here is a summary. He is a self-proclaimed communist, has been arrested several times as an activist, has on many occasions publicly accused whites of atrocities toward minorities, has promoted revolution and income distribution through the "green" movement and green jobs, and was closely associated with STORM which is a radical group explicitly committed to Marxist politics. (Update: Jones was dismissed from the White House when it became public he was a communist and is currently a regular commentator on MSNBC.)

Next let's look at John Holdren, the Science Czar. He once co-authored a book that advocated a "Planetary Regime" to control population growth and natural resources to protect the planet. The book advocated forced abortion and sterilization and advocated putting birth control in the water system as well as forcefully taking babies from single mothers and giving them to couples. He also came up with the idea to put particles in the atmosphere to reflect heat and control global warming. Remember the extinction of the dinosaurs? Wow, we could become dinosaurs.

Cass Sunstein is another interesting character. His book in 2004 discussed animals being thought of as humans and be given legal status to sue in order to stem animal abuse. How would you feel about being sued by your dog, your cat, or your pet hamster? Another book he wrote in 2004 stipulates that we need a second Bill of Rights to support FDR's unfinished revolution. His 2008 book, *The Nudge*, suggests that people need public and private organizations to help them make decisions since people make poor choices and look back in bafflement. He has also been credited as supporting the concept that emphasizes the young over the old in health and life decisions on the premise that the old are not discriminated against since they were once young themselves. Sure doesn't make an old man like me feel too good. And finally, Mr. Sunstein has said we should celebrate tax day and that without taxes there would be no liberty and no liberty without dependency.

Now we come to Carol Browner who is in charge of the White House Office of Energy and Climate Change and also known as the Energy or Climate Czar. The Washington Times reported in January that when she was appointed by Obama she was one of 14 leaders of a socialist group called the Commission for a Sustainable World Society which calls for global governance and says that rich countries must shrink their economies to address climate change. Obama's team responded that her association with this group was not a problem and her name was quickly removed from the organization's list of 14 leaders.

One of the most concerning Czars is Mark Lloyd who is the new Diversity Czar. He was recently appointed to the newly created post at the Federal Communications Commission as Associate General Counsel/Chief Diversity Officer. He has been quoted as saying that freedom of speech is a distraction. I have seen him on a video praising Chávez for learning the value of the media from the United States and how to control it to win revolutions. Scary. Obama has said he would not reinstitute the Fairness Doctrine imposed under FDR and rescinded under Reagan. But, Mr. Lloyd has determined there is more than one way to skin a cat. He has proposed a taxing scheme on broadcasters who don't follow certain guidelines as established through eight pods around the country to regulate political commentary and commercials. It would have the same effect as the Fairness Doctrine and would basically put conservative broadcasting out of business. He has been quoted as saying that he personally is opposed to private control of the media.

Also, it is worth noting that Mr. Lloyd is a Senior Fellow at the very liberal Center for American Progress run by John Podesta. Their web site says, "Progressive Ideas for a Strong, Just, and Free America. Their four Priorities are restoring global leadership, seizing energy opportunity, creating progressive growth, and delivering universal healthcare. Does that sound like a familiar agenda? It might be of great interest to note that Podesta was Vice Chair of Obama's White House transition team. Hmm? The Center for American Progress was funded by George Soros and has been said to be controlled by Hillary Clinton. Keep all this and Podesta in mind when we review ACORN and AmeriCorps. (Update: Podesta is currently chairman of Clinton's presidential campaign.)

Rahm Emanuel's brother Ezekiel Emanuel was appointed special advisor for health policy to the Office of Management and Budget and is Director of the Clinical Bioethics Department at the National Institute of Health. He has said he would phase out Medicare and Medicaid and give everyone a voucher funded by a value added tax. A value added tax is a tax that would be included in the price of all products we purchase. In Europe it runs as high as 25%. He has also expressed interest in taxing what he calls junk food such as soft drinks. Tax, tax, and more tax and proposing to intrude on our personal decisions and change behavior by taxing. What's next?

Emanuel advocates that a physician's duty is to work for the greater good of society instead of focusing on an individual patient's needs and has advocated national healthcare for a decade. He has said that the United States should, in a decision making body similar to the United Kingdom's rationing body, slow the adoption of new medications and set limits on how much will be paid to lengthen life. The New York Post reported in July that Ezekiel said, "Unlike allocation by sex and race, allocation by age is not invidious discrimination, every person lives through different life stages rather than being a single age". I bet he and Mr. Sunstein have some interesting conversations about us old folks. (Update: Ezekiel was the architect of Obamacare.)

Peter Orszag, Obama's new Director of Office and Budget (a new cabinet position), urged Congress in February to delegate its own authority over Medicare to a new, presidentially appointed bureaucracy that would be accountable to the public. Sounds like another White House attempt at increasing executive control to me. Read on. Interrogation of terrorists has been taken over by the Federal Bureau of Investigation (FBI) and the White House from the CIA. It has always been interesting to me how the government vilifies something before they attempt to take it over or do something bad to it. The CIA and insurance industry for instance. It was also recently announced that the Government is taking over Pell Grants for college education loans from the private sector. Why? And, it has been discussed that the Government be able to take over the internet "in case of emergency". There was even a hint of the Government bailing out the newspapers. After what they did to the banks and the auto industry, how would you feel about Government control of the printed news or, gradually over time, all the news?

Most recently there is discussion by the Government to control salaries of all employees of banks, even those without tarp funds, with assets over $1B. That equates to over 5,000 banks. Begs the question of what industry is next? Are these examples of a conspiracy by the radicals in Congress and more specifically in the White House for increasing significant control by Government? Draw your own conclusions. There are more interesting discoveries out there regarding these so called Czars and advisors, but as I said I'm not going to write a book. (Update:

My contempt toward the progressive onslaught to destroy America compelled me to the point that I had to write this book.)

Now, let's turn to some of the organizations that Obama was probably talking about that would assist in fundamentally changing America. Let's start with ACORN. Thanks to two young brave people, they have brought a very corrupt organization to the public forefront. ACORN was already being investigated in, I believe, 14 states for voter fraud and now the recently hidden camera interviews by these two young people have exposed ACORN even more for their corruption in the way they conduct their business. Six more states have now started investigations. Since the mainstream media has all but ignored this issue, we can thank Fox News and especially Glen Beck for pushing the issue and causing Congress to act to stop funding them and the Census Department from using them for our next census. Heaven forbid! It is worth noting that conservatives in the Senate and House have been trying to get their funding stopped for some time to no avail and several far left Senators and House members voted against stopping their funding even after the videos came out. And, as I write this, there are several far lefts in Congress fighting to keep the funding. Unbelievable! They have been government funded for years with tens of millions of dollars and were to receive approximately $8.5B in tarp funds.

Obama has had a long relationship with ACORN through his organizing work for affiliated groups in the 1980s and defending them as their attorney in the1990s. His campaign staff gave ACORN approximately $800,000 during his campaign. Why? I might also add that their founder's brother allegedly embezzled $1M and instead of going to jail he was terminated and went to work for SEIU. It has been reported that John Podesta is on their Board. I could not confirm it because that information is tightly held; however, the newspaper this morning quoted White House Press Secretary Robert Gibbs as saying that Podesta was a prominent ally of Obama and is on ACORN's advisory board and trying to clean up the mess. It would be interesting to know how long he has been on the advisory board, how and why he got there, and what he has actually done if anything to "clean up the mess". I won't even get into ACORN's roll in the housing crises, which was significant.

AmeriCorps is a similar organization as ACORN, but outwardly more legitimate in stature because it is a government organization which was created by Bill Clinton. Although the organization is not in the sleaze category as ACORN, the corruption could be as bad in the way they use taxpayers' money. In 1995 they gave a $1M grant to ACORN and eventually ACORN had to return it. They have been criticized because of their number of failed projects and the amount of money they have channeled to liberal advocacy groups. Most recently, Inspector General Gerald Walpin was fired by the White House for exposing that AmeriCorps gave money to the Mayor of San Francisco and Obama's friend Kevin Johnson who used it for personal and illegal purposes. Mr. Walpin settled with the Government out of court. Mr. Johnson gave the money back and to my knowledge nothing happened to him or AmeriCorps. In March of this year the Senate voted to increase funding to AmeriCorps to go from 75,000 positions to 250,000 positions at an additional cost of $6B over 5 years. Conservatives tried to stop it because they were concerned it was funding left-wing ideology groups. The liberals kept them from stopping the funding.

One of the more interesting organizations is the Apollo Alliance (the name was later changed to the BlueGreen Alliance which is not uncommon among these subversive organizations to make them harder to track). Most, if not all, of their 16 board members have significant liberal, union, and or radical backgrounds. Here are the more interesting ones: the President of the United Auto Workers; the Executive Vice President of SEIU; the President of the Labor International Union of North America; John Podesta; Carl Pope who is the President of the Sierra Club, a regular contributor to the Huffington Post, and has worked with his fellow board member from the UAW to form an alliance between their organizations; and, last but not least, former board member Van Jones.

Another interesting character with Apollo is the Director of their New York state office, Jeff Jones. Mr. Jones was a founding member of Weather Underground with none other than Bill Ayers and was involved in the bombing of government buildings. The current headline on Apollo's national web site states, "Labor Union's Green Efforts are Cause for Celebration". A weekly update on their site says, "Van Jones

Resignation (from the White House) Means It's Time for All to Work Harder". Harry Reid publicly thanked Apollo for their role in developing the stimulus plan and I understand they played a very significant role in writing both the stimulus plan and the cap and trade legislation where factories, utilities, and other businesses are given a carbon emissions target. Those entities that emit less than the target can sell the difference to another entity in the system. Each year the target becomes lower. I thought that was Congress' role? It is also interesting that Jeff Jones and his staff wrote the applications for New York to obtain stimulus funds. Convenient!

Now we come to SEIU. We might note that in many locations SEIU's offices are in the same building as ACORN. Without question, SEIU is one of the most aggressive unions in the country. Besides all the ties they have with these other groups we reviewed, their president (Andy Stern) has been a regular visitor to the White House. He visited many times on a weekly basis. He has bragged that SEIU gave Obama's campaign $60.7M. Wow! That does not count all the people they got to the polls to vote, which was huge.

Here are a few more tidbits. During our new Secretary of Labor Hilda Solis' four terms in Congress, SEIU gave her more than $900,000 in contributions. Former SEIU lobbyist Patrick Gaspard was appointed as the White House Political Advisor after he served in Obama's campaign. According to The Washington Post, Mr. Gaspard has a history with a George Soros' funded group (America Coming Together) as the National Field Director. This group was fined $775,000 by the Federal Election Commission for campaign finance violations. I wasn't going to spend much time on Mr. Soros (a multi-billionaire) but during my research I found that he plays a significant role in all of this. Soros, Hillary Clinton, and Harold McEwan Ickes who was Bill Clinton's Assistant Chief of Staff and son of the Secretary of Interior under FDR founded the Shadow Party which is a nationwide network of more than five dozen unions, non-profit activist groups, and think tanks whose agendas are ideologically to the far left and engage in campaigning for Democrats.

New groups are being formed in the Shadow Party all the time while others vanish, so it is hard to determine how many groups exist at any given time. The Center for American Progress originated here. Most of the groups in the Shadow Party are registered as "527 groups" for fund raising and campaigning. Their unofficial headquarters is in the same building as the Motion Picture Association of America in Washington (MPAA). Interestingly, I read the MPAA has enjoyed a close relationship with the Democratic Party as many high ranking Democrats have transitioned from government jobs into glamorous posts in the MPAA's upper management. Maybe this is part of the reason, besides being personally screwed-up, that so many Hollywood types trash our country, support socialist countries, and support countries with dictators. I have always said I would like to see them go to one those countries and live and see how they like it.

Another interesting thing I read was about Soros' connection to Arianna Huffington of the Huffington Post. He supposedly financed her Shadow Conventions in 2000 which were allegedly media events designed to lure news crews from the real party conventions that year and where most speakers pushed hard line far left ideology. Ms. Huffington, a former conservative, supposedly professed after these conventions that she had become radicalized. It has been reported that Soros and Hillary share an aversion to United States hegemony and both seek to subordinate U.S. interests to global interest, U.S. sovereignty to global government, U.S. law to global courts, U.S. wealth to global taxation, U.S. productivity to a scheme for global income redistribution, and a hostility toward Israel. Could this have Middle East implications? Their ideologies on these subjects appear to be alive and well in the White House among the president and his appointees. A coincidence? I don't think so. Like minds… It would be fascinating to have been privy to the Soros driven conversations behind the scenes during the presidential election regarding Hillary and Obama. I wonder who he really supported. Probably both.

One last thing I read about Soros, but found difficult to research and confirm, is that he has a long history in effecting regime change. Supposedly, he helped fund the 1989 revolution in the Czech Republic and by his own admission helped engineer coups in Slovakia, Croatia, Georgia, and Yugoslavia. They said that when Soros has targeted a regime change he begins by creating a shadow government-in-exile waiting to assume power when the opportunity arises. A Shadow Party? His own website did speak of donations to groups in these countries. Wow!

Before I read this stuff, I had wondered if Soros might be powerful enough to be the kingpin behind what I'm convinced is a conspiracy to change America to a far left radical ideology. His website said he was significantly influenced by Karl Popper and his book, *The Open Society and Its Enemies*. I can tell you Popper is one very intellectual and very weird dude. From what I read, Soros does believe in very liberal views and open societies that tolerate extreme new ideas and different modes of thinking and behavior. Obama is definitely playing a very key role in this conspiracy as president, but I believe he is only one of many. Neither he nor Soros are the kingpin. Most likely there is no one leader, but a symbiotic collaboration among many. But, if there is a leader, Soros certainly appears to be in the mix.

One last thing about SEIU is that in May of this year Obama cut funding to the Department of Labor for investigation of union fraud. In 2008 and 2009, three of Andy Sterns handpicked deputies had to resign over financial scandals involving cronyism, nepotism and embezzlement. Sad. I could write a book on SEIU from personal union experience during my career.

We still have the "Free Choice Act" or better called the "Lack of Free Choice Act" out there under consideration by liberals in Congress. This is an act that would do away with employee elections for unionization in certain situations and contains other pro union language. That would be a disaster for American businesses and employees so stay tuned. Dennis Hughes who is President of the New York AFL-CIO is the new Chairman of the New York Fed. How did that happen? And, last but not least, what role are unions playing in the government takeover of General Motors and Chrysler. I can assure you plenty. Obama's car Czar is Ron Bloom who worked for the United Steel Workers and had a reputation as a union hatchet man. I heard he is also the new Green Jobs Czar. Oh, by the way, the bills in Congress on healthcare reform give union workers a pass on paying penalties that non-union workers and employers would be paying. Does that surprise anyone? How much are unions running the country? My research shows they now have very significant influence in Congress as well as the White House and are "calling a lot of the shots". How does that make you feel?

One last interesting group I just learned about is called TIDES—another Soros funded group. I wonder how many more there are. Drummond Pike, TIDES' CEO, is Treasurer of Soros' Democracy Alliance. Wayne Rathke, who founded ACORN, is a former Chair of the TIDES Board. Supposedly TIDES paid back to ACORN the money that Rathke's brother stole from ACORN. ??? Apollo was a project of TIDES. TIDES website says, "TIDES was created to provide comprehensive flexible services and tools to those dedicated to lasting progressive change."

TIDES funded Annie Leonard's *Story of Stuff*, a controversial short movie she produced in December 2007 on her views of the effects of human consumption which is being shown in elementary schools and post graduate economic classes across the country. The film opens by saying, "It is the Government's roll to watch out for us, to take care of us. That's their job". It is very progressive and anti-capitalism. Parents who have found out their kids are shown this movie in school and given the accompanied test are outraged, as I would be. The part of the short story I saw also had inaccurate information obviously slanted to make her points.

I recently saw other video clips showing young children in school singing short songs and poems that praise Obama as if he is some kind of "holy-one". It is the kind of stuff you would expect to see in a country indoctrinating the children toward a totalitarian state. Quite frankly, I was shocked and upset. You certainly would never expect this in American schools. How is this stuff getting in our schools? Are our teachers becoming that liberal? I certainly hope not and hope these are just isolated cases. Even then, this needs to be stopped. We can't even pledge allegiance to the flag or say a prayer in class, but they can do this. Heaven forbid! Pun intended.

I want to end the organizational discussion with the following "web" of conspirators. Soros, ACORN and SEIU are funding and supporting Health Care for America Now which is a group supporting a national single-payer concept or in my view socialized medicine. In other countries socialized medicine has been the first step to socialized government. I have already reviewed Rathke's associations between SEIU, ACORN and TIDES; Pike's associations between Soros, TIDES and Apollo; and Podesta's board seats on Apollo and Acorn and his connection to the White House. SEIU has a seat on Apollo's Board along with other union-reps. Andy Stern has a seat on ACORN's Advisory Board. I think this "web" is the preverbal "tip of the ice berg".

One very interesting and disturbing thing is that most of these organizations have so many sub-corporations and you can't follow the money and what purpose it is being used for. That brings up how taxpayer funding for some of these groups that are not-for-profit is being used and any tax implications that might result for these groups if the truth were known. I have also wondered how money from these groups might have been channeled to Obama's campaign since there were so many small donations that were not traceable.

When thinking about Obama's comment about the civilian army, I never imagined he would be talking about the government itself. Three recent happenings are concerning. First, when opposition began to swell against his healthcare reform plans, the White House put a comment on its website that people should report suspicious activity and people also started getting info on his plan who did not request it. How? Sounds like George Orwell's 2009 instead of his *1984*. After much criticism, The White House took the request off its web site. Second, Yosi Sergant, a representative from the National Endowment for the Arts, held a conference call with about 70 to 80 member artists known to be Obama supporters and asked that they do something through their art to support Obama's agenda. Buffy Wicks, a former union worker who funneled hundreds of thousands of dollars to ACORN and is now the Deputy Director of The White House Office of Public Engagement under Valarie Jarrett, was on the phone and said this was just the beginning. They were just now learning how to bring this community together legally to speak with the government.

This was reported by one of the artists on the phone that felt threatened and spoke out about the call. I personally heard him discuss this on TV. Third, one fact lost by most of the news media in the recent hullabaloo about Obama's speech to the schools across the country is the controversy that started when the Department of Education was going to send a lesson plan to the children in advance that encouraged the children to write an essay after the speech and tell how they could help the President. After concerns were raised, the lesson plan idea was retracted and the person responsible was reassigned. One of these events by itself doesn't necessarily raise red flags but a pattern starts to define a culture within Obama's administration to support his comment on the civilian army.

When these government actions are combined with the multiple anti-American organizations and the progressive Obama Czars and White House advisors are put in context with Alinsky's book, you start to get the picture of what Obama really meant by his comment on October 30, 2008 when he said, "We are five days away from fundamentally changing America".

I don't think our founding fathers ever imagined, anticipated, or planned for the perfect anti-American storm where those controlling the Senate, the House, and the White House would adhere to a radical ideology that is in total fundamental contradiction to the Declaration of Independence and the Constitution. That is totally counter to the checks and balance system our founding fathers set up. Senator Byrd, a long term Democrat whose party is obviously in power, recently said that checks and balances were out the window. I don't know how the Supreme Court enters into the picture. That would be an interesting research and discussion topic.

In 1966 the Democrats controlled the House, Senate, and the White House and we didn't have this problem, but we didn't have radical progressives running the Democratic Party. There is even concern that the Supreme Court is in danger of being controlled by progressives as well. It is a conspiracy like no other in the history of our country. This has been in the making for a very long time. Actually, if you research it, you will find that not only does the ideology go back generations for some of these radical leaders, but there are significant connections between some of their families that go back generations as well.

So, what is the answer? The same as it has always been. America, stand up! Washington lawmakers in general, even without the radicals, are out of touch with Americans. Ego and power are blinding elements. They are grossly underestimating what they are seeing in the polls, at the Tea Party events in Washington, and around the country. What they are doing is against the principles that the vast majority of Americans believe in and I believe the American spirit will prevail.

We are also tired of the pork spending (the stimulus bill is laden with pork that is totally wasteful as are many bills) and the BS we get. For example, the Treasury Department came out in March with a report that said the proposed cap and trade bill would cost a total of $100 to $200 billion annually and would cost the average family $1761 per year in increased energy cost. Congressman Henry Waxman in April, in an attempt to sell his bill, said it would not cost more than 40 cents per day. Obama in June to promote their radical energy agenda said, "It would cost only that of a postage stamp per day".

Obama made several significant inaccurate statements during his speeches to promote his position on healthcare reform. Either he was disingenuous or didn't know what he was talking about. Either way, it was an irresponsible way to promote such an important issue. Americans are not stupid. And, don't forget increasing big government, increasing national debt, and the accompanying tax burden.

The Government just approved a loan of $529M to a Finnish car company backed by Al Gore to build a hybrid car in Finland that sells for $89,000. Lucky Al gets one of the first ones. That follows a $465M loan to a California startup company who are purveyors of a $109,000 British built electric roadster. (Update: This company is Tesla Motors Inc.) Both companies have contributed millions of dollars to the Democrats. Just plain old political corruption!

Republican Congressman Thaddeus McCotter from Michigan has introduced a bill in the House to allow up to a $3,500 tax deduction for pet care. Yes, you read correctly, pet care. And, from a Republican. Unbelievable! Our debt, if allowed to continue as aggressively as planned, without a doubt will drive us into socialism or worse.

I'm also astounded by the hypocrisy of all the lawmakers in Washington in the way they treat themselves to very rich "employee" benefits, large expense and travel accounts, and other perks when Americans are hurting, our debt is skyrocketing, and they want to tax us more. That is why people like us who have never demonstrated in our lives are standing up by hundreds of thousands and it appears by the millions to say enough is enough. (Update: This is in reference to the Tea Party rallies before the 2010 mid-term election.) We are taking our country back because the overwhelming majority of Americans believe in the Declaration of Independence, the Constitution, and what they stand for. We believe that our founding ideology is what has made this country the great country it is and will continue to make it so. We will find out in 2010 and 2012. (Update: We have found out and that is what the rest of this book is about.)

CHAPTER 6

The Un-News Media?

Before we proceed, I want to reiterate again that once you see one liberal and one conservative, you have seen one liberal and one conservative. Progressives are a "one-trick pony". What is important to correctly classify an individual to a specific political classification is the consistency with which that individual's core personality traits, beliefs, and behaviors fit that classification over time. There are examples of politicians and non-politicians who change from one classification to another classification or do they really? Were they confused or perhaps became more educated? That might be true in rare cases but I believe that political classifications are so aligned with our mental being that it is next to impossible to honestly move among them. I have seen politicians change classifications but in each case it was an attempt to get re-elected because they couldn't get re- elected if they stayed in their original classification. Pure dishonesty to attempt personal gain. Thus far, we have concentrated upon defining political classifications by using theory, opinion, and fact. We are now going to change directions and apply that knowledge to what is happening politically to our country, why it is happening, and to assess our country's future.

The mainstream news media should more correctly be called the mainstream "un-news" media as the title of the chapter denotes. It would also be correct to call them the politically biased media or the political agenda media or the political enabling media or the destroy-America-as-we-know-it media? Why are they doing this? I am convinced the vast majority of the mainstream news media is made up of very smart people who honestly believe they are doing the right thing. They are living proof of my analysis in chapter 2 regarding liberal core personality traits. The mainstream news media has progressives and conservatives in its ranks but the majority are non-progressive classic liberals. Most mainstream "un-news" is a result of progressives leading well-meaning liberals down the primrose path to assist them in their dastardly progressive deeds.

Let's take a look at a Gallup survey done in September 2014. The survey was reported in an article from gallup.com titled "Trust in Mass Media Returns to All-Time Low". The participants were asked, "In general, how much trust and confidence do you have in the media such as newspapers, television, and radio when it comes to reporting the news fully, accurately, and fairly. Do you have a great deal, a fair amount, not very much at all, or none at all?" Here are the results. The article said America's confidence in the media's ability to report the news fully, accurately, and fairly in 2014 tied its all-time low in 2012 at 40%. The report went back to 1997 and the highs were in the 51% to 55% range between 1997 and 2003 and averaged 53.4% during that time. After 2003, the numbers steady declined until they reached 40% in 2012 and in 2014.

The survey showed Americans perceive the following media bias: 44% said the media was too liberal; 34% said media was just about right; and 19% said media was too conservative. When the survey results were divided by party affiliation and ideology, the results were not surprising but interesting. Liberals perceived the following media bias: 15% said the media was too liberal; 49% said the media was just about right; and 33% said the media was too conservative. Moderates perceived: 35% as too liberal; 44% as about right; and 18% as too conservative. Conservatives perceived: 70% as too liberal; 16% as about right; and 12% as too conservative.

The article also said as the media expands into new domains of news reporting such as social media networks and new mobile technology, Americans might be becoming disenchanted with mainstream news media as they seek their own "personal veins" of getting information. I can understand that after writing this book. Although I used traditional print media and broadcast media extensively, I have been amazed by the ease and amount of information I can find on the Internet and I used that medium extensively as well. I found one has to be very careful and search out sources that can be trusted to communicate factual information. I used biased sources but compared that information with other sites I trust in my efforts to learn the truth. You know I am a conservative and wrote the book through my conservative eyes but I made every effort possible to assure information I deemed factual information to be true facts and not biased information or information that was sloppily obtained. My ideological beliefs and values expressed in this book is another matter. I firmly admit I am a conservative "blue blood" through and through, which is very obvious.

There are several conservative news outlets but they are in a significant minority when it comes to the mainstream news media that is the most watched and the most read by Americans. This gives the mainstream news media enormous power and opportunity to provide intentional and unintentional progressive propaganda that is politically biased to affect public opinion. I referenced Fox News as boasting to be fair and balanced. Liberals and especially progressives strongly accuse Fox News of being very conservatively biased and Fox's claim to be fair and balanced as totally false. I have already expressed my opinion on that one. I will admit that liberals and progressives are sometimes pushed hard to justify their statements by the Fox News hosts but that is OK as long as it doesn't affect the integrity of the discussion.

The Wall Street Journal is more conservative than liberal although the newspaper appears to be reasonably pragmatic and balanced in their approach to news. News Corp owns The Wall Street Journal and Fox News. I rarely listen to conservative radio or access conservative Internet to get my news even though that is where much of the conservative news comes from. I have used conservative Internet considerably in writing this book and to verify or obtain information. Conservative Internet sites present the information contained on them from a conservative viewpoint but I have also found them to be more accurate in their information than liberal Internet sites. I don't mean more biased. I mean more accurate. I believe that observation reflects my psychological analyses in chapters 2, 3, and 4. I wish I listened to Rush Limbaugh more often. He goes a little too far on occasion with his pontification on the issues but he is always spot-on. He can cut through the smoke and mirrors of a political situation like a laser to get to the root issue.

In order to keep some smattering of objectivity in my thoughts, I sometimes watch CNN Headline News and have watched MSNBC. It doesn't take long watching MSNBC before I have to change channels to keep my sanity. I would classify that station as progressive—super progressive. CNN is more middle road but still shows liberal bias. One of my favorite shows used to be 60 Minutes. I had to stop watching it several years ago because it became so liberally biased. They have gotten much better but have you ever seen them interview liberal politicians like Obama or Hillary Clinton? They don't go much beyond asking what their favorite color is or what they eat for breakfast. One cable TV show actually did ask Obama during the last presidential election what his favorite color was. It was as tough as any question he got on the show. Speaking of the last presidential election, the "softballs" thrown Obama's way on show after show were disturbing. The mainstream news media was not going to trip up Obama in any way. All they wanted to do was give him "rock star" exposure to the general public. It is similar with Hillary Clinton during her current campaign for president, although there is variation among the press depending upon the mood of the day regarding her honesty.

I need to update my comments about 60 Minutes. In October of last year, Steve Kroft did what I believe to be the best interview of Obama since he has been president. Kroft asked all the right questions regarding current domestic and foreign policy. Kroft did not let Obama off the hook with his usual non-answer answers. Kroft pushed hard and Obama was visibly frustrated and not too happy. I was proud of Kroft. It was real investigative reporting. Wow! How refreshing! I have seen several false starts by the media where they would begin with good reporting and then fizzle out.

Poor Mitt Romney was not so lucky with the mainstream news media as Obama and Hillary Clinton have traditionally been. One of the most egregious acts I have seen by the mainstream news media occurred during the presidential debate moderated by Candy Crawley of CNN News. Obama said that he called the attack on Benghazi a "terrorist attack" during his first news conference after the attack. Romney said that was not true. Crawley quickly blurted to Romney,

"Yes, he did." How inappropriate. Her job was to moderate, not to defend and support one of the debaters, especially when she was wrong.

I heard Obama's news conference on Benghazi at least twice in its entirety. He mentioned the words "terrorist attack" but not in reference to Benghazi. Obama referred to the attack on Benghazi as "a spontaneous attack because of a video" for weeks before the White House actually started calling it a terrorist attack. The sad thing is that when Crawly took up for Obama toward the end of the debate it took some of the fire out of Romney. That was a mistake by Romney. He should have correctly and forcefully defended himself. I thought he closed much weaker than he could have otherwise. I saw Crawley being asked about it later on a CNN panel show. She brushed it off and did not take responsibility. Not surprising but very disappointing.

I do want to recognize that there have been a few cracks on occasion that occurred in Obama's rock star armor with the mainstream news media. The Obamacare debacle got a decent rise from the mainstream news media in its early and troubled stages but the issue has faded in importance even though there are significant concerns still lurking out there. Other important issues have gotten as much and perhaps even more mainstream news media attention initially but faded from view rather quickly. I thought the mainstream news media was finally catching on to reality when they became somewhat critical of Obama before the 2014 midterm elections and seemed confused or disappointed by his actions. That also has faded from mainstream news reporting. There have been a few cracks in the Obama armor over time but there has never been any real investigative reporting.

The following are quotes made by some of our more notable founding fathers that give us great food for thought before we begin taking a close look at our un-news media.

- John Adams: Liberty cannot be preserved without a general knowledge among the people.
- James Madison: A popular government without popular information or the means of acquiring it is but a prologue to a farce or a tragedy, or perhaps both.

- Benjamin Franklin: A nation of well informed men who have been taught to know and prize the rights which God has given them cannot be enslaved. It is in the region of ignorance that tyranny begins.
- Thomas Jefferson: If we are to guard against ignorance and remain free, it is the responsibility of every American to be informed.
- George Washington: Truth will ultimately prevail where there is pains [*sic*] taken to bring it to light.

Here are four very important thoughts from these quotes. First. In order for a free society to remain free and avoid tyranny, it must be truthfully and fully informed. Second. Our mainstream news media is not keeping the people of our society truthfully and fully informed. Third. Our society is not holding the news media accountable and appears to be satisfied to live in a world of ignorant bliss. Fourth. This is a very dangerous situation for our free and prosperous society.

With those enlightening and sobering thoughts, lets get started exploring why the mainstream news media is the un-news media and the profound impact that has on our society. We will do that by analyzing actions by Congress and the Obama administration that were underreported, misreported, or not reported. How about Obamacare? It is the most profound piece of legislation in our country's history and has the potential of destroying the ideological foundation upon which our country was built. Until the Obamacare enrollment website became a disaster, the mainstream news media would have the public think Obamacare was just about perfect.

This administration had three and one half years to get the site ready and it literally shut down upon its initial use. They spent almost $300 million with two firms to develop it. Neither firm is headquartered in the United States. It was reported that one of these software companies had gotten over $2 billion in government contracts in the past and their work has always been "shoddy". One of them also got an additional $4.5 million contract with the Internal Revenue Service (IRS) after the Obamacare mess. You gotta be kidding me!

That $300 million doesn't count the cost in attempting to correct the problems, which was estimated to be approximately $200 million in the beginning and I have never seen a final number. Actually, they're still fixing problems. I did see total website cost numbers a few months ago of $834 million, $1 billion, $2 billion, and even $5 billion. The last number was said to include the cost of the state exchanges and their problems. Take your pick on the cost numbers. Who knows? Literally! The bottom line is that the implementation costs are extraordinarily expensive and out of control. How about the fact that no one has any idea of the true cost within billions? At least we are finally beginning to curtail the increasingly out-of-control cost of our incompetent healthcare system. Right? The bridge on sale for that one is absolutely beautiful, if you want it to be. It can take you to la-la land. I hear they have an incredible newspaper there called the La-La Land Gazette that reports all the important news one can't find anywhere else.

The government and therefore the mainstream news media last reported the Obamacare enrollment system is now working well. I hear it is still far from perfect. We have also learned that the government decided to stop distributing sensitive personal data from the system to private advertising and marketing companies. The government claimed distributing this personal data was meant to enhance the consumer experience. What the hell is that supposed to mean? The data included age, zip code, and income information. I find that very scary. This is unbelievable irresponsibility on the part of the Obama administration and the mainstream news media is fast asleep.

Obama said he did not know there were problems concerning the Obamacare rollout until after it began. If he did, it is very poor and dishonest leadership. If he didn't, it is only very poor leadership. Take your pick. How many times have you heard Obama say he heard it or read it first from the news media. "It" refers to several major events affecting our country from which Obama wanted to distance himself. He must eat a lot of California raisins. Obama gives new meaning to "I heard it through the grape vine". My leadership book would give him an F-minus as a leader if it were true that he first heard about these major issues from the news media. I honestly believe he was always aware of these issues and involved unless his staff shielded him from involvement. In any case, this administration is an extremely incompetent and dishonest leadership team.

In order to sell Obamacare to the public, Obama repeatedly said, "If you like your doctor you can keep your doctor and if you like your insurance plan you can keep your insurance plan." We all know now that was not true. What leadership grade would you give Obama on that one? Especially, since it obvious he was not telling the truth and knew better? Except for Fox News, the mainstream news left that one alone. Approximately 5 million people got their health insurance cancelled when it was time for renewal. Obamacare required coverage that was not in their old policies. For example, Obamacare requires eye and dental coverage for children under twelve even when people have no children under twelve. How about maternity care for people who for different reasons will not have children? Don't forget those parents that have children up to twenty-six years old can now keep those children on their insurance policies. At what age do you stop considering young people as children and subject to their own personal responsibility?

How about the controversial birth control and morning after pill coverage and the mandatory mental health coverage that is open ended? As a past healthcare system CEO whose organization had large inpatient and outpatient mental health and substance abuse programs, I can tell you that coverage with no criteria or restrictions is a huge black-hole-money-pit. Don't get me wrong. I feel strongly about mental health and substance abuse patients getting good care but not open ended care. There is way too much un-controllable abuse both intended and unintended. Why would the new law require coverage for these particular healthcare issues? Pure and simple—progressive politics! The progressives are appealing to women, young people, and liberals for votes. Obamacare could more appropriately be called Votes-care.

Obamacare is a taxation Ponzi scheme. The government wants to provide health insurance to the people that "they identify" as not being able to obtain coverage because they can't afford it or have pre-existing conditions. That can only work when those who currently have health insurance pay more and those who are young and healthy and currently do not have health insurance sign up for coverage. A sad component to this scenario is that many people who supposedly can't afford health insurance can afford it but make the decision to spend their money on other things. They want nicer cars, nicer housing, fun vacations, etc. I saw this several times during my career. How they spend their money is their choice but we should not have to subsidize their chosen lifestyle.

How about the multitude of people who truly cannot afford health insurance but had access to free or less costly healthcare through resources such as government funded or charity based health clinics? It has been reported that many of the estimated 1,200 charity-based clinics that treated almost 6 million patients annually are now having trouble staying open because private charitable donations are drying up. Prospective donors and past donors believe people who had no insurance can now afford Obamacare or get Medicaid that is 100% funded by taxpayers. Hospitals that accept Medicare and Medicaid, which is 100% of all community hospitals, have always been required by law to treat any patient in need of care regardless of their ability to pay. If a person puts one foot on hospital property, that hospital is required by law to medically treat them. This is the basis of the hospital's tax-exempt status and this cost was already built into the system. So much for the "Affordable" Health Care Act! Everyone who had insurance is paying more for less and private charity care is becoming a thing of the past.

Did you know that the Medicaid program pushed by Obamacare triggers a death tax on those who use it? I was in healthcare leadership positions for 37 years and I just recently found out about this law in The Wall Street Journal. I can understand it may not be public knowledge but I was stunned that I did not know about this as much as I have dealt with Medicaid in my career. In 1993, Congress mandated that states attempt to recover costs for certain Medicaid services such as long-term care. The states are also allowed to recover costs for most other services covered by Medicaid and about 40 states had passed laws to do so by 2014.

The funds are split on a formula basis between state and the federal government. This taxation scheme applies to the nearly 11 million people who have joined Medicaid since Obamacare began. I could not find data regarding how many people have been actually affected. The article said that some families are discovering they may have to sell the home or other assets of a deceased Medicare recipient to reimburse the government. The government can't seize assets of a surviving spouse, surviving children under 21, or survivors who are disabled. The survivors can also apply for low-income hardships. I can't believe I didn't know that. I have mixed feelings regarding the law depending on how I look at it. I don't think there is a right answer but it raises a very interesting discussion regarding government assistance programs.

I have heard many progressives attempt to "minimize" or "spin away" the problems with Obamacare. For example, they said "only" 5 million out of approximately 200 million people with private insurance initially lost their coverage and the coverage was substandard anyway. Ask the 5 million people who lost their less expensive and better coverage if their insurance policy was substandard? As of 2014, there were 1 million of those people still uninsured.

Supporters touted Obamacare would decrease the uninsured by 32 million people. That is not going to happen. The Congressional Budget Office (CBO) is projecting that the uninsured will decrease between 24 and 27 million people by 2025 but 31 million people will still be uninsured. I personally think those numbers are generous to Obamacare's potential success. The CBO said about 30% of that 31 million would be illegal immigrants who are ineligible for Medicaid or Obamacare subsidies (I would not be so sure about them being ineligible.); 10% will live in a state that choses not to expand Medicaid coverage; 15% to 20% will be eligible for Medicaid but will not enroll; and the remaining 40% to 45% will choose to not purchase insurance that is available to them.

Jeffery Anderson of The Weekly Standard posed an interesting thought regarding the CBO report. The CBO estimated that 5 million people lost their employer based health insurance plans and 4 million people lost individually purchased health insurance plans between 2013 and 2016. That is a total of 9 million people who have lost their private health insurance plans since Obamacare was implemented. Anderson said, "Indeed, based upon the CBO's own numbers, it seems possible that Obamacare has actually reduced the number of people with private health insurance." Potential negative consequences are the reason why Obama has continuously postponed the dates for certain elements of the law to take effect until after the 2014 mid-term election and now the 2016 presidential election.

We didn't hear much from the mainstream news media about the Obama administration's move to arbitrarily exempt unions from paying a $63 re-insurance fee for the vast majority of their members under their self-administered insurance programs as required by law. The fee applies to all businesses that provide health insurance to employees under self-administered self-insurance programs. Fortunately, due to their complexity, most big employers hire outside companies to administer their self-insurance programs. So far Obama has not exempted them and the unions were "hot under the collar". Imagine that! Do you think the unions will support progressives in future elections? Count on it. The unions will just have long memories and demand more the next time.

Do you know about the "high-risk corridor" where health insurance companies are subsidized on a sliding scale by the government if certain profits are not realized? The subsidy totaled $8 billion in 2014 according to The Daily Signal. Can you believe the anti-capitalistic and anti-free enterprise progressive politicians are giving money to private enterprise so they can make higher profits? I guess the progressives felt it was OK since they owe the insurance companies for their support to implement Obamacare. I think it is called a bribe.

In 2015, the congressional republicans aggressively studied the situation and were able to stop the funding, which The Daily Signal reported would have been $2.5 billion. In February 2016, The Daily Signal reported the Obama administration figured out a way to channel $3.5 billion to the insurers that was supposed to go to the U.S. Treasury. House republicans filed a lawsuit challenging the Obama administration's authority to subsidize heath insurers without obtaining appropriations from Congress. They won the first round in May of this year but, not surprising, there was an immediate appeal by the administration. The Obama administration has won their last two Obamacare cases at the Supreme Court if it reaches that level.

I feel compelled to make one additional comment regarding the insurers. Even though the insurers have received government funds as initially required by law, Obamacare was designed to put them out of business in the long term so the government can take over the healthcare industry. UnitedHealth Group, the largest health insurer in the country, has announced it is pulling out of Obamacare exchanges in 34 states and operate "only in a handful" because of financial loses. Humana, another major insurer, has also announced their continuation in Obamacare exchanges is iffy. The progressive plan is working.

No one and I mean no one has a clue what The "Affordable" Care Act is costing Americans. Unfortunately, we will never know. There are way too many hidden costs and we can't even figure out what the un-hidden costs are. So much for "Affordable"! I would love to see a side-by-side cost comparison of the total healthcare costs in the United States before and after Obamacare. In spite of reality, the Obama administration has and will continue to reassure us that they are doing what is right for us so we can be comfortable, supportive, and complacent. Investigative reporting is nowhere to be found.

We don't hear any news from the mainstream news media, as we once did, regarding the "death spiral". That is the name given to what would happen to Obamacare if too many healthy young people chose to pay their $95 fine rather than purchase healthcare insurance. This action, or rather lack of action, on the part of young people would prevent the infusion of adequate premium payments into Obamacare to make it viable. I have read a few isolated news reports that reported both it is a problem and it is not a problem. The latest report I read was in January of this year in The Wall Street Journal. It said the numbers are below the actuaries' estimates when the exchanges were set up but the percentages of new sign ups are trending upward. No opinion was given as to any effect this would have actuarially on Obamacare. Who knows?

A new and different "death spiral" arose in 2014. The Obama administration funded a study that concluded the elimination of premium subsidies would cause a 68% decline in enrollment and increases in premiums of 43% for those who remain. They did the study because of questions regarding the subsidies being valid in states that do not have their own exchanges. This is another scenario that proves Obamacare depends upon significant premium increases to those who are not subsidized to be viable. Obamacare is truly a tax upon Americans as the Supreme Court previously concluded.

The Supreme Court also decided it was lawful for the government to give subsidies to people who buy insurance in states that did not set up their own exchanges. This was in spite of the language in the Obamacare legislation that provides for subsidies in states "only where state exchanges have been established". The language was very clear and was intended to be an incentive for states to develop exchanges. Many, including myself, felt the Supreme Court inappropriately rewrote the law.

Thirteen states and the District of Columbia established their own exchanges and 37 states utilize federal exchanges. The government says 11.4 million people signed up for Obamacare for 2015. A little over 7 million of the 11.4 million people who signed up did so on federal exchanges. It has been reported that 87% of those signing up on the federal exchanges qualified for an average subsidy of $264 per month leaving recipients a monthly payment of approximately $82. Nice, if you can get it! I have also heard that eligibility requirements for these subsidies were not verified. Did you know you were subsidizing other people's insurance to that extent?

Forbes reported the CBO slashed 2016 enrollment estimates from 21 million to 13 million and for enrollment to peek at 16 million. This is significantly less than the March of 2015 projection of 24 million. They also reported Obamacare has reduced the percentage of Americans without healthcare insurance by 2.7 percent between 2008 and 2014. This means that Obamacare has only impacted 8.6 million people. That is a far cry from the 32 million projected by the White House in 2010. This information has not been widely reported by the mainstream news media.

In August of 2014, it was reported by some news media that approximately 310,000 people could lose their Obamacare coverage because they had to verify their U.S. citizenship or legal residency to keep it. How could they sign up in the first place? In addition to Obamacare's direct financial impact on taxpayers, no one knows the additional financial impact that Obamacare has created regarding Medicaid. Millions of new people are signing up for Medicaid under Obamacare. Medicaid patients' bills are paid by state and federal tax money. When I retired eight years ago, Medicaid paid about 60% of the patient's cost of treatment and Medicare paid about 80%. That "is cost" and "not charges". We had to pass the remaining cost on to our other patients. This is a hidden transfer tax on you. And, finally, I want to throw in another little tidbit. The IRS said 7.5 million households had to pay an average penalty of $200 for not having health insurance in 2014 as required by Obamacare. That penalty increases exponentially each year for the next two years. What a mess!!!

I had to do a reasonable amount of digging to find this stuff plus I worked in the healthcare environment for 37 years running hospitals. How does the average American have any idea what is happening to them? The most far-reaching piece of legislation affecting Americans in modern times and we have mainstream news media absent in investigative reporting. It seems we only hear information that supports Obamacare's successes. In many cases these success stories are false because only part of the truth is told.

Here is an example. Congressional progressives wanted to establish government run "public options" as a demonstration project to show how efficient and affordable government run insurance would be. Conservatives balked and as a compromise Congress came up with Consumer Oriented and Operated Plans (co-ops) in lieu of public option plans. These co-ops are run by boards controlled by policyholders and are non-profit. Liberally oriented Bloomberg news reported "Obamacare Co-Ops Defy Forecasts to Win Market Share". Conservative news oriented Forbes reported "Busted: Obamacare Co-Ops Are Underwater And Sinking Fast". Townhall reported "Virtually Every Remaining Obamacare Co-Op Is on The Verge Of Total Collapse". Are you confused?

The Bloomberg report is classic progressive BS. Here is the truth. Twenty-two of the 23 co-ops were losing money. They priced their insurance policies below their competitors to gain market share and were surviving on government loans totaling $2.5 billion. That equates to $17,344 per enrollee. How can they survive if they price their products below costs? They're not! Twelve of the 23 collapsed last year leaving more than 700,000 people looking for new insurance plans. Townhall said only 1/3 of the co-ops remain as of March 2016 and will probably all close by the end of this year.

The Daily Signal reported a co-op in Michigan collapsed in November 2015 that had received $71.5 million in government loans and had over 25,000 enrollees. Progressives complained that the reason the co-ops are in trouble is the government is only loaning the money and not giving it to them. Only in Progressiveland! How in the heck are we supposed to know what is really going on unless all the facts are presented by the mainstream news media to paint the total picture? We can't and the government is hiding the ugly truth about Obamacare and the news media is complicit.

When I first started writing this book, Obamacare was estimated to cost taxpayers an additional $1 trillion in the next decade. That number has now climbed to $2 trillion. These numbers do not include the cost of implementation. The Obamacare debacle is far from over and there are many more unfortunate surprises out there waiting for us. One thing is certain. After the dust settles, everyone will pay much more for less and we will have lost the best healthcare system in the world. I wonder what the progressive spinners will say then? More importantly, what will the mainstream news media say? Most importantly, what will the American public say?

I recently discovered answers to the first two questions. One of the key architects of Obamacare, Jonathan Gruber, spoke at a conference and let the preverbal "cat out of the bag". He said:

> This bill was written in a tortured way to make sure CBO did not score the mandate as taxes. If they score the bill as taxes, the bill dies. Okay, so it's written to do that. In terms of risk-rated subsidies, if you had a law which said that healthy people are going to pay in—you made explicit that healthy people pay in and sick people get money—it would not have passed... Lack of transparency is a huge political advantage. And basically, call it the stupidity of the American voter, or whatever, but basically that was really, really critical for the thing to pass. And it's the second-best argument. Look, I wish Mark was right that we could make it all transparent, but I'd rather have this law than not.

That is word for word what Gruber said. In other words, one of the key architects of Obamacare admitted the Obama administration lied to the public to get the bill passed, called the American people stupid, and justified lying to Americans because he would rather have the law than not. Gruber said later he spoke inappropriately and regretted making the comments but he in no way refuted or apologized for what he said.

The news media's response to that situation strongly supports the premise of this chapter. I saw the key architect in a video on Fox News making those comments. How many other mainstream television stations do you think reported these comments? One! Yes, one! The reporting consisted of a brief interview on a "little watched" show on CNN. Fox also showed videos of two other occasions when the key architect made similar comments. I was pleasantly surprised when I saw a syndicated article by The Washington Post that said, "'Stupid' voters remark draws fire". I was not so surprised, after I read it. The article included the comments about stupid Americans but it was basically about how "conservatives" were upset over the comments. The article did not report on the dishonesty or the elitism of this administration.

The article actually quoted Senator Angus King, an Independent from Maine, who caucuses with the democrats as saying, "Everybody knew that there were going to be additional taxes required to support the support for premiums under the Affordable Care Act. I don't see it as any deep, dark conspiracy." Senator King is another politician who was a democrat before he became an independent. By the way Senator, Americans did not know that additional taxes would be required for Obamacare and we do care! It is called the government lying to the American people!

The President and his administration lied to us to get one of the most impactful laws in our nation's history passed because they know better what Americans need. They also know how they can obtain the power and control they want. Progressive nudging! Our current government demonstrates incredible dishonesty and elitism and the news media is absent. How about the senator who is allowed to nonchalantly gloss over serious government deceit in a major newspaper?

Nancy Pelosi said in a news conference after this incident she did not know the person who made the comments regarding Obamacare. She said let's put him aside because he has withdrawn his comments. He did not withdraw his comments and I saw a news clip in which Pelosi quoted him in 2009. She has also put a report by him on her website in the past. That speaks for itself and she is the Minority Leader in the House. I should say the Progressive Leader in the House.

The Washington Post article did quote Rush Limbaugh as saying, "There you go, America. That is what the Democratic Party thinks of you. They think most people are incompetent and will make the wrong decisions if living a life of self-reliance." I wholeheartedly agree with Rush and this book repeatedly makes the same point. I would; however, make one change in what Rush said. I would substitute Progressive Party for Democratic Party.

Hillary Clinton pursued similar healthcare legislation during Bill's presidency that fortunately failed? I cannot emphasize enough that Obamacare is a Trojan horse to achieve national healthcare and national healthcare is a first step toward a Marxist governance model like socialism. The more our progressive friends can push America down that Marxist road, the more they have that power and control in perpetuity that is so important to them. If Obamacare is not repealed, it will be complicit in destroying the very foundation of our country.

It will be interesting to see if the mainstream news media follows Obamacare with any serious honest reporting as the legislation continues to unfold. There are several major pitfalls still ahead. The Obama administration has adjusted Obamacare legislation to fit their political agenda in more situations than one and the Supreme Court has allowed them to do it. The Supreme Court has become much too political, especially in today's progressive environment. What's it called when the reigning leadership of a country changes established laws at their pleasure to fit their political desires and gets away with it? I think leaders like Mussolini, Hitler, Mao, and Stalin called it totalitarianism. The Obamacare debacle is not going to dissipate anytime soon even though I have heard more than one Obama supporter say it is now old news and we need to move on. I think Obama himself proclaimed it to be old news and the mainstream news media "listens to their president". We will look further at Obamacare's negative effect on our society throughout the book, especially in chapter 8.

What is the responsibility of the news media in situations like Obamacare? When I assumed my last job as a healthcare system CEO, I was invited to visit with the news editor and publisher of our local newspaper because I was new in town. During our conversation the news editor informed me it was the newspaper's job to protect the public; therefore, they were always watching us closely. I explained to him that other than banks we were the most regulated industry in the country and he did not need to look over our shoulder. He told me that didn't matter and they would always monitor us to look out for the public's best interest. I was a little miffed that he would even insinuate his newspaper needed to look over our shoulder. But, in reality, isn't that a major if not the major responsibility of the news media to accurately and completely report information to the public as a means of protecting the public's best interest.

Public protection in government affairs by the news media has been there in the past through strong scrutinization of conservative politics and to a lesser but certain degree of liberal politics. The mainstream news media has become so biased since Obama has been in office that Americans have totally lost any protection regarding progressive liberal politics and conservative politics has become a target for unfair reporting. In fact, the mainstream news media protects Obama and progressive liberal politics by ignoring and in some cases covering up significant issues. Even Bill Clinton received more political scrutiny than Obama.

I don't have an answer as to why the Obama era is so special. I do see a correlation with the proliferation of progressivism in our country but that could just be coincidental. It could also be reflective of the cultural change taking place in America that we will discus in later chapters. What is important for this chapter is that the mainstream news media is allowing Obama and his administration to do as they please. This is extremely concerning and has consequences for our country even after Obama leaves office because this behavior by the mainstream news media appears to have become the new norm.

Remember the scandals involving the Obama administration that Obama called phony scandals? A scandal is defined by Merriam-Webster as "an action or event regarded as morally or legally wrong and causing public outrage". With that definition in mind, let's review Obama's so-called "phony scandals" and the reaction to them by the mainstream news media. We will also review a few other government scandals while we are at it.

Let's start with the 2012 attack on Benghazi. This is truly a tragic situation. Four Americans were killed in a preplanned terrorist attack after Obama had just announced before the presidential election that Bin Laden was dead and al-Qaeda was on the run. As an interesting side note, I heard the government knew for a long time where Bin Laden was but the White House was debating whether or not to go after him due to the risk of failure and embarrassment. It didn't look like it in Obama's photo-ops during the event and what he said after the event. The truth about the Benghazi attack would have been contrary to one of Obama's major campaign positions regarding his presidential accomplishments. He was claiming success in eradicating terrorism. If there was a terrorist attack on an American embassy killing four people including the ambassador two months before the election, that news event would not support his position. How convenient to blame the attack on a stupid video.

There was a demonstration at our embassy in Cairo, Egypt earlier that day because of a video mocking the Prophet Mohammad that was produced by a Coptic-Christian from Egypt who lived in the U.S. I read that an anti-American group used the video to stir up Egyptians to cause them to demonstrate. I assume that is where the idea of a video came from. After the attack, we reportedly spent about $70,000 on an ad in the Middle East apologizing for this video. I'm sure the ad had more success in informing people about the video than apologizing for something they knew nothing about. The video maker was arrested immediately after the attack and spent one year in prison because of a parole violation. Wikipedia said he is reported to now be living in a Los Angeles homeless shelter and working in a pizza parlor. I have to believe the entire Middle East was laughing at us when we said the attack was because of a video. The Prime Minister of Libya told the Obama administration and the world it was a terrorist attack immediately after it happened. He was miffed because they publicly contradicted him.

Many attempts have been made by Congress to get to the bottom of what happened to no avail. Documents have been requested and have not been received or have been heavily redacted. Judicial Watch deserves enormous credit for not giving up in obtaining pertinent records and has had good success. They have been able to get documents under FOIA that show the Obama administration knew from the beginning the attack had been planned 10 days in advance by an al Qaeda affiliate to "kill as many Americans as possible". An investigation by a group called The Accountability Review Board (ARB) chaired by two respected people was initiated by the State Department and nothing of substance was found. Why? Because their investigation was narrow in scope and did not get to the heart of the important issues. There was also an accusation by a State Department official that Clinton's Chief of Staff and Vice Chief of Staff orchestrated the purging of any documents that were unfavorable toward the State Department or Hillary Clinton prior to documents being turned over to the ARB. The ARB didn't even talk to Clinton as Secretary of State.

Obama publicly said he learned about the attack in the news. That statement in itself is farcical. We have an attack on one of our embassies in which an ambassador is killed and the president hears about it on the news? Sharyl Attkisson is an investigative reporter who broke this story and other stories that have been negative toward the Obama administration. Her major television network employer, CBS, pressured her to not be so aggressive in her reporting. She finally resigned. So much for investigative reporting by mainstream news! Oh, it might be of interest that the President of CBS News has a brother who works in the White House named Ben Rhodes. Is that name familiar to you? If not, it will be as you read the book.

Congress interviewed many people from the State Department and none of them gave any significant information. A Senate committee interviewed Clinton under oath and, after being pushed, she angrily said something to the effect, "Four Americans are dead. What difference at this point does it make whether it was a protest or a group of terrorists out for a walk who decided to kill some Americans? What is most important now is to figure out everything we can regarding how to prevent this from happening in the future." The mainstream news media said her response showed strength before republican congressional committee members who were out to get her. I personally saw political cover-up by both Clinton and her accomplice, the mainstream news media. I also saw a defiant, arrogant, and extremely inappropriate answer by Clinton in relation to the death of one of her ambassadors and three other Americans.

Speaking of political cover-up, how about the debacle regarding Clinton's emails when she served as Secretary of State? It is astounding to me that anyone in her position could have 100% of their work related emails on a server in their home when it is against government policy and against the law because of the classified information involved. No one is suspicious, not even the White House? The White House had to know. Obama said in an interview on CBS television he learned about this scandal on the news like everyone else. It's a good thing he reads and watches the news. He wouldn't know about any of his administration's wrong doings. His press secretary had to backtrack on Obama's statement regarding the Clinton emails when questioned at a daily news briefing.

A big unknown is why the White House allowed her to do it? Unbelievable! Will she go to the wood shed? I don't know. As this unfolds, she might be in serious trouble of indictment unless the White House bails her out and that is a question mark because of the significant strained relationship between the two as described in a book titled *Blood Feud* by Edward Klein. So far, Obama is endorsing her for president. I have heard pundits say Clinton has threatened to expose Obama regarding what he knew regarding the emails if he doesn't support her. I find it difficult to believe that would intimidate him. Stay tuned and let's see what happens regarding the FBI investigation.

Here is an update. As I am sure you know, the decision was not to prosecute her. I added comments on that decision in chapter 12.

Back to Benghazi. The most compelling testimony came from the Deputy Chief of Mission at the U.S. Embassy in Tripoli and a couple of others from the embassy who testified before congress in 2013. I watched their testimony. They were very emotional and appalled that their colleagues were dead and no one in government would stand up and tell the truth about what really happened. One of the questions they raised was why there was no effort to send military help. Even the few military who were in Tripoli were told to stand down. After their testimony, a great deal was been made of the term "stand down". Government sources adamantly denied that a stand down order was given to anyone during the attack. Several security personnel at the CIA compound in Benghazi and the Deputy Chief of Mission who was in Tripoli at the time said they were told not to go to the compound that was being attacked.

I saw three of the security personal based at the CIA compound being interviewed on several occasions by Fox News' Megyn Kelly and Bret Baier. The movie *13 Hours* was based upon a book they wrote. They consulted with the filmmakers during the filming so it would be a realistic story. They said after hearing the firefight in the distance, they went to the State Department compound against orders from their CIA superior who told them to wait. There was a difference of opinion among them if the actual term "stand down" was used but no difference of opinion that they were told not to go.

There were questionable statements from government sources that military support could not get there in time. Those in Tripoli could have gotten there fairly fast and the firefight in Benghazi went on for hours. Isn't it the American way to always give it all you have and sometimes do the impossible? How did the people calling the shots in Washington know how long the firefight would last? They didn't! The country and especially the families of those killed deserve to know why support was not sent. Oh, what happened to the survivors of the attack? I continually heard they were under a "nuclear blanket" to keep quiet as one person put it. Why? What could they have said? Wouldn't you like to know? I sure would.

This incident is an enormous White House cover-up. Here are two reasons why I believe that to be true. First, this incident took place two months before the presidential election and would have contradicted one of Obama's campaign positions that terrorists were on the run. What happens to public opinion if a terrorist group attacks one of our embassies and kills four Americans including the Ambassador before the election? We now know the White House knew it was a terrorist attack immediately and not a spontaneous demonstration as purported by Obama, Clinton, and Susan Rice. Second, Clinton knew she would run for president in 2016 and did not want that negative incident on her watch. The more the truth is discovered, the more the incident looks bad on her leadership ability and her honesty.

If the truth were to be known, I believe it would be worse than bad. Maybe she and Obama did a quid-pro-quo to help each other politically. Actually they supposedly did. Klein wrote in *Blood Feud* that at first Clinton felt Benghazi was Obama's problem and even thought of resigning rather than get involved in the video cover-up story. After discussing it with her husband, Bill, they decided she should involve herself in an attempt to obtain Obama's support for her presidential campaign in 2016 and to minimize political damage to her personally. The book said when Clinton makes up her mind in a situation like this; she is in 100% for the long haul. She sure put on a show. How could she say what she did at the funeral about a video knowing it was a cover-up? How could she one-on-one tell the families at the funeral it was because of a video and then later during her campaign deny she said that and accuse the families of lying?

In their September 2015 publication of The Verdict, Judicial Watch commented on new documents they had recently obtained through a FOIA lawsuit against the Department of State. Those documents show that Clinton and the State Department deferred to the White House for the official response to the attack. Ben Rhodes, the Deputy Strategic Communications Advisor, and Bernadette Meehan, a spokesperson for the National Security Council, were the key White House officials who determined the response. The documents also show the Obama administration involved domestic and foreign Islamist groups and foreign nationals to push the video narrative. The publication contained a copy of a memo from Ben Rhodes who stated one of the primary goals was "to underscore that these protests are rooted in an Internet video, and not a broader failure of policy".

No matter what the specific reason or reasons, it was a political cover-up plain and simple. We heard for a long time it was old news or a phony scandal. The investigative reporting by the mainstream news media not only was absent but they covered for Clinton and Obama in calling the investigation a right-wing conspiracy against the democrats. How can they in moral conscience do that? The leadership of our country dishonestly deceives the public on a matter this serious through a cover-up for political purposes, to hide incompetency, or both and the mainstream news media is absent.

Bill O'Reilly said on his Fox News show that no mainstream news media reported on the Benghazi attack the day it happened other than Fox News. One of our embassies is attacked, the ambassador is killed, three others are killed, and the mainstream news media does not report it? I do not have words or bridges for that one. O'Reilly did say CNN had a short report on the attack the next morning. Fox finally shamed the mainstream news into reporting the incident.

What is more important for public protection from government tyranny than a truthfully and fully informed society? We need you founding fathers? We need you to protect us from tyranny once again. Where is your surrogate, the mainstream news media? They are not only absent but are complicit in the cover-up by publicly protecting progressive liberal government leaders at the expense of not protecting society.

The news media eventually compared the Benghazi cover-up to Ronald Reagan and the Iran-Contra affair. The difference is Reagan did what he did to save American lives, waived executive privilege so his aids could testify, and people were held accountable. The Benghazi cover-up was to save political butts, everyone sang the company song, and no one was held accountable. What is the mainstream news media's end game? Don't they love America and believe in the Declaration of Independence and the Constitution? Are they all progressives? No. As I said before, they are not all progressives but the great majority are liberals who fall into progressive traps as a result of their liberal core personality traits as we discussed in chapter 2. How can they be blinded by their core personality traits to the point that complete and accurate critical news that Americans need and deserve to know is thrown out the window? I honestly don't know.

Here is a recent example to make the point. I learned from the Fox News show *Outnumbered* that between January 1st and June 7th of this year Donald Trump's controversies received 432 minutes on ABC, CBS, and NBC versus 105 minutes for Clinton's controversies even considering the ongoing FBI investigation regarding her email scandal. That is four times more coverage for controversies surrounding Trump than Clinton and 55% of Clinton's 105 minutes of controversial coverage was about her husband's infidelities. One can argue different reasons for the glaring difference in negative exposure for each candidate but the point remains regarding the disparity in unfavorable news coverage between a republican conservative candidate and a democratic progressive liberal candidate.

I read the following on a website for the Sedona Observer in Sedona, Arizona and was very impressed by what it said. It is the opening paragraph for their Journalism Code of Ethics. It said:

> Public enlightenment is the forerunner of justice and the foundation of democracy. The duty of the press is to further those ends by seeking truth and providing a fair and comprehensive account of events and issues. Conscientious journalists from all media formats and specialties will strive to serve the public with thoroughness, honesty, and integrity. As such, journalism becomes a sacred trust in which the public accepts information as the truth and holds journalists responsible for upholding it.

What a great statement for ethical reporting by journalists and for journalism in general. Shouldn't all legitimate news organizations adhere to those ethics and demand that their journalists do the same? I might add that the Sedona Observer is a liberal based non-profit online newspaper that has no advertising and operates on donations only

After I wrote the above review of the Benghazi attack, the report from the Senate Select Committee on Intelligence was released. It basically said the attack was preventable in that intelligence indicated the security situation in Benghazi was deteriorating and nothing was done to improve security. The report was very critical of the State Department and its inaction leading up to the attack. I would like to know why our military did not make a good faith effort to get to Benghazi and help our people. The congressional report said there were no military resources in position to respond to the attack. That may be true but I have two responses to that statement. My first response is that no one really knew how long the attack would actually last and it did last for about eight hours. My second response is that I can fly from the United States to Europe in eight hours. We had military resources much closer than that to Benghazi.

A quick look on the internet at flight times for different parts of the world shows the flight time from anywhere in Europe other than England is less than 3 1/2 hours. From England, one needs to add 30 to 60 minutes depending upon the starting location. Why couldn't the military reach Benghazi before the attack was over to help fight off the attackers, even if they were "not in position" whatever that means? Washington was notified immediately when the attack started. The military had no idea how long it would last and it certainly appears the military could have easily gotten there before the fight was even half over. It doesn't make sense, unless there was a sinister motive not to send military there to help.

Last December, after the Senate Select Committee released their report, Judicial Watch sent out a Weekly Update that reported on a Department of Defense email they obtained from a FOIA request. The email had been sent to the State Department about three hours after the attack began and stated, "We have identified the forces that could move to Benghazi. They are spinning up as we speak." The kind of forces that were spinning up (whatever that means) was redacted from the email. After Judicial Watch released the contents of the Department of Defense email, the Democrats on the Senate Select Committee filled in the blanks to their liking on the redaction thinking that would help their cause. Don't we all have the same cause—honesty and accuracy?

Why were forces not sent to Benghazi? In his 2013 testimony, the Deputy Chief of Mission said, "If we had been able to scramble a fighter or aircraft or two over Benghazi as quickly as possible after the attack commenced, I believe there would not have been a mortar attack on the annex in the morning because I believe the Libyans would have split. They would have been scared to death that we would have gotten a laser on them and killed them." Judicial Watch found out the forces referred to in the email were Special Operations Forces in Croatia and a Fleet Antiterrorism Security Team from Rota, Spain. The distance to Benghazi from Rota, Spain is 1,540 miles and from Croatia is 940 miles. Do the math regarding the time it would take to get help to Benghazi. I calculated 3 1/2 to 4 1/2 hours allowing for 1 1/2 hours to get the planes ready to take off. Remember, the attack lasted for eight hours and no one knew how long the attack would last. Why was help not sent? I think we know.

I saw the Deputy Chief of Mission being interviewed September 8, 2013 on ABC by George Stephanopoulos regarding his testimony on the Benghazi attack. The Deputy Chief said although he had maintained his pay and benefits he was "in limbo" concerning his career with the State Department and believed he was being punished. The State Department, not surprisingly, denied it. I cannot find any updates on the Deputy Chief and his career.

A New York Times editorial on the Senate Select Committee Report was appalling journalism even for a newspaper known for its liberal reporting. The editorial said the committee's report was the first report to implicitly criticize Ambassador Stevens for "his judgment and actions during the weeks before his death". What? How callous! The editorial stated, "The attacks were preventable based upon the extensive intelligence reporting on terrorist activity in Libya." The editorial then said, "The report does not cite in any specific intelligence warning about an impending attack." Which is it? The editorial's authors wanted it both ways to fit their ideology. The editorial also included a statement that said Clinton accepted responsibility but not blame. Clinton wants it both ways too.

The editorial's comments regarding Ambassador Stevens prompted an editorial rebuttal defending Ambassador Stevens in The Wall Street Journal by none other than the Deputy Chief of Mission. The short of a lengthy editorial is if Ambassador Stevens had accepted an offer by the military to beef up security in Libya for our State Department staff, the military would have control over the security forces rather than the State Department. Ambassador Stevens wanted to keep control within the State Department because the security forces would be shielded by diplomatic immunity. Otherwise, soldiers would not be shielded and risk being the subject of actions by Libyan authorities. Ambassador Steven's many requests to the State Department for improved security went unanswered. I'm just a hillbilly from Eastern Kentucky and this information was easy for me to find, so why did three professional editorial journalists not know these facts before they wrote such a misleading and callus editorial in a major U.S. newspaper? I don't have to tell you the answer to that one.

The New York Times editorial also said, "The report does not break any new ground on the issue of the administration's statements about the episode, or for a television appearance by Susan Rice." That is correct on face value regarding the Senate report, but let's add what House republicans found after they did a lot of digging and pushing hard for the truth. They found the White House and the State Department altered the accurate talking points drafted by the intelligence community to protect the State Department. How about protecting the White House? Judicial Watch has also confirmed this in their FOIA requests.

In an attempt to find the truth, House republicans voted to form a Select Committee on Benghazi chaired by republican congressman Trey Gowdy, a former long-term and successful prosecutor, to fully investigate the attack. This committee has more power than any previous committee studying Benghazi and hopefully they can finally get to the bottom of this travesty. There has been continued wrangling along party lines and stonewalling by government agencies but this is our best chance to get the truth. It has been a long process but I have confidence in Gowdy to direct the committee toward the best outcome possible. Not surprisingly, the democrats and mainstream news media raise the issue of the committee being nothing more than a republican biased witch-hunt against democrats every time the committee makes the news.

After 50 plus interviews over several months, they finally interviewed Hillary Clinton. You are probably aware that Clinton's campaign staff did everything possible to discredit the committee as a republican "witch hunt". No pun intended—seriously. The stupid comment on national television by republican House member Kevin McCarthy regarding the committee's discovery of Clinton's personal email server hurting her campaign did not help the committee's credibility. It probably cost him the Majority Leader of the House position.

My wife and I watched the 11-hour hearing. Actually, we recorded the hearing and fast-forwarded through the democratic questioning because I can't characterize the democratic questioning as questioning.

It was more like "praising" and was obviously a pre-determined set-up. There were even ugly outbursts toward chairman Gowdy by democratic congressman Elijah Cummings, the committee's ranking member. Other democrats attacked other republican committee members. You will read more about Cummings later in the chapter with regard to the IRS hearings. Whose side are these democrats on? They were obviously on their progressive party's side and not the side of the American people they were elected to represent. I see this all the time during congressional committee meetings and hearings. I find it disgusting for members of Congress to act in this manner. I cannot ever remember republicans acting this way unless they are provoked and I watch this stuff at lot.

The progressives and the mainstream press touted the hearing to be uneventful. Clintons campaign staff praised her answers and demeanor as showing cool-headedness and her innocence of any wrongdoing. The mainstream news media lapped it up like puppy dogs. An op-ed by Cal Thomas said USA Today, NBC Nightly News, ABC World News Tonight, CBS Evening News, and CNN Anderson Cooper were all gushing over Clinton's performance while trashing the republicans on the committee. A syndicated news article in my local newspaper by The Washington Post commented, "Throughout her political career, Hillary Clinton's greatest curse—the reaction she provokes in her adversaries—has also been her salvation. That was proved once again with her 11-hour inquisition by the House Select Committee on Benghazi, a republican-engineered train wreck from which she emerged without a scratch." This overwhelming political bias never ceases to amaze me.

I will give Clinton credit for keeping her cool and enduring 11 hours of questioning but here is what I saw and heard. Clinton used Libya in 2011 to promote herself in a positive political way by touting her success in the country's transition. She then lost interest in Libya. Ambassador Stevens sent 600 emails in 2012 asking for more security? Clinton said those appropriately went to her staff and not her. When asked why no one on her staff was held accountable, she responded that the ARB found there was "no breach of duty". There were 600 requests for security that were ignored when other countries pulled out of Libya for security reasons and there was no breach of duty? Why didn't we pull out? Clinton said Ambassador Stevens wanted to keep the Embassy open. What would Clinton's Libya success story have looked like if the United States had pulled out for security reasons?

The most damning evidence was the transcript of a telephone call between Clinton and the Prime Minister of Egypt the day after the attack that proved Clinton knew immediately the attack was a pre-planned terror attack. Clinton told the prime minister, "We know the attack had nothing to do with the film. It was a planned attack, not a protest. ... Based upon the information we saw today, we believe that the group that claimed responsibility for this was affiliated with al-Qaeda." Thanks to House republicans and Judicial Watch, we now have hard evidence that Clinton lied to us about the video. It was also discovered at the hearing that she emailed her daughter the night of the attack and told her it was a terrorist attack. Lying to the American people is extremely bad but Clinton lying to the victim's families during the victim's funeral and denying it later during her presidential campaign takes a special person and I do not mean that as a compliment.

To conclude my discussion on Benghazi, I want to share with you an interview I saw on Fox News with the commander and pilot of the airplane that took Ambassador Stevens, the three other deceased Americans, the wounded, and the non-wounded survivors of the attack to a military base in Germany. He had just retired from the Air force. With very watery eyes he described the scene when they landed in Germany and conducted a ceremony for the deceased. He said there was not a dry eye to be found. He also said they could have had the plane in the air from Germany in about 1 1/2 hours and been in Benghazi in 3 hours and 15 minutes. He said they could have gotten there easily before the attack was over to help. Perhaps more telling is he said 100% of the survivors they picked up knew it was a planned terrorist attack as soon as it happened and were confused by the reports of a video causing the attack. The survivors said the attackers actually used embassy cell phones to call their leaders during the attack. The commander was never interviewed by the ARB.

I have made a very big deal out of the Benghazi story and provided a lot of information and opinion. Why? I believe it was one of the most significant events during Obama's presidency and resulted in a disgraceful cover up. I truly believe both the State Department and the White House covered up the damning parts of the event to protect Clinton and Obama politically. I also believe the White House was involved in holding back the military after the attack started to avoid an international incident with terrorists.

If Clinton and Obama were not directly involved in that decision, they should have been. Where were they during this time? No one seems to know? It is unfathomable that one of our embassies is under a terrorist attack, an ambassador is killed, three other Americans are killed, no one knew what was going to happen next, and the Secretary of State and the president are "in absentia". They sure weren't absent from the Situation Room and photo ops during the attack on Bin Laden. This is a very sad story for America and one of extreme dishonesty and callousness on the part of our country's leadership. The Benghazi story involves a cover-up that would make Nixon and his henchmen look like schoolyard amateurs.

Well, here is the latest update on Benghazi and it supports what I just said regarding a cover-up. Gowdy's committee released their report in June. The democrats released their own report the day before the official committee report was released saying the committee found nothing new and verbally trashed the republicans for spending $7 million for nothing. I thought this was a joint committee of republicans and democrats. I saw the Chairman of the House Democratic Conference, Xavier Becarra (D., CA.), on Fox News echoing the Democratic Party's contrived story of "nothing new found". I found his comments troubling and appalling. Here was a congressman in a senior congressional position participating in a dishonest cover-up involving the killing of four Americans at an American Embassy including the embassy ambassador in order to support his political party. I did not expect anything else but I always find it disgusting every time it happens and it is always the progressive democrats doing it.

Here is what "is new" that was not uncovered previously. Secretary of Defense Leon Panetta gave the order to deploy military support three and one-half hours after the attack started. Panetta's order was changed and the deployment never happened. The committee could never find out who changed his order or why. There was a fast response military team in Rota, Spain ready to go. The team was told to change from military clothes to civilian clothes four times during the attack but was never allowed to go. Something was said about not offending the Libyans. A military pilot said he was on the ground in Italy and could have made it to Benghazi before the last two Americans were killed but was not deployed. The White House stonewalled the committee as to the whereabouts of Panetta and Obama. Clinton was in a meeting with senior White House officials three hours into the attack and the group issued a report in which five of the ten action items involved the infamous video. The committee found the video narrative had no basis from any of the reports received from Benghazi in real time. That information is not "nothing new found" and the White House's refusal to cooperate is inexcusable.

The next phony scandal actually got a decent rise from the mainstream news media because it affected some of their own. In 2013, the DOJ secretly obtained phone records for several Associated Press (AP) reporters. It was never determined whether or not the DOJ went through proper court proceedings. This action supposedly resulted from a news story regarding a foiled terror plot on a domestic airplane. The AP news story in question contradicted a previous public assertion by the White House that there was no credible evidence terrorists were planning an attack on the anniversary of Bin Laden's death. The AP staff asked the government source if the information obtained was classified and was told no before they printed it. DOJ guidelines require the department to attempt the obtainment of phone records direct from the entity before they are secretly acquired through subpoena. The only exception to this guideline is evidence that a crime was committed. Apparently, those telephone records were secretly obtained without a proper subpoena.

Shortly after this incident, it was discovered that the phone records of James Rosen, Fox News' chief Washington correspondent, and his parents were monitored because of an alleged information leak on North Korea's nuclear program. Eric Holder was Attorney General at the time. I saw Holder on television tell an audience that Rosen's leak was one of the worst breaches of national security he had ever seen. Really? The secret court order that was obtained to get Rosen's records requires Holder's signature. Holder, under oath, basically told Congress that he knew nothing about it. I watched his testimony on television. He did a lot of wiggling to avoid telling the truth. Obama asked Holder to investigate himself, which he did, and he said he solved everything with the news media. This would be laughable if it wasn't such a sad commentary. Any investigative reporting on the AP and Rosen stories is long gone and never got any real traction.

I will give Holder a complement. He is a very frugal man. He flew on a very small airplane rather the nice big airplanes we all get to fly on. He had to go on all those government, political, and personal trips on that little plane. My wife and I get to fly in real big airplanes. One was an Airbus A380. He flies in something called a Gulfstream V. His little G5 is only big enough to carry about12 passengers and our A380 carried over 500. And, his "government issue" plane only cost about $50 million and A380 cost over $400 million. I bet other cabinet members have to fly in these little planes too to save money with all that sequestration stuff.

Kidding aside, what hypocrisy! Our liberal and progressive friends in Washington politics and liberals and progressives all over the country are extremely critical of business executives flying in their jets when government officials like Holder fly in jets like G5's. The justification is the same for government officials as it is for business executives but government officials are flying on our tax money. Obama's trips on his Boeing 747 and his wife's use of other government airplanes is this issue on steroids.

You might remember Congress filed contempt of Congress charges against Holder during the 2012 Fast and Furious debacle because he would not turn over documents that were requested. Holder defended himself by saying they turned over thousands of records but in reality they were not the ones Congress asked for or were highly redacted. One of our border patrol officers, Bryan Terry, was killed with one of those guns. I bet Bryan Terry's family would like to know the truth about this incident as well as the rest of us. Where were you, news media?

A federal judge disallowed the contempt charge in October 2014 but ordered all "non-privileged" documents requested by Congress to be turned over along with a log of the privileged documents requested. That was done in November 2014. The press was absent on the outcome regarding Holder and the documents. The new Attorney General, Loretta Lynch, has been mum on the issue.

The whole Fast and Furious fiasco was one of the stupidest ideas I have ever heard. And then it got stupider when the DOJ tried to cover it up. Why didn't Holder and crew just tell the truth, admit stupidity, and move on? Everyone else would have moved on as well, including Bryan Terry's family. Wouldn't they like closure? Obama labeled it another phony scandal in attempting to save the White House from embarrassment over such a stupid and reckless idea. Not surprisingly, liberals blamed Bush for Fast and Furious when it came up in discussions on television. The concept did originate under Bush but was abandoned until the Obama administration took over and actually did it. This incident with Holder was the first time in history a sitting cabinet member has had contempt charges filed against them.

The last I heard, the government employee who leaked information to Rosen was being prosecuted by the DOJ. I could never find out what happened to him. I wonder how potential government whistle-blowers feel about this incident. I think the DOJ succeeded in what they were out to do and that is to shut them up. The AP reported there have been more of these whistle-blower cases against government employees under Obama than any other president. That is very troubling. We are talking about our country's Department of "Justice". That is Justice with a capital J. Sounds impossible, doesn't it? Well it is possible under progressive rule. How safe does that make you feel from government tyranny? Where was the mainstream news media after the initial hullabaloo between them and Holder? Oh, I forgot Holder solved it with the media. I guess it is old news—just a phony scandal after all.

Before we move away from Holder, the DOJ, and tyranny, I want to review Operation Choke Point. Thank you again mainstream news media. There is very little public awareness and this is one of the most intrusive efforts in history by the government to control segments of society "they" deem to be in disfavor with their ideology. The Obama administration's Fraud Enforcement Task Force started the program. That sounds like a good thing until you learn what actually happened. The program was started under Holder and the DOJ before Holder stepped down. After Holder announced he was steeping down he said the single failure of his tenure was his inability to enact gun safety laws after Sandy Hook. Looks like he found a clandestine way with Operation Choke Point and the Federal Deposit Insurance Corporation (FDIC) was brought in to enforce it.

Here's how it works. The Obama administration determines what businesses they deem to be "reputational risks" even though the businesses are legal and legitimate. The FDIC then puts pressure on banks to not work with these businesses. The FDIC regulates and audits 4,500 banks in the country. That can be a very powerful incentive to stop banks from working with these so-called "undesirable businesses" and it has been very effective. The businesses targeted include those dealing in pornography, short-term and payday lenders, firearms and ammunition merchants, coin dealers, tobacco sellers, home-based charities, dating services, lottery sales, on-line gambling, fireworks sales, get-rich products, and pyramid-type sales. From everything I have seen and read, Operation Choke Point is actually used to get rid of businesses that support ideology the Obama administration could not get laws or regulations passed to curtail or eliminate. The businesses that appear to be the most targeted are short-term and payday loans and, not surprisingly, firearms and ammunition dealers. If you can't get gun control legislation passed, put firearms and ammunition dealers out of business.

The Daily Signal reported in December 2014 on the House Oversight and Government Reform Committee's 20-page report that detailed their findings regarding Operation Coke Point. Chairman Darrell Issa (R., CA.) said, "Internal FDIC documents confirm that Operation Choke Point is an extraordinary abuse of government power. In the most egregious cases, federal bureaucrats injected personal moral judgments into the regulatory process. Such practices are totally inconsistent with basic principles of good government, transparency, and rule of law."

Reason.com reported in August 2014 that FDIC Chairman Martin Gruenberg told Congress that Operation Choke Point was finished. There is a belief among business owners it was just transferred to a newly created independent agency called the Consumer Financial Protection Bureau. You might be interested to know that this organization is the brainchild of ultra progressive Senator Elizabeth Warren from Massachusetts. They never quit "nudging". It's in their blood.

Here is an update I received from The Daily Signal in April of this year. The Senior Vice President and General Council for the National Sports Shooting Foundation said, "It is increasingly clear that the effects from Operation Coke Point are continuing to be felt, even if the administration has told Congress it has backed off from this campaign." This was based upon banks continuing to refuse banking services to firearms dealers. A bill was passed in the House in February of this year to defund Operation Choke Point and has been sent to the Senate. It is expected that Obama will veto the bill if it is passed.

My next comments are regarding an effort by Congress to reel in another inappropriate program started by the DOJ that is, without question, still in existence. The Daily Signal reported in June of this year that the Senate is considering steps to end a DOJ program that has channeled millions of dollars to progressive based groups outside of government such as La Raza, the National Community Reinvestment Group, and NeighborWorks America. The DOJ currently allows corporations found guilty of wrongdoing to donate a portion of their financial penalty to specific preapproved not-for-profit groups. In 2011, the DOJ directed $30 million to these groups. During the aftermath of the housing crisis the DOJ collected $575.7 million in fees from JPMorgan, Bank of America, and Citigroup. How much of that went to left-wing progressive groups? Senator Mike Lee of Utah said, "The Department of Justice is supposed to work for all Americans, not just whichever special interests are favored by whoever is in the White House." I find this extremely concerning, especially when it is combined with what I pointed out in chapter 5 regarding the government funding progressive oriented groups that are supporting and engaging in anti-American politics.

Am I being over zealous regarding the lack of transparency in our government? Obama did say he would have the most transparent administration in history. Actually, he does when he or his staff wants you to know something. How about when they don't want you to know something? Maybe we should ask the whistle blowers who have faced prosecution for talking to the press or all those potential whistle blowers who are still out there keeping their mouths shut. Let's see. Whistle blowers who provide information to the public that is purposeful White House propaganda are just fine while those providing damning leaks regarding this administration are dealt with harshly. Maybe they should change their transparency policy to the opaque policy. We can thank our mainstream news media for facilitating opaqueness in our government. How ironic!

Let's switch to the infamous phony IRS scandal? Phony? I have a very expensive bridge to sell over "retribution waters" that will keep anyone safe and sound from progressive harm who believes that. So, let's take a look at one of the most scary and disturbing un-phony scandals of all. During your lifetime, did you ever believe in your wildest imagination you would fear your government? I didn't—until Obama. I can tell you I have a degree of trepidation writing this book but if we don't stand up for our freedom, we are done for. Freedom is over. We become one of the multitudes of countries where political freedom and political dissension meets with government repression, harsh punishment, or worse. If anyone does not believe that can happen in America, I have an even bigger and more expensive anti-retribution bridge to sell. I see this phenomenon increasingly creeping into our country as the progressives obtain a stronger hold on our government.

What has been and might still be going on within the IRS is unthinkable and unprecedented. Richard Nixon and possibly other past presidents have used government agencies to target "political opponents" but I am not aware of any White House staff using government agencies to target "ordinary citizens" who are politically opposed to them until the Obama administration came into power. I strongly believe the White House was complicit in perpetrating or at minimum supporting the IRS scandal. Obama himself? I don't know but it is a very real possibility. He was certainly complicit after the fact.

Remember Obama's indignation when he "heard it on the news for the first time". He said he would not tolerate such behavior and would get to the bottom of it? That bottom must be really deep. How long has it been and he still hasn't gotten to the bottom. In fact he must have gotten lost in there somewhere. We have not heard anything from him since his indignation. Oops! My mistake. He did announce that the whole thing was a phony scandal. Bill O'Reilly interviewed Obama prior to the 2015 Super Bowl. Obama said people "made some bone-headed decisions" but there was "not one smidgeon of corruption" and blamed Fox News for the scandal continuing in the public eye. Let's review Obama's phony IRS scandal and see what you think.

The scandal was widely reported in the mainstream news media until it got to be old news. It was front and center for a period of time but only "the tip of the iceberg" was front and center. The mainstream news media kept their noses above that cold icy water rather than dive underneath to see how big that iceberg really was. Maybe they were afraid that icy water was really hot water and they didn't want to take a chance on getting their ideological bias burned. For example, I have personally heard many citizens who supported Romney, Tea Party groups, and other political oriented conservative groups talk on television about not only being harassed by the IRS but by other branches of government at the same time.

I heard one of the Koch brothers talk about how they were audited by the IRS for the first time in history after they contributed millions of dollars to Romney's campaign and had to spend tens of thousands of dollars to defend themselves. The same deputy director for the Obama campaign who accused Romney of being a felon also criticized the Koch brothers publicly in an ad. Could this action against the Koch brothers have been done to intimidate others to not make large donations to conservative candidates? Absolutely! A woman who tried to gain tax-exempt status for a conservative group that was against voter fraud had the IRS, FBI, The Bureau of Alcohol, Tobacco, Firearms, and Explosives (ATF), and Environmental Protection Agency (EPA) investigate her and her husband and their business at the same time. Coincidence? I still have that big expensive bridge over retribution waters.

In every case, the IRS asked these conservative organizations for their donor lists. Donor intimidation? Absolutely! I saw a person in a local restaurant eating breakfast and wearing an impeach Obama hat and t-shirt. I couldn't resist saying something to him. During our discussion I learned that he owns an accounting firm and was, for the first time ever, contacted by the IRS asking to see the list of organizations to which he has given donations. He had given money to one of the conservative organizations being scrutinized by the IRS. I can tell you he did not think it was a coincidence. Neither do I. Ironically, his accounting firm did tax accounting.

I heard on Fox News last year that 10% of tea partiers are audited by the IRS versus 1% of the general population. The National Organization for Marriage (NOM) that is opposed to gay marriage obtained a $50,000 consent judgment against the IRS. The Human Rights Campaign (HRC), an adversarial organization, made NOM's 2008 tax return and donor list public to progressive news media outlets such as the Huffington Post during January of 2012. The HRC president was announced as Obama's re-election campaign co-chairman that same month. Future presidential candidate Mitt Romany was on the NOM donor list. The IRS refused comment on the judgment citing privacy laws. Privacy laws? Is that a joke or what! Was there and is there a conspiracy by the Obama administration against those who politically oppose them and present a reasonable threat? Evidence is not hard to find to support there was. How about now? The mainstream news media is not playing Dick Tracy to find out—by choice!!!

This progressive administration has without question targeted conservatives and conservative organizations to diminish or negate their ability to exercise their right to free speech in political opposition. It's actually even worse than that. They appeared to punish the conservative individuals who were involved. The Obama administration was not alone in this IRS scandal or any of the other scandals for that matter. The progressives who serve on congressional committees investigating these scandals are practicing cover-up extraordinaire. One of the worst is our friend Elijah Cummings who is also the Ranking Member of the House Committee on Oversight and Government Reform, which is the committee that held the hearings on the IRS. After a brief showing of outrage at the revelation that the IRS targeted conservatives, he then took the position that liberal groups were also targeted, the IRS had solved the issues, and it is time to move on. As the hearings continued, he continually expressed that the investigation was a republican witch-hunt. I find this appalling beyond description. How can an elected official attempt to whitewash a scandal which threatens to infringe upon, if not destroy, the right to free speech for American citizens? Can progressives be that corrupt and insensitive to citizen's rights? Yes!

Congressman Cummings and his progressive colleagues' actions are appalling and dangerous for American freedom. This IRS scandal is the worst known breech of American trust in government history and almost the entire progressive laden Democratic Party is culpable in this atrocious political cover-up. To be totally correct in my comments, I will acknowledge there were three or four liberal groups that were held up in the process as well. That is three or four liberal groups versus over 300 conservative groups. You don't have to be a math major to figure out that one. Even the Treasury Inspector General who did the audit that started the investigation said only 30% of progressive groups were singled out for invasive questioning while 100% of conservative groups were. He said it was obvious conservative groups were specifically targeted.

During the congressional hearings, Fox News reported the IRS was continuing to target conservative groups at the same time the acting IRS Commissioner Daniel Werfel was testifying in Congress that the practice had stopped. Cummings referred to Werfel's testimony when he said the problem was solved and it's time to move on. Why would congressman Cummings do that? Remember my discussion on how Democratic progressives keep their flock in line and I said I bet that woodshed was pretty tough? I think congressman Cummings is proof of that statement but he is by no means alone.

Here are some updates on the IRS scandal I saw on Fox News, read in The Wall Street Journal and my local newspaper, and obtained from Judicial Watch after the chapter was written. Werfel's testimony was in July of 2013. The IRS proposed a new rule in September 2015 to make it optional to collect social security numbers of charitable donors who donate $250 or more. Why? So the IRS can collect more information in the future for political purposes? Have they really stopped? With progressives, who knows? A Senator proposed a bill to stop the new rule in December and the IRS dropped the proposal in January of this year. Interesting what happens when progressives meet strong opposition. It was also reported that correspondence was discovered indicating congressman Cummings coordinated with the IRS to target a conservative group fighting voter fraud. Supposedly, his staff also received confidential IRS information on the group.

You probably remember Lois Lerner as the person at the IRS who was in charge of auditing these conservative groups. She invoked the Fifth Amendment before the House Oversight and Government Reform Committee at her hearing and was held in contempt of Congress. The House committee asserted Lerner gave up her right to remain silent at the hearing when she declared her innocence immediately before she declared her Fifth Amendment rights.

The IRS told the House committee all of Lerner's emails sent to anyone outside the IRS from 2009 to 2011 were lost because of a computer crash and the IRS staff could not furnish those emails to the committee. The White House mantra was she acted alone and it was confined to the Cincinnati office. Since then we learned that six other employees supposedly had the same computer problem and their emails were also lost. It was no surprise that the FBI investigated Lerner and the IRS and found no wrongdoing. The Assistant Attorney General for Legislative Affairs said, "(He) uncovered substantial evidence of mismanagement, poor judgment, and institutional inertia; however, ineffective or poor management is not a crime." There is overwhelming evidence contrary to his findings.

The FBI agent who investigated the IRS and Lois Lerner contributed the maximum to the Obama campaign. Is that a conflict of interest? Here is one even better. The U.S. Attorney for the District of Columbia informed the House of Representatives he would not forward the House committee's contempt charge against Lerner to a grand jury. The U.S. Attorney did this on the last day he was in his position and mentioned his allegiance to Eric Holder saying he was a tremendous friend and mentor. An editorial in The Wall Street Journal said the U.S. Attorney's logic in the matter was very flawed and that it was up to a grand jury to decide whether or not Lerner should be prosecuted, not him.

Some employees did get a "slap on the wrist" for their political activity. The Hatch Act restricts political activity at work by government employees. Several employees supposedly got into trouble because of their political activity when the scandal was taking place. The Washington Times reported several IRS employees in Dallas wore campaign style pro-Obama stickers as well as having pro-Obama screensavers on their computers. In another case, an employee on the IRS telephone help-line urged the taxpayers she spoke with to re-elect Obama in 2012 by repeatedly reciting a "chant" based upon the spelling of his last name.

One employee in my home state of Kentucky actually told a taxpayer, "They are going to take women back 40 years. If you vote for a republican, the rich are going to get richer and the poor are going to get poorer." Can you imagine what would happen if republicans did this type of activity? The mainstream news media would make it a national scandal of major proportions. Oh, the employee in Kentucky got suspended for 14 days. In my organization, they would have been fired.

Through their intense FOIA efforts, Judicial Watch learned in August of last year that Lerner had another email account that was not "lost" and may contain pertinent information on this issue. There was an AP report that said the Chairman of the House Ways and Means Committee, republican Dave Camp, released some of Lerner's 2012 emails that show "disgust with conservatives". The emails in question were to a friend who did not work at the IRS. In the emails Lerner referred to some conservatives as "crazies" and others as "assholes". I heard there is a possibility that all the missing Lerner emails can be recovered but I have not heard any follow-up information.

Did mainstream news media widely report the new information regarding the emails potentially being recovered? I felt compelled to check. Remember what I said about my pragmatism and hating like hell to be wrong? It appears that CBS and ABC did report it but NBC and CNN did not. One of the worst (maybe the worst) breaches of citizens' rights and public trust in our country's history and it is haphazardly reported by the best protector we have—the mainstream news media. Was the U.S. Attorney's decision regarding Lerner's contempt charge reported? No, not at all. I found it only in The Wall Street Journal editorial.

In July 2015, Judicial Watch investigated an IRS probe of Wayne Root who has been a very outspoken critic of Obama for four years on national television, national radio, and through commentary in The Washington Times. Root was audited twice and had never been audited before. He said the agent on the first audit was very familiar with his conservative views as if he had done considerable research. After spending thousands of dollars and producing volumes of financial records he won his case in both audits. Root asked Judicial Watch to help him get to the bottom of why he was audited. The IRS stonewalled Judicial Watch until they were finally able to get pertinent documents. The Judicial Watch publication said, "The documents we finally obtained—some 950 pages—reveal a vindictive, out-of-control agency that makes the Nixon IRS shenanigans look like sophomoric hijinks."

A September 2015 Judicial Watch publication had some very troubling information on Lois Lerner's activities during the IRS scandal. Judicial Watch obtained documents that detailed an October 2010 meeting between Lerner, the Justice Department, and the FBI. The documents indicated the purpose of the meeting was to plan for the potential criminal prosecution of targeted non-profit groups that "lied" about political activities. I wonder who was going to determine whether or not they lied. Prior to that meeting, the IRS began providing the FBI with confidential taxpayer information on non-profit groups. Judicial Watch discovered an IRS document that shows the IRS supplied the FBI with 1.25 million pages of taxpayer records on 113,000 non-profit social-welfare 501(c)(4) groups. The publication also referenced a letter written to IRS Commissioner John Koskinen by Darrell Issa when Issa was Chairman of the House Oversight Committee. The letter said, "This revelation likely means the IRS violated federal tax law by transmitting this information to the Justice Department." That violation probably includes Lois Lerner, herself. I have not heard nor read anything further.

Judicial Watch President Tom Fitton said, "These new documents show that the Obama IRS scandal is also an Obama DOJ and FBI scandal. The FBI and Justice Department worked with Lois Lerner and the IRS to concoct reasons to put President Obama's opponents in jail before his re-election. And, this abuse resulted in the FBI's illegally obtaining confidential taxpayer information. How can the Justice Department and the FBI investigate the very scandal in which they are implicated?" Those are powerful comments by Fitton.

This is America? Just how dumb and passive do the progressives in Washington think we are? After what they get away with, can you blame them for believing we are that dumb and passive and will acquiesce to their nudging? Whose fault is that? The mainstream news media? The politicians? Ours? What do you think? I think all three!

Commissioner Koskinen may feel the fallout of Lerner being let off the hook for her actions. In October of last year, the House Government Reform Committee Chairman Jason Chaffetz (R., UT.) introduced a resolution to impeach Koskinen for "high crimes and misdemeanors". According to Judicial Watch the resolution focused on the "lies" and "obstructions" regarding Lerner's emails. The resolution says Koskinen: failed to comply with a subpoena resulting in destruction of key evidence; failed to testify truthfully and provided false and misleading information; and failed to notify Congress that key evidence was missing. The House Judiciary Chairman did not move forward with proceedings; therefore, three members of the House Freedom Caucus re-introduced the resolution in the House on the eve of this years' tax day. Stay tuned on this one. It might have some legs. Then again, look at the history. I always get excited when there is a chance to achieve some accountability in progressive Washington and then become very disappointed when nothing happens.

I do want to compliment representative Chaffetz. The Daily Signal interviewed him about the time they re-introduced the resolution on Koskinen and Chaffetz compared impeachment "to a muscle that has atrophied over time". He commented, "Get that muscle working again—this should be a common occurrence, this shouldn't be once in a century." There have only been 19 impeachment proceedings of federal officials in our history. The last time a federal official was impeached out of office was in 1876 when the Secretary of War was impeached for corruption. Chaffetz said impeachment "was a safety valve" and should be used "for somebody who's not serving the best interest of America". My hat is off to Chaffetz but he is a "lone voice in the woods".

Here is an update. In May of this year, The Daily Signal reported Koskinen agreed to appear before the House Judiciary Committee in June to answer questions. The Chairman of the Freedom Caucus Committee, Jim Jordan (R., OH.), said, "We're committed to impeaching Mr. Koskinen." Well, Mr. Koskinen did not attend the hearing. The committee voted for a bill to censure him and requested his resignation or dismissal and forfeiture of his pension. The National

Review reported Chaffetz said after the committee meeting if removing Koskinen requires impeachment that is what they will pursue. I sincerely hope this action succeeds and at least someone is held accountable. There should be a boatload held accountable.

Judicial Watch continues to push FOIA requests to find the "smoking gun" for this scandal. Let's hope they are successful. It won't be easy. There was an AP story in my local newspaper last year regarding a DOJ report that said the number of FOIA requests spiked from 558,000 in 2009 to 714,000 in 2014 since the Obama Administration has been in power. The backlog of FOIA requests has gone from 77,000 in 2009 to almost 160,000 in 2014. Requests increased by 28% while the backlog increased by 108%. Another issue with FOIA requests is the significant redaction of information on many of the documents that are released. The article also said people have waited years for documents only to find their request to be denied. This information resulted from a hearing by the House Oversight Committee.

I received a general email sent out by congressman Darrell Issa in August 2014 requesting a donation for the Republican Party. The email said 47 Inspectors General sent a letter to Congress to ask for help in obtaining information they need to investigate possible fraud, waste, or abuse within federal agencies. They said the Obama administration has been restricting, blocking, or delaying important information they need to do their jobs, which leaves the agencies "vulnerable to mismanagement and misconduct". You probably know me well enough by now to know I could not accept that on face value and went directly to the Office Of Inspector General website. Guess what? I found the letter from them to Issa. What Issa said was true. The only new information I found was that the letter to Issa as Chairman of the House Committee on Oversight and Government Reform only pertained to three agencies. The agencies were the Peace Corps, the EPA, and the DOJ. The Peace Corps may be a small time agency but the EPA and DOJ are big time.

The information I have shared thus far speaks loudly regarding the lack of transparency in this administration. What will Congress do about this problem? Nothing, except to rattle their swords and achieve no meaningful results. Will the mainstream news media do investigative reporting on the issue? I can assure you that the answer is no. Public outcry and indignation is the only hope for any accountability and we need mainstream news media investigative reporting to inspire that. Not very good odds to reign in this progressive behavior. If our next president is a progressive, this will only get worse and become entrenched as the Washington way.

How about the National Security Agency's (NSA) spying scandal? Can you imagine what the progressives could do with NSA information along with your IRS information? I heard James Clapper, Director of National Intelligence, mislead a congressional committee which was investigating Edward Snowden's assertions about NSA spying. You could tell Clapper was being less than honest because of his sheepish mannerisms. He admitted afterward he did mislead the committee, which is criminal perjury. I also heard General Keith Alexander, the Director of the NSA, interviewed by the same congressional committee and what he said to defend the NSA's data collection sounded grossly exaggerated to me. Interestingly, it was announced in October 2013 that Alexander was retiring and stepping down as director. The White House said it was his decision to retire. Who knows? What about Clapper? Nothing happened even though he committed perjury before Congress. Instead of having any accountability in Washington, we have the "law of loyal soldiers" I talked about in chapter 2. If you are a loyal soldier, nothing can harm you as long as it is for the cause—the progressive cause. We will discuss the NSA in much more detail in chapter 8 when we look at progressive domestic policy.

Speaking of spying, did you know the DOJ spies on millions of cars? According to The Wall Street Journal, they have been building a national database to track the movement of vehicles in the U.S. in real time. They claim the purpose is for the Drug Enforcement Administration (DEA) to seize cars, cash, and other assets to combat drug trafficking. Were you aware that local, state, and federal law enforcement could also seize personal assets for drug and other alleged crimes through what is called civil asset forfeiture? A citizen doesn't even have to be convicted of the crime. That is another story in itself that has resulted in abuse of American citizens. There has been talk of reeling in the abuse and a bill was introduced in Congress in May of this year to do so.

The Wall Street Journal said the DEA has spent years putting this database together and it is used for numerous other crimes from kidnappings to killings. Many state and local law-enforcement officials can track vehicles on major highways through license-plate readers. There are also devises on highways that can record visual images so clear that they can confirm one's identity. What else do we not know?

We have discussed many government employees who have been guilty of wrong deeds and none of them have been held accountable by the Obama administration. Not one! This is scandalous within itself. They have been given leave with pay, reassigned, and some even promoted. No one has lost their job or been penalized. Many government leaders say they can't do anything because of the employee unions. It takes months, if not years, and very egregious behavior to discipline or fire a union member. Employees who are non-union and loyal solders are protected by the Obama administration. There is no accountability and Congress is inept at doing anything to override this cloak of protection. All I hear is a lot of rhetoric by Congress and no action. What an industry!

Do you know what percent of government employees are unionized? According to The Heritage Foundation, union membership is at a one hundred year low nationwide and has been in decline for the past three decades. They reported union membership in the private sector is 6.6 %. How does that compare to union membership in the public sector? The Heritage Foundation said union membership in the public sector is 35.7 %. The public sector is the unions' shining star. Is government employee unionization influenced by the union's massive political contributions and union membership votes? Absolutely! How scandalous is that? Have you ever seen any news media reporting on this issue?

I don't have to tell you what happens in the private sector regarding employee accountability, union or no union. The government's lack of employee accountability is appalling. Whether it is a result of cover-ups, management incompetence, union contracts, political cover, political payback, or whatever; it is the most serious problem in government operations. It breeds incompetent decision-making, poor results, excessive costs, and corruption. This problem has always been in existence but, with the progressives and the growth of government, it is on steroids and is only getting worse as time goes on.

The only time any senior staff member has been fired is when they do not carry out Obama's wishes. A good example is Secretary of Defense Chuck Hagel. I actually know Chuck. He was Senator Hagel from Nebraska, which is the state from which I retired. His aunt worked for me and I met with him several times before and during his time as a Senator. On occasion, he wanted to come by and talk about healthcare.

An article in The Wall Street Journal said, "Officials at both the Pentagon and the White House signaled that Mr. Hagel's departure came amid mutual dissatisfaction over the renewed war in Iraq and the administration's wider approach to foreign policy." I think that means in plain English that Hagel "did not suck up" to Obama and his White House foreign policy advisors. After Hagel left, The Wall Street Journal had another article that quoted a senior defense official as saying, "What today confirmed for the (new) secretary (Ash Carter) is that the strategy is sound, the strategy is working. There are pieces of execution where I think he believes we can do better." Now, that "is sucking up". A syndicated article in my local newspaper by the Tribune Washington Bureau said two former defense secretaries under Obama, Leon Panetta (a democrat) and Robert Gates (a republican), have both complained in autobiographies about what they saw as the White House micromanaging the military. I have heard Panetta and Gates say the same thing on television during interviews.

My leadership book contains a great deal of material on organizational corporate culture. The CEO at the top of the organization establishes the corporate culture of that organization. Substitute government for organization and the principals are the same. It doesn't matter whether Obama is directly involved in scandalous government behavior or not. He sets the tone for the government's actions through his rhetoric, actions, policies, and administrative appointments; he is personally responsible and accountable for the result.

There has been a lot of rhetoric as to whether or not Obama is directly involved in the scandals he calls "phony scandals". Is Obama directly involved? I have to believe he is, at least in some of them, but only those people who are involved actually know? His staff could be protecting him by not involving him but I can guarantee you they are not acting against what they believe to be his wishes. If he was directly involved in his phony scandals, he participated in: political cover-up; dishonesty with the American people; suppression of free speech; and restriction of personal rights. It places a very problematic situation directly on the president that should result in his impeachment. If these issues can only be traced to the president's White House staff and not to the president personally, it throws presidential impeachment out the window but in terms of leadership responsibility it doesn't matter. Accountability is accountability and those responsible are responsible. The old saying is "the buck stops here" and "here" is the person at the top.

WE THE PEOPLE of the United States (as written in the Constitution) are being subjected to major deceit and cover-up by our government just like the citizens of Russia, China, Cuba, Venezuela, or other Marxists countries. That sounds harsh but think about it. I would not have felt that way unless I had put all the deceit and cover-up into one neat little package called *One American's Opinion: For Patriots Who Love Their Country* and looked at it in its totality. It is quite shocking when that is done. At least we are not like those totalitarian countries—yet. Truthful and fully disclosed investigative reporting by the mainstream news media is in absentia in all of those countries just as it is here. Actually, there is no mainstream news media in those or other countries because the government owns or controls all the news media. Take heed mainstream news media. Your own demise could be a product of protecting those who will destroy you. Ironic, isn't it!

Here is the basis of that last comment. Remember my reference in chapter 5 to Mark Lloyd who was a White House czar and then appointed Associate General Counsel/Chief Diversity Officer at the Federal Communications Commission (FCC)? He held both positions under Obama. He had been quoted as saying that freedom of speech is a distraction and that he personally is opposed to private control of the media. I also saw him in a video praising Chávez for learning the value of the media from the United States and then seizing control of it to win revolutions.

Well, Mr. Lloyd is gone but the FCC is alive and well and looking for new ways to control the media. The FCC proposed a government study called the Multi-Market Study of Critical Information Needs (MMSCIN) that was designed to gather information on how media organizations gather news. Under MMSCIN, the FCC would have researchers ask reporters, news anchors, and news managers at perhaps as many as 280 news organizations to describe such things as their news philosophy and how they selected news stories. The FCC claimed this research would assess whether or not the public's critical information needs were being met. They would accomplish this research by finding out the following processes from each organization: which news stories are selected; any perceived news bias; and the perceived responsiveness to underserved populations. I have another reason for this research. As you know, outside of Fox News and The Wall Street Journal, the vast majority of conservative news is found on the radio and the Internet. If the FCC can get their grips on these outlets, the government can basically control almost all of the political speech in our country.

The FCC is touted as an independent government agency. Is any government agency actually independent? Especially, under progressive rule. Three out of five FCC commissioners are democrats and you know as well as I do that the White House has its hooks into the agency. An op-ed in The Wall Street Journal quoted one of the republican commissioners who said, "The government has no place pressuring media organizations into covering certain stories." Fox News responded to the op-ed by saying the idea had frightening implications and raised the specter of government officials monitoring the nation's newsrooms. The republican House Energy and Commerce Committee Chairman said this was an attempt to control the political speech of journalists and urged putting a stop to this effort to engage the FCC as the "news police".

There was also a strong backlash from other conservatives who lamented this research could be an official effort by the current administration to intimidate or second-guess journalists. In response to this enormous pushback, the FCC announced in February 2014 that it would suspend (not abandon) the study. This is a dead issue for now but stay tuned on this one. It is far from over. Think of what the progressives could and would do with that kind of power and control.

Are you familiar with net neutrality? It's another progressive attempt to control information to the public. Some say it is another version of the 1949 Fairness Doctrine and FDR's 1934 Communications Act, which was labeled by the conservative website Breitbart to be enacted by the most far left Congress in U.S. history. Interestingly, it was reported the net neutrality regulations adopted by the FCC in a 3-2 vote (not a surprise) were taken from FDR's act to avoid congressional input and not have to divulge the new regulations until after the committee vote. In defending the secrecy, the FCC said there was ample public input and support based upon the four million public comments that were submitted to the agency. Did you send in your comments? Did you even know about net neutrality? I can guarantee you four million other people didn't either. There probably is some obscure basis for the comment but it would not be based in reality. That is the progressive way.

Any time you see progressives referring to one of their programs as neutral, you know it is just the opposite. The Chairman of the FCC said the regulations insure Internet providers will allow data to move across their networks without interference. He also said regarding the vote, "Today is a red-letter day for Internet freedom." I wonder if he was referring to the color red as in communist red. Where is Paul Harvey and "the rest of the story"?

We don't have Paul Harvey but here is the rest of the story from "people in the know". A republican FCC Commissioner was very critical of the net neutrality plan. Actually, a congressional inquiry was made regarding net neutrality because of the secrecy surrounding the vote and the concern that the Obama administration was underhandedly gaining control over the Internet. The FCC is "supposed to be independent" from the White House but how about the three appointed democrat commissioners who are in the majority?

The republican FCC commissioner quoted earlier said the 332 page document containing the regulations was a secret Obama document designed to micro-manage the Internet and extract billions in new taxes resulting in higher prices and hidden fees for consumers. He also said net neutrality saddles small independent businesses and entrepreneurs with heavy-handed regulations that will push them out of the market and Americans will have fewer broadband choices. The republican FCC Commissioner also remarked, "Net neutrality was designed to enforce the progressives' ideas of honest, equitable, and balanced content fairness as described in the 1949 Fairness Doctrine and as determined by the progressive controlled FCC Commissioners." We all know what that last statement means.

A second op-ed in The Wall Street Journal said the liberal chairman of Google who lobbied for net neutrality called the White House to complain when he learned the regulations micromanages the internet rather than what it was touted to do and he was told to "buzz off". Several other liberals have also complained publicly about the regulations, which were based on the regulations developed to regulate a 1930s telephone system. The op-ed said until Congress or the courts block net neutrality, innovation would come to a halt.

I saw still another op-ed in The Wall Street Journal titled "From Internet to Obamanet". Couldn't be said better. Remember Obama said if you like your doctor and your insurance you could keep them under Obamacare? Glen Beck's website reported Ben Sasse, the recently elected republican Senator from Nebraska, said the term net neutrality is misleading and it is in reality a new government Department of the Internet. Sasse continued, "This is a government bureaucracy in search of being an Orwellian solution for problems that don't exist. The Federal Trade Commission already has laws that would prohibit the things they say they're trying to guard against." Verizon has filed a suit to stop net neutrality. They won the first round but lost in appeals court. The issue is headed to the Supreme Court. If you like your Internet and freedom of speech, stay tuned!

How about if you like Twitter and freedom of speech? Listen to this. The only other republican FCC Commissioner wrote a commentary in October 2014 that was syndicated by The Washington Post. Here is a summary of that commentary. The National Science Foundation (NSF) is a federal agency that states its mission is to: promote the progress of science; advance national health, prosperity, and welfare; and to secure the national defense. Well, the NSF decided to do something else. It decided to control your speech with a new program called

"Truthy". Do you know what "memes" are? I didn't. I learned through the commentary they are ideas that spread throughout pop culture. The purpose of Truthy was to detect what the NSF deems "social pollution" and to study what they call "social epidemics" including how memes propagate. They targeted political smears, astroturfing, and other forms of misinformation based upon their determination. The NSF planned to use a sophisticated method to distinguish between memes that arise in an "organic manner" and those that are "manipulated into being". That's certainly interesting.

The focus was on political speech and to keep track of which Twitter accounts are using hashtags such as "Tea Party" and "Dems". The system was designed to estimate users partisanship and evaluate whether accounts are expressing positive or negative sentiments toward other users or memes. The project's leaders wrote a paper that referred to a "highly active, densely interconnected constituency of right leaning users using Twitter to further their political views". The republican FCC Commissioner said, "Hmm. A government-funded initiative is going to 'assist in the preservation of open debate' by monitoring social media for 'subversive propaganda' and combating what it considers to be 'the diffusion of false and misleading ideas? The concept seems straight out of a George Orwell novel." You hear about George's books a lot in this book. As I write, I often wonder how far the progressives have gone in areas where we are clueless and one day we will wake up and say, "What the hell happened?"

After the NSF spent almost $1 million developing the Truthy project, it was cancelled. Fortunately, enough people found out about it and the "howls of protest" from across the political spectrum caused the FCC to scrap it. The republican FCC Commissioner commented, "The episode reaffirmed that the American people, not the government, determine what their critical information needs are and that the First Amendment means the government has no place in the newsroom." His statement applies to all government actions, not just those involving freedom of speech. I do not know whom the people were who protested against this outrageous project. I didn't even know about it until I read the commentary. The point to be made here is that Americans pushing back works and this is the only way we can take back our country before it's too late.

I wonder what it would be like in Washington if the republicans had not retaken the House in 2010? There would have been more Obama administration scandals and the progressive Congress would have continued out of control. How many new Obamacares or failed stimulus programs would we have? How about the mainstream news media? They would be in "donkey heaven".

Do you know how the donkey became the symbol of the Democratic Party? When Andrew Jackson was running for president in 1828 his opponents called him a "jackass" so he put a picture of a donkey on his campaign posters to represent "strong will". Cartoonists began using a donkey to represent democrats in political cartoons. Over time the donkey symbol stuck and the rest is history. The cartoonist who gets the most credit for aligning the donkey with democrats is Thomas Nast. He is also the cartoonist who gets credit for crafting the American version of Santa Clause.

That's interesting. Maybe the connection with Nast is why the democrats are so aligned with being known as "Santa Clause"? I know. That's enough. Can you possibly imagine what it would be like to have progressives in perpetual control of Congress and the White House? The term "checks and balances" would be relegated to one's bank account for those lucky enough to have any money left after all the new taxes to pay for their out of control spending.

The progressives had total control of Congress and the White House for two years from 2009 to 2011. Look what happened. We got a lame $831billion economic stimulus bill that was a monument to pork spending and creating union jobs that did absolutely nothing for the economy. And, we got Obamacare. They are two of the worst pieces of legislation in our country's history and the mainstream news media acted like a pack of progressive lap dogs.

Well, I have to be honest. There were other things that happened too. For example, Obama was able to add approximately 18 million people to the food stamp ranks. We now have more than 46 million. How can that be? According to mainstream news, Obama has solved the unemployment problem and the economy is significantly improving.

That is hard to understand. Why are food stamps in such need in this robust economy? It's the conservatives' fault. What? Just ask the mainstream news media that routinely covers for Obama's failed economic policies.

Brian Williams said a year ago on his NBC nightly news show the reason for so many food stamp recipients was because conservatives do not support raising the minimum wage for workers in the fast food industry. These workers were demanding their minimum wage be more than doubled. Williams said taxpayers are footing some of the bill for low wages because more than half of fast food workers received government benefits like food stamps. This is a perfect case of "don't confuse me with the facts". When this issue was hot news, I read several articles by conservative sources that debunked this thinking with the facts. We will cover those facts in chapter 8. It seems Williams has had a lot of trouble with the accuracy of his reporting. Many others in the mainstream news media have also expended great effort to divert attention away from Obama regarding our country's economic problems.

Obama may not have solved our economic problems but he did take 5 million people out of danger. These people were in danger because they did not have a cellphone. The cellphone program called LifeLine Assistance was initiated to provide communication with emergency and government services. It is now affectionately called the "Obama Phone". Some even have multiple Obama Phones. Those people are extra safe. Obama did not start this phone program and neither did Bush as progressives have said in defense of Obama. Poor Bush again. Divert and switch. Actually, the program started in 1985 under Ronald Reagan. Wait a minute! Reagan was a strong conservative. He is not supposed to care about people in need; he is supposed to only care about people who are rich and big corporations. Oh, I get it. Reagan must have been supporting the big corporations in the telephone industry. See how easy it is to be a progressive! Just alter the truth to fit your ideological narrative.

After Obama became president, the number of phones increased from 7 million in 2008 at a cost of about $800 million to 12 million phones in 2012 at a cost of $2.2 billion. Obama Phone or Reagan Phone? You decide. Actually, they should be called "Hidden-Tax-Phones". Why hidden tax? You pay for these "free" phones through your phone bill. If you look, you can find a small charge disguised on each monthly bill for this program. The Wall Street Journal reported only 1 in 20 households who get these free phones actually need them. Was this reported in your newspaper? What other hidden taxes might we be paying and don't know we are paying?

Speaking of taking people out of danger, this progressive administration has funded and is funding billions to companies involved in manufacturing alternative energy products and electric cars that are run by progressive supporters who are struggling to survive or in danger of going out of business. The 2011 Solyndra scandal got some decent mainstream news and then—nothing. What they really got was $536 million in stimulus money even though one government agency recommended against it. After Solyndra declared bankruptcy, the company's owners came under investigation because they were suspected of fraudulently reporting their finances to the government to obtain the money. What finally happened to them? The owners received between $875 and $975 million in tax benefits in 2012 from their bankruptcy proceedings and we taxpayers got $0.00. The investigation is continuing.

As I am editing, I found an update. An August 2015 news story from U.S. News and World Report quoted the Energy Department's Inspector General saying, "In our view the investigative record suggests that the actions of the Solyndra officials were, at best, reckless and irresponsible or, at worst, an orchestrated effort to knowingly and intentionally deceive and mislead the department." Early last year the DOJ notified the inspector general's office they were not going to pursue criminal prosecution of any Solyndra officials. The DOJ based their decision on an FBI report that the U.S. News article described as faulty. To my knowledge, there was no general reporting on either the bankruptcy outcome or the results of the investigation in the mainstream news media. How about some investigative reporting to truthfully and fully inform the public about the entire debacle? I guess we all need to subscribe to the La-La Land Gazette on that one.

Here is another government subsidy more concerning than Solyndra and the mainstream news media is again absent. This subsidy is ongoing and involves liberal entrepreneur Elon Musk who founded Tesla Motors and SpaceX. SpaceX is the company the government is contracting with to furnish rockets to our space program. I found the following in an August 2015 article from The Daily Caller. Musk receives about $5 billion from the government for his electric car and space adventures. Yes, billion. According to his calculations he loses $4,000 on each Tesla he sells. Reuters reported that if Tesla used generally accepted accounting principles like those used by GM or Ford that loss would be $14,758 per car rather than $4,000. How many businesses could stay in business losing thousands of dollars on each unit of product sold? Only those receiving your unapproved investment through the brokerage firm called the United States Government.

Tesla buyers have qualified for Federal tax incentives totaling $284 million. Remember, Tesla sticker prices start at about $70,000 and usually sell closer to $100,000 when buyers add on all the bells and whistles. Why are we subsiding $100,000 cars? California alone gave buyers rebates totaling $38 million and the Los Angeles Times reported the state has committed $126 million to Tesla for companies that develop energy storage technology. The Times also reported that Nevada has committed $1.3 billion to Tesla to build a battery factory. Don't forget, we American taxpayers are paying for all of this. Musk has said they will have a car on the market by 2018 for $35,000 less government incentives. Government incentives? For what! I wonder what I would have to do to get government incentives for my bridges? Actually, I don't want to know. I doubt I would like the answer.

How do you feel about the government saving the owners of so-called environmentally friendly companies with your money? I wonder if these people donated money to progressive Washington politicians before they got in trouble, after they got in trouble, or both? From what I understand through reading conservative news sources, yes and yes. We need campaign finance reform big time! Will we ever get our remaining $20 billion taxpayer investment back from bailing out General Motors and Chrysler Motors? I believe the unions did. Good for them. How did Ford Motors make it without our help? I guess they were just lucky. Whatever happened to mainstream news stories regarding these rockets, cars, and progressive government bailouts with your money? They seemed to have gone into the abyss. Maybe these news stories were relegated to the La-La Land Gazette as well.

Here are three other interesting news stories about our progressive government that never made mainstream news. That La-La Land Gazette must be a big newspaper. The government subsidizes electric car manufactures with government grants and electric car sales with tax credits but very few electric cars have been sold to date. The government did; however, create significant interest in golf cart sales. Democratic Congressman, Charlie Rangel, got the Energy Improvement and Extension Act of 2008 passed to give tax subsidies to purchasers of electric vehicles. Fox News's John Stossel said he was very happy about the Act because he got an electric golf cart for free after a $2,000 discount by the golf cart retailer and a $6,400 tax credit. He said retailers were advertising this deal like crazy and were selling out all over the country. If you know Stossel, the ultimate libertarian, you know he was being facetious about being happy. I don't think the countless other people who took the deal were being facetious about being happy. Unfortunately for golfers, it ended in 2009.

At Obama's State of the Union address in 2011, he pledged $2.4 billion in grants to manufacturers with a goal of having 1 million electric cars on the road by last year. Those grants are expected to reach $7.9 billion by 2019. How did Obama do in reaching his goal? In February 2015, CNS News, a conservative online news source, reported the Washington based Electric Drive Transportation Association said there were 286,390 plug-in vehicles on the road. That is a far cry from 1 million. Most of the 118,773 electric vehicles sold last year were sold in California because of their strict emission standards and government rebates. CNS News also reported the AP calculated it would take 5 years to recoup the difference in price between an electric Ford Focus and the gas powered model even with the 16% sticker price discount and the $7,500 federal tax credit that is available. There is also the problem of driver inconvenience in that few electric cars can go more than 100 miles before recharging.

As I said in Chapter 2, I totally agree with spending money on valid research for battery powered cars but these cars should not be shoved down our throats at taxpayer expense before they are ready for prime time. And, clean energy government grants like those given to Solyndra and Tesla Motors are reckless, irresponsible, and out of control, especially in light of our national debt problem.

How about the government rebate given to people in 2009 who got rid of their old gas-guzzlers to buy new and more gas efficient cars? That program only cost taxpayers $3 billion. A study showed the cost of the program outweighed its benefits by approximately $1.48 billion. It may not have worked for gas efficiency but it sure was an efficient way to clean out junk cars from empty lots and people's back yards. The program unfortunately supported the Japanese and Korean automobile manufacturers in car sales over American manufacturers. But what the heck, the Japanese and Koreans need jobs as much as Americans. Besides, our progressive politicians will always take care of us. The more we need them, the more they like it, and they just give us more and more.

Are these progressive actions we just discussed actual scandals or just bad decision making? Sometimes they are both and other times I can't tell the difference. In any case, these news stories need to be reported truthfully and fully to the taxpayer by mainstream news and not relegated to the La-La Land Gazette.

Lets get back to more recent major scandals the mainstream news media actually covered and I'll start with the Veterans Administration (VA) scandal. At least Obama did not call this one a phony scandal. We have heard horror story after horror story of veterans not being given timely appointments at VA hospitals. In most cases, the veterans had to wait for months. Hospital management covered up this atrocity in order to receive their financial bonuses. There is also the potential that many veterans died because they did not receive timely care. This problem was recognized under the Bush administration and actually began several presidents ago. The progressives have a hard time blaming Bush for this one although I have heard a few try. Obama's transition team was made aware of the problem and Obama publicly vowed to fix it when he first took office.

The pressure on the VA system increased significantly after Obama took office because of our troupes coming home and problems at the VA got much worse. A well-respected retired military general who had been Army Chief of Staff was appointed Secretary of the Veterans Health Administration by Obama to fix the problem. Under his leadership or lack of leadership, the problem escalated enormously. I wonder if the problem escalated because the general was not competent to do the job or the government bureaucracy is so complex that no one can effectively run the VA.

This begs the question about privatizing the VA health system. How many other agencies could save money and have much better results through privatization? The potential for government corruption with private contracts would exist and already exists far too often; however, potential corruption is cheaper than exorbitant financial waste in the VA system and the lack of competence and accountability resulting in the death of our veterans. If we had accountability in government, these problems would be greatly minimized. Does this VA scandal make you feel secure about your future healthcare needs as the government moves to take them over in totality with national healthcare?

It takes months and many times over a year for veterans to get non-medical benefits that are owed to them? I find it interesting that entitlement payments don't take months to receive for the millions of people who sign up for them. Explain that one. Maybe I can. Veterans usually vote conservatively and those on entitlements vote for those who give them entitlements. I'm just thinking out loud. The mainstream news media got pretty exercised over this VA problem at first but, not surprisingly, the issue has now become "old news" even though the problems are far from being solved. How do I know that? I saw a Fox News interview the new secretary for the VA health system, Robert McDonald, who was CEO of Procter & Gamble. He admitted that there were still significant problems but he said he has a new team and they are making progress.

He just recently made news headlines that cast doubt on any progress made or his ability to run the VA. He said publicly, "When you go to Disneyland, do they measure the number of hours you wait in line? What's important is: What's your satisfaction with the experience?" He appropriately received major public criticism but there was no reporting on the status of the current wait times. Why not?

The next scandalous situation also concerns the military. Remember, a scandal can be defined as an action or event regarded as morally or legally wrong and causing public outrage. This scandal is not as serious as the VA problem but it is just as repulsive. Obama traded five top Taliban prisoners from Gitmo for a U.S. soldier named Bowe Bergdahl. Bergdahl was a hostage in Afghanistan and has been labeled an Army deserter. I assume you remember this incident. I don't know how you felt when you heard about it but I was appalled. I wasn't the only one appalled. As I watched Fox News contributors who were connected to the military and republican politicians express their feelings about the matter, I was surprised but not surprised at the degree of negative emotion this event conjured toward Obama and the White House staff who were involved. It even got several liberals riled up.

All the evidence points to the soldier being an Army deserter. I watched soldiers who were serving with him at the time he disappeared being interviewed and they said he deserted. There were six soldiers who were said by many to have been killed looking for Bergdahl during the first 45 days after he went missing. Other soldiers were wounded. There was quite a bit of controversy over these killings and injuries. Some of his fellow soldiers said their military maneuvers changed because they were told to search for Bergdahl as they carried out their missions and these changes resulted in dead and injured soldiers. Others in and out of the military said the deaths and injuries were not directly attributable to searching for Bergdahl. My guess the truth is somewhere in between.

A general was assigned to investigate the case. It is unusual for a person at the rank of general to do so. The defense claimed Bergdahl suffered from mental illness. The investigation began in June 2014 and it was announced in December 2015 that Bergdahl would be tried for desertion and misbehavior before the enemy. It has been reported the final decision on Bergdahl's future is being drawn out on orders from the White House. I assume they believe the longer they postpone the decision the older the news gets and looks less bad on Obama for making the controversial trade and bragging about it in the White House Rose Garden with the soldier's parents. Obama did not notify Congress about the prisoner swap as is statutorily required, which also caused uproar. There were even rumors that our government paid a ransom through the Qatar government in addition to trading the Gitmo prisoners.

I know Obama wants to close Gitmo for his legacy but how far is he willing to go to make a legacy for himself? The United States historically has not swapped prisoners of war for civilian hostages or our own prisoners of war because it invites hostage taking. This case is worse. Fellow soldiers of Bergdahl have said he walked off the base looking for the Taliban. I have heard compelling evidence that supports that premise. From what I have heard about him, he is a troubled individual and may have even tried to aid the Taliban in his defiance of America. He is definitely not someone Obama should be grandstanding for on national television in the White House Rose Garden.

In my opinion, the situation was an excuse to release the worst of the worst at Gitmo so getting rid of the rest of the prisoners would not be as difficult. It was also suggested it was done flamboyantly to divert some of the VA scandal criticism away from the Obama administration by appearing to support soldiers. That would indicate the White House as being out of touch with reality, if true, but what else is new? The White House has been to congress several times in the past to release these five prisoners with negative results. What's that old saying? It is easier to ask for forgiveness than permission. I think that is what happened here.

There is also the question of legality in releasing the prisoners without giving Congress thirty days notice. This behavior by the White House toward Congress is symptomatic of a bigger issue that we will discuss in the next chapter but that is not the main issue here. This is another cover-up like Benghazi. The cover-up involves the White House lying to Congress and the public. We have heard Bergdahl was in very bad health and they had to get him out. We have heard there was credible intelligence that he was going to be killed. We have heard Congress was not told about the swap because they feared an intelligence leak, although supposedly up to ninety people in government outside of Congress knew about the prisoner swap before it happened. Then we heard they didn't have time to tell Congress. Pick your lie. When the White House lies to Congress, they lie to us. Just scandalous! Tyranny fodder? You bet.

What were the responses of the mainstream news media regarding his hearing and upcoming trial? Any reporting on his hearing was hard to find and the announcement of his trial was on mainstream news but given minimal coverage. It appeared to me that some mainstream news stories were actually sympathetic to Bergdahl. I saw a John Stewart video that was the worst. A lot of young Gen Xers and Millennials watched Stewart before he retired and listened to what he said on his show as current news even though he is a comic satirist. He enjoyed much more respect for his news reporting by young people than he deserved. In the video, he did something he loves to do—trash Fox News. I think he did that to support his progressive ideology and for higher television ratings.

He gave a lengthy diatribe showing Fox News clips where Fox pundits were being critical of Bergdahl's apparent desertion, the death of the six soldiers, and Bergdahl's father's physical appearance. Stewart was satirically berating Fox pundits accusing them of extreme bias in their reporting. Stewart was extremely hypocritical in that he was personally doing the same thing he was accusing the Fox pundits of doing. The difference is that Stewart was obviously editing the Fox clips to alter what was being said to fit his narrative. Classic progressive behavior. Unfortunately, young people listen to and believe this stuff.

As I was searching the Internet, I found comments by one of the soldiers who was severely wounded during the search for Bergdahl. He blamed Berghdal for his injuries. His comments were in a Breitbart article regarding Bergdahl's last hearing. The soldier also expressed frustration that the recent Bergdahl legal proceeding received only "scant media attention". He said, "I think it is telling that this hearing isn't a blip on the radar of todays news. Its all about Donald trump and the political circus." I agree with the soldier. I'll bet the founding fathers I quoted earlier do too.

I want to end this Bergdahl story with some quotes I took from a well-publicized Bergdahl letter I located on Wikipedia that was supposedly the last letter he wrote his parents before he deserted his unit. He wrote, "And life is way too short for the damnation of others, as well as to spend it helping fools with their ideas that are wrong. I have seen their ideas and I am ashamed to even be american ([sic] and probably intentional). The horror of the self-righteous arrogance that they thrive in. It is all revolting. ... I am ashamed to be an american ([sic] again). And the title of US soldier is just a lie of fools. ... The

US army is the biggest joke the world has to laugh at. It is the army of liars, backstabbers, fools, and bullies." The letter also said, "There are a few more boxes coming (he sent his personnel belongings home). Fell free to open them, and use them." There was more but this is enough.

This was written by the soldier we traded 5 top Taliban prisoners for, was praised as a hero on national television by our president in the White House Rose Garden, and could have been responsible for the deaths of up to six of his fellow soldiers and injuries to more? I have no doubt he has significant emotional problems but I also have no doubt he is an army deserter that deserves appropriate punishment. Stay tuned on this one. It will be very interesting to see if they adjudicate the case before Obama leaves office and the mainstream press covers it. Don't hold your breath.

Here is an update after I wrote that last paragraph. It was announced in May of this year that Bergdahl's trial would be postponed until February 2017 to allow time for trial preparation. That is almost three years since the Rose Garden speech by our president announcing his release. Whose preparation is this for? Is it to give Obama time to leave the White House? The answer to those two questions is an easy one.

Here is a more recent scandal regarding Obama releasing prisoners and paying ransom money. As I said, the United States historically has not swapped foreign prisoners for American prisoners because it invites hostage taking. Well, he did it again; however, this time it was for civilian hostages and not for a deserter. Within hours after we released the $100 billion to Iran as a result of Obama's nuclear deal, the Obama administration announced they were going to exchange seven Iranian prisoners for four Americans. Charles Krauthammer, a Fox News contributor and syndicated columnist, said the timing was "brilliant" because it was timed to overshadow the official lifting of the sanctions against Iran.

In addition to lifting the sanctions, we gave Iran $1.7 billion in additional funds. The Wall Street Journal reported a key Iranian military official stated the money was a prime factor in Iran releasing the Americans. The Obama administration claimed the $1.7 billion was the settlement of an Iranian lawsuit against the U.S. We sold Iran arms in 1979 under Jimmy Carter's presidency that were never delivered because of the Islamic revolution. This had been in arbitration court in The Hague since 1981. We paid principle of $400 million and interest of $1.3 billion. Obama was quoted as saying, "Iran will be returned its own funds, including appropriate interest, but much less than the amount Iran sought." Appropriate interest? Obama needs to take a refresher course in debt repayment. Do countries ever pay up regarding these situations? I don't remember any before now, do you?

According to The Wall Street Journal article, the Iranian military official said the following regarding the $1.7 billion payment, "Taking this much money back was in return for the release of the American spies and doesn't have anything to do with the (nuclear) talks. The way to take our rights back from arrogants (Americans) is to become powerful, and we must grow stronger and stronger ever day." When the nuclear deal closed, John Kerry said, "Today marks the first day of a safer world." Who do you believe—Kerry or the Iranian military official?

Iran is playing Obama and his administration like a "string fiddle". Unfortunately, it is American citizens who pay the piper. I am very happy the Americans were released but at what price? The conservative news stories I read online used the word "ransom". What precedent does this set? We will find out in the future. In researching this topic, I saw an Internet video of a CNN news report regarding this hostage deal and the news report completely mischaracterized the event. Non-conservative news stories were hard to find. Our interactions with Iran will be discussed later in much more detail.

The next scandal is another one of those scandals the mainstream news media was all over in the beginning and then very little follow-up since. It appeared overnight in the news as an enormous issue and then disappeared just as fast. Thousands of children and adolescents, many of them unaccompanied by a parent or other adult, are pouring into the U.S. illegally. Most are from El Salvador, Guatemala, and Honduras. They come here to join family members, escape violence, and to find a better life. The immigration system is overwhelmed and the situation creates a shocking travesty.

When they arrive, they are interviewed and sent to a holding area for processing. In the past, some were put on buses and sent throughout the U.S. to join family already here after they promised to check in after they met up with their family members. I have a freeway bridge on sale that can cross the Rio Grand but it certainly is not free! Others were sent to holding areas in U.S. cities or army bases in Texas, California, and Oklahoma. I recently learned a large number of these illegal aliens are still sequestered in government camps, have no place to go, and are becoming a huge problem.

I heard one border patrol agent say on television during the scandal's peak news cycle that seventy-four kids crossed into McAllen, Texas by themselves in one day. There have also been reports that a child sex trade has resulted. What is the federal government going to do about this problem? They don't have a clue and basically have let the problem overpower them with no solution in sight.

Different versions of the so-called Dream Act that would give young people under the age of 18 a path to citizenship failed in Congress on several occasions between 2006 and 2011. There have been problems in the past regarding young people crossing the border illegally. This new massive problem began after Obama, through executive order, issued his own Dream Act by giving amnesty to any young person who was not a U.S. citizen but under the age of 18. In November 2015, the U.S. Court of Appeals for the Fifth Circuit struck down Obama's executive order. Unfortunately, the damage was already done in encouraging these young people to cross the border into the U.S. illegally. It is estimated approximately 6,000 children and adolescents were crossing the border per year before Obama announced his executive order. It is believed between 75,000 and 100,000 children and adolescents entered the U.S. in 2014 and 95% of them said they were here to receive amnesty.

The Daily Signal reported in December 2015 more than 10,500 children and adolescents crossed the border by themselves in October and November, which is a 106% increase over those same two months in 2014. An additional 12,500 family units, usually consisting of a mother and her children, crossed the border during the same time period. That is an increase of 173% over 2014. This is still less than its peak in the summer of 2014 when more than 10,600 unaccompanied minors crossed the border in June alone. A December 2015 syndicated news story by The Washington Post reported the Secretary of HHS wrote to Congress urging them to grant a request for a contingency fund of up to $400 million in addition to the already requested $950 million. This was in case the number of unaccompanied minors crossing the border continues to grow.

The Daily Signal reported in February of this year that more than 152,000 unaccompanied minors and family units are projected to cross the border in 2016. Some estimates top 177,000. This would be roughly a 30% increase over 2014, which was the biggest year in past history. The report said about two-thirds of the minors are between 15 to 17 years old. The Commissioner of Customs and Border Protection said, "We could very well be seeing the new normal."

The Daily Signal also quoted a Border Patrol agent as saying. "I would say it (referring to faster detention releases) is a major reason we're having the surge because people know we won't detain them and are going to release them." He also said women and children actually seek out the Border Patrol when they cross the border and ask for asylum protection because they claim to have a "credible fear" of returning to their home countries. In other words they know how to "play the system". I should say, "Obama's system."

News media in Latin American countries promoted the United States as a "land of milk and honey" for young people prior to our government running ads to discourage them from coming. Our government ads obviously did not work. As a result, kids as young as three years old were sent alone to the U.S. for a safer and better life. I cannot imagine sending my children to another country by themselves for any reason but obviously I'm not in their shoes and cannot understand what they are experiencing or how they think. The bottom line is they are doing it with "reckless abandon" both in numbers and manner. Are Obama and his "reckless pen" responsible? Absolutely! More importantly, what the heck do we do now to address the problem? It is a gigantic travesty for these kids and a catch-22 for our country.

Here is a real travesty. I read a syndicated article by the AP in January of this year that told of many children incurring the same issues in the U.S. that they were trying to escape from in their native countries. The AP found the system is overwhelmed and the Department of Health and Human Services has lowered its safety standards causing the children to be recklessly placed into foster care. The AP identified more than two-dozen children who were subjected to sexual abuse, labor trafficking, or severe abuse and neglect; some even with their own relatives who were already here. A researcher on this topic at Harvard University said, "This is clearly the tip of the iceberg." This situation is so out of control, I cannot think of words to describe my feelings regarding these innocent children.

We discussed the AP and James Rosen scandal. In addition to that scandal concerning news reporting, I have another one about a news reporter that should scare the hell out of us. Sharyl Attkisson is the investigative reporter who broke the story regarding the State Department's purging of Benghazi documents. She watched information on her computer disappear before her very eyes line by line in a split second. The Daily Signal reported in 2014 a security specialist examined Attkisson's computer and said he found key evidence of a government computer connection to her computer. She also had problems with her telephones, television, and alarm systems that are part of a bundled Internet system. She had someone look around the outside of her house and they found a stray fiber-optic line dangling from her bundled Internet access box.

Attkisson claimed she found three classified documents on her computer that she had no knowledge were there and could be used to frame her. She also expressed concern her Skype system had been hacked and used as a listening tool. The very progressive news media watchdog, Media Matters for America, reported security experts suggested the delete key or backspace key on her computer was stuck. I have a cheep drawbridge for sale that is "stuck", if anyone is interested. Media Matters is the organization that reportedly received a $1 million donation from George Soros in 2010 to go after Fox News. In isolated cases like Attkisson's, *1984* is already here. Remember, her ex-boss's brother works in the White House and made his displeasure known, as did the White House, regarding her investigative reporting that was critical of the Obama administration. She also had stories nixed at CBS that were critical or appeared to be critical.

This is scary stuff in anybody's book. If you are interested in more information on this story, she wrote a book published in 2014 titled *Stonewalled: My Fight for Truth Against the Forces of Obstruction,*

Intimidation, and Harassment in Obama's Washington. When this story is combined with what the DOJ did to the AP reporters and James Rosen, one can understand why some mainstream news reporters and journalists could feel personally threatened and might be cautious and reluctant to report any negativity toward our progressive friends. Even though this reluctance might be found in isolated cases, I believe that it is political ideology that primarily drives journalistic behavior for the mainstream news media. My hat is off to Attkisson who did the right thing. She not only ignored the threats but she pushed back.

One can never underestimate the danger of tyranny when the government monitors, intimidates, and punishes citizens who openly express opposition. Ask our founding fathers. There is another form of tyranny lurking out there that is a foreseeable time bomb regarding intimidation and danger for Americans. That is radical Islam. There is no question Islamic terrorists do not like who we are or how we think. These radical Islamists want to eradicate Western culture and the Judeo-Christian faith to accomplish caliphate for Islam. The scandal is that Obama and his administration will not recognize radical Islamists even exist and refuse to take action necessary to protect Americans from radical Islamic aggression. As usual, the mainstream press is complicit in aiding this delusional Obama administrative policy. I will begin to talk about this issue here and will continue in chapters 7 and 9 as radical Islam is intertwined in the subject matter of those chapters.

Although there are several Islamic terrorist organizations throughout the world, ISIS (Islamic State in Iraq and Syria) is currently posing the biggest threat to American security. The government calls the organization ISIL (Islamic State of Iraq and the Levant). ISIS began its notoriety by taking over a large geographical area in Syria. They moved into Iraq and now control a large area in that country. Their goal is to form a caliphate or Islamic state. These terrorists are so extreme and brutal that Al Qaida disavowed them in the beginning but have warmed up to them because of their success. The leader of ISIS has been referred to as the next Bin Laden. The Iraq army's ability to effectively fight ISIS has been suspect based upon past experience but appears to be improving. The Iraqis were able to take back Fallujah.

We have thousands of Americans in Baghdad including our embassy staff who were very concerned about their safety in the beginning. That concern had settled down but after the last terrorist attack, I don't know. ISIS started isolated bombings in Baghdad to put pressure on an unstable Iraq government and the most recent attack killed over 250 people and injured hundreds. Before ISIS stopped their territorial aggression in Iraq, they took over Mosul in June of 2014. Christians left Mosul and went 20 miles south to Qaragosh, which is Iraq's largest Christian city. In August 2014, ISIS took over that city. CNN reported the French Foreign Minister said there were "horrible acts of violence" by ISIS.

I researched that further and found a video on the Internet of a CNN news interview with a representative of a group called Ending Genocide in Iraq. The representative had just been to Washington to report the following. ISIS is targeting Christians in Mosul and Qaragosh. Christians either convert to Islam or pay a fine. If they don't, ISIS is hanging the men, raping and killing the woman, and beheading the children. He said there were the heads of children on sticks in a park in Mosul. They have bombed six churches and put a red "N" on the doors of Christian homes. I have no doubt that ISIS would love to come to the United States and do the same thing? It was difficult to hear him speak of these atrocities; however, it was no surprise.

The CNN reporter doing the interview looked and acted like he was in disbelief. What planet did he come from? This is ISIS's standard procedure and is not new. This reporter's reaction supported my view of the mainstream news media's lack of in depth reporting regarding ISIS but at least CNN reported this horrific story.

CNN also reported in March of this year the House of Representatives voted 393 to 0 to pass a resolution labeling the ISIS atrocities against Christian groups in Syria and Iraq as genocide. I was very impressed by that vote. Wow—393 to 0! The resolution was non-binding but was meant to put pressure on the Obama administration to label these atrocities what they are—genocide. Not surprisingly, the State Department ignored the resolution. Can you imagine the power of the news media if they took on this issue?

Obama acted as if ISIS was a new aberration when they took over Iraqi land even though he was warned over five years ago when our troops were pulled out of Iraq that this would happen. Ex-Speaker of the House, John Boehner, said Obama was "taking a nap" as this developed. Senator John McCain said all of Obama's security advisors should be fired and replaced. Good idea, but I wouldn't stop there. I would clean out all of Obama's administrative staff starting at the very top. Now, that would be a "dream act". Hopefully, we can call it the White House Dream Act of 2016.

Obama gives the news media gobbledygook answers regarding our country's position on ISIS and terrorism. He has routinely said all options are on the table. And, what happens after that? Basically nothing. We send a drone to kill a few terrorists who have big titles in their terrorist organizations and a couple of jets to drop a few bombs and that is our strategy. We do send a couple hundred troops from time to time but no one seems to know why. Obama asked Congress early in 2015 for a new war powers bill to wage military operations against ISIS. He said there would be no "boots on the ground" and limited the fight to three years. I wonder if he consulted with ISIS before he sent that request to Congress. Who announces to their enemies what their plans are before they carry out those plans? Obama does! I believe the bill literally died for lack of enthusiasm on the part of Congress and Obama. I honestly think it was a paper tiger reaction by Obama to significant criticism that he is not taking a stronger leadership position to protect U.S. security.

Iran doesn't dilly-dally in that region and certainly is not a paper tiger. An Iraqi official said the United States was supporting Iraq "on paper" and Iran was supporting Iraq "on the battlefield". Ask John Kerry and his negotiating team about Iran. They got their butts kicked hard by Iran in the nuclear negations. It should be called the nuclear capitulation. Iran announced early on they were going to send troops into Iraq to help and did. They signed a formal agreement with Iraq to help rebuild the Iraq army. I thought Obama sent troops to Iraq to do that? This alliance between Iraq and Iran has significant implications for Middle East stability. Now Russia has entered the picture and taken over influence we had in the region. Thank you Mr. President! Ben Laden is dead and Al Qaida is decimated! I thought about sending Obama a free Iranian bridge but he has probably bought enough bridges already?

Obama was in Palm Springs raising money and playing golf, as the ISIS issue in Iraq was first unfolding. I doubt he had much time to consider what to do until he got back to Washington. After Obama got back, it was reported he said Iraq would not get any help from us unless they can "resolve their sectarian differences". I assume that meant Obama was blaming the ISIS issue on the historical fight between the Sunnis and the Shiites and not the real issue, which was a significant and successful terrorist uprising. Not surprisingly, the uprising actually began in Syria after Obama refused to help in the overthrow of Assad. Have you ever imagined what the world would be like today if Obama had demonstrated strong leadership? I certainly have and my bridge company would be out of business.

Obama's position on Iraq was not reality. It was a case of divert and switch. He had to save face for his ill-fated decision to pull all of our troops out of Iraq instead of orchestrating a treaty with Maliki, which would have left adequate troops for Iraq's future stability and prevented the proliferation of ISIS terrorists. Nero may be in danger of losing his reputation as the most famous fiddler in history

Since Obama's 2011 announcement of our troop withdrawal schedule in Afghanistan, the same problems started to appear there just like they did in Iraq. Obama met with Afghan President Ashraf Ghani in March 2015 and told him he would leave 9,800 troops in Afghanistan until the end of 2015 and pull out all troops by the end of 2016. The Washington Post reported that before Obama and Ghani met, several former senior officials from both the Obama and Bush administrations released an open letter that said the war in Afghanistan was a stalemate.

Ryan Crocker, Obama's former Ambassador to Afghanistan, and Michele Flournoy, a top choice as defense secretary under Obama, were among those that signed the letter. The letter said in part, "The Taliban is intensifying their pressure on Afghan civilians. Meanwhile the political and economic situation is fragile." The twenty-three experts who signed the letter said the planned withdrawal would "unnecessarily put at risk hard-won gains of the last 13 years". Sound familiar, like in Iraq? You would think Obama and his advisors would learn from past experience. You don't tell your enemy your plans and then stick to those plans come hell or high water even in the face of defeat. Obama just announced again to slow down the troop withdrawal—until he is out of office, of course.

When the key Afghanistan city of Kunduz fell to the Taliban last year there was a news article in my local newspaper that said, "The fast-moving assault took military and intelligence agencies by surprise as the insurgents descended on the city, one of Afghanistan's richest, and the target of repeated Taliban offenses as the militants spread their fight across the country following the withdrawal last year of U.S. and NATO combat troupes." This is yet another example of world destabilization as Obama and his advisors dither about America's future in the Middle East.

Afghan troops reportedly took Kunduz back a few days later. Evidently there were Taliban troops still in the city and our airplanes were dropping bombs to help the Afghanistan soldiers root them out. It was extremely unfortunate that the airplanes bombed a Doctors Without Borders Hospital and killed 22 people including staff, adult patients, and patients who were children. The Obama administration couldn't get its stories straight. They first said there were Taliban in the vicinity and then said Taliban were using the hospital as a shelter. The hospital said there were no Taliban in its facility and made telephone calls to get the bombing stopped to no avail as the airplanes kept on bombing. They also said they had previously provided the hospital's GPS position to prevent something like this from happening. Even if there were Taliban in the hospital, why in the hell would you purposefully bomb a hospital with innocent staff and patients? As a retired hospital CEO, I am mystified and shocked that this could happen.

I am familiar with Doctors Without Borders and they are a great organization doing great work all over the world. I think we actually donated medical supplies and equipment to them before I retired. The hospital was destroyed and the Doctors Without Borders left Kunduz. Defense Secretary, Ash Carter, said it was a "complicated and confused issue" but they will get to the bottom of it. Obama was quoted by the AP as saying he expected a full accounting of the circumstances surrounding the bombing and that he would wait for those results before making a judgment. Waiting is one of Obama's principal governance strategies.

The AP reported Obama did apologize to the leader of the organization and pledged a "transparent, thorough, and objective accounting of the facts". He said the U.S. would look for better ways to prevent such accidents. I assume the heat got too great and the administration wanted to put this to bed as quickly as possible.

This is the power of the mainstream news media when they exercise it. A more recent news report said those in the military involved in the attack were suspended as they await disciplinary action that could include criminal charges. Is this action another cover-your-rear-end move by the Obama administration or an honest attempt to appropriately address the issue? I do not know and we probably will never find out unless the mainstream news media does follow-up investigative reporting. Don't hold your breath.

Well, I was wrong on this one. There was an AP story, albeit a small one, after I wrote the above. The report was six months after the attack and said about 16 people received administrative punishment including a two-star general. No criminal charges were filed. They said full details of the attack were forthcoming. The AP story did say the accident was human error and chances to avert the incident were missed. I hate to be so cynical but I wonder if the disciplinary action was appropriate for the situation or was nothing more than a slap on the wrist to put the issue at rest. I also wonder if the AP would have followed up on the story if the government had not released new information?

Obama has his own take on the news media. In February 2015, Fox News reported quotes by Obama regarding the news media in his interviews with The Hill and Vox. The heading said "Obama Faults Media Hype For Terror Fears". Obama was quoted as saying, "What's the famous saying about local newscasts, right? If it bleeds, it leads, right? You show crime stories and you show fires, because that's what folks watch, and it is all about ratings. And, you know the problems of terrorism and dysfunction and chaos, along with plane crashes and a few other things, that's the equivalent when it comes to covering international affairs."

Obama was also quoted as saying there was not going to be a lot of interest in stories showing positive progress on issues such as infant mortality or improving productivity for farmers. "It's not a sexy story",

Obama declared. Obama continued, "And climate change is one that is happening at such a broad scale and at such a complex system, it's a hard story for the media to tell on a day-to-day basis." Another reported quote by Obama was, "It is entirely legitimate for the American people to be deeply concerned when you've got a bunch of violent, vicious zealots who behead people or randomly shoot a bunch of folks in a deli in Paris. We devote enormous resources to that, and it is right and appropriate for us to be vigilant and aggressive in trying to deal with that—the same way a big city mayor's got to cut the crime rate down if he wants that city to thrive."

Obama lives in another world from the rest of us. Do you think Obama is covering for himself or actually believes what he said? You will discover in the next chapter I believe he believes this stuff and it's not a cover. The Fox News report also contained comments by John Kerry and a top White House official. The two said the U.S. strategy to defeat the Islamic State is working, despite warnings from other members of the Obama administration that the terror network is spreading. Were Kerry and the White House official covering for the White House or do they believe what they said? Your guess is as good as mine. The one thing we can always believe is that this outfit consistently says things and does things to cover their inept progressive rear ends.

I want to comment on some "loose end" media reports I have collected. The Rolling Stone magazine gave rock star status to the Boston bomber, Dzhokhar Tsarnaev, on the cover of their August 1, 2013 issue and doubled their sales over the same month the year before. How could a magazine do that to the victims' families and their country? Worse, how could the people who bought the magazine support that rock star status and make the magazine's decision successful? There is a troubling underlying message about our young society here that will be discussed later.

There was an AP article in my local newspaper that said in the opening paragraph, "Pope Francis arrived Tuesday on the first visit of his life to the United States, bringing his humble manner and his 'church of the poor' to a rich and powerful nation polarized over economic inequality, immigration and equal justice." Did the national press try to make the Pope sound anti-American and a supporter of Marxist ideology? Why did the AP open their coverage with that statement? It doesn't stop there. The next comment in the article said the Pope was "accorded a rare honor" when Obama, Michelle, and their kids met the Pope at the bottom of the steps as he exited his airplane. The article continued, "Presidents usually make important visitors come to them at the White House." Talk about the mainstream news media allocating "rock star" status to Obama. The AP article supported Obama's political agenda and the polarization in America. The article did not mention Obama has created polarization through his own actions. The AP made Obama look like the "holy one" over the Pope by saying he accorded the Pope a rare honor. The article was astonishingly biased.

Here is an August 2015 report by The Daily Signal that is very troubling regarding the lack of openness by the Obama administration. Current and former State Department officials have been quietly called to testify behind closed doors before Trey Gowdy's committee on Benghazi. Diplopundit, a pseudonymously published blog that follows State Department management and leadership, said there are now new department rules. The blog said official or unofficial employee testimony regarding department matters may be subject to review and employees should "consult with the Department of State's Office of the Legal Advisor or Office of the General Council as appropriate to determine applicable procedures".

The blog commented, "We think this means that if you get summoned to appear before the House Select Benghazi Committee and are testifying in your personal capacity as a former or retired employee of the State Department, these new regulations may still apply to you and you may still need clearance before you testify." Chaffetz, as Chairman of the House Oversight and Government Reform Committee, said it's an absolute overreach and indicated this would have an effect on future testimony before his congressional committee by State Department staff.

A State Department deputy spokesperson said the reason for the revisions to State Department rules was to "underscore that the Department encourages employees to engage with the public on matters related to the nation's foreign relations". He continued, "The revised policies and procedures are more protective of employees speech as they establish a higher bar for limiting employees' writing or speaking in their personal capacity, while also recognizing changing technologies in communication, such as social media." That is progressive speak for keep your mouth shut regarding anything that will make the Department or the Obama administration look bad or you will regret it.

Also written into the regulation was something the deputy spokesperson forgot to mention. It said, "Noncompliance may result in disciplinary action, criminal prosecution and/or civil liability." A former State Department official who asked to be anonymous told the person who wrote The Daily Signal article that at the very least, this regulation will have a "chilling effect" on current and former employees. Oh, by the way, who wrote The Daily Signal article? Someone named Sharyl Attkisson. Could our mainstream media learn a few things from her! The article concluded with a comment by Chaffetz who said this penalty clause is "threatening and over the top".

Ironically, there was an article in my local newspaper the following October about information being leaked by Secret Service employees to two news services regarding Chaffetz being turned down for employment at the Secret Service. They said it was because "better qualified candidates existed". It was also reported that Chaffetz's personal record had been accessed 60 times by 45 employees. Chaffetz said he was undaunted by the Secret Service employees' attempt to get back at him after he convened a meeting of his committee titled "Holding the Protectors Accountable" that reviewed significant problems with the Secret Service. The Secret Service Director finally admitted to Congress that he had known about employees accessing Chaffetz's personal record but not about the leak to the news media.

I saw a news story on Fox News regarding the government's alteration of military intelligence reports to present a watered down picture regarding terrorism. In the process of obtaining more information on the story, I found a website called theconservativetreehouse.com. I had never heard of the site before and found it interesting. The site is very professionally done and is titled The Last Refuge. It had a tagline that said "Rag Tag Bunch of Conservative Misfits". There was a picture of Andrew Breitbart dressed up as Uncle Sam at the top of the home page with a large caption that said "I Want You To Be Andrew Breitbart". A smaller narrative with the picture said Breitbart was irreplaceable, one person could never fill the void that Breitbart left behind, and it will take thousands. You might remember that he died March 1, 2012 of heart failure at a young age of 43.

I bring up this website because, other than PragerU, it is the only information source I have ever seen with an analysis of the difference in how conservatives think and how liberals think. Obviously, I was very curious. The site offered a somewhat different perspective than chapters 2, 3, and 4 but nothing in conflict with my analysis. For example, the site said that fear was at the core of liberalism and love and trust was at the core of conservatism. It went on to say liberalism is about control and conservatism is about self-empowerment. The analysis of liberalism versus conservatism is found under "about us" on their website and is worthwhile reading. Their analogy fits well with a quote I ran across by Winston Churchill that said, "Socialism is a philosophy of failure, the creed of ignorance, and the gospel of envy, its inherent virtue is the equal sharing of misery."

Here is the report from The Last Refuge on the news story regarding the alteration of military intelligence reports. They said The Daily Beast reported intelligence analysts in the military central command accused senior officials of altering their reports on ISIS and al Qaeda's branch in Syria to make the situation look better than it was in the beginning and is now. The complaints prompted the Pentagon's Inspector General to launch an investigation. Two senior analysts at CENTCOM made a written complaint to the Inspector General in July 2015 alleging the reports portrayed the terrorist groups to be weaker than the analysts believed. Some of these reports were supposedly briefed to Obama. Fifty other analysts supported the allegations. Eleven of the analysts anonymously told The Daily Beast that analysts have been complaining about the politicizing of these reports for months.

The writer of the story on The Last Refuge said the following, "Many people will look at this devastating sunlight upon the U.S. Intel Community as a political embarrassment for the Obama administration. However, I would disagree. The entire exposition smells more like a deflective shield targeted to give the White House an excuse for terrible Mid-East policy. This 'revelation' protects the White House more than it causes embarrassment; it gives Obama excuses for his failures...."

and you'll note this is surfacing at a time when Russia is entering Syria under the auspices of needing to fight ISIS, because the U.S. has failed. There's an obvious transparency to the timing…" I think the writer with The Last Refuge nailed it. In dealing with the Obama administration, it seems as if we are constantly with Alice in Wonderland where things are not always as they seem.

Here is a more recent story regarding government employees speaking out. The Wall Street Journal reported in June of this year that 51 State Department Officials signed a document protesting against U.S. policy in Syria. These officials called for military strikes against the Syrian government and urged regime change as the only way to defeat ISIS. The article called this a "scalding internal critique" of our U.S. policy against taking sides in the Syrian war. After what I wrote above, why would these officials feel comfortable to sign such a document? The document was on the department's "Dissent Channel" which allows employees to express opposing views and retaliation against them is expressly prohibited. I think that was still a brave thing to do and I also think there is a much deeper message of frustration here. I wonder what would happen if all government departments had a Dissent Channel? I think we know!

Scandals just keep coming and coming under the progressive Obama administration. They remind me of the Energizer Bunny that just keeps going and going. It seems I can't finish writing about one without learning of another. It is extremely concerning that so much turmoil has developed at home and abroad so rapidly under Obama's presidency. Past government administrations haven't been perfect but the progressive Obama administration takes imperfection to a new high. It gives us great insight into what a future progressive America would be like if this progressive behavior continues after the 2016 election. How about world affairs? I heard a guest contributor on Fox News bring up the Cloward and Piven theory in relation to these disruptive scandals. I found that very interesting since I assumed only progressives knew about Cloward and Piven's theory. I guess there are a couple of us non-progressives too.

Well, mainstream news media; I am bringing your chapter to an end. Here is a message to you from me. I know it was brutal but it was brutally honest. Did I hit a nerve with my ranting or did I just make you mad? Do you not agree with my editor friend that it is your job to protect the public? How do you feel about the ethical statement by the Sedona Observer? There are many more ethical statements for journalism out there just like that one.

How about the Code of Ethics for the Society of Professional Journalists? For you non-journalists, the society is one of the oldest organizations in the United States representing journalist with approximately 300 chapters across the country? Here are excerpts from that code of ethics:

> Under the Preamble it says, "Members of the Society of Professional Journalists believe that public enlightenment is the forerunner of justice and the foundation of democracy. Ethical journalism strives to ensure the free exchange of information that is accurate, fair, and thorough. An ethical journalist acts with integrity." The Code of Ethics continues by saying, "The Society declares the following four principles are the foundation of ethical journalism and encourages their use in its practice by all people in all media." (1) Seek Truth and Report It—Ethical journalism should be accurate and fair. Journalists should be honest and courageous in gathering, reporting, and interpreting information. (2) Minimize Harm—Ethical journalism treats sources, subjects, colleagues, and members of the public as human beings deserving of respect. (3) Act Independently—The highest and primary obligation of ethical journalism is to serve the public. (4) Be Accountable and Transparent—Ethical journalism means taking responsibility for one's work and explaining one's decisions to the public.

I am sure your news organization has its own code of ethics. How about the quotes from our founding fathers? Do you not support the Declaration of Independence and the Constitution as written and intended? I will admit you were present in varying degrees for these progressive scandals but where is the hard hitting investigative reporting and outrage for inappropriate, incompetent, and dishonest behavior by our progressive government that is not in the best interest of the American people? I am not talking about every one of you. I applaud and thank those of you who strive for unbiased accuracy and are true investigative news reporters like Sharyl Attakisson. Without you, the ballgame was over before it started. Thank you Fox News, The Wall Street Journal, conservative Internet sites, The Heritage Foundation, Judicial Watch, Rush Limbaugh, Glen Beck, other conservative radio and television hosts, and those in the mainstream news media that speak out against and counter the progressive deception in mainstream news.

Here is a great example of mainstream news that countered progressive deception. It is an article that was in my local newspaper and syndicated by The Washington Post to highlight Columbus Day. It took up the entire first page and one-half page inside the newspaper section that covers such things as editorials, travel, and books. There was a one-half page picture of a statue of Columbus on the first page and the headline said "Man vs. Myths" with a subheading that said "Dispelling 5 misconceptions about Christopher Columbus". The five topics covered were: 1) Columbus proved the "flat Earth" theory wrong; 2) Columbus was Italian; 3) Columbus was a successful businessman and a model leader; 4) Columbus committed genocide (the progressives won't like this presented as a myth); and 5) Columbus believed he had discovered America.

I cannot tell you how wonderful and refreshing it was to read such an extensive article about Columbus in the mainstream news media that was totally void of any political ideology. It was simply a fascinating and educational story about one of the most famous people in our history. I can't thank The Washington Post and the author enough for such a rare and refreshing experience from the mainstream news media. The author was Kris Lane who holds the France V. Scholes chair in colonial Latin American history at Tulane University. You can find the article on the Internet if you are interested. Eat your hearts out, progressives. They are not always in your web of deceit.

I enjoyed the article so much; I emailed Kris, told him how much I enjoyed it, and thanked him for writing it. He emailed me back and said, "Choosing a posture is always easier than doing the work necessary to search for the truth. I must admit I was hesitant to write this piece knowing what a polarizing figure Columbus is, but I decided to take a stab at updating the story without being too academic." Great job, Kris!

The vast majority of you mainstream news media are very intelligent, strive to do a professional and accurate job, and care about your country. I understand political ideological differences, but news should not be politically biased and should be reported truthfully and fully to protect society. As an industry, you are turning your back on pragmatic reality and I struggle to understand why. I can only look back to chapter 2 and my discussion of liberal core traits and beliefs and behaviors. I will leave you with one last thought. This problem is real and extremely problematic for the long-term success of "our" country—yours and mine. Think about it.

CHAPTER 7

Progressive Washington!

In writing this chapter, I want to say up front that I have no formal experience in politics. I have never been a politician but I have personally had to deal with political and non-political politics on a frequent basis during my career. My wife and I vote in every election for our informed choice of political candidate or political issue but we have never gotten involved in political campaigns and I have never been intrigued or enamored with governmental politics except when it infringed upon or enhanced something I valued. What I see happening to our incredible country falls heavily into the category of infringement. We discussed progressive core personality traits and progressive beliefs and behaviors in chapters 2 and 4 and we discussed how progressives practice those beliefs and behaviors in chapters 5 and 6. This chapter will focus on how our federal government operates in Washington under progressive rule.

I only remember specifics of presidential terms back to John F. Kennedy. His assassination and philandering are still topics today. Lyndon Johnson was certainly an opportunistic character. It has been intimated by a few that he might have been part of a conspiracy in Kennedy's assassination. I also saw a documentary that said he could have won the Vietnam War but chose not to because what he had to do to win would have been such a political "hot potato". Who could forget "Tricky Dick" (Richard Nixon) and his Watergate Scandal? Gerald Ford? Several years ago, I was playing golf on the golf course where he lived in Palm Springs. I saw him through a window sitting at his desk in his den. He still looked presidential—especially since there were two Secret Service men walking around in the yard. I tried to not act suspicious but I couldn't help but stare. He was born in Nebraska where I spent the last twenty-one years before my retirement. I guess I should also mention he announced the Vietnam War had ended when he was president but he certainly was not a major player in the war as were the presidents before him.

I vaguely remember Jimmy Carter but I will never forget paying a 15.5 % interest rate on my home loan when he was in office. I see similarities between Obama and Carter and I'm not the only one who makes that comparison. Both are seen as very naive and inept leaders both domestically and internationally. Ronald Reagan corrected Carter's mistakes and got the country on a strong conservative and successful course. Bill Clinton was a strong liberal but I would not classify him as a progressive. I can't say the same for his wife. Clinton had his bouts with ethics and honesty but tended to go with the "political wind" even if it meant that he moved to the political center or even a little center-right. Contrary to what some say, I remember the Bushes as good Presidents. I don't remember much about George H. W. Bush except that I liked him. I had the privilege of attending a relatively small campaign event when he was running for re-election and heard him speak. All I remember about that event is the Secret Service staff was all over the place including the roof of the building. It looked like something you would see in a movie.

I can still see George W. Bush on television announcing the invasion of Iraq as the bombing of Baghdad was unfolding. The bombing was quite a "fireworks show" for the world to see. What a way to let the "bad guys" know that you don't mess with a stable world order, America's closest friends, or America! You do and you get your ass kicked. Sometimes you need to kick ass (with reason of course) just to remind the bad guys of that fact. Our current policy is to do a lot of kissing rather than kicking. This change in policy will be the basis of our discussion in chapter 9 on foreign policy. George W. was a conservative but on occasion he was a little too liberal for me. I still liked and respected him for standing up and doing what he believed was best for the country even if what he did was sometimes controversial like Iraq. He and his dad had that trait in common.

It is obvious that my recollections and impressions of past presidents are very limited. We human beings are all subject to our short memories and what recorded history imparts upon us. This dynamic not only pertains to past presidents but also for American politics and American history. Writing this book has reinforced with me that what we hear and read regarding the historical context of our country is many times not historical reality. Sometimes that is intentional and sometimes not. Many times, historical pundits contribute to or create this situation by "cleansing and distorting the facts" to support their political biases.

The Wall Street Journal contained an op-ed that provided a good example of this dynamic. What do you think of Herbert Hoover who was president from 1929 to 1933? Before I read the op-ed, I really had no opinion but my feelings were generally positive. After all, he has a famous dam named after him. The op-ed said legend stipulates the Great Depression resulted from the stock market crash of 1929 but that is not true. The market was recovering nicely in 1930 and the Great Depression actually resulted from Hoover's bad economic policies. I read in Wikipedia that those policies also resulted in Hoover loosing the election in 1932 to FDR and his New Deal. Even calling the dam Hoover Dam rather than Boulder Dam was very controversial at the time. As you read, keep this important dynamic in mind. As I said, what we remember is not always reality and sometimes historians create falsehoods to push their agenda. These two dynamics have enormous impact on our society's beliefs and political attitudes.

Washington has never been so progressive in ideology, so divided by politics, so corrupted by politics, and so driven by decisions based solely on politics until President Barack Hussein Obama II. That includes the presidential terms of FDR and Wilson. I can't necessarily say Obama is more progressive than FDR and Wilson but without a doubt Obama can have a greater impact on America because of the size and power of the federal government today versus when FDR and Wilson were presidents. That is a very profound indictment but it is true. We have, in the past several months, begun to hear similar rumblings from conservative Washington politicians and national political pundits. Actions and comments by some liberals indicate they are feeling that way too but they will not overtly say so. Look at the deceit, corruption, and anti-American decisions and actions coming out of Washington. Look at how we Americans are so divided among ourselves because of this progressive political turmoil. I have never observed such divisiveness in our country since the civil rights un-rest that I remember from the 50s and 60s or the Vietnam War during the 60s and 70s. This tumultuous progressive politicization of Washington is what this chapter is about.

Do you find it as interesting as I do that no one ever says Hussein and you rarely here Barack in referring to Obama? He is almost always referred to as President Obama or just Obama. Do you know the origins of and the meaning of the two names? Barack is Hebrew in origin and means "to shine" or "lighting". The name is mostly found in Israel. Hussein is Arabic and was first used by the Islamic Prophet Muhammad as a name for his grandson. The name means "good", "beautiful", or "handsome". Obama can be either Mandarin Chinese meaning "to lean or bend" or a Japanese surname for "little beach". I do not think his names necessarily mean anything to take note of except it does show some insight into his mother's thinking which we will discuss later in the chapter. One name being Jewish and the other Islamic is certainly ironic and interesting.

Although our society is rapidly changing, the majority of Americans still believe in the values upon which the Declaration of Independence and the Constitution are based and the principles contained within them. Our founding fathers obviously believed in those values and principles. The early colonists and immigrants who came to America for a better life had those values and came here to achieve that better life through the principals expressed in those two documents. We discussed in chapter 2 that classic liberal democrats genuinely support the values and principals of the Declaration of Independence and the Constitution but the progressives—that is a "donkey" of a different color so to speak.

Progressive politicians in Washington do not support the Constitution even though they take the following oath to do so:

> I do solemnly swear (or affirm) that I will support and defend the Constitution of the United States against all enemies, foreign and domestic; that I will bear true faith and allegiance to the same; that I take this obligation freely, without any mental reservation or purpose of

evasion; and that I will well and faithfully discharge the duties of the office on which I am about to enter: so help me God.

For progressives, this oath is only a meaningless ticket to get into office and destroy the very thing they pledge to support. How could these anti-American and self-serving radicals possibly get into power? Let's begin to answer that question by going back in time. My family was considered middle class but we didn't have even close to what middle class families have today. For example, we were lucky to have one television rather than multiple televisions. I remember when our little town first got television and we were one of the first families to have one. It was stunning black and white. If I had gotten a car when I turned 16, I would have had to work to pay for it. I never left the country until I was in college and that was with a bunch of guys driving to Mexico for a week during spring break. I never left the continent or flew in an airplane until I was an adult. How many televisions on the average do middle class or even poor families have today? My kids got their own cars when they got their drivers license. My son went to Europe once in high school and twice in college. How about smartphones, computers, and electronic games? Look at Facebook, Twitter, and Google. We had nothing like this when I was growing up. I am not going to play curmudgeon and say these advantages are bad. They're great! They're great individually and for society in general.

But, there is a "but". These wonderful "material things" and our current "good life" are distracting Americans more and more from the appreciation and understanding of how we got to where we are and how to continue down that path of success. This phenomenon began with the actual founding of our country and has increasingly escalated over time as our country has developed and prospered. We Americans are victims of our own success and it can destroy us. The definition of "strive" is to make great efforts to achieve or obtain something or to struggle. We used to be a nation of want, strive, and get. We are rapidly becoming a nation of want and get. We are losing appreciation for the conservative values and principals expressed in the Declaration of Independence and the Constitution and we are forgetting it was those conservative values and principals that provided to us what our society and we personally have achieved.

This disconnect is particularly true for younger generations: Gen Xers born in the sixties and seventies and Millennials born in the eighties and the nineties. Some analysts include Baby Boomers who were born in the mid-forties to the mid-sixties as being disconnected but that is a stretch in my book. I am a Baby Boomer and the vast majority of Baby Boomers I associate with are as conservative and as appreciative of our Declaration of Independence and Constitution as I am.

The majority of young people look at politics from a utopian influenced ideology rather than the conservative ideology that is the basis of our prosperity and success. I read about two studies reported by the Tribune Washington Bureau and the Los Angeles Times that support my supposition. One study indicated the Millennial Generation is less religious, less likely to be patriotic, and significantly more liberal than past generations. The study proposed that Gen Xers fall somewhere in between Millennials and Baby Boomers in this regard. In another study, employers expressed that Millennials have a poor work ethic, are easily distracted, and have unrealistic pay demands.

The Dallas Morning News recently reported Millennials are 81.1 million strong and represent the largest single age group in the U.S. The genesis of the Dallas Morning News article was that Millennials have enormous influence on major chain restaurants through their buying power and these restaurants are gearing up to acquire their business.

What does this say about their voting power? I read a syndicated article by the Los Angeles Times about this issue. The article reviewed a poll by Harvard University's institute of Politics on the current presidential election. It said Millennials prefer a democrat to a republican by a margin of 61% to 33% and exit polls show socialist candidate Bernie Sanders consistently beat Hillary Clinton, sometimes by 4 to 1. That is not surprising. Sanders consistently promised "free stuff". He promoted want and get. About 50% said healthcare was a right and should be paid for by the government. I often think they don't think. Who is the government in this case? It is the taxpayers. It is pay me now or pay me later at a much great greater expense for less care than is available through private insurance. We have already discussed that extensively in the book and will talk about it later in this chapter and the next.

The study showed the Millennials support more government spending to reduce poverty (which actually increases poverty as we will discuss later) and for measures to curb climate change (which is a progressive ruse). They said these expenditures should be made even if it costs jobs. They really can't mean that. I do not know if they don't understand what they are saying, do not see themselves as taxpayers, or just flat out don't care. I guess it depends on the Millennial and his or her situation in life.

I regularly watch Jesse Watters who interviews young people on *Watters' World* for Fox's *O'Reilly Factor* and also for his own new show on Fox. His interviews are meant to be entertaining but they are also very telling. I will admit that some of his interviewees are in the "offbeat" category but they are still young people in our society. He often interviews college students who are not offbeat. It is shocking that the great majority of these young people, offbeat or not, do not have any idea what is happening in American politics, in America in general, or around the world. It is more shocking that many don't seem to care. I will share some of his and others interviews with these young people later.

The environment we live in today, which has been morphing over the last several decades, has three scenarios that have diminished society's interest and especially our younger generations' interest in supporting and maintaining conservative values and principles. The first scenario is this. My generation grew up during a time when Americans remembered the hard times and the struggles their parents, grandparents, great-grandparents, and/or other generations endured. Many remembered when their relatives immigrated to America to achieve a better life. We greatly appreciated conservative values and principals and embraced what we had politically, socially, and materially.

Because we didn't have a lot of material things when we were young and had to work hard for what we did have, we gave our kids more than we had and made life easier for them. That practice combined with the fact that families on the average have increasingly gained more wealth over past years has made our society become a society of haves and expectations. Even with the poor economic conditions during the last eight years, younger generations take for granted what they have and have high expectations for "getting" rather than "striving for" what they want. It is a scenario of entitlement versus hard work and excess versus sufficient.

Pickles is one of my favorite cartoons. In a recent cartoon, Earl was at a playground with his grandson, Nelson, who was playing on the playground equipment. Earl said, "Life was a lot more dangerous when I was a kid. We did not have playgrounds. We played on railroad tracks and farm equipment. It is a wonder any of us survived. To get by we had to grow up fast. How old are you, son?" Nelson responded, "Six." Earl then said, "When I was your age, I was eight and a half." I can identify with that.

The second scenario is that the new electronic age, geographic mobility, and more permissive societal norms have given our society and especially our young people opportunities and distractions we didn't even imagine when we were growing up. This has not been kind to a strong family unit, close personal relationships, and the conservative values and principles that result from that interpersonal unity with family and friends.

I regularly see families in restaurants with their children sitting there intently using their electronic devices and no family interaction taking place. That's not exactly family time. Here is another cartoon that makes the point. Blondie is not the best cartoon in the newspaper but I still enjoy it because it has been a classic since 1930 and I like the characters. Five-year-old Elmo is camping in the back yard with a friend. Dagwood says, "Wanna sing some camp songs, Guys?" Elmo says, "We already downloaded music on our iPads, Mr. B." Dagwood then says, "How about a scary story?" Elmo replies, "Thanks, but we have the Headless Horseman on our Kindles, Mr. B." Dagwood then goes into the house and Blondie says, "I thought you were helping with the campout." Dagwood replies, "Nope! They lost me at virtual s'mores." Later, Dagwood and Blondie are setting up in bed talking. Elmo and his friend walk into the bedroom and ask, "Mr. B., what's your Wi-Fi password again? We want to download a virtual campfire!" Dagwood turns to Blondie and says, "See what I mean?" Blondie replies, "Don't worry about it, honey. It's the new age." It certainly is!

Baby Blues is also one of my favorite cartoons. A recent one has Zoe asking her mom how she and her dad met. Zoe asked, "Did you meet dad on line?" Wanda said, "We met in college." Zoe then said, "Not on the internet?" Wanda replied, "Nope. We had some classes together and just started talking to each other." Zoe responded, "On Facebook?" In frustration, Wanda said, "NO! In person!" Zoe concluded, "I have some real concerns about this relationship." Enough said. I am seeing more and more cartoons depicting electronic interaction between people versus human one to one interaction as the basis of their humor. This is a sign of how ingrained electronics are becoming in our lives and in our society.

Even Dear Abby has gotten into the act regarding families and electronic devices. A letter she put in her newspaper column interestingly involves adults and electronics rather than children and electronics. The letter said it would be a long time before Disconnected in Midtown, Tennessee will invite their adult kids and grandkids over to their house again. That sounds a little tough to me but I wasn't there. The letter explained that the grandparents who wrote it had a family birthday party. They looked after the grandchildren, cooked, waited on everyone, and cleaned up afterwards while the adult parents sat texting or playing on their cell phones. The grandparents wrote that the adult parents spending time on cellphones rather than socializing was rude and signified that the grandparents' and grandchildren's company was not valuable. They continued to write neither they (the grandparents) nor the adult children's own children are important enough for their attention and teaches young children that it isn't necessary to be social, offer help to clear the table, or be gracious and appreciative when someone prepares a meal for you.

Abby responded by asking if the grandparents told their adult children who were "sitting on their fannies", they needed help, their own children needed minding, and their behavior was rude? Abby then said the behaviors they experienced did not happen overnight and the grandparents might be partly responsible. Abby concluded, "If you say what is on your mind, you might startle them into better behavior for their own children before it is too late." Here are the lessons to be learned from this Dear Abby story. Putting electronics above human relationships is rude. Family discipline and family values are an important part of the family unit and the maturation of children as they are growing up. Finally, it demonstrates family relations are not easy and need constant attention and work to achieve the positive results in life that strong healthy family relations provide.

I found an unusual story in my local newspaper on this topic. The headline was "Hitting a Low Note—Piano stores closing as fewer children taking up the instrument". The news story said piano sales were tops in 1909 when approximately 350,000 pianos were sold. Sales have now fallen to between 30,000 and 40,000. The reason? A piano consultant concluded it is because of the change in society. He was quoted as saying, "Computer technology has just changed everything about what kids are interested in. People are interested in things that don't take much effort, so the idea of sitting and playing an hour a day to learn piano is not what kids want to do." The key here is "things that don't take much effort".

I have one last and very telling example. I was taken aback by a photo and accompanying text in the February 2015 issue of the Conde Nast Traveler magazine. A large photo shows a young couple in Paris sitting on a concrete wall next to the Seine River romantically hugging and kissing. The text included the following. "Back then (Paris 1962), everyone was kissing in the streets," recalls Hans Mauli who was the Swiss photographer who took the photo. The 77-year-old Mauli, who now lives in California, still believes Paris is a city that inspires romance. He said, "Everything is beautiful—the light, the architecture, the river." But, Mauli isn't sure there are as many displays of public passion these days. He continued. "So many people are looking at their smartphones instead of looking at each other."

There are numerous statistics regarding marriage and divorce for our younger generation. Some of the statistics are in conflict depending upon what source is used but there is one clear trend. The concept of marriage is diminishing and divorce is on the rise, particularly among young people. That trend was summarized in a recent Lockhorns cartoon. Leroy was sitting at the kitchen table drinking his coffee and reading the newspaper. He said to Loretta, "This younger generation is smarter than we were … It says 63% of them never plan to marry." I did read a story in The Wall Street Journal that had a positive note to it. The headline for the story was "Coming Soon: More Married Millennial Parents". The story said, "Demographic Intelligence predicts that ultimately around 60% of the children of Millennials will be born to married parents, up from around 45% today."

Our young people are experiencing significant wants and expectations, diminished traditional social norms, and progressive political ideologies without the benefit and pressure of traditional conservative family values and principles. This disconnect is exacerbated by the impact of decreasing church attendance and connection to Christianity. There was a Rasmussen poll a couple of years ago that said 37% of American adults believe it is possible to have a healthy community without churches or religious presence. I am surprised and not surprised. Of those polled, only 57% disagreed and said it is not possible to have a healthy community without churches. This scenario has not been kind to our conservative society. The dissolution of close relationships within the family unit and with each other coupled with the decline of Christianity is increasingly allowing radical societal norms and progressive ideologies to be accepted by our young people as being more rational and realistic than tradition conservative norms and ideologies.

I commented in chapter 1 that, when I was a young person, everyone went to church. I do not believe one must go to church to be a Christian. I also do not believe everyone has to be a Christian to be moral. I do believe a society has to be moral to survive and morality has to be based upon Judeo-Christian beliefs or a religion of like values. This is a major problem in our American society today. I do not go to church as I once did but I believe in and practice Christianity and Christian morals. I do attend a Christian based men's fellowship in the community where I live. A minister who was a key member of a national committee in Washington studying our prison systems spoke to our fellowship group. He said the kinder and gentler approach to reform our young people who are incarcerated has not worked and they are now going back to the "boot camp and farming hard work" approach. He said the "tough love" approach has proven to be the most successful in achieving discipline of the mind and body.

The same experience can be found in the classrooms of our schools. The students are much more successful in classes where discipline is practiced than classes where discipline is absent. I have always said, "Tough love is the best love in the world." This is good advice for our society that is creeping out of disciplinary control. Our universities could certainly heed that advise as well. We will discuss that in chapter 10.

Scenario three involves progressive government practices to solicit and maintain power and control. Politicians have increasingly become more and more progressive and have increased the government's roll as a "sugar daddy" to gain political favor and votes. As this has occurred, government has increasingly gained more influence over our lives. The government gets bigger and bigger and we have more and more rules and regulations. During Obama's reign, the concept of "political sugar daddy" is on steroids in buying votes through entitlements and executive mandates to please and grow the progressive political base. This is particularly true concerning women, minorities, the poor, the middle class, and younger voters. The progressives and especially Obama have used Saul Alinsky's principals to perfection to deceive society in implementing progressive laws, policies, and practices. Remember, Obama taught community organizing using Alinsky's principals. Massive entitlements, deception, cover-up, corruption, and news media bias are powerful political tools and the progressive politicians are masters at it.

These three scenarios explain how the anti-American and self-serving progressive radicals got into power and are having significant success in changing our society from traditional American values to a society that embraces a Marxist based political philosophy. Can we stop this evolution and preserve the principles of the Declaration of Independence and the laws of the Constitution for the future? That is what the rest of this book is about.

I have referred to George Orwell's book titled *1984* several times. It was required reading in school when I was growing up. I assume everyone has read it or at least is aware of what it is about. Here is a quick synopsis. The story takes place in a fictitious land that is run by the privileged inter-elite government headed by *Big Brother*. The book was published in 1949 and the fictitious land called Oceania is thought to be socialist Great Britain. The book raises doubt that Big Brother even exists since no one outside the Inner Party ever sees him. The Inner

Party is the privileged inner-elite upper ruling class that is 2% of the population. There is also the Outer Party that represents the middle class and is 13% of the population. Proles are 85% of the population and are the uneducated working class.

The government proclaims they rule for the greater good but they persecute individualism and independent thinking. There is total surveillance on citizens and the government practices public mind control. Historical accounts of the past are revised to support the party line. The Ministry of Love oversees torture and brainwashing. The Ministry of Peace oversees war and atrocity. The Ministry of Plenty oversees shortage and famine. And lastly, the Ministry of Truth oversees propaganda and historical revision. Keep *1984* in mind as you read this book. The resemblance between the fictitious government in Oceania and our own evolving government imposing its will on the American people is scary as hell and disturbing.

With our three scenarios in mind and the enlightenment provided by George Orwell, let's analyze progressive Washington. Politico reported on an August 2015 Quinnipiac poll that said 71% of Americans are dissatisfied with the direction our country is going. When asked specifically about the federal government, 49% expressed "dissatisfaction", 27% expressed "anger", and 21% said they were "satisfied but not enthusiastic". Only 2% said they trusted government "almost all of the time". Only 13% said they trusted leaders in Washington "most of the time". Fifty-one percent responded they "sometimes trusted" government and 34% said they "hardly ever" did. I heard Jesse Watters say the following on Fox News' *The Five*, "A gaff in Washington is when someone tells the truth."

The AP reported on a poll that was jointly done in April of this year with GfK research that covered the same topic. The poll said almost 8 in 10 Americans say they are "dissatisfied or angry" with the way the federal government is working while the same percentage say they are "satisfied or enthusiastic" about their personal lives. The report commented that republicans are more likely to be angry. The participants said their anger wasn't driven so much by political ideology as it was by distain for a political system that doesn't seem to be working.

It is not surprising we hear and read how dysfunctional and inept Congress is on a regular basis. I cannot remember the last time any meaningful legislation was enacted. I saw a Beetle Bailey cartoon that portrayed it well. Major Greenbrass is conducting a meeting with General Halftrack and four other officers. The Major says, "All in favor say 'aye'." Everyone says "aye" and the motion passes. General Halftrack says, "Who says we can't get anything done!" Someone asks Miss Buxley, "What did they vote on?" Miss Buxley said, "To postpone the vote on reducing the budget." Sounds like Congress to me.

We have an immense congressional ideological divide between conservatives and progressives. Progressive democrats defend their positions to a fault with no compromise and republicans have been "missing in action" since the last time they got their butts kicked by progressive democrats and the president. You can think what you want about Bill Clinton but as I said, when he was in office he acted like a liberal and not a progressive. There were also more liberal democrats versus progressive democrats in Congress who were willing to compromise with the republicans and they did along with Bill. Things got done! Maybe not exactly what either side always wanted but "stuff happened". Bill watched the daily public polls like a bird watcher looking for rare birds and reacted accordingly.

Today, progressives are dominating congressional democrats. Progressives Harry Reid and Nancy Pelosi are leading them or I should say controlling them. Until the democrats lost the House and then the Senate, it was Reid and Pelosi's progressive way or out to the "woodshed". There was no compromise. When the republicans took control of the House, Reid and Pelosi still had their way. Reid would not let any republican sponsored bill come to the Senate floor for a vote though it probably would not have passed anyway. Reid excused his behavior by regularly blaming the billionaire Koch brothers for influencing congressional republican votes with their political donations. Is that the "pot calling the kettle black"? The democrats have many more wealthy donors influencing Congress than do the republicans. How about the donor who personally gave $50 million to the democrats and promised to raise $50 million more if they would stop the Keystone XL Pipeline? I guess Reid overlooked that one.

Have you ever looked at the "shady stuff" that Reid has done for Nevada. After all, Nevada is a "hot and sunny" place. The Los Angeles Times reported a few years ago that Reid "sliced a little pork" to fund an $18 million bridge from Nevada to Arizona that is within miles of property he owns. This property is reportedly a great place to develop housing and other projects. At least it wasn't a "bridge to nowhere". I need to send him one of my bridge catalogs. Breitbart said Reid also rushed U.S. visas through DHS for foreign investors so they could invest $115 million in a Nevada gambling casino. His son was hired to do the legal work. Is there anything wrong with a father helping his son?

Even though republicans now control the House and Senate, Reid and Pelosi still continue to have power because the progressive Senate democrats will not let a bill they do not support get to the Senate floor for a vote. There are 54 republicans, 44 democrats, and 2 independents. In order to end a filibuster and bring a bill to vote, which is called cloture, 3/5ths or 60 Senators have to vote "yea" to do it. Obviously, the republicans do not have the votes to end filibusters; therefore, Reid still has a degree of control.

How many Americans know about cloture and truly understand the democrats or I should say the progressives still have significant control in Congress even though republicans are in the majority. Not many. They believe the republicans now control Congress and still can't get anything done. There is a degree of truth to that because of the infighting between congressional republican factions. During an interview on CNN, Obama blamed congressional gridlock on Rush Limbaugh and the Tea Party. He said republicans have told him privately they are afraid to do what is right for the American people and break gridlock in congress because Rush Limbaugh and the Tea Party will say something bad about them. Maybe I should sell "whopper" bridges on the Internet for this one. I wonder if net neutrality would allow me to do that?

We now have a new Speaker of the House in republican Paul Ryan from Wisconsin. The mainstream news media had a field day in degrading the Republican Party when Californian Kevin McCarthy withdrew from contention because he didn't have the votes to win. I saw many of the reports. They were like a bunch of vultures feasting on the dead—the Republican Party. There were rumors he withdrew because someone in DHS posted on Wikipedia that he was having an affair with a female representative from North Carolina. I have no idea if that is true or not. I honestly think his lack of votes was a result of his snafu by commenting that the Benghazi committee's discovery of Clinton's personal email server was hurting her campaign. In any event, he did not have the votes.

When Boehner announced he was stepping down, I was fascinated that every newspaper article I read and every news report I saw on television said the "conservatives" took Boehner down. A headline in The Wall Street Journal said "Opposed By Right, Boehner To Quit". Excuse me! Who does the Republican Party represent—the left or the right? Unfortunately, that is a good question! These comments are a sad commentary to the Republican Party. It will be very interesting to see what happens under Ryan's leadership. This is a golden opportunity for the republicans to bring the party together. We need someone to shake it up and work toward party unity even though some say it will cause chaos and ruin the Republican Party.

The congressional republicans haven't taken a firm stand on controversial issues for a long time. They simply walk away from tough issues. Lets only hope that changes under Ryan's leadership. Boehner became an ineffective Speaker after the going got tough with the progressive democrats. He doesn't know how to fight and win in that environment. It is difficult to do but can be done with specific goals, honesty, openness, pragmatism, tenacity, and perseverance. The republicans need to adopt those qualities in a mature and pragmatic manner and go after the progressive democrats. Republicans either win or lose but their effort would be based upon honesty, hard work, and a defined set of political beliefs and behaviors.

Obama constantly blames republicans for the failure of Congress to get anything accomplished. He took congressional republicans out to a social dinner twice and touted he was working with them in an effort to get things done. He also held a few behind closed-door meetings and attempted to badger and blackmail them into submission. Obama publicly advocates his positive effort to co-operate and compromise when in reality the opposite is true. I even heard Obama say in a nationally televised news conference the republicans have decided to make "denying twenty-five million people access to healthcare their holy grail". He also said that was the only thing the republicans could agree upon among themselves. How self-serving and disingenuous for Obama to act in this manner and then put forth the appearance of trying to do what is best for the American people! Obama's behavior does not motivate any congressional republican to compromise with him when it is his way or the highway. I guess Obama gets compromise and capitulation confused.

To no one's surprise, Congress consistently gets very low marks on its performance in public polls. More recent polls show the public has become slightly more pleased with Congress but not by much. At the beginning of 2015, a poll showed 11% of likely-voters believed the current Congress was doing a good or excellent job. That is the first time since October 2012 that the number was in double digits. These numbers are dismal at best. The House and Senate have never been perfect but with Obama it isn't entirely their fault. Obama with the support of his progressive congressional cohorts have, in effect, shut down any meaningful congressional legislation. How irresponsible but it's the only way Obama knows how to make decisions—autocratically. He is not a leader who works with diverse political groups and brings them together for the good of the people.

Obama is an organizer type who makes unilateral decisions and then attempts to manipulate people to jump on his bandwagon to support those decisions. This is very obvious as he constantly travels around the country speaking to, or more appropriately preaching to, live audiences in front of television cameras to promote his agenda. I have had considerable experience with unions and union organizers. Obama is a classic organizer. They will promise or say anything to achieve what they want. After they achieve their agenda, what they promised or said may or may not materialize depending upon how it fits their true agenda. Other terms come to mind as I write this—oppressor, tyrant, autocrat, and dictator. Congress is vilified as inept and unworkable; therefore, the only choice left in getting things done for America is for Obama to do it by himself through executive order. During his State of the Union address in 2014, he said that he would get things done through his telephone and his pen. Sounds dictatorial to me.

A Rasmussen poll said 55% of likely voters believe Obama should do only what he and congress agree upon. Thirty-five percent said Obama should take action alone if Congress does not agree with him and 10% were undecided. Another Rasmussen pole said 60% of likely voters think the president should not have the right to ignore federal court rulings and 26% said he should. I find this shocking. In effect, 45% of American voters in one pole and 26% in another pole do not understand the Constitution, don't believe in the Constitution, or don't care. That starts to eat away at my position regarding Americans still predominately believing in and supporting the Constitution but I think it is more ignorance and ideological blindness than intent. Unfortunately, there is no difference in the outcome regarding a segment of our society giving backhanded support to autocratic rule.

Did you ever think in your wildest imagination that America would be governed like a dictatorship? Checks and balances have being attempted by Congress but have not been successful. Don't forget, oversight by Congress is nothing but phony scandals and Obama's pen is mightier than the law. The Supreme Court was involved in two cases concerning Obamacare overreach by the Obama administration. Their decision in one case did not support the Obama administration's position but in effect allowed it to stand. In the second case they did uphold the Obama administration's position and from my standpoint, allowed the administration to re-write the law to suit their purposes. A new appeal was filed with the Supreme Court in October of last year contending the law violates the provision of the Constitution that requires tax-raising bills to "originate" in the House. The House originally passed the first bill but it was gutted by the Senate and sent back to the House. My guess this appeal has a slim chance of succeeding, especially since the death of Justice Scalia. Opponents say the law is unconstitutional in several ways and they will be back to the Supreme Court with more litigation if this attempt fails.

The Supreme Court has a different role than Congress in the scheme of government checks and balances. They are the law of the land and not in an official law making and oversight position like Congress. Even then, they receive Obama's scorn when he perceives they disagree with him. I will never forget the time he chastised the Supreme Court to their face. It was on national television during a State of the Union address regarding a decision they rendered that he did not like. He actually misrepresented their decision in his comments. That was extremely inappropriate. Are we now, in reality, different from Cuba, Venezuela, China, or Russia? We are in degree but how about in principle? If a progressive obtains the presidency in the 2016 election, that degree is going to blur much more than we see now. One significant difference between those countries and ours is that those countries control the mainstream news media for their propaganda purposes and Obama doesn't have to control ours as we discussed inordinately in the last chapter.

> Before the death of Justice Scalia, the Supreme Court did render a decision nine to zero (yes, nine to zero) that said Obama did not have the power to determine when Congress was and was not in session in order to make recess appointments. That decision negated three recess appointments that Obama made to the National Labor Relations Board when "he" proclaimed Congress was in recess. He did that because he knew Congress would not approve them. A glimmer of hope but we are a long way from solving Obama's overriding the Constitution and the separation of powers.

This progressive behavior by Obama was very effective during his first several years as president but started to finally wear a little thin during the last two years. His approval ratings always go up and down as they do for every president but his overall trending started downward, especially with regard to effectiveness and trust. Unfortunately, his ratings have recently slipped back to about where they were. His tactics have worked in the past and continue to work without major public criticism because the mainstream news media not only give him a pass on his actions and performance but also have his back with their unwavering support. If the mainstream news media followed the ethical statement published by the Sedona Observer, followed the Code of Ethics of their professional society, and listened to the quotes of our founding fathers; Obama and his administration would be in desperate trouble even to the point of discussion of impeachment.

Obama started to feel pressure when his approval ratings slid to 41% and he began to fight back. I saw him on the news when he was in Minneapolis during June of 2014. He had a backdrop of green grass and beautiful trees in a park with his sleeves rolled up. He looked like a regular "good old boy". It was labeled a town hall meeting but it was a highly loyal crowd. In an effort to improve his falling ratings, he defended himself by drawing a sharp contrast between himself and congressional republicans. He told the crowd not to loose faith that things can get done. Here are his exact words:

> These are just Washington fights. They're fabricated issues. They are phony scandals that are generated. It's all geared towards the next election or ginning up a base. You guys are the reason I ran. You're who I'm thinking about every single day. And just because it's not reported in the news, I don't want you to think that I am not fighting for you. I don't want you to be cynical. Cynicism is popular these days but hope is better.

It was an "organizer speech". Obama's speech reminds me of something a personal friend and member of my board used to say about such rhetoric. He said, "Its like a mushroom farm. Keep them in the dark and feed them a bunch of shit." A little crude but says it well.

Here is what I heard during Obama's weekly radio address after his speech. He said he spent a couple of days in Minneapolis meeting with some people about their lives, concerns, successes, and hopes for the future because he got a letter from a young mother that said things are better economically for her and her family but she wanted things to be even better. Really? You fly to Minneapolis to speak to a few people about the economy? Wouldn't it be cheaper to fly them to Washington and then you could have more time to do some actual work on improving the economy? Weren't there a couple of fundraisers that you attended in Minneapolis as well? Is that dishonest to say you went there to talk to citizens?

It gets better. He also said in his address that the republicans in congress only cared about and passed laws that support the rich. He continued to say republicans were blocking everything he was trying to do for the middle class such as minimum wage increases, unemployment benefits, and improvements in educational loans. He stated he was going to do his job and as long as the republicans insisted on supporting the rich and legislating against the middle class, he was going to keep taking actions on his own like he has already. How convenient! Sounds like a good reason to be dictatorial to me. He did say he would welcome help from the republicans. I have to keep replenishing those bridges in my inventory.

His strategy was obvious. Change the subject and attack your adversaries as the "real" villains. Actually, his radio address "was a hoot" if it wasn't so tragic. I watched his entire radio address on the Internet. I found it fascinating that you could see Obama's presidency in its totality very clearly in three or four minutes. It was all there. His behavior and tactics were his way of getting the scandals and negativism off his back.

After denouncing these scandals as phony scandals and fabricated issues, he went back on the speaking circuit promoting a better economy for the middle class. Speaking circuit here is synonymous with community organizing activity. It was a tactic to get his constituency and his mainstream news media buddies to change the subject from scandals to the economy. The economy was the most important concern he expressed in his last election platform and as soon as the election was over so was his concern. He has done nothing about the economy other than talk about how good it is and indulge in self-praise. In actuality, his administration has done great harm to the economy through restrictive and costly rules and regulations and through government uncertainty; all of which stifle economic growth.

I want to go back to what I quoted from The Last Refuge website. The site said "fear" was at the core of liberalism and "love and trust" was at the core of conservatism. It also said liberalism is about "control" and conservatism is about "self-empowerment". I had never thought of progressives using rhetoric based upon fear to gain liberal support.

I started listening to Hillary Clinton, Bernie Sanders, congressional progressives, and Obama from the standpoint of fear mongering. The fear mongering was so obvious I was embarrassed I had missed it before now. I always viewed their rhetoric as fabricated progressive Marxist propaganda. That is true as well but it is also based upon fear, i.e., fear of losing income, fear of losing healthcare coverage, fear of women being treated like second-class citizens, fear of not getting an education, etc. It's like the "fear of the week". Whatever is in vogue at the time? In other words, if you don't vote for us progressives, those mean old conservatives will take everything away from you and keep it for their rich selfish selves.

Even my beloved Wall Street Journal is complicit in aiding an effort to spew political fear. A recent article semi-supporting Marxism appeared in their weekend Review section. I will admit this section is not one of hard news and is more cultural in nature but, nevertheless, the article took up the entire front page of the section and two thirds of the next page. It was even equipped with a large photo of Karl Marx. Yes, Karl Marx. The headline for the article said "The Middle Class Squeeze". The narrative under that headline said, "Over the past few decades, the western world has increasingly become a society of 'have lesses,' if not yet of 'have nots.' If we want to disprove the dire forecasts of Karl Marx, we had better do some creative thinking about how to make the middle class more prosperous and secure." It is interesting that the terms "have lesses" and have nots" are basically straight out of Alinsky's book *Rules for Radicals*. A bolded insert in the article said, "Many members of the middle class now see themselves as prisoners of the system they helped create." Sounds like fear to me. It is also total hogwash.

As I read the article it became increasingly clear that the author was Marxist even though he claimed not to be. At the very end, the author stated he was not a late convert to Marxism but at the same time criticized a pure capitalist approach to business ownership and said "Marx did have insight about the disproportionate power of the ownership of capital". Which is it Mr. Author? Are you a Marxist or not? You can't have it both ways? The author is Charles Moore from Great Britain and is the former editor of The Daily Telegraph.

I understand good journalism presents different points of view on issues, even political issues. Unless one took the time to read this very long article, they got the Cliff's Notes version from the headline and bolded text that promoted fear and supported Marxism. How could you do that Wall Street Journal? You are one of my few sources of accurate conservative news.

It is hard to keep the book's contents current on Obama's scandals and his divert and switch tactics. That has been especially true in latter months with so many new scandals and news updates continuing to happen. Scandals and divert and switch have become such a trademark of his presidency. For example, he announced they captured the terrorist leader in the Benghazi attack and patted himself on the back saying we never stop searching for those who harm us until we bring them to justice. I find it more than curious it had been two years since the attack and all of a sudden when Benghazi starts to heat up again with the House Select Committee and the Bergdahl situation blew up in his face (not to mention the VA, the massive illegal border crossing, Iraq, and Islamic terrorism situations) that our government finally arrested the leader of the Benghazi attack. During the two years after the attack, several news reporters interviewed him. It's not like he has been hiding in a cave somewhere and couldn't be found. Divert and switch? Self-bolstering? Both? Absolutely!

The day after they arrested the leader of the Benghazi attack, Obama and his security staff called for Iraq's Prime Minister Maliki to go. They said Maliki is unable to resolve differences between the Shiites and the Sunnis. Obama stated his ouster would diminish ISIS influence and power and stop them from controlling Iraq. Really? This is a laughable divert and switch. Maliki has created problems during his leadership but being responsible for the ISIS surge is not one of them. Who is responsible? Responsibility goes to Obama and his political advisors who either overlooked or didn't care about the negative effect of pulling all of our troops out of Iraq. Obama was living his political ideology and playing to his political base versus making sound decisions that were in the best interest of our country. Maybe we should put vice president Joe Biden in that category too since he said publicly that Obama's handling of Iraq may be the shinning accomplishment of his presidency.

Maliki eventually resigned in 2014. With the new government in power, who will ultimately control Iraq? ISIS? Iran? Both? How about Russia's entry into the equation? We will explore those implications in chapter 9. Iran is significantly influencing and militarily supporting the Iraqi government and ISIS controls a portion of the country. Iran and ISIS are at odds for two reasons. Iran is predominately made up of Shia Muslims. ISIS is Sunni Muslim because they believe the Sunni form of the Muslim religion is the most pure form and the one upon which they want to base their caliphate. Iran is supporting Iraq in fighting ISIS because they are both Shia and because Iran wants to control a new Persian Empire in the region. ISIS is a problem on both counts.

When ISIS's presence in Iraq was originally blowing up in Obama's face, he sent 300 elite troops into Iraq to act as military advisors. What for? Does anyone really know? Does Obama really know? It is another example of much too little and much too late. After significant criticism of Obama being asleep at the switch while Iraq was falling apart, there was an announcement that Obama had authorized a "secret plan" a couple of years before to aid Iraq but the Iraqis screwed it up. Poor Obama. Everything he does to save America and the rest of the world blows up in his face because of all the incompetent republican leadership he has to deal with in Washington as well as incompetent leadership around the world. This bridge is the most expensive bridge in my inventory for anyone who buys it.

I have heard many progressives say it wasn't Obama's fault that we couldn't leave U.S. military forces in Iraq to maintain stability because he could not obtain a status of forces agreement with Maliki. I have also heard several military and foreign policy experts discuss how Obama bungled the agreement on purpose so that no troops would be left in Iraq. We left tens of thousands of troops in Europe, Japan, and South Korea after major wars as well as place tens of thousands of troops elsewhere around the world. I wonder what impact those troops have had on world security? I don't remember seeing anything in the news about any further uprisings in these areas and that goes back to WWII in the mid 1940s. I wonder what kind of respect and power that had given America throughout the world before Obama? How about our own national security?

Compare that scenario to our current policy of apologizing to the world for our existence. We look like a wimp on a world playground being overrun by bullies. Iraq and the resulting escalation of Islamic radicalism is an enormous foreign policy failure as well as a significant homeland security threat. This failure occurred because of Obama and his progressive cohorts' liberal ideology of globalism rather than our historical American exceptionalism approach to foreign policy. Our exceptionalism approach has had an enormously positive effect upon world affairs and our own national security. I constantly wonder what will happen next? I have never observed such dangerous activity in the world, as we are experiencing today. I can assure you whatever Obama and his progressive cohorts do in response will be what they perceive to be in their political best interest and what concurs with their radical ideology. It will be in the best interest of our country only if our country's and their interests line up.

One of the most stunning revelations in Obama's ideological thinking is his refusal to call Islamic terrorism what it is—Islamic terrorism. He calls it violent extremism, which has been mystifying to many Americans including many liberals. We will analyze Islamic terrorism, its threat to America and the world, and Obama's approach or lack of approach to combat this threat when we specifically discuss foreign policy, which I have appropriately dubbed "Progressive Foreign Lack of Policy". That discussion will have more meaning after we examine Obama's ideology, leadership ability, and personal background as presented in this chapter.

Obama, as president, is the CEO of the executive branch of the federal government. The president should appropriately influence the legislative branch but not control it. The judicial branch is totally independent from the president except for his role in nominating new judges to the Senate for approval when vacancies occur. In addition to being influenced by and responding to what is happening in our country and around the world, the president has significant pressures from his or her political party and other influential people. World leaders, congressional leaders, political donors, and a multitude of other influential people traditionally influence their decisions.

Obama is an anomaly. He has made himself into an island and listens very little to anyone accept his top advisor, Valerie Jarrett, and maybe his wife, Michelle. His top White House "political" advisors influence his decisions but all evidence points toward Valarie Jarrett being the "queen of the mountain" regarding influence. Have you ever noticed how many of his chiefs of staff have left? Jarrett is supposedly the reason. This narrative is heavily supported in Kline's book *Blood Feud*. I sometimes wonder if Jarrett is really our president through Obama as her surrogate. Some of the major democratic donors have influenced Obama like the one who stopped the Keystone XL Pipeline with his personal political donation and fundraising. Surprisingly, he doesn't always appear to "cow down" to the unions, which have probably been his biggest political donor as a group.

Who is Obama and what is his ability to lead America? He has no clue how to effectively lead. I am trying to think of even one success story in true leadership during his presidency. I can't. This is obviously an enormous issue for our country and the world. His approach to everything he does is "organizing" based, not "leadership" based. He has never done anything in his career but teach constitutional law (which is interesting considering his constant attacks on the Constitution), practice civil rights law, and teach and practice community organizing. I guess he was an Illinois State Senator and U.S. Senator but his record in those endeavors is uneventful.

How could Obama become president? He certainly had a meteoric rise. Did you ever see the 1979 movie titled *Being There*? It was about a simple-minded gardener played by Peter Sellers who as a result of his employer's death and subsequently being accidentally hit by a car became involved with the Washington elite. Because of his simple-minded approach to everything, he was thought to be a genius by people in Congress and the president. He was so highly thought of by them they picked him to be the next President of the United States. Is there more truth than fiction here?

Here is Obama's story. He seemed to be in the shadows during his rise to power but was always in the hunt. The first time I ever saw or heard of him was when he spoke at the Democratic National Convention as a rising star. The next thing you know he is our president. I read another book by Klein titled *The Amateur* that talked about how he constantly worked the political power base in Chicago to achieve higher and higher political aspirations. Obviously, he was very good at it. After that compliment, I am going to compliment Obama again. I don't think there has ever been anyone in the history of American politics that has the ability to use community-organizing skills the way he does to achieve personal political success. Having said that, I want to emphasize he could not have done it without the strong support of the mainstream news media and a few very bright political strategists. I also believe he was in the right place at the right time. Unfortunately for America, this was a very effective combination to give him the success he strived for.

I have a theory regarding his mental being that made him the radical progressive he is and provided to him the desire to achieve the ultimate job to put his radicalism into practice. It is interesting that some of the information I learned about Obama, his childhood, and his family when he was first elected in 2008 is difficult to find today. It appears that the Internet has been cleansed to a degree. That's an interesting observation—keep in mind *1984*. Here is a summary of what I can still access on the Internet and remember from before.

Obama's childhood was very chaotic. I obtained the following timeline from Wikipedia. His mother and father were going to college in Hawaii. They were married in February 1961 and he was born in August of that year. Obama and his mother went to Seattle a few months after he was born and his father stayed in Hawaii to finish college while his mother took classes at the University of Washington. In June 1962, his father left Hawaii to attend graduate school at Harvard University. Obama and his mother moved back to Hawaii in January 1963 and she returned to the University of Hawaii. She filed for divorce in January 1964. Obama's mother then met a man from Indonesia and they were married in March 1965. Obama's stepfather moved back to Indonesia in June 1966 and Obama and his mother moved in with her parents in Hawaii.

Obama and his mother moved to Jakarta in October 1967 to rejoin his stepfather and his stepsister was born in August 1970. After attending the 1st through the 4th grades in Jakarta, Obama moved back to Hawaii to live with his grandparents in mid 1971 and started the 5th grade. In

1971, Obama's biological father visited him for one month and Obama never saw him again. In August 1972 his mother returned to Hawaii with his stepsister and they lived together from the 6th grade to the 8th grade. After his mother graduated from the University of Hawaii in December 1974, she moved back to Jakarta with his stepsister. Obama chose to stay with his maternal grandparents and finished high school at the private school he had attended for grade school and middle school.

Wow! That is a lot for a young kid to digest. His early life was chaotic, insecure, and confusing and he struggled with his mixed race heritage in the Hawaiian culture. This life would be very difficult for any young person. Remember, I said who we become (our mental being) is a product of our genes and the first few years of our lives. There is no doubt Obama inherited high intellect genes from two very intelligent people. His mother and father's unstable lives might or might not be indicative of some dysfunctional gene issues but, in any event, his parents did not provide a stable environment for Obama's early childhood.

When Obama's biological father went back to Kenya, he became a government economist to support income redistribution through higher taxes and to express his mistrust of capitalism by quoting Karl Marx. Obama's paternal grandfather had done the same thing many years before. The British government supposedly imprisoned Obama's paternal grandfather and tortured him for his Marxist based activism. Could this be why Obama gave the bust of Churchill in the Oval Office back to Britain when he took office? Dinesh D'Souza's film *2016: Obama's America* said Obama might have sent it back due to the anti-colonialism attitude he learned from his father and paternal grandfather.

I saw the movie. It was extremely well done and thought provoking. Not a big crowd at the theater and, unfortunately, they were all conservatives. I wish non-conservatives had seen the movie, if for no reason other than to provoke thought and discussion. D'Souza made another movie titled *America*, which was based upon "loving our country not because it is ours but because it is good". That movie was also excellent and dispelled a lot of progressive myths. My wife and I actually met D'Souza several years ago before his first film was made.

He is a very savvy person who is fighting for the country he loves by forcefully fighting progressivism.

Are you familiar with what happened to D'Souza after he produced his films and has spoken regularly about Obama's shortcomings on many national television shows? The FBI investigated him for violating campaign donation laws. He pleaded guilty to giving $20,000 in donations through straw donors to a New York senate campaign and admitted his actions were misguided and wrong. He received five years probation, eight months in a community confinement center, and a $30,000 fine. The judge also mandated psychologically evaluation.

In a recent hearing by the same judge that originally sentenced him (who was appointed by Bill Clinton), D'Souza was told he must continue community service for four more years and continue psychological counseling even though two psychologists have said there is nothing wrong with him and cleared him from further counseling. The judge said he was trying to be helpful in ordering more psychological counseling. He appears to be continuing punishment of D'Souza even though D'Souza has met his sentencing requirements. Progressive judges don't want to be confused with the law.

What D'Souza did was wrong and he should receive fair punishment. The overriding issue for me is the question of whether or not the FBI targeted him in retaliation for his aggressive fight against Obama and other progressives. A secondary issue is the judge continuing to punish D'Souza at his whim and without legal reason or authority. I don't know how the judge can do that? I find the judge's actions to be extremely inappropriate and troubling.

Let's get back to Obama and his childhood. Basically, his maternal grandparents raised him in Hawaii. The grandparents supposedly attended a communist leaning church when they lived in Seattle, Washington before they moved to Hawaii. The church is called "The Little Red Church on the Hill". A very significant influence in Obama's life while he was in Hawaii was a man named Frank Marshal Davis who was a journalist and writer. The story regarding Davis is that Obama expressed concern to his grandparents about his dark skin. His grandfather then introduced Obama to the strong personality of Davis who was a black man with very dark skin. Davis was a role model and mentor. By all accounts, Davis was a staunch member of the Communist Party USA and Obama referred to him several times in his book *Dreams from My Father*.

When I was researching this connection, I ran across two other very interesting connections that were discussed in a book by Dr. Paul Kengor titled *The Communist: Frank Marshall Davis, The Untold Story of Barack Obama's Mentor*. Kengor said Davis worked with Valarie Jarrett's grandfather and father-in-law in organizations that were fronts for the communist party. When I think of Jarrett's interest and praise in communist Van Jones and Kengor's book's comments regarding her family's communist history, I wonder if Jarrett is influencing Obama and the White House staff to adhere to communistic ideology? On second thought, I wonder if she even has to do so? Interesting but troubling! Kengor's book also said David Axelrod who was Obama's chief campaign strategist was mentored by a couple whose family had deep ties to communist organizations. Kengor said it was Axelrod who first recognized Obama as a rising star. Axelrod said Obama was Lincoln-esque. It was also Axelrod who proposed the phrases "Hope and Change" and "Forward" for Obama's presidential campaigns. The slogan "Forward" has its roots in Marxism and is commonly used by communist and communist organizations.

I could not find a connection to Marxism for the slogan "Hope and Change" but it sure sounds like it should have one. I was getting to the point that my research did not surprise me anymore because it was constantly proving what I already believed. I have to admit; however, the connections between Jarrett, Axelrod, and communism were surprising and concerning. How does it make you feel that our president's top campaign advisor and his top White House advisor have such strong communist backgrounds? It raises the question of what else is out there. How about Obama himself?

Obama's mother had a political background that is very interesting; however, it is somewhat difficult to get an accurate picture of her political ideology because it is complicated. Here is a synopsis of what I found. There is no doubt that his mother was far left in her ideology. How far left is the question. She has been said to be socialist, Marxist, and communist. Supposedly, one of her friends said they were "fellow travelers", which would mean they both were sympathetic to communism but not openly. That friend supposedly also said they were practitioners of "critical thinking" which means they believed in neo-Marxist philosophy. No matter what Obama's mother's political ideology, it appears to have been in significant conflict with traditional American values. This is very important since Obama has said that his mother was the dominant figure in his formative years and was the touchstone for his politics.

We will cover neo-Marxism and critical thinking extensively in chapter 10. When I was researching the material for chapter 10, I was stunned by what I found regarding the evolution of Marxism in America. It caused me to change the course of my writing this book. I went from writing the book strictly to support a conservative political outcome in the 2014 mid-term election to rewriting the book to reflect my opinion regarding the future of America based upon the cultural and political evolution of our society. You will understand what I mean when you read the chapter.

Let's now switch to adult Obama. When Obama ran for president in 2008, he was attending the church of Jeremiah Wright. I saw several videos of Wright's sermons. They were extremely anti-American. I saw Wright in one video say, "God damn America". How offensive! That was just the tip of the iceberg for his continuous anti-American sermons. He is still at it. I saw Wright on television speaking on the same stage with the radical America hater Louis Farrakhan last year at the 20th anniversary of the Million Man March in Washington.

How about Bill Ayers holding a fundraiser for Obama in his home in 1995 which was said to have launched Obama's political career? Whether it did launch his career or not—a fundraiser in Ayers' home? Ayers and his wife were founding members and leaders in the radical Weather Underground that blew up buildings and killed police. I saw Ayers on Megyn Kelly's show a few months ago still putting down America and saying that under certain circumstances America would deserve to be attacked. Can you believe Ayers is a retired professor who until only recently taught at the University of Chicago? Actually he was called a distinguished professor. You kidding me? Distinguished for what? Hate for America!

His wife is currently a law professor at Northwestern University. Another Weather Underground member, who served time in prison for murder, is now a professor at Columbia University. All of these universities are recognized as top-tier schools and these are the people they are hiring to teach our kids? Progressives might say that I am "cherry picking" radical professors to make my point but it doesn't take much research to discover this is a growing problem in schools all across the country.

Obama and his campaign staff denied the fundraiser at Ayers' house but Ayers has repeatedly said it was true. Obama and his campaign staff also threw Reverend Wright under the bus. Obama distanced himself and his family from Wright even though the Obamas were married by him, their kids baptized by him, they regularly attended his church, they contributed a lot of money to his church, and Obama supposedly called Wright one of his closest advisors. How could someone do that to his or her long time minister and close family friend? Obama did. Also, Obama said he never heard that anti-American stuff when he was in church. Obama must snore very loudly and often during Wright's sermons because his sermons are very loud and forceful. It would be very difficult not to hear him if you are in attendance. Here is one of the biggest bridges of all for sale cheap but you might find someone under it. I guess that should be a bus and not a bridge and I don't have any of those.

A very interesting and telling observation is the title of Obama's book *Dreams from My Father*. Notice the book is called dreams "from" my father, not dreams "of" my father. This says to me these dreams are Obama's dreams not Obama's father's dreams and indicates the significant influence Obama feels from his father. Also, in his book, Obama comments that he chose his friends carefully and included Marxists professors in his short list at Occidental College.

One of the mysteries about Obama is how he developed his vehement support for Islam. I have tried to figure that one out with little success. I have theories but no facts. His middle name, Hussein, is Muslim in origin but I doubt he is an Islamic sympathizer just because of his name. We know he went to a Muslim school in Jakarta but not very long. It appears his mother was an agnostic or an atheist and his dad was raised Muslim but became an atheist before he met Obama's mother. Obama's paternal grandfather was a Muslim. It could be that he is playing to his paternal grandfather but I doubt that.

I hear progressives say why does it matter that he refuses to put Islam and terrorism together? It does matter. How do Americans know what he is trying to accomplish regarding the Muslim culture unless we know his motives. The Fort Hood mass murder was workplace violence? The Muslim terrorists who have targeted the United States and other countries are not radical Islamists? Muslim terrorists who are apprehended on U.S. soil are tried in civilian court? The Guantanamo Bay prison where Muslim terrorists are confined is a country club compared to other prisons in our country and he continuously attempts to permanently close it?

We negotiated a totally one-sided deal with Iran in their quest for nuclear weapons when Iran is regarded as a rogue Muslim country and known supporter of Islamic terrorists. These nuclear weapons will be able to reach the United States when they develop their intercontinental ballistic missiles (ICBMs). The Obama administration literally gave away the store. Iran has said more than once they want to wipe Israel off the face of the Earth. Israel is our biggest and only true ally in the Middle East. Obama treats Israel as if the country is a nuisance to him and acts as if he doesn't care if Iran does destroy them? I saw an editorial by Charles Krauthammer, one of my favorite pundits, titled "A Holocaust Today Would Take Just 1 Iranian Nuclear Weapon". What has Iran repeatedly said about the United States during and after these negotiations? Death to America!

I received an email from a friend who proposed we now have a Muslim government in Washington. I won't go that far but I did discover some very troubling information. The email listed several Muslim individuals who work in high-level positions in the Obama administration and others who provide significant advice. Some are known to advise Obama personally. Several of these individuals are reported to have ties to Muslim organizations that provide support to or sympathize with radical Muslims including Islamic terrorists' groups.

I spent considerable time trying to confirm what was in that email and other emails I have received on the topic. As I researched the Internet, I found a number of websites regarding connections between the Obama administration and radical Muslim organizations. Here is what I found that I felt confident in sharing with you. Even though Valarie Jarrett was born in Iran, she moved to Chicago with her parents at age 5. I found no evidence that she is a Muslim as she was accused of being. John Brennan, Director of the CIA was accused of converting to the Muslim faith when he worked for the CIA in Saudi Arabia. He did give a speech in 2010 to a group of students from the Islamic Center at New York University that was very fraternizing. I watched a video of his speech.

He said he had felt the tremendous warmth of Islam culture and Islamic societies and Islam preaches tolerance and diversity. He spoke in Arabic for part of his speech since he learned to speak it fluently when he attended the American University in Cairo, Egypt for his junior year in college. He spoke very glowingly about Islam but that does not make him a Muslim. It does: however, paint him as a Muslim sympathizer. His version of Islam is in significant conflict with what I read and hear about the Muslim religion. Everyone is entitled to her or his opinion but he is the current Director of our CIA at a time when radical Muslimism is presenting a significant threat to our country. Is he biased in that role?

The Muslim Brotherhood and the Council on American-Islamic Relations (CAIR) appear to have Obama's ear as well as many other ears in Washington and wield more power than is in our country's best interest. My research shows both organizations have significant ties to terrorist groups. Glen Beck had a very interesting and informative report on his website in March of last year regarding the Muslim Brotherhood and its founder Hassan al-Banna. Prior to the 1930s, many Arab leaders supported Jews moving to their ancestral homeland. In the early 1930s, Egypt was in economic hardship and al-Banna blamed the situation on Western civilization and the Jews. Al-Banna was a master community organizer and recruited hundreds of Muslims to the cause of rejecting western influence, establishing the caliphate, and death in jihad for Allah. Thus, the Muslim Brotherhood was born on a "platform of hate".

In 1921, the British were trying to appease the Arabs so they appointed an Arab who was a prior fugitive named Amin al-Husseini to be the Grand Mufti of Jerusalem; which was the highest Islamic position of the time. In 1933, al-Husseini initiated contact with the

Germans to ask them for their help in eliminating Jews from Palestine. In return, al-Husseini promised Hitler a "pan Islamic jihad" or Islamic caliphate that would be in alliance with Hitler against Jews around the world. Al-Husseini collaborated with Germans like Adolf Eichman, who orchestrated the holocaust, and Heinrich Himmler, who was head of the SS, to have European countries send the Jews they deported to Auschwitz in Poland rather than Palestine. Radical Islamic ideology is similar all over the world because everyone had the same teacher—al-Husseini. Between al-Husseini's inspiration and the Muslim Brotherhood's community organization skills, the Muslim Brotherhood grew from about 1,000 members before the Arab uprising in 1936 to hundreds of thousands by the end of WWII.

Al-Banna and al-Husseini influenced all the major names and groups associated with radical Islam and the jihadist of today. Yasser Arafat, head of the PLO for many years before his death, was al-Husseini's cousin. Abdulla Azzam who was a member of the Muslim Brotherhood founded Hamas. Bin Laden and Azzam fought Russia in Afghanistan and their goal was to train fighters to return to Palestine and fight the Israelis. What was the name of their organization? Al-Qaeda. These actions were the birth of modern day jihad but were not any different from what al-Banna and al-Husseini started in the 1930s.

On June 28, 2014, Abu Bakr al-Baghdadi officially announced the Islamic State of Iraq and al Sham or ISIS. This is the dream that was started in the 1930s by al-Banna and al-Husseini, progressed with Azzam and Bin Laden, and made a reality under al-Baghadi. Another very interesting tidbit is that Iran's Grand Ayatollah Khomeini was a follower of al-Banna's and al-Husseini's teachings; therefore, modern day Iran was founded upon the anti-Semitic and jihadist principals of the Muslim Brotherhood and al-Husseini. Khomeini became the Grand Ayatollah of Iran in 1979 when the Shah was overthrown and maintained that position until his death in 1989.

Glen Beck said:

> ISIS is attempting to purify the world before the final
> battle. To do that they're willing to call anyone that
> doesn't convert and pledge allegiance to the caliph an

apostate. That carries with it a death sentence. This includes other Muslims. This is a significant evolution and divergence from modern day jihadism. Not even al-Qaeda was willing to go that far. They believed they were preparing for the days leading up to the re-establishment of the caliphate. ISIS has declared that the caliphate has returned and it's time to prepare for the next stage…the end.

The modern jihadist movement has morphed over several decades, is very intertwined among several current Muslim organizations, and jihad as a concept goes back several centuries. The Muslim Brotherhood is not the innocent and well-meaning organization the White House makes it out to be and its leaders are not the innocent and well-meaning Muslims that I hear them personally proclaim on television. CAIR is also a known radical organization. A book written by John Guandolo titled *Raising a Jihadi Generation: Understanding the Muslim Brotherhood Movement in America* said the following, "The Council on American Islamic Relations was created in 1994 by the Palestine Committee in the United States (Hamas) to be the 'Political' arm of Hamas here in America." These are the people advising the White House on Muslim relations. I find what I have just shared with you to be of great concern and suspicion. What else is out there that we do not know about? Oh, I forgot, this is the most transparent administration in history. How much are those see-through bridges worth?

I said, "What else is out there we do not know about?" Well, I found one and it's a doozy. After I wrote the above, I received my February 2016 issue of The Verdict from Judicial Watch and learned the following. Obama fired a staffer named Robert Malley in 2008 from his campaign when the British Times reported Malley had meetings with Hamas. Israel's largest news site, Ynet, reported these meetings went on for months. Malley said that was part of his job when he worked for the International Crisis Group. He was also a special advisor to National Security Advisor Sandy Berger under Bill Clinton at the same time. Malley has been an advocate for the United States to negotiate with terrorist groups like Hamas, Hezbollah, and Muqtada al-Sadr.

His Egyptian father was a key figure in the Egyptian Communist Party and a close friend of Arafat. His parents were strongly anti-Israel and supporters of several leftist revolutionary movements and especially the Palestinian cause.

Are you setting down? In 2015, Malley was appointed as a senior advisor to the National Security Council. In November 2015, Malley was named Obama's new czar in charge of countering ISIS. His official title is Senior Advisor to the President for the Counter-ISIL Campaign in Iraq and Syria. That's a heck of a title. I wonder what it means? White House Press Secretary, Josh Ernest, said the president has directed Malley to, "... strengthen our partnership with Iraq and to support our reinvigorated diplomatic tract toward a political transition in Syria, and an end to its civil war, which continues to fuel ISIL." You can't make this stuff up. Your guess is as good as mine as to what that actually means. Malley is another example of a very disturbing trend with people around Obama. Many have family ties, if not personal ties, to communism?

Obama's speech at the National Prayer Breakfast last year caused a firestorm among conservatives as well as among some liberals when he said "lest we get on our high horse" in referring to the Crusades, the Inquisition, and Jim Crow, which he said all happened in the name of Christ. Besides being inaccurate, it was a significant put down to Christians and America as a Judeo-Christian based nation in an attempt to justify his and his administration's refusal to use the term Islamist in identifying terrorists' groups.

Obama gave a speech at the Muslim Society of Baltimore in February of this year. It was his first speech at a mosque. He quoted phrases from the Quran, praised American mosques as a crucial part of American history, and also praised American mosques as being vital to America's future. What kind of future is he thinking of? He said he was speaking to "fellow Christians" (really, fellow Christians?) when he said an attack on one faith is an attack on all faiths. This was extremely inappropriate on the part of an American president, especially since Fox and other news sources reported that at least one previous imam who served the mosque from 1983 to 1989 and from 1994 to 2003 is a member of the Muslim Brotherhood and another organization that has known ties to Al Qaeda and the Taliban.

Even though Obama's family and his childhood schooling have Muslim ties, he has always gone to a Christian based church as far as I know even though his last one was extremely anti-America. Is he really a Muslim in a Judeo-Christian cloak? I don't think so. I honestly don't think he is religious at all. Is it another way for Obama to apologize for and diminish America in the eyes of the world in his war on American exceptionalism? This is a plausible explanation and I believe to be one reason for his behavior but I also have a theory to explain his behavior and will share it with you when we take a closer look at Obama as a person. No matter what the real reason or reasons, the extent to which he supports Islam and Muslims is contradictory to protecting, defending, and standing up for America.

Who is Obama? I want to begin answering that question by providing you with some background information that supports my two theories regarding Obama. We humans are very fragile creatures, even those with huge egos and overpowering personalities. In fact, those who act the toughest are the weakest inside that tough outer shell. I wrote extensively about this in my leadership book. I find biographies fascinating and they are very telling regarding why we are who we are. I have learned about the lives of many famous and successful people through their biographies. Entertainers have the most telling biographies of people who seek public adulation and acceptance. With few exceptions, the following holds true. They have experienced a dysfunctional childhood and as a result have a needy mental being. It is common for entertainers' parents to be divorced, absent, dysfunctional, and/or abusive. Many times a parent or parents pressured the entertainer during childhood to live the life in the entertainment industry they always wanted.

Whatever the reason or reasons, many entertainers did not receive the love, attention, and security they needed growing up and developed a "needy" mental being in efforts to fill that void. In addition to their environment during the early formative years, there is also the potential of inherited dysfunctional family genes. A majority of entertainers continually have chaotic interpersonal relationships throughout their lives. It is my unscientific conclusion that their mental being is unconsciously searching for comfort and fulfillment through fame and adulation from their admiring fans. Their mental being also clings to being a savior of the world because it makes them feel relevant and important. This is why so many entertainers are far left and support progressive ideology.

These people are continually and subconsciously searching for that elusive love, attention, and security they never had. That is a very big, empty hole to fill. The fallacy of their subconscious desire and resulting behavior to fill this void is that only their parents or a reversal of their childhood experience, which is impossible, can fill that hole. If inherited genes are also at work in creating dysfunctional behavior, the situation is even more complex and improbable to resolve.

No matter what the reason or reasons, that hole is always there throughout life searching for fulfillment. Look at how many successful stars perform on and on and on in their lives. Why don't they retire? Most of them don't need the money. They need the adulation and feeling of relevance. The 2015 Academy Awards show was a menagerie of what I am talking about. It was a continuous collection of self-indulgence and political correctness eruptions including the show's host coming on stage in his underwear. I can do without this idiotic self-expression and this is the reason why I haven't watched the show for the past several years and only saw the underwear stunt because it was on the news. I read the 2016 Academy Awards was worse.

You're probably familiar with the movie *On Golden Pond* staring Henry Fonda, Jane Fonda, and Kathryn Hepburn. In the story, the daughter (Jane) never pleases her dad (Henry). This is traumatic for the daughter and she strives throughout her life to obtain from her dad the love and attention she desires. I understand this was also true for them in real life. People like Jane Fonda do not consciously understand what is driving them and they never quit searching in life to fill that deep hole. I call it the "On Golden Pond Syndrome". One of my best examples is Jack Lemmon. He is one of my all-time favorite actors. I heard him say during a talk show interview that he was always disappointed that he never reached the success that he desired. Jack Lemmon—not successful? I believe Lemmon was suffering from an unfilled emotional hole that resulted from personal needs his parents never fulfilled. My On Golden Pond Syndrome is a deep and unproven theory but pond-er it. Pun intended.

I surprisingly discovered an op-ed in The Wall Street Journal that supports my theory. It was by Raymond Siller who is a television and political writer and was a long time head writer for Johnny Carson and The Tonight Show. The editorial was to honor Joan Rivers after her death. Siller said, "Stand up comedy is not for the faint of heart; nor do comedians go into the business for the money. They are driven by an insatiable need for applause as they wrap themselves in the warm blanket of audience acceptance and approval. The irony is that most of these people, like Robin Williams, are unhappy souls, scarred by their past. For them, the sound of laughter is a drug that can never erase those slights from long ago. Perhaps they were childhood losers. Perhaps a parent didn't love them enough. Or, maybe they were isolated in high school. Rarely were they the popular kid. Prom queens and quarterbacks have no future in comedy."

The editorial quoted Rivers as saying, "Comedy only comes from a place of tragedy or anger or being hurt. The worst thing that can happen to a female comedian is to fall in love and be happy. You're screwed." Siller also said, "To get up there it takes guts and a broken heart." This editorial was about Joan Rivers and comedians but without question the same narrative is applicable to most entertainers.

Even though entertainers inspired my theory, it isn't limited to entertainers. They are just the most apparent examples because their lives are on public display. If you look at Obama's chaotic childhood, I believe he suffers from my On Golden Pond Syndrome. Even though his parents are deceased, it doesn't matter. That deep hole lasts a lifetime. I believe Obama, through his presidency, is unconsciously trying to please his father and mother to achieve that love, attention, and security he never had.

Here are some examples to support my theory as it pertains to Obama. At the end of Obama's first election campaign he said in five days we are going to fundamentally change the United States of America. This is in keeping with his parents' philosophies. Obama expounds a Marxist based ideology by tearing down the upper class, promoting income redistribution, and pushing the country in a Marxist direction. He consistently works around Congress through executive fiat in dictatorial fashion and strives to avoid accountability for his actions, which is prevalent in Marxist based countries. Obama's approach to foreign policy is consistent with the anti-colonialism philosophy of his dad and grandfather as depicted in one of D'Souza's films and he takes extreme measures to present an anti-colonial and anti-exceptionalism image of America throughout the world. A friend of his mother was quoted as saying they were communist sympathizers and practitioners of "critical thinking", which means they believed in neo-Marxist philosophy. This last comment is extremely important if my theory is true. Keep this in mind when you read chapter 10. It goes a long way in explaining Obama's ideology and behavior.

Is this enough evidence to say that Obama is suffering from my On Golden Pond Syndrome and subconsciously using the presidency to please and gain the favor his parents posthumously? As I said, I am not a clinical psychologist but he exhibits behavior that leads me to believe that is exactly what he is doing. Why is this theory so important in Obama's case? If I am correct, he is in a groove of political ideology and political actions that he cannot change. He will always think the way he does and cannot grow and mature ideologically. Nor can he develop into a successful leader from "on the job" experience as he carries out his duties as president. The leadership issue is exacerbated by the fact that he has core personality traits that support organizing behavior versus leadership behavior. As his presidency winds down, he will only become more assertive in implementing his Marxist and anti-American based progressive ideology to achieve his goals to leave as his legacy.

There is another behavioral issue that needs analysis regarding the manner in which Obama performs as president. During past months, I have heard more and more commentary from news pundits and politicians regarding Obama being in his own world and his responses to issues not befitting the situation at hand. Not only have we heard comments from conservative news pundits and politicians but we have also heard comments from the liberal side, as they all seem mystified by some of Obama's approaches to issues. I have felt this way for a long time. I just don't know why it took so long for these pundits to come to this conclusion, especially the conservatives.

I read an editorial in The Wall Street Journal by Bret Stevens that is a great summary of what I hear others saying. Stevens said:

Not enough has been said about the bald certitude of its (referring to the Iran deal) principle sponsor (Obama), or the naked condescending distain with which he treats his opponents. Mr. Obama has the swagger of a man who never seems to have encountered a contrary point of view he respected, or come to grips with the limits of his own intelligence, or figured out that facile arguments tend to be weak ones, if for no other reason than the world is a complicated place, information is never complete, and truth is rarely more than partial. One might have thought that, by now, the president and his advisors would be chastened by experience. Al Qaeda is "on the path to defeat" (2012). Bashar Assad's "days are numbered" (2011). "If you like your current insurance, you can keep that insurance. Period, end of story" (2009). Russia and the U.S. "are not simply resetting our relationship but are also broadening it" (2010). Yemen is an example of a counterterrorist strategy "we have successfully pursued … for years" (2014). And so on—a record of prediction as striking for the boldness of its initial claims as it is for the consistency of its failures. Doesn't Mr. Obama get this?

Well, Mr. Stevens, if my next theory is correct, he does not. Not only does he not get it, he can't. It is impossible for him to do so. During my career in healthcare, I gained a reasonable amount of clinical knowledge regarding mental health. Obama's behavior leads me to believe that he very possibly could have what is called a narcissistic personality disorder. This disorder is well defined by the American Psychiatric Association and includes the following behavior as described in the Mayo Clinic website: having an exaggerated sense of self-importance; expecting to be recognized as superior even without achievements that warrant it; exaggerating your achievements and talents; being preoccupied with fantasies about success, power, brilliance, beauty or the perfect mate; believing that you are superior and can only be understood by or associate with equally special people; requiring constant admiration;

having a sense of entitlement; expecting special favors and unquestioning compliance with your expectations, taking advantage of others to get what you want; having an inability or unwillingness to recognize the needs and feelings of others; being envious of others and believing others envy you; and behaving in an arrogant or haughty manner.

All successful people have egos and are narcissistic to some degree but there are major differences between the majority of successful people and those with narcissistic personality disorders. Those with narcissistic personality disorders do not deal in reality and value themselves at the expense of others. They are psychotic and lack empathy for other human beings. They are able to compartmentalize reality that does not fit their fantasies into a mental lockbox or they can transpose that unwanted reality into false narratives that support their fantasies about themselves and their agendas. This is personal behavior that the individual cannot rationally control.

The more I have observed Obama the more I feel he meets the criteria of having a narcissistic personality disorder. I questioned if my conservative passion was driving me to make a false judgment, so I decided to explore the Internet to see what I could find that might support my theory. Was I surprised! The Internet was loaded with support. I thought my theory was unique but I quickly learned I was in a very large crowd. The several websites I examined were not akin to the "far left destroy-your-adversary websites" but were websites that took a pragmatic approach to aligning Obama's behavior with the clinical definitions of narcissistic disorders. Most used the term narcissistic personality disorder in describing Obama's behavior.

I will share a summary of a 42-minute YouTube video that I watched involving an interview between Peter Boyles, a Denver radio talk show host, and Dr. Sam Vaknin who is an expert on personality disorders and author of the book titled *Malignant Self Love*. I also listened to another interview of Vaknin that supplemented the Boyles interview with more detail regarding his evaluation of Obama's narcissism. There is no doubt in Vaknin's mind that Obama suffers from narcissism. He said after studying over 1,200 hours of Obama's behavior that he believes Obama is in the category of psychotic versus neurotic narcissism, which he said is very dangerous for America for the following reasons. Obama sees himself as being on a global historic messianic mission as the messiah of the second coming. Yes, he really said that and gave his rational to support his conclusion. Interestingly, David Axelrod's book titled *Believer: My Forty Years In Politics* quotes Obama as saying, in reference to running for president, "It may not be exactly the time I would pick but sometimes the times pick you." That certainly supports Vaknin's comment regarding Obama being on a messianic mission.

Vaknin also said narcissists like Obama become "God like" by creating unpredictability resulting in instability. It is like the "eye of the storm". Everyone around them is uncertain and fearful and this gives them their power since they are the only one that has the certainty to fix it. He said society has a propensity to develop mass psychosis resulting in mass hysteria and this is what happened to America when the economy became so chaotic at the end of Bush's presidency. Obama took advantage of the situation and stepped in with his promises of "Hope and Change" that was like a blank canvas for American society to read into it anything they desired to want and believe. He said it was as if Obama was invented by a group of psychiatrists to become president. I found that very interesting. Are we doing the same thing again in 2016?

Vaknin also said something very interesting with regards to Obama's approach to world affairs, especially to the Middle East. He said it is impossible to obtain hard facts on Obama's history and it is typical of narcissists to paint the picture as they want it to be and not necessarily like it truly was. He said this results from the psychosis factor that developed during Obama's dysfunctional childhood. I also wonder about his inherited genes since both his mother and his father lived chaotic and dysfunctional lives. Vaknin said Obama's self-directed biography describes him as an orphan, a lonely child, of mixed race, a supporter of world peace, and a supporter of crossing the divide of Eastern and Western cultures. Is this why he is so defensive of Islam? He sees himself as the savior and healer of the world. Is it globalism on steroids and he sees himself as the messiah to make it happen?

I believe Vaknin is correct and for the first time Obama's approach to the Middle East and Islam makes rational sense to me. He sees himself not just responsible for the United States but for the world.

This means he would throw the United States under the bus in order to save the world. This is a very scary thought. Vaknin said, and it is iterated in the classic definition of narcissistic personality disorder, that people with Obama's disorder lack emotion and empathy and cannot empathize with people or put themselves in other people's shoes. They are anti-social, exploit others, and lie incessantly. They are Superman. Because of this, their behavior always ends in disaster. He did say Obama currently has the ability to rejuvenate himself if his narcissistic behavior hits a dead end.

Vaknin concluded his analysis by summarizing what happens when narcissists in Obama's position begin to lose power and do not have the ability to rejuvenate their narcissism. He said they usually destroy themselves and those around them because narcissists consume what they sell to others. He called it "narcissist supply". Narcissists need crises to feed their narcissism because in their minds it makes them feel important and indispensable in solving or believing they have solved them. When this "narcissistic supply" starts to break down due to a series of reality events or the narcissist's popularity plummets, the narcissist moves to his last phase of narcissism. They develop a defense to negate the pain for themselves by blaming everyone else for these events and they begin to act out and pull everyone down with them. It is a case of you are too stupid and do not deserve me; therefore, I will ruin all of you and take you with me.

This behavior is a final attempt to restart their position of power by creating fear and instability. Vaknin said this has routinely been the case in history involving narcissistic leaders. He says Obama is in his final stage. Vaknin suggested the crisis used by Obama might include a congressional crisis involving the Constitution, an economic crisis, or a war. This comment by Vaknin is a stretch for me at the time of this writing; however, I have seen signs of this behavior when Obama's popularity is in free fall like when he gave his self-adulation speech in Minneapolis and then touted during his weekly radio address how he was saving Americans from the republicans.

I found a very interesting quote written in 1920 by a journalist, satirist, critic, and registered democrat named H. L. Mencken (1880-1956). He said, "As democracy is perfected, the office of the president represents, more and more closely, the inner soul of the people. On some great and glorious day, the plain folks of the land will reach their heart's desire at last and the White House will be occupied by a downright fool and complete narcissistic moron." Is he correct? Are we there?

Fortunately, Obama cannot by law run for a third term and he will not be able to get that law changed, as have narcissistic leaders in other countries. However, we do have several months left under his reign. I find this to be somewhat concerning in light of what Vaknin said regarding the stages of narcissistic behavior. Vaknin also said Obama was inordinately dangerous because he is the leader of the most powerful country in the world. The question is how far is he willing to go to feed his narcissism before his presidency is up and how serious could the implications be for our future?

You can make up your own mind whether or not you believe what Vaknin said about Obama's narcissism. You can also make up your mind whether or not you believe my theories. I have researched the heck out of Obama's behavior and I believe Vaknin has it correct and my theories are valid.

Here are some examples to support these theories. We learned Obama's political ideology very quickly after he took office. He was very far left of center and opposed to American exceptionalism. After observing him over time, it became more and more obvious that he was a Marxist sympathizer. His anti-America rhetoric became front and center after he took office. His approach to foreign policy progressively diminished our country's national security and weakened our past alliances with other countries. His disregard for the Constitution and the law became stronger over time.

His actions made America look weak in the eyes of the world. Do you remember when Obama bowed to King Abdullah of Saudi Arabia? I was stunned. I think Abdulla was too because he just stood there like "what the hell are you doing"? Here is the president of the most powerful country in the world bowing to a Saudi King. That is unheard of! When has an American president bowed to any other leader in the world? Respectful greetings—yes, but bowing—no! How about Obama's speeches in Berlin, Cairo, and the U.N. where he diminished the United States and what it stands for?

How about his support for the overthrow of Gaddafi and his cool response to Egypt after the Arab Spring? Why did he throw Israel and Prime Minister Benjamin Netanyahu under the bus when Israel is our biggest ally in the Middle East? Why does Obama refuse to call Islamist terrorists Islamist terrorists? Why does he not have a strategy to defend America against these terrorists? Why did Obama tell then Russian President Medvedev to tell current President Vladimir Putin he would have more flexibility after his re-election? Why did Obama allow Russia to run over Ukraine, support Assad, and toy with NATO and member countries? Why does he ignore aggression by Russia, China and North Korea? Why was Obama so hell-bent on getting a nuclear treaty with Iran at all costs?

Does Obama not care about our National Security or our image and relationship with our world allies? Why is he so careless with government spending and our spiraling national debt? Is he a reverse racist who wants to create civil strife in our country? Is he really that dishonest, deceitful, and scandalous to do whatever it takes to satisfy his political base, support a progressive Marxist government for the future of America, and feed his insatiable narcissistic appetite? Does he obsess for dictatorial rule by ignoring his Constitutional obligations and the laws of our country?

I could go on and on but I am preaching to the choir here. These actions by Obama do not make rational sense because they all seemed to be in direct opposition to the best interest of America and himself as president. They do make sense when they are put into perspective with my theories and Vaknin's analysis. I had a startling epiphany on this issue when I observed what happened regarding Obama and Netanyahu's re-election.

It was widely reported that Obama opposed the re-election of Netanyahu. It has also been widely reported that Obama does not support Israel. A special Senate committee is investigating a $350,000 donation by the State Department to a not-for-profit group in the United States. There were reports that some of Obama's previous political henchmen went to Israel to assist in getting voters to the polls to vote for Netanyahu's opposition. I also heard a report that millions of dollars were secretly given to the opposition from unknown sources in the United States. Is there a connection between these occurrences? I don't know but that would be quite an accusation.

Why would Obama oppose Netanyahu and Israel? I do not believe Obama opposes Israel. I believe he opposes Netanyahu. He opposes Netanyahu because Netanyahu stands in the way of his dream. Vaknin said that Obama sees himself as the messianic savior to bring world peace and cross the divide between Eastern and Western cultures. Netanyahu is in the way. Netanyahu, more than anyone in the world, will fight any agreements with Iran or any other Middle Eastern country that remotely threatens Israel's existence. Iran has said many times they will wipe Israel off the face of the Earth. Other Middle Eastern Muslim countries profess either openly or privately to support similar positions.

Netanyahu does not oppose world peace but he will always be resolutely opposed, including military opposition, to any agreements that would be necessary for Obama's messianic goal of bridging the divide between East and West at Israel's expense. Any action by Obama in the Middle East to achieve his dream would most likely be in a direct conflict of interest with Israel. Netanyahu's political opponent took a much more passive stance to Obama's actions in the Middle East than did Netanyahu and I believe Obama felt he could exercise more control over Netanyahu's opponent if he were to win.

Former New York City Mayor Rudy Giuliani took a lot of criticism for saying that Obama "does not love America". I believe Obama does love America but he loves "his America", not "our America" because our America stands in the way of his dream. So does Netanyahu. Doesn't Obama realize that his actions are not just detrimental to Israel but to the United States as well? The more power the Muslims obtain, the greater the threat to our Western values and our national security. How about Iran's nuclear ICBMs once they get the nuclear bomb? Obama doesn't see that. How can that be when it is so obvious? Remember the definition of narcissistic personality disorder? Obama doesn't think like you and me. He only listens to what he wants to listen to and believes what he wants to believe. That is why there is confusion, even among liberals, regarding his comments and his actions when he does not do what would commonly be expected. He appears to be in his own world and oblivious to the real world and he literally is.

How can he do that? That's easy for people with narcissistic personality disorder. They can lock away in their minds any unwanted facts or opinions or rationalize away any reality that does not fit their narrative. This is how Obama can be so wrong and so naive about domestic and foreign policy that does not make rational sense. This is how he can be so involved in the many scandals we have discussed and justify them or rationalize them away. He is going to make America the wonderful Marxist country that his family envisioned. It is going to be a racist free country because of his black heritage and everyone is going to be equal because he does not like being a black minority in a white dominated world.

He is going to make the world a perfect world by waving his utopian wand regardless of what the bad guys or other leaders in the world do because he is omnipotent. America will no longer be the most powerful country in the world and exercise that power economically and militarily to keep the world in balance. Obama will be the savior of the world by brokering peace and prosperity with world leaders through idealism, charm, and narcissistic naivety. Unfortunately, this is not the real world and all the bad guys and opportunistic world leaders are using this opportunity to manipulate Obama to support their dastardly deeds. My epiphany provides a rational and practical look at Obama's behavior and actions and puts them into perspective with the behavioral theories presented in this chapter, including why he will not call Islamic terrorists Islamic terrorists.

Did you ever believe that you would witness a time when almost all of the information coming out of the White House is significantly altered if not totally altered to accomplish their political agenda or to "cover their behinds". I am not talking about putting your best foot forward or presenting bad information as positive as possible as all administrations have done. I am talking about out and out perpetual dishonesty. I know people are not always honest with the press in order to cover up undesirable information. I also know that sometimes information is spun so far it becomes misinformation. What I am referring to here is the magnitude of dishonesty that prevails with this administration.

I watch portions of the White House Press Secretary's daily briefings on Fox News fairly often. As I listen, I feel I am trapped in a fictional land created by Obama and his White House staff and I can't change it or get out of it. I feel great frustration. I said in the last chapter that it seems as if we are constantly with Alice in Wonderland where things are not always as they seem. I should change that to America in Obamaland. I get the same feeling I experienced when I was forced to debate a group of progressive political radicals on television, in the newspaper, and at public meetings for over a year. They would say anything to accomplish their ideological goals. If you said blue, they would say red. If you said red, they would say blue. It drove me crazy. What they said was rarely based upon reality and they routinely contradicted themselves when they were caught being untruthful, which was most of the time. I learned how to counter them by overtly correcting their falsehoods, making sure what I said was accurate and simple to understand, and pounding it home.

This practice of dishonesty is common with the press secretaries in all departments of the Obama administration. Many times they say they "don't know" or refer the reporter to another department, which is also a form of dishonesty to hide the truth. It is obvious these people spend time preparing for their press conferences to determine how to spin the truth or what lies to tell to cover up what the administration does not want us to know. I can't understand how anyone can knowingly be so dishonest. I assume they rationalize the dishonesty in some manner that allows them to live with themselves. Maybe they think they are "saving the country" or it's their obligation to "protect the president". Remember Obama said during his presidential campaign that his administration would be the most transparent in history? Well, as Gomer Pyle would say, "Surprise, Surprise, Surprise!" Welcome to Progressive Wonderland or Progressive Obamaland. Take your pick.

Our country is going-to-hell-in-a-hand-basket at "warp" speed (pun intended) considering we are only 240 years old. In terms of ancient societies, we are just beginning to evolve and we are already on a path toward self-destruction. What can we do to turn this situation around and get back on track? There is very little we can do until the next presidential election. There have been three things; however, that have seemed to slow Obama down but unfortunately not stop him. First, he seems to react to public opinion polls when they indicate disapproval of him. I assume this plays to his narcissism and his White House political advisors have a degree of panic attacks.

Second, when the press firmly stands up to Obama on issues, he seems to listen and modify if not change course. I think that is because his top White House advisors are so political in their decision-making and influence him accordingly. Unfortunately, the press corps is usually an enabler versus a watchdog. It is the only way a person with Obama's dubious background and lack of experience could become President of the United States. Obama was very clear in his books about his politics and whom he had associated with such as his mentor Frank Marshall Davis. Obama's history with Bill Ayres and Reverend Wright was open knowledge until it was suppressed at election time. His radicalism was there for all to see and judge. If I remember correctly, the mainstream news media actually downplayed the warning signs.

Third, his legacy is extremely important to him. Anything that would appear to get in the way of that legacy would influence him. The real question is how does that happen? The mainstream news media is not going to do anything. Public outcry is not going to happen. Congress has paralysis. Liberals are not going to do anything. When the conservative Tea Party rallies took place after he first took office, they didn't accomplish anything except make us all feel good. I can only hope Congress will wake up and stand up with Paul Ryan's arrival as Speaker of the House and the Supreme Court can hold his outlandish actions to a "moderate" roar (pun intended again) until he leaves office. That could be difficult with Scalia's death.

How does Obama's progressive ideology impact the operational aspects of our government? Let's take a look. Obama has surrounded himself with like-minded people when it comes to ideology. That is not unusual. All presidents do. One would have to be a strong progressive to work in Obama's top administration. I don't think a conservative or perhaps even a non-progressive liberal could handle the onslaught to their personal value system for a long period of time, even if they were opportunistic.

As president, Obama is "The Boss" with a capital T and a capital B. He is responsible and accountable for anything that happens under his watch—period! He can't absolve himself of responsibility by saying he heard about it on the news or it was some staff member under him and he is not accountable. He can't "talk away" his responsibility by announcing his unmitigated concern over a problem issue and his intent to get to the absolute bottom of it; then later call it a phony scandal or fabricated issue and do nothing. He cannot absolve himself of responsibility by saying "there is not one smidgen of truth" when it is blatantly obvious it is is a cover-up. The same goes for all those in leadership positions under Obama as responsibility and accountability trickles down through his administration layer by layer.

How many times have you heard the term "close enough for government work" to denote the lack of quality outcomes due to poor leadership, poor employee productivity, and/or poor employee accountability? This has always been an issue in Washington but under Obama "government work" takes on a whole new meaning. We have covered several Obama administration scandals that have had negative effects outside of government operations. Now, I want to share with you a few internal workplace scandals that affect operations inside government. I am sure similar scandals have occurred within other presidential administrations and can also be found outside of government in private industry. The difference between the Obama administration, other administrations, and the private sector is the magnitude and frequency of these scandals, which is a product of the management culture created under progressive leadership.

Let's take a quick look at the federal workforce in terms of number of employees, pay, and discipline policy. When I wrote the initial draft of this chapter, I wrote the following from memory, "Tens of thousands of new employees are being hired to carry out new and expanded government programs and the $100,000 plus salary club has grown significantly." To my surprise, when I researched this for verification, I discovered that it was only half true and even that depended on how one looked at the data. When I wrote that initial statement, I remembered hearing and reading about how the number of federal employees has grown over past years and especially how they have grown under Obama. That is not true according to the U.S. Office of Personnel Management. According to their statistics, the number of federal employees has actually decreased since the seventies. Federal employees totaled 2,726,000 in 2014 and averaged 2,887,000 annually in the seventies. These numbers include full time, part time, temporary, and intermittent employees but do not include the military in uniform. I find this hard to believe but I could not find any evidence to dispute it. That is why good research is so important.

I was more correct regarding the $100,000 club. The information I found on this issue was inconsistent but collectively supports the point. The reason for the inconsistency is that every information source I found used a different database for their reports. A 2012 Breitbart article said, "Federal government workers reportedly average more than twice the salary and benefits of an average private sector worker." The article reported there were 459,016 federal employees making over $100,000, which equates to one in five federal workers. A 2015 report by FedSmith, a digital news service for current and former federal employees, said the number of federal employees making $100,000 or more increased from 282,605 in 2010 to 308,734 in 2014 resulting in a 9.25% five-year increase. It also said that trend has been down for the past two years. The report showed 417,783 in 2012 and 375,843 in 2013. I could not find any explanation for the higher numbers in 2012 and 2013 or the lower numbers in 2010 and 2014. These FedSmith numbers do not include the Department of Defense or agencies involved in national security.

The Washington Post reported in February of 2012 the average salary for a full-time federal employee was $76,231 as of September 2010. The report said as of September 2011 423,000 federal employees made less than $50,000, 1 million federal employees made between $50,000 and $100,000, and 420,000 made more than $100,000. Of those making $100,000 per year, more than half make between $100,000 and $130,000 and roughly 13,000 make $180,000 or more. These salary numbers exclude part-time and other non-fulltime federal employees. My sources are like comparing apples to oranges and are not as current as I would like but they were the best I could find. They at least give some sense of reference.

You can make up your own mind what these numbers mean to you. The bottom line for me is a lot of federal employees make $100,000 or more per year and it is excessive. The Breitbart article said it well,

"The corrupt cycle works like this: Democratic politicians negotiate rich wages and benefits for union members with taxpayer cash; the union members then pay union dues; the unions use that money to re-elect the Democratic politicians. Everybody wins, except the taxpayers."

A friend sent me an email containing a video on this topic that looked at the implications from a different standpoint. The video was from the Government Gone Wild series and made a very important point. The video said there were 21,300,000 government workers. For verification of that number, I researched another source. That source said there were approximately 21,995,000 federal, state, and local government workers in the U.S. at the end of 2015. The video made the point that as government employees grow in number they are becoming a formidable voting force against any efforts to curtail government spending. The video said government employees are currently 16% of our total work force and when you add interested parties like spouses that number doubles to 32% or more who will vote against government spending cuts or any politician who supports government spending cuts. This is a very interesting and sobering thought. Remember what happened in Greece where the government employs about half the population and they tried to implement austerity measures.

We discussed that employee accountability in this progressive administration is a big problem and that is particularly true for those "loyal soldiers" who support the Obama administration's deceit and corruption involving "phony" scandals and other dastardly deeds. There are government employee policies and procedures to prevent unfair political firings and I totally agree with that. There are union rules regarding discipline and firings that I do not agree with. My research shows it is almost impossible to fire a unionized government employee for almost any reason. This situation is out of control and is in desperate need of new legislation and union re-negotiation. How about just getting rid of the government unions through congressional legislation? You and I know that will never happen with all the union money pouring into political elections.

With that background, let's get into workplace scandals within government operations. A member of the House introduced a bill in February of last year for new legislation to prevent government employees from watching pornography on the job. What? Yep, that's true. Here is the story that prompted the bill if you haven't heard it. An EPA employee was found to have 7,000 porn files on his computer and had been watching porn for two to six hours per day since 2010. He said he did it "out of boredom". When we caught a night employee in our computer department at my last organization watching pornography, we fired him immediately. When we caught a night nurse watching a non-pornographic movie he brought from home while he was supposed to be watching patient monitors, guess what we did? We fired him immediately.

So, what happened to the EPA employee? He continues to work while he has filed an appeal to retain his job. Unbelievable! Maybe we should not judge him too harshly. An employee at the Treasury Department was reported to have 13,000 pornographic images on his computer. He said he was aware it is against government rules but he often does not have enough work to do. We also have the unbelievable story of paralegals at the U.S. Patent and Trademark office that were paid $80,000 per year plus an annual bonus of $3,500 to stay home, watch television, and wash clothes. They did this because they had "little work to do" and booked the hours under "other time". Their supervisors were fully aware of this practice.

When you think it can't get any worse, guess what? If watching pornography on taxpayer time is bad, how about engaging in prostitution on taxpayer time? Remember the 2012 Secret Service prostitution scandal in Cartagena, Colombia? We now have a new scandal that is even worse than government employees watching pornography at work or participating in a sexual tryst with prostitutes while on the job. An Inspector General's report found that agents in the DEA were involved in dozens of "sex parties" with prostitutes over a period of years in Bogota, Columbia dating back to perhaps 2001. Columbia must be a very interesting place. Actually, my wife and I were just there and it seemed like a very nice foreign country to us.

The prostitutes were paid for by the drug cartels the agents were supposed to be combating. You, the taxpayer, paid for the residences where the parties were held. I watched the administrator of the DEA testify before Congress that her agents' behavior was not acceptable.

Wow, what a revelation! She went on to say she "hoped" the additional training provided to the agency's staff would prevent similar incidents from happening in the future. Training? What kind of training does she have in mind? That's laughable! In addition to the training, those involved got a whopping two-week suspension. She defended her actions by saying she could not impose a stronger punishment because civil service protections for government workers prevented her from doing so.

After the congressional hearing, the DEA administrator announced she was departing. What does departing mean? Resignation? Retirement? These people never get fired. Think Lois Lerner. Is there any accountability in Washington for personal behavior except for those low-level employees who get fired for doing something the progressive government doesn't like such as leak information to the press that holds the administration accountable. You can't make this stuff up.

What are the implications to our country resulting from this risky behavior by these agents? Well, lets see. The Secret Service was in Cartagena to protect the president. At least the Bogota police who set up the prostitutes did watch the agents' weapons, computers, and smart phones while the parties were going on. Was there any potential for coercion, extortion, blackmail, or data breach? You know I'm not an Obama fan but to potentially put his life or well-being in danger? That's inexcusable! The record of the Secret Service during the past couple of years certainly does not breed confidence in presidential safety. I am sure the majority of Secret Service agents are hard working and competent agents. It is unfortunate that there are those who give the rest a bad name.

Maybe the IRS should subcontract some of their work to these other government departments that don't have enough work to do. IRS Commissioner, John Koskinen, has said on several occasions, including a congressional hearing, the department cannot function at one hundred percent with all the cuts it has incurred due to budget restraints. He said this would be most noticeable with the IRS call service during 2015 in that 50% of the taxpayers who called for help would not reach a live person. He also commented they have: reduced their employees by 13,000 since 2010; are currently under a hiring and overtime freeze; and must find a 1% pay increase for all employees that is deserved and mandated by the 2015 Omnibus Spending Bill. Let's have another Paul Harvey moment.

This story sounds dire and concerning until one hears the "rest of the story". Here is a compilation of several reports I researched concerning the IRS. In 2011 and 2012, more than 2,800 employees under disciplinary action were paid more than $2.8 million in monetary bonuses and received more than 27,000 hours in time-off awards. In 2014, the IRS paid $1 million in monetary bonuses to employees who were tax-delinquent. In 2011, the IRS monetary awards program paid almost $92 million in cash and almost 520,000 hours of time off to 70,500 of its 104,400 workers. The numbers for 2012 were $86 million in cash and almost 490,000 hours of time off to 67,870 of the department's 98,000 workers. These time-off awards are a significant waste in productivity. Add that time-off program to the issue of employee inefficiency that occurs in government bureaucracy. They said no executives who were subject to discipline received any awards. An IRS spokesman commented they are "considering" a similar policy for the entire IRS workforce. The policy would be subject to negotiations with the National Treasury Employees Union. Considering? Are you kidding me! Considering? Where in the "Sam Hill" is management accountability?

Just so you know, here are the most recent reported numbers on tax delinquency for the entire federal government. There are 318,462 federal employees who owe $3.3 billion in back taxes. That includes 4.87% of the House of Representatives employees and 3.24% of the Senate employees but here is the big one. There are thirty-six or 2.06% of the employees in the executive office of the president who are delinquent in their taxes. There is no real effort or interest that I am aware of to install management discipline and accountability in any federal agency, Congress, or the White House.

Did you see the Star Wars video staring IRS management? That only cost about $60,000; however, that does not include the rumored $4 million they paid for the studio where the video was made. I guess they're going to make some more videos. How about the Gilligan's Island skit? Did you see that one? They are easy to find on the Internet and are educational—not to learn about management or employee skills but to learn how your tax money is being wasted. The video approach is cheaper than the estimated $49 million in conferences and retreats during 2011 to 2012. I thought Koskinen said they were under severe budget restraints and could not function at 100%.

I wonder how many more telephone calls they could have personally answered if they had given up their acting careers. Considering the number of employee training events (a government euphemism for lavish employee retreats) required by all the government departments and agencies, the IRS could show them how to save money by making movies and skits to train their employees rather than participate in lavish out-of-town retreats. Our government employees are certainly very well trained, or is that entertained?

It seems to never stop with the IRS. Koskinen had to again address a congressional hearing to explain why he blamed the IRS's 2015 poor customer service performance on budget cuts when there were no budget cuts from 2014 to 2015. I obtained the following information from several news services but my primary source was an article by the Weekly Standard that was a summary of an April 2015 report by the House Committee on Ways and Means. I actually went directly to the House Committee report to verify any information that was vague in the article. This book must be getting to me. Approximately $134 million in funds were deferred from providing service to taxpayers for other activities and employee bonuses. Did you know that roughly 500,000 hours of employee time you paid for with your tax money went for union activities? I guess that is why they didn't have any time to collect any delinquent taxes from federal employees. That's correct, no delinquent taxes were collected from federal employees and that included their own IRS employees.

After I wrote this, I read an op-ed by a Virginian-Pilot reporter who said in 2013 more than 200 IRS employees worked 573,319 hours on union work at a cost of $23.5 million. Many of those employees were in that $100,000 club. What happened to the union dues that should pay for those union activities? Union dues have to go to political campaigns to keep government employees unionized. The Virginian-Pilot op-ed said the National Treasury Union that represents the IRS employees gave $583,912 to federal candidates in 2012 of which 94% went to democrats. No surprise there.

In addition to their $11 billion budget appropriated by Congress, the IRS receives $400 million in user fees for services like rulings, opinions, and advice they render outside the agency. For some reason that I could not find, the IRS allocated $183 million in user fees to customer service in 2014 and only $49 million in 2015. If the way they use their money sounds complicated and confusing, it is. It seems everything a government agency does is smoke and mirrors, especially under progressive rule. That way, you can't "follow the dots". I don't see how they function. Many of them don't as we have discussed throughout the book. A viable explanation for the "smoke and mirrors" accounting in the IRS is that they spent over $1.2 billion through 2014 on Obamacare and planned to spend $500 million last year. Looks like we found more hidden taxes to support Obamacare?

The 2015 House Committee report also said the IRS paid out $17.7 billion in 2014 in improper Earned Income Tax Credit payments which are meant to help low income families. I calculated from the report that between 2010 and 2014 the IRS averaged improper payments of $15.4 billion per year. The House Committee report estimated the IRS paid an additional $6 billion to $7 billion in improper Child Tax Credit payments in 2014. These overpayments have been a long-standing problem for many years. Can you fathom non-government organizations allowing this ineptness to happen?

The republican controlled Congress used the most recent federal budget to address some of these issues. The budget prohibits the making of videos unless approved in advance by a special board, bonuses cannot be given to employees who owe back taxes, personal email accounts are prohibited for work, Congress must be informed regarding how much taxpayer money is spent on salaries for union work, and groups cannot be targeted for their political beliefs. This is ridiculous. All of these issues should be dealt with at the administrative leadership level and should never happen in the first place.

Koskinen reported in January of this year that only 38% of those calling the IRS last year had a chance to reach a live person after waiting 30 minutes and he "hoped" this year that number would increase to 60%

after 20 minutes. If this were a non-government business, heads would roll or the business would go out of business so what did Congress do to address the issue? The Wall Street Journal said they gave Koskinen $290 million to hire up to 1,000 additional people. Only in "government work".

I want to end my review of the IRS with one of the oddest stories I found. In 2011, the IRS decided to require the approximate 300,000 independent tax preparers to take a $116 exam and pay $63 for a personal tax ID number. This was an effort to regulate the tax preparation industry. The only problem was the IRS needed a law to do it. Well, they found one. They were going to use the Dead Horse Act of 1884. That's not a misprint. After the Civil War, citizens were filing claims against the U.S. government to be reimbursed for their horses that were killed during the war. Some of the dead horse owners' agents were unscrupulous, so a law was passed to license them in an attempt to separate the honest agents from the dishonest agents.

The IRS was trying to use this Dead Horse Act to regulate the tax preparers. I guess the IRS thought you "can't beat a dead horse to death". Maybe I could sell them a covered bridge. I wonder how many other outdated and ridiculous laws are still on the books and need to be rescinded? The owner of a small tax preparation business sued the IRS and won in district court and on appeal in circuit court. The IRS decided not to appeal it to the Supreme Court. Regulation is a major issue in progressive Washington domestic policy. We will hit this topic hard in the next chapter.

Let's go back to the concept of whether our government employees are being trained or entertained. Think about the picture that went viral depicting the regional Government Services Administration (GSA) director in the bathtub drinking wine at your expense. Maybe not! His eight pre-planning trips for that conference cost about $130,000. At least that cost included the bathtub experience and wine. The conference cost almost $1 million and they sure didn't learn very much. Do you know how much property the government owns that is sitting empty and costs almost $2 billion per year for the GSA to maintain? I'm not sure they know. Why not sell the empty property to pay off their extravagant conferences? How about selling it to reduce our taxes? If I remember correctly, the bathtub director pleaded "the fifth" and shortly after being put on administrative leave he retired with full benefits. He probably is now buying liquid "fifths" with his retirement money— our tax money. Enjoy!

Speaking of employee accountability, what happened or I should say what didn't happen to employees who were implicated in some of the scandals we discussed. The employees that were implicated in Fast and Furious were reassigned. The whistle blowers who were involved in the scandal were fired. The State Department employees who were found to make bad decisions on Benghazi security were either given promotions or reassigned. Our friend Lois Lerner who was the key witness in the IRS scandal and took "the fifth" before Congress was put on leave with full pay. There's that "fifth" again. A federal judge dismissed Eric Holder's citation for contempt of Congress regarding the Fast and Furious scandal and Obama asked Holder to investigate himself regarding the scandal with the news reporters.

Maybe I should drink the preverbal Kool-Aid and not worry about this untruthfulness and lack of accountability stuff I'm writing about since it doesn't affect me directly? Or does it? Hmm? OK, here I go. Gulp! Ugh, I was wrong. It taste terrible and disgusting and has long term effects. How do those progressives do it? As a side note, Kool-Aid started in my wife's hometown of Hastings, Nebraska. Her father's law firm did the inventor's initial legal work. The firm was offered cash or stock and the firm took cash. Bad decision but who would have thought some colored flavored powder would become such an American icon.

While we are looking at day-to-day operational issues, let's take a quick look at a few other ridiculous examples involving operational accountability. I do not know if these problems are because of sloppy employee performance, sloppy systems, sloppy management, sloppy government policy, or all four. It really doesn't matter. The outcomes are the outcomes and I found no effort to fix them.

Social Security's Inspector General released a report in March 2015 that said there are 6.5 million social security numbers for people who are 112 years old or older. Some dated back to before the Civil War. The report went on to say that, at a minimum, tens of thousands of illegal immigrants are using those social security numbers. You may or may not know that illegals who use these social security numbers to file income tax returns can get an earned income tax credit and receive a government check in an amount up to $6,145. How about fraud and identity theft issues? Close enough for government work, I guess.

This next one is hard to believe but it is true. I read a syndicated article by The Washington Post last year in my local newspaper that said DHS was affected with the lowest morale of any large government agency. They did a study costing over $1 million to assess the morale problem and when the study was done, it was put in a drawer and guess what they did? They did another study. At least it cost less but it said the same thing. The leadership of the department was still confused so guess what they did then? They ordered two more studies. Some of the officials inside the department admitted they should spend less time studying and more time fixing. The article said this problem was endemic across all government departments. Here's Gomer Pyle again. Surprise, Surprise, Surprise! This problem is not unique to government leadership. It is just much worse in government and significantly much worse under progressives. Progressive leadership focuses totally on what is in the best interest of themselves and their politics rather than what is in the best interest of the employees.

The Baltimore Sun reported in July 2014 that The Social Security Administration spent $300 million to develop a computer system to increase the speed of processing disability claims because beneficiaries have been waiting months and sometimes years to receive benefits. The last progress report I could find was March of last year and the problems were still there. I guess that is understandable since the department had been working on the project for six-years with no success before the new system was installed. An independent analysis commissioned by the agency said the project had been mismanaged and poorly executed. These agencies sure do a lot of independent studies. How about some good old-fashioned effective leadership? Maybe rather than try to sell them some of my bridges, I should sell them some of my leadership books. Actually, I would give the books to them if they would read them, learn from them, and practice the great leadership I wrote about.

I strongly believe the vast majority of our 2,726,000 government employees are well-meaning and hard working employees. They deserve the tools and leadership needed to support them. Unfortunately, many of our progressive government leaders are the epitome of bad leadership resulting from of a combination of putting self-interest first, political influence, management incompetence, organizational complexity, and union influence. Bad leadership also encourages the bad employee behavior that we talked about. Our good government employees and the American public deserve more.

I want to close our discussion of day-to-day operational issues by touching on spending accountability? You continually hear about the massive expenditures throughout government that are necessary to keep the government operating. We used to hear government expenditures in terms of millions. We now hear expenditures in terms of billions and occasionally we hear the term trillion. I understand inflation, but! The total federal budget for 2016 is $3.871 trillion. I tried to break that down into operational expenses versus entitlement expenses but could not find a source to do so. The only government department for which we ever hear any serious spending cuts is the Pentagon and that is the last place I would be cutting in today's dangerous environment.

You are well aware of the government's spending insanity but I want to share with you a few examples that demonstrate this insanity. Did you know that in 2013 you, as a taxpayer, paid almost $1 million for 13,712 government bank accounts that had no money in them and were inactive? The Washington Post article from which I obtained this information quoted a watchdog group called Citizens Against Government Waste as saying, "It's just lack of attention to detail and poor management. And, clearly the fact that no one gets penalized for paying money to keep the accounts open." The Office of Management and Budget said the problem was down from $2.1 million the year before. The newspaper article also reported the Pentagon once paid $435 for a hammer and commented, "But at least in that case they got a hammer."

I guess we need a new embassy in London. I don't know why but the government says we do. Do you know how much you are going to pay for it? $1 billion! I read it didn't even meet current security standards. Speaking of billions, The Fiscal Times reported the government "blatantly wasted $30 billion" in 2013. I believe the $30 billion is low. The Washington Post reported in April 2014 that the State

Department's Inspector General found contract documents totaling $6 billion over the past six years were incomplete or missing. The Inspector General concluded the situation posed significant financial risk and demonstrates a lack of internal control. That was during Hillary's watch. Sounds like she has problems properly keeping all kinds of records.

Here is my best story on government spending. How much do you think a gas station in Afghanistan should cost? Think again. Fox News reported in November of last year that the Department of Defense (DOD) spent $42,718,739. That's right—$43 million! That same gas station in Pakistan cost $500,000. The gas station was built under the Task Force for Stability and Business Operations (TFBSO). The special inspector general for reconstruction in Afghanistan (SIGAR) found the gas station cost $12.3 million in direct cost and $30 million in overhead costs. The DOD refused to answer the SIGAR's questions about the TFBSO program. The SIGAR said, "Frankly, I find it both shocking and incredible that DOD asserts that it no longer has any knowledge about TFSBO, an $800 million program that reported directly to the Office of the Secretary of Defense and shut down only a little over six months ago." The SIGAR said he intends to pursue this. Good luck. Sounds to me like a good way to "channel money" for influence. We do it and so do other countries. It is the "cost of doing business" in foreign lands. It seems to me; however, there should be a better way to do that than spend $43 million for a gas station.

My last story in this chapter is a very fishy story. This story demonstrates the dysfunction of Washington politics in general. In 2008, the Senate added a catfish inspection program to its Farm Bill to improve the inspection of catfish imported from outside the U.S. The FDA has traditionally inspected catfish, as it does all imported seafood, at a cost of $700,000 per year. The USDA said it would cost $30 million to set up the new Farm Bill catfish inspection program and $15 million per year to administer it. What an imbroglio! OK, I admit I had to use my thesaurus to find a suitable word to describe this "extremely confusing, complicated, and embarrassing situation" involving the Senate

The honest reason for the new inspection program is to restrict the importation of catfish from Asian Pacific countries. A senior republican (yes, republican) senator from a southern state supposedly wanted to protect his state's catfish industry from foreign imports. This situation points out that we can't blame the progressive democrats for everything. The Senate and the House are at odds over this issue as are some individual members of the Senate. The Senate will not give in because they say the tougher USDA inspections mean safer catfish. In fact, the Senate voted again in 2014 to reaffirm their position even though the GAO has said there is not an inspection problem.

My wife and I visited catfish farms when we were in Vietnam in 2013. The catfish industry is extremely important to the area's economy. In fact, the farms looked like "the economy" and were well maintained. They are not going to risk exporting tainted fish. The FDA has kept us safe and is significantly less expensive to do the job. My research indicates this issue is still not resolved and there is ongoing debate among lawmakers. Many catfish producing countries say this Senate action is in conflict with international law and The Vietnam Association of Seafood Exporters & Producers was in the process of a mounting a legal challenge through the World Trade Organization. I could find no update. I wonder how much this issue will cost us to defend and how much the price of catfish will increase if the Senate plan eventually prevails?

Doesn't the government have more important things to do? Think about how much we could reduce our taxes if ridiculous regulations, laziness, incompetence, and corruption could be cleaned up and spending accountability instilled in the government? I have thought about it but can't fathom what the savings would be. Some say, "That's just the government." Really? We should never accept that as an excuse. There are probably a million stories like these out there that are just as ridiculous and wasteful at a time when our country is spending or is that spinning out of control in debt. The federal government is notorious for unnecessary and wasteful spending on programs and projects that contribute little or nothing to society and it only gets worse as the government becomes more progressive and grows bigger and bigger.

Government has historically grown exponentially in regulatory authority, complexity, and size under every president since George Washington. Government control over our lives was much less and much simpler when I was a kid and we survived very well. We will never change back to where it was in our past because government is like a giant amoeba. The more it grows and changes form, the more it grows and changes form. The only thing certain is that government will be increasingly more intrusive in our lives as it gains power and control, which in turn gives it more power and control, which in turn makes it more intrusive in our lives. This is why decisions made in Washington are increasingly having a bigger impact on us no matter which party is in power.

A Rasmussen pole taken in April of this year reported 62% of Americans say government has too much power. Unless progressive Washington is stopped, it will push government control much closer to *1984* levels in the future for our kids and grandkids. Would a non-progressive Washington be significantly better regarding power and control? The answer is a resounding yes but then the next question is by how much? That is a good question to ponder. Don't forget the fish story and the politicians pushing it were not progressives.

Speaking of a giant amoeba, the common classifications for amoeba are Chaos carolinense and Amoeba proteus. We could call Congress Chaos washingtonense and the president Amoeba potus. On second thought it would be much simpler and as accurate to name Congress and the president simply *The Blob* after the 1958 science fiction film in which a giant alien amoeba from outer space engulfs and dissolves every citizen in its path. Ok, you have probably had enough. After working on this subject matter long and hard, I have to become a little goofy to keep my sanity.

Before we proceed to the next chapter, I want to go back to what I said in my epistle in chapter 5 regarding who is leading this progressive movement in progressive Washington. There is no one leader. Not even Obama. It reminds me of *Rosemary's Baby*. The progressives are the devil's cult and Obama is the baby. There is a multitude of people who play a part in assuring that the progressive movement moves forward and they are always looking for that next "baby" to lead the way. They have different agendas and different ideas of what exactly the movement should be—socialism, communism, Marxism, fascism, or anarchy. Marxist theory has somewhat different definitions depending upon the person interpreting

Marx's theory. I adhere to the simple definition that Marxism begins with socialism and moves toward communism. I saw a letter to the editor once that said we got rid of the communist and socialist threats by renaming them progressive. The one thing they all have in common which keeps them focused in unity is their motivation to destroy the America we know. As I say that, I am reminded that it is becoming more and more the America we knew. Under Obama's presidency they are having enormous success. It makes me very sad to say that.

That concludes my chapter on progressive Washington. We are rapidly losing our country. America has to remember that it voted for Obama and his promise of "Hope and Change". I didn't vote for him. How about those who didn't vote at all? If an American citizen doesn't do their homework and vote for the person who represents the best interests of our country, they deserve what they get. The great misfortune is that the rest of us don't.

CHAPTER 8

Progressive Domestic Policy— Votes, Rule, and Perpetuity!

Progressive domestic policy is very simple. Do whatever it takes to obtain the votes you need to rule over the country in perpetuity. Always be skeptical of what progressives say in their quest for power. It is interesting as well as troubling that whatever progressives say to influence society or the vocabulary they use to name or describe something is usually the opposite of reality. This is one of their methods of duping society. For example, do you know the official name of North Korea? It is the Democratic People's Republic of Korea. By definition, a democratic republic's ultimate power and authority is derived through its citizens. North Korea is arguably the most oppressive country in the world and its government calls the country a democratic republic?

I dealt with three radical employee unions during my career but the most contentious radical group I had to contend with was when we bought the city owned hospital. The organization was called the Nebraskans for Peace. Their website states "A statewide grassroots advocacy organization working nonviolently for peace through community building, education, and political action". Their Wikipedia website uses the terms progressive, promoting peace, and social justice in describing them. There are many well-meaning people involved with that organization that are duped by its radical leadership.

When I dealt with that leadership, the organization's primary purpose was not to promote peace. What does buying a hospital have to do with peace? The organization is a front to advocate for Marxist ideology through progressive behavior. The term "peace" was only to disguise their efforts to tear down traditional American values and promote their radical ideas. They came after me personally in the public arena for eighteen months and were very disruptive to the process of purchasing the hospital. It became very ugly. Our local newspaper designated the story as the number one news story for the year. After we purchased the city hospital and carried through with all of our promises, they quickly disappeared and took on a statewide public issue. The leaders I dealt with in this organization were similar to radical leaders in many progressive organizations. It doesn't seem to matter what they are opposing as long as they are opposing something. It is in their mental being to be radical activists and I have always found their beliefs to center around Marxist ideology.

There are a multitude of national organizations like the Nebraskans for Peace and there is great variation in their radical intensity. There are those like PETA, Code Pink, and Greenpeace that are overtly radical in their actions but are not violently destructive. There are Marxist and anarchist organizations like those that participated in Occupy Wall Street and the more recent community riots that are violently destructive. Then, there are radical organizations like the Center for American Progress and Media Matters that are not as overt in their methods but their radicalism is equally the same. They just go about their business in a more muted but no less forceful way.

As I said in chapter 5, be aware and beware of the behind the scenes connections between a great number of these radical organizations. It is a powerful force moving toward a Marxist America and becoming stronger and more integrated every day. Actions by the Obama administration and the Democratic Party are not as overt as most of these radical groups but the intent is the same and there are many informal connections between them. Progressive domestic policy is akin to being in Wonderland, a.k.a. Obamaland, where things are not always as they seem.

Before we begin the review of specific Washington progressive domestic policies, I want to share an email with you that was widely circulated. It's titled "How to create a social state by Saul Alinsky". All my research says Alinsky did not write it. Some have attributed it to

Cloward and Piven. My research says they are not the authors either. Here's what is true. It is an interesting and valid summary of progressive strategy. Tom White, editor of varight.com, wrote, "Liberals easily cast this off as a lie by claiming that Alinsky didn't write this. And while that much is true, the actual plan is real. It was inspired by Alinsky and enumerated by Cloward and Piven. It has been refined and updated, but it is still the road-map to the 'fundamental change' Obama has been implementing." White claims to be a recovering republican who has finally had enough of the war on conservatives and with the leadership of the Republican Party. He is a man after my own heart. Here is what was attributed to Alinsky. There are eight levels of control that must be obtained before you are able to create a social state and the first is the most important. The eight levels are:

1) Healthcare: Control healthcare and you control the people.
2) Poverty: Increase the poverty level as high as possible, poor people are easier to control and will not fight back if you are providing everything for them to live.
3) Debt: Increase the debt to an unsustainable level. That way you are able to increase taxes and this will produce more poverty.
4) Gun Control: Remove the ability for citizens to defend themselves from the government. That way you are able to create a police state.
5) Welfare: Take control of every aspect of their lives (food, housing, and income).
6) Education: Take control of what people read and listen to. Take control of what children learn in school.
7) Religion: Remove the belief in God from the government and schools.
8) Class warfare: Divide the people into the wealthy and the poor. This will cause more discontent and it will be easier to take (Tax) the wealthy with the support of the poor.

Whether this was written before Obama took office or after, it doesn't matter. This is scary as hell because it is exactly what is happening and it's working. We have discussed the impact of Obamacare on our society. We will begin our look at progressive domestic policy with a continuation of that discussion and look at Obamacare's contribution in making our free society less free. We will also talk about how our welfare system is increasing poverty and strengthening the power of government. Our debt continues to pile up at the fastest rate in history and our out-of-sight-out-of-mind approach to that debt will have a very significant impact on future taxes if not the collapse of our economy. We have already talked about gun control in chapters 2 and 3 and how gun control legislation takes away people's rights and is not effective in stopping violence.

We discussed the efforts by the government to control television, radio, and the Internet in chapters 6 and 7. Chapter 10 provides extensive discussion on progressive influence in our schools, eradicating Judeo-Christian religion in our society, the promotion of racial turmoil, creating class warfare, and promoting violence in our streets. I need to add one more issue to this list and that is our abysmal record in foreign policy that threatens our national safety, our economy, and our image and influence in the world. That will be covered in the next chapter.

The summary narrative that was included with the above eight points said, "Alinsky merely simplified Vladimir Lenin's original scheme for world conquest by communism, under Russian rule." Lenin was the ruling leader of Russia from 1917 to 1922. The summary continued, "Stalin described his converts as 'Useful idiots'. The Useful idiots have destroyed every nation in which they have seized power and control. It is presently happening at an alarming rate in the United States. It is difficult to free fools from the chains they revere." Joseph Stalin took over as the ruling leader of Russia after Lenin had his second stroke in 1922 and was in power until he died in 1953. The summary concluded, "If people can read this and still say everything is just fine ... they are 'useful idiots'." My research indicates the term "useful idiots" has been historically attributed to Lenin but that has never been proven.

Are we useful idiots? Let's take a look. Healthcare was deemed to be the most important of the eight levels of control that must be obtained before a social state can be created. Was it a coincidence or intentional that the progressives' first priority when they controlled Congress and the White House was to get Obamacare implemented?

The economy was in shambles and what did they spend their time on after their idiotic stimulus failure? Obamacare. Why? There is no question that Obamacare was extremely important to progressive domestic policy as a major step toward a progressive style government. Once a country converts from a totally private healthcare system to one controlled by the government, the government gains so much power over the citizenry it becomes the stepping-stone to socialism and beyond. Those eight steps may not have been originated by Alinsky or Cloward and Piven but they are "spot on" in bringing about a Marxist society.

Obamacare is regularly touted as Obama's signature accomplishment. The "Affordable" Care Act is the biggest oxymoron in government history. As I discussed in chapter 6, The Affordable Care Act was never intended to reduce the cost of healthcare to make it affordable to everyone. It is a ruse for progressive control and as Cass Sunstein would say, "nudge" us toward Marxist control. There was an attempt at "Hillary Care" when Bill Clinton was president to do the same thing. That effort fortunately failed. The reason Hillary Care failed is because of the backlash that occurred due to the secrecy of the committee meetings chaired by Hillary in developing it. Sound familiar as in Hillary's secrecy involving her emails while she was Secretary of State? This is certainly a trend with her. How secret would she be as president?

A bigger question is why must she always be so secretive? The answer to that question is no secret. A friend recently sent me a YouTube video of all the scandals with which she has been associated, beginning when Bill was Governor of Arkansas. I knew about most of them but the video was still stunning to see them all together. The video was 19 minutes long and hit each one quickly and moved on to the next one. Think about that—19 minutes to list her scandals! And, she is the leading democratic (progressive) candidate for President of the United States.

Putting the government in control of healthcare has been a cornerstone of progressive philosophy for decades. Obama, Pelosi, and Reid not only knew the Affordable Care Act would not save money for Americans but that it would be more expensive. The justification and projected cost savings were nothing but smoke and mirrors to accomplish their dastardly deed. Their only concern was to ram it through congress before anything could happen to stop it. Like Pelosi said, "We need to pass it to find out what is in it away from the fog." Can you imagine anything more irresponsible than that? One of the most, if not the most, significant laws passed in the history of our country and no one in Congress who voted for it even read it. At least not one republican voted for it. Our progressive democratic friends can take 100% of the credit.

Here are excerpts from a White House review of Obamacare I found on whitehouse.gov written in September of 2010 by Nancy-Ann DeParle who was Director of White House Office of Health Reform at the time. DeParla said:

> The numbers are yet another reminder that the passage of the Affordable Care Act came at a critical time. The (Census Bureau) data show that the number of Americans without insurance increased by 4.4 million since 2008, with a total of 50.7 million uninsured Americans. The Affordable Care Act makes a crucial turning point for our healthcare system and will help make affordable, high-quality care accessible to millions of Americans. Under the Affordable Care Act, millions of Americans will be able to purchase better coverage in the new competitive private health insurance exchanges where individuals and small business will be able to choose coverage from a range of insurance options—the same options members of Congress will have (Update: What happened to that one? When Congress found out how bad Obamacare was they had an exemption carved out for themselves and their staff so they could keep what they had. That is the height of hypocrisy even for the republicans who voted against Obamacare. For democrats, it's just the progressive way.). The law also helps cover millions of Americans who have been priced out of the market. Taken together, the provisions in the law will expand coverage to 32 million Americans.

What happened in reality regarding the White House's declaration? Well, let's see. My wife and I used to get insurance premium increases of about 3% per year on our Medicare supplemental insurance and in 2014 our increase was 15%. It went back down last year. Many Americans were not so lucky. The Daily Signal reported in June 2015 that 2016 rates were going to increase by 51.6% in New Mexico and over 30% in Maryland and Tennessee. How about other states? The Wall Street Journal reported in October 2015 that the second-lowest-cost midrange "silver plan" is a key metric for premiums around the country and will increase an average of 7.5% across three-dozen states. The article did not say if that increase was based upon a subsidized increase or total increase. As you know, Washington tends to use a lot of smoke and a lot of mirrors when they quote Obamacare statistics. The article also said premiums for the silver plan would raise an average of 31.5% in Alaska, 22.9% in Oregon, and 35.7% in Oklahoma. I obtained my most recent information from The Daily Signal in March of this year. It quoted rate increases of 25.1% in Kentucky, 14% in Ohio, and almost 11% in Michigan. They estimated the average increase across the country for 2016 to be about 15%.

I read in my local newspaper in September of last year that the premiums for our Florida Healthy Kids Insurance plan are doubling for families that are not eligible for subsidized premiums or Medicaid. In order to qualify for subsidized premiums of either $15 or $25 per month, a family of four must have an income under $48,000. A Florida mother said it was like "a punch in the stomach" when she was notified the premiums for her children were increasing from $153 to $299 per child per month. She said, "I cried a lot last week. We can't afford $600. My (children's) insurance just doubled in the blink of an eye. You think you are making headway with bills and they slam you again." The state blamed the increase on the benefit requirements under Obamacare. I thought the progressive politicians were for helping the middle class? Cost increases like these are just the beginning. Some elements of the Obamacare have not yet taken effect. If the law had been implemented all at once, there would have been a rebellion by Americans. Mr. Alinsky was right.

The Department of Health and Human Services (DHHS) estimates 7.7 million Americans currently receive subsidies. The Daily Signal reported in March 2015 that by 2025: 31 million people will remain uninsured; subsidies for exchanges will cost over $1 trillion; and the expansion of Medicaid will cost an additional $920 billion. They said there would be 18 new or increased taxes between 2013 and 2022 totaling almost $800 billion. These taxes are imposed upon medical device companies, pharmaceutical companies, health insurance, individual and employer mandates, and payroll tax increases on high earners for Medicare and investment income. The Associated Press reported in December 2015 that healthcare spending for that year "grew at the fastest pace since Obama took office". They said after five years of historically low growth, expenditures increased by 5.3 % in 2014 reaching $3 trillion or $9,523 for every man, women, and child. The increase in 2013 was 2.9%.

It is more than interesting that the new tax on "Cadillac" health insurance plans doesn't take effect until 2018 after Obama and many democrats who voted for it leave office. The employer mandate was postponed until this year. I am sure they were postponed for the purpose of getting some of the other bad stuff and the mid-term elections out of the way before these two big hits occurred. You probably remember the employer mandate requires employers with 50 or more employees to offer health insurance to all employees who work 30 hours or more per week. Many, including me, believe that will be harmful to employees and the economy because small business employers will adjust hours and number of employees accordingly to cut cost. Making cost cutting adjustments could be a matter of survival for some small businesses. How about the big employers? They will be required to provide health insurance subsidy based upon the employee's income. Some believe that there will be large employers who will pay the penalty rather than increase their current subsidy, which will result in pushing employees out into the insurance marketplace and incur higher premiums. Will taxpayers have to subsidize them too? Absolutely!

And finally, how about those who choose not to purchase health insurance? I found the following on healthcare.gov. In 2014, those without health insurance had to pay a penalty to the government equal to the higher of 1% of total income or $95 per person over 18 years old and $47.50 per child. The maximum fine was $285. In 2015 that penalty went up to 2% of total income or $325 per person over 18 years old and $162.50 per child. The maximum fine was $975. In 2016 that penalty increases to 2.5% of total income or $695 per person over 18 years old and $347.50 per child. The maximum fine is $2,085. There is a $10,150 income exemption for these fines. The Associated Press reported last October that approximately 7.5 million households paid $1.5 billion in penalties for the 2014 tax year. That equates to an average of $200 per household.

Like I said in chapter 6, Obamacare is a taxation Ponzi scheme that results in income redistribution. I received an email from a friend regarding Obamacare that I really enjoyed. The author of the email's content is unknown. The content is as follows:

1. In order to insure the uninsured, we first have to un-insure the insured.
2. Next, we require the newly un-insured to be re-insured.
3. To re-insure the newly un-insured, they are required to pay extra charges to be re-insured.
4. The extra charges are required so that the original insured, who became un-insured, and then became re-insured, can pay enough extra so that the original un-insured can be insured, so it will be "free-of-charge" to them.

The email concluded, "This, ladies and gentlemen, is called 'redistribution of wealth'." I couldn't say it better or in a more amusing way. The only problem is that income re-distribution is not amusing.

I learned there are no checks and balances to catch "cheaters" in any aspect of Obamacare. A recent review by the DHHS Inspector General said he found significant unresolved data discrepancies concerning both income and U.S. citizenship requirements. This lack of operational accountability is very convenient for progressives in using Obamacare to facilitate income redistribution and buy votes and support. Surprise, surprise, surprise! Gomer is very popular in my book.

I wrote a section in my leadership book articulating my condensed analysis of Obamacare and what effective government policies could and should be implemented to address healthcare costs. Here is that section from my book:

> This is one that I could write books on and have written newspaper editorials about. Here is the short version. We have the best health care system in the world. The numbers you see quoted regarding clinical outcomes in America not being as good as in other countries are numbers reflecting socioeconomic issues, not quality outcomes of our healthcare system. The Affordable Care Act will not reduce costs and is not needed to provide care to those who supposedly can't obtain care. For a variety of reasons, the act will actually result in billions of increased costs to Americans. There are many hospitals and community medical clinics for the indigent and people who can't afford health insurance that are financially supported by the government and private sources that you never hear about that already exist. In addition, a private hospital is legally required to provide care to anyone who needs healthcare services, and each state has a Medicaid program for the indigent. These costs are already built into the system. And, how about all the people who use personal income that could be used to buy health insurance to buy newer and nicer cars, bigger and nicer places to live, better vacations, or whatever. Those choices are their choices, and society should not be burdened with the extra expense of providing them health insurance because they chose not to purchase it. There are ways to reduce our health care costs. People expect and want what they want when they want it regarding medical care. As long as people have no meaningful out-of-pocket costs to consider in their decision making to access services, health care will always be excessively expensive and will become more so as technology continues to increase. Out-of-pocket costs drive people to be more prudent in making access decisions and looking at alternatives. Restructuring

insurance programs to put more responsibility for payment of services on the individual would be one of the biggest cost saving measures available. Pushing a healthier life style is admirable, but it doesn't work. Structuring lifestyle into insurance plans could have some impact by requiring, for example, people who smoke or are overweight to pay higher premiums. A very significant way to decrease costs is tort reform for malpractice and medical products suits. This is a huge issue that adds significant costs. This issue coupled with people wanting what they want when they want it are the two issues adding the most costs to the system. End-of-life decisions also play a part. Significant costs occur during a person's last years in life, mostly at the end of life. Living wills are important, and everyone should decide his end-of-life desires and put them in a living will. Families, sometimes over the objections of the patient, want the patient to hang on as long as is medically possible during that final period. This can be a significant moral as well as cost issue. It puts providers at risk of legal action, even if the patient's desires are different from his or her family's demands. I strongly believe that a person should decide what her or his wishes are, and those wishes should be honored. This is another argument for legal reform. National healthcare does not work. I have studied several countries, and there is not one example where it works. Even in the countries where national health care worked fine for years (their healthcare still did not compare to ours), it is now falling apart from cost, quality, and access standpoints, not to mention the long waits for and the rationing of services. The government simply can't run a business as well as private industry can. We can improve the costs of healthcare, but one thing society has to accept is that healthcare, as we want it, is and will always be very expensive.

I want to elaborate on my above comment regarding the rationing of services. It is not uncommon for national healthcare in other countries to ration services for the elderly and anyone with certain diseases. Remember from chapter 5 that Ezekiel Emanuel, who was the architect of Obamacare, said, "Unlike allocation by sex and race, allocation by age is not invidious discrimination, every person lives through different life stages rather than being a single age." There is provision for a specific committee and funding for end-of-life planning contained in the law that has collectively been referred to as the "death panel" which the Obama administration adamantly denies.

They adamantly deny a lot of things that come true. For example, I read recently where a 90-year-old man had heart valve surgery, a 91-year-old women got a new hip, and a 94-year-old man is receiving cancer treatments. All three are living good quality lives. Unless the progressives are ousted from power in Washington and Obamacare is repealed, I can assure you these 90-year-olds are lucky to be in need of medical care today and not in the future because it would not be available to them. We see it coming with the new Medicare rules that just came out regarding hip and knee replacements on patients with medical conditions that place them at a higher risk of complications. These new Medicare rules are designed to discourage care to this high-risk population. This is the government's first effort to restrict care to the elderly. There was a symbolic repeal of Obamacare by the republican dominated Congress in January of this year that Obama naturally vetoed. We need more than symbolism.

Here are three very interesting insights into healthcare and progressive domestic policy. First, the progressives consider healthcare as a human right and that every citizen should be covered by health insurance through legislative fiat. This is their position even though there are adequate public and private medical care resources for those who "legitimately" can't afford healthcare. Unless one has a need for "life-saving" medical care, isn't food and shelter more critical for survival? Why haven't the progressives declared food and shelter a human right? Yes, there are government entitlement programs and private sector organizations that provide for those who can't afford food and housing but healthcare also had entitlement programs prior to Obamacare for those who couldn't afford it. Why haven't the progressives demanded legislation to provide specific levels of food and housing for all Americans as they did for healthcare? That would put progressives in "control heaven". Maybe I shouldn't say that. Sometimes, when you say weird things, they come true.

Progressives haven't declared food and housing to be a right, yet, but they are doing their best to control what we eat and provide their definition of adequate housing for those they deem in need. What can we expect next? Maybe a more appropriate question is, "What isn't under their thumb?" Try to name an aspect of your life that doesn't in some manner have an element of government control out of progressive Washington. I bet you can't. The real question is how much control is truly necessary to achieve the best interest of society and how much control is only in the best interest of those controlling it?

Here is my second interesting insight. We have constantly heard about healthcare expenses spiraling out of control and approaching 20% of Gross Domestic Product (GDP). Let's take a quick and simple look at this. Progressives in Washington say health insurance cost individuals and families thousands of dollars per year and is too expensive; therefore, the government must step in and fix it. Let's compare healthcare costs to other costs in a family's budget. The U.S. Department of Labor Bureau of Labor Statistics did a consumer expenditure survey in 2013 of 125,670,000 households and here is a summary of the results. The gross income of those families ranged from $565 (not a typo) to $131,945 for an average of $63,784 before taxes or $56,352 after taxes. Here are the average expenditures per family by category in rank order: housing, $17,148; transportation, $9,004; food, $6,602; personal insurance and pension, $5,528; healthcare, $3,631; entertainment, $2,482; contributions, $1,834; clothes, $1,604; and other, $3,267. Where is healthcare spiraling out of control? It is well below expenses for housing, transportation, food, and future retirement. It is closer to what people spend for entertainment and only twice what families spend on contributions.

We need cars for transportation, which is the second highest expense in the average family budget. We never hear the progressives tell us that our cars are too expensive and the government has to fix it. We hear cars use too much gas and omit too much pollutant and the government has to step in and fix that, but not that they are too expensive. I read an article by The Heritage Foundation that said in 2009 the Obama administration and the democratic controlled Congress began implementing stricter Corporate Average Fuel Economy standards (CAFE). Congress originally promulgated CAFE in 1975 because of the Arab oil embargo; not to control emissions.

The article said these new stricter standards are adding thousands of dollars to new cars. Prices had been falling but started rising after 2009. The average price per car is now $6,200 more. Prices are predicted to continue to rise by at least $3,400 per car through 2025 unless these 2009 standards are eliminated. The article concluded that the increase in car prices would force millions of lower income households out of the new-car market. Don't be surprised if the progressives initiate an entitlement program to buy new cars. Electric cars are already heavily subsidized.

Here is my third insight. The progressives spent billions of dollars to bail out the automobile industry because they said it would be disastrous to our economy if it failed. What percent of our economy does the automobile industry represent? It represents less than 5%. Now lets see. Hospitals are almost always the largest employer in any American community. That does not count physician offices and other medical based businesses like physical therapy centers, outpatient labs, pharmacies, etc. How about industries that support healthcare providers like medical supply companies, medical device companies, medical equipment companies, drug companies, local suppliers, repair businesses, construction companies, etc.? Here is an interesting tidbit that might surprise you. Even though my healthcare system was not-for-profit, we were one of the top five businesses in the county paying property taxes because of the taxable property we owned. The progressives say it is critically necessary to bail out and keep intact an industry that provides less than 5% of our GDP but wants to tear apart and diminish an industry that is 20% of our GDP and the largest employer in the country. Absolutely amazing!

What does all this mean for America? I know I sound like a broken record but Obamacare was never designed to provide more affordable healthcare to all Americans. It was designed to force the conversion of our healthcare system into a government run system. The more the progressives can lock American citizens and illegal aliens into their government dependency model they gain more control over us, they can keep their power in perpetuity, and they can continue to replace our traditional American values with their Marxist ideology. Obamacare is but one of their Trojan horses to accomplish those goals. Obamacare is their strongest and fastest Trojan horse but they have a stable full of strong Trojan horses we have yet to see.

Where does our economy stand under progressive Washington? Does anyone really know? The rhetoric changes on a continuous basis. It usually depends upon the economist and their political ideology or how the government wants to spin it on a particular day. The government has also changed the way they report some of the economic indicators. Hey! If the numbers don't make you look good, change the way you calculate the numbers. That works! You hear from the progressives that millions of new jobs have materialized, less people are seeking unemployment benefits, and the economy grew by x-amount. This is all hogwash.

One of the tactics the government uses that I would find laughable, if it were not so serious, is quoting how many millions of people have been employed since Obama took office. I heard Obama say on television during his State of the Union address last year that 11 million new jobs have been created since he took office. Even my favorite singer got into the act. According to The Daily Signal, Barbara Streisand penned an op-ed titled "Have You Heard The Good News?". She said in her op-ed, "President Obama's administration, with only opposition from republicans, has steadily helped put more than 11 million Americans back to work in the private sector." She is the greatest singer on the planet but an economist she is not. As hard as I try, I cannot understand how very bright and accomplished people like Streisand can be so blinded by their ideology. They don't seek the honest truth and blindly follow what they want to believe like "puppy dogs".

When Obama quotes employment numbers, he conveniently forgets to compare those numbers with statistics regarding those who have lost their jobs and are now underemployed or unemployed. He also forgets how many additional new workers are needed to enter the workforce on a regular basis just to replace those that left the workforce for reasons such as going back to school, retirement, death, etc. The numbers he quotes on new jobs have no meaning without putting them into perspective with the total picture.

There is also a credibility problem with the official unemployment rate reported by the Bureau of Labor Statistics (BLS). The officially reported unemployment rate only includes people who have been seeking employment during the four weeks prior to the unemployment rate being published. They are the only unemployed people who are still technically considered part of the labor force. Does that surprise you? It surprised me and is very misleading. How many people in the general public do you think know this? I can assure you that very few, if any, know it.

After people have been on the list for four weeks and are no longer considered unemployed or in the labor force, the BLS labels them as marginally attached. Some of the marginally attached have quit looking for work and are sub-labeled discouraged workers. After 12 months, those still on the marginally attached list are deleted from the list and are no longer included in any category. Part-time workers who have indicated they are looking for a full-time job are deemed by the BLS to be underemployed. All part-time workers not indicating they are looking for a full-time job are reported as employed. If this sounds confusing, it is. The BLS obtains this data for their reports by surveying 60,000 households or about 110,000 people on a rotating basis. What are the true unemployment numbers? No one really knows because the Obama administration constantly uses smoke and mirrors to make the numbers look better than they actually are.

In addition to their officially reported unemployment rate the BLS does publish a more accurate number that includes the marginally detached and underemployed workers. That number is called the "real" employment rate and you have to hunt to find it. Here are some interesting statistics. The official unemployment rate for January 2008 before the Great Recession hit in late 2008 was 5.0%. The real unemployment rate was 9.2%. The highest January official rate since 2008 was in 2010 at 9.8% while the real rate was 16.7%. In January of 2015 the official rate was 5.7% and the real rate was 11.3% and in 2016 the rates were 4.9% and 10.5% respectively. The Great Recession is the longest downturn in the economy since the Great Depression. It has been over eight years since the Great Recession began. It took 10 years to recover from the Great Depression and unemployment reached 25%. The lowest rates we have had in the last 20 years was in 2000 at an official rate of 4.0% and real rate of 7.1%.

I will admit I have no technical expertise in understanding these numbers other than my ability to read and offer un-educated opinions. With that in mind, here is an interesting look at the numbers. The January 2016 official unemployment rate is basically equal to that of January 2008 while the real rate is 1.3% higher. The official rate is improving faster than the real rate, which says to me there are more marginally attached and discouraged workers as well as underemployed workers now than there were before Obama's so-called economic recovery plan. These numbers do not include those workers who have quit looking for work for 12 months or have accepted a job with less responsibility or less work hours than they had before the Great Recession begin, which I believe is a very significant number of workers. What would the official and real unemployment rates be if they were included?

After I wrote the above, Bret Baier addressed this issue in May of this year on his Fox News show. It was in response to Obama praising his accomplishment of improving the economy and creating jobs in a televised speech in Indiana. I saw part of the speech on television and scanned it on whitehouse.gov. It was a classic organizer speech. It reminded me of the union organizers I had to deal with during my career. Bret said only 62.6% of the workforce was working. The number of people not working in May of this year was 94.71 million versus 77.36 in May of 2006. Obama should listen to Bret and Fox News more often. Actually, Obama said during his speech he "had not turned on Fox News or listened to conservative radio today" as if he does so every day. He blamed conservative news and republicans for lying to Americans about the great things he and his progressive cohorts have done for the economy. His speech was nothing but a self -adulatory progressive democratic campaign speech based upon falsehoods.

Here are some of the highlights. He said the economy was not only better than eight-years ago; it was the strongest in the world. He said he has cut the deficit by 75% and fewer families are on welfare than in the 1990s. He quoted health insurance premiums are $2,600 less than they would have been without Obamacare. He said he has issued fewer regulations than his predecessor and he was not over regulating. He commented that illegal border crossings are less than they have been in 40 years. He also said he cut taxes by $3,600 for middle class families and the wealthy are paying less than they used to pay. And, of course, he blamed Congress for opposing everything he has tried to do. My book disproves every statement he made. How can he lie like that? He is our president. All presidents put their best foot forward but I have never heard any president in my lifetime lie like that to the American people. It is further proof of my theories on Obama in the last chapter.

The Chairman and Editor-in-Chief of U.S. News and World Report, Mortimer Zuckerman, wrote a July 2014 op-ed in The Wall Street Journal on the topic. He said only 47.7% of workers are full time, 2.4 million workers have become discouraged and dropped out of the workforce, and 44% of all employment growth since unemployment hit bottom in 2010 is in low wage industries (3.8 million jobs). He concluded, "The great American job machine is sputtering. We are going through the weakest post-recession recovery the U.S. has ever experienced, with growth half of what it was after four previous recessions. And that's despite the most expansive monetary policy in history and the largest fiscal stimulus since World War II. We are not in the middle of a recovery. We are in the muddle-through and there's no point in pretending that the sky is blue when so many millions can attest to dark clouds."

There has been improvement in the economy since Obama took office but after 9 years we are still nowhere near where we were before the Great Recession. Stephen Moore of The Heritage Foundation said in January of this year, "On almost every measure examined, the 2009-2015 recovery since the recession ended in June of 2009 has been the meekest in more than 50 years." He based his statement on economic data from the Bureau of Labor Statistics and the Joint

Economic Committee of Congress. Has the Obama administration's actions promoted or hindered economic recovery?

Let's start answering that question analyzing Obama's economic recovery plan. The only problem is that Obama doesn't have a plan for economic recovery. Name one effective action he has taken to improve the economy. You can't. His only approach along with his progressive Washington colleagues is the progressive plan. The progressive plan is to get as many people on government "hand out" programs as possible, choke the free market with regulations, push income redistribution through taxation and other means, give lip service to improving the middle class, and spend-spend-spend.

There are two very opposite theories for economic recovery. Keynesian economics, the theory advocated by John Maynard Keynes, advocates that it is necessary for the government to facilitate economic recovery through government spending. The second theory is by Milton Friedman. His approach is to leave economic recovery to the free market system and the government stays the heck out. History supports Friedman and so do I. One only has to look around the world at other countries like Greece to validate that opinion. It is progressive economics (Keynesian) versus conservative economics (Friedman).

Let's take a look at these two theories by looking at the economic approaches of some of our states. The Daily Signal published reports in April and October of last year that were written by Stephen Moore that make a compelling point. Moore said, "The so-called 'progressives' love to talk about how their policies will create a worker's paradise, but then why is it that day after day, month after month, year after year, people are fleeing liberal blue states for conservative red states?" Census data shows the top seven states with the biggest percentage of in-migration from other states are in rank order: North Dakota; Nevada; South Carolina; Colorado; Florida; Arizona; and Texas. All of these states are red except Colorado, which is purple (split between liberal and conservative). The leading exodus states are: Alaska; New York; Illinois; Connecticut; New Mexico; New Jersey; and Kansas. All of these states are blue except Alaska and Kansas. Moore gave an example that showed Florida gained $8.2 billion in adjusted gross income from new residents in 2013 while New York lost $5.2 billion when 112,236 taxpayers left the state.

Moore's report indicated almost a net of 1,000 people each day are leaving blue states and moving to red states. He referenced a book titled *How Money Walks* by Travis Brown that shows two of the leading factors behind this movement of "human capital" are whether or not the state has a right-to-work law and how high the top income tax rate is in the state. The 10 states with the most highly regressive tax had "population growth" that was 4% higher than the U.S. average. The reason given for this growth was that states without state income taxes have twice the "job growth" of states with high tax rates. He said most American's think fairness means having a job versus progressives imposing higher taxes on higher income earners. Moore referenced a study at Ohio University that compared the income gap in states with higher tax rates, higher minimum wages, and more welfare benefits than states that are in the opposite policy spectrum. The study concluded that there was no evidence the poor were any better off in the states with these liberal policies. In fact, it was found that income inequality in these liberal oriented states was worse than those states that were more conservative.

Moore said, "I've never met a democrat who could come up with even a semi-plausible explanation for why families and businesses are hightailing it out of blue states. They are leaving states with high minimum wages, pro-union work rules, high taxes on the rich, generous welfare benefits, expansive regulations to 'help' workers, green energy policies, etc. People are voting with their feet against these liberal policies." Moore said he debated Paul Krugman who is an economics professor, author, and op-ed columnist for The New York Times. He asked Krugman why this migration was happening and said, "His lame explanation for the steady migration from the liberal north to the conservative south was that 'air conditioning' has made the south more livable. Americans are evidently moving because of the weather." Moore commented that California had 1.4 million people leave the state during the decade ending in 2013 and North Dakota had the biggest percentage population gain in the country in that year. When I researched Krugman on the Internet, I learned that he is a strong proponent of Keynesian economics. I am sure "progressive" is an accurate description as well.

Next, we will explore progressive actions and attempted actions that are very repressive toward America's economic future and personal freedoms. Let's began by looking at the beliefs and behaviors of the young people who are the future of America and how that plays into this equation. According to a Pew study published in July 2014, the unemployment rate for Millennials in 2010 at the height of their unemployment was 12.4%. It dropped to 7.7% during the first quarter of 2014, which was much better but not great. These numbers are the "official rate" and not the "real rate". Better yet, how about an "actual rate" that is not calculated by the BLS or anyone.

Here is an interesting statistic from the study. In 2007, 22% of Millennials lived with their parents. That number grew to 24% in 2010 and to 26% in 2015. This percentage increase may not sound significant at first blush but the number of Millennials increased by 3 million during that time as well. Unemployment is going down and living at home is going up. This trend is not necessarily economic related. It aligns with the studies I referenced in the last chapter regarding our young people having a poor work ethic, being easily distracted, having unrealistic pay demands, and having high expectations for "getting" rather than "striving for".

The Daily Signal published a story in January of this year regarding Generation Opportunity, which is part of a network of organizations that were founded in 2011 by Charles and David Koch. Generation Opportunity is an advocacy group founded to increase opportunity for young Americans through limited government. The organization said Millennials "face record high levels of student debt, higher unemployment and poverty levels, and lower personal income than the previous two generations". They concluded, for the first time in U.S. history, a younger generation might be left worse off than the one preceding it.

Here's how Pickles would respond to the group. In a recent cartoon, Earl's daughter, Sylvia, asked him, "Did you know that my generation is the first generation to be less well-off than their parents?" Earl said, "Really?" Then Sylvia said, "Yes, really! And, it's not fair!" Earl said to his wife Opel, "I heard that her generation is the first generation to be whinier than their parents."

I agree that the current economic situation and government intrusion is very problematic in starting out in life on your own but the report does not address the bigger and more important point. When I graduated from both undergraduate and graduate school, I did not even think about how I stacked up to other generations or what the government was doing. I had no choice but to work my butt off to find a job, personally pay off debt for "two" college degrees, and work my way up the ladder of success through hard work and personal sacrifice.

I read a January 2016 newspaper article in The Wall Street Journal regarding 7,500 student loan borrowers that owed $164 million who had applied during the past six months to have their student loans "expunged" under an obscure federal law that had only been used three times in the past. The law forgives loans for students who can prove their schools used illegal tactics to recruit them. The students said their schools deceived them by promising a well-paying career. How irresponsible and dishonest to not pay off his or her debt! If the claims are legitimate, the students should have their degrees "expunged" for lack of intelligence and common sense in falling for such promises and having such expectations.

There is significant difference in student attitudes when I went to college and the attitude of many college graduates today. For example, there was a syndicated article by the Chicago Tribune, also in January, which said, "The Spartan college dorm is out. The luxury student apartment is in." The article talked about student luxury apartments that rented between $855 and $1,500 per month in downtown Chicago. Recently, when I was at the University of Kentucky and the University of Nebraska, I saw very nice student apartment buildings next to both campuses that were non-university owned. I do not know the rental cost but I am sure it was close to or in the range quoted for Chicago. I don't know if it's fair to connect The Wall Street Journal and Chicago Tribune articles together but it certainly raises the issue of unrealistic expectations on the part of today's young people.

The Daily Signal report concluded, "As government continues to grow, young Americans (referring to Millennials) are beginning to believe the American dream is dead." That depends upon what their American dream is. Where is the traditional American independent pioneer spirit and fight for traditional American values among Millinnials? The majority of Millennials are actually in opposition to the traditional American and conservative values that would bring them the success they say they desire and are supporting more government handouts which will do the opposite of what they say they want. Parents are also complicit in promoting this attitude. A Wall Street Journal/NBC poll taken in August 2014 said 76% of adults lack confidence that their children's generation will have a better life than they do. Millennials as a group have a very soft and distorted view of real life. I greatly admire those millennials who don't.

An op-ed by Cal Thomas published in May of this year quoted a Harvard University study that found 51% of Millennials between the ages of 18 and 29 do not support capitalism. Only 42% support our free enterprise capitalistic system. Thomas said, "Just 42% support the economic system that has allowed even the poorest American to live better and to have more opportunity for advancement than most of the rest of the world." Reality does not allow her or him to "have their cake and eat it too". I also read that 33% of the Millinneals in the study supported socialism although they were not sure what socialism was. Not surprising but very alarming.

How about the economy in general? Even though the stock market has recovered (thank goodness for us old retired folks), the economy has not. Some of our progressive friends have equated the economy to the stock market. That is not accurate. There is a correlation but business and industry can do very well in a bad economy, if they adjust accordingly and maintain strong profitability. That is exactly what has happened and overall stocks are doing well. The lack of economic growth does ultimately catch up with business and industry and would eventually affect the stock market negatively.

What is the current state of our economy and what is the foreseeable outlook? You probably know that the Gross Domestic Product (GDP) is the indicator used to measure the overall economic performance for the country and is published by the Department of Commerce Bureau of Economic Analysis (BEA). The GDP for the first quarter of 2014 was a minus 0.9%. That is the worst decline since the Great Recession began. We are considered to be in a recession when there are two consecutive quarters of negative GDP growth. The GDP was up 4.6% for the second quarter. The third quarter GDP was 4.3% but dropped in the fourth quarter to 2.1%. The GDP numbers for 2015 did not do as well. They were: 0.06% for the first quarter; 3.9% for the second quarter; 2.0% for the third quarter; and 1.4% for the fourth quarter. The GDP for the first quarter of 2016 was the worst in two years at 0.5%.

The first quarter number for 2016 is the advanced estimate. The other quarterly numbers reflect the third estimate. There is also a second estimate. Sound confusing? It is. The BEA publishes an advanced GDP, a second GDP, and a third GDP. They commonly vary to some degree and sometimes vary to a great degree. I make the point because the government can use numbers that are technically accurate to make their points that do not always portray the true picture in order to make themselves look better.

We hear from the Obama administration how great the recovery is going when the GDP numbers are good and then total silence when they are not. The GDP should ideally fluctuate between 2% and 4%. Less than 2% means a stagnant economy and growth more than 4% is too fast and most likely will create an economic contraction. In reality, none of us outside of government bureaucratic bean counters and the White House have a clue where the economy or unemployment truly is because of all the smoke and mirrors economics. I often feel that no one, even our most brilliant economists, truly knows. I will say this. I believe the economy is in "languish" mode and there are many polls that show Americans agree with that assessment in spite of the numbers put forth to the contrary by our progressive friends in Washington and their supportive liberal economists.

Progressive Washington is showering business and industry with regulations and control that is very stifling for economic growth. What happened when countries like China and Russia lessened government control and moved toward a capitalistic free market system? Even though they have had a few "hiccups", China's economy has flourished and Russia's has vastly improved. We are going in the opposite direction.

The Obama administration is required by law to release plans for new regulations twice per year. It is no surprise that they are always released before major holidays. The last release was just before Thanksgiving 2015. According to The Daily Signal, over 2,000 regulations were released and 144 were deemed "economically significant". The designation of being economically significant means the regulation will cost Americans $100 million or more. That is a record for the number of new economically significant regulations. Guess which administration holds the old record? You got it! The last record of 136 was by the Obama administration in the spring of 2015. They have two releases to go before Obama leaves office.

The Daily Signal reported in May of this year that the new regulations imposed by Obama in 2015 will cost Americans $22 billion per year in additional costs. Obama has imposed 20,642 new regulations since he was elected at a cost of $100 billion annually. When this report came out there were comments on Fox News regarding the untold number of government staff that convert these regulations and laws into language for implementation and it is that language that actually determines the cost, not the president or Congress.

This reminded me of what I learned when I was Chairman of the Nebraska Hospital Association Board in 2000 and we were "schmoozing" our Nebraska congressional delegation staff in Washington. I was very unhappy with the National Institute of Health's (NIH) 1999 report titled "To Err is Human" that concluded at least 44,000 and up to 98,000 patients died each year from medical errors in hospitals. Because of my experience and knowledge, I did not believe the report. President Bill Clinton and the President of the American Hospital Association (AHA) appeared on national television together proclaiming improvements must be made to curtail the problem. I was so vocally critically of the report and the lack of support for hospitals by the AHA that I received a call from the President of the AHA. We agreed to disagree but I felt good that I pushed back on something I strongly believed in and "hit a nerve".

Here is what I learned from our state's congressional staff. First, the NIH report was not a study. The congressional staff told me it was a book review. The data was extrapolated from two studies that took place in two different cities many years prior. There was no way the data was even close to being accurate because of the small sample and its age. Always be leery of government reports that make a political point. Second, the congressional staff told me it was not uncommon that the language written by government staff to implement the laws passed by Congress does not conform to the laws' original intent.

We have talked about the negative impact of Obamacare on business growth and hiring? It has created great uncertainty, which has caused a wait and see attitude among big and especially small business and industry. These progressives are regulating fools. The current unofficial motto of the Obama administration is "if you can't legislate, regulate". It would take another book to go through all the regulations that Obama and his progressive appointees have imposed or want to impose on business and industry. Let's highlight a few to make the point.

The energy and financial sectors are great examples of business and industry that have been clobbered with new regulation. The United States could be 100% energy independent from the rest of the world if Washington would allow sufficient oil drilling at home. The oil is there. What would that do to our economy? It would mean lower energy costs, more employment, and more foreign trade opportunity? The Organization of Petroleum Exporting Countries (OPEC) lowered their price per barrel to curtail our oil production when the United States started infringing upon their traditional turf and profits. When this plays out, we all know what will happen. Wouldn't it be nice if we had control over production and price and not care what OPEC does?

The EPA is one of the worst agencies, if not the worst agency, in government when it comes to over-regulation. We have discussed the lack of proof regarding "man made" climate change and its purported impact on our Earth. The progressives are using climate change as a hammer, actually as a sledgehammer, to propel the EPA to impose arbitrary and stifling regulatory control on the energy industry. My home county of Harlan in Eastern Kentucky is economically decimated because of what the EPA has done to the coal industry.

In October of last year, Bret Baier reported on his Fox News show that the EPA has about 200 public relations staff members and spent $160 million on public relations between 2000 and 2014. The data came from an in-depth study on EAP expenses by a group called Open the Books. I actually went to the Open the Books website and read the report. Very interesting. This public relations expense sounds bizarre to me. A government agency needs to spend $160 million and maintain a staff of 200 employees for public relations?

On second thought, maybe its not so bizarre when one looks at the 2015 Animas River Disaster in Colorado where the EPA was responsible for the Gold King Mine "blowout" that dumped 3 million gallons of toxic waste into rivers in Colorado, Utah, and New Mexico. They were warned about the potential blowout and did not take proper precautions. I read the clean up of the spill could cost taxpayers $1 billion. What would happen if a non-government entity caused an environmental problem that big? They would be vilified and condemned in the mainstream news media and receive a huge fine from the EPA. Where is the accountability for the EPA? Two hundred employees and $160 million will take care of that. Oh, and a progressive administration. How do you spell hypocrisy?

Progressives are obsessed with controlling any emissions in the atmosphere they deem to be pollutants. Remember the following from my epistle? The Treasury Department came out in March of 2009 with a report that said the proposed cap and trade bill would cost $100 billion to $200 billion annually in the U.S. resulting in a $1,761 annual increased energy cost for the average family. Congressman Waxman, in an attempt to sell his bill, said it would cost the average family no more than 40 cents per day. Let's see. Forty cents times 365 days equals $146.00. Obama said, "It would cost only that of a postage stamp per day." OK, lets calculate this one. I think postage stamps when he said that were 44 cents. That would mean an annual increase of $160.60. Was this bad math or deplorable dishonesty on the part of Waxman and Obama in attempting to achieve their goal? It was absolute deplorable dishonesty!

Obama and Waxman could not get cap and trade legislation passed through Congress so the EPA is attempting to impose emission standards on coal-fired power plants through rule changes to existing legislation. The Supreme Court temporarily clipped the progressive wings of the EPA in June 2015 but unfortunately they got their wings back. The New York Times published a good accounting of what happened. Industry groups and 20 states challenged the EPA's decision to regulate emissions of mercury and other toxic pollutants from coal-fired power plants because the EPA did not take into account the cost benefit of implementing their rules. The industry groups said the new rules would cost $9.6 billion annually and create only $6 million in benefits. The government claimed tens of billions in benefits. Sound familiar? The case wound up at the Supreme Court. Justice Scalia wrote in the majority opinion, "It is not rational, never mind 'appropriate' to impose billions of dollars in economic costs in return for a few dollars in health or environmental benefits. Statutory context supports this reading." The vote was 5 to 4 to remand the case back to the lower court requiring the EPA to show cost benefit.

The Supreme Court was asked in March of this year to stop the EPA from implementing the new rules until the case was resolved. Chief Justice John Roberts wrote an order refusing to do so without referring the question to the full Court. The New York Times said this was the courts' way of saying they do not want to be inundated with cases like this one. The Supreme Court had struck down another EPA rule on global warming called the Clean Power Plan only three weeks before. In April of this year, the lower appeals court ruled the EPA had revised their cost benefit and left the new rules in effect while the EPA revises the way it calculates compliance costs. In June of this year, the Supreme Court refused to take up another appeal to block the EPA from implementing the rules. Reportedly many utilities have already complied with the new standards.

We are really going to miss Scalia. The Supreme Court is the only protection we have to stop Obama or any future progressive president's dictatorial overreach. I can't see the republicans ever attempting impeachment. Based upon the Bill Clinton experience, it wouldn't pass anyway. We better hope we get a conservative in the White House before a new Supreme Court Justice appointment is made. Otherwise, welcome to the progressive "kingdom" and say goodbye to American "democracy". The Senate has said they will not go through the confirmation process for Obama's recommendation before the end of his term.

Justice Sotomayer is proclaiming we need more diversity on the court. I thought the Supreme Court 's job is to interpret the Constitution and settle legal cases they accept directly or have been sent to them through the lower courts. That takes a good, independent, and objective legal mind and has nothing to do with diversity.

After I wrote this, I read an editorial in the Wall Street Journal critical of Justice Sotomayer for bringing race into a Supreme Court case that had nothing to do with race. The editorial said she "went off the deep end" about police misconduct, Ferguson, and race in America. She was quoted as saying, "Although many Americans have been stopped for speeding or jaywalking, few may realize how degrading a stop can be when the officer is looking for more…it is no secret that people of color are disproportionate victims of this type of scrutiny."

Her dissent had nothing to do with the case in question and the person the case was about was white. The editorial concluded, "This dissent continues her habit of wandering far from the law or precedent to decide cases based on her personal political and policy views." This is a hint of what is to come if a progressive gets into the white house in 2016. In all likelihood that president will have opportunity to appoint more Supreme Court Justices than just one to replace Scalia. Even a conservative Senate majority will not be able to stop placing progressives on the Court if we have a progressive democrat president. This is really scary. If we are no longer a nation of laws, we become a nation of totalitarianism.

Can you even imagine the speed with which America would become a socialist based country or worse if progressives win the next congressional and presidential elections and take over the Supreme Court? Stay tuned! This is a realistic possibility. Taking over the presidency, Senate, and Supreme Court would probably do it without controlling the House of Representatives. This honestly makes me nervous as hell just sitting here writing about it. This is the most critical year for national elections in our country's young history and the prospect for a good outcome is shaky at best. More about that in chapter 13.

Our friends at the EPA want to regulate you individually as well. They are claiming new power to garnish your wages if you break one of their out of control pollution standards. These penalties can run into tens of thousands of dollars. According to a July 2014 news report by The Washington Times, a Wyoming homeowner was threatened with fines up to $75,000 per day for building a pond on his own rural property. The report said fines by the EPA increased from $96 million in 2009 to $252 million in 2012. That is a 40% increase in three years. The Daily Caller reported in September of 2014 that 35 people were fined an average of $12,490 for relatively minor paperwork violations involving lead paint. They do give you a hearing. They pick the hearing officer and the burden is on you to prove them wrong. I thought in America we were innocent until proven guilty. Not with the EPA.

It gets better. The Washington Times report said the EPA claimed in 2014 that the Debt Collection Improvement Act of 1996 allows them to garnish non-federal wages to collect delinquent non-tax debts owed to the United States government without first obtaining a court order. Just before July 4, 2014 (a major holiday) the EPA announced in the Federal Register they were proceeding to do so. The Heritage Foundation reported that due to adverse public reaction the EPA withdrew their proposed rule on July17[th]. The power of public reaction! Both the House and Senate introduced bills to stop any such future action by the EPA. The house bill has been working its way through two committees since July 2014 and, according to congress.gov, appears to have been buried in a sub-committee on regulatory reform since September 2, 2014. The Senate bill has been in the Committee on the Judiciary since September 15, 2014. The speed of government! This story is only one example of a growing number of government over-reaches that control and diminish our freedoms.

Here is an interesting side note. The republican Senator who introduced the Senate bill is from Nebraska. He was the mayor when I had to contend with the Nebraskans for Peace and their radicalism, so I know him pretty well. The real reason for the Nebraskans for Peace radical behavior was not because they opposed our purchase of the city hospital. Their opposition was a ruse to politically attack the Nebraska senator when he was our mayor running as a conservative republican for governor. He won the governor's race and obviously was also elected to the Senate. As I consistently say, you can't trust what progressives do or say when it comes to the reality of their intentions. The Nebraskans for

Peace loved the public attention and publicity they got from their efforts in opposing us. They also got their kicks from publicly attacking me personally as "a rich capitalist who did not care about the community". I proved them wrong.

Before we end our discussion on the EPA, I want to share a report I got from The Daily Signal in June of this year. The report said "environmental justice" was born during the Clinton years, was dormant during the Bush years, and has now become an "overreaching political commissar-style ideological mandate" during the Obama years. It surmised as many as 15 executive agencies are complicit but focused the report on the EPA and Department of the Interior.

The report commented the Obama-era environmental justice initiative "tracks, analyzes, and reviews regulations to insure they are environmentally just". The report said, "It also plays a hand in issuing public tax dollars in the form of grants to all sorts of community groups and agenda driven environmentalist to educate the public in the form of political protests and campaigns against private industry". The author of the report concluded, "In short, the limited statutory authority of executive agencies to do the work of regulating has been trumped by the political. Formal actions by agencies are increasingly judged through the political prism of the Orwellian 'environmental justice' movement, now cloaked with government power."

The Dodd-Frank Wall Street Reform and Consumer Protection Act (Dodd-Frank Act) is a piece of government regulation aimed at the financial industry that is stifling the economy. It was touted to save us from those mean greedy financial institutions and prevent another Great Recession. I read the bill creates two hundred and forty-three rules, conducts sixty-seven studies, and issues twenty-two periodic reports. For what? Will this act save us from another Great Recession? No! It just means more government bureaucracy, more government employees, more government expense, and more consumer cost. In reality, it creates more control over us and more uncertainty in the marketplace. It's another Trojan horse from the progressive stable.

I read an recent op-ed in The Wall Street Journal by Peter J. Wallison who is a senior fellow at the American Enterprise Institute and author of the book titled *Hidden in Plain Sight: What Really Caused the World's*

Worst Financial Crisis and Why It Could Happen Again. Wallison said, "America's economic recovery since the recession ended in 2009 has been the weakest in decades, principally because the 2010 Dodd-Frank financial law suppresses risk taking."

Chris Dodd and Barney Frank played a significant roll in the Great Recession. What irony! They co-sponsored a legislative bill that is supposed to prevent a future occurrence of a problem in which they played significant roles in causing. Let me explain. Fannie Mae was formed by the government in 1938 as part of the New Deal under FDR. Freddie Mac was formed by congressional legislation and signed by President Nixon in 1970 to compete with Fannie Mae in an effort to help relieve a housing shortage during a time of high interest rates.

The problems that led to the Great Recession began with The Community Reinvestment Act that was signed into law in 1977 by Jimmy Carter. It was intended to reduce discriminatory credit practices against low and moderate-income neighborhoods, which are defined as geographic areas that are 115% under average median income. The law said the people obtaining housing loans under this legislation must be without adequate housing but able to afford home loans. Is that an oxymoron? This law also encouraged banks to provide home loans to these people even though their credit was questionable. I could have sold them my bridge to failure. You can think of your own words to describe the stupidity of this practice and its inevitable collapse.

Frank consistently covered for Fannie Mae and Freddy Mac as they made a multitude of questionable loans. I believe his behavior primarily resulted from his progressive ideology but, as a point of interest, it was widely reported that Frank obtained a job at Fannie Mae for his live-in companion, Herb Moses. Frank wrote in Politico, "Herb and I were also the first openly gay congressional couple." Moses became Director of Product Initiatives at Fannie Mae and was reported to have had influence regarding Fannie Mae making sub-par loans. The relationship between Frank and Moses raises the question of whether or not their relationship influenced the outcome at Fannie Mae regarding those loans.

I also read that Fannie Mae and Freddy Mac donated $205,000 collectively to homosexual groups while Frank was in office. I have nothing against donations to homosexual groups but that is not appropriate for these two quasi-government organizations. And, Frank and Dodd reportedly received over $130,000 and $40,000 respectively in campaign contributions from Fannie Mae and Freddy Mac. Even Obama was reported to have gotten around $106,000 in campaign contributions during his stint in the Senate. These questionable contributions by Fannie Mae and Freddy Mac are out of line.

The executive leadership of Fannie Mae was enjoying a financial windfall while things were going to hell-in-a-hand-basket at the organization. The executive compensation plan provided bonuses based upon company performance. During the 1990s, Fannie Mae improperly deferred $200 million in expenses resulting in excessive compensation for James Johnson, the CEO. A book written in 2011 titled *Reckless Endangerment: How Outsized Ambition, Greed, and Corruption Led to Economic Armageddon* accused Johnson of being one of the key figures responsible for the Great Recession. One of the authors commented during a television interview that Johnson was corporate America's founding father of regulation manipulation and earned over $200 million in executive compensation during his seven years at the helm after changing Fannie Mae's executive compensation plan to one based upon volume.

The next CEO at Fannie Mae was Franklin Raines who was the Chief Operating Officer under Johnson when the expenses were deferred and the compensation plan was changed. He reportedly received over $90 million in salary and bonuses during his five years as CEO and was said to have orchestrated inflated earnings at Fannie Mae somewhere in the neighborhood of $9 billion to $10 billion. CEO salaries at Fannie Mae and Freddy Mac are still controversial today. I recently read that the House Financial Services Committee approved a bill to limit the CEO's pay for each organization to $600,000 per year. This was after the Federal Housing Finance Agency Director approved a $3.4 million raise last year for the CEOs. The article I read did not mention anything regarding their bonuses.

I intended to write a brief summary on this topic from memory and shore up that memory through some cursory research. What I found was far more involved and much more extensive than I could have ever imagined. For that reason, I want to make a disclaimer. I am comfortable that the information I have provided to support my opinions on this topic are reasonably accurate. I must admit; however, practically every reference I reviewed took me down more convoluted paths than I was able to fully research. I knew Fannie Mae and Freddy Mac were instrumental in causing the Great Recession but it was astounding what I learned from my research regarding how entangled these two organizations are with not only our federal government but with outside progressive organizations and individuals. The following is what I am talking about.

Fannie Mae and Freddie Mac are government-sponsored enterprises, which means the government establishes them but has no formal management or legal responsibility. There is an oversight agency for Fannie Mae and Freddy Mac called the Office of Federal Housing Enterprise Oversight (OFHEO). There is also an implicit guarantee that the government would not let Fannie Mae or Freddy Mac fail or default on their debt and the government will back them as they did in the Great Recession. This supposedly saves Fannie Mae and Freddie Mac about $2 billion per year because this implicit guarantee gives them favorable interest rates and their securities get high prices. I have always read this implicit guarantee was a significant reason why the financial institutions took as much risk as they did on the housing loans.

Can someone explain to me how a government-sponsored enterprise that operates under a government oversight agency can donate money to members of Congress who have significant influence on the future of these entities? How can this not be a direct conflict of interest? Dodd was even reported to have received two preferential home loans from Countrywide Financial. Were the House and Senate Ethics Committees asleep? Yes, especially since the progressives controlled Congress. The OFHEO did file civil charges against Franklin Raines because of his dishonest shenanigans at Fannie Mae. They also filed charges against two other Fannie Mae executives. These executives were sued for $110 million in penalties and for another $115 million to return their bonuses. These civil charges resulted in payments to the government of about $3 million total from all three. And, guess what? They didn't pay one dime of it. It was paid by Fannie Mae's insurance policies.

Raines did agree to give the proceeds from his sale of $1.8 million worth of Fannie Mae stock to charities that supported home ownership. He also agreed to give up his stock options that were valued at $15.6 million when they were issued. This was a farce because they had no value at that time he agreed to do that. I guess the OFHEO was embarrassed by their lack of results and claimed Raines gave up $5.3 million of other benefits and cash. Raines denied it. The OFHEO tried one more time to file a lawsuit. They worked with a state attorney general to file a class action securities fraud suit in a state court. The judge dismissed the suit. So much for the OFHEO's oversight ability.

Bill Clinton played a part as well. The Clinton administration pushed banks to make bad housing loans to unqualified people. We also have our friends at ACORN jumping into the "Act" (pun intended) by holding demonstrations in front of banks in an effort to harass them into making sub-prime loans. The rest is history.

George W. Bush and his Secretary of Treasury, Henry Paulson, got the blame but it was Dodd and Frank and their compatriots that truly deserve it. Paulson warned Congress about a potential serious problem in home financing but nothing happened. Why? Frank was chairman of the Financial Services Committee in the House from 2007 to 2011. Dodd was Chairman of Banking, Housing, and Urban Affairs also from 2007 to 2011. That was an unfortunate combination. Because of their powerful positions they were able to circumvent efforts by Paulson and Bush to reign in Fannie Mae and Freddy Mac. I read the two organizations collectively purchased $1.9 trillion in mortgages made to borrowers with credit scores below 660, which is considered subprime. That represented 54% of all mortgages purchased.

Should Paulson and Bush have seen the potential for the Great Recession and taken a tougher stance with Congress in an attempt to prevent it from happening? Absolutely, but Bush's economic policies did not cause the Great Recession. The financial industry did some stupid things to profit from the situation but without the opportunity provided by the government, they wouldn't have had the ability to do so. There is plenty of blame to go around for everyone but Congress deserves the lion's share of blame by setting the stage for the Great Recession to play out. We can primarily thank progressive ideology, progressive politicians, and progressive legislation for allowing this mess to happen.

One would think that after this disastrous debacle there could never be another one that resulted because of the same reasons. As Einstein said, "The definition of insanity is doing the same thing over and over again and expecting different results." Well, insanity happened. In 2014, Fannie Mae, Freddy Mac, their regulator, and lenders reached an agreement to do it all over again. They relaxed their standards on credit scores, down payments, and turn around times. Not all lenders went along but it appears most did, especially the big ones. The Wall Street Journal said the Urban Institute estimated these changes would open up 1.2 million new loans. Stay tuned on this one.

Before we move past Fannie Mae, lets go back to cap and trade. Did you know that Fannie Mae co-owns the patent for the method to identify and quantify reductions in residential emissions and converting that into a tradable commodity? The patent also comprises the steps of measuring energy savings and calculating the emissions reduction resulting from those savings. Yes, that's correct. Fannie Mae co-owns the patent that would be used to calculate the information needed for residential cap and trade. This is an important discussion for two reasons. One is to expose the real reasons behind cap and trade legislation and the other is to expose the potential corruption associated with it. In doing my research, I went down as many or more endless paths as I did for the Fannie Mae and Freddy Mac debacle. I was also astounded how complicated, involved, and messy cap and trade is. There is enormous potential for government control over our lives and political corruption.

Here is the Cliff's Notes version of what I am talking about. As a "side note", Cliff lived in Lincoln, Nebraska and was good friends with one of my board members. While Franklin Raines was CEO of Fannie Mae, he obtained the patent for the system needed for residential cap and trade. The patent is co-owned by CO2e.com, LLC that was under the umbrella of the investment banking and brokerage firm Canter Fitzgerald. The CEO of CO2e.com, LLC was probably the brains behind the guts of the patent. He has gotten similar patents in the past.

His name was Carlton Bartels. Unfortunately, he was killed in the 9/11 attacks and Fannie Mae purchased Bartels' rights to the patent from his widow. While I was researching this, I ran across a very sad statistic. Canter Fitzgerald lost 658 employees out of a total workforce of 960 in the 9/11 attacks. I can't imagine what it must have felt like to be a surviving employee of that company.

The patent lists Raines, Bartels, Bartels' widow, and five others whom I believe were Fannie Mae executives and consultants as the inventors. I could not find any information on the contractual and financial relationship between the owners (Fannie Mae and CO2e.com) and any of the inventors. I am certain there is one that could potentially be very lucrative for the people I just referenced in addition to the potential financial windfall for Fannie Mae. The CBO estimated the federal government would be hauling in an extra $104 billion per year if the cap and trade bill titled the American Clean Energy and Security Act of 2009 (ACES) had passed in the Senate after its narrow passage in the house. I shudder to think what would have happened if the bill had passed. Don't you love the names that are coined for legislation? This act would have been more appropriately named the American Outrageous Tax and Enormous Government Control Act. I believe the estimated $104 billion windfall for the government would have been low. Perhaps, very low.

It gets better. I read the financial windfall for the people involved in managing and investing in the cap and trade system would have easily been into the billions. Yes, in the billions. I also read that the exchange would have eventually become a $10 trillion industry. As that old saying by Senator Everett Dirksen goes, "A billion here, a billion there, pretty soon it adds up to real money." I guess that saying shows his age. He lived between 1896 and 1969. If he were alive today he would say, "A trillion here, a trillion there, pretty soon it adds up to real money." As hard as I tried, I could not find information that would put all the players and their financial relationships together in a neat little understandable package. I believe that is on purpose. I will share with you the tidbits that I did learn and let you decide what you think.

Let's start with the founding of the Chicago Climate Exchange (CCX) that was to be the exchange for carbon emissions trading.

The founder of the exchange was Richard Sander. I found no direct connection to the people I have discussed thus far but did find the following that is certainly interesting. He is a lecturer at the University of Chicago Law School and it was announced in 2013 that he and his wife are the principal donors to a $10 million endowment at the law school. It was reported that he received more than $90 million from the $622 million sale of CCX and its sister European Climate Exchange to the Intercontinental Exchange that does carbon trading in the European market.

CCX was founded by $1.1 million in grants from The Joyce Foundation based in Chicago. This foundation has also funded the Center for American Progress and the Tides Foundation. Hmm, remember them from chapter 5? Both are organizations that push very progressive ideology. Ironically, the Joyce Foundation's endowment began in 1948 from the fortune of a staunch republican who made his wealth from the lumber industry. After his niece and sole survivor of the family fortune died in 1972, the foundation was taken over by the professional staffers who began to channel the organizations funding away from past non-political philanthropic practices toward social engineering schemes and social justice activists' organizations. Would you like to guess who was on the board of the Joyce Foundation when these grants were given to CCX? Barrack Obama. I don't know if there is a connection between Obama and Sander but I do find that both Sander and Obama have connections to the University of Chicago, The Joyce Foundation, and cap and trade philosophy. Very interesting.

What else is interesting involving CCX? After the grants were given to CCX, Joyce's president left to become CCX's first executive vice president. That's convenient. Al Gore was a major investor in CCX through a firm he co-founded named Generation Investment Management (GIM). Now we know the real reason he has been such an advocate for fighting climate change. Would cap and trade mean millions or billions for Al? The other co-founder of GIM was a past CEO of Goldman Sachs Asset Management. In my research I found several references to connections between Goldman Sachs, their executives, and CCX. These connections raised my interest but all I could discover is that they were opportunists and nothing else. The day after the democrats took control of Congress in 2006 the patent for the residential cap and trade carbon exchange system used by CCX was approved after pending for two years. Coincidence? When cap and trade legislation failed in Congress, all of the CCX investors quickly sold out and ran.

The investors still made a nice profit by selling to the Intercontinental Exchange. Does that give you some idea of what investment returns they expected if the cap and trade legislation had passed? Europol, the European Union's (EU) law enforcement agency, announced in 2009 that in some EU countries upwards to 90% of the carbon-trading volume was fraudulent; costing the EU members 5 billion EUR (approximately $7 billion) over the prior 18 months. The GDP for the EU and the United States is roughly the same. I read the potential cost of fraudulent trading in the United States was expected to be much higher than in the EU countries.

Here is another curious and potentially very troubling connection to Fannie Mae involving the residential cap and trade patent. A Fox News story on the Internet dated July 2010 reported an unnamed source close to Fannie Mae said a plan was in place to funnel future earnings from the patent to a non-profit housing organization called Enterprise Community Partners. The article went on to say that Raines as well as a Goldman Sachs executive was on their board. I did my own Internet review of the organization including their website and their 2013 annual report. James and Pattie Rouse founded the organization in 1982. He was a developer and philanthropist. Raines was listed as a senior advisor. An executive of Goldman Sachs was on their board but so were several other executives of major banks and investment companies. There was a Freddie Mac executive on the board and the donor list included Fannie Mae in the $100,000 to $499,999 category. That was the only connection to Fannie Mae that I could find.

Enterprise Community Partners is a 501(c)(3) not-for-profit organization that invested $2.5 billion dollars to create 16,800 affordable homes during 2013. I did not find anything significant on the Internet that would raise alarm as to their mission or indicate they were a radical progressive organization. The only thing I discovered that indicated any potential radicalism was the organization's original name—Robin

Hood Inc. That is perhaps a clue to their intended mission. Keep this in mind as we continue.

The Fox News report went on to say that in December 2009 The Joyce Foundation gave Raines and Enterprise Community Partners a $200,000 grant to launch the Emerald Cities Collaborative. I could not find any connection between the Emerald Cities Collaborative and Enterprise Community Partners on either of their respective websites or the Internet but I did discover the Emerald Cities Collaborative is a very far left progressive organization with lots of tentacles. The Fox report said Joel Rogers headed up the Emerald Cities Collaborative. Remember the radical Apollo Alliance organization in chapter 5 that changed its name to the BlueGreen Alliance? The Fox report also said Rogers was a co-founder of the Apollo Alliance.

The BlueGreen Alliance website confirmed that Rogers was a co-founder and its first chairman. He is currently on their advisory board for what they call the Apollo Alliance Project. I reviewed the Emerald Cities Collaborative list of board members. The organizations represented on its board were the usual suspects for radical progressive organizations. There were several union executives and a multitude of people from other progressive organizations. Most of the progressive organizations sounded pretty radical. And, guess who is listed as a board member? Mr. Rogers and not the Mr. Rogers that we all knew and loved on television who passed away in 2003. Did you know that Mr. (Fred) Rogers was an ordained Presbyterian minister. I don't think he would have ever served on this board or any board like it. It is amazing, but not surprising, how intertwined the leadership is of these radical progressive organizations.

I will finish my review of the Emerald Cities organization with what they said was their vision. Their website said they wanted to green our cities through deep retrofits of America's metropolitan regions toward energy efficiency. The vision continued to say they wanted to build our communities through training, jobs, and labor standards to support the growth of a well paid workforce and sustained local economies. Finally the vision said they wanted to strengthen democracy through coalitions that support our metropolitan regions in a way that are accountable and equitable.

How do phrases like "green our cities through deep retrofits" and "strengthen democracy in ways that are accountable and equitable" grab you? You know what those phrases really mean. They mean radical progressive endeavors to accomplish their agenda for social justice. If this Fox News report is accurate, this is a clever way to channel millions if not billions of dollars from government controlled programs into non-government progressive organizations to carry out their progressive Marxist agenda including income redistribution. As you have read, this would not be uncommon.

I will admit that I had trouble connecting the dots between these organizations but I trust Fox News to be pretty darn accurate in their reporting. I believe this Fox report is accurate regarding the relationships between Fannie Mae and these three organizations. The information I found during my personal research was consistent with what was included in their report.

Before we close this discussion on cap and trade let's review what the patent owned by Fannie Mae could mean personally for our families and us. The title of the patent is Method for Residential Emissions Trading. I thought that cap and trade was all about controlling these big out-of-control utility companies and big business. Didn't you? I am going to provide a Paul Harvey moment again. I did not read the bill or the detailed language of the patent but I promise you I would have read the bill if I had been in Congress when it was under consideration and had to vote on it. With that acknowledgement, here is what I have learned from my research that tells me we dodged a bullet. On second thought, not a bullet but maybe a nuclear rocket.

Fannie Mae has the exclusive rights for identifying and measuring energy savings in our homes that can be packaged and sold as credits on the carbon exchange. There is language in the patent that talks about replacing older appliances with newer and more energy-efficient appliances, upgrading water heating systems, modifying lighting, switching heating methods, renovating with more energy efficient insulation and windows, etc. The patents would have allowed Fannie Mae to establish an energy baseline on your home through electronic means like "smart meters" and by onsite visual inspection by the government. The house version of the cap and trade bill contained federally mandated energy efficient building regulations that overrode all state and local codes and would be enforced by federal inspectors. The author of one of the articles I read called the onsite inspectors the "green goon squad".

Once your house is up to code you would receive a certificate as part of the Energy Performance Labeling Program. The house bill stated the goal of this certification was to have 90% of our homes certified within 5 years. The EPA and Department of Energy (DOE) were to receive about $100 million in funding to administer these provisions of the law. I could not find anything that said what would happen if you did not achieve certification. I will leave that one up to your imagination but you know as well as I, it would be some type of punitive action.

Think about what I have just said and its potential impact on you. It makes that $1,761 per year additional cost look cheap. The technology to monitor energy usage for specific energy using components in the home is already available and would allow the government to monitor our homes in any manner they wish. For example, utilities could install smart monitors that can tell them how much energy you are using in heating, air conditioning, hot water heaters, refrigerators, freezers, clothes washers, clothes dryers, and other home appliances. What if you exceed your government allowance on a specific appliance like your refrigerator?

Under the defeated cap and trade legislation, the government could have required you to buy a new more energy efficient refrigerator, sold you more credits, or charged a penalty if you did not comply with your pre-set allowance for energy usage for that component. Would the EPA have garnished your wages? That law hasn't passed yet! How much would it have cost you to cook like you like to cook, cool and heat your house the way you like to cool and heat your house, or take hot showers the way you like to take hot showers? Seem far-fetched? Not at all, they can do it now. All they need is the authority to do it and cap and trade legislation would have given them that authority.

Actually, California tried in 2008. The state wanted to mandate every new heating and cooling system include a non-removable FM receiver that would allow public and private utility companies to send price signals and adjust the temperature up or down four degrees. The receivers were also capable of controlling other electrical appliances and apparatuses such as water heaters, refrigerators, pool pumps, computers, and lights. There was no allowance for people with special needs and no ability to override the control. If contractors and homeowners did not comply, their building permits would be denied. After conservative news service WND exposed the state's plans, public outcry stopped this regulation from being enacted.

If you think I am getting too far-out, lets look at a March 2015 story by Newsmax, a conservative Internet site. Evidently, the EPA likes to give out $15,000 grants to colleges for research on their "creative" ideas. Not much grant money but it seems to work. The EPA says showering counts for almost 17% of residential water use. That equals about 30 gallons per household per day and 1.2 trillion gallons per year. The EPA gave the University of Tulsa's chemical engineering school one of those $15,000 grants to develop a low cost wireless device to monitor water use by hotel guests when they take their showers. An associate professor at the school said, "(He) hopes to see the devise adopted by all major hotels, used across the country, and believes getting hotel guests to limit their showers to seven minutes is just the beginning." What does "just the beginning" mean? Here's a possible example. You better sit down for this one. Well, maybe not. Stanford University and the University of California each got one of those $15,000 grants to design a waterless toilet that uses a reusable cartridge for the "safe removal of human waste". This gives a whole new meaning to cleaning toilets and it could "just be the beginning"?

Here is a real life personal experience. In April of last year, the DOE required all new water heaters above 55 gallons to be hybrid heat pump models. Our 80-gallon water heater went out in January of this year and was under warranty. To replace it would have normally cost $650 dollars in labor costs. The new hot water heater now required by the federal government cost $1,960 after our plumber got a $300 rebate for us from the wholesaler. Because of the additional installation requirements for the new water heater, our plumber charged $1,080 to install it and my builder charged $750 to oversee the installation and make a minor modification to our house to accommodate it for a total cost of $3,790. We did receive a $450 check from the manufacturer of our old water heater since it was under warranty. Our net increase in cost due to the new government requirement was $2,690.

Our water heater manufacture's website said we could expect energy savings up to 30%. That sounds great but first I need to calculate how long is it going to take to get back our $2,690 and begin to see those savings? Let's see. Florida Power and Light estimates the electricity cost for our old water heater was $216 per year. A 30% savings would equal $65 per year. If you divide $2,690 by $65, that equals 41.4 years to break even on the additional cost of our new hybrid heat pump water heater before any true savings begins. Neither the water heater nor my wife or I will last that long. At least I do not have a smart monitor on my new water heater. Or, do I? If I do, the government can't monitor my hot water usage—yet!

I support the EPA and the DOE in looking at ways to reduce consumption of natural resources and curtail environmental pollution. I do not trust them to make sound rational decisions in their ineffective and authoritarian attempts to save energy that respect our cost of living and our individual rights. I also believe there is a psychological element of control that is pervasive in government—progressive or not.

Until I studied this cap and trade issue, I had no idea how far reaching and intrusive it could be. What if Americans didn't comply with government established goals or mandates? What would the government do to us? Would they eventually tell us what appliances we can and can't have, what the temperature in our homes would be, how many hot showers we can take, or when to empty the toilet? That would make sense to the power hungry and controlling progressives. Don't ever forget that we common citizens make stupid decisions, the progressives know what is best for us, and they need to "nudge" or, if necessary, "control" us in the right direction.

Cap and trade legislation is not dead. It is just in progressive hibernation like healthcare legislation was between the failure of Hillary Care and the implementation of Obamacare. It is too important to the progressives to give it up. They have the Dodd-Frank Act to control the financial industry and the FCC has adopted net neutrality regulation to control communications. If they convert Obamacare to the government run healthcare system they want, accomplish cap and trade legislation, and attempts to control communications become successful; America will become a "mushroom farm". Progressive Washington will no longer work for us; we will work for them. Sounds like the *Animal Farm* we will discuss in chapter 13 as well as a "mushroom farm".

It doesn't tale a Rhodes' scholar to figure out what happens to American citizens under this scenario. The progressive government could play us all like puppets, which would give a whole new meaning to the words "nudge" and "control". In implementing their Marxist based model, how far would these Washington progressives go? Would they take us to an authoritarian communistic style model? We would never go that far, would we? Look how far we have gone during the last 7 years. We never thought that would happen either, did we? Once these progressives taste that much power and the control, anything is possible. It would be the death of the America we know and love. We are getting closer and closer at an increasing pace.

Here is one last piece of surprising information before we move on. At least, it was surprising to me. Did you know that three state coalitions have organized cap and trade consortiums on their own? One is the Midwestern Greenhouse Gas Reduction Accord that had an agreement between six states and one Canadian province in 2007. Three states in the sponsoring Midwestern Governors Association and one other Canadian province took a wait and see approach and did not sign. Those three states and the Canadian province knew what they were doing. The accord adopted a plan in 2010 to begin in 2012. Never happened and the accord is now defunct.

The second consortium is the Regional Greenhouse Gas Initiative that organized in 2003 and began operation in 2008. The consortium is composed of ten states in the Northeast and Mid-Atlantic and three Canadian providences. They are still in existence and are participating in cap and trade involving fossil fuel power plants. All the original states are still involved with the exception of New Jersey that backed out in 2011.

The third consortium is the Western Climate Initiative. It was started in 2007 with five western states. In 2008 the consortium expanded to seven states and four Canadian providences. When I looked at their website, there are currently only the state of California and two

Canadian provinces remaining in the initiative. California appears to be going strong. That's not surprising. Long live progressive California. Let us always hope that what happens in California stays in California!

An economy based upon free market capitalism depends upon opportunity, risk taking, entrepreneurship, and hard work. That is the American way. In order to take those risks, corporations and entrepreneurs need to know the rules that affect them so they only have to cope with the variables associated with the risk itself. When the government is constantly threatening to change the rules and do change the rules, corporations and risk takers become more risk-adverse. Business in a capitalistic market flourishes during government certainty and reasonable freedom from government control. I don't mean freedom from laws and regulations that govern ethical behavior or protect the public from risks associated with dishonest practices, health issues, and personal injury. I am talking about overbearing government intrusion into business that stifles creativity, stifles business operations, and significantly increases costs.

If the general public truly understood the benefits they receive from free market capitalism and how it actually worked, they would be dumfounded by and unaccepting of the untruthful and misleading progressive propaganda they are bombarded with. For example, polls showed more than 60% of Americans supported raising the minimum wage when Obama proposed to raise the minimum wage from $7.25 to $10.25 per hour. He said it would bring millions of Americans out of poverty. The truth is that the CBO estimated it would raise the wages of 16.5 million Americans and lift 900,000 out of poverty but it would also cost 1,000,000 jobs because businesses may not be able to pay the increased wages. I take significant issue with the CBO's comment regarding increased wages bringing Americans out of poverty and I will discuss that untruth in chapter 10. After the CBO information was made public, another poll showed that 57% of those polled said it was an unacceptable trade-off. That is a significant turnaround after a more realistic story was known but what is the other 43% thinking? The problem is they're not. People! Aren't we a curious wonder?

There have been many demonstrations in major cities for a new minimum wage of $15 per hour at fast food restaurants such as

McDonalds and retailers such as Wal-Mart. What is the reason behind this minimum wage push across the country? In actuality, it has nothing to do with increased wages for low-wage earners. It is driven by a perverse progressive ideology to gain votes and by the unions to gain new members. The low-wage earners who are demonstrating are only pawns in this endeavor. I'll bet, if the truth were known, most if not all of the demonstrators have union ties and are not low-wage earners at the businesses where these demonstrations are taking place.

Here is an example of what I am talking about. The Daily Signal reported in September of 2014 the Los Angeles County Federation of Labor (Union) was successful in obtaining an exemption for union workers in Santa Monica's $15 per hour minimum wage proposal. This was after the same union supported the $15 per hour minimum wage increase. James Sherk of The Heritage Foundation said, "This proposal would force any worker in Santa Monica whose labor is worth less than $15 an hour to purchase union representation in order to hold a job. Unions should not be able to selectively exempt themselves from the harmful consequences of the minimum wage hikes they lobby for." The union said businesses and employees should have the ability to negotiate a wage below the law's mandated minimum in exchange for other benefits.

The Los Angeles City Council refused to go along with the union. The Los Angeles Times wrote, "This is hypocrisy at its worst. It plays into the cynical view that the federation is more interested in unionizing companies and boosting its rolls of dues-paying members than helping poor workers." So, what else is new? Sounds like standard union philosophy to me!

In October 2015, The Daily Signal reported Seattle voted for a $15 per hour minimum wage that will be phased in. The minimum wage went to $11 per hour in May 2015 and will increase to $15 per hour in 2017. The Seattle Metropolitan Statistical Area lost 700 restaurant jobs in 2015 between January and September while restaurant jobs were "booming" in the rest of the state with an increase of 5,800 new jobs. Between January and September in 2012, 2013, and 2014, restaurant employment in Seattle had increased by almost 4,000 employees. Is the 2015 decrease in jobs a coincidence? You decide.

The Daily Signal published a follow-up report on the topic in January of this year. Data showed a downhill economic trend for the cities of Chicago, Oakland, San Francisco, Seattle, Los Angeles, and Washington, D.C. where minimum wages were hiked to $10 or more per hour in 2015. The report said Chicago, San Francisco, and Oakland have sunk to five-year employment lows in the leisure and hospitality fields. Another example given was Washington, D.C. where suburban restaurants increased staffing last year by almost 5,000 workers while the city decreased by more than 200 jobs.

It appeared that McDonalds was hit the hardest by demonstrations nationwide. The vast majority of people who work at places like McDonalds are there for part time or temporary work, to supplement their retirement, or to supplement income from another job. Most are young people. This is not their career job as the demonstrators suggest. If it is, they need to re-think their careers and go back to school to gain a new set of skills. I don't mean to sound harsh. I am just being a pragmatist and a realist. Here is what our progressive friends and their $15 per hour wage are going to do to these young people and their future employment at fast-food restaurants. A friend sent me an email that contained a picture showing the new McDonald's touch-screen self-service kiosks. The email said we now have touch-screen cashiers and McDonalds plans to implement them in 2,000 U.S. locations. I could not verify that comment but found several websites that said they are installing or have installed 7,000 kiosks in Europe.

One liberal website I read said not to worry because 70% of McDonalds' business is drive-through business and the kiosks are all indoors. What naivety, dishonesty, or both. It won't be long until we will see kiosks at fast food drive-through windows as well. Subway is already experimenting with them. What can one expect when employees would be making $31,200 per year at $15 per hour and the restaurants have such low profit margins? Self-service kiosks or going out of business? Easy choice!

Not to be outdone, Governor Jerry Brown of California signed into law a bill to pay a minimum of $15 per hour and Governor Andrew Cuomo of New York has agreed to do the same. Don't these governors read the news or study the issues? They need to read my book. It really wouldn't make any difference. They are both progressives blinded to facts by their ideology.

I read a great April 15, 2015 article in The Blaze by Matt Walsh who calls himself a blogger, writer, and "professional truthsayer". His picture indicates he is a young person. The article is too long to quote in its entirety but here is one of Walsh's comments. He said:

> So, real talk: Your job isn't worth 15 bucks an hour. Sure, as a human being, you're priceless. As a child of god, you are precious, a work of art, a freaking miracle. But your job wrapping hamburgers in foil and putting them into bags—that has a price tag, and the price tag ain't anywhere close to the one our economy and society puts on teachers and mechanics. Don't like it? Well, you shouldn't. It's fast food. It's menial. It's not supposed to be a career. It's not supposed to be a living. … It isn't paying enough? OK, get another job. Get a second job. Get a third job. Get a different job."

Speaking of mechanics and obtaining a new set of skills, I have a wonderful story I saw on television to share with you. A blind man went to auto mechanics school at a New Mexico State University community college and became a mechanic. He has a genetic disease he inherited from his mother. His 15-year-old daughter has the disease and he did this to be a roll model and encourage her for the future. He said he felt like he was "living a dream" and was looking for a job. This was in June of 2014. I could not find an update whether or not he found a job but wow, what a story of courage, determination, and success. He puts these "whiners who demonstrate for un-deserved entitlements" to shame.

Here is an op-ed on the topic by an economist whom I greatly admire. He is a black conservative and his name is Thomas Sowell. He is a Senior Fellow at the Hoover Institute at Stanford University. He is one of the smartest purveyors of common sense that I know of and is an incredible pragmatist. The headline for the op-ed reads, "Is the simple act of thinking obsolete in modern America". The op-ed contains a series of common sense looks at issues of the day. One of the issues he covers is minimum wage. He pointed out a news story in the San Francisco Chronicle that said a local non profit would not be able to serve as many low-income minority youths if they had to pay a higher wage. He commented the same thing happens to "profit based" businesses when the minimum wage is increased. They hire fewer inexperienced young people.

Sowell then said Switzerland is one of the few countries in the world that does not have a minimum wage and quoted The Economist magazine in stating that Switzerland's unemployment rate has been consistently below 4%. The most recent quoted unemployment rate was 3.2%, which he said was typical. Sowell concluded by saying, "Does anyone think having minimum wage laws and high youth unemployment is better? In fact, does anyone think at all these days?" I fully understand that there are more complexities involved in this minimum wage discussion than a simple comparison to Switzerland but I completely agree with Sowell's last comment.

Reckless progressive regulation negatively affects all business and industry that in turn negatively affects the economy. In the end, that negatively affects all of us. Our economy is dead in the water due to increasing government control and the blatant marketplace uncertainty that continues to proliferate under this administration's progressive domestic policies. Remember, "they" know what is better for us more than "we" do. Like our progressive friend Cass Sunstein said in his book, "People make poor decisions and look back in bafflement." I am often amazed how many Americans are clueless about the real reasons why the economy is so lackluster. I will give the progressives credit for successfully sticking the blame on Wall Street, big banks, big business, and those greedy selfish rich people.

Did you know Sunstein's wife is Samantha Power who is our Ambassador to the U.N.? She replaced Susan Rice of Benghazi fame who became Obama's National Security Advisor. That job as Ambassador must be very strenuous. After only 19 days on the job Ms. Power took a personal trip to Ireland according to the State Department. I guess it was some R&R away from her new stressful job. I read where one person suggested she went to see the Charlie Chaplin Film Festival. The timing would work for the festival but she was also born there so maybe she was just relaxing with friends and relatives to relieve job stress. Good thing she had staff at home to participate in the emergency U.N. meeting that took place while she was gone to discuss the beginning of the crisis in Syria. We will get into this foreign policy mess in the next chapter.

Let's get back to progressive Washington and the economy. Where is the national debt? Do you know? Have you heard anything lately? Maybe not since the last presidential election? Just for fun, I looked up the National Debt Clock on the Internet. It said $19,354,101,5??, ???. The last five numbers were changing so fast I couldn't write them down. That's a lot of debt. Our poor kids, grand kids, great grand kids, and beyond. They will never be able to pay it off. It equates to $59,575 for every man, women, and child and $161,187 for every taxpayer. Taxes will have to rise just to keep up with the interest.

The only president I have heard mention the national debt since 2008 is President James Heller (William Devane) of *24: Live Another Day* fame who advertises investments in gold and silver on television for Rosland Capital. Even he isn't that optimistic about our economy's future but he is, after all, selling gold and silver investments. The national debt is undoubtedly one of the most serious domestic policy problems facing our country and absolutely nothing is being done about it. The EU recently gave us a preview of what could happen until they kicked it down the road—again. I wonder how long their road is? If Greece continues to dilly-dally with real and effective austerity measures, the road won't be that long for Greece or the EU. It will be interesting to see what effect the Brexit will have.

How long is our road? Here is what I recently read in The Daily Signal. Obama has added $7.5 trillion in debt since he became president. Singer Taylor Swift made $80 million in 2015. She performed 55 concerts. She would have to perform everyday for 3 years to pay "one day of interest" on the national debt. Boxer Floyd Mayweather, the country's highest paid athlete, made $300 million in 2015. He fought in only two fights. Wow, $300 million in two fights? He would have to fight everyday for over 331 years to pay off the national debt. Here is one for you football fans. Aaron Rogers is the highest paid football player and averaged being paid $1.29 million per game during regular season. He would have to play 406,752 games to pay one year's interest. I save the best for last. As you know, Bill Gates is listed as the world's wealthiest person (at least that we know about). His net worth is listed as $79.2 billion. It would take 229 times his lifetime earnings to pay off the national debt. I thought if we taxed the rich our budget problems would be solved.

Congress passed the Bipartisan Budget Act of 2015 and Obama happily signed it. Everyone, except "true" conservatives, danced around the table celebrating their great accomplishment in preventing a government shutdown and reaching a budget compromise. I just misspoke. What compromise? Here is what the budget act accomplished. There is a spending increase of $85 billion in the next three fiscal years. Then, beginning in 2020, the budget spending will begin to decrease each year with the vast majority of the decrease, $33 billion, taking place in 2025. This is worse than sad or laughable. It is appallingly irresponsible. Everyone in Washington, including the rest of America, will have amnesia in three years (probably before) and the government will be begging for more spending increases. Why are most republicans claiming success in working out a budget compromise and avoiding a government shutdown when what they did is such a failure? We will cover that in chapter 12.

Lets look back at the republicans' last failure. The debt-ceiling debacle in 2013 was inconceivable but it happened. Can you believe Obama and his progressive cohorts released convicted felons and punished American citizens in an attempt to make republicans look bad in front of the voting public? Obama said sequestration was going to be disastrous for the country? The Daily Signal reported the Obama administration claimed 34,000 illegal immigrants cost an average of $122 per-bed-per-day resulting in a daily cost of $4.15 million or an annual cost of $1.5 billion. One of the first things the Obama administration did was to release 2,226 illegal immigrants three weeks prior to sequestration that included 617 convicted criminals. Some of those criminals were felons. About 1,450 additional immigrants were released the weekend before sequestration. This information was released to the public by the Obama administration in a manner to maximize embarrassment for the republicans. It is unbelievable what the progressives are capable of doing to "beat up" their competition at America's expense.

Remember they closed the White House (which is really Our House) for tours? None of us are so dumb as to think there weren't alternatives to meet the requirements of sequestration without doing that. If I remember correctly, Obama was flying around the country at that time politicking for the Democratic Party. How much was it to operate that plane? About $228,000 per hour. Wouldn't that pay for a few hours of security so we could visit and see our house, especially for kids on field trips to Washington? They also tried to use airport controllers to slow down air traffic but that went too far and it backfired. They always find money for what they want including extravagant parties. Uh, I mean employee educational meetings.

Obama blamed sequestration on the republicans when it was actually his idea. When the republicans offered to amend sequestration to allow government departments to use their own judgment on how they cut expenses, Obama and his progressive friends wouldn't do it. Why? They wanted to use sequestration as a big club to beat the republicans over the head and they did it at the expense of American citizens. Republicans stood their ground on the national debt in the beginning and received a lot of criticism in that 2013 debacle because they got outsmarted, outgunned, and caved in to the progressives. I thought progressives didn't like to use guns. I guess it is only the metal kind they don't like. They sure shot enough bullets at the republicans to make them run to the hills and take shelter. The republicans rattled their swords and then succumbed to the democrat's pressure and made a half-wit compromise. I guess you could say the gun is mightier than the sword.

Obama has done absolutely nothing to address the national debt. When he took office he said he would reduce the national debt by half during his first term. What happened? The national debt has grown to over $19 trillion under his presidency and he has roughly six months to go. Since he took office in January 2009, our national debt has almost doubled from $10.6 trillion. That is a far bigger increase than under any other president. How can we be in so much debt? Obama, his progressive administration, and the progressive leaders in Congress said they had taken effective steps to address the issue over the next ten years. Isn't it interesting it always takes ten years for something to happen in government? How about doing it this year? BS, BS, and more BS from Obama and his progressive colleagues. And, BS does not stand for Boy Scouts.

Obama has kicked the national debt down the road to become someone else's problem after he is out of office. It will continue to get worse and will be increasingly more difficult to solve. In reality, the president apparently doesn't give a hoot about the economy or the national debt as long as he is able to have the money to do what he wants. The only thing he has done to address the economy is that idiotic stimulus program which was a total failure. I said earlier that, in reality, it was a stimulus program for his progressive friends and the unions that supported his election. Everything he and his administration have done has created an increased burden on our economic future. Addressing the economy and the national debt is somewhere between Washington and the Milky Way. And, it's much closer to the Milky Way.

Ronald Reagan has two great quotes on big government. He said, "Government's view of the economy could be summed up in a few short phrases: If it moves, tax it. If it keeps moving, regulate it. And if it stops moving, subsidize it." He also said, "The most terrifying words in the English language are: I'm from the government and I'm here to help." Milton Friedman provides the quote with the best visual image. He said, "If you put the federal government in charge of the Sahara Desert, in 5 years there'd be a shortage of sand."

It is no surprise that progressives do not like Reagan's philosophy and presidential success. We hear conservatives, classic liberals, and even progressives refer to him in respectful ways. I guess Hollywood had enough of hearing praise for Reagan. They recently tried to distort his presidency by proposing to make a comic film depicting Reagan as a demented person with Alzheimer's disease during his last year as president. How crass. His family and public outrage stopped it, at least for now.

Obama and his progressive colleagues really care about the American people, don't they? Well, actually, they don't even profess to do so. They routinely profess to only care about the middle class. How many times have you heard Obama and his progressive cohorts say they want to strengthen the middle class? Hillary Clinton repetitiously says it during her campaigning. It's a "bread and butter" motto for the progressives. Where do the poor and the rich stand? Don't they count? Well, let's see. I'll start with the poor. They believe they can buy the poor vote with entitlements—and do. Did you know that 50 million people are now below the poverty level? Approximately 48 million people are on food stamps, which is a 70% increase in food stamp recipients since Obama took office. The progressives argue that these high numbers are a result of the economy. I have a very long and very unstable bridge for that one.

The official mantra of the Obama administration is that if it were not for their actions, the economy would be much worse. Really? Exactly what actions are they referring to? I have heard and read numerous reports that say when someone visits a welfare office or signs up for Obamacare they are encouraged to sign up for more entitlements. I should also add they are encouraged to sign up to vote if they are not already registered. How convenient. Sign up for more free stuff and then go vote for those who gave it to you so you can get more free stuff. No wonder the progressives push hard against photo IDs for identifying legitimate voters. How many votes would they lose if the voters had to prove who they really are?

Entitlement programs are totally out of control. Here is an example I saw on Fox News. The Chicago Public Schools were doing automated robocalls to encourage parents to sign up for low-cost health insurance and food stamps. The recording stated there were 68,000 students not signed up for these benefits and their child was one of them. The parents were told to call and find out if they were eligible. This type of activity is classic for progressives. It is all about giving more people more stuff for more votes. As I write this, it raises a very interesting question in my mind. I wonder what the impact would be on reducing the cost of government entitlement programs if the government did not push them on people and forced people to come to the government and provide proof of need? We will never have the actual monetary answer to that question but we know what the answer would be in theory.

The especially devilish aspect of this atrocity is the more the government pushes entitlements on the poor, the poorer get poorer and the poor population grows larger. Joe Cortwright and Dillon Mahmoundi did a research study regarding poverty in the country's 51 largest metropolitan areas in 2014 for the City Observatory. The study showed the number of high-poverty neighborhoods where poverty tops 30% nearly tripled from 1970 to 2010 (1,100 to 3,100) and the number of people living in these high-poverty urban neighborhoods doubled from 2 million to 4 million. This is during a period of time when government handouts grew to an all-time high.

How many times have you heard the progressives say that the rich get richer and the poor get poorer? Did you know that is a catch phrase from the 1800s used to criticize free market capitalism? The phrase infers the inevitability of what Karl Marx called the Law of Increasing Poverty? Marx's Law of Increasing Poverty is not reality in America. The Minneapolis Federal Reserve Bank did a study a few years ago. The study indicated the lowest twenty percent of income earners moved up forty-four percent between the years of 2001 and 2007 while the highest twenty percent of income earners moved down thirty-four percent. The study said there was no evidence that the top one percent of earners gained any wealth at the expense of the middle or lower class. In fact, it has been a contention among many experts over the years that the poor and middle class are pulled up the economic ladder by the increased wealth of the rich. If this is true, it doesn't matter if the rich are growing their wealth at a higher rate than the poor or middle class? Everyone benefits and not at anyone's expense. I should also add that eventually our progressive friends in Washington, in addition to taxing top money earners at much higher rates, get a big chunk of the rich's earned money through estate taxes upon their death, which is double taxation. We never hear about that.

Even if the rich were taxed at 100%, it would not help the middle class, help the poor, or stop the national debt from increasing. The Pew Research Center categorizes the top 21% of the population as upper class, the middle 50% as middle class, and the bottom 29% as lower class. According to The Wall Street Journal, the Tax Policy Center reported the following for the 2014 tax year. The top 20% of taxpayers paid 83.9% of all taxes, the next 40% paid 19.3% of all taxes, and the bottom 40% was a minus 3.2%. The upper and middle class pay almost 100% of the federal income taxes. Look out middle class. If the upper class is now paying roughly 85%% of the federal income tax, the government has no option but to look to you to get additional money to pay the poor to stay poor.

According to the Tax Policy Center, 43% of Americans paid no federal income tax in 2013. In February 2016, The Daily Signal reported that number was 24% in 1962, 12.6% in 1969, 34.1% in 2000, 49.6% in 2009, 44.7% in 2011, and has stayed a steady 44% ever since. The report also said an astounding 33.67% of tax returns are filed only to claim benefits and not to pay any taxes. That number is up from 18.64% in 1990. Forbes reported this year the Tax Policy Center estimates 45.3% of American households will not pay taxes for 2015. They said this does not mean more Americans moved off the tax rolls since 2013 but the 2015 estimate is more accurate. The Daily Signal reported the last accurate data published by the IRS and the U.S. Census Bureau was in 2013 and the percent of Americans not paying any taxes was 44.2%.

I frequently found discrepancy in statistical numbers because there is often variation in data depending upon who is reporting it. In this case we have the Tax Policy Center and the IRS and Census Bureau. I have found these discrepancies often in researching data for this book and have made every effort to be as accurate as possible to present a correct picture. I find those reporting data often use the same primary source but interpret or express it somewhat differently. Sometimes it is only minor and their true intention is to present an accurate picture. Other times, the data is intentionally presented in a skewed and distorted manner to justify an ideological point. When that is done, it is almost always associated with progressive reporting. No matter which number is used to express how many Americans do not pay taxes, it proves our current progressive tax and tax credits championed by progressives effectively results in one of their major ideologies—income redistribution.

Here are three examples of income redistribution through refundable tax credits that are paid to taxpayers even if the taxpayer pays no taxes. We discussed the Obamacare health coverage tax credit in chapter 6. I roughly calculated that redistributes about $2 billion per year. I could not find any official numbers. Wonder why? The second refundable tax credit is the Earned Income Tax Credit (EITC). A single parent taxpayer can qualify for the following: $6,044 for a household making less than $46,227 per year with three or more children; $5,372 for a household making less than $43,038 per year with two children; and $3,250 for a household making less than $43,210 per year with one child? A married couple can qualify for the same tax credit if they make less than $51,567, $48,378, and $43,210 respectively. I could only the find direct cost for the EITC for 2012 and it was said to be about $56 billion. If you remember from the last chapter, it was estimated that EITC "improper payments" totaled approximately $18 billion for 2014 and I estimated the improper payments averaged $15.4 billion from 2010 to 2014, which equals about 26% of the total EITC benefit payout.

The third refundable tax credit is the Additional Child Tax Credit that is available to those who qualify and make less than $130,000 per year. What! $130,000 per year! Now, don't get your shorts in a bundle! A full credit is only available to those families who make less than $100,000 per year and it is limited to a maximum of $1,000. Geeze! The Treasury Inspector General for Tax Administration only estimated that between 25.2% and 30.5% of those payments were improper for a total somewhere between $5.9 billion and $7.1 billion.

Does it surprise anyone how income redistribution encourages single parent households, unemployment, and increased poverty as it is defined by the government? We desperately need tax reform to bring about a fair tax structure for all Americans and encourage people to be self sufficient and responsible for themselves. There has been a lot of talk during the presidential campaign about a flat tax. We should convert to a flat tax where everyone and I mean everyone should have "skin in the game" and pay something even if it's only a minimal amount per year. Everything I read says a flat tax is very feasible and workable if the bureaucrats and Congress had the b _ _ _ s to do it.

The progressives are a broken record with their continuous political mantra of income inequality where the rich get richer, the poorer get poorer, and the middle class is getting clobbered financially. I hear Hillary Clinton literally "screaming" concern for the middle class over and over to her campaign audiences. In reality, she is screaming, "Vote for me!" She has no plans of substance to do anything different from what is happening today.

Let me share with you an op-ed I read in The Wall Street Journal last November by Phil Graham, a former republican senator, and Michael Solon who is a visiting professor at the American Enterprise Institute and ex-budget advisor to Senator Mitch McConnell. Solon is now a partner with US Policy Metrics. The op-ed indicated the progressives could be basing their income inequality mantra on a famous study by Thomas Piketty and Emmanuel Saez who are professors of economics at the Paris School of Economics and the University of California Berkeley, respectively. That is, if the progressives are basing income inequality on anything but ideology. Piketty and Saez claimed their study indicated the rich get richer and the poorer get poorer. The problem with their study is their method was highly flawed because of they way they dealt with taxes, non cash compensation, social security, Medicare, Medicaid, employer based pensions, and multiple other government programs. They also used data from individual tax returns and ignored multiple earners.

The op-ed discussed a new study by economists Philip Armour and Richard Burkhauser from Cornell University and Jeff Larrimore of Congress's Joint Committee on Taxation that was published in the Southern Economic Journal. Their study corrected Piketty and Saez's study and the result was significantly different. The new study showed a 31% increase in income for the bottom quintile from 1979 to 2007 instead of a 33% decline. The second quintile which is the so-called working class rose by 32% rather than 0.7% as reported by Piketty and Saez and the income of the middle quintile, the middle class, increased by 37%, not 2.2%.

The op-ed said income is 24% less equally distributed in the U.S. than the average distribution of income in the 34 member countries of the Organization of Economic Co-operation and Development (OECD). The OECD members include 24 European countries, 10 countries from other parts the world, and the United States. Their stated purpose is to help governments foster prosperity and fight poverty through economic growth and financial stability. I had never heard of the OECD until I read this op-ed and looked at their website. OECD figures show the following for the U.S. in comparison to its other members: per capita GDP is 42% higher; household wealth is 210% higher, and median disposable income is 42% higher. The op-ed concluded, "How many Americans would give up 42% of their income to see the rich get less?"

Here are four great quotes on income inequality and income redistribution by three of my favorite people and one who is not a favorite. The first quote is by Margaret Thatcher. She said, "The problem with socialism is you eventually run out of other people's money." Winston Churchill said, "Socialism is a philosophy of failure, the creed of ignorance, and the gospel of envy, its inherent virtue is the equal sharing of misery." Ayn Rand said, "The difference between a welfare state and a totalitarian state is a matter of time." Vladimir Lenin said, "The goal of socialism is communism." My research for this book proves again and again these quotes to be true.

The rich count as important Americans in a progressive's book only if they provide opportunity for income redistribution or they are big political donors. The rich do not provide very many votes as compared to the middle class or lower class. I received an email from a friend that said, "Only in America...could the rich people, who pay 86% of all income taxes, be accused of not paying their "fare share" by people who don't pay any income tax at all." That email also said, "Only in America could politicians talk about the greed of the rich at a $35,000 per plate Obama campaign fund-raising event." I have heard that some fundraisers attended by Obama have been as much as $50,000 per plate.

How about the fundraiser for Hillary Clinton in Los Angeles this year sponsored by George Clooney? Attendees paid $2,700 direct to Clinton. Additional money was raised for the Hillary Victory Fund, the Democratic National Committee, and state democratic parties. Attendees paid $33,400. Co-hosts paid $50,000. And, co-chairs at the head table sitting with Clooney and Clinton paid $353,000. How about the hundreds of thousands of dollars Clinton was paid to speak to Wall Street groups and refuses to release the transcripts of those speeches to the public? Total hypocrisy!

The government needs more of your money and there are other ways to take your money besides income tax. Think Obamacare. What if cap and trade had passed? There has been discussion regarding a VAT tax like they have in Europe. Think about the increased business costs that get passed along to you as a result of increased government regulation. How much has excessive EPA regulations or the Dodd-Frank Act cost you? We haven't seen the costs of net neutrality yet. How many hidden fees do you pay for entitlements like free phones? What other "hidden taxes" are out there we do not know about?

What happens when more and more corporations leave the United States because we have the highest corporate tax rate in the world? Who picks up the difference in lost tax revenue? We taxpayers do. I have read articles in The Wall Street Journal during the past several months regarding major U.S. corporations that are in the process of moving or proposing to move their corporate offices out of the United States. They are not the first and will not be the last. I read that fifty firms have left the United States in the last ten years and most of those have left since 2008 when Obama came into office.

Treasury Secretary, Jack Lew, said congress should immediately enact legislation to stop this tax abuse of "our system" by these fleeing corporations. Whose system? America's or the progressives'? How about being competitive in the world regarding corporate taxes? Do they not get it or don't they care? I don't know the correct answer to that question but the result is the same. It seems that everything the progressives do to solve a problem does just the opposite of the stated goal. Lew's approach will drive more corporations out of the United States and make the problem worse. More regulation—less economy!

The progressives are intent on taxing the hell out of our personal income. Isn't opportunity and reward for hard work part of the fabric of America? Without an excessive and unfair tax structure they could not accomplish their mission of income redistribution. Let's talk about income redistribution and its impact on our standard of living and more importantly its impact on the poor. Obama said in a 2013 speech that a child born in our country in the bottom twenty percent income level has a less than five percent chance to move to the top income level and is ten times more likely to stay where he or she is. Obama said it was worse in America than in any other industrialized countries like Canada, Germany, and France. He said the combined threats of growing inequality and lack of upward mobility is "the defining challenge of our time" and poses a "fundamental threat to the American Dream".

Really? Let's talk about that. My wife and I have had the privilege of traveling to several so-called industrialized countries as well as so-called developing countries during the past few years. When we travel, we spend a lot of time talking to people who live there and studying their culture. Here is what we have found. We have seen a lot of beggars in industrialized European countries but do not remember seeing many people or very much housing that we would classify as poor. That doesn't mean it was not there. It just means we didn't see it. I cannot say the same for the developing countries we have visited. It could be that the percent of population in the middle class category for industrialized countries far exceeds ours and the percent of poor in those countries is much less than ours. That would actually make sense because of their socialistic approach to life.

Am I proving your point Mr. President? Let's see. I can tell you the disparity between the middle class in those countries and in the United States is profound. We all know the standard of living of the middle class in America. In the industrialized European countries, my wife and I observed clothes hanging on the balconies of middle class condos and apartments. Most can't afford houses. We were told the living facilities were either too small to have a dryer or they could not afford one. We were also told that it took two people working to have a small place to live and to buy a small automobile. I might add that none of these automobiles had an automatic transmission and the cost of gas was about double ours. A vast number of people ride motor scooters rather than drive cars? I can go on but you get the message. The industrialized countries you referred to that we have visited include France, Italy, Spain, Greece, Turkey, the United Kingdom, and several smaller countries along the Adriatic Sea. The difference in the standard of living for the middle class in our country versus the standard of living in those countries is astounding and the standard of living of those countries is where you and your progressive buddies want to take us.

Lets take a close look at the poor. Robert Rector of The Heritage Foundation wrote a critique of a book published in 2010 by Irwin Garfinkel, Lee Rainwater, and Timothy Smeedlig titled *Wealth and Welfare States: America a Laggard or Leader?* The critique was published this year in the National Review. Rector asserted that conventional wisdom says the United States has a smaller social welfare system and far more poverty compared with affluent European nations. Rector's critique of the book shows that to be wrong.

The book said social welfare spending in the U.S. differs from European nations in that we depend heavily upon both public and private resources where even the upper middle class in Europe depends mostly on government controlled resources and benefits. The examples of private resources being used in the U.S. for social welfare were healthcare, retirement benefits, and higher education. The U.S. still has the third highest level of per capita government social welfare spending among affluent nations and Rector said this was striking considering government spending in the U.S. is more tightly targeted to benefit the poor in contrast to European countries. When private sector contributions to healthcare, retirement, and higher education are added to our social welfare spending, the U.S. social welfare spending per capita rises to nearly twice the European average. Only Norway spends more per person.

Progressives consistently expound that the U.S. has a much higher poverty rate than the socialist based European countries. Rector says the progressives use a "relative poverty standard" that defines the poor as those whose income is below 50% of the national median. The median income in the U.S. is substantially higher than in European countries; therefore, the poverty in the U.S. falsely appears statistically higher. There was a study in the book that compared "apples to apples" and found the U.S. poverty rate was lower than the United Kingdom and only slightly higher than the other European countries. The U.S. rate was 8.7 % compared to 7.6 % for the others. This comparison did not include healthcare, education, or the high taxes paid by low-income families in Europe. An adjustment was made for these differences that showed the U.S. actually had a slightly lower poverty rate than affluent European countries.

The misconceptions about the poverty rate in America are also driven in part by flawed Census Bureau poverty reports that do not take into account the roughly $1 trillion per year that the government spends on means-tested welfare aid. Rector said the actual living standards of the poor in the U.S. vary significantly from perceptions. I have read this same observation in other articles. For example, government data shows the typical poor family in the U.S. has air-conditioning, a car, cable or satellite TV, 50% have computers, 43% have internet, and 40% have a wide-screen plasma or LCD television. The U.S. Department of Agriculture reported that only 4% of poor children were hungry for even a single day in the past year because of no money for food. The critique also said only 7% of poor in the U.S. live in crowded conditions and the average poor American family has more living space than the average non-poor family in Sweden, France Germany, or the United Kingdom.

All the information I have just presented is 100% in sync with the observations and dialog with the locals my wife and I have experienced during our travels in the last few years and provides a very strong case to debunk all the related gobbledygook being spewed out by the progressive runaway propaganda train. Let's look at this in a way that you might think is a little wacky but I find interesting. This discussion reminds me of Darwin's theory of natural selection and raises the following question. Is it better to allow the most successful society on Earth to continue that success socially and economically by natural selection or is it better to socially engineer that society to a much lower standard by taking social and economic success from the "fittest" and providing it to the "weakest"? Think about it.

Lyndon B. Johnson (LBJ) said in his January 8, 1964 State of the Union address, "This administration today, here and now, declares unconditional war on poverty in America." I wonder what LBJ would say now regarding the success of income redistribution in social and economic improvement for society? He is another president who tried to eliminate poverty by re-distribution of wealth through entitlement programs he referred to as the Great Society. The Great Society resembled FDR's New Deal and was a continuation of John F. Kennedy's New Frontier.

The Great Society is not any greater today and the poor are worse off. The Daily Signal reported in January of this year the official poverty rate has "hovered" between 10% and 15% during the past 50 years but the official statistical level of poverty does not include government entitlements and we know these entitlements have increased significantly since LBJ initiated his Great Society plan. Robert Rector was quoted as saying, "Taxpayers have spent $22 trillion on Johnson's war. Adjusted for inflation, that is three times the cost of all military wars since the American Revolution."

The Daily Signal report said marriage and work are the most important contributions to self-sufficiency. Since the 1960s those two institutions have declined. In 1964, only 7% of children were born out of wedlock. Today, that number is more than 40%. Even in good economic times, work rates among the poor are problematic with only an average of 16 hours worked per week per household. Entitlements drive people statistically further into poverty because people become less self-supporting but are able to maintain or improve their standard of living. Income redistribution does not drive people out of poverty. It makes them more dependent upon poverty.

I quoted Obama earlier in this chapter as saying the combined threats of growing inequality and lack of upward mobility is the defining challenge of our time and poses a fundamental threat to the American Dream. Robert E. Grady, an economic advisor to Gov. Chris Christie and Chairman of the New Jersey State Investment Council, wrote an op-ed in The Wall Street Journal in December of 2013 regarding Obama's statement. He said, "Here is the bottom line: In periods of high economic growth, such as the 1980s and 1990s, the vast majority of Americans gain, and have the opportunity to gain. In periods of slow growth, such as in the past four and a half years since the recession officially ended, poor people and the middle class are hurt the most, and the opportunity is curbed." He went on to say, "The point is this: If the goal is to deliver higher incomes and a better standard for the majority of Americans, then generating economic growth—not income inequality or the redistribution of wealth—is the defining challenge of our time."

Another Wall Street Journal op-ed written in March of this year by Lawrence B. Lindsey, a former economic advisor to George W. Bush, also addressed the issue. He said, "In 1968, government transfer payments (redistribution of income by the government) totaled $53 billion or roughly 7% of personal income. By 2014, these had climbed to $2.5 trillion—about 17% of personal income. Despite the redistribution of a sixth of all income, inequality measured by all three of the Census Bureau's indexes is far higher today than in 1968. Transfer payments under Mr. Obama increased by $560 billion. By contrast, private-sector wages and salaries grew by $1.1 trillion. So for every $2 in extra wages, about $1 was paid out in extra transfer payments—lowering the relative reward to work." He said two family earners have been the backbone of the middle class. Research has shown when families with children making between $20,000 and $50,000 per year attempt to have a second family member go back to work, the effective tax rate is between 50% and 80% when you account for lost government entitlement benefits. This has created a "working-class trap" instead of a "poverty trap" that is increasing inequality and keeping household income lower than it would be otherwise.

Obama and his progressive crew never quit coming up with new ideas to make those traps bigger. According to The Daily Signal, they announced a proposal in January of this year to provide free lunch to millions of children who lose access to subsidized meals when school is out for the summer. The children will receive an electronic benefits card loaded with $45 per month per child to buy groceries. This is in addition to approximately one dozen programs currently providing food to low-income families. If Congress accepts this proposal in Obama's 2017 budget request, it would add $12 billion over 10 years to the current 80 welfare programs that already cost $1 trillion. Congress' track record in vetoing these ridiculous entitlements is not stellar, even with the republicans in control.

Lindsey said the number of two-earner households decreased during Obama's first six years in office while the number of single-worker households increased by 2.6 million. This is the reason the middle class has shrunk and inequality has increased. He concluded that unless we increase the number of people wanting to work and increase the number of jobs available through economic improvement, inequality would only increase. I enjoyed one of his ending statements in the op-ed. He said, "The appeal of redistribution is understandable, but voters who think the progressives running today are going to reduce inequality are falling into the same trap as people entering into fifth or sixth marriages—the triumph of hope over experience." Well-said, Mr. Lindsey!

The problems of the poor result from socioeconomic issues, not lack of opportunity. No country in the world offers people, poor or not, the opportunity to improve their economic status like America—not even close! That opportunity is there for the taking. That is still true in our current economic situation. I said in my leadership book that personal success is achieved through honoring and respecting those around you, always being ethical, channeling your motivation and desires toward specific career and personal goals, and being willing to pay the price of achieving those goals through sacrifice and hard work. Unless she or he has a mental or physical challenge that prevents them from doing that, any American can be successful. Being poor has nothing to do with it. I would love to see a chart showing how many financially successful people started out being poor. It would be amazing. Being poor might make it harder for some people to be successful but that is life. There is always someone who has it harder in life and someone who has it easier. That is true for all of us, no matter what socioeconomic status we inherited.

Even those who are mentally challenged can often overcome their disabilities to be economically successful. For example, the grocery store chain where we shop hires several mentally challenged people who bag our groceries. One mentally challenged person is a cashier. Even if they receive government entitlements, they are working and don't depend upon the government for their entire livelihood. I might add that they do a very good job and are proud of what they do. I always enjoy interacting with them when I check out, as do they.

Mr. President, let's go back to your original premise that a child born in our country in the bottom twenty percent income level has a less than five percent chance to move to the top income level and is ten times more likely to stay where she or he is. What you said is probably true but your premise reflects the outcome of the problem and not the problem itself. Income redistribution is the problem and encourages people to remain in poverty rather than encourage them to fight their way out. It's as simple as that.

We have already discussed the impact entitlements have in the decline of two-worker families and the resulting impact on inequality. Entitlement programs also encourage single women who live in poverty to have children to obtain greater benefits, which in return creates a vicious cycle of socioeconomic issues that impact inequality. The Heritage Foundation did an analysis that indicates children raised in the increasing number of single-parent homes are four times more likely to be living in poverty than children raised by married parents with the same education level as the single parent. Children who grow up without a father in the home are more likely to suffer from a number of social and behavioral problems. As these children progress into adulthood they are three times more likely to end up in jail and fifty percent more likely to be poor adults. Then what happens? The cycle continuously repeats and the number of people affected proliferates on an increasing basis.

The Heritage Foundation also reported a study in October of last year by the American Enterprise Institute and the Institute for Family Studies that supports what was just said from a different perspective. The study found that states where most parents are married are better off than those where they are not. These states have $1,451 more per capita GDP, 10.5% more upward mobility for low income children, a 13.2% decrease in child poverty, and $3,654 more in median family income. The researchers controlled other socioeconomic factors and concluded, "The states share of married parents is generally a stronger predictor of economic mobility, child poverty, and median family income than education, race, and age."

Here is a sobering thought. The Cato Institute did a study in 2013 that showed welfare benefits pay more than the minimum wage in 35 states. They found the welfare benefits in 13 states equate to more than a $15 per hour wage. Maybe those McDonalds demonstrators should move to those 13 states. The author of the study concluded, "One of the best ways to climb out of poverty is taking a job but as long as welfare provides a better standard of living than an entry-level job, recipients will continue to choose it over work."

The Daily Signal said in May 2015, "The more we spend on the poor, the harder it seems for them to attain decent, productive lives in loving families. The government has spent $22 trillion on anti-poverty programs since the beginning of the war on poverty in 1965 (LBJ's Great Society) but the poverty rate is nearly the same rate today as in 1969, fluctuating between roughly 11% and 15%." The article went on to say, "Thomas Jefferson and Benjamin Franklin believed government has an obligation to the poor. But any aid policy, they insisted, would include work requirements for the able bodied." Benjamin Franklin said, "I think the best way of doing good to the poor is not making them easy in poverty but leading or driving them out of it." The article concluded, "Among the most destructive features of the post-1965 welfare regime has been its unintentional dismantling of the family. By making welfare wages higher than working wages, the government essentially replaced fathers with a government check. The state is many families' primary provider."

I want to close this discussion with two other reports I received from The Daily Signal. They reported in October 2015 the state of Maine has announced that they have reduced their food stamp recipients by 22% from 255,663 to 199,157. How did they do that? They implemented a policy that required adult recipients to work 20 hours per week, volunteer for about one hour per day, or attend a class in order to maintain food stamps beyond three months. A policy director with the Maine Equal Justice Partners said, "I hear language that says this is a good thing because it is forcing people to work. People don't need to be forced to work. People need to be helped to find a job." Progressives! You can't make this stuff up.

In April 2016, The Daily Signal reported Kansas instituted a work requirement and 40% of the food stamp recipients found work within three months and 60% found employment within a year. One person who has been unemployed for four years found employment in the publishing industry and now earns $45,000 per year. The state's food stamp caseload dropped 75% and the state's expenses for food stamps went from $5.5 million per month to $1.2 million per month for able-bodied adults.

So, Mr. President, the more you push entitlements on the poor, the more you are enslaving them into poverty for their entire lives. Is that what you want? Didn't you learn from your fellow democratic compadre LBJ? I opine that it is what you want because entitlements for the poor result in progressives obtaining votes and power in perpetuity from those who get the entitlements and you progressives obtain support from well-meaning classic liberals because of their unwavering liberal ideology. These classic liberals do not understand your true motives.

I have heard many successful people who grew up in poor neighborhoods give the same advice on how to address the issues of the poor. One, wean the poor from entitlements and force personal accountability. That doesn't mean that you don't provide economic assistance to those who are "truly in need". Two, help the poor find economic opportunity. Three, stick to one and two and don't "backslide". Backslide is an old expression I learned as a kid in the Baptist church that means to "relapse into your old bad ways". It is economic opportunity and motivation, not entitlements that wipe out poverty and improve the financial position of the poor. I would also add that emotional support is needed as they make this transition.

We just discussed how progressive economic redistribution will not improve the socio-economic status of the poor and will only pull down the middle class in America to that of Europe or worse. The same will happen to the rich if we continue down this progressive Marxist road. The rich will become less in number and corruption will become much more commonplace among those who strive to be rich. In countries with Marxist style governments, job opportunities are less in number, personal success is more difficult to realize, and income levels are lower than we enjoy in America. It is commonplace around the world for those who strive to be rich in Marxist countries to become rich by giving political and monetary support to the government and government officials in order to obtain the opportunity for economic success that all Americans enjoy today because of our Constitution and traditional American values.

We discussed the fallacy and hypocrisy of how the progressive elite professes to be profoundly concerned about the economic well-being of the poor and middle class and expound how the rich benefit economically at their expense. Part of the discussion was the very expensive fundraisers where the progressives court rich democrats and non-democrats to raise campaign money. I wonder how much that fundraising cost taxpayers including the middle class when those favors are returned?

The real big hitters don't even come to dinners. Did you know that Obama entertained children of billionaires at the White House? Was he looking for advice on how to improve the economic well-being of their fellow Millennials or was he looking to improve the economic well-being of his party? The latter is illegal when it is done in the White House. Our president plugs up the Keystone XL Pipeline that creates jobs and provides energy independence and the Democratic Party supposedly gets $100 million from a donor opposed to the pipeline—$50 million direct and another $50 million in his fundraising efforts. That is a pretty good return for plugging a pipe. Solyndra's corporate executives and investors were significant campaign contributors to Obama and the democrats and we know the rest of that story. How much does Elon Musk contribute? Our friends at Planned Parenthood do disgusting quid pro quo campaign contributions.

These examples are only the tip of the iceberg. Those who give the progressive politicians money are not poor or middle class but they sure get a lot of income opportunity in return. This must be a surreptitious component of the progressive's income redistribution plan to redistribute income to themselves. Like I said, the further a country's government goes down the Marxist path; the more intense this pay to play issue becomes.

How about union contributions? It was reported that Obama received hundreds of millions of dollars in campaign contributions from the unions during his presidential campaigns. That doesn't count the huge amount of time spent by union members campaigning for him or union members voting for him. The leaders of the unions got unfettered access to the White House after his election and the Obama administration showers them with favorable legislation and government rulings. This is another example of the surreptitious progressive politician income redistribution plan. That must be one heck of a plan.

Here is the biggest hypocrisy by the progressive elite involving income and it doesn't even involve progressive politicians. It involves the entertainment industry. I personally have "zero" patience with the multitude of entertainers who bad-mouth our country by putting down the principles of our Constitution, trashing our capitalistic free market system, and criticizing the rich. It is particularly hypocritical for them to be criticizing the rich in corporate America. I especially despise entertainers who criticize our country during photo ops in countries run by dictators where the people are suffering. This is hypocrisy on steroids! When I see them criticizing our country on television, I blurt out loud, "If you don't like America, get the hell out and move to the country where you are doing your photo op and see how you like it!" It really hacks me off just writing about it. How do they make "their" money? Aren't they rich because of free market capitalism and the Constitutional governance they condemn?

Here is an interesting look at the entertainment industry's hypocrisy. I put sports figures in the category of entertainers. I was reading a USA TODAY newspaper on an airplane and ran across an article listing all the salaries of professional baseball players. Do you know how many players make over $1 million per year? I counted 374 players. Their average salary for 2015 according to the Associated Press was about $4.25 million and that is for part-time work. The highest paid player was reported to make $31 million. These salaries do not count the enormous amount of money many of them make on advertising endorsements. What do they do for a living? They entertain us and provide a place to buy hotdogs and beer. They also give us a means to exercise our core personality traits of pride and ego and espouse our anger trait when we are not pleased with the outcome.

How much do players in other sports make? Plenty! At least as much, if not more! How much does the National Football League (NFL) boss make? He made $11.6 million in 2011, $29.5 million in 2012, $44.5 million in 2013, and $35 million in 2014. His salary in 2013 included a one-time payment of $9 million but he must have really excelled in performance between 2011 and 2012 to get an $18 million raise in one year.

How much money do movie stars make? It is in the millions for most and the tens of millions for many. My research on the Internet found the top twenty movie star incomes during recent years ranged from $30 million to $156 million per year. Five of them made over $100 million. Information on musical entertainers' income was the hardest to find and what I found was somewhat contradictory but I think one can get a sense of their earning power from three sources I reviewed. One source was Billboard that said the 2014 annual income for the top 40 musicians was in the following ranges: 1 at $40 million; 4 between $26 and $35 million; 11 between $16 and $25 million; and 14 between $5 and $15 million. Celebrity Net Worth said there were 50 musical artists with net worth over $125 million. The top net worth on the list was $1.2 billion. TheRichest's list of top 100 richest musical entertainers based upon net worth ranged from a low of $40 million to a high of $1.2 billion. There were two people listed at $1.2 billion; one was an entertainer and the other was a musical arranger. Successful sports figures, movie stars, and musical entertainers are very well paid.

Not very scientific but I couldn't resist comparing middle class salaries to movie star salaries as presented in Parade magazine's annual report for 2016, which was included in my Sunday newspaper. My calculations showed the average salary of 28 middle class jobs was $76,000. The average salary of nine entertainers was $24,000,000. This is a great example of the entertainment industry's hypocrisy in criticizing the rich versus the poor and middle class.

Here is an interesting group—models. They may not exactly fit the category of entertainment but let's throw them in for good measure. Their job is to influence us on what we wear and to accessorize our personal wardrobes. They also influence us on what makeup to use, how we want to smell, and various other products. Many times they have to be practically naked to do their jobs. Sometimes they are naked. They also have to learn how to pose and walk down those narrow runways. Not everyone can be a model depending upon his or her appearance and physical stature. Where is the progressive politically correct condemnation on that one?

I accept the fact that it is a demanding career but how much is a job like that really worth when considering its importance to the well-being of our society? Forbes reported in August of 2014 the top 21 models made a combined income of $142 million for an average of $6.8 million. The top model made $47 million and her NFL superstar football player husband made only $31.3 million. There is no gender income inequality in that family. They made a total of $78.3 million together. The rest of the models in the list made an average of $4.75 million.

Now that we have an idea of what entertainers and models make, let's take a quick look at those greedy no-good overpaid corporate executives in business and industry. I bet they make a hell of a lot more. My Internet research discovered the following. One site said the average CEO salary for all CEOs was $740,000 including bonuses. The 90th percentile average was $1,065,794. That didn't seem high enough based upon what I hear and read from the mainstream news media and the progressives regarding the huge salaries of overpaid corporate CEOs so I decided to look further. Another source said the average CEO salary for the S&P 500 in 2011 was $9.6 million. I thought the average salary should be more than that since these are the biggest companies in America so I kept looking. A Bloomberg website showed most of the top 250 CEO salaries in the S&P 500 for 2012 to be in the $10 to $30 million range including benefits.

That still seemed low based upon the rhetoric from mainstream news media and progressives. After my extraordinary persistence, I finally found some of those real super greedy CEO salaries. Now we're getting somewhere. I found Bloomberg data that showed a total of four CEOs in the S&P 500 that made over $50 million. One made, oh my gosh, $137 million. Those salaries are almost as much as some of those entertainers who bad-mouth our country and tear down our capitalistic free enterprise system.

Who deserve higher salaries; people who entertain us and influence our clothes, jewelry, and perfume purchases or those who lead business and industry that powers the economic engine for America's future? Actually, if it were not for the leadership of our country's economic engine these entertainers and models would not even have a job because no one could afford to watch them entertain or buy the clothes, jewelry, and perfume they advertise.

This hypocrisy in the entertainment industry does not apply to all entertainers, particularly sports entertainers, but it includes a significant number. Taken as a group they deserve the designation of being hypocrites. They need to join their hypocritical progressive friends in reciting the following every day: We (can only in America-the land of opportunity) hold these truths to be self evident, that all men (and women) are created equal, that they are endowed by their Creator (that is more and more coming under intense fire) with certain unalienable Rights (that is more and more only for those in minority positions), that among these are Life, Liberty and the pursuit of Happiness. What I just said is word for word from The Declaration of Independence with my personal additions in parentheses. These people who put down our country should be grateful to be Americans and what America has provided to them. They should not expound anti-American rhetoric and utopian nonsense based upon skewed and unrealistic personal ideology.

Let's now explore another very serious topic—American freedom, progressive ideology, and the National Security Administration (NSA). George W. Bush and not our progressive friends started the NSA monitoring system but he went through Congress to do so. How far should the government go in protecting our national security in relation to infringing upon our freedoms? That's a very good question. I recently heard one of the sponsors of the bill that created the NSA spying program say the current practices far exceed the original intent of the bill. These spying practices increased significantly after Obama took office and intended checks and balances have become loosey-goosey (not a very technological phrase but it makes the point).

Obama established a so-called independent panel of knowledgeable experts to oversee the NSA to prevent abuse of information. The panel was to be established by James Clapper, Director of National Intelligence. Yes, Clapper is the same person who lied to Congress about what information the NSA was collecting. After some backlash, the White House clarified that Clapper would not be leading the panel. Guess who is on the panel? Our friend Cass Sunstein. Progressives watching progressives! It's like the fox watching or I should say feasting in the hen house. Remember, Sunstein advocated that we are bunch of bumbling idiots that look back in bafflement on our stupid decisions; therefore, we need the government to make decisions for us. How much confidence does that give you that there is any serious intent to protect our privacy and personal independence? Sunstein is no different than any other progressive leader. At least he is honest about his feelings.

The panel released their recommendations in January and July of 2014. They basically said the collection of telephone call records should end because it does not comply with the law but the government could continue to conduct warrantless searches for communications data. That is the last information I could find on the topic. I guess any follow-up reporting was in the La-La Land Gazette.

Where does this lead regarding the NSA collecting information for national security versus collecting information on all citizens to see what we are doing? It takes us straight to George's *1984*. Remember the Utah Data Center? The center has faded from public view but construction was completed late in 2014. Remember the big controversy regarding the center's ability to spy on us? This is another news story that was relegated to the La-La Land Gazette. I went to the NSA site on the Internet to see what I could find and here is a summary of my findings. The facility is 1 million square feet and cost $1.5 billion. The site talked in terms of exabytes, zettabytes, and yottabytes. I did learn that one yottabyte is equal to one septillion bytes of storage. Hope you understand that. I don't. All I know is that the computer that I'm using to write this book has 256 gigabytes of storage.

The future storage capacity of this facility is beyond the comprehension of computer neophytes like myself. The site addressed the privacy concerns that were so controversial during the debacle surrounding the Edward Snowden NSA leaks and the NSA congressional hearings. Under the heading Openness and Transparency - Our Cooperation with Privacy Groups was the following statement, "As proof of our genuine concern for privacy protection, we recently gave permission for several privacy groups to fly their little blimp over our massive data center. We would like to thank these airborne privacy pioneers for the stunning photo below of our impressive facility. By allowing harmless publicity stunts like these, we can have our data and store it too." What is that supposed to mean? Absolutely nothing! It actually sounds arrogant and sarcastic but appeared it was meant to be serious. I find their comment to be quite concerning.

Here is something I read on Wikipedia. I did not check multiple sources to confirm the information but it is commonsensical. The website said that the Utah Data Center is alleged to be able to process all forms of communication including the complete contents of private emails, cellphone calls, personal data trails, parking receipts, book store purchases, and other digital "pocket litter". The site also commented on a NSA clandestine surveillance program called PRISM. PRISM was launched in 2007 and is supposed to collect Internet communications of foreign nationals from multiple major U.S. Internet firms. Documents were leaked to the media in 2013 that raised concern that PRISM was doing electronic surveillance on live Internet communications and was storing information that exceeded their intended scope of surveillance and legal authority. They easily have the capability to do that and that capability is increasing as evidenced by what I learned on the NSA website.

Think about how sophisticated the Internet is even without the capability of the Utah Data Center. Here are personal examples of what I am talking about. I was in the process of verifying information that I included in this book. To do so, I Googled a reference that was included in the bibliography of my leadership book. The fourth Internet site down was my book. I was mystified and amazed. I clicked on that site and my bibliography came up from Amazon books. There are probably millions of books out there and my bibliography shows up within a couple of seconds on the Internet.

I discovered a more profound example after I experienced this one. My wife and I were planning a trip to England and France. One of her favorite places in France is Giverny where Claude Monet's garden and home are located. As we were planning our trip, I went to the Google Maps website to determine how far Giverny was from Paris. I was more than surprised when the map popped up showing the route, distance, and the route's starting point in Paris with the name of our hotel and the dates we were staying there. The same thing happened when I looked up the route in France between Nice and Vence, which was our next destination. Again, the hotel we were staying at in Vence showed up with the exact dates we were staying there. How is that possible? We booked the hotels by telephone direct with each hotel chain's reservations staff.

Obviously, the information was obtained from my email confirmation from the hotel chain, my computer, or both. You figure. I can't. If this can happen, it is unthinkable what the government can do with the NSA and its probing tentacles.

I'm going to sound paranoid when you read my next comments and I am. An eventual priority in data collection for progressive Washington politicians, if they achieve their ultimate goal, would be to obtain information to affect election results that would keep them in power in perpetuity. How would they do that? Easy. They can find out personal information including contacts with certain organizations (think IRS scandal) and either encourage or punish (I mean nudge) individuals toward progressive ideology and progressive politicians or shut individuals down if their political preference is in opposition. The same scenario applies to organizations. How about personal manipulation (I mean nudge) to make us better citizens and do what is best for the whole of society as "they envision it"? Why not? They know what is best for us. If you do anything that is not in the best interest of society (in their eyes), you can be punished or rewarded depending upon their choice to effect a behavior change. Remember the electrical shock experiments on rats you studied in Psychology 101? Basically, it's the same thing.

It has been reported that the NSA has already monitored several individuals who had nothing to do with terrorism or national security. It remains unclear why they were monitored. Think about the intensity with which the government can monitor us with the new NSA facility? How you vote? Who do you associate with? Do you support the government in power or not? What if you don't? What happens to you then? Do you get a government appointed hearing officer to whom you have to prove you allegiance to the government or face punishment? What is the punishment if you can't prove allegiance? Will there be re-education camps like those in Vietnam during and after the Vietnam War? I saw a well known legal expert on television recently say in response to this NSA revelation that if the government looked hard enough they could find something on every citizen that could be considered illegal and subject to punishment. I don't know about you but that scares the hell out of me. It is exactly what Orwell warned about and here it is right before our very eyes.

I want to make an extremely important point. If anyone doesn't think the information collection capabilities of the federal government is a potential forerunner to "big brother" watching us, I have a superabundance of bridges. This concern is applicable to Washington no matter what ideology is in power but it obviously goes without saying that there is a much greater concern with progressives. How far the progressives would go if they were to continue to retain power in Washington is unknown. You don't know until you know but I can assure you it would be very intrusive in our lives and used for their political and personal benefit.

Here is my answer to the earlier question of how far the government should go in protecting our national security versus intruding upon our rights and freedoms. Personal rights and freedoms should always out-trump intelligence for national security unless our country or we individually are in imminent danger or there is a reasonable suspicion of imminent danger. If you don't believe me, ask the estimated 100+ million citizens that Mao, Stalin, and other progressive ideologues put in their graves for the sake of supporting Marxist based ideological control. Personal rights, freedom, and security should be a balance and reasonable common sense should prevail.

A good example is the conflict between Apple and the FBI in obtaining information from the San Bernardino terrorist attacker's iPhone. This is a big to do about nothing. Just use common sense and do what is best for society. Apple was wrong in their position. The FBI should have been able to get a court order to obtain the information and Apple should have cooperated for the safety of Americans. I will admit this was a difficult issue for Apple. I understand their loyalty to their customers and they have to deal in some countries where the government system is corrupt but that is life and Apple should do the right thing. They should deal with each information privacy issue on its own merits and make the "morally and legally correct" decision even if it means they may loose business for that decision.

How do we prevent losing our personal rights and freedom? It is reasonably easy but not commonly done since only about half of Americans do it. The answer—vote and vote informed! It is unbelievable to me that only about half of eligible voters actually vote. We need to vote politicians into power who value personal rights and freedoms and adhere to and practice our personal values. How do we do that? Do your homework and vote 100% of the time you have an opportunity.

We touched upon immigration in chapter 3 and addressed the issue of young kids poring over the border from Central America in chapter 6. It needs further discussion under progressive domestic policy. Obama asked Congress last year for $3.7 billion to take care of these illegal kids, improve border patrol, and to hire judges to process the kids once they get here. The White House said this legislation would process an additional 55,000 to 75,000 cases per year. Part of the money was to go toward efforts to repatriate and reintegrate migrants back to Central America and to mount a media program to explain the dangers of migrating from Central America to the United States. If Obama and his administration were so concerned about these kids coming to America, flooding our system, and putting themselves in danger then why did they not take action months ago instead of turning their heads until it became public knowledge?

Obama says many of these immigrants will be repatriated but he has to follow the existing law and give them due process in the U.S. Really? That's a new approach. I guess following the law works when it's convenient. Why doesn't he just ask Congress to amend the current law so Central Americans would be treated like Mexicans and Canadians and automatically be sent home? The next step would be to give the border patrol the support and authority they need to do their job and actually enforce the law by sending home those crossing the border illegally. That would stop it. Congress did not approve the $3.7 billion. Judicial Watch reported in April of this year that the Obama administration is spending $19 million to provide free instruction to illegal immigrants so that they can become citizens. Judicial Watch said, "… the obvious goal is to register more immigrant voters because they tend to be Democrat." Judicial Watch is absolutely correct.

Well, the government did fly about 40 mothers and children home to Honduras. I assume that was a token response to the criticism that ensued when this situation become public. We could lease a lot of airplanes for $3.7 billion and send them all home first class. I can guarantee that would stop this influx of illegals when people in those countries learn spending their life savings will go for naught. How can families even send their kids to America with these awful human "coyotes" that are known to abuse these kids physically and sexually? I know things are tough in those countries for young children and their families want a better life for them but it can not be worse than what many of them are enduring coming to the United States?

Progressives want to promote the reason these children are leaving their home country is to avoid violence, which allows them to be classified as refugees. There is violence in those countries but is that the real reason? Is it because of economic opportunity? I have tried to understand why these families subject their kids to such potential abuse and to physical and emotional abandonment but I honestly do not know. Some of these kids do have family in the U.S. but many have none. Whether these kids have family here or not, I can't imagine abandoning your children for any reason and knowingly subjecting then to such danger.

The progressives will tell you this whole issue is George W. Bush's fault (poor George again) because he signed the current law into effect in an effort to stem sex slavery involving kids. How ironic that this law actually created child sexual abuse under Obama. There is a slam-dunk easy fix and Obama would never do it. Rescind the law. He would rather spend billions of our dollars to house and process these kids for the future of the Democratic (Progressive) Party and not provide any real solution to stem the future tide.

Not all of these illegals are innocent kids. Judicial Watch reported in September of 2015 that DHS told them many of these immigrant kids have ties to street gangs. The most notorious gang is Mara Salvatrucha or MS-13. They are renowned for such crimes as drug distribution, murder, rape, robbery, home invasion, kidnappings, and vandalism. The Justice Department's National Gang Intelligence Center said street gangs like MS-13 are responsible for the majority of violent crimes in the U.S and are the primary distributer of illicit drugs. The Judicial Watch report said, "MS-13 went on a recruiting frenzy at U.S. shelters housing the illegal immigrant minors and they were using Red Cross phones to communicate." What a mess!

Our immigration policy pertaining to these kids got worse a few months ago. Obama offered them free airline transportation. That's correct. Free for them at a cost to you. They are no longer officially termed Unaccompanied Alien Children. They are now officially deemed Central American Minors. Judicial Watch said DHS is accepting applications from "qualifying parents" for children from the same Central American countries as before—El Salvador, Guatemala, and Honduras. The kids are then granted a special refugee parole status. That includes such things as a free education, food stamps, medical expenses, and living expenses. A U.S. based parent will initiate the application for the child. To qualify the parent must be a permanent resident, a parolee himself or herself, or a beneficiary of Obama's recent amnesty program. They do have to pass a DNA test to prove the relationship. Based upon our past history in such matters, I wonder how successful the criteria will be in determining legitimacy? Judicial Watch said most of these parents have lived in the U.S. illegally for years.

A disturbing fact brought out by Judicial Watch is that only organizations and individuals friendly to the program were invited to the briefing announcing it. The press was not invited. Wonder why? I bet the La-La Land Gazette was there. The people at the briefing were told this was a family reunification program that was completely funded by American taxpayers, there was no idea how much it will cost, and they wanted to make sure it was open to as many people as possible. That is so insane that I have no comment.

Do future votes by these immigrants and their relatives really matter that much to the progressive politicians? You bet they do. No one really knows the number of current or potential votes that are involved but it is significant and 100% of those votes go to the progressives that will take care of them. A survey done by Old Dominion University last year indicated there are currently more than 1 million voters who are not citizens and vote illegally. How can they vote? Easy! We routinely learn about how progressives vigorously fight proposed voter laws that identify those who are not eligible to vote because they say these laws are discriminatory. They sure are. They discriminate between those voters who are legal and those who are not.

The Daily Signal reported last year the federal agencies responsible for immigration and naturalization routinely fight efforts to compare voter rolls with lists of known non-citizens. An agency specifically mentioned was The Election Assistance Commission, which is a small government agency responsible for printing the federal voter registration form. The forms are state specific and this agency routinely denies instructions or request for information on the forms that would be used to identify non-legal voters. The American Civil Rights Union, a conservative based advocacy group, has requested the Supreme Court to take on a case involving Kansas and Arizona in an effort to overturn a decision by the 10th Circuit Court of Appeals that blocks these two states' efforts in preventing illegal voting.

A May 2015 survey by Rasmussen indicated 35% of voters believe tax-paying illegal immigrants should be allowed to vote, 60% said no, and 5% were undecided. Politically, it broke down like this: 53% of democrats said yes; 21% of republicans said yes; and 30% of independents said yes. What do you think? To me, illegal is illegal. It doesn't matter if illegal immigrants pay taxes or not.

Illegal immigrants are not the only illegal voters in the country. California is one of, if not the worst, states regarding illegal voting by dead people. A May 2016 story by The Daily Signal said, "Hollywood has always loved making films about the walking dead, but in Southern California it appears they have a real life problem with 'zombie' voters." The story told of hundreds of deceased voters who vote in Southern California. Here are two examples provided in the story. One person died in 2006 but voted in 2008, 2010, 2012, and 2014. Another example was a woman who died in 1988 and has been voting for 26 years. Illegal voting is nothing new in our country's history but it should never be condoned for political advantage and every effort should be made to prevent it.

We are not enforcing existing immigration laws and haven't since the progressives have been in power in Washington. The White House and the Department of Justice make up the rules as they go to meet their political objectives. They say the border is secure. It is not. They say we need a comprehensive immigration law when following the existing law would go a long way toward solving our immigration problems. How about sanctuary cities? How can they override federal law? They do it because the Obama administration not only allows them to do so but also assists them. The Daily Signal said in October 2015 there are now 340 sanctuary cities in the United States and they release roughly 1,000 detained illegal immigrants each month. Judicial Watch obtained information in 2014 from DHS that showed ICE has released a total of 195,900 known criminally convicted illegal aliens throughout the United States. Information obtained indicated, in 2013 alone, ICE released 36,007 illegal aliens with the following convictions: 193 homicides; 426 sexual assaults; 303 kidnappings; 1,075 aggravated assaults; 1,160 stolen vehicles; 9,187 for dangerous drugs; 16,070 for drunk or drugged driving; and 303 for flight escape.

When a crime like the Kate Steinle tragedy happens in a sanctuary city and involves a "released" illegal alien, no one is ever assigned blame for the illegal alien being on the loose. The local officials blame the federal officials and the federal officials blame the local officials. They are all to blame but primary accountability has to fall on the Obama administration because federal law trumps local law and the federal government allows sanctuary cities to exist. Judicial Watch said former House Judiciary Committee Chairman, Larmar Smith (R., TX.), issued a statement terming this situation "the worst prison brake in history". Congressman Smith was quoted as saying, "It was sanctioned by the president and perpetrated by our own immigration officials … The administration's actions are outrageous. They willfully and knowingly put the interests of criminal immigrants before the safety and security of the American people."

Here is a reasonable and effective conservative approach to illegal immigration. First, enforce existing laws. If they need updating, do it. Second, tighten border control to the hilt. With all the *Star Wars* type technology available today, it could reasonably be done. Third, there should be a sensible and firm immigration process to provide amnesty to those currently in our country illegally and have not committed felonious acts. Common sense goes a long way in reaching sound decisions that have a chance of working in a reasonable manner.

It is very unrealistic to think we can send millions of immigrants home. Even the Greyhound and Trailways Bus Lines combined don't have that many buses. It's just not going to happen and shouldn't. We are the ones to blame for letting this issue get out of hand, not the illegal immigrants. There has been a lot of rhetoric about giving citizenship to an illegal immigrant's extended family not currently residing in the United States. If the illegal immigrants want to live with their extended family, they can go back where they came from or the extended families can apply for "legal" citizenship.

I want to salute all those people who want to be Americans and do it legally. I have met several and I welcomed them as fellow Americans. I am so proud of them. There was an article in our local newspaper with the headline "This is like a dream". Fifty-one local people had just become American citizens. There was a large picture showing a woman with a huge smile on her face and holding a big bouquet of roses containing American flags. She was quoted saying, "I can pursue the American dream now." One's quest for citizenship doesn't get any better than that and she used our current law. America has always been a beacon for immigration because of our incredible opportunity to achieve success in life. Our progressive friends are doing their best to make America the land of opportunity to achieve a life of entitlements to support progressive politics. What the progressives are doing is totally unfair to those who become citizens legally.

Here is an inconceivable immigration issue that has been kept under the radar by the Obama administration. Did you know that this administration allowed 1,519 foreigners into the country in 2014 who had known ties to terrorism and gave them full rights and benefits of a U.S. citizen? That's right! Known ties to terrorism! How could they do that? The administration has the discretion to do so and tweaked a federal law titled the Immigration and Nationality Act.

Before it was tweaked, the law would have required zero tolerance for these immigrants and they would have been kept out. More than half of these immigrants were known to have provided material support to terrorist organizations. The others received military-type training from terrorists, provided medical care to terrorists, and solicited money or recruits for terrorist organizations. The DHS Secretary, Jeh Johnson, determined after a case-by-case review these terrorists only participated in these activities "while under duress" and used his discretion to let them in. I cannot think of words sufficient enough to describe the idiocy and danger to Americans regarding this action. We can thank Judicial Watch for discovering and publicizing this.

Judicial Watch reported that a frustrated senator said the Obama administration appears to also have a "hands off list" that permits individuals with extremist ties to enter and leave the country as they wish. Here is what I found when I dug into the story. The comment was based upon email information between ICE and Customs and Border Protection (CBP) obtained by Senator Chuck Grassley (R., IA.). Both ICE and CBP are agencies under DHS. Grassley's website contained information on the topic including a letter he sent to Jeh Johnson at DHS requesting an explanation. The best summary I found addressing the total story was a May 2014 report by The Washington Free Beacon. Based upon several emails between ICE and CBP, it was learned that a disagreement occurred in 2012 within ICE and CBP regarding the admittance of a Canadian Islamist leader who praised suicide bombings and is close to Hamas, Hezbollah, and other terrorist groups.

These emails also revealed an internal campaign by DHS and former Secretary Janet Napolitano to purge the records of hundreds of foreign terror suspects including the individual in question. No reason was given for the purge. The Washington Free Beacon said individuals tied to terror groups have gained entrance to the United States multiple times over the past few years. An example involved a member of the Egyptian Islamic Group, a U.S. designated terror organization, who met with the Obama administration in 2012.

The Washington Free Beacon report concluded by saying Napolitano told members of Congress they should expect members of terror groups to be admitted to the United States "for meetings". Really? Now, I don't want to sound paranoid and I do not oppose "calculated communication" with our enemies or "clandestine intelligence gathering" but does this report bother you after reading the connections in the last chapter between the Muslim Brotherhood, CAIR, other radical Islamic groups, and the White House? I'll admit I do not have all the information but I find what I do know to be very troubling.

Progressives in Washington have a very simple policy on education; control the nation's educational system in order to indoctrinate students to progressive ideology and support teacher unions to keep those political contributions coming in. My 2009 epistle in chapter 5 talked about the indoctrination of students beginning in grade school. I was curious to see if the *Story of Stuff* is still around. It looks alive and well to me. They actually have a website that says "From a Movie to a Movement". Under that heading it says 5 years and 40 million views later we are a community of 500,000 change makers worldwide. I can't judge how true that is but they did show photos of several staff members and they promoted a high school program that consisted of ten lessons.

The movie is easy to find on YouTube. I couldn't resist watching it again to see if the propaganda was as bad as I remember. It was worse. If you haven't seen it, I would suggest you do so to get a feel for the anti-American propaganda our school kids are being taught. The video is fairly typical of the progressive indoctrination that is widespread in our nation's educational system. Chapter 10 provides an extensive look at what is happening in our schools.

I have tried to understand why progressivism has become so pervasive in our schools and here is the best explanation I can come up with. When I was a kid, most teachers were women. They went into teaching or nursing because of the lack of opportunity in other fields. Thank goodness that is not the case today and women have endless opportunity. This change in opportunity has left the door open for female and male teachers who have a progressive oriented ideology. They are attracted to the current union environment that includes the security of tenure, good salaries, and good benefits for their level of productivity. I really question whose future becomes most important with these people—the children or theirs. Don't get me wrong. Everyone should look out for her or his future but he or she should secure their future by constantly working toward "doing a good job", not by constantly working toward "keeping their job".

I have great admiration for teachers who adhere to conservative and classic liberal ideology and hang in there because they love to teach and care about our children's future. Our schools desperately need more of these teachers. Where are they? Maybe if we revamped the way our schools are run and got rid of the unions, we would find them.

Colleges are attracting more and more progressive minded professors who are intellectual elitist, do not want to work or cannot work in the real world, want the security of tenure, and want the great long-term benefits. The Daily Signal reported in January of this year that college professors have noticeably become more liberal (I say progressive.) during the last 25 years. The Higher Research Institute at UCLA did a study in 2014 that indicated 60% of college professors identified as liberal or far left. Only 42% identified as liberal or far left in a 1990 study. The number of professors that identified as conservative or far right between 1990 and 2014 fell 6% while those identifying as moderate fell 13%. A graph in the report showed a 5 to 1 ratio of liberal or far left professors over conservative or far right professors.

Daniel Klein, an economics professor at George Mason University, said the 5 to 1 ratio was not very meaningful. He said when one looks at the imbalance between professors who vote democratic and republican, the imbalance is between 9 to 1 or even 10 to 1. A May 2016 editorial in The Wall Street Journal by Jason Riley supports Klein's position. Jason is on the Journal's Editorial Board. His editorial quotes political scientists Jon Shields and Joshua Dunn Sr. from their new book titled *Passing on the Right*. They said, "Progressives rule higher education." Their book states that surveys show 18% of the college professors in the humanities and social sciences are self-described Marxists. That is double the number of self-described republicans. Their book also mentions how leftist faculty and college administrators closely monitor outside speakers invited to campus, which sends a message to students that people who challenge the liberal dogma are not welcome.

Jason said he is invited to approximately 15 college campuses per year to give an alternate perspective to the 25% of sociology professors who identify as Marxists. He was just recently disinvited to speak at Virginia Tech University. The president of the university claimed the entire situation was an internal error in miscommunication and now Jason is going to speak. I heard Jason say on television it was because of outside pressure on the university.

I want to emphasize there are many great conservative and classic liberal teachers at all levels of education who are teaching because they love to to teach and care about the students they are teaching. I taught hospital administration as a college adjunct professor and loved it. I admire those in education who are there to educate because that is their passion. This is a key element to a successful society. I am sure the conservative and classic liberal educators become very frustrated at times with an educational system that is becoming progressively worse (pun intended).

We have looked at what the union environment is doing to government competence and accountability and the same thing is happening in our educational system. Why does Obama always talk about adding more teachers, police, and firemen when he talks about unemployment and jobs? They are all union jobs that feed the progressive financial war chest and generate votes. Several months ago, I saw a news clip regarding the 2015 mayoral election in Chicago. Rahm Emanuel was third in a poll with two others that were thought to be candidates for mayor. One can think what they want about Emanuel's political ideology or his ability to run Chicago but I admire him for taking on the teachers' union.

One potential candidate in the poll said she was not going to run and the other person had basically announced her candidacy. She was the president of the teachers' union. Remember the Chicago teacher's strike in 2012? The main issues between Emanuel and the teachers' union during the strike involved how teachers are hired, evaluated, fired, and tenured. They finally reached a deal after Emanuel stood up to the union and some very nasty union protests. Emanuel was re-elected in 2015 but it took a run-off election to do it.

Can you imagine what would have happened if the union president had been elected mayor? The Chicago school system is not known for its educational prowess. Would the kids become only a conduit for more union jobs and all the union "stuff" that goes with those jobs? In all likelihood, the kids would have become a human commodity used as a bargaining chip in union negotiations. Our kids deserve better. Especially in tough deprived areas where education is one of their best chances of getting out of poverty and crime. We have talked about the enormous influence of home life on these kids and their future. Schools are another important influence. Throwing more money and more teachers at them does not help as the progressives would like you to believe. They need roll models, a disciplined learning environment, and someone to care. What I have just described is not just a Chicago issue.

How about Detroit? A teacher's "sick out" closed dozens of schools earlier this year and kept 46,000 kids out of school. That number of students is down from 300,000 students in 1966, which is another story in itself regarding the failure of progressive government. All the teachers and the superintendent are unionized. The teachers said they were upset because of over-crowded classrooms, poor school conditions, and the growth of charter schools. I read a report in The Daily Signal that said the following regarding the Detroit school system. It is likely that only 4,000 of those students can read and only 7 in 10 will graduate. The school system spends $16,000 per student and 75% of the annual budget goes toward teachers salaries. The school system is $3.5 billion in debt, which includes unfunded pension liabilities. The school system received a new $7,450 grant per-pupil this year and $4,400 will go toward paying debt service that includes benefits for retired teachers. Multiply this fairly common scenario across the country in communities with similar problems and it is staggering.

How about community schools unlike Chicago where the family unit is predominately strong and poverty and crime is minimized. Teacher's unions are strong and progressive teachers are there as well. I have immense concern regarding the lack of support for traditional American values and American history being altered in these schools to support the progressive way? I brought up Common Core in chapter 4. There is no doubt the progressive purpose for Common Core is to shift power from local governments to the federal government by establishing national standards for education. If state governments do not adopt Common Core standards they risk losing their federal funding. Why would Washington want to do that? Here is Gomer again. Surprise, surprise, surprise! Remember what the progressives love—control and power. Fortunately, many states have not adopted Common Core and its future is still up in the air. Let's hope when it comes down, it comes down in a colossal crash.

State government is not the only push back Common Core is getting. The Associated Press reported thousands of students in Atlanta are opting out of Common Core testing and the practice of opting out is growing in other parts of the country. For example, tens of thousands of students recently set out the first day of testing in New York. If fewer than 95% of the school district's students do not participate in the testing, federal funding can be withheld. The U.S. Department of Education said the withholding of federal funds has not happened. The act of Americans pushing back against Common Core is certainly encouraging and would be very successful in fighting all progressive attempts at government control if it were practiced more frequently before it becomes too late. A Rasmussen poll taken in December last year indicated that only 20% of the population felt the federal government should set education standards. Forty percent said the state should set the standards and 31% believed it should be local government. Where are you 71%?

We have already talked about the federal government using Title IX to threaten colleges and universities that do not adhere to the Obama administrations progressive ideology concerning sexual assault. The latest hot button using Title IX is transgender equality. We will look at this issue in more detail in chapter 10.

I can't end discussion on progressive domestic policy without commenting on what has happened to the National Aeronautics and Space Administration (NASA). What a source of national pride, a source of new technology, a source for world leadership, and potential source for national security before Obama curtailed its function and mission. The entire world looked up to the U.S. as the world leader in space exploration. I remember Sputnik. It was the first satellite in space and Russia did it. It was a downer for Americans. In 1961, President John F. Kennedy challenged Congress that the United States would put a man on the moon by the end of the decade and by golly we did on July 20, 1969. I still remember watching it on television. It was in the middle of the night and I was glued to the TV set. What a show! The United States was now the "super star" of space. Pun intended. We only got better and stronger in our efforts and left Russia in "space dust" until Obama took us down. We now buy tickets on the Russian rocket ships for millions of dollars each. They are in total control of our manned space efforts. I guess we are back to sputnik days. Sorry John. What happens if they don't sell us tickets any more? Is that a problem? Well, with Putin's current toying with Obama, it's his call. How about all the technology we gained from NASA and the space program that benefited our entire society? That's gone too.

How about national security? That's a big one. Maybe I read too many outer space oriented comic books or saw too many Flash Gordon TV shows when I was a kid but I strongly believe that someday the entity that controls outer space will militarily control the world. Think lasers or some weapon we don't yet know about. For example, I recently read in The Wall Street Journal we now have a new type of gun that is called a railgun. Instead of the projectile using gunpowder or explosives, electromagnetic rails accelerate the projectile to 4,500 miles per hour or one mile per second. The projectile's velocity is so powerful it can destroy ships, tanks, and level enemy camps without explosives. They referred to it as a battlefield meteorite. The projectile is only 24-inches long and weighs 25 pounds but the gun that shoots it is not small at 32 feet. The technology will only improve and the gun will increasingly get smaller and the projectile more powerful.

I have seen and own all the James Bond movies so I am well educated on the subject of using outer space for military purposes. Maybe controlling outer space weaponry is how the one world order is accomplished that progressives talk and salivate about. The only problem for these progressives is that the leader of that world order will be somebody from Russia, China, or some country yet to be determined if the United States continues in the direction we are going. It sure as hell won't be us and "us" stands for a very diminished "U.S.".

I know we have Space X but that is a privately owned company that is subject to the whims of a single individual who is known to be subject to whims. That gives me no confidence. I actually find it scary. I did read the other day that Boeing is going to be involved in building rockets for NASA in addition to Space X and will be ready to launch its first rocket by 2017. The latest news is that NASA is looking to reach Mars "with the aid from European friends". What happened to U.S. pride and leadership? That's easy—progressive dominance. What a downer! Watching what is happening to NASA is sad. NASA is one of our national treasures that have provided so much national pride, respect in the world, technological improvement for society, and potential national security. We need the old NASA back to serve the best interest of our country.

Speaking of national security, how secure are we under progressive Washington rule? It has diminished significantly under Obama. We have let our allies down and severely tarnished our image. We are inviting terrorism around the world and that includes our homeland. Obama's news conference at the G20 Summit in Turkey last year was very telling about his approach to countering terrorism. Here are some of his responses at the news conference during unusually strong questioning by the mainstream news media, which was nice for a change. We know the news media can do it. The terrorists' attack on Paris was only three days earlier. Obama said the following: our strategy is working; we have ISIS contained; Paris is a setback; and he sarcastically said that anyone who has better ideas than his Chair of the Joint Chiefs of Staff and people on the ground are welcome to share their plan with him.

His responses were unbelievable. He showed no anger or emotion regarding the Paris terrorists' attack but did show anger toward those (mainly republicans) who criticized his approach to terrorism. The press appeared to be dumfounded by his comments when they reported them on all the mainstream television news shows afterwards including MSNBC. Bill O'Reilly called Obama delusional during opening comments on his Fox News show. I saw several military analysts including high-ranking retired military officers talk on television about the stupidity of his remarks. During his news conference, Obama also responded to state governors and those in Congress who are opposed to his plan to allow 10,000 refugees to come to the U.S. from Syria. His response was very un-presidential. A Rasmussen survey indicated that 63% of likely voters opposed Obama's plan, only 23% supported it, and 14% were undecided.

Our Secretary of State's response to the Paris attack was worse. John Kerry was actually speaking in Paris and casually said the recent attack was different from the Charlie Hebdo attack because it was indiscriminate whereas the Charlie Hebdo attack had legitimacy. He immediately caught himself and then mumbled out he meant there was a rationale to which you could attach yourself. People in France and the U.S. found what Kerry said to be appalling. This naive behavior by the

Obama administration emboldens terrorists to increase their size and strength and to attack our allies and us. Lt. Colonel Ralph Peters is a frequent news contributor on Fox News and is one of my favorites. His reaction to Obama's and Kerry's comments was that he would not be surprised if Obama called Eric Holder out of retirement to lead a new movement called "Jihadi lives matter".

Obama did it again after the Brussels attacks in March of this year. Over 300 people were injured and 35 people died including four Americans and three attackers. What did Obama do immediately after the attacks? He spoke for less than one minute on the attack and then went to a baseball game with Castro and did the "wave". He followed up that behavior doing the tango at a state dinner in Argentina that was televised around the world. What does that say to Americans? What does that say to the rest of the world? He said he did not want the Islamic terrorists to think their actions would impact his activities and others should respond in the same way. How about showing concern and compassion for the victims and their families and not acting so callus? Remember what I said in the last chapter about those with narcissistic personality disorders lacking empathy? The White house did say Obama called the parents of two victims.

Within 5 days of the Brussels attack, Islamic terrorists killed 65 people and injured over 300 people in Pakistan on Easter day. Obama was nowhere to be found. John Kirby, spokesperson for the State Department, did release a statement that said in part, "The United States condemns in the strongest terms today's appalling terrorist attack in Lahore, Pakistan. This cowardly act, which targeted innocent civilians in Gulshan-e-Iqbal Park, has killed dozens and left scores injured. The United States stands with the people and Government of Pakistan at this difficult hour. Attacks like these only deepen our shared resolve to defeat terrorism around the world, and we will continue to work with our partners in Pakistan and across the region to combat the threat of terrorism." I bet his comments had the Islamic terrorists "shaking in their boots". How did the Pakistanis and other countries in the region feel about America after hearing "standard State Department BS" that contained nothing of significance? Oh, and the State Department statement forgot to mention the Islamic terrorist attack was at an Easter gathering of Christians.

John Kerry had declared just before the Easter attack that he had determined the Christians, Yazidis, and Shiite groups in Iraq and Syria are ISIS victims of genocide and crimes against humanity. This was after Congress and humanitarian groups were pressuring him to do so. What does that mean? Kerry said he hoped that the groups he cited as being victimized would take some comfort in the fact that the "United States recognizes and confirms the despicable nature of the crimes committed against them". It means absolutely nothing, just like what John Kirby said means absolutely nothing.

During the three months after those March terrorist attacks, we have seen 45 people killed and 239 people injured at Istanbul's airport, 23 killed and 50 injured at a coffee shop in Bangladesh, approximately 55 army soldiers and army recruits killed in Yemen, over 250 killed and hundreds more injured at a Baghdad mall, and our own Orlando attack killing 49 people and wounding 53. There are hundreds more who have been killed in Syria. As this book is being readied to go to press, 84 people were killed and 303 people injured in Nice, France and over 60 killed and 200 injured in Kabul by terrorist attacks. What do we do? Our State Department and our president offer more rhetoric condemning these terrorists' attacks. I saw Kerry's Deputy Secretary of State, Tony Blinken, say on television that we have taken away ISIS's territory, fighters, and resources and these isolated terror attacks are proof that we are winning and they are desperate. I am totally speechless on that one.

Fox News conducted a poll in June after the attack in Orlando that asked how Americans feel about our ability to prevent terrorist attacks and compared the results with a July 2005 poll. In 2005, 50% were nervous and that number is now 84%. In 2005, 30% were confident and now that number is 11%. In 2005, feelings were mixed for 15% but now the number is 2%.

I believe Obama is in denial on Islamic terrorism for three reasons. The first reason involves his proclamation to the world that Osama Bin Laden is dead, terrorism is on the run, and ISIS is junior varsity. For Obama to admit "reality" would prove him wrong. As we discussed in the last chapter, being wrong is not in Obama's vocabulary. Here is the second reason. If Obama admits the world's terrorism results from radical Islamic fighters and condemns the countries that support the radical Islamic movement, then he has no chance to achieve his messianic dream to pull the world together as one big happy family. If what I hypothesized in the last chapter regarding Obama's behavior is true, Obama is oblivious to the reality of this dangerous situation. In June 2014, Obama attended the Young Southeast Asian Leaders Initiative in Burma. The following is an excerpt from whitehouse.gov articulating his comments at the initiative that supports this point:

> People don't remember but when I came into office the United States in world opinion ranked below China and just barely above Russia and today, once again, the United States is the most respected country on Earth and part of that, I think, is because of the work we did to reengage the world and say that we want to work with you as partners with mutual interests and mutual respect. It was on that basis we were able to end two wars while still focusing on the very real threat of terrorism and to try to work with our partners in Iraq and Afghanistan. It's the reason why we are moving in the direction to normalize relations with Cuba. The nuclear deal that we are trying to negotiate with Iran.

The above comments are very telling in explaining much of Obama's behavior that doesn't make sense to us and supports my hypotheses about his behavior. The third reason is that he does not want anything that could be labeled "Obama's war" connected to his legacy. Why would his administration support him? Remember, they are progressives who think in terms of successful political image for their movement and war is not in that ideology. Also, never forget the power of the presidential office over people, especially over those who aspire toward a successful political future themselves. I often wonder how much Valarie Jarrett influences his actions regarding terrorism. I have never seen or heard anything regarding her position on terrorism but I have to believe it is significant.

The Islamic terrorists aren't the only ones watching Obama's diminished support for a strong military defense. How about Russia, China, North Korea and now Iran? Who knows what other countries are lurking in the shadows? Have you read or heard about all the military officers who have been let go or forced to retire. I saw a list that had about 100 top officers including generals and admirals that were retired or terminated during the three-year period prior to 2014. I read there were about 200 retired or terminated during the five-year period prior to 2014. I heard several officers were notified they were terminated while they were on the battlefield in Afghanistan. What a morale downer for them and those around them. How callous and stupid. These numbers are staggering and scary.

I Googled a newscast in November 2013 by Diane Sawyer on the firings of military officers and the reasons given to her for the terminations were lame—very lame. Bret Baier did a Fox special on this topic in March of this year. The report said that when Obama took office, he inherited a professional, world-class, battle-toughened military. Now, experts see our military as a "tattered and demoralized" organization. This change was attributed to billions of dollars in cuts, radical social change forced upon the troops, and a foreign policy that breaks with decades of tradition. The report said this leaves us in a world more dangerous than ever. Bret interviewed Robert Gates, former Secretary of Defense, who said he was in a meeting where Obama ignored his entire security team and listened to three junior "back benchers" in deciding to let Egyptian President Hosni Mubarak fall. One of the junior members reportedly said, "Mr. President, you need to be on the right side of history". What does that mean?

We have lost significant military experience and expertise. Retired officers spoke out about this issue on television news shows and said that anyone who does not agree with Obama's and his progressive cohorts' viewpoints is at risk of termination. Unbelievable but this is a pattern we see over and over! Where does that put our national security? It puts us at great risk. I have always had great confidence in our military protecting our national security. No matter what the situation, they have prevailed under any circumstance. What do "yes people" do? They do nothing until they are told what to do and they don't buck what they are told even if they disagree. How secure does that make you feel when Obama and his progressive minions protect our national security with inexperienced "yes people" making our military decisions? It scares the hell out of me.

Here is an email I received from a friend that provides a thought-provoking common sense look at what we have discussed in this chapter. The author is unknown. The email started by defining the word "conundrum" as "something that is puzzling or confusing". The following are what the email calls "six conundrums of socialism" in the United States:

1. America is capitalist and greedy and yet half the population is subsidized.
2. Half of the population is subsidized and yet they believe they are victims.
3. They believe they are victims and yet their representatives run the government.
4. Their representatives run the government and yet the poor keep getting poorer.
5. The poor keep getting poorer and yet they have things that people in other countries only dream about.
6. They have things that people in other countries only dream about yet they want America to be more like those other countries.

The email also contained the following interesting thoughts:

1. We are advised to not judge all Muslims by the actions of a few lunatics but we are encouraged to judge all gun owners by the actions of a few lunatics.
2. It seems we constantly hear about how Social Security is going to run out of money but we never hear about the welfare or food stamp programs running out of money. What is interesting is that the first group worked for their money, the second did not.

3. Why are we cutting benefits for our veterans, no pay raises for our military, and cutting our army back but we are not stopping the payments or benefits to illegal aliens?

With these sobering thoughts on progressive domestic policy, I'm getting out of this chapter before I think of something else that I don't want to think about. I always thought that our president was the President of the United States, which includes all Americans. That's not true with progressives. A progressive president picks and chooses for whom he or she wants to be president in order to advance her or his agenda. The rest of us are just plain out of luck. I guess we are president-less. We patriotic Americans are also becoming homeless. Think about that for a minute.

CHAPTER 9

Progressive Foreign Lack of Policy!

Even in light of our economic woes, foreign policy is arguably the most critical issue facing our country because of its effect upon our national security and our personal safety. There is international conflict in Israel, Iraq, Syria, Afghanistan, Pakistan, Yemen, Libya, Iran, and Ukraine. North Korea is always seeking relevance and is governed by a ruthless maverick dictator who is a "loose cannon". China is issuing threats with their burgeoning nuclear weapons arsenal and newfound military might, not to mention their attacks on our cyberspace. Russia is having a field day wielding its military sword and invading surrounding countries. Islamic terrorism is spreading throughout the world and wrecking havoc. An unsettled world is coming at us fast from multiple directions.

Can you articulate our foreign policy? I would say our foreign policy is to voice illusionary and delusional rhetoric to world issues, duck our heads when the "stuff" flies, use a lot of red disappearing ink, and continuously boast of imaginary success. In other words, the United States' foreign policy is no foreign policy. It is a combination of Obama's "duck and run" world leadership, his grandiose image of himself, and progressive globalism ideology on steroids. That is a far cry from our past exceptionalism roll as the social conscience and protector of the world. I might add that we were damn good and successful at it. I feel like the world is literally falling apart around us since Obama and the progressives took over. It gives me a strong feeling of loss and sadness when I think about it. There is that word "sad" again. I seem to use it a lot in describing what is happening to our country under progressive rule.

After the fall of Rome, the Dark Ages set in. If America falls permanently to progressive ideology, America and the rest of world can look forward to the darkness of the Progressive Ages. When Obama first became president, he went around the world apologizing for the abhorrent things he accused the United States of doing in the past. Not only is this mantra in the progressive songbook, I believe Obama's strong indictment toward the United States goes back to his childhood and his relationship with his parents, grandparents, and his mentor who were not supporters of American philosophy. Like I said in chapter 7, I believe it is his unconscious or perhaps his conscious way of pleasing them posthumously. It also fits the narrative by Vaknin in that Obama is acting out his messianic vision of himself and his belief that it is his calling to bring the world together as one. What better way to accomplish those goals than to profess the evils of America's exceptionalism and global influence and change the way America relates to the world. It is very misguided thinking but fits the narrative I have painted to explain his behavior.

When Obama is trashing America, he conveniently fails to remember the numerous times the United States has "saved other countries' bacon" during the past several decades after hostile forces invaded them and how grateful they were then and now. There is WW I, WW II, the Korean War, the Vietnam War, and the Iraq war before Obama pulled out. During my trip to Vietnam, people in Saigon told me that if the United States had not intervened in the Vietnam War that their entire country, north and south, would have become another North Korea. Even though we pulled out of the war and let South Vietnam fall, I still observed an enormous difference in the standard of living between Hanoi and Saigon. Interestingly, the signs in and around Saigon say Ho Chi Minh City but everyone I met there still calls it Saigon.

Military intervention isn't the only thing the United States has historically done for other countries. Obama even ran into George and Laura Bush during his Africa trip where the Bushes were still working on the AIDS/HIV program George started when he was president. Bush isn't the first American president to perform humanitarian deeds like that. I guess Obama is so involved in creating our new progressive based economy, his unrestrained political travel, his family vacations de jure, and propping up the declining golf course industry that he hasn't had time to do those things yet.

We have also routinely given aid in past decades to other countries for military and humanitarian purposes. OK, so it is mostly bribery to gain influence with their leaders but other countries around the world do it and it unfortunately works. If you don't do it, you are out and others are in. Like it or not, it's the way much of the influence in the world operates. It's not a lot different than lobbying in Washington, is it? I challenge Obama to name even one country that has historically done more for the world to keep it safe and to help people in need than America.

Our military presence around the world is a significant issue for progressives like Obama to come to grips with. The United States has kept the world a much safer place because of our military might. It doesn't matter if our military might is sitting home twiddling its thumbs waiting for military action or is somewhere "kicking butt", bad guys around the world know our military might is there and fear it. If that fear is gone, these bad guys act out and people get hurt as we see happening today. There is no way to go back and measure our historical positive influence in the world. We could only do that if history could repeat itself without our presence. Since Obama took office; however, we are getting a taste of what would have historically happened in the world without us when one considers the Islamic terrorism throughout the world, Iran's quest for power over the Middle East, and with Russia's and China's new aggression. And, that taste is pretty bitter.

Let's review some of Obama's more profound foreign policy blunders. After Obama went around the world apologizing for our atrocities, he proceeded to placate his liberal base and himself by pulling all of our troops out of Iraq and starting the process to do the same in Afghanistan. He did this without regard to the potential impact that is now taking root in the Middle East. In response to a UN Security Council Resolution, Obama involved the United States, in tandem with several other nations, in the overthrow of Gadhafi. We did not take the lead in that endeavor and the outcome certainly has had undesirable results since nothing was done to maintain stability. Islamic hardline militias including those that attacked our embassy in Benghazi have basically taken over Libya and are forming another terrorist dominated country.

Are you aware of what Obama did recently in an interview with The Atlantic magazine to our friends and colleagues—now probably our ex-friends and colleagues—in Great Britain and France to cover his rear end regarding Libya? Obama blamed British Prime Minister David Cameron for creating a mess in Libya because he was "distracted by a range of other things" and not invested in the follow-up after Qaddafi's defeat. He said then French President Nicolas Sarkozy "wanted to trumpet the flights he was taking in the air campaign despite the fact (the U.S.) had wiped out all the air defenses and essentially set up the entire infrastructure". Obama went on to say he warned Cameron that the "so-called special relationship between Great Britain and the United States" would end if their government did not commit 2% of their GDP to defense. Obama commented, "Free riders aggravate me." Those comments are unthinkable! Especially, to be said on the world stage about perhaps our two best allies in the world. Actually, Obama's actions are not too surprising and reinforce our discussion about him suffering from narcissistic personality disorder. How about Yemen? Shortly after Obama called Yemen a success story in fighting terrorism, our embassy staff had to flee the country in a hurry from what—terrorists!

Obama's approach to stop Iran from obtaining nuclear weapons involved his participation with other countries in negotiating a so-called nuclear arms agreement. Technically it's a treaty but then Obama would have to get congressional approval and we know how he feels about the Constitutional process. Imposing tough sanctions brought Iran to the table. Some of those sanctions, worth billions of dollars to Iran, were lifted to supposedly keep Iran negotiating. That was a ruse on Iran's part and very poor judgment on ours. One doesn't give up their biggest bargaining chip at the height of negotiations and expect to have any future bargaining power unless getting any deal at any cost is more important than not getting a deal at all.

As you know a deal was finally announced by all parties. The elements of the deal that I thought were most comical were: Iran would only curtail its overall operation and not shut down their most important weapon's grade uranium enrichment facility; Iran would do their own inspections; the International Atomic Energy Agency (IAEA) inspectors whose job it is to monitor Iran's compliance would not have unfettered access to any of their enrichment facilities; and the agreement only lasts for a maximum of ten years. I really don't think what is in the agreement matters anyway since Iran has historically not honored any agreements they have made on any issue.

Iran's leader, Ayatollah Ali Khamenei publicly proclaimed "death to America" during these negotiations. Obama shrugged off the Ayatollah's comment saying it was rhetoric intended for internal domestic political audience. It doesn't matter. What matters is that he said it to the world. The world hears death to America from a leader that we are kowtowing to. To add insult to injury, Iran also constructed a crude life-size model of one of our Nimitz-class aircraft carriers in the Strait of Hormuz and blew it to smithereens with their military ships and airplanes and then bragged they could take down all of our military ships in 50 seconds. A video of the attack can be seen on several websites and it was shown on television news across the world. After the nuclear agreement was announced, Iran tested a ballistic missile capable of carrying a nuclear warhead that was in violation of a UN ban on such activity. Iran also convicted a journalist from The Washington Post of espionage who by all indications was innocent.

An October 2015 news article in The Wall Street Journal contained the following quotes. Obama said, "We, together with our partners, must now focus on the critical work of fully implementing this comprehensive resolution that addresses our concerns over Iran's nuclear program." John Kerry said adopting the deal is, "… a critical first step in the process of ensuring that Iran's nuclear program will be for peaceful purposes."

In order to seal the deal, an assessment had to be made by the IAEA, which was completed in January 2016. The assessment stated Iran had conformed to all the requirements imposed upon them to complete the transaction. I heard that the IAEA did not get full cooperation from Iran and, contrary to what the IAEA said, Iran has already cheated on their commitments in the agreement. The Wall Street Journal article reported that a senior U.S. official said the final assessment by the IAEA is not a perquisite for implementation of the agreement anyway.

This one requires a "railroad" bridge and we know who got railroaded. The Obama administration has made a horrifically bad deal with Iran and totally washes their hands of any future responsibility. What a mess. This is a very unfortunate example of our total lack of foreign policy leadership. A Rasmussen poll taken in September of last year pointed out 62% of likely American voters said it was unlikely that Iran would honor an agreement (39% of those said it was not likely at all), 35% said somewhat likely, and 8% said Iran is very likely to honor a deal. I put that last 43% on my mailing list as potential customers for my newest bridges. They probably already have several old ones but appear to be in the market for a new one.

Here is a stunning but not surprising update. Obama's Deputy National Security Advisor, Ben Rhodes, admitted in a New York Times Magazine interview in May of this year that the Obama administration deceived the American people about the Iran deal. Most pundits I heard said Rhodes' ego got the best of him as he portrayed the White House press corps as young naive reporters who are spoon-fed what the White House wants them to print and the reporters do so without any investigative reporting. The pundits also portrayed Rhodes as young and inexperienced himself to be in such an important White House position. They surmised Rhodes was part of the problem at the White House regarding the national defense decision making that Hagel, Gates, and Panetta talked about.

It was no surprise that Rhodes and the White House walked it back after the uproar in the news media. Is this debacle shades of the Jonathan Gruber debacle we talked about in chapter 6 where the White House misled the public to get Obamacare passed? An effort to have Rhodes testify before Congress failed because he evoked executive privilege. I heard our friend Elijah Cummings performing his usual democratic rant against the republicans at the committee meeting for even inviting Rhodes to come.

Cummings is consistently a mouthpiece for the progressives. I wonder how he sleeps at night considering his responsibility as a public servant to the American people for truth and justice? I wonder how all progressives in Congress sleep at night the way they assert their progressive lies and cover-up to support their ideological agenda. I consistently see it 100% of the time in congressional hearings and when they are interviewed by the news media. The congressional republicans demonstrate conservative ideology but not dishonesty. I just sit there and shake my head in amazement and disgust. The uproar over Rhodes was short lived and the White House lying to the American people about serious issues is again old news.

Before we leave the topic of Iran, I want to share another Iran story I find more than concerning. I first heard about it on Fox News in March of last year. Jenna Lee reported it on *Happening Now*. When I researched the story for the book, I found several related articles on the Internet. Did you know that Iran is gaining significant influence in Latin America? Countries mentioned were Cuba, Venezuela, Argentina, Chile, Brazil, and Bolivia. A 2013 news report by U.S. News and World Report said Obama signed into law the Western Hemisphere Act in 2012 to provide an in-depth look at Iran's growing operations south of our border. The Washington Times reported the study concluded "Iran is not supporting active terrorist cells in the Western Hemisphere" and they have "far less influence and activities" in the region than commonly believed. The U.S. News and World Report said Our State Department's assessment is vastly at odds with that conclusion.

Then House Foreign Affairs Committee Chairwomen, Ileana Ros-Lehtinen (R., FL.) made the case that Iran's regional alliances "can pose an immediate threat by giving Iran—directly through the IRGE (Iranian Revolutionary Guard), the Qods force (responsible for IRGE extraterritorial operations and a U.S. designated terrorist group), or its proxies like Hezbollah—a platform to carry out attacks against the United States, our interests, and allies". How about Iran placing their soon to be ICBMs with nuclear warheads that we handed to them "on a silver platter" at our doorstep? U.S. News also reported that Michael Leiter, the former director of the National Counterterrorism Center, told the House Homeland Security Committee that Iran represents a threat to the U.S. through our porous borders and there are Hezbollah and Iranian Revolutionary Guard active operations within the U.S. today. Why wasn't this a major concern during the negations with Iran?

It gets worse. I read a syndicated article by the Los Angeles Times in December of 2015 that said, "The southern border has become a flash-point in recent weeks as Syrian families, along with Cuban and Central American migrants, have arrived to seek asylum." They quoted Representative Henry Cuellar (R., TX.) who said 80 Syrians were apprehended at the border last year. How did they get to the U.S. border from Syria and how many did not get caught?

It gets much worse. Here are some headlines from articles I received from Judicial Watch: 1) ISIS Camp a Few Miles from Texas, Mexican Authorities Confirm (April 2015); 2) Team led by Middle Eastern Women Caught Surveilling U.S. Facility on Mexican Border (December 2015); 3) New State Department Intel Confirms Arab Smuggling "Cells", al Qaeda Leader in Mexico (January 2016); and 4) State Department Records Confirm Arab Smuggling Cells, al Qaeda In Mexico (April 2016).

Where are you mainstream news and investigative reporting? More importantly, why is this not a major issue with you, Mr. President? How about you, Mr. Secretary of State? Why doesn't Congress "blow a gasket"? They all know about it. Are there secret efforts going on to address this national security problem? If we are approaching this problem like we approach our other national security problems, then the answer is no. I often wonder who, if anyone, is protecting us? As I write this, the answer is no one. The military's hands are tied. The Obama administration is flying by the seat of their pants hoping to stay lucky. Congress holds inquiries, "rants and raves" about our lack of security, and does nothing. I worry that San Bernardino and Orlando are the "tip of the iceberg" and another 9/11 is out there waiting. I sincerely want to be wrong on this one and I have told you I hate like hell to be wrong.

I repeatedly read and hear all that of our old friends in the world have lost confidence in America because of our approach to the Iran debacle, our weak approach to terrorism, and our red lines that always seem to disappear into thin air. We are becoming the laughing stock of the world. Here is a great example. Last year, Obama invited six Gulf States Middle East leaders to a summit at Camp David. Only two showed up and the other four sent junior leaders. The most notable absent leader was Saudi King Salman after originally accepting an invitation. This is a significant snub and indicates Obama's lack of respect in the Middle East because of his Middle East policies. This snub would have never happened with any past U.S. president. Obama pledged America's "iron clad commitment" to those who were there to help protect their security. I don't think those Middle East leaders are going to buy any of my bridges.

Here is a more recent example of the impact on our credibility and stature in the world as a result of the Iranian deal. Daniel Henninger wrote an editorial in The Wall Street Journal in January of this year titled "The Humbling of the West". Henninger's story was based upon three photographs that were included in the op-ed. The first photograph showed white boxes covering several nude statues in an art museum in Rome. Why the boxes? Iran's president, Hassen Rauhani, was visiting and the Italian government had the boxes placed upon the statues out of respect for "his sensibilities". During the same visit, there was not any wine served at dinner because Rauhani will not attend a meal where alcohol is served. No wine at an Italian meal?

While Rauhani was in Italy, Italian businesses signed about a dozen deals with the Iranians worth $18 billion. This could not have happened before the nuclear deal was signed. Would Rauhani have been "kowtowed to" like that before we gave Iran the ability to do business in Italy and increase their economic worth? Absolutely not! What are they going to do with the money they obtain from their newfound ability to do business in the world? No bridges on that one either! Henninger said, "Italy's repudiation of its own heritage to accommodate Iran's president is a significant symbolic event." We are going to see a lot of significant symbolic events involving the Iranians in the future.

The second photograph showed Rauhani with Pope Francis. They both are smiling as if they are enjoying themselves. What kind of propaganda photo-op is this for Rauhani to use for self-serving reasons? Why isn't the Pope lecturing Rauhani on Iran's support of terrorism around the world and the poor human rights treatment of its citizens? What is the Pope going to say when Iran explodes its first nuclear bomb? What would the Pope say if Iran bombs Israel as they have said they would?

The third picture depicts ten American sailors on their boat kneeling with their hands behind their heads like what happens at an

ISIS execution ceremony. Remember the incident last January? Iran captured ten personal and their two boats in the Persian Gulf between Bahrain and Kuwait. The Iranian government used the propaganda opportunity to publicly humiliate the United States on the anniversary of the overthrow of the Shah. Is there a connection in timing here? Looks like it to me.

The Iranian people along with the entire world were shown pictures and video of the following: all of our sailors kneeling with their hands behind their head; one of the sailors crying after being captured; one admitting wrongdoing and reading an apology; and all of them all sitting on the floor in a room looking very dejected. The only female in the group had a piece of her clothing over her head like a scarf worn by a Muslim woman. Ayatollah Khamenei met with the Iranian Revolution Guard and told them, "This event should be considered God's work." Really? So, what did we do? Nothing! Absolutely nothing!

The story hit all the news media outlets big time, the Obama administration gave some lame "lip service" to the disastrous event, and it quickly fizzled out. We never learned if the boats were in International waters or in Iranian waters as Iran claimed. We never learned if there was engine trouble as some in the administration hinted might have happened or the boats were hunted down and commandeered by the Iranians. The sailors were never allowed to talk to the media.

What was our official response? Our illustrious Secretary of State, John Kerry, said, "I think we can all imagine how a similar situation might have played out three of four years ago. It is clear that today is a testament to the critical role that diplomacy plays in keeping our country safe, secure, and strong." Secretary Kerry, I can imagine what would have happened before Obama became president. We would have "kicked their butts" diplomatically and militarily if necessary. Actually, this event would have never taken place before Obama became president because Iran would not have felt the confidence to do what they did without fearing retaliation. Remember the Iran hostage crises under Jimmy Carter? Fifty-two Americans from our U.S. Embassy were taken hostage for 444 days. The hostages were released on the same day that Ronald Reagan took office. There is a strong message there. I just realized that I have used the word "butts" a lot, haven't I?

Congressman Randy Forbes (R., VA.) is a member of the House Armed Services Committee. I recently saw him on television commenting that classified details of this event from both the Iran side and our side would likely "shock the nation". He said he could not elaborate and it would be a year or more before the details are released. A few weeks after Forbes' comments, the Navy released a report that said their investigation found the captured sailors failed to report they were behind schedule and decided to take a shortcut, which took them into Iranian waters. After the sailors were captured they did not meet our code of conduct when they exchanged dialog with the Iranians, gave them passwords to their laptops and cell phones, and disclosed sensitive information about their ships. Three officers and six sailors were punished.

The Navy also said Iran broke international law by: impeding the boats' innocent passage; boarding, searching and seizing the boats; and photographing and videotaping the crew. Is this the report Forbes was talking about or was it something else? Who knows? The Navy said the lessons learned from the incident would be taught to all sailors and to future generations of officers and enlisted sailors. My friend Ralph Peters said the military is spending too much time on political correctness training and not enough on military training.

Adding Iran and now potentially other Middle Eastern countries to the current nuclear arsenals of Russia, the United Kingdom, France, China, India, Pakistan, Israel, North Korea, and Israel could foster one hell of a fireworks show sometime in the future and give the movie "Planet of the Apes" a whole new meaning. It just takes one wacko moment for something unthinkable to happen and start a nuclear war and there are a lot of wacko's leaders in countries with nuclear weapons.

Let me give you an example. Kim Jong-un, the leader of North Korea, reportedly has ordered the execution of 70 senior officials since he took over in 2011. Fifteen of those took place last year. The most recent official Kim had killed was his defense chief who reportedly was charged with treason for disobeying him and falling asleep during events when he was present. How was the officer executed? He was shot with an anti-aircraft gun at a firing range in front of hundreds of people. I read this was not the first time that has happened. An anti-aircraft gun is not a nuclear weapon but think about what Kim did to that human being in front of all those people. Within a few days of the execution it was reported that North Korea launched its first newly developed ballistic missile from a submarine capable of reaching the United States.

Remember that "red line" Obama imposed upon Syria? Many countries including the United States and the U.N. said there was evidence the Syrian government used chemical weapons on its people. Obama said if the Syrian government crossed the red line in using chemical weapons it would be a game changer regarding the United States getting militarily involved and destroying their chemical stockpiles. After Obama's red line announcement, I saw a news-alert on television that a new chemical weapons' attack had just occurred. The attack came up at the daily White House news briefing and the deputy press secretary said the UN would be asked to investigate.

After being questioned rather hard by several press members about the president's previous comments on the red line, the deputy press secretary gave rambling answers that in reality were not answers but pure gobbledygook. The mainstream news media actually reported the White House was dancing around the issue and those reports got some traction with the Obama administration. If the press was not so deep in the progressive tank and routinely practiced honest investigative reporting, much traction could be had in preventing or improving outcomes of many of these Obama administration fiascoes?

After a few days, Obama announced at a press conference that he had made a decision to attack Syria. I was watching the press conference and I was astonished and rejoicing that we might finally make a strong statement to our enemies. He then immediately commented that he would seek approval from Congress although he felt he did not need their approval. My astonishment and joy immediately faded and I realized it was the same old same old. As usual, Obama did not make a decisive decision? It was an attempt to cover his previous comments on the red line and then "punted" to Congress. Actually, he did more than punt following that press conference. I heard that Obama met with

David Axelrod and some of his other campaign staff buddies during the following weekend and then Obama threw a total "pass interception".

After he had previously, without any doubt, stated his position was to attack Syria if they crossed the red line, he said he did not draw a red line. He said that he was only echoing the red line that was drawn by the world. Unbelievable! The world is a pretty nebulous entity to assign responsibility to but it is convenient when you are being dishonest in attempting to "cover your butt". Prior to Obama, when America spoke, the world listened with respect and trepidation. Now, when America speaks, the world shakes in its boots because they are laughing so hard. News media, oh news media, where were you on that one regarding the red line?

Chuck Hagel gave an interview to Foreign Policy, a print news magazine and news website, after he was fired as Secretary of Defense. He said he had approved plans to strike Damascus with a barrage of missile strikes after Syria crossed the red line and there were also naval destroyers on standby ready to fire. Obama called him while he was having dinner with his wife at a northern Virginia upscale restaurant and told him to "stand down". Hagel said, "There's no doubt in my mind that it hurt the credibility of the president's word when this occurred." Hagel went on to say that his counterparts around the world told him their confidence in our government had been shaken.

Even if our military had attacked the chemical weapon stockpiles, we gave the Assad regime time to move their chemical weapons into zones that were safe from attack such as civilian neighborhoods. We also gave them ample opportunity in conjunction with radical Islamist groups to mount significant propaganda attacks against the United States and that is exactly what they did. Eventually, under pressure from Russia (not us), Assad supposedly turned over his remaining chemical weapons to the UN and the Organization for the Prohibition of Chemical Weapons (OPCW). No one really knows for sure if all the chemical weapons were actually turned over. There were allegations months after that announcement was made that Assad stockpiled a different kind of chemical weapon in case he needed them to save himself from an internal attack. Accusations have been made that Assad continued to use chemical weapons on his people.

We should have militarily supported the Syrian rebels in the beginning. We would have saved a lot of lives, prevented sexual abuse and slavery of women and children, prevented the current refugee problem, shown strength to our allies, and made a defining statement to Iran and other Middle East countries. There is a strong argument we would have also curtailed the ISIS evolution. At least we would have maintained some respect in the world. We have lost so much respect in our foreign affairs fumbles. Now it's a no-win. If we do anything to diminish the Assad regime, we are de-facto supporting radical Islamists. What a mess and it could have been avoided with true leadership in the White House. Sad—truly sad.

Our friend, Mr. Putin, was the one who persuaded Assad to pledge he would turn over his chemical weapon stockpile to the UN and OPCW. Putin's caveat in doing so was that the United States not take military action against the Assad regime. Obama's address to the nation after the agreement between Putin and Assad was announced was a mish-mash of positions on the issue and Obama left military action on the table. In response to Obama's address, Putin put an op-ed in the New York Times. The op-ed said if the United States attacked Syria, it would cause more innocent victims and unleash a flurry of terrorist attacks upon us. He said Russia supports peaceful dialog to resolve the issue—not military action. You gotta be kidding me! One of America's greatest adversaries is chastising us in one of our own national newspapers and purporting to be the powerful world peacemaker that we once were.

Obama handed Putin this opportunity on a silver platter. Why in the world would Obama do that? The answer is obvious. It is his lack of ability to lead and his focus on political ideology and self-image. Afterwards, Putin was "temporarily shot in the foot" on the world stage by the accidental Russian missile strike on the Malaysian airplane flying over Ukraine but the issue of Putin gaining world power over Obama is far from over. Sad, isn't it? I wish I could stop using that word. Actually, "sad" applies to the entire chapter.

I have repeatedly chastised the press in accuracy of reporting and even absence of reporting that involved negativity toward the Obama administration? This next story involves another example of the mainstream news media fabricating the news to support them. After John McCain and Lindsey Graham met with Obama to discuss an attack on Syria, they held a press conference. I read reports by USA TODAY, the AP, and The New York Times regarding the press conference that said McCain and Graham supported Obama in his approach to Syria and they urged Congress to support him as well. There were probably other news outlets that said the same thing. I watched the entire press conference, and those mainstream news reports were totally out of context.

Here is what McCain and Graham really said. They were very critical of Obama on the following fronts. Obama should have acted early on to support the true rebels instead of waiting until radical Islamists were involved. Obama should have acted unilaterally as both republican and democratic presidents have in the past and kept Congress informed. He should have not asked Congress for permission because if Congress denied permission, it would be very problematic for Obama to move forward. If Obama does not move forward, he has emboldened Iran and probably other countries to ignore the United States and for Iran to continue the development of nuclear weapons. How correct McCain and Graham were. They also said not to act would be catastrophic for United States credibility throughout the world. Right again. They concluded Obama should abandon his narrow scope approach to only attack chemical weapons and go after the ouster of Assad. It is no wonder the majority of Americans live in a "mushroom farm" on political issues. Whose fault is that? Is it the news media's fault or is it ours for not demanding more from them?

The mainstream news media reported on the power struggle between Obama and Putin. That reporting was somewhat honest but they still gave Obama a pass in reporting public opinion polls that pitted Obama against Putin. Three different news sources put out very different messages. Breitbart, a conservative news and opinion website, published a poll that said 78% of the respondents saw Putin as strong versus 45% for Obama. The poll also said 8% saw Putin as weak versus 29% for Obama. The Huffington Post, a progressive news and opinion website, presented the situation differently using the same pollster. Their poll discussed whether Putin or Obama would win at certain games and they said it was a stalemate. The games included chess, poker, Twister, Monopoly, checkers, and Hungry Hungry Hippos. Hungry Hungry Hippos? Our national security and image in the world is not a game of Hungry Hungry Hippos. USA TODAY, which is arguably liberal, said voters were evenly divided at 42% each for Putin and Obama as to which was stronger. Even if a draw between Putin and Obama was accurate, it does not impress me. Does it impress you? I will vote for Breitbart being right on this one.

What is our foreign policy toward Egypt? There isn't one unless "wishy-washy" is a foreign policy. Did we support the Egyptian military or the Muslim Brotherhood during and after the Arab Spring? Who do we support now? How about the Coptic Christians who were slaughtered and had their churches torched and blown-up by the Brotherhood? How about the 10-year-old girl who was murdered by the Brotherhood as she was walking home from a Bible study class? Why did we not take a stand? I thought the Obama and the progressives were all about human rights. We haven't had a firm foreign relations policy regarding Egypt since the Arab Spring occurred. Last year, Obama did allow military aircraft and other weaponry to be sold again to Egypt plus he reinstated the $1.3 billion in military aid. That was only because of the terrorist upheaval in the Middle East and not a firm policy toward Egypt. It is difficult, if not impossible, for Obama to articulate a firm policy decision on any foreign policy issue.

My wife and I were in Egypt during November of 2013. Here is what we learned from talking to a number of Egyptian citizens. The citizens we met included a woman who was a professor at the American University in Cairo and one of the members of the Egyptian Parliament who resigned in protest when Mohamed Morsi took office. She was collaborating with other Egyptians to oppose Morsi and the Muslim Brotherhood. Do you know how the Egyptian uprising started in the first place? Wealthy and middle class students at the American University begin demonstrating for improved conditions for the poor. Other well-meaning Egyptians joined in.

The Muslim Brotherhood joined the demonstrations for their own self-serving purpose. They initially said they had no intention in having a Muslim Brotherhood member run for president and they were only there to support the people. The election was a farce the way it was manipulated. We were told the Brotherhood made many promises and gave money and food to the poor before the election. After the election, Morsi and the Brotherhood pushed hard to implement a sharia based constitution and accompanying laws. This upset many Egyptians. They felt they would go back in time and lose their personal independence. Every person we talked to told us the same thing.

Tourism is the biggest industry in Egypt and the majority of people depend upon tourism to survive. Did you know that most Egyptians eat meat only twice a year during religious festivals? Many can't afford meat even then and have never had it at all. When we were there, tourism was down significantly. Vendors told us they had no money. They begged us to buy something from them much more assertively than normal, which even in good times is aggressive. They had not had public garbage pick-up in Cairo for over two years because there was no money to do so. There was trash everywhere except in affluent neighborhoods where people could afford private trash pickup.

So, why am I sharing this with you and what does this have to do with the United States? The Egyptian people blamed Morsi for trying to take their freedoms away and as importantly they blamed him for the decrease in tourism and the resulting economic demise. Guess whom else they blamed? They blamed Obama! The people of Egypt despised him. We heard this over and over from everyone we met when they found out we were from the United States. I mean they volunteered it without our asking—even after that great speech he gave in Cairo. I would strongly suggest you go to the Internet and look up the New York Times website that has Obama's Cairo speech in its entirety and listen to him trash the United States and praise Islam and Muslims. I have nothing against law-abiding Muslims but I have great resentment for our own president demeaning the United States and at the same time building up the Muslim culture.

Our continuing lack of firm foreign policy toward Egypt is one of the biggest mistakes today in American foreign policy. Here are the reasons why. Egypt's president, Abdel Fattah el-Sisi, is the only political or religious leader in the Middle East who has been outspoken against radical Islam and pushing for a more moderate approach to

Islamic teachings to combat radicalism. There is no question that radical Muslims believe in a caliphate, which means Islamic law and a single caliph will rule the community of Islam. So, what is the community of Islam as defined by radical Muslims? The Middle East? The Middle East and southern Asia? The world including the United States? I read that Ayman al-Zawahiri, who is currently the leader of al-Qaeda and an Egyptian, stated Egypt would become the rallying point for Islamists in leading "jihad against the world". Last time I looked at a world map that included us.

Egypt has traditionally been one of our biggest allies in the volatile and dangerous Middle East and now we are wishy-washy about our relationship and influence with them. The Saudis, who are our friends when it is to their advantage, and our Russian adversaries, who continually kick dust in our face, have told Egypt they are waiting in the wings to take our place in giving them financial support and becoming their new best friends. Israel must be enthralled by that potential. Egypt has historically been Israel's best if not only friend in the Middle East since the 1978 Camp David Accords. I guess Jimmy Carter deserves credit for something. If the Saudis and/or Russians replace us with Egypt, our past close relationship with Egypt will more than likely end.

What happened when Egypt initially tried to broker a treaty to stop the most recent major onslaught by Hamas from the Gaza Strip on Israel? Secretary Kerry ignored Egypt and flew off to Paris for some lame idea for peace conjured up by Qatar and Turkey who are both known to support Hamas. I am sitting here trying to think of some smart-alecky reaction to what I just said and I am speechless. Pelosi said during a television interview that the Qataris have told her repeatedly that Hamas is a humanitarian organization and we need to confer with the Qataris to obtain peace between Hamas and Israel. When she was repeatedly asked if Hamas was a terrorist organization, Pelosi kept hedging her answer even though the United States has officially declared Hamas a terrorist organization. She finally under her breath said, "mm hmm". Life is so much easier for progressives who have the ability to believe what they want to believe regardless of the truth.

To Egypt's credit, they re-entered the picture and we supported their negotiations. Actually, we had no choice but to either support or not support them because we were not invited to actively participate. Kerry was told to stay out of it because Egypt thought they would have more success without him being involved. I wonder how Jimmy Carter feels about that turn of events. I am sure the negotiated cease-fire is only temporary. In reality, nothing is ever going to work for peace between Hamas and Israel. It will be a lifelong conflict between the Palestinians and Israel. It is a very unfortunate situation for a lot of innocent people.

Israel has historically been our best ally in the Middle East. There is also a strong tie between our countries because of the large Jewish population in the United States. We have already discussed what the Obama administration allegedly did during the recent Israel elections. News reports say that Netanyahu and Obama have very strained and tense discussions when they speak on the telephone. Washington publicly criticized Israel's bombing of Gaza and the resulting loss of innocent lives including many children. Israel does not want the loss of innocent lives. Hamas intentionally creates that situation in order to mount world condemnation against Israel. They know they can't defeat Israel on the battlefield so they try to defeat them in world opinion. We fall right in line with Hamas like a puppy after a dog biscuit in the Obama administration's attempt to accomplish their nefarious goals. It is inexplicable to me how this administration can consciously throw our best Middle Eastern ally under the bus to accomplish their political ideology. Like I have said over and over, it is the progressive way.

Putin would love to take Obama's place as the most influential leader in the world and he is certainly making progress. Did you see Putin and Obama's demeanor during their news conference at the G8 summit in Northern Ireland in June 2013? You could cut the air with a knife, as both appeared very tense toward each other. During the September 2013 G20 summit in Russia, every country except France refused to support Obama in an attack on Syria after Obama's red line debacle. As you know, Putin supports Assad. That is what happens when you dither and look weak. You give traditional allies ample time and reason to turn on you rather than stand back in amazement and awe and support you. Did you hear about the tweet sent out in 2014 by Russia's deputy prime minister? It contained a picture of Putin with a leopard lying in his lap and a picture of Obama holding a small fluffy dog. The tweet said, "We have different values and allies."

We know Putin is power hungry but how about the Chinese? Decades ago they were basically isolationists. In order to improve their economic state, they adopted a "quasi" free-market approach for economic growth. This change has enabled them to exercise enormous economic influence in the world. I say "quasi" because the Communist Party of China continues, in reality, to control the economy. China's market works like our free enterprise system because the government allows it, manipulates it, and can shut it down any time they wish to do so. In fact, China did that last year. The Shanghai Stock Exchange went into a nosedive. Instead of letting the market make adjustments on its own as the market should, China's leadership panicked. They added stocks to their exchange and placed limits on selling.

This maneuvering by the Chinese government was seen by most knowledgeable observers as a move to protect its image and security rather than an effort in earnest to correct the market, which would have eventually corrected itself. The moral to this story is that you can try to mimic the free-market approach to economic success but unless you have the ideological underpinning to support it, you are always flirting with economic danger.

Isn't it interesting that traditional communistic countries like China and Russia have modified their economic approach to be more like ours in order to become more successful and the progressives want us to be more like them? Progressives never learn? Or do they and don't care? Never confuse progressives with the facts when their goals of power and control are involved. Since Obama has been in office, China's strong-arming of foreign companies doing business there is on steroids. Just ask our U.S. based companies.

Obama is working on a 12-nation Trans-Pacific Partnership free-trade deal to economically compete with the Chinese. There has been considerable controversy surrounding the proposed deal because of the secrecy in which it was negotiated and some of the specifics contained in it. The House Ways and Means Committee reportedly started hearings on the proposed agreement in March of this year and its passage in Congress is in doubt.

The proposed trade bill is so controversial that Hillary Clinton has done a flip-flop on the bill during her campaign. It was reported that she publicly supported the trade bill 45 times since 2010 but then turned against the agreement when Bernie Sanders started receiving support for being against it. Interestingly, this is the first time she has publicly opposed Obama on any issue since she became Secretary of State. This is a great example of how fickle politicians can be in trying to obtain votes for their political future. Politicians are entitled to change their minds for a variety of reasons but flip-flopping for their own interest is not one of them. One can compare politicians who flip-flop to "tumbleweeds in a western movie". After they mature and become dry (no longer feel the need to honor their campaign promises) they detach from their roots (their constituency) and are always at the whim of which way the wind blows.

Since Hillary is the progressive's choice for president, lets talk about how she might approach our country's foreign policy toward countries like China and Russia if she were elected and would it be different from Obama? After her official speech announcing that she was running for president, she only participates in tightly controlled interview situations and attempts to avoid any potential situation in which she might say anything that would mar her candidacy. But, Hillary is Hillary. Remember when she told Diane Sawyer during an interview how poor she and Bill were before and after his presidency? Hillary said, "We struggled to piece together the resources for mortgages for houses." Houses—plural! That comment raised eyebrows and then the press quickly allowed it to became old news. I can forgive the press for that one but they missed the bigger and more important question. How did she and Bill pay for those "houses"? I believe the answer to be very telling in explaining how she would handle foreign policy as president. Let's take a look.

There is a very good reason why Hillary might have used a private server for her communications and it is not for her convenience as she said. There were damning revelations in a book by Peter Schweizer titled *Clinton Cash* regarding the millions upon millions of dollars Hillary and Bill's foundation have received and the suspicious deal-making involving the Clintons that were linked to some of those donations. I saw a documentary on Fox News regarding Bill, Hillary, and their foundation. The actions of the Clintons that resulted in immense personal financial gain were compelling, if not out and out fraud. I could not keep up with the content it was so extensive. It sounded like they had their own personal foreign policy as a past president and as Secretary of State. That foreign policy is called pay to play. Although this is common political practice throughout the world, I do not know of any past U.S. public officials who have held the Clintons' lofty government positions and participated in such activity. Maybe I am naive but I don't think so.

Here is a quick update. Judicial Watch reported in the June 2016 issue of Verdict that information obtained from a previous Judicial Watch lawsuit forced disclosure of documents that "provided a road map for more than 200 conflict-of-interest rulings that led to at least $48 million in speaking fees for the Clintons during Hillary Clinton's tenure as Secretary of State".

When the issue regarding their foundation was first exposed, it had legs in Congress and with conservative watchdog organizations. The mainstream news media was in its usual state of sleep. The issue is still asleep except for Fox News, The Heritage Foundation, conservative websites, and Judicial Watch. Judicial Watch has filed a FOIA lawsuit to uncover information on Hillary's involvement in what they call the Hillary Clinton-Russian Uranium Scandal. That's the most compelling scandal exposed in Schweizer's book. This scandal is so egregious; I cannot understand why it was not a major issue with the mainstream news media. It potentially has criminal implications and the FBI is supposedly investigating it in conjunction with the classified information found on her private server. It will be interesting to see how this issue finally plays out and if it affects Hillary's campaign.

Here is a compilation of reports from The New York Times, which was one of the few news sources that did report on the matter. The Russian atomic energy agency purchased controlling interest in a uranium mining company that owns 20% of the weapons grade uranium mined in the U.S. and a significant amount of what is mined worldwide. I read somewhere it was approximately 50%. This occurred while Hillary was Secretary of State and she was involved in approving the deal. The mines are located in Kazakhstan, Africa, Australia, and the

U.S. The Clinton Foundation got $2.35 million in donations from the uranium mining company now controlled by the Russians. I know Bill is a good speaker but is he worth the $500,000 he additionally received for a speech in Moscow paid by a Russian investment bank involved in the deal?

The foundation also received $31.3 million from the Canadian who originally started the uranium mining company. The original company was started by obtaining the ownership of mines in Kazakhstan through Bill's influence with the President of Kazakhstan. Bill's involvement was reportedly in conflict with American foreign policy. The Clinton Foundation was promised $100 million more in the future from the originator of the Canadian company. This is one of many stories in Schweizer's book involving Clinton Foundation donations, speaking engagements by the Clinton's, and deal making by the Clintons. I might add that that the Moscow speech was one of thirteen in which Bill received outrageous fees. Eleven of them took place while Hillary was Secretary of State. Judicial Watch filed a lawsuit in October 2015 seeking communications between Clinton and the U.S. Department of the Treasury on this matter. Stay tuned.

Before we leave this topic, I want to share two more tidbits I learned about the foundation. I read between 2009 and 2012 the foundation's IRS filings showed they raised over $500 million. Only $75 million or 15% was spent on charitable activities. More than $25 million was spent on travel expenses and about $100 million was spent on salaries. I am sure there were some additional expenses but what happened to the other $300 million? Evidently, the foundation has to re-file their IRS returns for 2010, 2011, and 2012 because they forgot to include some of the foreign donations they received. Is it a coincidence that these are the years the Russian uranium deal was taking place?

It doesn't take a lot of imagination or genius to connect the dots on this one. Should we have like concerns regarding Obama's upcoming "top secret" free-trade deal? Why do I say that? Which is worse, selling out your country for personal monetary gain or selling out your country for personal ideological gain and establishing your legacy? Selling out is selling out and the American people lose? This topic gives insight into how lucrative foreign policy decisions can be for those who are in a position of power. They can chose to enrich themselves financially or emotionally at the expense of the American people even though they are bound by law and ethics to represent our best interest. I have thought many times what Hillary and Bill might do for personal enrichment if she were to become president. It certainly provides insight as to what Hillary's foreign policy might be if she were elected?

We just talked about Bill and Hillary's quest for power, let's now go back to China and take an in-depth look at their quest for power. China has now become the world's second largest economy behind the United States. They trail us by approximately $7 trillion and are predicted to significantly narrow that gap to around $2.5 trillion by 2030. China is the largest holder of our debt at $1.25 trillion. I was never comfortable with that. In the past, they have held that issue over our head. Japan is the second largest holder at $1.13 trillion. The U.S. owns $12.9 trillion and other countries own $3.8 trillion. Our total debt today stands at a little over $19.3 trillion. Our national debt was $1 trillion in 1981 under Reagan. In order to put $1 trillion in perspective, Reagan said a stack of $1,000 bills 4 inches high in someone's hand equals $1 million but it would take a stack of $1,000 bills 67 miles high to get $1 trillion. That's an imposing thought.

International acquisitions and mergers is another economic power move by the Chinese that I find very troubling. The Wall Street Journal reported in March of this year that a Chinese company named the Anbang Insurance Group made an all-cash offer of $14 billion to buy American owned Starwood Hotels and Resorts Worldwide Inc. This was their second attempt to outbid American owned Marriott International, Inc. For some unknown reason, Anbang walked away. The newspaper article said Anbang has "exploded into the international scene in recent years by spending billions to acquire insurers and hotels throughout the world". They are the same company that bought New York's Waldorf Astoria for approximately $1.95 billion. That transaction raised eyebrows because the Waldorf Astoria is where our diplomatic corps stayed when they came to visit the U.N. and the sale created concerns regarding espionage by the Chinese. Our diplomatic corps no longer stays there. Anbang said their goal was to become a "top 10 global financial empire".

So, why does this trouble me? I am troubled for two reasons. First, Anbang is not the only Chinese company expanding through global buyouts. The Wall Street Journal said this bid "highlights the newfound muscle of Chinese companies in the high states global business of mergers and acquisitions". Fortunately, the Chinese have had trouble closing mergers and acquisitions in the U.S. I do not like a totalitarian country like China increasingly becoming more aggressive militarily and obtaining such a powerful economic footprint in the world, especially in our own country.

Secondly, Anbang was deemed by the article to have an "opaque structure". What does that mean? The article commented that the company is owned by a "mash of corporate shareholders with multiple layers of holding companies registered all around the country". Anbang responded "they are owned by more than 30 corporate investors who don't participate in the company's daily operation". It sounds like something out of a James Bond movie. At least their corporate name is not SPECTRE. I do not want major companies in my country owned and controlled by "opaque structures" from a foreign country that is aggressive toward us both economically and militarily.

Here are two other troubling issues regarding China and our economy. They involve cyberspace. Do we have any idea of the number of trade secrets stolen from United States businesses by the Chinese? The answer is no. I recently learned of another cyberspace issue involving the Chinese and our business community—cyber-theft. There was an article in my local newspaper by the AP regarding Chinese cyber-thieves who stole over $3 million from Mattel, Inc. through the Internet by deception. The article said, "Mounting evidence indicates that China is becoming a global banker for the criminal economy according to interviews with police officials, court records in the U.S. and Europe, and intelligence documents reviewed by the AP." The State Department said the Chinese government is not cooperating in financial investigations, which adds to China's appeal as a money-laundering hub.

How about the Chinese and their cyber-espionage against the U.S. government? Ask our roughly 21,500,000 government and non-government employees how they feel about the Chinese hacking personal information including their social security numbers. The government initially tried to cover up the seriousness of the attack. No surprise there. Anyone who thinks these tactics by the Chinese are not supported by or endorsed by the Chinese government is a candidate for one of my newer bridges. I'm thinking the red one with a few gold stars.

James Clapper, Director of National Intelligence, said he was not optimistic that the Chinese will stop their cyber intrusion. I even read that someone hacked into the personal email accounts of 20 U.S. officials including CIA Director John Brennan and DHS Secretary Jeh Johnson. What is in our future regarding cyber-espionage? Is this administration doing anything to develop a cyber defense system for Americans, American businesses, the U.S. government, or the U.S. military from cyber attacks? I don't have a clue. They appear to give lip service and then develop amnesia. I call it my "ostrich syndrome". First, bury your head in the sand and pretend it's not there. Then, hope it will go away if you keep your head in the sand long enough. I often believe the White House is an ostrich farm.

I have always had confidence that our country had the ability to develop any technology needed to counter any national security threat that might come our way. I knew there were brilliant and dedicated people working in a secluded basement somewhere, or in research compounds like the Lawrence Livermore National Laboratory in California and Los Alamos National Laboratory in New Mexico, developing incredible "secret stuff" to keep us safe and secure. I have driven through Los Alamos where the atomic bomb was developed. The buildings are spread over several miles and are very impressive. As I drove through Los Alamos, I was a proud American and I felt a comforting sense of safety and security as I thought about the innovations they have developed in the past.

I have lost that comforting sense of safety and security under the Obama administration. The following graphic comes to mind as I ponder these insecure sentiments:

> This administration is taking us very fast to the progressive political Milky Way and is so clueless about effectively leading our country in a safe and prosperous way that we are drifting into a black hole of danger

while the bad guys are taking a thrill ride around the
Earth in their new found rocket ship of evil

I can only hope that all of the brilliant and dedicated people in these
government operated and funded scientific facilities are still working
hard on secret projects needed to keep us safe and secure in spite of the
Obama administration's seemingly lack of direction.

Becoming the world's second largest economy and moving toward
number one does not satisfy China's thirst for power. They are also on
a quest to be a military might, if not an expansionist nation. They are
significantly expanding the military capability of their air force and navy.
The South China Sea includes some of the busiest trade routes in the world
and China is claiming most of the South China Sea as their territory. That
puts them in dispute with Malaysia, Vietnam, Brunei, Taiwan and the
Philippians. Several of these countries look to the United States as a friend
and ally who would protect them from China intrusion. We actually have
a defense treaty with the Philippians, South Korea, and Japan.

Are you going to take a cruise in the East or South China Seas? If
so, you should wear a flack jacket at all times and insist that your ship
practice avoidance drills? In order to demonstrate their power and
authority, the Chinese navy performed ramming drills on Vietnamese
ships when Vietnam was protesting China placing an oil rig off their
coast. This ramming took place just after Obama visited the area in
2014 and expressed his support for our allies who are involved in this
territorial dispute with China. Coincidence? China then claimed the
Vietnamese rammed their ships 1,400 times at the oil rig. The few
reports I found regarding China's allegation were not very convincing.

I read in The Wall Street Journal that Vietnam turned to Japan to
form an alliance as a result of China's continuing aggression. This was
after Vietnam's General Secretary came to Washington and visited with
Obama and other top U.S. officials. I assume the General Secretary
came up empty handed. Seems this pattern is becoming the norm in
our foreign lack of policy. Are we going to have any alliances left in the
world by the time Obama leaves office? After I wrote this, I was very
pleased Obama told the Vietnamese during his visit in May of this year
the United States would lift our ban on selling arms to them. I believe

this deal was more important to Obama to gain support for his free-trade deal than to send a message to China. Sounds like an opportunity to sell a legacy bridge to me.

Three months after China rammed the Vietnamese ships, a Chinese fighter plane "barrel rolled" over one of our Navy anti-sub airplanes. The Chinese fighter plane supposedly came within 20 feet of our airplane and was very threatening. A news report said, "The risky incident was one of the latest in a series of near-misses between Chinese and American ships and aircraft as both countries have sought to assert their military might in the East China and South China seas". China is building a network of facilities in the South China Sea by increasing the size of existing reefs that could be used for military operations. These facilities include the capability for military aircraft.

During Obama's September 2015 visit to Alaska, China sent five navy ships to the Bearing Sea to cruise off the coast of Alaska while he was there. They had never sent ships to that area before. The exercise was an unbelievable "in your face" from China to Obama. These "in your face" shenanigans are something both China and Russia have wanted to do to America for a long time but, before Obama, they were afraid to do so. Now, they are having a field day.

The Obama administration publicly criticized China for its actions in the South China Sea. Two high-ranking Chinese military officials responded by stating their actions fall well within the scope of their sovereignty. They said what they are doing with the reefs "could be used for military purposes" but it is primarily for maritime search-and-rescue, oceanic research, and environmental protection. How could I have been so cynical and suspicious—silly me! If the Chinese honestly think our country and our allies are that gullible, I have a transoceanic bridge to sell them that reaches from the China mainland to those reefs they are building up. Unfortunately, they are much too smart to be interested in that ocean bridge. They are just "toying" with Obama and his administration.

Here are a few more moves the Chinese have made as they strive to increase their world power. I read in The Wall Street Journal that China has negotiated with the east African nation of Djibouti to build its first overseas navel instillation and potential air base. It is very interesting that we currently have a military base in that small country. China also announced they plan to build more army and navy bases around the world and they have begun efforts to obtain world influence by providing financial aid to other countries that have traditionally been in in our camp?

Here is a great example. China announced a plan last year to spend $46 billion in building energy and infrastructure improvement projects in Pakistan. The plan is called the China-Pakistan Economic Corridor and China states the plan's purpose is to open new trade routes to central and south Asia. NBC News reported in May of this year that the plan's purpose is about more than simple trade. The report said the massive plan is about bolstering Pakistan's economy, giving China's navy access to the Indian Ocean, strengthening both countries against India, and hedging against U.S. influence in the region. The NBC report commented, "A 30 by 45-foot Chinese flag draping the port authority building here (referring to Gwadar, Pakistan) projects an unmistakable message: Pakistan and Chinas are now self-declared "iron brothers" and "all-weather friends".

China has circled the Earth with manned space flights since 2003 and launched an experimental spacecraft in 2014 in preparation for their first unmanned space flight to the moon. Will they catch up with or surpass our decimated space program? Are there national security implications here? Can you imagine China and Russia aiming their "Star Wars" laser guns at us from outer space while we are dilly-dallying around throwing our space program under the proverbial bus? Laser weapons would make nuclear missiles antiquated. Maybe the Obama administration knows something we don't and that is why they continually find false rationale to get rid of our nuclear missile stockpile. I say that tongue in cheek because I really don't think this administration listens to or takes seriously any national security information they have access to.

I commented on NASA and our national defense in the last chapter. After I wrote those comments and the comments in this chapter regarding Chinese aggression, I read a syndicated article in my local newspaper from The Washington Post that supported the concerns I have expressed and made me feel a little eerie. Here is what the article said:

Picture this: A Chinese fighter jet accidentally crashes into a Navy P-8 Poseidon surveillance plane while attempting to buzz over the South China Sea, killing all on board both aircraft. Fearing U.S. retaliation, China goes a relatively unexpected route. It uses surface-to-air missiles to shoot numerous U.S. satellites out of the heavens in quick session. Very quickly, the Navy is forced to navigate the Pacific with little use of GPS and degraded communications, causing chaos and uncertainty. The Chinese strikes also have knocked out some of the Pentagon's ability to control its arsenal of precision-guided weapons.

The Washington Post article obviously said that none of this has happened but it did say this hypothetical scenario points out the reliance the Pentagon has on space and its importance to military technology. It mentioned a report put out by the Center for a New American Security that highlighted the vulnerabilities of the Pentagon in space and chided them to make a shift in strategy to prepare for conflict there. Particular reference was made to China and Russia as potential threats in this regard. The report also said, no matter what steps the military takes, it is "unlikely that the United States will have unchallenged dominance in space again". I have to use my "sad" word here.

If anyone thinks our national defense being controlled from outer space will never materialize and is off the wall, let's take a quick look at some history. Pioneers like Daniel Boone, Davy Crocket, and Lewis & Clark couldn't imagine automobiles, jet planes, televisions, computers, and cell phones when they were living? That was only 175 to 210 years ago? How about characters from the American Wild West such as Wild Bill Hickok, Billy the Kid, and Jessie James who lived from the early 1800s to the early 1900s? That was only 115 years ago. It is astonishing to me that the development of the sophisticated inventions we enjoy today, which these explorers and cowboys could never imagine, took place in such a short period of time. This is especially true when one considers the world's evolutionary timeframe regarding civilization. How old is our common light bulb that we take for granted? Thomas

Edison's first public demonstration of the light bulb was only 136 years ago. How about Alexander Graham Bell's telephone? That was in 1876—141 years ago. Here is a big one. The first commercial computer was on the market in 1950, 66 years ago, and Hewett Packard sold the first mass produced desktop computer in 1968—only 48 years ago. What has happened with computers during those 48 years is mind-boggling to me.

The more exponentially technology grows, the more exponentially it grows. Our civilization is lucky we have pioneers to blaze the trail for us not only geographically but also technologically. I often wonder what it will be like in another 100 to 200 years. I can't imagine. Will military Star Wars exist? Probably will. For our national safety, we need to do everything possible to insure that America continues to lead the world in the technological boom. Unfortunately, that is not a priority with our progressive friends. What are they thinking? They're not! Remember chapters 2 and 4.

I obtained the following from a variety of news reports. Although it has not been confirmed by U.S. intelligence, China is now believed to have submarines carrying nuclear-armed missiles. These missiles have the capability of hitting the United States. China's navy chief said, "This is a trump card that makes our motherland proud and our adversaries terrified. It is a strategic force symbolizing great power status and supporting national security." The commander of the U.S. 7th Fleet said in response, "They were very clear with respect to their messaging. We're a professional navy, we're a professional submarine force, and we're global. We're no longer just a coastal-water submarine force." A retired Chinese Major General said in response to a question regarding their submarines causing another cold war, "We're not that stupid but we need enough nuclear submarines to be a credible force—to have some bargaining chips."

Not to be outdone by the Chinese, the Russians have done "in your face" exercises as well. During the Ukrainian rebel uprising, they sent 150 pure white unmarked trucks into Ukraine supposedly for humanitarian aid purposes. Why white? Was that some kind of symbolism? Internationally, the white flag stands for truce, ceasefire, and surrender. Were these trucks a Trojan horse or a laugh by Putin toward Obama and our allies? Russia did not follow the rules that were established by Ukraine for the trucks to enter their country and received severe criticism by the North Atlantic Treaty Organization (NATO). NATO suspected the Russians were sending supplies to support the pro-Russian Ukrainian separatists. I wonder how many of those separatists are in reality Russian soldiers? What country is the most powerful country in NATO and also the de facto leader? Of course, we are! One could easily and most accurately conclude that when Russia challenges NATO they are in reality challenging the United States.

A syndicated Los Angeles Times news story reported in August of 2014 that Putin denied the Kremlin sent troops and tanks into Ukraine and countered Western threats of Western sanctions by saying "it is best not to mess with us". Three months later, The Wall Street Journal reported that Russia announced a new initiative to spread Moscow's messages by radio and Internet in 30 different languages that will be run out of offices in 25 major cities around the world including Washington, D.C. This is an effort to intensify their information war with the West. In the beginning their website was to be only in English and featured U.S. bashing news columns such as "Presidential crimes. Then and Now." that likened the Department of Homeland Security to the Nazis' Gestapo secret police.

Did you know, according to Wikipedia, Russia already has satellite and cable television news, commentary, and documentary programing in German, English, Spanish, French, and Arabic that is broadcast around the world by satellite, cable, computer, mobile devices, and You Tube? I had no idea this was taking place until I found it researching The Wall Street Journal story. The television network is based in Moscow and has 21 news bureaus in 16 countries and 9 channels. Its name is RT and stands for Russia Today. There are bureaus in Washington and New York that support their international and American channels and in Miami and Los Angeles that support their Spanish channel. According to RT, they reach about 700 million households in 100 countries. They claim they reach 85 million households in the United States.

Wikipedia says RT is the most watched foreign news channel in the U.S. after BBC World News and is the number one foreign network in five major urban areas. It was noted that the network rates well among

Americans less than 35 years of age and in inner city areas. In 2012, Pew Research found that RT was the most popular news service on YouTube. Fox News was second. In 2013, RT reached a total of 1 billion viewers on YouTube. In 2014, RT was reported to have 1.4 million subscribers on its English YouTube channel. The most popular video of Putin was in 2010 when he sang Blueberry Hill at a St. Petersburg charity event. I watched his video. I give him a lot of credit for "giving it a whirl" but Fats Domino he's not.

I was concerned about the introduction of Al Jazeera's intro into the U.S. market and spreading anti-American propaganda. The discovery of RT was an unwelcomed surprise. Especially, after I looked on RT's web site that has the headline "Question More" and read some of its propaganda. RT is available on Time Warner Cable, Cox Cable, Comcast, and Verizon FiOS as well as the Internet. This gives Russia an enormous opportunity to provide negative propaganda to our young people and our disenfranchised population to influence them against America. Unbelievable! Al Jazeera's cable news channel that was bought from Al Gore shut down in April of this year and will expand its digital presence. According to Al Jazeera they are going to "bring new global content into America". What the heck does that mean? I guess we will find out.

Researching RT, I discovered Press TV, which is a 24-hour English language news and documentary network operated by Iran. Iran? Yes Iran. They have offices and bureaus around the world including London, Beirut, Damascus, Kabul, and the Gaza Strip. Thank God I could not find any in the U.S.—yet. We cannot get their television feed but we can get their website. It makes RT look tame. For example, I saw a big headline on their website that said, "Trump says our friend Israel funds Daesh (ISIS) terrorists." It was in response to Trump's comment that our allies send money to terrorist groups. I read the article and it "assumed" Trump included Israel in his comment. This is only one of many distortions of the facts on their website and the website is rife with propaganda. The Press TV website was a big surprise. I should get out of my cave more often to discover what is happening and so should everyone else who is concerned about the future of our country.

I found these revelations about RT and Press TV to be stunning and more than concerning.

After I wrote the above, I updated the list of recent terrorists attacks to include the one in Kabul, Pakistan and I became even more stunned. When I went to the Internet to research the number of casualties in the attack, the featured news source at the top of the page of listed websites was the RT website. I have never seen that before and, as you know, I have done enormous research on the Internet during the past three years. I never thought I would see a Russian news service get top billing like that. I think it is a hint of what is to come. It is a very scary thought and I believe the progressive onslaught to destroy traditional American ideology has opened the door for this to happen. The Obama administration's progressive actions have invigorated our adversaries to be more aggressive and use their Marxists propaganda against us. The progressives like it because it supports their cause. Diabolical but very possible.

These adversarial countries hate America for a variety of reasons and are selling "bridges of enlightenment" to gullible, misguided, and vulnerable Americans and unfortunately many people in our society are buying them. This is not only an American problem but is a world problem. How about ISIS and their worldwide recruitment propaganda? Our president going around the world and putting America down instead of portraying America as a beacon of hope only exacerbates the problem. Deteriorating relationships with our long time allies and friends aren't helping the situation either.

Russia didn't limit their "in your face" campaign against NATO and the United States to Ukraine. Russia's military aircraft have been making routine flights that abut the airspace of our NATO allies. This intrusion toward NATO airspace only began last year and has not happened to this extent since the cold war. They also test fired an ICBM missile capable of a nuclear warhead from one of their submarines. It was reported that Russian military planes flew into Alaskan airspace multiple times last year and their navy ships chased one of our submarines out of their territory in the Barents Sea. Russian attack jets repeatedly buzzed our Navy destroyers in the Baltic Sea in March of this year. We did nothing except voice rhetoric that their actions were "unsafe and unprofessional". How does that affect the morale of our military and what message does that send to Putin and the rest of the world?

After requests during the past several months by Ukraine for U.S. assistance in their civil strife with Russia, we finally announced we were going to provide training to their troops and monetary aid for military hardware. This is another one of our many foreign policy examples of too little too late. Russia's affronts toward the U.S., NATO, and our other allies have been bad but this next one really hits home. Russia socked it to us by stepping on one of our biggest international symbols of "world power". The Russians accused McDonald's of sanitary violations and inspected over four hundred McDonald's restaurants across their country. Some of them were shut down for alleged violations. There are obviously more options than the military to say "in your face". I wonder how Ronald felt about taking a fall for Obama. OK, I can't prove the Russian affront against Ronald wasn't legit but I am sticking to my story. After all, this is an opinion book.

If what we have discussed so far hasn't gotten your attention regarding our national security, the following should. It certainly got mine. Russia has announced it will send long-range strategic bombers on regular patrol missions to the Arctic Ocean, the Caribbean, and the Gulf of Mexico. Russia has never flown bombers in the Gulf of Mexico, even during the cold war. They also said they were going to expand their worldwide military presence and would seek permission in Latin America, Asia, and other regions of the world for their ships and airplanes to use sea ports and airplane facilities for repairs and re-fueling. Sounds like the Chinese. The countries they are supposedly talking to include Algeria, Cyprus, Nicaragua, Venezuela, Cuba, Seychelles, Vietnam, and Singapore. This Russian activity makes the Cuban missile crises look like child's play. What do you think would be the result if we could compare how John F. Kennedy would handle this situation versus how Obama is handling it? I can guarantee you that if John F. Kennedy was president instead of Obama, we would not have this situation to talk about and remember I am a staunch conservative.

When the world leaders were at the 2014 G-20 summit in Australia, Russia sent four warships to international waters off the Australian coast. Australia's Prime Minister said, "Russia was being more assertive now than it has been for a long time." Russia said their Pacific fleet was testing its range and could also be used for security for Putin. I think it was an in-your-face moment against Obama and the United States in front of 20 of the world's top leaders.

Did you know that Russia lifted their self-imposed ban on supplying Iran with a powerful missile air-defense system while we were trying to close negotiations with Iran on the nuclear agreement? This air-defense system will make it much harder to mount a militarily attack on their nuclear facilities. Coincidence? You tell me. There is no doubt this decision by Russia has an odor to it.

Before we move on to ISIS and Islamic Terrorism, I want to share the essence of an editorial in The Wall Street Journal that I find fascinating and applicable to this discussion. Russia signed a deal with China to supply them with $400 billion worth of natural gas over the next 30 years. The two countries also made plans to set up ground stations on each other's land for their satellite global-positioning navigation systems, made agreements for an ice-free port in Russia's far eastern region, and agreed to build a railway bridge over their common border. I have a great railway bridge to sell them to connect their countries that brings together adversaries that have a common goal. I don't want them to know the bridge eventually implodes when each realizes they can only reach their individual goals when the other is no longer in the way. Maybe I could greatly shorten that bridge and sell it to them by putting a two-way picture of Obama in the middle. It would be like two bulls charging a matador's cape from opposite directions except they don't realize they are actually charging each other until it's too late.

Surprisingly, my plan may not work. The editorial said the Chinese people are fascinated with Putin and that books about him are "flying off the shelves". A biography on Putin made the top 10 non-fiction bestseller list in the Beijing News newspaper. A Chinese poll said Putin's approval rating in China was 92% after Russia invaded Crimea in March of 2014. An expert on China-Russia relations at Shanghai's Fudan University said, "Putin's personality is impressive—as a man, as a leader. Chinese people find that attractive. He defends Russia's interest. China and Russia can learn a lot from each other." Are these comments another affront against Obama?

The editorial commented that many Chinese call Putin "Putin the Great". The more I think about this, the more I still believe my railroad bridge will work. The egos for Putin and the Communist Party of China are too big not to clash at some point. It is the same scenario as with our progressive groups who have a common cause but a different agenda. They are all for one and one for all until they no longer have a common enemy at which time their own agenda's take over and clashes begin. I can never imagine Russia and China forging long-term harmony and solidarity. Their individual quests for power are too much at odds.

Military cat and mouse incidents like those carried out around the globe by Russia and China are not new and occurred pre-Obama but they were never so frequent and so blatant. The Wall Street Journal reported two Chinese and three Russian defense companies are now in the global top 20 in size and the double digit growth in defense spending has allowed their defense companies to grow faster than average. Our Lockheed Martin and Boeing defense companies still top the list but their revenues have been shrinking during the past four years. No surprise there. The Wall Street Journal had another article that said India announced they were going to spend $8 billion on new "war ships" and their prime minister called upon the world's arms makers to manufacture more weapons in India. Everyone might as well jump into the fray. They may have to before the world calms down. That is going to get increasingly harder to do unless we jump in the ring with "fists up" and shout "stop it". Unfortunately, we are now going to have to bloody some noses to get our credibility back.

Before Obama, the world's bad guys did not observe the President of the United States make some idle threat toward them and then immediately head back to the golf course to finish their golf game. Remember that one? The incident took place when Obama gave his public response to the beheading of American journalist James Foley, briefly talked with his family, and immediately went back to playing golf? How crass! In response to the public criticism he received for his behavior, Obama said the following during an interview with NBC News, "Part of this job is also the theater of it. Well, its not something that always comes natural to me. But it matters. And I am mindful of that. I should have anticipated the optics." Theater and optics when an American was just beheaded? How about empathy, remorse, and anger?

Obama also commented that he was "heartbroken" and it was hard for him to hold back tears when he spoke to the family. Really? I saw him at the golf course on television immediately after he got back. He didn't look too heartbroken to me. Obama partially blamed the press for his criticism because they follow him everywhere even when he is "supposed to be on vacation". Well Mr. President, the President of the United States is never "totally" on vacation just like I was never "totally" on vacation when I was a CEO. Stuff happens and it's the leader's responsibility to deal with it even on vacation. I can tell you that I did multiple times. That's just part of the job. Obama's actions in this situation showed a lack of sensitivity and a lack of empathy. Again, this behavior is indicative of someone with a narcissistic personality disorder.

I can assure you bad guys like Russia, China, and terrorists are "shaking in their boots" because they're laughing so hard. The rest of the world and foreign leaders who have been our close allies are also "shaking in their boots" but not because they're laughing. We have lost our credibility on the world stage. It breaks my heart that our once powerful and highly respected country is now being reduced to a pile of smoldering whimpering ash in the eyes of the world. Congratulations Mr. President. You have had great success in fundamentally changing America.

What I just said was very evident on my trip to Europe last year. The newspapers and television news shows were full of negativity toward United States foreign policy. There was concern expressed in one newspaper about Russia flexing its military muscle in the Baltic Sea to intimidate its European neighbors from seeking energy independency from them. This was in spite of several U.S. Navy vessels in the area. I might add that the countries being intimidated by Russia were members of NATO. There was also a significant amount of news in the newspapers and on television regarding ISIS becoming increasingly stronger despite efforts by the United States and our allies to combat them.

I watched a television news interview in which Kurdish soldiers openly, without any disguise, blamed the United States for the ISIS upheaval. I read one rather lengthy article about Michelle Obama that reported on her comments regarding racism in America. The article quoted her expressing the pain she felt due to the way Barack Obama has been treated because he is black, the criticism she has endured as First Lady, and the overall racism that is prevalent in America. As an American in a foreign country, it was extremely embarrassing. If what she said was true, how can we have a black president and black First Lady? And, our black president was elected twice!

One newspaper had a cartoon showing a U.S. National Security Administration employee on a computer saying, "We need to hack into China's computers so we can get more information on Americans." There was continuous economic news about China and its increasing influence on the world economy. One article said, if the United States did not sign the Trans-Pacific Partnership, Washington's already weakened position in the Pacific would further deteriorate enhancing China's growing power. A Japanese university professor said, "If this (partnership) collapses, Pacific Rim countries will be aghast. China is pushing and if the U.S. just stands aside, it would be a tragedy."

The newspaper story that pushed me over the edge in feeling very sad (yes, again) as a proud American was an op-ed written by well-known British journalist, Jonathan Freedland. It was published in the largest selling British Sunday newspaper. It was titled "Set your watch to Beijing time: the US is clocking off". One could say the op-ed was anti-American rhetoric by a journalist who does not like us but everything he said is supported by my research for this book. He said Washington is fearful of the Chinese buildup in the South China Sea as they watch the "rise and rise" of China. He went on to say this fear is just the latest in a "series of worries" to affect the U.S. foreign policy establishment. He said "they tremble" (referring to the United Sates) at the daring and technical skill of Beijing's army of cyber-hackers, "watched with alarm" as Britain and others ignored Washington's pleas and signed up to join China's new Asian Infrastructure Investment Bank, and "have noted" China's never-ending scramble to buy up the world's natural resources.

This will make you feel even better. Freedland referenced a recent poll taken in 40 countries by the U.S. based Pew Research Center and said the results were "stark". He commented the poll shows people around the world are generally convinced that China will eventually replace the United States or has already replaced the United States as the world's leading superpower. He said 59% of Britons believe that. He also said it was not surprising that people in Europe, the Middle East, and Africa believe it but 55% of American's believe America's days as "top dog" are numbered. I was so stunned at what I read, I went to the Pew Research website to look for myself and I found what Freedland said was accurate. I found only minor differences in the published survey results on the Pew website and Freedland's op-ed and the differences did not dispute his comments. What does that do for your American pride? How about your confidence in our and our descendants' future?

Freedland's op-ed also offered insight into the future. He said the world has grown up with Coca-Cola and Hollywood. If China took over, what would we eat and what movies would we watch? He said Oolong tea and dim sum are not going to replace Cokes and Big Macs but then he said something interesting. He said the household names we now enjoy would not change; just the ownership of those companies to Chinese based companies. He then said something not only interesting but very troubling. He said our Hollywood movies that one would see in a cinema owned by Beijing would have its script approved by China. Think about that one for a minute. It is bad enough now with the progressives' political correctness movement.

Freedland offered a few other observations that I feel are very possible. The world's workdays and calendars (including the United States) will change to fit Beijing rather than New York City. Major world events will cater to China's television audience and not the U.S. audience. You will love this one. He said, "If pumpkins and face-masks have crossed the Atlantic for American-style Halloween, who's to say red lanterns and roast-duck-in-a-bag won't make a similar journey?" If that were to happen, I wonder what our progressive friends would find wrong with it so they can practice their political correctness. Oh! That is not possible in this scenario. Political correctness is not allowed in the communist controlled Chinese culture.

Freedland remarked the things he said in the op-ed seem fanciful now and it is hard to imagine a world different from today's when fashion, culture, and habits are often originated in New York City or

Los Angeles. He then gave the analogy that Britons could not have imagined the world today when it was assumed that the British Empire would "rule the waves forever more" and yet London lost its dominate place in the world and another country took over. He concluded that the same thing could happen again. Unfortunately, it is. Thank you Mr. President and your progressive accomplices for fundamentally changing, or more appropriate, fundamentally destroying America.

Which is most threatening to us—Russia, China, or international terrorism? They are very different scenarios. Russia and China are most likely never going to attack us militarily unless we do something really stupid which unfortunately is a possibility with this or some other progressive administration. It is likely; however, that Russia and China will continue to increase their military might and significantly diminish or replace our position as the world's most militarily powerful country unless we significantly reverse our course.

China is in a position to replace us as the dominant economic force in the world but Russia, not so much. Russia has not adopted the economic "quasi-free enterprise model" as aggressively as the Chinese. According to a story in The Daily Signal in November 2015, the number of Chinese billionaires has now passed the number of U.S. billionaires. There are now 596 Chinese billionaires as opposed to 545 in the U.S. At least the Chinese billionaires are worth less than U.S. billionaires. China's 596 billionaires are worth $2.1 trillion versus $2.34 trillion for the first 400 billionaires in the U.S. The most stunning difference in wealth is that our per capita GDP is $53,101 and China's is only $9,844. Think about the implication of that statistic for a Marxist based society versus a capitalistic free market society and individual freedom of opportunity. This is a progressive's nightmare to defend.

The Daily Signal concluded that China's strict business policies and lack of development in rural areas inhibit China's potential for continued growth. The report concluded that without economic freedom reforms, China would not surpass the United States any time soon. That last comment is somewhat in contrast with my other research and I hope The Daily Signal is right. I give China's government two points, Russia's government one point, and the United States government zero points in the game of "Who Wants To Be the Most Powerful Country in the

World". It doesn't mean we would be decimated if this would ever occur. It just means we would no longer be "King of the Mountain" and would be subject to the whim of China and perhaps even Russia. The economic, cultural, and national security benefits we now enjoy through American exceptionalism would be significantly diminished.

Is the above scenario with China and Russia more threatening to America's future than Islamic terrorism? Islamic terrorism is not an overt threat to our economy like China but it is a much greater threat to our national security and personal safety than China or Russia. There is an estimated 1.6 billion Muslims in the world, which equates to 22% of the world's population. Our government estimates there are between 2 and 7 million Muslims in the United States. The Pew Research Center estimates there are roughly 13 million Muslims in the European Union countries and projects Muslims to make up about 8% of Europe's population by 2030. Their research listed the top four European countries with Muslim populations as Germany with 4.7 million, France with 4.7 million, the United Kingdom with 2.9 million, and Italy with 2.2 million. Their research showed Russia with 14 million.

I find that stunning about Russia. Actually, I found the number of Muslims I personally observed during my recent visit to the United Kingdom and France to be stunning. Women wearing headscarves were everywhere in London, especially in a popular area of the city where our hotel was located. Several wore burkas. The situation was surreal to me. I found the same situation in Paris, which was not as surprising after my experience in London. I was surprised; however, to see so many Muslim women in a small town of 20,000 people where we rented a house in the hills of France above Nice. I expect the vast majority of Muslims I see in the Middle Eastern cities I visit but not the significant number I see in European cities.

Did you know the United States was at war with Muslims during the 1800s—twice? They were called the Barbary Wars and occurred from 1801 to 1805 and in 1815. The Barbary States of Tunis, Algiers, and Tripoli in Northern Africa routinely pirated merchant and passenger ships for ransom. According to Wikipedia, between 1 and 1.25 million Europeans were captured by the Barbary Pirates and sold as slaves between the 16th and 19th centuries. The first Barbary War ended in a treaty being signed after the U.S. defeated the pirates. The second Barbary War also ended in defeat of the pirates and effectively ended piracy and the practice of "paying tribute" for safe passage through the region. If you are interested, Brian Kilmeade of Fox News wrote a book on the subject titled *Thomas Jefferson and the Tripoli Pirates.*

The Muslims who have joined radical Muslim terrorist's organizations are undoubtedly disenfranchised from society and/or their families and feel these radical organizations can fill that void in their lives. They have most likely become disenfranchised because of one or more of the following reasons: deep-rooted mental dysfunction resulting from their family's gene pool; dysfunctional behavior resulting from family and/or environmental influence; or a feeling of hopelessness resulting from poverty and/or lack of education. Terrorist organizations give the disenfranchised a feeling of belonging and purpose. Contributing to the appeal of terrorist organizations is the significant difference in Western and other non-Muslim cultures that are in conflict with the religious values expounded by the Muslim religion, which has been paramount in their lives. The Muslim terrorists proclaim the fundamental interpretation of Islam as the true Muslim religion. The difference between Western culture and fundamental Islam gives these converts to radicalism impassioned motivation to destroy us in supporting and defending fundamental Islamic ideology.

A good example is the 24-year-old Muslim terrorist shooter in Chattanooga, Tennessee who killed five military personnel. It was reported his mother filed for divorce from his father in 2009 because the father repeatedly beat and sexually abused her in front of the children and threatened to take a second wife as permitted in Islamic law. Once, she was beaten so severely, she went to a crisis center for help. The father also beat the shooter and his siblings. This was obviously a very dysfunctional home with significant potential to create mental issues for the shooter and disenfranchise him from society. In fact, it was reported the shooter had suffered from depression since he was 12 or 13 years old and had a history of drug and alcohol abuse.

The shooter wrote in his blogs, "Everyone of them (referring to the Companions of the Profit Mohammad) fought Jihad for the sake of Allah. This life we are living is nothing more than a test of our faith and patience. It was designed to separate the inhabitants of Paradise from the inhabitants of Hellfire, and to rank amongst them the best of the best and the worst of the worst. Don't let the society we live in deviate you from the task at hand. Brothers and sisters don't be fooled by your desires, this life is short and bitter and the opportunity to submit to Allah may pass you by."

What a tragic story for those military servicemen who were killed and for the shooter who was killed. The shooter and his family obviously were living a life of hell. The shooter took his life of hell and brought it down upon innocent people in the name of his religion. Is this really any different from other mentally ill shooters like the 20-year-old who killed 20 children and 6 adult staff at the Sandy Hook Elementary School in Connecticut or the 27-year-old that was convicted of killing 12 people and injuring 70 more at the movie theater in Aurora, Colorado? The answer is yes. The difference is the Sandy Hook and Aurora killers' motivations were not connected to and in support of radical fundamental Muslim ideology, as was the shooter in Chattanooga. What the shooters did have in common was the desire to act out and kill others that resulted from mental instability acquired through family genes, learned dysfunctional behavior, or a combination of both.

Let's analyze that last thought through the prism of radical Muslim terrorism. I am not personally familiar with the Muslim faith. Everything I hear and read about Islam; however, indicates it is authoritarian in governing the lives of its followers. This includes, for example, giving the male gender dominance over the female gender and discrimination toward and violation of the personal rights of the LGBT community. Islam does not allow significant flexibility in how Muslims live within their society and anyone who does not follow the teachings of Islam is considered an "infidel" and subject to rebuke, violence, or death. There are Muslims who are more moderate in their beliefs but they appear to be in the minority.

The Quran is the book of religious teachings for Muslims as the Bible is the religious book of teachings for Christians. The Quran is taken very seriously and followed very closely by all devout Muslims. There is variation in strength of devotion to the Quran in the Muslim faith but there is nowhere near the variation practiced by those in the Christian faith with regard to the teachings of the Bible. The Quran is not only used to guide Muslims spiritually but also to stipulate the laws of Muslim society that are faithfully and strictly followed by the vast majority.

I know Muslims in general are considered to be good and peace loving people but what I have just articulated regarding the Muslim religion combined with what I learned about the Chattanooga shooter raises a question in my mind. Are dysfunctional families more common in Muslim households than in non-Muslim households because of the powerful and restrictive impact of Islamic teachings? I honestly do not know the answer to that question but it leads to two other interesting questions that are built off the first one. Are young Muslims more prone to become disenfranchised from society versus young non-Muslims because of the controlling power of their religious ideology over their lives? And, are young disenfranchised Muslims who join radical fundamentalist Muslim terrorist groups more prone to thinking if they commit suicidal jihad for the sake of Allah against the infidels; they will go to Paradise (heaven) and rid themselves of any distress or dissatisfaction they are experiencing here on Earth?

Here is another story I read in The Wall Street Journal regarding the radicalization of a young Muslim man. The young man's father was a member of the Jordanian parliament. In January of last year, he joined his father in protesting the capture of the Jordanian pilot who was eventually burned to death by ISIS. The pilot was a childhood acquaintance. Nine months later he was one of three suicide bombers who died when they drove explosive-rigged cars into an Iraqi army barracks. How can that happen? The father said his son's interest in ISIS apparently began after January as he was cultivating new relationships while attending medical school in Ukraine. It appears he began to associate with Muslims who were radical in thought. He also became married during this time. There was nothing in the article about his wife's religious beliefs. One has to wonder; however, about his wife's religious beliefs and influence after what we learned regarding the wife's influence over her husband in the San Bernardino attack.

The young man would come home to Jordan and the family would debate whether or not ISIS was a terrorist organization and Jordan's role in fighting them. The father said in the beginning his son appeared to be "repulsed" by ISIS and commented "there must be something wrong with them". A few months later, when the son came home, the father said he "recoiled" at his son's long beard and unkempt hair. He told his father he wanted to become a martyr and go to heaven. He then cut off communication with his father and only spoke to his mother and brother. He told his brother that his father was an "infidel" because he drafted laws in parliament against "God's law".

The last thing the family heard from him before he died was that he had joined ISIS and was "living and sleeping comfortably". The father said, "I wanted to bring him back, even if it meant he goes to prison. Now my son is gone and it's over." This is another tragic story. We obviously do know the son's life story, including his emotional relationship with his family and his personal life outside his family, but it begs the question of how a seemingly normal young person with a good life ahead of him succumbed to radicalization.

After I wrote this, I saw an article in my local newspaper regarding the father. ISIS supporters had recruited a 25-year-old Jordanian woman on Facebook and she was in the process of being mentally trained at a secret compound in Turkey to become a terrorist. The woman's father is a retired army officer and asked the Jordanian parliamentarian to try and save his daughter. He was able to convince her to return to Jordan and give up her radicalization. I am sure that was bittersweet for the parliamentarian.

Young Muslims are immersed into their faith at a very young age and that influence strongly continues throughout their lives. I have observed this devotion when I visited Muslim countries and heard the call to prayer five times per day over the loud speakers on the minarets at the mosques and personally talked to Muslims about their commitment to their religion. The idea that young Muslims have a greater propensity than non-Muslims to become hostile toward a society that is counter to the ideological power of their religion is a very real possibility. It is also very possible that young Muslims are more prone to become disenfranchised from society versus young non-Muslims because of the controlling power of their religion over their lives. And finally, it is very possible that young disenfranchised Muslims who join radical fundamentalist Muslim terrorist groups are more prone to believing if they become martyrs for Allah they will go to Paradise and rid themselves of any distress or dissatisfaction they are experiencing here on Earth.

The young Jordanian's comment and the Chattanooga shooter's blogs are evidence of these possibilities. I cannot confirm my hypothesis based upon two individuals but how many of you know a Baptist, Methodist, Presbyterian, or Catholic radical terrorist? Even disallowing my hypothesis, mental health professionals say that one in four people are in need of mental health counseling. I think that percentage is low. That is a lot of young people, Muslim or not, who have potential to act out in an effort to alleviate mental dysfunction.

The Center for Security Policy (CSP) sponsored a project called the Mapping Sharia in America Project. This project was tasked with conducting undercover reconnaissance at mosques, Islamic centers, and Islamic schools in the U.S. The project report was published in the Middle East Quarterly in the summer of 2011. The founder of CSP is Frank Gaffney, a former assistant Secretary of Defense under Reagan. He is very controversial among progressive and Islamic publications and they label him a "notorious Islamophobe".

I took a hard look on the Internet at Gaffney and CSP and firmly believe the project report to be correct in principle if not correct in actual content. The CSP project found that almost 80% of the Muslim mosques and facilities they studied in the U.S. preach anti-West extremism and exhibit a high level of sharia compliance and jihad threat. Religious sermons in those mosques included the following language: women are inferior to men and can be beaten for disobedience; non-Muslims are infidels and inferior to Muslims; jihad or support for jihad is a Muslim's duty; suicide bombers and martyrs are worthy of the highest praise; and Islamic caliphate should one day encompass the United States.

According to the CSP study and several websites I reviewed, one does not have to go too far from our nation's Capitol to find a very radical mosque. It is the Dar al-Hijrah Islamic Center and is one of the largest mosques in Washington. A radical imam who had been at the Baltimore mosque where Obama gave his speech became an imam here after he left Baltimore. Al-Awlaki was also an imam at this mosque. You might remember him as a senior recruiter for al-Qaeda. Al-Awlaki was also a spiritual advisor to terrorists including at least two of the 9/11 attackers on the World Trade Center and the Army psychiatrist involved in the Fort Hood shooting. The mosque has supported several terrorist organizations, especially Hamas. Leaders of the Muslim Brotherhood reportedly run it. WND reported investigators for the CSP study said this is one of the mosques they studied that has the goal to turn the U.S. into an Islamic state governed by sharia law. The more I read the more I find out how intertwined these mosques are around the country.

Three members of the House of Representatives joined Virginia state lawmakers (the mosque is actually in Falls Church, Virginia) for a prayer service at the mosque after the San Bernardino and Paris attacks to "counter anti-Muslim rhetoric" and encouraged other House members to do so as well. According to The Blaze, one of the House members said, "We come today to say that we stand in total solidarity with you and we represent millions more." Fox News reported the director of the Los Angeles chapter of CAIR said the following after the San Bernardino attack, "Let's not forget that some of our own foreign policy, as Americans, as the West, have fueled that extremism." He doesn't sound very American to me and he talks like our progressive friends in the White House and Congress.

Here is another situation that raises questions about the relationship between radical Muslims and some of our government officials. I found the following on the Internet as I was doing research. The website for the U.S. government administered Smithsonian Institute, Smithsonian.com, listed a story titled "The Statue of Liberty Was Originally a Muslim Woman" as number one on their list of most popular stories. When you read the story it explains their reasoning but the rational is a stretch and very misleading.

Why would a U.S. government-controlled entity like the Smithsonian Institute make such a controversial statement? That statement disparages the international symbol of American freedom and revises that symbol to support Muslims who live under strict Islamic law that is the antithesis of freedom. Only in progressive Washington could that happen. I found it disgusting as I did the comments of the members of Congress at the Falls Church, Virginia mosque and the director of the Los Angeles chapter of CAIR.

The actions of the lawmakers at the Virginia mosque beg several questions. First, why are our elected national and state lawmakers supporting a mosque that has such a strong reputation for supporting terrorism? Second, why were they supporting the feelings of Muslims in lieu of supporting American terrorism victims and the families of those victims? Third, why are they supporting Muslims and Islam at the expense of supporting American national security with regard to Islamic terrorism? And fourth, why did they put the feelings and rights of Muslims above those of non-Muslim Americans? They were only three people from Congress and a few elected state officials but their actions are representative of all progressives in and out of government including our president and his administration.

I watched Obama's televised speech after the San Bernardino attack as he attempted to reassure Americans on terrorism. This was only his third speech from the Oval Office in 7 years. I might add that his approval polls were tanking which may be the real reason for the speech. He spent more time criticizing America for violence and our current gun laws than he spent on terrorism. He still did not use the term Islamic terrorists. In fact, he said we cannot "turn against each other" in a war between America and Islam. He said that's what ISIS wants. Really? As Mike Gonzalez said in The Daily Signal, "The Obama administration is, in fact, making the case that the proper response to current threats from ISIS is to tighten gun control laws, reduce carbon emissions, and double down on political correctness." Our president's entire speech toward terrorism was absolutely farcical and it was a big "thud" with both republicans and democrats.

Here is what Obama said regarding his approach to fighting terrorism. He praised his strategy as the right one by mounting air raids, supporting local troops, and sending Special Forces. Let's take a quick look at each one of these. We are currently doing "hundreds" of air raids versus the "thousands" we did during the Iraq war and we don't always drop bombs during the raids he bragged about. We spent approximately $500 million to train Syrian rebels and we can only account for 4 or 5 rebels who were trained. We sent 50 Special Forces last year and the

Secretary of Defense recently said no more than 200 would be sent early this year. We actually sent 250 troops. That oughta scare em! Maybe not! During the Iraq war, we had an average of 150,000 troops on the ground and during the surge that total went to about 170,000 troops.

As I said, ISIS is certainly not "shaking in their boots" unless they are laughing hard with all the rest of the bad guys. A political cartoon in my local newspaper makes this point. A very diminutive Obama with a stern smirk on his face is standing at the door of a house on Halloween with a trick or treat bag. The door is being held open by a Halloween jack-o-lantern. There are two very large ISIS terrorists answering the door and one says, "Get the camera. This is just too cute. He's getting set to scare us with another lecture."

At the same time as Obama's speech, a new intelligence report commissioned by the White House was released that said ISIS is not contained and would continue to grow in numbers and gain ground unless they experienced significant losses in Syria and Iraq. This is after there were government leaks that intelligence assessments on ISIS were being watered down and the president ordered military officials to get to the bottom of it. I wonder who caused the watered down reports to happen in the first place and why? Did I say White House? Did I say to cover their butts? According to The Wall Street Journal, Obama said he did not want intelligence "shaded by politics" or a "desire to tell a feel-good story". That's certainly new! Looks like the White House shot themselves in the foot on that one.

I heard a guest contributor on Fox News say something very profound. He asked why Obama gave his terrorism speech in the Oval Office rather than travel to San Bernardino to give the speech after he visited with the victims who survived and their families and the families of the victims who were killed? Ouch! The second largest terror attack in U.S. history at the time and the president doesn't appear in person to show his concern for the victims and their families? I did hear on the news that Obama was seen at an event wearing his tux after his speech. I guess he had other important things to do. Sounds like a repeat of James Foley and golf course incident? He sure has a lot of time to travel around the country for golf, vacations, political fundraisers, and ideological speeches. Why not the victims of an Islamic terrorist attack and their families? Would he have gone if it had been a Baptist, Methodist, Presbyterian, or Catholic terrorist attack?

After I wrote the above, Obama announced he was going to San Bernardino and meet with the surviving victims and all the victims' families. It was a little over two weeks since the attack and he saved us taxpayers' money. Rather than make a special expensive trip to California, he stopped by on his way to his annual Christmas vacation in Hawaii.

I guess Obama learned a lesson from San Bernardino. After the horrific "lone wolf" Islamic terrorist attack on the gay nightclub in Orlando, Florida, he and Joe Biden went to Orlando to meet with the victims and families and pay their respects to the 49 people who died. It was the largest mass shooting in U.S. history. After he came back to Washington, Obama met with his national security team and then gave a nationally televised speech. He, as usual after such tragedies, could not resist promoting gun control. He also went on a diatribe putting down congressional republicans and Donald Trump as the republican presumptive nominee for president. He then defended his position in not using the term "radical Islam".

I saw part of his speech and his demeanor appeared angry and defensive. He said he had been clear regarding how extremist groups have "perverted" Islam to justify terrorism (That is not what I have learned in writing this book.) and how he has "called on our Muslim friends and allies at home and around the world to reject this twisted interpretation of one of the world's greatest religions (Where are they???)". Obama said there has never been a time during his entire presidency when not using the term "radical Islam" prevented them from pursing a strategy or using the term would "turn this whole thing around". Obama angrily said, "So, there is no magic to the phrase radical Islam. It is a political talking point. It's not a strategy (That's not how most Americans and I see it, especially those with military and foreign service experience and those who are true moderate Muslims.)." Obama concluded that if we imply we are at war with Islam, we will be doing the terrorists' work for them in recruiting more terrorists (Looks like they have done very well without our help.).

Obama reminded me of the union organizers I had to deal with several times during my career. He was anything but presidential. Obama wasn't alone in not living up to public office responsibilities. Speaker of the House Paul Ryan called for a moment of silence on the House floor to honor those killed in Orlando. Several democrats demanded the speaker consider gun control legislation as they walked out of the room during the time of silence. I saw this on television and was stunned and angered at the inappropriateness and total disrespect for the victims shown by the democratic members of Congress who walked out. I read later that some of those who walked out tweeted their actions were justified. They have a right to ask for gun legislation but not in that manner. Ryan's spokeswoman said, "It's shameful that anyone would try to use a moment of silence honoring victims of a brutal attack to advance their own political agenda." Only a progressive can do that.

Our democratic congressional friends in the House did not stop there. They later staged a sit-in on the House floor (literally) for approximately 26 hours to push for gun control legislation. Not to let a good opportunity go by, they also used the opportunity to do political fundraising. Speaker of the House, Paul Ryan was obviously irritated and called it "a publicity stunt and a fundraising stunt". I think it was a disgusting stunt by progressives to use the worst mass shooting in our country's history to push their ideology and raise money.

Our Attorney General Loretta Lynch appeared on the Sunday morning talk show circuit. I watched her say they were going to be transparent as possible and release many of the transcripts of the 911 calls made by the Orlando shooter. She did say some of the information would be redacted. You probably know they redacted any reference to Islam, Islamic terrorism, or ISIS. After significant criticism, the DOJ re-released the transcripts that included those references with the exception of substituting God for Allah. Why would they do that? I think it was an organized attempt orchestrated by the White House to gloss over the fact that the attack was a lone wolf terrorist attack brought about by the shooter's dedication to Islamic terrorism and ISIS. That narrative does not fit the White House narrative and makes the Obama administration look bad. I saw Ms. Lynch being pushed by the press at a news conference as to who ordered the redactions and she refused to answer. The whole thing reminded me of the Benghazi cover up.

How about Muslim refugees coming into our country? On MSNBC's *Morning Joe* show, Bloomberg columnist Margaret Carlson said the following regarding Muslim terrorists sneaking into the United States disguised as Muslim refugees as compared to European countries, "… maybe they become Americanized, maybe the anger goes away. Maybe what they snuck in to do they're not going to do because we do have an acceptance of these people … they are more patriotic because they are here and work harder." She and Morning Joe supported these comments based upon America's long-standing immigration experience versus European countries. I do not have a bridge big enough to hold that one. This rhetoric is preposterous but I have watched several clips from other news shows and read several articles in the newspaper and these two individuals are not isolated in their thinking. These two are the kind of people who blissfully go along in their idyllic world until they wake up one day and say, "What the hell happened?"

This brings up a very important point regarding refugees being brought into our country by the government to escape terror in their homeland. The Obama administration makes it sound as if it is no different than our founding colonists and early immigrants coming to America. They say our country was founded upon immigration. That's true, but! Colonists and early immigrants came here for freedom and opportunity to succeed in life. They were hard working opportunists who took risks and made many sacrifices to get here and to stay here. They were not brought to America by the government and provided handouts to live. Don't get me wrong. I admire and welcome immigrants who come to America and apply for legal citizenship for the same reasons as our founding colonists and early immigrants. I feel very badly about the tragedies experienced by the refugees in trying to escape terror. Their plight is horrific. I also feel badly about the problems experienced by the Latin American illegal immigrants seeking a better life. But, we cannot save the world by destroying our country in the process. Why do the progressives do this? This immigration supports their utopian ideology and increases the progressive voter pool!

I received an email from a friend that listed all the cities in the United States where our government reportedly placed Muslim Refugees in 2015. The list showed 76,972 refugees were sent to 190 cities in all the states except Montana and Wyoming. The number of refugees sent to each city ranged from 5 to 2,660. The references for the list included US News, WND, Breitbart, and Refugee Resettlement Watch.

Wikipedia said officially there were 69,933 refugees brought into the U.S. in 2015 from all over the world under the U.S. Refugee Resettlement Program. The estimate for 2016 is 85,000. Obama said he would bring 10,000 Syrian refugees into the country this year. John Kerry said we are going to bring in a total of 85,000 refugees from around the world this year and 100,000 in 2017. During my research, I ran across across a significant amount of unverified information on the Internet claiming the government is "covertly sneaking" thousands of refugees into the country on chartered UPS jets. If that is true, what kind of vetting is being done, if any? What financial burden and safety risk does that put on Americans? We have no clue as to what the Obama administration is doing in this regard but I bet if we did, we would be extremely concerned. Where is the news media to help us find out?

I have tried to make sense of the political correctness afforded Muslims by our president, his administration, members of Congress, mainstream news media, progressives, and many classic liberals at the expense of all Americans who are not Muslim. I can only defer to chapters 2,3,4, and the next chapter to even begin explaining this behavior. Given the fact that progressives are looking for votes, it is still beyond rational thinking. If Muslims in the United States are as supportive of America as they say, why do we not hear public outcries from American Muslims and their religious leaders condemning Islamic terrorism? Except for a few, they are silent.

I was very happy to see a report in The Daily Signal in April of this year that said there is an organized effort in Houston to "develop innovative solutions to defend their communities against the threat of extremist ideology". The leaders of this movement said other communities in the U.S. are doing the same but none were mentioned by name. The report also said Congress has appropriated $10 million for grants to states and local communities to do the same as Houston. DHS, the DOJ, and the FBI have organized a joint task force to determine how they can assist in these efforts. I want to be hopeful these efforts will be successful but I have great doubt. There was also a very interesting chart in the report from the Pew Research Center showing age statistics on Muslims in the U.S. The chart said 15% are Baby Boomers, 31% are Gen Xers, and 51% are Millennials. Does that surprise you how young the Muslim population is? It certainly did me.

Here is something very interesting regarding political correctness I found on the Internet when I was researching the Dar al-Hijrah mosque. When I accessed the mosque's website, I could not access its content until I deleted a document that was covering the home web page. It was dated December 2, 2015, the date of the San Bernardino terrorist attack, and labeled "For Immediate Release". Here are the opening comments from that document:

> Description: Northern Virginia Mosque, (Dar al-Hijrah), opens its doors after the recent Islamophobia attacks, with a Unity Walk and Interfaith Coat and Blanket Drive for Syrian and Iraqi refugees. In this current climate of intolerance, we open our hearts in prayer, service, and solidarity as we mourn the loss of life and suffering caused by those whose true religion is hatred and intolerance—not Islam. We commemorate our resilience and common beliefs as 'One nation' that will not be split apart but unified by our love and freedom and the right to practice our faiths together and live justly in peace with our neighbors of all convictions.

The above is in reference to the event attended by the members of Congress and Virginia state officials. Here is my opinion on the document, especially after my research and the CSP report. Islamophobia is a fabricated situation. There have been minor incidences but I have not seen or heard of any significant backlash against Muslims in America. On the other hand, Americans have overwhelming reason to be concerned about Islam in America creating home grown radical terrorists. Unless we accurately understand and acknowledge the issue we are dealing with, how can we fight it? I agree with the mosque's comment that the true religion of terrorists is hatred and intolerance but where do terrorists get that mindset? They get it from the teachings of Islam carried out in mosques like Dar al-Hijrah. If the Dar al-Hijrah mosque believes American Muslims and non-Muslims should be one nation as they stated on their website, then why don't they stand with the rest of America and openly condemn Islamic terrorism rather than stay mum and claim Islamophobia.

There was an article in my local newspaper after the San Bernardino attack that contained interviews with two leaders of local Islamic entities. An imam of a local mosque said, "What is wrong with these people? They are sick people really. They have something wrong with their psyche. Islam is innocent in this. It teaches the opposite. They will receive their punishment by God very soon. Some wicked people interpret it the way they want to interpret it. They commit terrible acts in the name of God. It is very sad." The leader of a Muslim outreach organization said, "Our priest gave a very tough talk on this. Nobody has the right to take the law into his or her own hands. An organization like ISIS, they are a disgrace. Any sane person agrees. Our sympathies are with all other Americans. This is a very hard situation."

What these two Islamic leaders said could not be said better. The exception to their comments is that the teaching of fundamental Islam is not innocent. The important question here is whether or not these Muslim leaders are telling the truth. Do they fall into the 20% or the 80% category as described in the CSP study. I am not alone in that line of thought. A Rasmussen poll published in December, on the day before the San Bernardino attack, said 49% of likely voters believe Islam as practiced today encourages violence more than most other religions, 29% say that is not true, and 21% say they are undecided.

This brings up a serious question for our American society regarding all Muslim organizations in the U.S. and their leaders. Do we institute tough measures including some degree of selective profiling and take appropriate action based upon what we learn? Profiling is something I do not support except in dire times and we are in dire times concerning our national security. We need to be aggressive but use common sense.

I read the following in The Wall Street Journal. After the Paris attack, French authorities used sweeping emergency powers to shut down four mosques that were "suspected" of nurturing Islamic radicalism and raided more than 2,200 homes and businesses. The raids included the homes of several leaders from one of the mosques. French officials commented, "We must not cut ties with loyal Muslims of good faith." But, they continued, "We will be totally firm against all those who preach hate in France."

Our U.S. government could take a page from France's playbook. Political correctness is never correct, as we will review extensively in the next chapter. The current political correctness regarding Muslims in America is putting Americans at significant risk of harm. We do not want to wake up one day and say "What the hell happened?" after it's too late because we were asleep in the land of the politically correct. We need to search out that 80% or whatever the true percentage is and forcefully deal with it. Several neighbors of the San Bernardino terrorists observed strange behavior in the terrorists' garage and did not report it because they were afraid of being labeled Islamophobic. DHS has a saying, "If you see something, say something." Their website says, "It takes a community to protect a community." Political correctness won and the community lost in San Bernardino.

A Rasmussen poll taken in November 2015 said 32% of likely voters believed individual Muslims should be monitored, 52% disagreed, and 16% were undecided. This is a higher percentage in favor of profiling than I thought it would be and this was before the San Bernardino terrorist attack. Another Rasmussen poll, also taken in November, said 60% of likely voters believed we are at war with radical Islamic terrorists, 24% shared Obama's position, and 16% were undecided. That same pole said 92% of all voters regarded Islamic terrorism as a "serious" threat to our national security. A third Rasmussen pole taken in December 2015 after the San Bernardino attack said 66% of likely republican voters and 46% of all voters favor a temporary ban on Muslims entering the United States until the government improves its ability to screen out potential terrorists. Just 24% of republicans and 40% of all voters are opposed. The rest are undecided.

A study titled "ISIS in America: From Retweets to Raqqa" was released in December 2015 by The George Washington University. The study quoted U.S. authorities as saying there were 250 Americans who have traveled or attempted to travel to Syria and/or Iraq to join ISIS and they have 900 active investigations against ISIS sympathizers in all 50 states. I think that is the preverbal "tip of the iceberg". The report said seventy-one individuals have been charged with ISIS related activities since March 2014 and 56 of those 71 were arrested during 2015. Here is the profile of those arrested: the average age is 26; 86% are male; their activities took place in 21 states; 51% traveled or attempted to travel abroad; and 27% were involved in plots to carry out attacks in the U.S. The profiles of those arrested were very diverse in race, age, social class, education, family background, and motivation for involvement. The study found that face-to-face relationships are involved in cultivating and strengthening interest in ISIS. Social media plays a critical role in radicalization and mobilization of these people and they are particularly active on Twitter.

Whatever their personal reasons, there are tens of thousands of young Muslim men and women from around the world who have joined the Muslim terrorists. A thought to remember as we discuss Islamic terrorism is there are an estimated 1.6 billion Muslims in the world. Even if Muslims are not prone to disenfranchisement or violence more than any other segment of society, there is arguably a minimum of one in four who have mental health issues significant enough to put them in danger of becoming radicalized. You can do the math.

If Islamist terrorists are outliers in the Muslim faith as decried by so many Muslims, then why don't Muslims in America and around the world frequently and openly renounce radical Islamist jihad and caliphate? Why is it extremely rare that any Muslim leaders in any part of the world openly condemn Islamic terrorism? Why don't Muslims renounce mosques, religious centers, and schools that are havens for radicalization in Muslim and non-Muslim countries including the United States.

Why do isolated and very secretive Muslim communes in several of our states claim to be religious in nature and to carry out humanitarian work around the world but not allow entry into their communes by outsiders? It has been reported there are 22 of these communes in the United States operated by Muslims of the Americas. Could it be that Muslims of the Americas is a branch of Pakistan based Jamaat al-Fuqra that is known for terrorist activities? I read it was. I have also read these communes act as ideological and military style training camps for very young Muslims as well as adult Muslims. How many other communes are there like these that we do not know about? The Clarion Project says there are many of them across the United States. The good thing is The Clarion Project says these training camps are not widely supported by the general Muslim population.

I do not have any informed answers for these questions but I do have three theories. The first theory is there are countless numbers of Muslims who are closet jihadists and want to bring about caliphate to support Islam. This list includes Muslim religious leaders, Muslim organization leaders, and ordinary Muslims who support and encourage Muslim men and women who have the propensity to join Islamic terrorist's organizations to do so but do not get involved themselves. The Muslims in this category are also educating young and very young Muslims in radical Islamic ideology for the future. The second theory results from the oppressive nature of Islam. Muslims who do not support Islamic terrorists are afraid to speak out because of the fear of risking condemnation if not retaliation. My third theory is there are those in life, Muslim or not, who avoid personal involvement in any controversial situation.

Breitbart reported in May 2015 there was a survey done by the Internet website for the Al Jazeera Arabic television channel that asked, "Do you support victories of the Islamic State in Iraq and Syria (ISIS)?" According to Breitbart there were 38,000 respondents and 81% said yes. A poll published in May2015 by Saudi Arabia's Al-Hayat news said 92% of Saudis believe ISIS conforms to the values of Islam and Islamic law. I also found a March 2015 analysis done by The Clarion Project. Based upon opinion polls taken in 11 Arab states, they estimated 8,523,803 people strongly support ISIS. They extrapolated that percentage to the remainder 11 Arab states and that number became 21,460,000 people or 5.8% of the population strongly supporting ISIS. When you add the people in the Clarion survey who said they somewhat support ISIS to those that strongly support ISIS, that number is 24,454,228 for the 11 Arab states surveyed and 42,550,000 or 11.5% for the entire Arab world. The total population for these 22 Arab states was estimated to be 370,000,000.

Glen Beck published a book titled *It Is About Islam*. He quoted a June 2015 poll from the CSP study that showed 51% of Muslims in the U.S. embrace sharia law over the U.S. Constitution. Almost one in four Muslims polled believed "it is legitimate to use violence to punish those who give offense to Islam by, for example, portraying the prophet Mohammed". The study also showed that one in five respondents agreed "the use of violence is justified in order to make sharia the law of the land in this country", while only 39% believed Muslims in the U.S. should be subjected to American courts. Beck used a Pew Research estimate of three million Muslims in the U.S. and concluded that roughly 500,000 Muslims in the U.S. believe that "acts of terror and murder" are legitimate ways to replace the Constitution with sharia law.

Based upon what I just said, which one of my theories do you believe is accurate? There is no question in my mind after researching the subject. Although theories two and three have some validity, there is no doubt theory one is the most dominant reason and it is especially true for those in Muslim leadership positions. This is also consistent with the CSP study.

We hear over and over that Islam breeds peace loving Muslims who wish to live in harmony with non-Muslims. The statistics I just quoted do not support that thought but let's say for argument's sake that the overwhelming majority are totally peace loving, want to assimilate into other cultures, and want no part of radical jihad and caliphate as practiced by Islamic terrorists. Here is reality. Muslims follow a religion that is very controlling and domineering and does not allow the separation of church and state nor protect individual rights as required by America's Judeo-Christian based Constitution. This also applies to other Western cultured non-Muslim countries dominated by Christians. The Bible teaches us how to live from our hearts—from the inside. The Quran, from what I understand, teaches how to live through sharia law—from the outside. This is a very important distinction between the two cultures. Western culture is much more permissive in all respects than is allowed by the Quran

The majority of Muslims will never be able to truly assimilate into our American culture or any other Western culture. I often see this dynamic take place on Fox News. There are moderate Muslim news contributors that debate on television with devout Muslims and the dynamic is profound. The moderate Muslims are true Americans who have assimilated into American culture and still practice their religion. It is obvious the devout Muslims will never be able to assimilate into American culture and most appear to be anti-American even though I assume they are American citizens.

How do Muslims rectify this issue? I saw an article that described no-go zones in the United Kingdom where sharia law is followed and overrides local laws. I could not find much on the Internet regarding the subject, so I decided to ask people about it while I was in London last year. Here is what I learned. Apparently there are not any "known" no-go zones in London but are in other parts of the United Kingdom. The people I talked to said they did not believe there were courts in those areas imposing sharia law. How do they know? With what I know about the autocratic culture of Islam, I think sharia law could easily be imposed and followed behind the scenes without those on the outside knowing. I was told Muslims have taken over control of the schools in these no-go zone areas.

Here is a tragic story reported in August of 2014 regarding tolerance in the United Kingdom toward Muslims. At least 1,400 young people were victims of sexual exploitation in and around the city of Rotherham since 1997. Rotherham is a city of about 260,000 people. The young people were said to be from working class families and many were from troubled homes. The British government launched an investigation that reported children and teens, mostly girls, were raped multiple times, threatened with personal harm, and made to witness violent rapes. They were also trafficked to other towns. Those accused of this horrific crime were said to be Pakistani Muslims and others of Asian origin. The article said five men were convicted in 2010 who were involved in these crimes but did not mention any convictions regarding the many others who were involved. The government report said senior city officials ignored the "politically inconvenient truth" because they were fearful of appearing racist toward the Pakistanis who made up only 3% of the population. In my opinion, these city officials are as guilty as the perpetrators.

Members of the local Muslim community condemned these crimes but at the same time justified them due to the alleged lax social mores of the northeast England region. I can't even suggest a bridge for such an abominable excuse for such a heinous crime. The police district commander did apologize to the young people who were victimized. He said, "they did not receive the level of service they should expect from their local police force and they fully acknowledge their previous failings". His comment is despicable. I have not read or heard anything about what has happened since. I guess in the vernacular of our progressive friends, it's old news.

Well, I discovered an update during my editing of the book and it is shocking. Roughly 300 suspects were identified in 2015 and in February 2016 and four more men were prosecuted in Rotherham. Similar crimes were reported in West Midlands and South Yorkshire. The problem in South Yorkshire was reported to be worse than Rotherham. If that is not shocking enough, here is one bigger. I discovered that this problem is endemic in the United Kingdom and all across Europe. Countries specifically mentioned were Holland, Sweden, Norway, Belgium, and France. Canada and Australia were said to be "seeing their fair share" as well. How about Minnesota, Tennessee, Michigan, and Ohio? The American Thinker reported two years ago that 29 Muslims were convicted in 2010 for kidnaping, raping, and prostituting non-Muslim women and children between 2000 and 2010 in Minneapolis and Nashville. They had been operating there for 10 years and were mainly from Somali. It has been reported that this activity is happening in other parts of the U.S. as well.

The Muslims who do this are called Muslim Grooming Gangs. Government officials, police, and others around the world commonly refer them to as "Asians" rather than Muslims to avoid being labeled as Islamophobic and/or racist by the left and Muslim groups. I did not know this when I read the Rotherham story, which said the perpetrators were Pakistani Muslims and others of "Asian origin". Also,

I did not realize the lack of awareness in the U.S. regarding Muslims and the Muslim culture being a worldwide problem. This would be an interesting study but too time consuming for this book.

The American Thinker said this crime is motivated by Islamic doctrine that calls for the capturing, raping, and prostituting of non-Muslim women and children after battle and keeping or selling them as sex slaves. This practice goes back to the time of Mohammed and is carried out by ISIS today. I also read these Muslim groups prefer "white girls" because of they way they look, the way they dress, and the fact that they are not Muslim.

Sweden appears to be the European country most affected by this practice. I saw headlines on the Internet that said "Sweden buckling under Muslim immigration" and "Sweden—Rape Capital of the World". Sweden has historically been one of the most, if not the most, liberal countries in Europe. They have welcomed mass immigration, mostly from Muslim countries, with open arms. They are now paying the price by losing their country. I read on wmd.com there is contempt by Muslims toward their adopted country, no-go zones are common, and the Swedish government is losing control. Doesn't socialist Bernie Sanders want us to be more like Sweden?

I first learned about the Muslim Grooming Gangs and Sweden's plight when I watched a video presentation by Paul Weston, Chairman of the Liberty Great Britain (political) Party at this year's Conservative Political Action Conference (CPAC) meeting. In reference to London's new mayor being Muslim, he said Great Britain was on the verge of being taken over by the Muslim population. He said it would take place in about 10 years at the rate the Muslim population is multiplying in his country. He commented Sweden is gone and urged the United States to wake-up before it is too late.

After I wrote the above, Great Britain did wake up and voted to take back their country from the EU and uncontrolled foreign immigration. Although it has caused a firestorm within the United Kingdom, it was the only choice they had to be a sovereign country. For example, they were paying about 24 billion British Pounds more into the EU than they gained back economically and they were losing more and more control over their laws including immigration.

This brings up a very important point. We human beings tend to look at everything through our own paradigm, which often results in self-deception. This is especially dangerous when devious factions want to achieve end goals that are very different from our goals and use dishonest manipulation. Remember *Rules for Radicals*. This is happening in America today with regard to the progressive push toward a Marxist society and the defense of the Islamic religion. If you do not believe this can happen in America, ask Sweden. It is imperative that America heeds Mr. Weston's advice and wakes up before it is too late if we want our children, grandchildren, and subsequent generations to live in the America we know and love.

Here is a great example of what I am talking about. According to Breitbart, Islamic Tribunals like those reported in the no-go zones in the United Kingdom are starting to happen in Texas. The Muslims involved in setting up these Tribunals that use sharia law say participation is voluntary and is devoted to non-binding dispute resolution. I saw this being discussed on television by some of those devout Muslim leaders I mentioned. The Muslim leaders significantly downplayed the Islamic Tribunals and said people who questioned the Tribunals were overreacting and Islamophobic. They were playing to our traditional American paradigm in that Islamic Tribunals are foreign to us and we non-Muslim Americans would never conceive of doing what they are doing. When I listened to these Islamic leaders, I personally had no doubt they were being dishonest and doing exactly what they said they were not doing. That camel's nose just gets deeper and deeper into the tent until one day—bam, here I am!

The Breitbart story also said a BBC Panorama documentary went undercover in the United Kingdom and found 85 Sharia courts operating as a parallel legal system in the Muslim communities and an extensive abuse of women's rights was uncovered. As I write this comment on women's rights, an interesting thought comes to mind. I wonder how our progressive politically correct friends will deal with Muslims and Islam as that culture continues to proliferate in our society and increasingly comes into conflict with our basic American values including women's rights? Probably the same way they do other issues that both fit and conflict with their ideology. They will defend what they agree with and deny and ignore what they don't. Remember their core personality traits pointed out in chapters 2 and 4.

After I wrote the above, I saw an op-ed in my local newspaper by Cal Thomas on the same subject. The op-ed talked about a British scholar who was quoted in The Independent, a British left-leaning newspaper, who said she attended 15 hours of testimony at The Islamic Sharia Council in London and the Birmingham Central Mosque. The Islamic Sharia Council consists of 16 locations across England that serves as an arbitration council primarily for marriage and divorce issues but they also cover religious and business issues. Although what the Sharia Council decides is not legally binding in the United Kingdom, I read what the Council decides is invariably followed. The scholar reviewed more than a dozen cases and concluded that most of the Islamic judges are always in favor of the man.

The United Kingdom's House of Lords passed a bill last summer making it illegal for Sharia Councils to treat "the evidence of a man as worth more than the evidence of a women." I thought the Sharia Councils were only advisory and did not have legal standing? Why did the House of Lords do that? There is a school of thought that these Sharia Councils are in actuality arbitration courts and their rulings can be legally binding. Don't forget that Muslims are starting these councils in Texas.

An editorial in The Independent said the following, "Can a healthy, harmonious multicultural society tolerate private legal systems? Not if that means the subjugation of women in abusive and indeed dangerous marriages, a form of imprisonment in all but name sanctioned by their local religious leaders." That is a good question but the wrong answer. The right answer is "no and hell no" under any circumstances. No country can have parallel legal systems in any fashion and not create significant moral and legal problems. The only way to have long-term success in avoiding conflict and chaos as Muslims migrate into our Western Christian based society is to assimilate together. Muslims can maintain the worship of their faith but they have to adhere to our cultural mores and laws. They cannot create a parallel society. Otherwise, as the number of Muslims grows in our culture, we will have increasing conflict and chaos. I said earlier that assimilation could not happen because of the significant conflict in religious doctrine. Where does this leave us? We are going to find out over time and the answer is not going to be a pleasant one.

Thomas concluded his op-ed by addressing that issue. He questioned if those of us who practice a different faith or no faith at all would be required to adhere to sharia law if the Muslim population became a majority? He said carved into the facade of the Supreme Court building are the words "Equal Justice Under Law" but "how equal can justice be" if that law becomes sharia law either in a parallel law or a dominate one that forces all other laws to succumb? Thomas concluded, "The question is more than academic and theological. The answer could determine the future direction of the world." I could not have said it better. Jay Sekulow of the American Center of Law and Justice said, "One of the most impressive aspects of the building (The Supreme Court) is the depiction of great lawgivers carved into the marble. Each time I enter the courtroom, I glance up at those lawgivers, including Moses holding the Ten Commandments written in Hebrew." That is a very telling picture of our country's legal heritage.

When one thinks of this issue, they need to remember we humans live in only a teeny-tiny speck of time. We cannot just think in terms of our life span or that of our ancestors we have known or know about. Look what has occurred throughout the world during the last few thousand years. The United States is only 240 years old. For comparison, the Roman Empire lasted 1,500 years and Ancient Egypt survived 3,100 years. Think what could happen during the next few hundred years to the United States and the world if we do not stand up for our way of life?

A Pew Research study released in April of 2015 predicted Muslims will grow more than twice as fast as the overall world population between 2010 and 2050 and will likely equal the number of Christians in the world by then. What will happen to that balance after 2050? Currently there are 3.1 babies being born for each Muslim woman, while Christian women average 2.7 babies per women. The average for women in other religions is 2.3 babies per woman. Muslim women have the youngest median age at 23 years old, while non-Muslim women were at 30 years old. Pew predicted the Muslim birth rate coupled with the Muslim median age will "accelerate" future Muslim population growth. Consider what I have just shared with you regarding the world's timeline for the evolution of civilization; the growth of the Muslim population; the Islamic concept of sharia law, caliphate, and jihad versus Christianity. Just think about it.

A friend of mine sent me an article titled "A German's View on Islam". The author is unknown. The article makes a comparison of Islamic rule and Nazi Germany and quoted a German citizen involved in the Nazi takeover of Germany who said, "Very few people were true Nazis but many enjoyed this return of German pride and many more were too busy to care. I was one of those who just thought the Nazis were a bunch of fools. So, the majority just sat back and let it happen. Then, before we knew it, they owned us, and we lost control, and the end of the world had come. My family lost everything. I ended up in a concentration camp and the Allies destroyed my factories." The article concluded it is the fanatics that rule Islam and the peaceful and silent majority is "cowed and extraneous". This article is tremendous food for thought for all Americans as we talk about the evolution of progressive power and control and their push toward a Marxist society. How about the evolution of Islam in future centuries? This can't happen in America? My bridge for sale on this one is the biggest yet. It is a whopper!

I received an email from another friend that said, "When you hear the extremist are only a small percentage of Muslims, remember only 7% to 10% of Germans were Nazis." There are many current and historical examples of societies around the world where the people living in those societies just want to live peaceful lives and millions of innocent people have been killed because of the whims of autocratic tyrants in political control. I'm not an alarmist but I am a pragmatist and if what we are seeing in the Muslim world doesn't alarm you, I do not have a bridge in my showroom big enough to sell to you. Muslim culture is not compatible with Western culture, Christianity and other religions, freedom, or democracy. So, what happens when these cultural differences clash? We are going to discuss that next and it ain't pretty.

I have repeatedly said Obama and his administration's refusal to associate terrorism with the Islamic faith is a disastrous foreign policy position. It puts the world at risk for Islamic terrorist attacks and that is exactly what is happening in the Middle East, Africa, Europe, and the

United States. What areas of the world are next? The Islamist terrorists want to use jihad to accomplish a worldwide caliphate. This is nothing new. A worldwide caliphate has been an Islamic goal for hundreds of years and, based upon my research, is possible in time. Islamic terrorists could realistically gain control of a significant part of the Middle East and Africa within the foreseeable future. How far they can go to achieve their goal and in what time period will depend largely upon the actions of the United States during the next decade or two and that will be heavily influenced by the upcoming presidential election. These Islamic extremist groups have made tremendous strides while Obama has been president. If they ever were junior varsity, they are now major college and becoming NFL.

Our mainstream news media is also complicit in supporting radical Islam and misinforming the American public. I was channel surfing on my television in May of this year and ran across a news documentary on CNN titled "Why They Hate Us". The documentary was hosted by CNN personality Fareed Zakaria who was born in India to a Muslim family but now claims to be completely secular. The documentary implied Islamic terrorism is basically America's fault. The documentary did say Islamic terrorists hate the entire modern world and there was recognition that modern Islam is "a cancer of backwardness and intolerance".

Here are the highlights I remember. The documentary opened by saying radical Islam began when an Egyptian student named Sayyid Qutb was going to school at a university in Colorado and dropped in on a church party in Greeley in 1949 where young people were dancing and he "was horrified" (poor guy). The documentary said he wrote later that young Americans were "lips to lips", "breasts to breasts", "legs were swirling", and worst of all was "the outline of breast in tight sweaters" (wow!). The documentary said that situation caused Qutb to go back to the Middle East and condemn this behavior. Qutb's condemnation was said to have inspired Osama bin Laden's radicalism, create al-Qaeda, and begin the radical Islamic movement (really?). Zakaria said less than one percent of Muslims support Islamic terrorists (not according to my research).

Zakaria also said about 30,000 people were killed by Muslim terrorist in 2014 but most of those killed were also Muslim (He failed to mention religious divide was the basis of radical Sunni Muslims killing Shia Muslims and Middle East Christians in Muslim countries.) The documentary insinuated Muslims throughout history have had periods of war and peace as if during the times of peace everything was great (Ask Muslim women and children and the men they conquered how peaceful it was during the "peaceful times" after their conquest.). Although Zakaria did address some of the Muslim issues in Muslim countries around the world, I felt he squarely placed blame on American citizens for U.S. issues between Muslims and non-Muslims. He chastised us non-Muslims for not being more tolerant and working with Muslims to solve our mutual issues. Where are the Muslims in the U.S. hiding who want to do the same? I would personally welcome Muslims who want to blend into and support American culture but I only see a small minority in that category compared to the total U.S. Muslim population. He also said there was no sharia law in the U.S (He needs to read my book.).

I did not hear Zakaria's documentary mention Qutb's father was a political activist, Qutb was active in the radical Egyptian Muslim Brotherhood, and Qutb was hanged for plotting the assignation of Egyptian president Gamel Abdel Nasser. Qutb's writings were influential with Bin Laden and al-Qaeda but his American experience did not cause al-Qaeda and radical Islam. Qutb was radical not because of America but because it was in his mental being to be so. Wikipedia said Qutb published a book titled *The America that I Have Seen*. In the book he was critical of the following things he observed while he was in the United States: materialism; individual freedoms; our economic system; racism; brutal boxing; poor haircuts (The government needs to adopt stronger barber school laws.); superficial conversations and friendships; restrictions on divorce; enthusiasm for sports; lack of artistic feeling; "animal-like" mixing of the sexes; and strong support for Israel. There isn't much left.

He really did not like us, did he? The real question is, "Did he like anything that did not support his radical thinking?" I would put up my most expensive bridges on that one for anyone who would want to take my bet. This documentary was totally irresponsible reporting by CNN that inaccurately informed their audience regarding a critical topic that has serious implications for the future safety and well-being of all Americans.

CNN is not alone in dishonestly misleading Americans regarding progressive ideology. Katie Couric recently made a documentary on gun control titled *Under the Gun*. She was interviewing a group called the Virginia Citizens Defense League that proclaims it is for firearm rights and is pro-liberty. Couric asked them a question regarding the need for more background checks and the film showed the group's members sitting there in a stupor as if they had no answer for her question. The group released an audio tape they made of the interview that proved several of their members did answer the question. Couric's director had edited the film to make the group look bad and to distort the message. After significant criticism, Couric and her director "sort of" apologized. After this story broke, another person who was interviewed by Couric for a documentary on surgery drinks and obesity titled *Fed Up* said the same thing happened to him.

When I researched the gun control documentary by Katie Couric, I ran across another CNN special aired in November of last year that was said to have dishonestly supported progressive ideology. The special was centered on an independent film documentary about college sexual assault titled *The Hunting Ground*. I found several websites that claimed the special was dishonest. There was also significant push back regarding the film from universities like Harvard and Florida State. They said the film was very one sided and inaccurate.

Wikipedia had an example of an email sent to students recruiting them to participate in the movie. The film's producer was reported to have sent an email that said in effect, "*The Hunting Ground* is very much in the corner of advocacy for victims, so there will be no insensitive questions or the need to get the perpetrator's side". Wikipedia said a crewmember of the movie also made changes on the movies' Wikipedia site prior to the CNN special that made the site's content more in line with the content of the movie. The filmmakers disagreed they did anything wrong and said they complied with Wikipedia's principles and values.

My last example involves my local newspaper, which was recently bought by Gannett. Gannett is in expansion mode and refers to all its newspapers as the USA TODAY Network. My newspaper had a rather lengthy news article syndicated by the USA TODAY Network titled "Hundreds allege: Trump doesn't pay his bills". There is nothing wrong with the subject as a news story. The problem is with the reporting. Rather than a news article, it was basically an editorial presented as news. For example, the article said, "However, the circumstances laid out in those lawsuits and other non-payment claims raise questions about Trump's judgment as a businessman, and as a potential commander in chief." That is editorial judgment, not news reporting. I can assure you there would not be a syndicated negative editorial by USA TODAY Network disguised as a news story regarding Hillary Clinton's email scandal and she and Bill throwing our country under the bus by using their connections with the U.S. government to make financial deals that channeled millions and millions of dollars into their foundation.

We talked about news bias in chapter 6 and throughout the book but there is a difference in bias and dishonesty. I read a definition that said bias is "a matter of selectively revealing or suppression of information" to make your point. Dishonesty is "intentionally changing the facts" to make your point. Bias can be unintentional but dishonesty is always by intent. There is a significant difference in the two with regard to one's moral principles. These four examples of dishonesty disguised as news by CNN, Couric, and USA TODAY Network, are surprising to me. I expect more from them. My findings beg the question of what else is out there spewing dishonest progressive propaganda to our society. Let's get out of here and get back to Islam before I find more.

I have learned enough about Islam to realize that I am not an expert on the subject of the Islamic religion but here is the little bit I do know. There are two major denominations of Islam—Sunni and Shia. The split took place after the death of the Islamic prophet Muhammad. The Sunnis believe that Muslims should be under a caliph, a political and religious successor to Muhammad, who is chosen by God and is a descendant of Muhammad. The Shiites believe Muslims should elect the caliph. The remainder of both groups' religious beliefs is very similar. The difference regarding the caliph coupled with the fundamentalist beliefs of the Sunnis is sufficient enough to create a major divide between the two that results in the hostility toward each other we read and hear about on a frequent basis. ISIS is Sunni as we discussed in the last chapter. Shias as well as Christians are the recipient of ISIS brutality as they take over territory. It also drives the alliances among the countries and territories in the region.

When it comes to the brutality of murderous jihad and human beheadings, ISIS and their affiliates interpret elements of the Quran in a manner to justify their actions. I honestly don't know if that is an accurate fundamental interpretation of the Quran or not. I have heard and read arguments both ways and I am not knowledgeable enough to know. The Quran was written almost fourteen hundred years ago and is very much open to interpretation. In the beginning it was reported that ISIS was so brutal that other Islamic militant groups like al-Qaeda disavowed any connection with them. It is amazing what success can do. After the success of ISIS, the division between ISIS and al-Qaeda is now a thing of the past. They are united against their targeted enemies.

Before Obama, these terrorist organizations saw the United States' aggressive foreign policy regarding national security and our military might as a significant threat and deterrence to pursuing their goals. As we have repeatedly discussed in this book, that is no longer true. ISIS and their terrorist buddies are making significant headway. They are capable of causing worldwide chaos and mounting attacks on the United States that could wreck havoc. We constantly hear on the news about the vulnerability of our power grid. They could also mount attacks that could result in mass causalities even greater than 9/11; like a "dirty bomb" attack in a highly populated city. We know how porous our borders are and supporters of terrorism have access to nuclear material. How about multiple coordinated terrorists attacks across the country at the same time?

The Muslim faith promotes the preservation of that faith by any means necessary including violence. Think about what would happen if Islamic terrorists who reside in our country successfully recruited Muslims who are willing to demonstrate and riot for Islam and also recruited radical progressives who will demonstrate and riot at the drop of a hat for any cause like those who have demonstrated recently in our cities regarding race relations. I will let your imagination provide the picture for that one. What a disastrous formula for demonstrating and rioting in the streets of America against the status quo!

Pew Research predicts that Muslims will outnumber Christians around the world after 2050. At least in the United States, Christians are predicted to remain number one with about two thirds of the population. Muslims will be number two. How long will it be before those numbers are reversed? Remember, 240 years is less than a teeny-tiny spec in time. A January 2015 poll by Rasmussen showed that 64% of Americans believe there is a global conflict in the world today between Western civilization and Islam. Should we feel comfort in that 64% of the U.S. population realizes this conflict or should we be concerned that 36% don't?

With these unsettling thoughts in mind, let's take a look at what Islamic terrorists are doing to people around the world who are in conflict with their Islamic beliefs. According to Wikipedia, ISIS beheaded approximately 300 people during 2014 and 2015. As you know, many of these beheadings were videoed and put on the Internet for propaganda and recruitment purposes. That number includes three Americans. A Jordanian pilot was videoed being burned alive. Men, women, and children who are suspected to be in opposition to ISIS politically or religiously are rounded up and killed. Often the women and children are captured and sexually abused, enslaved or sold as slaves. When Ramadi fell, it was reported that hundreds of residents were killed in the streets and tens of thousands had already fled the city to avoid the same fate.

This barbarous behavior is not limited to ISIS. I read that the Taliban rushed a school in Pakistan in December of 2014 and killed over 140 school children by shooting each one in the head and set a schoolteacher on fire in front of the students as they yelled "Allahu Akbar" or "God is great". Their stated reason was retaliation for a Pakistan military operation. It seems that Boko Haram, the Islamic terrorist group in Nigeria that aligns itself with ISIS, routinely kills people and rapes women and children for sport. I read they have killed over 12,000 people and forced over 1.5 million people from their homes during the past six years.

A syndicated article by the Los Angeles Times published in July 2015 reported ISIS beheaded two women for sorcery in northeast Syria. The article said ISIS has now carried out over 3,000 executions in Syrian territories in the past year and the methods have included beheadings, stoning, crucifixion, and throwing people from buildings.

I have seen television interviews with men who escaped and have no idea what has happened to their wives and children. They say they just hope and wait. Can you possibly imagine how they feel? The pain and anguish that could be seen in their faces as they talked was very telling. There must be hundreds of thousands who have been driven from their homes and are living in refugee camps and have lost everything. It is beyond my comprehension to fathom the cruelty by Islamist terrorists toward human beings and the horror these people are going through.

I saw Melissa Francis on Fox News' *The Five* recently and I loved what she said about ISIS. Melissa was referring to a comment she heard by an ISIS fighter who said he was jealous of a suicide bomber because the suicide bomber was going to heaven. Melissa said, "We have the same purpose. They want to die and we want to wipe them out." Great thought!

Here is a very surprising side note. I learned during my research that 110 people were beheaded in Saudi Arabia from January through August of 2015 for criminal punishment. Their record is 192 beheadings in 1995. That had nothing to do with ISIS. It is amazing what we do not know until we find out. I wonder how many other Muslim countries use beheadings as punishment?

I remember hearing many years ago that World War III would take place in the Middle East. I found that pronouncement interesting but it was something that I did not understand and took with a grain of salt. That grain of salt has turned into a salt mine. The person or persons who made that prediction knew a lot more about the dynamics of the Middle Eastern Islamic cultural than almost anyone understood. Whether an official World War III breaks out or not, it is a more serious world conflict than any we have experienced since World War II. Iran's former chief commander of their Revolutionary Guard was interviewed in December 2015 on Press TV. Remember, Press TV is Iran's English language news and documentary network. He commented the region is now "poised for a big explosion" and "the ground may also become prepared for the Third World War". Does he know something we don't? I am sure he knows plenty we don't know but what? Actually, when I think about it, we are in World War III. It is just that no one wants to call it that—especially our president and his White House advisors who try to link terrorism and our national security to climate change.

That last observation regarding terrorism, our national security, and climate change is highlighted by Obama's speech at the United States Coast Guard Academy Commencement in May of last year, which I honestly found very strange. In his opening remarks, Obama said as a nation we face many challenges including the "grave threat of terrorism". That was an appropriate comment but then he quickly turned to climate change as the reason for that terrorism. Remember, he is addressing a group of graduates from a specialized college that teaches students how to defend the coastline of our nation from outside threats but certainly not from climate change. I was stunned but not surprised. He said science was indisputable that the fossil fuels we burn release carbon dioxide into the atmosphere and are at the highest level they have been in 800,000 years. I wonder who measured our carbon dioxide 800,000 years ago? I assume climate scientists can technically do that but I don't trust the ones who do. He also said that we could be proud that our carbon pollution is near its lowest levels in almost two decades. You can't have it both ways in order to pat yourself on the back.

Obama continued, "This is not just a problem for countries on the coast or for certain regions of the world. Climate change will impact every country on the planet. No nation is immune. So I am here today to say that climate change constitutes a serious threat to global security, an immediate risk to our national security, and, make no mistake, it will impact how our military defends our country. And so we need to act—and we need to act now." He added, "That's why confronting climate change is now a key pillar of American leadership." At least he also said, "Understand, climate change did not cause the conflicts we see around the world." But then he said this, "Yet what we also know is that severe drought helped to create the instability in Nigeria that was exploited by the terrorist group Boko Haram. It is now believed that drought and crop failures and high food prices helped fuel the unrest in Syria, which descended into civil war in the heart of the Middle East."

Which is it? Is it climate change causing terrorism or not? Obama said nothing about threats from ISIS, al Qaeda, Russia, China, North Korea, or Iran. Maybe I just don't get it. I bet Mr. Alinsky could explain it to me if he were alive. Obama did, however, say something in his speech that got my undivided attention. He said, "Climate change, and especially rising seas, is a threat to homeland security, our economic infrastructure, the safety and health of the American people. Already, today, in Miami and Charleston, streets now flood at high tide." Wow! That's close to home—just 120 miles across Alligator Alley.

I was very surprised that I haven't read anything about the Miami flooding in my local newspaper or seen anything on local television. Next time I drive over to Miami, I'll look for myself. Actually, I did look it up on the Internet. Flooding does happen in low-lying areas of Miami Beach when there is a supermoon at high tide. This occurs about every 14th full moon, which means it happens about every 13 to 14 months. A supermoon is when the moon is closest to Earth and its effect on tides is at its greatest. I read the effect is only a few inches. Obama's comments were a gross exaggeration and not accurate. What else is new for climate change supporters!

Maybe Obama and the government would like to buy some of my bridges to help solve the problem. As I read his speech in its entirety, I asked myself whether or not Obama really believes this stuff or is it just an effort to excuse his inept approach in fighting terrorism or is he using the opportunity to push the liberal agenda. I can't answer that. If I had to give an answer, I would say all three.

Obama ended his commencement address by honoring the first black woman to join the Coast Guard. She was in the audience. She is 100 years old and deserved to be honored. I thought that was very appropriate and her story was impressive. Then, Obama blew it. He used the situation to publicize racism in America. He said, "In 1921, in Tulsa, Oklahoma, when she was just six years old, her African American community was attacked by white mobs—it was a horrific racial incident and hundreds of innocent African Americans were killed. The mobs destroyed her father's clothing store. They looted her house. They even burned the little clothes for her doll." Using her honor to promote racism in America was extremely wrong, ill-judged, and disgusting. Obama has never let a good opportunity to expound his "reverse racist" views go to waste. We will talk about that in depth in the next chapter.

Let's now switch to a very controversial foreign policy issue being pursued by Obama and his administration—the normalization of relations with Cuba. This announcement has created significant controversy between conservatives and progressives and between old guard Cubans and young Cubans who live in Cuba and in the United States. The basis of this controversy is as follows. The young see this move as potentially opening up new opportunities for them. Conservatives and the old guard see this as manipulation by the Castro brothers to improve their image and to obtain money for their government and personal coffers. Cuba needs to replace the substantial funding previously provided to them by the Venezuelan government. According to Wikipedia, Venezuela provided Cuba with $18 billion between 2008 and 2011 in loans, investments, and grants before Chavez died in 2013.

The progressives tout this as a good move toward improving the lives of the Cuban people and reversing a strategy that has not been successful in helping Cubans in the past. That is rather naive if they think the Castro brothers are going to do anything different than they have for the last 55 years. The Castro brothers are in tight control of everything in Cuba including the income and standard of living for all citizens. In addition, Cuba puts those in opposition to the government in jail to keep them in line.

Pope Francis visited Cuba last year in September. Prior to the Pope's visit, I read the government was going to pardon 3,500 prisoners. The pardon excluded prisoners that were there for homicide, rape, drug trafficking, and cattle rustling. The pardon also excluded, not surprisingly, political prisoners. This is the third time in 17 years the Cuban government has pardoned prisoners as the result of a visit by the Pope. If the Pope can't change behavior toward political prisoners, how can Obama. I read a comment by a Cuban dissident regarding our normalization of relations with Cuba and I think he got it right. He said, "Castroism has won. Today, Fidel must be smiling and lighting up a large El Rey del Mondo cigar in his Havana palace."

None of the money we would give them or the economic opportunity we would provide is going to wind up in the Cuban citizens' pockets or be spent for infrastructure improvement unless the Castros want it to. I would not hold your breath on that one. I thought of taking a tour of Cuba with Tauck Tours. I watched a video on Tauck's website taken by someone who had recently traveled with them to Cuba. I was taken aback at the significant control exercised upon the Cuban citizens by the government. For example, salaries are paid to the government and then the government pays the employee. Breitbart says that the government keeps about 92% of the wages paid to Cuban citizens by businesses owned outside Cuba. No wonder the Castro brothers welcome economic investment from the United States. Talk about pay to play!

From everything I have read and seen, conservatives and the old guard Cubans are right. It appears we are the ones giving up everything to the Cuban government; i.e., the Castro brothers. Neither the United States nor the Cuban citizens are going to get anything in return. Just to throw a little more negativity on the pile, I saw a picture on a January 2015 front page of The Wall Street Journal showing a Russian intelligence ship in the Havana harbor the day before a top U.S. diplomat arrived to start negotiations between us and Cuba. How is that for an "in your face" by both Russia and Cuba. Remember that Cuba is on Russia's list for harbors to refuel and repair their ships that are to maneuver in the Caribbean.

While we are at it, let's add one more national security concern regarding Cuba to the list. Remember earlier in the chapter where we discussed Iran expanding their influence in Latin America and their potential to use the Iranian Revolutionary Guard or its proxies like Hezbollah as a platform to carry out attacks against the United States, our interests, and our allies. It was also discussed that Iran represents a threat through our porous borders and there are Hezbollah and Iranian Revolutionary Guard active operations within the U.S. today. Judicial Watch reported in February of this year they uncovered a 2011 email to then Secretary of State Hillary Clinton that said Hezbollah had opened an operational base in Cuba designed to support terrorist attacks throughout Latin America. Brietbart reported in February of this year

442

that Asharq Al-Awsat, an Arabic international newspaper headquartered in London, published a story saying members of Hezbollah are "moving freely within the United States" courtesy of Venezuelan passports issued by a Cuban company. Brietbart said Hezbollah was also using Cuban Passports to come here.

The February Judicial Watch report also said Obama announced to Congress in May of last year his intent to rescind Cuba's designation as a state sponsor of terrorism because they "meet the statutory criteria for rescission". He based his decision on the premise that Cuba had not provided any support for international terrorism during the previous six months. Six months??? Obama also said Cuba assured us they will not support acts of international terrorism in the future. That is not what was reported in the above paragraph. In my opinion, this is an example of Obama blindly undermining the best interest of the United States in his effort to build his legacy. I deeply wonder if America can ever be as safe in the future as it was before Obama was elected?

As I write about Cuba, I am reminded of a guest commentary in my local newspaper written by an old guard Cuban who is strongly opposed to our normalizing relations with them. I found the commentary very emotional. The writer came to the United States over 50 years ago after he was released from one of what he calls Castro's Gulags where about 200 people literally slept on top of each other. The bathroom consisted of a bucket in the corner of the room. The food was whatever you could get from relatives, which was inconsistently allowed by the guards. Prisoners shared their food because that was the only way they could survive.

Torture was a daily event and included sleep deprivation brought about by lights being turned on and hearing taped speeches by Castro 24 hours a day. They got used to that but not the more severe torture that varied from day-to-day. Some days they were striped naked, electric cattle prods were placed on their private parts, and current was applied to the prods. Other days they were hit with a baseball bat while being questioned. It was not uncommon to have six of the prisoners lined up in front of a firing squad. One of the guards would have a real bullet in their gun and the other five would not. Obviously five lived and one died. He said that really broke down the prisoners. He said only his faith in God kept him from breaking down.

Che Guevara came a couple of days per week to watch the torture. One day a prisoner could not take it anymore and challenged Guevara. He told Guevara to take his pistol off and fight him like a man. Guevara took his pistol out of his holster, walked over to the prisoner, placed the pistol against his forehead, and pulled the trigger. The writer of the commentary had to clean up the bloody mess. The writer ended the commentary by making his argument against normalizing relations with Cuba and concluded by saying, "The sad part for us (the United States) is that we are going to pay with our money (taxes) for Cuban's influence expansion in Latin America, while the Cuban people will continue suffering this ruthless regime."

Che Guevara is well known for his brutality. He is not the great revolutionary freedom fighter he is often portrayed to be. He is known for taking his gun out and shooting people on impulse if they did something he did not like, yet it is not uncommon to see his picture on t-shirts as a folk hero who cared about freeing people from repression. On my last cruise, I saw a man in his mid-to-late 60s with picture of Guevara on his shirt that would be similar to a logo on a golf shirt. It was all I could do to not say something like, "Do you know who he really is?" With the help of my wife, I am learning to keep my mouth shut more often as I age.

The day after the Pope arrived in Havana my local newspaper had a very large photograph on the front page showing the Pope and Fidel Castro shaking hands. This was one of the rare times I can remember the newspaper placing a photograph of international nature in that spot. They always have a local interest picture. A smaller but also prominent picture on the front page showed the Pope arriving at the Revolution Plaza to celebrate Mass. The photograph was taken in front of a government building that has a huge multistory iron stylized relief sculpture of Che Guevara attached on the front. Is that an oxymoron! Putting the Pope, who is arguably the most recognized symbol of humanitarianism in the world, in the same picture with one of the worst inhumane monsters who ever lived?

I guess our president did not want to be outdone by the Pope. During his recent trip to Cuba, The Wall Street Journal published a picture of Obama in the Revolution Plaza with that same relief of

Guevara behind him as he was honoring another Cuban revolutionary named Jose Marti. There was one big difference from the picture of the Pope. Obama was standing at attention with his hand over his heart. Was that symbolic or coincidental?

Back to the Pope's visit. There were no pictures in the newspaper of the Cuban dissidents who were taken away by security and not allowed to protest. The pictures that were in the newspaper were credited to the AP. Was the picture depicting the Pope and Guevara together a coincidence or on purpose? There was a tagline under the picture in the newspaper calling Guevara a revolutionary hero. It is not surprising that Guevara called Karl Marx his ideological inspiration. I believe the picture was taken purposefully to make a statement comparing the two as fighters for freedom and humanitarianism. If I am correct, what a warped belief expressed by that photographer, the AP, and my local newspaper? Remember, never confuse progressive ideology with the facts.

The Obama administration announced that we would open an embassy in Cuba and they would in turn open one here. Opening an embassy in Cuba will cost several million dollars not including ongoing expenses. These expenditures have to be approved by Congress. Republican members of Congress have said they will not approve the expenditures. Well, I don't know what happened but the government did open an embassy in Havana in August of last year. The building was actually our old embassy and it did appear to be more symbolic versus our embassies in other countries. Cuba re-opened their old embassy in Washington as well. Stay tuned on this one.

In order to fully normalize relations with Cuba, the current trade embargoes will have to be lifted by Congress. Republican members of Congress have said that will not happen. Learning the final outcome of Obama's efforts to normalize relations with Cuba might take a long time and is not in Obama's best interest. He only has a few months left to finalize his legacy. It seems Obama has been doing a lot of that lately. How about Gitmo? It gets very concerning, wondering what he might do (or not do) before he leaves office. How about him just doing the right things it takes to make our country safe, economically strong, and minimizing the discord he and his progressive friends have created? In other words, returning America to America. It's not rocket science. Oh, that's a legacy he will not claim—the diminishing of the NASA space program. Sorry, I got carried away. It's so easy to do nowadays.

Before we leave Cuba, I want to share with you a March 2016 Daily Signal article written by Lee Edwards that I find very powerful. It is titled 6 Questions Obama Should Have Asked Castro. Here is a summary of the six questions:

1. When will you allow free and open elections as promised?
2. When will you open your government's archives to allow historians and others to document how many Cubans have been executed? The Black Book of Communism estimates between 15,000 and 17,000.
3. When you release all political prisoners, especially the husbands, sons, fathers, and friends of the Ladies in White? The Black Book of Communism estimates that 100,000 Cubans have been placed in prisons and forced labor camps for political reasons.
4. When will you allow the free market to truly operate in Cuba so that the average worker will be able to earn a decent wage rather than the $20 per month they currently receive?
5. When will your brother Fidel admit that Che Guevara (admired by many Americans) was not a high-minded revolutionary but a cold-blooded murderer who functioned as Fidel's personal executioner?
6. Isn't it true that Cuba is not a socialist paradise but a troubled third world country ruled by a communist regime that discourages religion, denies freedom of the press and free speech, bars legitimate elections, treats the judiciary as a lapdog, and reveres the Communist Party above all things?

Those questions are so powerful. They speak for themselves and need no comment from me. Let's let them close our discussion on Cuba and move on.

In the last chapter, I mentioned Bret Baier's recent Fox News special regarding our military. The special reported that experts see our military as a "tattered and demoralized" organization. Let's take a quick look at our foreign policy and military defense. Our national security is significantly impacted by our domestic policy that drives the military budget but it is our foreign policy that drives domestic policy. The two are tightly integrated. Obama has consistently apologized to the world for our past atrocities. He and his administration would like to supply our troops with alms instead of arms. One of the first things Obama did when he took office is abandon the NATO missile defense system that George W. Bush had negotiated with Poland and the Czech Republic. That decision did not do us any favors regarding our credibility with our allies. Especially, after they stood up with us against robust Russian opposition to the plan.

Obama not only abandoned that missile defense system but also gave up military strength by agreeing to significantly reduce the number of missiles we had stockpiled based upon a similar commitment by Putin. It was no surprise that Putin only paid lip service to that agreement and has never honored any part of it. In fact, Russia has announced they are increasing their missile capability by 40 new intercontinental ballistic missiles. We gave up significant national security assets and diminished our international credibility and they added military strength.

Here is an update on the NATO missile system. After the missile system proposed by Bush was abandoned, Joe Biden announced that we would build a smaller NATO system over a longer period of time. The first missile site was just opened in Poland and the entire missile system is to be completed by 2018. Russia is still complaining.

A few months ago, it was announced that the Obama administration was going to reduce our troops by 40,000 soldiers and move the aircraft carrier that is currently in the Persian Gulf elsewhere for routine maintenance and give those manning the ship some R&R. It was reported that this will be the lowest troop level since 9/11 and there could be more reductions. The report said the carrier might be replaced in a couple of months but it depends upon having the funding to do so. We called France to see if they could put an aircraft carrier in the area in the meantime.

It is several months later and there is no carrier in the Persian Gulf. I heard a military contributor on Fox News recently say the aircraft carrier was sitting in San Diego (since November 2015) with a big hole in the middle and it's nuclear reactor removed. What a message these two decisions send to our enemies. On the same day of the announcement, the Chairman of the Joint Chiefs of Staff, General Joseph Dunford, testified before Congress that Russia was the biggest threat to the United States followed by China, North Korea, and then ISIS. I wonder where he puts Iran?

Our FBI Director, James Comey, told congress at the same time that ISIS is "not your grandfather's al Qaeda". He said that ISIS has 21,000 English-speaking followers on Twitter using encrypted messaging to communicate with each other and the FBI cannot decode what they are saying. Comey said he was concerned that the recruiting of followers and the planning of attacks are taking place and the FBI can no longer monitor this activity.

As these two testimonies were taking place before Congress, Obama made a rare visit to the Pentagon and said the U.S. led coalition was gaining ground in a long fight against ISIS. What coalition? Many months ago, the Obama administration claimed there were 60 countries in the fight with us. Who are they and where are they? I think the two or three that were doing air strikes with us in the beginning are now absent. Russia has dropped a few bombs on ISIS for show in an attempt to alleviate criticism for bombing Syrian rebels instead of ISIS and France has done a few air strikes for show after the attacks on Paris and Nice.

Obama reiterated from the pentagon, as he continuously does, that we are not in a war with Islam and most of the victims have been Muslims. He concluded by saying patriotic Muslim Americans are "partners in keeping this country safe". I agree with him that most victims have been Muslims but commenting that patriotic Muslim Americans are our partners in keeping us safe? Please explain that one! As we discussed earlier in the chapter, there are very few Muslims who speak out against Islamic terrorists and only a small number have joined our military. ABC News reported last December the Department of Defense said there were 5,896 self-identified Muslims in the U.S. military out of a total of 2.2 million active-duty and reserve members. Add the streamlining of the military to what I wrote concerning military officers being fired or retired who disagree with this administration. Then add that to the information I have covered regarding all the potential threats to our national security and how safe do you feel? This combined scenario reinforces the ineptness and cluelessness of the Obama administration in pushing their progressive agenda at the expense of putting all Americans in danger of great harm.

As I repeatedly say, many times when you think things can't get worse, look out! After I wrote the above, I read a story in The Wall Street Journal in June of this year that gives ineptness and cluelessness new meaning. In the past, the Pentagon bought almost all of the custom made chips used in our most sensitive weapons systems from two heavily guarded IBM plants in Vermont and New York. The article said, "The plants where chips are assembled have long been viewed by the Pentagon as a vulnerable part of the military supply chain. The biggest concerns were over technology theft and any insertion of elements that could be remotely triggered to access equipment or so-called kill switches that render equipment useless." The Pentagon signed a new seven-year deal with the two plants even though IBM just sold them to GLOBALFOUNDRIES Inc. Who owns GLOBALFOUNDRIES Inc.? The Emirate of Abu Dhabi. You can't make this stuff up. This is worse than turning over our space program to Russia and Elon Musk's Space X.

I have often wondered what Obama had in mind when he told Russian President Dmitry Medvedev he would have more flexibility after the 2012 election. I think we dodged a bullet on that one. We can thank Putin for being aggressive toward Obama before Obama could negotiate away our military power to Russia through his naive actions and; therefore, negotiate away our national security. I think Obama still believes that significantly diminishing our military will result over time in adversarial countries not fearing us any longer and become our "bosom buddy" friends. This is naivety on steroids but what else is new. I thought Russia's and China's latest military aggression around the world might temper Obama continuing to militarily disarm America but not so.

What does Obama think countries like Russia, China, Iran, North Korea, or terrorist groups like ISIS are going to do as we diminish our military power and exceptionalism? Our national security is not predicated on a bow to world leaders or a warm handshake with our adversaries who are clever, cunning, totally self-serving, and power hungry. Our national security depends upon our adversaries worrying about our ability and willingness to kick their butts—not kiss them!

Our military might and foreign policy based upon United States exceptionalism has kept our country safe since 1776. No country in the world has enjoyed our level of security and safety. Our military might has also provided a police force to the world and kept the bad guys from taking over. For example, in 1957, President Dwight D. Eisenhower announced to the world that the United States would intervene militarily and economically in response to the spread of communism. Remember, he was a five-star general in the U.S. Army before he was president and was not a person to back down from a challenge. We wouldn't have to guess what he would do about the spread of terrorism. George Washington once said, "There is nothing so likely to produce peace as to be well prepared to meet the enemy."

We have always had bad guys being bad. Think what the world would have been like in past decades if our military might hadn't been around. Well, we are starting to find out. Until Obama, when America spoke, the bad guys listened and respected and feared us. Our influence has quickly diminished during the Obama administration and the bad guys are putting their bodies in the water, rather than their toes, to test our resolve. ISIS is using a powerboat, Putin is using the diving board, China is wading deeper and deeper, and Iran is now taking swimming lessons. I am surprised that Kim Jong-un is only still playing in the water with his toes. I guess we need to give him time since he is the youngest. We will never be able to truly measure the positive impact our military might has historically had on world peace and the prevention of many global atrocities that would have happened otherwise. Since the bad guys have tested the Obama administration's resolve and overwhelmingly won, the world is turning more and more into an unsettled "snake pit" and atrocities in human rights are proliferating.

You know by now my great respect for Thomas Sowell. I want to close this chapter with a brief summary of an op-ed he wrote. Sowell said when Winston Churchill looked back on the magnitude of carnage and destruction brought about during World War II, Churchill said there had never been a war easier to prevent if Hitler had been militarily opposed early on before the German forces became so strong. Sowell said France was militarily capable of "stopping Hitler in his tracks" and preventing World War II. Politically, the French government would not do so because World War I was painfully vivid in the minds of the French people and they wanted no part of war. Sound familiar? Hitler grew stronger militarily and invaded France at a time of "his choosing". It has been reported that 50 million people lost their lives and one only has to look at old World War II pictures of bombed-out European cities to visualize the destruction. Sowell concluded, "Obama has done more than anyone else to promote the dangerous illusion that we can choose whether to have a war or not. But our enemies have already made that choice."

CHAPTER 10

Progressive Political Incorrectness!

One of the things I like about writing is the extraordinary learning experience. It is not only extraordinary from the new knowledge you uncover but also from provoking new thinking and new ways of looking at old thinking. Researching and writing this chapter resulted in new knowledge that had a profound impact on me personally and on the book's content and conclusion. Do you know where the term "political correctness" comes from? I didn't until I researched this chapter and what I learned turned my political knowledge upside down.

Until I discovered differently, I thought political correctness was the naive liberal practice of taking actions to alleviate perceived discrimination against minority groups. There is; however, a significant distinction between being politically incorrect and preventing discrimination. No person or group should ever discriminate against a minority person or minority group because of race, ethnicity, social status, political status, religious status, mental status, gender, sexual orientation, or whatever minority status they have. The practice of political correctness is, in actuality, reverse discrimination by suppressing and limiting of the rights of the majority.

Ironically, the rights of the minority that political correctness is supposedly protecting also become suppressed in the long run. Political correctness is progressive Marxist aggression under the guise of protecting minority groups. The affected minority groups and well-meaning classic liberals are deceived into actively supporting politically correct practices which give the progressives the power and control they seek over all members of society. This point will become increasingly clearer as the chapter progresses.

Christian religion is one of the concepts most under attack. For example, substituting the word "holiday" for "Christmas" and taking prayer out of schools to diminish or eradicate God and Christianity in American society. Progressives say this practice is promoted in order to not offend the atheists or the non-Christian minority. Does this behavior not offend the Christian majority? An April 2015 Rasmussen poll said two out of three Americans believe in Christianity, Jesus Christ is the Son of God, and Jesus was resurrected on Easter Day. Another April 2015 Rasmussen poll indicated 39% of Americans believe Easter Day to be an important holiday, only 19% believe Easter Day to be among the least important, and 38% place the holiday in between. In December 2015, a Rasmussen poll showed that 59% of American adults consider Christmas to be one of the country's most important holidays while only 6% said Christmas is the least important. Thirty-three percent said Christmas is somewhere in between.

American patriotism is also strongly under attack. I saw a cartoon depicting a student apathetically sitting at his classroom desk with his arms crossed on his chest and his feet crossed upon the desk. The rest of the class was standing with their hands over their hearts looking at the American flag. The teacher and a soldier in a wheelchair were in the front of the room. The teacher said, "Kevin, you have the right to not stand for the pledge but let me introduce you to this soldier who can't stand because he was defending that right." It was a powerful cartoon and much more powerful to look at than what I can describe here. The Pledge of Allegiance to the flag has been under constant fire because of the words "under God"; however, the reference to God is not the only issue with the Pledge of Allegiance. It is the pledge to America itself that is under attack as is evidenced by politically correct practices against the values America stands for. The assault on Christianity is thought to be separate from the assault on traditional American values but the Declaration of Independence and the Constitution are both based upon Judeo-Christian principles and there is an important connection. More about that later

I read an outstanding op-ed on this topic by Cal Thomas. Thomas commented, "The framers of our Constitution clearly understood that in order to put certain rights out of the reach of government, whose power they wished to limit, those rights had to come from a place government could not reach. Thomas Jefferson understood this well enough to write in the Declaration of Independence that our rights to 'life, liberty and the pursuit of happiness' are endowed by our Creator." He added that the purpose of government is to "secure these rights". Thomas then said, "When government believes it can create or take away rights, it becomes a god into itself and potentially endangers those rights. The only way to preserve them for ourselves and our prosperity is to acknowledge they come from a higher place." Thomas concluded his op-ed by saying, "Secular progressives believe in a 'living Constitution' that constantly 'evolves' to serve the people. The founders believed the people are best served when they conform to laws established by God. One doesn't have to believe in God for this to work but the alternative potentially puts the rights of everyone in peril should one group or class fall out of favor."

I had never heard that before. I don't know if that was Cal Thomas' own analysis, it came from someone else, or was articulated by our founding fathers. What a powerful rationale for putting God in our country's founding documents. Our constitution and our way of life are under siege by the progressives and the progressives are winning. Political correctness is one of their most powerful weapons. Thomas also had a quote in his op-ed by a famous liberal that might surprise you. It did me, in a nice way. The quote said, "The rights of man come not from the generosity of the state but from the hand of God." Who said that? John F. Kennedy said that in his inaugural address on January 20, 1961. Was John F. Kennedy a classic liberal or a progressive? I think his quote answers that question. That was over 50 years ago. What are our kids and grandkids going to remember about our Constitution as intended by our founding fathers 50 years from now? Good question! It doesn't look good!

If progressives and other anti-American factions want to destroy Christianity and individual rights in our American society that get in their way to accomplish their goals, then let them change our

Constitution as it legally allows. They can't do it. The majority won't let them. So, they resort to circumvent the rights of the majority through progressive politically correct behavior. It is ironic that these minority groups are successfully doing to the majority what they accuse the majority of doing to them. It is hypocrisy on steroids but goes much deeper than that! Political correctness is only a facade for the real purpose. Progressives want to eradicate traditional American culture. In reality, political correctness is the most powerful method to convert our traditional American society into a Marxist society. No, I'm not loony-tunes. Now, you know why I was so shocked when I made this discovery. If you are doubtful of my conclusion, hold that doubt until you finish reading the entire chapter.

The term political correctness is a colloquialism that first came into being in the early 1900s. Socialists used the term to negatively criticize members of the Communist Party who dogmatically proclaimed their positions on political ideology to be correct regardless of the resulting morality of the those positions. The term did not become commonplace in the United States until around 1990 but using political correctness as a means to infuse the Marxist philosophy in the United States started in the 1960s.

Remember the phrase "make love-not war"? That's an American hippy phrase—right? Actually, it is an American Marxist phrase. Or, at least, the Marxist movement perpetrated it. Do you know what Marxist ideology actually is? I thought I did until I researched the term and learned that I did not fully understand it. Simply put, it is an ideological philosophy that all members of society share equally in economic output and social classes do not exist. Karl Marx and Friedrich Engels wrote in their 1848 book titled *The Communist Manifesto* that poverty and starvation were products of the evil that resulted from a capitalist society. The book proposed that the evolution of Marxist theory begins with socialism and progresses to communism. It was written over 160 years ago at a much different time and in a much different culture than the American culture we enjoy today.

Let's go back to the Democratic Party versus the Whig Party in the 1850s. Was the Democratic Party adhering to Marxist theory then, either knowingly or unknowingly? Remember, I said in chapter

3 that the Democratic Party stood for "sovereignty of the people" and "majority rule" as the general principal of governing. The Whigs advocated the rule of law, an enduring unwavering written constitution, and protections for minority interest against majority tyranny. I concluded that while these two political philosophies sound very similar, they were not. If one investigates the true meaning of "sovereignty", it means supreme power or authority. I believe when the democrats said they stood for "sovereignty of the people", they meant everyone should be equal in our society or, in other words, a Marxist based philosophy.

The philosophical foundation of the modern day Republican Party honors our individual rights as provided in the Declaration of Independence and the Constitution, which are the basis of our American values and the antithesis of Marxism. Over the years, the Democratic Party has become much more progressive and gone much further down the Marxist path. The more I write the more I realize there are only two basic underlying ideological principles in political theory. There are people who believe in individualism as advocated by traditional American culture and people who believe in collectivism as advocated in a Marxist style culture. All the other elements of one's ideology revolve around those two concepts in varying degrees. As we discussed at the beginning of the book, people whose ideology leans toward individualism exhibit more personal independence and people whose ideology leans toward collectivism are more idealistic, utopian, and susceptible to authoritarian manipulation.

Ironically, Marxist ideology is based upon collectivism that results in a totalitarian state. That is the opposite of what Marx and Engels intended. How can that be if Marxist ideology is based upon economic and class equality? Ask Marxist based leaders like Stalin, Lenin, Mao, Pol Pot, Castro, and Chávez. How can Marxist leaders be above society when there is economic and class equality? The answer lies in the fact that Marxist based societies are a utopian fallacy. One thing I have learned about Marx and other individuals over the years that expound these utopian philosophies is that they are highly intellectual and well-meaning philosophers who don't have a clue in understanding the true nature of people and society. They are intellectual wackos. They look at human nature through naive glasses and are totally unrealistic about societal dynamics

There are human beings in every society on Earth who are narcissists who cannot control their desire to rise above and control society in either a neurotic or psychotic way. Utopian based Marxist ideology becomes a perfect vehicle for monsters like Stalin who killed an estimated 62 million people under his rule, Mao who killed an estimated 49 million people under his rule, and Pol Pot who killed only an estimated 2 million people under his rule to implement their narcissistic totalitarian psychotic fantasies on the people they controlled. Stalin is quoted as saying, "Death is the solution to all problems. No man—no problem." That quote is unreal!!!

A society with a Marxist foundation breeds the culture and norms that dumb down society through manipulation into a submissive culture that allows narcissists to thrive and control society in varying degrees. Our traditional American culture and system of governance does not allow that to happen. The more our American culture can be pushed toward a Marxist based culture; the more our traditional system of governance breaks down and progressives can increasingly gain control. The last 7 1/2 years make the point.

As I said before, my wife and I have had the wonderful privilege to travel throughout the world. We went to Cambodia a couple of years ago. We visited the Killing Fields of Choeung Ek where the Khmer Rouge, under Pol Pot, killed over one million people. The most common means of killing adults was beating them with blunted hoes to preserve bullets. They killed babies by holding their ankles and slinging them against a big tree. We saw one of the trees. This is unthinkable! How can human beings do such things? One of our guides told us a sad and touching story. His dad was one of those killed. There was a memorial on the grounds that contained a very tall glass enclosed showcase with multiple levels containing 8,000 skulls. Our guide said he comes here often hoping to hear his dad's voice. His emotion showed on his face and we were having trouble hiding ours. This is Marxist inspired communism at its worst.

Not quite as murderous are the Marxist countries of Cuba and Venezuela that also reflect the failure of Marxist ideology. We discussed the current happenings between the U.S. and Cuba in the last chapter. Castro and his buddy Che Guevara murdered anyone who got in the way of their revolution but the real story for communist Cuba is its disastrous economic downfall after the revolution. It is a beautiful romantic country with wonderful people. It wasn't perfect before Castro and Guevara but it got the %!@?&# kicked out of it by these Marxist revolutionaries.

I know someone who was a primary care physician in Cuba. She is now in the United States working as a nurse. I asked her why? She told me when she worked as a physician in Cuba she made $25 per month. That's right, $25 per month. Remember, Lee Edwards said the average worker in Cuba makes $20 per month. By working in the United States as a nurse, she does not have to make financial decisions each month such as what personal grooming products to buy now or put off until the following month. We are not talking about Channel or Hermes. We are talking about Proctor & Gamble type stuff. She also told me she had to learn to use her instinct and judgment as a physician in Cuba because sophisticated medical equipment was not available. That is not the picture Michael Moore painted against the American medical system in his propaganda-laced documentary *Sicko*. Who is the real sicko in this picture?

I read an article in The Wall Street Journal regarding Chávez's continuing power over Venezuela. Even though he is dead, his legacy lives on. The article talked about Chávez's socialist government nationalizing hundreds of private companies to empower the working classes against "savage capitalism" so the workers could prosper. Now, the workers say the "state" is the new "big boss" and has taken over everything including worker's rights. Inflation is hitting 60% and workers complain about a monthly salary of approximately $200. They also said they face lapsed contracts and government troops when they protest, which results in trumped-up charges and arrests. I read those same government troops have been stealing goats because they have no food. The article reported that workplaces are unsafe and that corruption has confiscated much needed investment money. I read 1 in 10 citizens between the ages of 18 and 25 are seeking to leave the country. Most of them are middle and upper class citizens.

Here is an update. Since the recent elections won by "the opposition", the country is in political turmoil. The Marxists are doing everything possible to stay in power including forming a "parallel government" to maintain control. Problems in Venezuela are moving fast toward an explosive economic disaster and they have the largest oil reserves in the world. There is no food and people are at the breaking point. It is a very volatile situation. This is a great tribute to Marxist ideology in action.

I have been in several semi-socialist, socialist, and communist countries where the Marxist ideology is practiced in varying degrees. There are only 5 countries in the world today that officially call themselves communist: China; Cuba; Laos; North Korea; and Vietnam. It is not important what a country officially calls itself. What's important is how a country governs its people in reality. One profound observation during my travels is that I haven't seen any country that claims a Marxist based political structure to be a classless society in which all the people equally share in the economy. Not one! They all have a class system in spite of their self-proclaimed adherence to varying stages of Marxist philosophy.

I have observed that the wealthy in Marxist based countries enjoy much greater individual wealth than citizens in other income levels when compared to the differences between the wealthy and those in other income levels in the United States. The number of wealthy individuals in Marxist countries is also much less on a percentage basis of the population when compared to the U.S. This is especially true in communist or communist like countries where an authoritarian style government is in tight control. These realities are because Marxist based countries have much greater economic and political corruption depending on the degree of autocratic leadership. My observations in Marxist based countries do not sound very classless or demonstrate economic equality to me. This is further proof there is no such thing as a Marxist society as Marx intended and the intellectual elite push for. Like I said, it is utopian fallacy. It is a ruse that takes any society moving in the direction of Marxist theory down a black hole toward autocratic ruin.

Communist's countries like China, Vietnam, and Laos are moving toward a free-market capitalist ideology. Must be a reason! I wouldn't hold my breath; however, waiting on any of those governments to give up any serious control. They will only go so far in order to improve their economies that were in shambles before they brought in quasi-capitalism. When I was in Laos a couple of years ago, a Laotian told me the Laotian people were very happy they could now own property. I feel I should add Russia to the list of communist countries although they are now officially the Russian Federation and no longer considered a communist country. I don't think much is politically different since the change took place. Putin, who has been in power since 2000, runs the country in an autocratic manner as was done under communist rule.

During my travels, I have discovered a technically unsophisticated but very telling observation that always impresses me regarding the dichotomy of wealth differences between social classes in our country and those of other countries. That observation is the multitude of big yachts in their harbors. This observation is especially telling in semi-socialist Europe. Many middle class citizens have shared information with my wife and me that points out it is impossible to obtain an American middle class standard of living in any of these countries even with two incomes. Here is a great example. During a recent trip to France, I asked our private tour guide what the average salary was in France. She said about $18,000 per year. We then discussed housing and other expenses and it was obvious that the math did not work. For example, she said a 700 sq. ft. apartment would rent for about $1,000 per month depending upon location. Now, I will admit we were in a very affluent part of France but the majority of the population who lives there full time are certainly not wealthy. I asked her how anyone does it? She gave a very interesting answer. She said, "It's complicated." I asked her again how someone can make it financially and got the same answer—it's complicated. She did say that college tuition was free in that it only costs 100 euros per year for her son to go to college.

She told us their VAT tax, which is the same thing as our sales tax, was 20.6%. I researched what other taxes French citizens pay. They pay all the same taxes we do; i.e., income taxes, gasoline taxes, local taxes, etc. I do not know the specific tax rates they pay but I certainly found out how expensive their gasoline tax is when I filled the gas tank on my rental van. I paid over $6 per gallon of which almost half of the cost was tax. They do have one tax that is different from us in that they have an additional tax called a wealth tax. I saw a 2014 tax table showing families with a total wealth (not income) of 800,000 euros or more paying an additional tax on top of all the other taxes. The tax rate started at .5% of total wealth and progressively went to a cap of 1.5% at 10,000,000+ euros. The only good thing I read about France's tax structure is that the absolute total tax on any one family subjected to this wealth tax is capped at 75% of income and doesn't go up to 100 % of income.

Income tax on all other citizens is capped at 45% of taxable income but how about all the other taxes to which they are subjected like VAT and gasoline taxes? Aren't these European countries the ones the American classic liberals and progressives say the United States should emulate? When Obama, Clinton, and Sanders talk about freebies like college tuition to the American people and give examples of other countries providing these freebies, they conveniently leave out the extraordinary high tax rate the citizens of these countries are faced with and the difference in "their" and "our" standard of living. For example, Obama conveniently forgot to tell us about all of the significant hidden taxes that we incurred to support Obamacare? I wonder how much college tuition really costs the French people?

I discovered a recent article on the Internet by the Christian Broadcasting Network (CBN) titled "France's Reckoning: Rich, Young Flee Welfare State". I found the article very interesting based upon my recent visit to France and what I know about their labor and tax laws. The first two sentences said, "France's day of reckoning has arrived: Its wealthy, best, and brightest are saying goodbye to a nation they believe doesn't want them to succeed or become affluent. According to one poll in Le Point, half of all young adults in France would leave the country if they could because the future looks so bleak." I wish the Gen Xers and the Millennials in our country could have the learning experience of the French young people regarding the results of progressive Marxist ideology. Maybe Obama should pay for an educational experience in France for all of our Millennials rather than subsidize their college tuition. That would be an education worth paying for. They would certainly be much wiser regarding the benefit and rewards of American traditional values over progressive Marxist ideology. There is nothing like a dose of reality for a good wake-up call.

I wouldn't limit that experience to young Millennials because there are those who are older and should be wiser who also fall for this progressive nonsense. The CBN article went on to say France suffers from a "toxic Marxist heritage" and the French left hates what it calls "Anglo-Saxon capitalism". The French need to wake up regardless of their political ideology. The article provided statistics that showed 26,000 French families left the country in 2010 and 35,000 families left in 2011. I doubt that trend has stopped. The article then commented that London has become France's sixth largest city. I thought London had its own problems in being too socialistic. I guess it's all relative.

The CBN article referenced a French tax lawyer who wrote a book in which he claimed that more than half of France's workforce is living off the state through government jobs or welfare. The lawyer had a warning for Americans. He said the United States is following in the steps of France with Obamacare and our exploding welfare state will be unsustainable. The article concluded, "The French can teach Americans a thing or two about the trap of the welfare state and how hard it is to escape."

I found it interesting that people we hired to do things for us while we were in France wanted "cash". Doesn't take much to figure that one out. After doing research on the French economy and from my personal experience, I am beginning to understand what my friend meant by "it's complicated". One last comment on France and I will move on. Upon our return home, several people asked us if we found the French to be rude like their reputation. I can honestly say that we found every French person we encountered to be exceptionally nice.

I don't want to be overly harsh on semi-socialist Europe. Russia's class differences appear to be worse. For example, a 38-year-old Russian billionaire entrepreneur recently built a 394 foot $300 million yacht. But wait! His isn't the biggest yacht owned by a Russian billionaire. The biggest is a 535 foot $500 million yacht and was the largest yacht in the world until recently. I wonder how many more Russian billionaires there are? There was a lecturer on our recent cruise to South America who was an expert on Russia. He acknowledged he could not prove it but was fairly certain that Putin was the richest person in the world at approximately $200 billion. He said there were three groups of billionaires in Russia. There were government officials, legitimate business oligarchs, and the Russian mafia.

According to Forbes, there were officially 88 Russian billionaires in 2015. That is a drop from 111 in 2014. They were third in the world in number of billionaires behind the United States and China but now also trail Germany and India. There are still boatloads of them. Pun intended. Forbes reported there were 1,826 billionaires in the world last year with a total of 290 new names on the list. Forbes added 198 more for 1016.

Do we truly know how many billionaires there are in the world? I'm sure we don't. I read a lengthy article in a British newspaper during my recent visit to London about the ex-wife of a Russian billionaire who divorced her for a younger woman after more than 30 years of marriage. The ex-wife said she and her husband were penniless when they were first married and she was instrumental in helping him build his fortune. She stated she was going to take him to court to obtain half of his wealth that she is entitled to under Russian law. The article reported he has several billion dollars from investments in a Russian company that he can't hide but that is probably only a small portion of his true wealth.

The story said there was no way for the wife to accurately determine how many billions her ex-husband has. The conclusion was that even if she could discover his total wealth, it is very difficult, if not impossible, for ex-wives to obtain their share of wealth in such divorces because of the influence these billionaires have with the Russian government and with Russian courts. The news story said this is not an isolated case. This is yet another example of the failure of Marxist utopian culture that Marx envisioned and Russia embraced where the concept of a classless society and commonly shared economy resulted in ideological deception.

Here is some justice for the Russian middle and lower social classes. I said a Russian had the largest yacht in the world until recently. After three years of having the honor, the Russians lost that distinction to the President of the United Arab Emirates (UAB) and Emir of Abu Dhabi. His yacht is 591 feet long and cost an estimated $600 million. Take that Russian upper class! The UAB does not claim to have a utopian Marxist government ideologically based upon a classless society and shared economy. The UAB is labeled an authoritarian regime, as are other Middle Eastern countries and they make no bones about it. Is the Emir going to buy a bigger yacht after he sells us all of those custom made chips for the military?

Speaking of yachts, I did a cursory survey of the countries where the owners of the 50 largest yachts in the world were from. Most owners were capitalistic money-grubbing awful rich upper class people from the United States. Right? Wrong! Of the yachts that I could determine ownership, 13 were from the authoritarian Middle East (not surprising), 10 were from semi-socialist Europe (I thought there would be more), 9 were from Russia (Marx and Lenin would not be happy), 7 were from the free market capitalistic United States (we need more billionaires who like yachting), 11 were from other countries, and 10 did not list ownership.

I will be the first to admit that yacht ownership is not an accurate measure of the rich upper class in any country. It does; however, support Marxist ideology as a myth that many classic liberal and progressive Americans buy hook, line, and sinker as evidenced by their politically correct behavior. Fortunately, not all classic liberals fall into that Marxist trap. It depends upon where they are on the liberal dial we talked about in chapter 2.

I often wonder how many classic liberal Americans fully understand the Marxist principals behind the progressive political correctness movement. Progressives dupe classic liberals to gain their support for their agenda. We know from chapter 2 classic liberals are vulnerable because of their idealism and dedication to their ideology. There are several progressives in the United States who have studied Marxist theory and knowingly use political correctness as a means toward progressive change to enhance their power and control. For example, I read a telling article in our local newspaper about Hillary Clinton. Clinton spoke at an Iowa Democratic fundraiser and she, "Implored democrats on Sunday to chose 'shared economic opportunity' over the guardian of gridlock." Clinton was referencing the republicans doing nothing in Congress to help the American people whereas she will help everyone get ahead if she is elected—except the rich, of course. We have already discussed the fallacy of that one. It doesn't leave much to the imagination as to where she stands on Marxism in America. Unfortunately, it is easy to dupe people if you tell them what "they believe" they want to hear.

It sure would be interesting to read Clinton's sequestered senior thesis at Wellesley College, wouldn't it? I have read it is about her interviews with Saul Alinsky and is also a critique of his principles. It is widely reported that they communicated with each other. I actually saw a copy of a letter on The Blaze Internet site that Hillary sent him asking when his book, *Rules for Radicals*, was coming out. There was also the warm response from Alinsky's secretary saying he would like to see her when he returned from Asia because she (the secretary) knew his (Alinsky's) feelings for her (Hillary). What did that mean? Who knows?

I have a great counter story to the issue of progressives pitting the middle class and the poor against the rich. I live in Naples, Florida where a great number of these "rich people" have homes. The vast majority are second or greater homes. In my development that number is greater than 80%. My local newspaper had a recent article regarding the assessed value and resulting tax liability on some of these properties. The homes they highlighted were valuated in the tens of millions of dollars for tax purposes and obviously many of the owners paid taxes in the hundreds of thousands of dollars. The highest valued home was valuated at $54.725 million. The tax assessment was $487,416.95. I wonder how much the owner pays to the government in "total taxes" each year? Where do the middle class and poor who get sucked into this Marxist utopian scam think "shared economic opportunity" comes from? As we discussed in chapter 8, it comes from the rich who progressive Marxist say they want to "take down". If the rich are not there to provide this income redistribution, where does it come from? It doesn't!

Oh, the person who owns that house I mentioned? He is rich today but he started with basically nothing. He used to be a lineman for a cable company. He built a new company through entrepreneurial sprit, risk taking, and hard work. The name of that company is Cablevision. I can tell you that all the rich people I have met and read about in Naples are self-made. I have never known of anyone here who was born rich and had their wealth handed to them on the proverbial silver platter. I thought that was the American dream. Not to the progressives. The American dream to them is to put us all in their neat little utopian package and rule over us with their ruse.

How does this discussion regarding the proliferation of Marxism in America make you feel? I find it very disturbing and scary as hell for America's future. I was totally oblivious how ingrained Marxist ideology is becoming in our society until I wrote this book and I am a legitimate news junkie.

With this cheerful observation in mind, let's go back to the concept of "make love-not war". I'll start with the history of how this phrase evolved. In 1914, during World War I, Marxists in Europe thought the working class would rise up against their "bourgeois governments" and overthrow them. They would then combine into one Marxist society. That didn't happen. People rallied to each of their country's needs and went off to war to defend them. Marxists believed it couldn't be the Marxist theory that failed so after the war they started uprisings in several countries. That endeavor also failed. The Marxists had a problem implementing their ideology and began to look for a solution. In 1919, two Marxists named Antonio Gramsci and Georg Lukacs said workers would never realize a "Marxist paradise" and its benefits until they were freed from "Western culture and religion". I assume when they said religion they meant Christianity.

In 1923, a "think tank" was established in Germany at Frankfurt University to transition Marxism from economic to cultural terms. Originally, it was to be called the Institute for Marxism. The Marxists decided their efforts should not be openly identified in any way with Marxism so they decided to formally call their Marxist think tank the Institute for Social Research. Informally, it became the Frankfurt School. In 1930, the school acquired a new director named Max Horkheimer who was considered a Marxist renegade. Under his leadership, the Frankfurt School combined the theories of Marx and Sigmund Freud and came up with a theory they called Critical Theory. I could not find any evidence that Freud was personally involved with Marxist ideology.

The basis of Critical Theory is to "criticize" existing society in the most destructive way possible to bring "liberating change" as opposed to merely presenting a Marxist political alternative, which had been proven to be unsuccessful. The purpose of Critical Theory is to bring down Western culture and religion in order to replace free market capitalism with a Marxist based society. Critical Theory concentrated on touting society's repression of women, gays, and blacks. Another theme touted by Horkheimer that became a primary concern at the Institute was environmentalism to counter what he called man's domination of nature. Sound familiar? Critical Theory is now referred to as "political correctness". This Marxist movement of Critical Theory started in the 1930s and hasn't changed in 80 years—only the name.

Two other key people at the Frankfort School were Erich Fromm and Herbert Marcuse. They introduced the sexual element, which is central to political correctness. Marcuse's writings promoted a society of "polymorphous perversity" in which a person can "do their own thing". He wrote extreme material regarding the need for sexual liberation. Horkheimer promoted the bourgeois culture as being excessively devoted to labor. He expressed his demand for human sensual happiness that he claimed the bourgeois inherently had treated with hostility. We routinely see this today as progressives push laws and regulations that diminish personal responsibility and independence and promote leisure and entitlement. Our social norms are being attacked to permit a society of excessive permissiveness. These acts combined make society easier to manipulate and control. A society out of control is much easier to control than a society in control.

I said two of the prime goals by Gramsci and Lukacs to accomplish the implementation of Marxism throughout in the world were to take down Western culture and religion. I read a very interesting take on that topic in The Daily Signal in October 2015 by Paul Kengor. He hypothesized that the push in America to support same-sex marriage is part of that effort by progressives. He said the Communist Party of America heralded the Supreme Court decision in June of 2015 on same-sex marriage along with classic liberals and progressives. Kengor referred to Marx and Engle's book, *Communist Manifesto*, where he said the two wrote about "the abolition of the family". Kengor said it was Engle who was most opposed to marriage and family and quoted Engle as saying the "bourgeois claptrap" of marriage was merely a "system of housewives held in common". Kengor also referred to the efforts of Lukacs, Marcuse, and the Frankfort School to fundamentally transform the culture of a society through "Freudian-based Marxism" that would obliterate traditional religious understandings using cultural evolution achieved through institutions, especially academia.

Kengor said, "For the far left, same-sex marriage is the Trojan horse to secure the takedown of marriage it has long wanted, and countless everyday Americans are oblivious to the older, deeper forces at work. And even more delicious for the left, same-sex marriage is serving as a powerful tool in attacking what the extreme left has always hated most; religion." Kengor also said, "As for communists, they couldn't care less whatever tags or hashtags or slogans or colors the majority culture uses to redefine marriage and family. To them, the larger objective remains the same: to reject and abolish a traditional Judeo-Christian understanding of marriage and family." He went on to say they are getting what they wanted, and they could not have done it without the support of mainstream Americans.

I have said that I support gay marriage but obviously not to take down traditional Judeo-Christian marriage and family. Until I read Kengor's article, I did not see any connection between gay marriages, the destruction of the traditional family unit, and religion. After reading his article and knowing what I know about the Frankfort School and Critical Theory, I believe he is right. What a conundrum!

When the Nazis came into power in 1933, they shut down the Frankfort School. The members of the school fled to New York City and the school became affiliated with Columbia University. Their focus shifted from German society to American society. Thanks Columbia! During World War II, Marcuse went to work for what became the CIA. Are you kidding me? Horkheimer and another Institute leader moved to Los Angeles. We know what happened there! Honestly, I do not know if he had anything to do with developing the Marxist Hollywood crowd but I do wonder. One interesting tidbit regarding the Frankfurt School is that all the founding members were German Jews. I found that curious, interesting, and surprising. I discussed it with a Jewish friend of mine and learned why they were the leaders in this deep ideological endeavor. He told me the German Jews were a very intellectual group and were elitist among European Jews. That would make sense why they would be involved in such deep thinking. I guess I should say deep "critical thinking".

Next comes the Vietnam War and open rebellion in the 1960s among young radicals who opposed the draft and the war. They needed an excuse not to serve their country. Marcuse gave it to them. He saw an opportunity to utilize the Critical Theory that the Frankfort School had developed. Marcuse's book titled *Eros and Civilization* became the bible of the Students for a Democratic Society (SDS), other student rebels, and draft dodgers as they embraced his philosophy. In his book, Marcuse argues that a capitalistic society is repressive and results in people with hang-ups and neuroses because their sexual instincts are repressed. Marcuse said he could envision a future in which people can liberate their Eros and their libido and have a world of "polymorphous perversity", if our repressive capitalistic society could be destroyed. In his world, there would be only play and no work. That is exactly where our progressive friends want to take us and are having significant success. They are especially having success with young Millennials.

Marcuse's theory is vastly irresponsible and unrealistic but doesn't sound too bad on the surface. Especially if you're a young person in the uncertain 60s who has never had to worry about anything and your world was just turned upside down with huge potential responsibility in a scary war. Whether a young person was radical or not, they were not prepared to fight. I was one of those young people and I remember it well. Once my friends and I graduated from college, it was a given that we would be drafted into the military unless there was some legitimate reason not to be. We saw the dramatic pictures on television and were all scared to death we would wind up on the front lines in Vietnam. Even in light of that fear, we all took our responsibility to our country seriously and none of us were draft dodgers. Marcuse gave those that did not take their responsibility seriously an excuse. He told them what they wanted to hear. He told them things like: do your own thing; if it feels good do it; and it is OK to avoid the draft. He told them to "make love, not war"! Now, you know where "make love, not war" came from.

After researching this chapter and learning the true meaning and purpose of political correctness, I was astounded our country's conversion to Marxism has crept so deep into our culture and Americans don't have a clue. I was so stunned by my discovery; I spent another year and a half re-writing the book to encompass what I learned and how it will affect our future. I'll bet Horkheimer, Fromm, Marcuse, and the other original philosophers from the Frankfurt School are grinning from ear to ear in their graves. Their Critical Theory is working in America.

Political correctness is growing at an increasing rate. Our progressive politicians in Washington are making it easier and easier for society to get more and more free stuff without earning it. Those same progressive politicians are autocratically picking and choosing which laws they enforce, ignoring the Constitution, and increasingly implementing policy and regulation that should be controlled by Congress. There is aggressive demonization of the upper class. The mores of our society are increasingly becoming more permissive and irresponsible. Marxist ideology is taking hold.

If the progressives take total control, what happens to us? Will we be the first country in the history of the world to achieve a successful utopian Marxist society? Do we live in this wonderful utopian world where everyone is treated equal, we have no material needs in life, the Earth's environment stands still the way we want it, and we live our lives in polymorphous perversity? Let's take a quick look at Marxist history. We know what happened when Marxists like Stalin, Lenin, Mao, Pol Pot, Castro, and Chávez came into power. How about Hitler and Nazi Germany? I read somewhere that he was a closet Marxist once he got past his Aryanism. Hitler's political party was originally called The National Socialist German Worker's Party. How about the Marxist based societies without authoritarian rule? No country, Marxist or not, has ever provided even close to what Americans have with regard to freedom, security, equal rights, economic status, personal opportunity, and quality of life? There never has been nor ever will be. And, there never has been nor ever will be a country to achieve the goals set out in Marxist ideology, which is utopian fantasy.

It is preposterous to think America can become a Marxist country! We never have in past attempts and we are 240 years old. Besides, Americans will not stand for it. OK, let's see. We looked at progressive Washington in chapter 7 and the enabling media in chapter 6. Chapter

8 talked about what the progressives are doing to stay in power in perpetuity. Chapters 2, 3, and 4 talked about well-meaning liberal naivety and the deception by progressives to lead classic liberals down their progressive "primrose path". And finally, where in the Sam Hill are the conservatives we discussed in chapter 3?

I'm an informed conservative who watches and reads conservative news every day. I have gone to Tea Party rallies and I do my homework and vote informed in every election. I knew America was under attack by the progressives but I did not fully understand their intended goal and I had no idea regarding the success they are having. I did not know Marxist culture has invaded American culture as deeply as it has. If any American takes the time to do the research I did on political correctness in America and still doesn't believe that traditional conservative values and the Constitution of the United States are in serious jeopardy, I don't have a bridge big enough to sell him or her.

Is there still hope to save America as we know it and love it? In my heart and in every part of my body I want to believe there is hope but look at what I have discovered regarding Critical Theory. Lets take a look at some of the political correctness issues we face today and their impact on traditional American culture. Critical Theory targeted women, gays, blacks, environmental issues, and religion to create the illusion of the victimization of minorities and environmental ruin in order to disparagingly attack existing social norms and laws to convert a non-Marxist society to Marxism. I want to emphasize the phrase "creating the illusion" because that is exactly what it is. It is a ruse to accomplish the progressive mission of tearing down a society in order to build it back with Marxist philosophy. In writing this chapter, I feel a deep sense of frustration and sadness for my country. I want to yell from the highest mountaintop for America to wake up. This book is my mountaintop.

I find it fascinating that the same political correctness issues pushed by Critical Theory over 80 years ago are still the same major issues pushed by progressives today. Does time stand that still? When it comes to basic human nature, it does. I wrote about this in my last book. For example, women have come a long way in society regarding their rights and equality since the 30s but don't confuse that fact with the narrative spun by progressives for their own gain. Political correctness worked very successfully for the democrats during the last presidential election by pushing a narrative portraying a republican war on women and it has continued to work in supporting Obamacare and other democratic agendas. It is still alive and well for the upcoming presidential election.

Be damned the truth. Progressive democrats say anything that fits their politically correct narrative to accomplish their goals. Repression of women's rights, lack of opportunity, birth control, and you name it is on the table to portray women as victims. Mitt Romney was even trashed after one of the Presidential Debates because he referred to a "folder of women" he used in determining the women he considered for leadership positions. As ridiculous as it is, his reference to a folder of women created a lot of negative news against Romney. The progressive democrats used it to accomplish their mission of demeaning him by using political correctness. Now I am not naive enough to believe that there is still not opportunity for improvement regarding women's issues but really—victims of the Republican Party?

If the Democratic Party is so concerned about women's rights, why haven't they done anything to resolve their assertions? It is almost eight years later and they are still saying the exact same things. They have controlled the White House the entire time, controlled both the House and Senate two of those years, and controlled the Senate six of those years. It is nothing more than false political hype to win votes. Women's rights aren't the only campaign issue that falls into this situation. We hear the same issues again and again every election cycle. Helping the middle class is another one. I even heard them bring up slavery at this year's Democratic National Convention, which also seems to be a reoccurring theme for progressives. Whatever works to stir up the liberal psychic we discussed in chapter 2 to achieve their nefarious ends. Voters have short memories.

Do republican men victimize their wives, daughters, mothers, sisters, female friends, and female colleagues and republican women victimize other women? It seems to me that the progressive democrat's record on victimizing women is more pronounced than the republicans' record when one looks at past scandals.

The stand by progressive democrats regarding birth control is ridiculous and their stand on abortion laws is disturbing. The politically correct feel that all women deserve to get the type of birth control they desire through their employee insurance policies even if those who own the organization do not believe in that type of birth control because of religious reasons. The most notable example is the Hobby Lobby case. The politically correct vigorously came after Hobby Lobby. They said, "Hobby Lobby did not want to offer birth control in their health insurance policies." When Hobby Lobby won in court there were outrage and demonstrations. The political correct either didn't care to know what they were talking about or were dishonest. I would pick both. In reality, Hobby Lobby did not ban birth control from their health insurance policies. They banned four pills that were "morning after" pills and that is what the court upheld. Hobby Lobby still had almost 20 different birth control pills included in their employee health insurance policies.

How about the Sandra Fluke debacle during the last presidential election? She was perhaps the Democratic Party's "poster child" to demonstrate the republican's war on women. Ms. Fluke, a law student at Georgetown University at the time, was invited by the Democratic Party to speak at a congressional hearing where she testified it cost Georgetown students $3,000 over three years to purchase birth control because the Catholic school refused to offer the coverage required by Obamacare due to religious beliefs. That equates to about $83 per month. She said 40% of the female students at Georgetown have struggled financially because of this policy and she had seen the faces of students on campus who were affected by the lack of contraceptive coverage. She also said some of these students had told her they were incurring financial, emotional, and medical burdens.

Fluke told the story of a fellow law student who was standing at a pharmacy counter and felt embarrassed and powerless when she learned that her health insurance did not cover birth control. The law student then had to go without contraception. I saw a rebuttal to Fluke's testimony on the Internet that said any student without insurance could have bought birth control pills at a CVS Pharmacy two blocks from campus for $33 per month and at a Target pharmacy three miles from campus for $9 per month. I did some quick checking that supported these numbers as reasonable costs for birth control pills.

Think about this for a minute. A student can find a way to pay tuition and living expenses at a very expensive private university and can't afford to pay $9 to $33 per month for birth control? Maybe they should make a choice between birth control and a few beers, a few glasses of wine, or whatever they consume for pleasure. Life is full of necessary choices. One choice I don't like is the progressive's choice to force me to pay for their birth control through my insurance premiums rather than they taking financial responsibility for themselves. Sounds like Marxism at work to me—equality for everyone through a shared economy. I share my wealth and they share their expenses.

Oh, by the way. Would you allow a lawyer to represent your interest who didn't do reasonable due diligence on their own insurance coverage and when a pharmacy employee explained it to them they felt embarrassed and helpless. Helpless and lawyer is an oxymoron in my experience with lawyers. This whole testimony on women's rights by Fluke is silly and ridiculously exaggerated. She spoke at the Democratic National Convention with the same silliness and exaggeration to support the Democratic narrative of the Republican war on women. When it comes to reality, one should never confuse political correctness with the truth.

I am appalled at the progressives' politically correct stand on abortion. Remember Dr. Kermit Gosnell who was convicted in Philadelphia for performing abortions that killed babies who were taken from the womb alive? This case brought scrutiny to many abortion clinics across the country for similar practices as well as for unsterile environments. Progressive politically correct abortion supporters came out of the woodwork to defend these rogue abortion clinics. Our mainstream news media was absent, not surprisingly, on such a tragic and illegal situation but were not absent on the support that arose for these illegal and unsafe abortion clinics.

The most recent controversy involves Planned Parenthood which is many times front and center in these controversies. A physician group called The Center for Medical Progress (CMP) released several undercover videos last year. No, it is not associated with the Center for American Progress. Far from it. One video was between the Senior Director for Medical Services for Planned Parenthood and undercover representatives of CMP. The people representing CMP were posing as representatives of a research company interested in buying tissue and organs from aborted babies. The representative from Planned Parenthood was very cavalier in discussing how they clinically abort fetuses to preserve and sell specific organs of fully developed fetuses. She said this was done on a regular bases.

The liver was the most common organ sold but they also sold hearts, lungs, legs and other organs. They sold them for $30 to $100 each. The Planned Parenthood representative also discussed how they did this quietly because of the legal concerns expressed by their legal department. Selling body parts from an aborted baby is punishable by up to 10 years in prison and/or a fine of up to $500,000. How about a felony murder charge? It was arguably the most disgusting interview I have ever heard and I am pro-choice.

In the second interview, a Planned Parenthood physician was haggling over the price of fetal parts with the undercover representatives joking that she wanted to buy a Lamborghini. A third video showed Planned Parenthood staff talking to the undercover representatives in a disgusting manner regarding a mutilated fetus lying on a table in front of them. In a fourth video, a staff member basically admitted what they were doing was illegal and they made efforts to cover it up. She made reference to an intact fetus being "just a matter of line items" and talked about a diversified revenue stream. In the latest video, a representative of one of the companies that purchased fetal parts said there were times when the fetal parts were taken without the women's consent, which is illegal. Obviously, Planned Parenthood denied the accusation saying that individual was not one of their employees. I understand there is more to come if CMP can get past the temporary restraining orders that were issued by a California judge to stop their release. A Federal Appeals Court has gotten involved.

The judge's actions are very disappointing but not surprising. It gets worse. A grand jury in Texas investigated Planned Parenthood and let them off the hook but indicted the director and another employee of CMP for using fake California drivers licenses during the making of their videos. The director was also charged for allegedly trying to buy body parts. A judge dropped that last charge against the director but the other charges are still pending. It was reported there was collusion between the prosecutor's office and Planned Parenthood. Several other states conducted investigations on Planned Parenthood and most investigations are closed without any further action.

I found these undercover videos extremely disgusting and it appeared to me they exposed illegal activity. How can these politically correct people portray to support women's rights and be holier-than-thou in political correctness and then support clinics that do these things to women and babies? Its abhorrent hypocrisy at its worst in pushing their political agenda!

I saw the President of Planned Parenthood, Cecile Richards, testify before the House Oversight and Government reform Committee. Not surprising, it became a political contest between the progressive democrats and conservative republicans. The Daily Signal had a good summary of the hearing and I watched a good part of the hearing on television. Richards said the allegations made by the committee republicans were "outrageous", "offensive", and "categorically untrue". The republicans focused upon Planned Parenthood finances and the $528 million the government gives them. Democrats defended the organization and criticized republicans for going too far. Our friend, Elijah Cummings said, "You threaten to shut down the government, you ousted your speaker, and now you really want to set off another select committee to investigate. Do you really want to do this? Do you really want to align yourself with extremists?"

Who are the extremists here? Those who support an organization that performs illegal abortions, illegally sells body parts for research, and receives hundreds of millions of dollars of our tax money to do it or those who oppose this illegal activity? I have watched all the videos that have been released, researched the Roe vs. Wade decision, and researched the law regarding the selling of body parts. There is zero doubt in my mind that Planned Parenthood was engaging in illegal activity and our government was paying them to do it. In all probability, this is still going on.

I have said over and over that progressive politicians will do anything for power, control, and votes. Planned Parenthood has a lobbying arm called the Planned Parenthood Action Fund. I will give you three guesses which politicians and political ideology that organization supports and the first two don't count. The organization's tax returns indicate Planned Parenthood has given their political arm $21,576,629 in grants and they share employees, facilities, equipment, mailing lists, and other assets. Richards's salary is also partially paid by that organization. The chairman of the house committee pointed out Planned Parenthood sent over $31 million outside the United States during the past five years including the Republic of Congo, which is under U.S. sanctions. Where are you IRS, DOJ, and FBI on the Planned Parenthood Action Fund?

Republican committee members pointed out the high salaries received by Richards and others. Richards received $590,928 in 2013, four others made between $387,000 and $460,000 and more than 40 executives earned a least $200,000. That met with a stern and emotional rebuke by democrat Gerry Connolly from Virginia. I watched him do it and I thought he was going to burst a blood vessel in his head and start crying at the same time he was so emotional. He alternated the following comments back and forth between Richards and the committee, "Look at how you have been treated as a witness: intimidation; talking over; interrupting; cutting off sentences; criticizing you because of your salary. How dare you? Who do you think you are? Making a professional salary as a head of a premier national organization, and daring to actually make decisions as the head of that organization? Lord almighty, what's America coming to? The disrespect, the misogyny rampant here today tells us what's really going on here."

It seems the progressives always plant a committee member to do a "diatribe" like this when hearings are controversial and not in the progressive's best interest. They always know how to pick them for dramatics. I have seen congressman Cummings be the one, more than once. The republicans also pointed out the organization spent $5 million on travel in 2013. Some of those expenses were spent on first-class and charter travel. Richards responded that she did not travel first-class but did not dispute the claim. It was also pointed out that Planned Parenthood spent $43 million to purchase corporate office space in New York City.

One argument we constantly hear from mainstream news reports and from progressives is that indigent women would not get the healthcare they need if the government did not fund Planned Parenthood. Breast cancer screenings are always brought up as a big deal. Conservative committee members presented reports that show breast cancer screenings at Planned Parenthood were down by 50% between 2009 and 2013. None of their clinics have mammography equipment. All of their screenings are manual breast cancer screenings and they send their patients to other clinics for mammography.

A report by The Heritage Foundation said abortions in the U.S. decreased by approximately 20% between 2000 and 2011. Abortions performed at Planned Parenthood during that period increased from 197,070 to 333,064 per year. That increase doubled the percent of U.S. abortions they perform from 15% to 32%.

Richards said the proposal to defund them would, "Deny people on Medicaid the ability to go to a provider of their choice and many of them do go to Planned Parenthood for a variety of reasons." The republican committee members pointed out there were approximately 13,500 Federally Qualified Healthcare Centers (FQHC) as opposed to the approximately 700 Planned Parenthood clinics and argued those clinics can provide better and more comprehensive healthcare to indigent women. The Daily Signal reported Planned Parenthood served 2.7 million patients in 2014 versus 21.1 million patients being served by the FQHCs.

I know the community health system extremely well. Planned Parenthood is primarily a birth control clinic that does abortions. These other community healthcare clinics are far superior to Planned Parenthood for the continuum of women's healthcare. This issue is a great example of all the progressive core personality traits wrapped up in one. There is idealism, rationalization, the end justifies the means, actions justified to a fault, inordinate ideological bias, divert and switch, and denial; not to mention just plain old flat out dishonesty. Whatever it takes for self-serving power and control.

It is a sad commentary but not surprising that the progressive democratic politicians in Washington are supporting Planned Parenthood and not the defunding of Planned Parenthood after the organization's disgusting and illegal activity was exposed. Guess who else is complicit in supporting Planned Parenthood? Our friends, the mainstream news media. They provided only minimal coverage of the story and it certainly could not be classified as investigative reporting. For example, a recent headline in my local newspaper said "Senate blocks anti-abortion bill; new showdown set". There were two issues in the bill and neither was anti-abortion as indicated in the headline. One issue was to ban late-term abortions in an effort to try stopping atrocities as Gosnell was doing. The other was to defund Planned Parenthood. The killing of Cecil the lion in Africa by a Minnesota dentist got considerably more news and outrage than the mutilation and selling of fetuses by Planned Parenthood. I heard one news source say the Planned Parenthood story was a right-wing conspiracy by Fox News. It would be comical, if not so serious.

I want to end this review of Planned Parenthood with an interesting observation and question for you. I read that 70% of their abortion clinics are located in minority neighborhoods and they performed 327,653 abortions during their 2013/2014 reporting year. I am a fan of Millard Fillmore cartoons, which are almost always political in nature. One had a picture of an unborn fetus in the womb holding a sign that said "Our Black Lives Matter Too". The bottom of the cartoon had the following comment, "African Americans comprise 13% of the U.S. population, 35% of abortions."

You may or may not know that Planned Parenthood was founded by a very controversial figure named Margaret Sanger (1879-1966) who has been labeled as a "birth control activist and racial eugenicist" who once spoke before the Ku Klux Klan. Do you think the location of these clinics in minority neighborhoods reflect intent by Planned Parenthood to offer clinical services to those who are in most need of free birth control, including abortions, or does the location of these clinics reflect a more sinister motive? Maybe both? Just a thought.

Actually, it is more than a thought. After I wrote the above, I read an August 2015 news story from The Daily Signal that said, "Many of the group's founding directors were actively involved in the 'eugenics' movement, which held that certain classes or colors of people were 'lesser' and 'unfit' for humanity and shockingly should be eliminated.

Included in these targeted 'unfit' groups were black Americans." Another group targeted were those with disabilities. If this is true about eugenics and Planned Parenthood, which I believe is a strong possibility; it is hypocrisy on steroids again and extremely sinister for both the Planned Parenthood organization and the progressives who support it knowingly or unknowingly.

I have four more disturbing situations to share with you involving birth control and sexuality. Remember, I said if you think it can't get worse, it can? If you are not sitting down, I suggest you do. This information is from a report I received from Judicial Watch. They found that poor children as young as 10 years old are getting taxpayer-funded birth control in the state of Washington by inserting intrauterine devices (IUD's) without the knowledge or permission of their parents. The largest age group to receive them in 2013 and 2014 was 17-year-olds. A total of 2,336 IUDs were inserted in minors between the ages of 16 to 17. Four 11-year-olds received IUDs during this two and one-half year period, as did more than 100 girls between 12 and 13 years old. There were 364 fourteen-year-olds and 744 fifteen-year-olds who received IUDs.

The Daily Signal published a report in June of this year regarding a parent who learned the Washington state public school system was sending guidelines to schools on teaching gender identity and sex education in kindergarten through the 5th grade. Parents were never specifically notified of these guidelines. Although the guidelines are publicly published, it was in reality done behind the parent's backs. I read the guidelines. They included teaching these very young children about self-gender identity, HIV prevention, and reproduction. The guidelines were very specific and very difficult for children that age to reasonably comprehend. For example, from kindergarten through the first grade they are taught there are many ways to express gender. In the second grade they are taught there is a range of gender roles and expression. In the third grade they are taught that gender roles can vary considerably. It is extremely inappropriate to teach these topics in public schools without parental knowledge and approval. How about the variation in teacher quality and ideology on such a sensitive and complicated subject?

The risk of inappropriately teaching children subject matter contrary to the parent's wishes or values far outweighs situations where parents do not teach their children that subject matter and those children find out the information somewhere else. The Daily Signal report contained an opposition video that called this activity "a social experiment that does not belong to the government". This is the tip of the proverbial iceberg for a government controlled by progressives and this type of activity is becoming more and more prevalent throughout our society.

I learned that Planned Parenthood has also gotten into the act of furnishing school age children with birth control. The Daily Signal reported in October of last year that Planned Parenthood became involved in a school board recall election in Jefferson County (Denver) Colorado. The recall was an attempt by an organized group to oust three republican school board members in the middle of their terms over a disagreement on educational policies. The Planned Parenthood message was contrary to the one being pushed by the recall group but they seized the opportunity to promote their agenda on sex education and birth control. Planned Parenthood supporters boasted of advancing Colorado's youths' rights to "real sex education and reproductive healthcare" and their campaign mantra was "Vote in the Election on November 3rd for Real Sex Ed!". The group that organized the recall does not support (at least publicly) the Planned Parenthood slogan. The recall group said their campaign is about "educating kids", not about the "sex education of kids".

What is Planned Parenthood's motive? They have, for some time, been pushing to get rid of a state law that requires parents of children under the age of 18 to be notified within 48 hours prior to an abortion. More compelling is the fact that Planned Parenthood is selling "Birth Control Training Kits" to schools in that county and the surrounding area. The kit contains eight kinds of contraceptives for both male and female including a controversial birth control shot. I had never heard of many of the contraceptives and had to look them up on the Internet to understand what they were. I must be getting really old. The kit also contains lubricants, cycle beads for natural family planning, and a "faux" morning after pill to familiarize the kids with them.

The Daily Signal report concluded, "At $125 per kit per student, it stands to reason that Planned Parenthood may view access to schools not simply as an opportunity to educate but rather as a lucrative business opportunity. According to the National Center for Education Statistics, the population of children enrolled in school is expected to increase 6% through the school year 2024/2025—from 49.8 million to nearly 53 million. In border states and near-border states, the increase is even higher at upwards of 10 percent and 15 percent growth. Not a bad business model, if you can get it." I do not know the circumstances when the kids are given these kits but I would be willing to bet it doesn't include parental permission. If I were a parent in Washington state or Colorado, I would be livid!

Here is a follow-up on the Colorado recall election. The Washington Post reported the recall was successful by a vote of 2 to 1 against the three republican school board members who favored educational reforms that included weakening the teacher's union, boosting charter school funding, and supporting market-driven policy changes for public schools. The voter turnout was 40%. Where in the heck is the other 60%? Voter turnout is a major problem in our country that the progressives exploit and the conservatives do a miserable job of improving.

Chalkbeat Colorado reported after The Washington Post article was published, the three school board members were defeated primarily by the teachers' union and "well connected parents" whatever that means. A Colorado administrative judge cited the not-for-profit group that launched the recall, Jeffco United for Action, for not disclosing their donors. They were fined $1,000, made to register with the state as a political organization, and disclose their donors. I'll bet that list would tell an interesting story? Do you think the teacher's union and/or Planned Parenthood are listed as donors? Maybe they channeled money through individuals. It doesn't matter now. They won.

As bad as the Washington story is, the next situation reported by Judicial Watch is worse. I said if you think it can't get worse, it can. Here we go again. The state of Oregon made it legal for minor children to undergo radical treatment for gender dysphoria without parental permission. I have great trust in Judicial Watch but I was so stunned I did an Internet review of the topic including a state government website. Judicial Watch was 100% correct and here is a synopsis of all that I found including their report.

The Health Evidence Review Commission in Oregon approved the program without any public debate and it begin in January of last year. The co-founder of the Portland-based Active Gender Center petitioned the commission to approve the plan. The treatment for gender dysphoria includes sex-change operations, cross-sex hormone therapy, and puberty-inhibiting medications.

Oregon state statute proclaims the minimum age for surgery consent is 15 without parental permission. Oregon teens can by law, without their parents consent at age 15, have sex, obtain birth control, get pregnancy tests, get an abortion, and now have sex-change surgery; however, they are unable to smoke cigarettes or marijuana, drive alone, send or receive sexts, vote, work more than 18 hours per week, get tattoos, eat unhealthy foods, take aspirin at school, or use a tanning bed. Judicial Watch obtained official documents that showed between January and September of last year that 7 children receiving therapy were less than 9 years of age, 22 were between 10 and 14, and 27 were between 15 and 17. One site I found, medicaldaily.com dated July 13, 2015, said they reviewed a state government FAQ sheet that indicated zero teens and 10 adults have undergone sex-change surgery under the taxpayer funded Oregon Health Plan since the program started that January.

Are you as mystified and speechless as I am? Are these stories examples of modern day eugenics and the usurping of parental rights and authority by our progressive friends who believe our society needs "nudging" because we make bad decisions and look back in bafflement? How about Critical Theory and polymorphous perversity? Very troubling. Usurping parental rights and authority is a major thrust by progressives because it gives them power to end-run parental influence and authority and also gives them the power to brainwash our younger generation. There are numerous examples of their end-runs around parents in this book. This practice is very dangerous and proliferating at a faster pace.

The Daily Signal published an article written by a transgender person that begins by saying, "Many Americans are unaware of the serious problems that face transgender persons." The author commented, "As a former transgender person, I wish the guy who approved me for gender surgery would have told me about the risks." The article said transgender individuals are never subjected to any objective test to diagnose their gender dysphoria because no such test exists and medical professionals are too quick to reach such a diagnosis and recommend immediate therapy when the individual may be suffering from something else.

The article quoted a study published in JAMA Pediatrics in March of this year indicating a high prevalence of psychiatric diagnosis in a study sample of 298 young transgender women that were between the ages of 16 and 29. More than 40% had coexisting mental health or substance dependency diagnoses and 1 in 5 had two or more psychiatric diagnoses. The study said the most common problem was major depressive episodes and non-alcoholic substance use dependence. The author quoted several other studies indicating a high percentage of transgender young people have psychiatric and/or developmental comorbidities. He said further investigation of traumatic childhood experiences and their correlation between transsexualism and dissociative identity is needed.

The article commented on research studies in 2009 and 2013. None of those studies indicated there is an abnormal transgender gene different from a normal male gene or normal female gene that causes someone to be transgender and the studies did not conclude that improved access to bathrooms, hormones, or surgery is urgently needed. The author said, "Without sufficient research and consensus on treatment of children diagnosed with gender dysphora, and knowing over half have coexisting disorders, any invasive treatment, even if recommended by the current guidelines, is simply an experiment. It's time to stop using children as experiments."

The author concluded that transgender individuals need psychotherapy rather than access to "cross-sex" restrooms, showers, and dressing areas. He said blaming society for the problems of transgender people would not improve their diagnosis and treatment. The article ended by saying true compassion is acknowledging the mental health issues of transgender persons, stop pretending they are born that way, and to provide effective treatment to slow the number of suicides rather than rush to perform irreversible surgeries. The author is obviously a person who has gone through a traumatic transgender experience and is warning others diagnosed with gender dysphoria and society in general to tread carefully.

That last article is a good lead into the controversy that is taking place today regarding gender identification in bathrooms and locker rooms? The Daily Signal reported in February of this year that the U.S. Department of Education is threatening schools with revocation of funding through Title IX if they do not identify students the way they wish to be identified according to their "internal sense of gender" and treat them accordingly. I can tell you, if my kids were still in school, they would not be going to the bathroom, changing clothes, or showering where boys and girls in the traditional sense are mixed. When I was in school, that would have created mega-problems and today would not be any different. I support "reasonable accommodation" as many schools are doing but I do not support a practice that threatens the safety and privacy of our children.

The city of Houston and the state of South Dakota have both passed laws to prevent this from happening in their jurisdictions in anticipation of federal intervention. The Daily Signal said those who are transgender have more options than those who are not; however, this does not placate the progressives who are trying to bully South Dakota into reversing course under the charge of discrimination.

Look out! This is just the beginning. It was widely reported in April of this year that PayPal backed out of a $3.6 million global operations center in Charlotte, North Carolina because the state was the first to pass a law requiring people to use bathrooms or locker rooms in schools and other public facilities that match the gender on their birth certificate rather than their gender identity. As this book is being readied to go to press, the National Basketball Association cancelled their plans to hold the 2017 All-Star Game in Charlotte. Several well-known entertainers have also refused to perform in the state. Reuters reported this action by North Carolina was "widely interpreted as an attack on LGBT rights". How about the rights of the majority? The founders and chief executives of more than one hundred companies including Apple and Twitter urged the conservative governor to repeal the law. Why would they do that?

The lieutenant governor, who is also a conservative, said, "If our action in keeping men out of women's bathrooms and showers protected the life of just one child or one woman from being molested or assaulted, then it was worth it." My hat is off to the governor and lieutenant governor of North Carolina. They stood up to this progressive nonsense and are great examples for all of us to follow. This is one of those issues where common sense needs to prevail in respect to all parties.

After the above took place, the DOJ threatened to pull $1.4 billion in educational funding under Title IX and possibly $800 million in federally backed loans if the state did not rescind the law. The state responded with a lawsuit against the DOJ stating the DOJ made a radical interpretation of the Civil Rights Act. I'm sure this will wind up at the Supreme Court. A group of students at the University of North Carolina along with parents and students at elementary, middle, and high schools have also filed a lawsuit against the DOJ and the Department of Education. A nonprofit Christian legal group called Alliance Defending Freedom represents them.

Here are some more recent happenings. A federal court in Virginia overruled a school that attempted to accommodate a transgender student rather than allow the student access to the school facilities of their choice. Fifty-one families in Illinois filed a lawsuit to prevent a high school from allowing a transgender student to use girls' locker rooms, bathrooms, and other "sex specific" facilities. The court in Virginia used Title IX as the bases for their decision and the U.S. Department of Education mandated the school policy in Illinois.

The Obama administration sent out a directive that every public school in the country must provide transgender access to the bathroom of their choice or face loss of federal funds. The progressive federal government is using federal law to coerce states to comply with their progressive agenda. It is Critical Theory on steroids. The Chicago schools announced as of May 2nd this year students and staff must be granted unfettered access to intimate school facilities based on their chosen gender identity. Where are the parents and the outcry on this one? Texas and 10 other states did speak up. They are suing the Obama administration because of their directive. According to The Wall Street Journal, the eleven states said, "The directive is a massive social experiment running roughshod over common-sense policies." I could not say it better! Where are the other 39 states?

I saw Cal Thomas as a guest on Fox News' *America's Town Hall*. He expressed my sentiments on transgender bathrooms perfectly. He said transgender bathrooms are not the issue. The issue is that our culture is moving in one direction very rapidly to tear down our society by tearing down all of our traditions, values, and religious beliefs. I wonder if he is aware of Critical Theory?

The Wall Street Journal reported in January of this year that the federal government is also using Title IX to "dictate" to colleges and universities how they should address the issue of sexual assault on campus and the newspaper questioned if this practice exceeds the federal government's legal authority. We have seen a significant uptick recently regarding sexual assault being a major campus issue. Even one campus sexual assault is one too many and deserves condemnation and attention but is the federal government using campus sexual assault to create another issue regarding women's rights to support Critical Theory? I would vote yes.

Michelle Obama gave an address to the U.N. regarding women's rights and women's equality. Boy oh boy, is that a group that knows a lot about women's rights and women's equality. Uh-oh, I shouldn't have used the idiom boy oh boy! Maybe I should use boy oh girl or better yet use girl oh boy. What is gender neutral for that? OK, enough silliness but it makes the point. Our First Lady said, "Women are still woefully underrepresented in government and in senior ranks of our corporations." She continued, "We still struggle with violence against women and harmful cultural norms that tell women how they are expected to act." Notice she said "our" and "we". Not surprising that she puts our country down in front of countries that are despicable when it comes to women's rights and women's opportunity.

If Michelle Obama is so concerned about violence and harmful cultural norms against women, why doesn't she crusade against a real and extremely serious problem of violence and harmful culture against women and young females—sex slavery? Reliable information is impossible because of the nature of the problem but it is estimated 800,000 women and children are trafficked between countries around the world each year for sex and labor. Eighty percent are said to be involved in sex trafficking and 80 percent of those are divided equally between adult women and adolescent girls. The average adolescent involved is between 12 and 14 years old.

Human slavery is the third largest crime in the world behind illegal drugs and arms smuggling. No one has a clue as to the total number of human slaves worldwide. I saw numbers on the Internet ranging from 2.5 million to 27 million.

I read a news article in the Lincoln, Nebraska newspaper that was the impetus for me to write about this. One would expect cities like Los Angeles, Houston, New York, Atlanta, and Miami to be involved in sex trafficking but how about smaller cities like Omaha, Nebraska? The Omaha Child Exploitation Task Force rescued more than 100 women and young girls from sex trafficking between 2010 and 2015. Human service agencies across the state of Nebraska identified sex trafficking victims younger than 17 years old at least 176 times during 2015. I feel very badly for those victims. The stories I read and see on television about their lives are sadder than sad. They are manipulated by their pimps into the business, imprisoned in servitude, and physically beaten on a regular basis to keep them in line or if they are not producing their earnings quota. Nebraska is a rural low-population state with strong values. Multiply Nebraska's sex slave numbers across the entire country to states with much larger populations, more diverse populations, and more diverse values. This is stunning to me.

The Lincoln news article said an estimated 300,000 men, women, and children are victims of sex and labor trafficking in the United States and sex trafficking alone was a $9.5 billion industry. This is one of the biggest travesties in our American society. If the progressives and our First Lady are so concerned about how women are treated in our country, why don't they do something about this? They don't because it is a very real and extremely difficult problem to attack. It also doesn't fit the narrative of Critical Theory in exploiting mainstream women to identify with fabricated issues that result in support for the progressives and their political movement.

I read a response to Michelle Obama's U.N. address on The Heritage Foundation website that I thought was very appropriate and telling as in "telling the truth" rather than spinning political correct propaganda. The response said a Pew Survey showed 51% of women interrupted their careers in order to have a family even though it hurt their careers and they were glad they did. Rasmussen published a poll on Mother's Day this year in which 60% of the women polled said motherhood was a women's most important role. The Heritage Foundation website also referred to research that showed women routinely have different interests and choose different career paths than men.

Thomas Sowell wrote in an op-ed this year that he discovered many women choose to work fewer hours than men and used physicians as an example. I personally welcomed all new physicians to our medical staff one-on-one in my office. About 50% were young women and they routinely told me they intended to eventually go part time and raise a family. Sowell also said women receive more than three-quarters of the degrees in education while men receive more than three-quarters of the degrees in engineering. He concluded the outcome of these choices affects the jobs women obtain and how much they are paid.

The Heritage Foundation said the reality is that men and women will never be represented equally in corporations or government because of personal choices and that should not bother us. The article concluded by asking, "Are women obligated to be equal to or outdo men?" The author of The Heritage Foundation article was a young woman.

Before I retired, roughly sixty-five to seventy percent of our 5,000 employees were women. I can assure you there are significant laws and regulations regarding equal treatment and opportunity for women in the workplace. I can also assure you women aren't bashful about filing Equal Employment Opportunity Commission (EEOC) claims. I can't speak for other organizations but we strictly followed the laws and regulations and it was a rarity for us to lose a discrimination case. If we did, we always felt comfortable we had not done anything wrong as accused. No matter how right you are, you don't always win. We were not perfect but we followed the law to a T.

We followed the laws and regulations, not because we were afraid not to, but because it was the right thing to do. It is not a perfect world and women can be and are treated wrongly in spite of EEOC laws but it is the exception and not the rule. Based upon historical societal norms, women are probably discriminated against more in our culture than men but don't think unfairness doesn't happen to men as well? Men are not immune from bias and discrimination. There are cultural norms that pressure men to act in certain ways the same as there are for women. Here is an interesting Rasmussen poll taken in May 2012. Seventy-three percent of those polled did not know of anyone who had been discriminated against at work. Nineteen percent said they knew of someone who had been discriminated against. The results were the same as a poll they had taken in November 2010.

I want to share an interesting bit of news. My local newspaper reported the median CEO pay for women exceeded the median pay for their male colleagues in the 2016 Equilar pay study for the 100 top paid CEO's. The female CEOs average salary was $22.7 million per year compared to a median salary of $14.9 for males. There were eight female CEOs in the study. That is about the same ratio of women to men for the top 200 CEOs they reported last year. The newspaper also reported a research company named Catalyst said 19% of board seats and 25% of senior management were women. USA TODAY reported in May 2015 the top 21 female CEOs in the S&P 500 were paid an average of $18 million, which exceeded their male counterparts. USA TODAY also said the highest paid female CEOs were Yahoo CEO Marissa Mayer at $42 million, Oracle CEO Safra Ada Catz at $37.7 million, and Lockheed Martin CEO Marillyn Hewson at $33.7 million.

Safra Ada Catz must have gotten a big raise. The Wall Street Journal reported a compensation study in April of this year that showed her salary was $53.2 million and I guess the article blew my theory on equal pay for woman. It said Catz's co-CEO, Mark Hurd, made $1,500 more. I am sure our progressive friends can make something out of that without even knowing why. Out of curiosity, I looked on the Internet and Catz and Hurd's salaries were reported to be the same on all the websites I looked at. I guess the $1,500 is a rounding error since 98% of their salaries are in stock options. The Wall Street Journal said 15 out of 17 women in the group studied were above the S&P median. Woman represented about 6% of the group. You can make out of these studies what you want. It tells me that women make up a little less than

10% of corporate CEO's and their salaries are higher than their male counterparts. It also tells me the number of women in large company CEO jobs, board seats, and top executive positions could be higher but, considering men and women in general have different goals in life, this democratic "war on women" baloney is just that—baloney. The real war on women is not by the republicans but by the democrats themselves. Progressive male and female democrats intentionally and aggressively downgrade women to selfishly promote their agenda.

How about gay rights? The politically correct do have a stronger case for gay rights issues than for women's rights issues but political correctness is not the solution. Our society is making progress but still has work to do. We can be proud; however, that we are making faster progress than most other parts of the world. The Washington Post published a study that said homosexual acts were illegal in 66 countries and punishable by death in 12 others. Same sex marriage is allowed in only 22 countries in addition to ours. Human beings are human beings and our Constitution gives every human being in our country equal rights. I said earlier that homosexuality is not a personal choice but rather a choice of God, nature, or however one wants to describe where we came from. It is no different than being a male or female. It is not our choice.

This is another example where society on both sides of the fence needs to use commonsense and practice understanding, tolerance, and maturity. Gay "marriage" is the biggest issue for those who express opposition to gay rights. In almost all cases, this results from her or his religious beliefs and other people and the courts should honor those religious beliefs. They should not be disrespected as progressives are doing.

I feel a strong degree of empathy for people like the young couple in Oregon who lost their bakery and were ordered to pay $135,000 in damages for refusing to bake a wedding cake for a gay couple. Their lives and the lives of their five children have been significantly affected. They didn't prevent the wedding from taking place. There were other options. Where are their rights? That same gay couple had been regular customers in the past and the bakery owners treated them like any other customer. It was the marriage issue that made the difference.

The director of the state government agency responsible for determining and enforcing the penalties on the bakers appears to have been heavily influenced by Basic Rights Oregon, which is a powerful LGBT organization that has contributed to the director's election campaign. When the bakers began to get national support and funding to help them pay the fine, this government agency director slapped a gag order on them. The couple has refused to pay the damages and the agency that fined them is researching ways to collect the money. This is true politically correct injustice by the government against innocent people.

Another example is a 70-year-old flower shop owner in the state of Washington. She had never refused to sell flowers to gays in the past and felt a close friendship with the gay customer who asked her to do the flowers for his wedding. The Daily Signal quoted the flower shop owner as saying, "I put my hand on his and said, I'm sorry Rob, I can't do your wedding because of my relationship with Jesus Christ. We talked a little bit, we talked about his mom (walking him down the aisle) … we hugged and he left." She immediately had charges filed against her and was fined $1,000 and $1 in court costs.

She is fighting these charges in court. The lower courts have ruled against her but the Washington Supreme court has announced they will hear the case. She said her legal fees would put her shop out of business. The Daily Signal also quoted her as saying something else that is very telling. She said, "There won't be anything left. They want my home, they want my business, they want my personal finances as an example for others to be quiet." A GoFundMe site was set up for her and after about $175,000 was raised, the site was shut down. GoFundMe said the site was in violation of its terms, whatever that means. A GoFundMe site for the Oregon bakers had also been shut down after they had raised approximately $110,000.

It is the progressive way to make examples of those who oppose their objectives in order to intimidate others who might do the same thing. These two situations are classic examples of the progressive "tail-wagging-the-dog" with the dog representing the rights of the majority and its tail representing the minority. It will be interesting to see how these two cases eventually turn out.

Remember the young lady who owned a pizza shop with her dad in Indiana who told the press (when they came into the pizza shop unannounced with cameras rolling) they would "hypothetically" refuse to serve pizza for a gay wedding because they were a Christian establishment but would otherwise serve them as customers? If you do remember, then you also remember the very negative reaction toward them by the mainstream news media and progressives. That reaction included death threats and they closed their shop for safety reasons. I was very pleased when they received over $840,000 in donations from supporters on GoFundMe, which shows there is a still a large contingent out there who believes in religious beliefs and individual rights. If I remember correctly, they eventually opened back up and used some of the money to make their pizza shop look nicer. GoFundMe got a lot of heat over this fund and I think that is why they decided to shut down the bakers and the flower shop owner.

The state of Mississippi just passed a law in April of this year that says the government cannot force ministers, religious organizations, or private business owners to participate in activities that violate their religious beliefs. It does not conflict in any way with the recent Supreme Court ruling on same-sex marriage. It just supports First Amendment rights. It is no surprise that the progressives went bonkers.

We are all concerned about the rights of our fellow man or should I say fellow man and woman? Just kidding. Merriam-Webster defines "fellow man" as "a person other than yourself: a fellow human being". See how easy it is to become politically correct. How about the politically correct rights of "man's best friend" and other lovable animals? Let's take a look at politically correct animal rights activists and organizations like The People for the Ethical Treatment of Animals (PETA) that claim to protect animals for their well-being or is it the activists' well-being?

I will give you an example of animal political correctness gone amuck in my own community. Nosey the elephant was scheduled to perform at the local Shriners Circus. After local animal activists threw a "hissy fit" and made multiple public accusations against Nosey's owner, the Shriners voted to cancel Nosey's performance. Fortunately, they did not notify the owner in time and he showed up with her at the circus. Nosey was allowed to perform and the chairman of the circus was quoted as saying, "He (the owner) laid out all of his licenses, current vet reports on the elephant, and everything appears to be above board. And, I'll be honest, the elephant looks happy and healthy."

The animal activists had complained about the horrible treatment Nosey got from her owner and what bad physical shape she was in. Obviously, they were wrong. I find example after example how radicals practicing political correctness make up their own narrative to push their progressive ideological agenda regardless of reality. It is dishonest as hell. The end always justifies the means. We all know what recently happened to the Ringling Bros. and Barnum & Bailey Circus elephants. They were retired because some local governments were passing anti-elephant and anti-circus ordinances and the circus was being driven from performing in those communities. What gave these local governments the right to do that? Did the community vote on the issue?

Here is the most ridiculous animal political correctness example of all. Remember the White House Czar and Harvard University law professor in chapter 5, Cass Sunstein, who advocated that animals be given the right to sue in order to protect animal rights? Well, guess what? A group called the Nonhuman Rights Project went to court in New York State to do just that. I kid you not! This group went to court to get Tommy, a chimpanzee, released from his cage. They argued that animals with human qualities like chimpanzees deserve basic rights including freedom from imprisonment. There was no evidence that the owner was mistreating the chimp. The group lost the case but appealed. The appeals court denied legal human rights to Tommy saying that a human is any being whom the law regards as capable of rights and duties. The court wrote in their opinion, "Needless to say, unlike human beings, chimpanzees cannot bear any legal duties, submit to societal responsibilities, or be held legally accountable for their actions."

At least there is some sanity left in the courts in opposing politically correct nonsense. The animal rights group said they would appeal to a higher court and find other cases to pursue. This was not their first case. They lost all the others as well. I might add that Tommy's owner said Tommy lives in a seven-room enclosure and has "lots of toys and other enrichment". Sounds like Tommy lives a lot better than many human beings. I can't believe I am going to say this but I am glad these people spend their time doing these ridiculous radical things. Can you imagine what it would be like to work with these people in our everyday lives? Actually, we unfortunately do, don't we?

Here is one last observation regarding ridiculous animal rights activism. You probably know the activists finally got SeaWorld through their disruptive activities and the movie *Blackfish*. The AP reported SeaWorld is phasing out their orca shows and breading program by 2019. The AP article I read said many marine scientists are disappointed because they will "lose vital opportunities" to learn things that would help killer whales in the wild. The article also said no marine park in the world has SeaWorld's experience in maintaining or breeding orcas in captivity. PETA and the Whale and Dolphin Conservation (WDC) said SeaWorld's research has not been helpful to orcas in the wild. PETA's director of animal law was quoted as saying SeaWorld has done no useful research. Who is right on this one? Is it the marine scientists or PETA and WDC? That's an easy one. As I routinely say, these progressive activists never confuse their radical positions with the facts.

I have passionately expressed my thoughts on climate change, which is a 21st century lightening rod for Critical Theory. I will add to my previous ranting an announcement released by researchers in 2014 that was organized by the U.S. National Oceanic and Atmospheric Administration (NOAA). They have concluded they can now associate specific weather events with man-made global warming. They gave specific heat waves, intense rains, and severe droughts in different parts of the world during 2013 as examples. They did say they could not connect a specific early South Dakota blizzard to global warming. Wow, these guys are good even if they did fail in South Dakota. I thought these scientists changed from "global warming" to "climate change" because recent evidence did not support global warming. I saw the co-founder of *The Weather Channel* in a television interview totally trash global warming and climate change.

The Daily Signal had a story in May of this year that contained a graph showing temperature changes for the last 500,000 years. I still do not know how scientists can do that. The graph showed temperature variations about every 50,000 years that averaged roughly15 degrees

Celsius, which is about 60 degrees Fahrenheit. The story said, "The 'science thought police' insist that even though none of the temperature variations for the first 499,950 years had anything to do with human activity, virtually none of the temperature increases of the past 50 years had anything to do with nature. Got it?" Sure do! Oh, by the way. Where did the graph come from? A study report released by NOAA.

Don't forget the narrative of climate change resulting from man's assault on the environment keeps progressive grant money flowing to these climate change scientists and keeps them from needing a real job. A great example is a revelation I read in March of this year in The Daily Signal concerning a climate change professor at George Mason University who is accused of "double dipping" his salary from the university and his taxpayer-funded climate change research center. His salary in 2014 was $511,410 and he has earned more than $5.6 million since 2001. Enough said. At least he is under investigation.

Political correctness through climate change is another ruse by progressive Washington to tear down capitalism through regulation and excessive costs and to achieve control over society. This next one should get your undivided attention. The Daily Signal, as well as many other news outlets, reported in March of this year that Attorney General Loretta Lynch told the Senate Judiciary Committee she is considering civil actions against "climate change deniers" and has sent an inquiry to the FBI to determine whether or not it would meet criteria to take action. Democratic Senator Sheldon Whitehouse urged Lynch to prosecute those who "pretend that the science of carbon emissions is unsettled". He gave the example of the DOJ winning a RICO suite against the tobacco industry under President Clinton. Climate change is not the same as the tobacco issue. The tobacco industry hid "verifiable research" from the public that showed without question the dangers of smoking cigarettes. Our federal government and climate change researchers have distorted and fabricated data to support their climate change assertions?

The Daily Signal concluded any civil action by the DOJ regarding climate change would be a "fundamental violation of the First Amendment". Progressive shenanigans don't shock me anymore but I have to admit that I was shocked by Lynch's comment. The Daily

Signal said, "This absurdity would be laughable if it were not so serious and dangerous". The writer also said it reminded him of the old Soviet Union where Stalin prosecuting anyone whom he believed had incorrect scientific views.

It gets better. It was reported in The Daily Signal in April 2016 that a coalition of 15 state attorneys general and the attorneys general for D.C. and the Virgin Islands "will pursue to the fullest extent of the law" any business that commits fraud by lying about the dangers of climate change. They call themselves the "AGs for Clean Power". This is so far fetched it is difficult to believe. The states are California, Connecticut, Illinois, Iowa, Maine, Maryland, Massachusetts, Minnesota, New Mexico, New York, Oregon, Rhode Island, Vermont, Virginia, and Washington State.

No surprise the attorneys general are all democrats (progressives) except for one who is an independent who I am sure is a progressive in independent clothing. I find the actions by Lynch and these attorneys general astonishing and more than scary. The Daily Signal said the attorneys general for California and New York have begun investigations into ExxonMobil for allegedly funding research that questions climate change. Exxon has emphatically denounced the accusations. Guess who was on the stage during the news conference to announce the group and their mission? Our climate savior, Al Gore. I guess he hasn't made enough money or gotten enough attention from his climate change hooey.

The Daily Signal equated this situation to the Spanish Inquisition in 1478 that silenced any citizen who held views that did not align with the king's. The report said that one of the lasting effects was the stifling of speech, thought, and scientific debate throughout Spain. Many brilliant individuals were silenced and the development of new ideas stopped and Spain became a "scientific backwater". The Daily Signal also reported that when New York's Attorney General was pressed at the news conference on the effect their actions would have on free speech, she responded, "Climate change dissenters are committing fraud and are not protected by law". Is she referring to corporations, individuals, or both? She didn't make a distinction.

I am speechless and you know by now that is hard for me. This is potentially the most flagrant violation of American rights and the Constitution that I have reported in this book. Every American should be livid these 17 top state law enforcers have taken the law into their own hands to silence those who do not agree with their progressive movement. It is inconceivable the top law enforcer in the land is contemplating doing the same. Which one of their politically correct movements will be next? Looks like *1984* is moving faster than I predicted. Wow! What I have just written is hard to believe.

What is harder to believe is they are getting away with it. I wrote this 10 days after the coalition's news conference and the news media is absent. I found very few reports on liberal and conservative news websites, one news story by The New York Times, some reporting on Fox News, and nothing else. Where are the other newspapers, television news shows, and the rest of the news websites? The entire news media is not doing their job on this one. Where are our conservative congressional representatives? They all should be screaming from the mountaintop and so should we. If they get away with this, "you ain't seen nothin' yet". This is the tip of the proverbial iceberg. It's progressive heaven on steroids.

I read the George Mason University professor under investigation for double dipping his salary was a big supporter of legal action against those who provided contrary research to man made climate change. No surprise there. I believe if we all knew the entire truth regarding research on man made climate change and its associated activist activity, it would be quite a story of self-serving deceit and corruption.

I have a great update. The Daily Signal reported later in April that The Competitive Enterprise Institute (CEI) launched a counter attack against the Virgin Islands Attorney General after the Attorney General subpoenaed documents relating to their research on climate change. The attorney general said he intended to "make it clear to our residents as well as the American people that we have to do something transformational" regarding climate change. CEI's attorney wrote him a letter that said the following, "Your demand on CEI is offensive. It is un-American, it is unlawful, and it will not stand. You can either withdraw (the subpoena) or expect to fight … the law does not allow government officials to violate Americans' rights with impunity."

In May, The Daily Signal reported the attorney general revoked his subpoena to CEI after CEI ran a full-page ad in The New York Times and the republican attorneys general of Texas and Alabama filed motions to block the investigation. CEI's attorney said, "CEI is going forward with our motion for sanctions because Walker's (the Virgin Islands' Attorney General) withdrawal only strengthens our claim that this subpoena was a constitutional outrage from the very beginning, violating our right to free speech and our donor's right to confidentially, and threatening the right of all Americans to express views that go against some party line." I applaud CEI for holding the Virgin Islands' Attorney General accountable. It really felt good to read the CEI attorney's comments.

Pushing back with authority is the only way we can stop politically correct intrusion in our lives. We need to see much more push back and holding the politically correct accountable. Except for a few, conservatives and classic liberals who do not agree with this politically correct onslaught are standing back and only complaining. This emboldens the progressives to inflict their warped ideas upon us. They will not stop until they meet stiff resistance.

Let's jump out of the fire (American freedom) into the frying pan (race relations). Political correctness regarding race is a major issue that is very destructive to all of society as well as to the specific race in question. The targets for the politically correct are American Indians, Hispanics, and blacks. I always use the descriptor "blacks" for black Americans. How can black Americans be African Americans when they are born in America? I bet very few American blacks have even been to Africa. I do not call myself a white American. Do the politically correct discriminate against the white race like they accuse the white race of doing to all other races? Absolutely! So basically, every person in our society is being subjected to politically correct discrimination. That doesn't make sense on the surface but not much of anything the political correct do makes sense. Let's make some sense out of it.

Let's start with the most ridiculous—American Indian political correctness. Any sport team that has an American Indian based nickname and/or mascot is fair game. I mentioned earlier that I live in Florida. The Florida State University Seminoles were under attack until they got the endorsement of the Seminole tribe. I had personally hoped they would have to give up their Indian nickname because of the obnoxiously irritating Indian chant they do during their ballgames from beginning to end. Just kidding but only about the nickname and not the chant. The chant does drive me crazy.

The Washington Redskins has been a big issue. A couple of well-known announcers stated they would not say Redskins anymore and just say Washington. They should be fired for being too politically one sided and not doing their jobs as announcers. At the very least, they should get a life. There have been lawsuits against the team in an effort to get rid of the name. The last lawsuit was to nullify the patent on the Redskin name, which the complainants won. It's under appeal. The owner of the Redskins said if these politically correct people are so interested in helping the Indians, why don't they go to the Indian reservations and honestly help them.

The owner brings up a good point but this is not the narrative these people are interested in. What they say is not what they mean. Whether they personally realize it or not, the underlying goal is to tear down society as we know it—Critical Theory. A Rasmussen poll showed 60% of those surveyed agree the Redskins name should not be changed. In the same poll, 61% think America is too politically correct and 12% think we are not politically correct enough. That 12% are in need of help. The poll also showed that 79% see political correctness as a serious problem while 16% does not. I do not know how many people overlap in that 12% and 16% category but they could go to group therapy together to learn about the real world.

In May of this year, The Washington Post conducted a poll of Native Americans that showed 9 out of 10 were not offended by the Washington Redskins name. A 2004 poll by the Annenberg Public Policy Center found the same result. That same article quoted a 2014 ESPN poll that concluded 23% of those Americans polled felt the Redskin name should be retired because it was offensive to Native Americans. This article makes the point that only 23% of those polled by ESPN were offended by the Redskin name and even that small number is more than double the number of the Native Americans who said they were offended. This Redskin issue is politically correct nonsense at its worst. It is another classic example of "never confuse the politically correct with the facts".

The reference to the Redskins honors the Indian race. It is in no way disrespectful. Anyone who has at least minimal intelligence and does not succumb to the politically correct mentality would realize that no team owner would name their team after anything they or the fans disrespected. The owner, the players, and the fans are proud of and honor the Redskin name. The Redskins are their heroes. Good grief! Are we going to change the names of our cities, our states, our other favorite sport teams, and who knows what else to satisfy these loonies. What would we call Oklahoma? Sioux Falls, South Dakota? Omaha, Nebraska? Alabama? Tucson, Arizona? The Mississippi and Ohio rivers? Miami, Florida? Kentucky? Missouri? Alabama? Manhattan, New York? Is the U.S. Military going to have to get rid of their Apache helicopters?

OK, I understand that these names don't reflect a skin color but come on; there are literally hundreds, if not thousands, of references to the Indian heritage in our country and none of them are disrespectful, including the Redskins. I'm called a white person and my skin is not white. If it was, I would be dead! What is going to happen to the Kansas City Chiefs, the Atlanta Braves, and the Cleveland Indians? Are the atheists going to go after the New Orleans Saints and the Los Angeles Angels? Do the Oakland Raiders, the Tampa Bay Buccaneers, and the Minnesota Vikings offend peace lovers? Where does it end? It doesn't! It just depends what "issue of the day" a radical group chooses to push their politically correct agenda for their own nefarious purpose.

A friend sent me an email that said the following, "Daniel Snyder, owner of the NFL Redskins, has announced the team is dropping the word 'Washington' from the team and it will henceforth be simply known as 'the Redskins'. It was reported he finds the word 'Washington' imparts a negative image of poor leadership, mismanagement, corruption, cheating, and lying, and is not a fitting role model for young fans of football." Enough said.

One of the most serious and troubling politically correct issues being thrown at our society today is racial unrest. The progressive politically correct politicians and non-politicians concentrate on pitting the black race against the white race, which is very destructive to all Americans. It hypocritically promotes the stereotype of blacks it purports to admonish. It also gives certain members of the black race an excuse to be victims rather than stand up as equals in our society. The racial debacles in Ferguson, Missouri and Baltimore, Maryland speak to these issues, as do many other unfortunate situations that were also tragic but less volatile for their communities. There were no winners in any of them. These incidents pose an important question regarding racial unrest in our country. Is our president, the Department of Justice, progressive politicians, and self serving race-baiters perpetrating racial inequality through political correctness that suppresses and marginalizes the black race in order to promote the progressive Marxist agenda, secure votes, and personally profit financially?

If this is true, and I have no doubt it is, then the mainstream news media is surprisingly complicit in this endeavor. They routinely report these tragic stories from the perspective of "racism in America" and ignore the true facts of the matter. Here is a great example of what I am talking about. After the Ferguson situation occurred, there was a lengthy article in my local newspaper in August of last year that began with full-page coverage on the first page of the editorial section. There was a very large picture of a white policeman talking to a young black boy in Ferguson who was holding a sign saying "Hands Up! Don't Shoot!". Under the picture was the comment that the policeman was talking to the boy "in an effort to foster some good will". Under that was a very large headline that said, "Root of the Problem". Under that headline was a smaller sub-headline that said, "Suburban ghettos like Ferguson, Missouri are ticking time bombs."

Two reporters from The Washington Times wrote the article that was syndicated across the country. The first paragraph said the following, "The current turmoil in Ferguson, Missouri, follows the trajectory of urban riots in Newark, Detroit, Cincinnati, Miami, Oakland, Los Angeles and elsewhere. They typically began with an incident of racially tinged police abuse. Outraged members of the black community organize protests, the police overreact, and the protests become more violent and threatening." The article went on to say that major issues such as unemployment, homelessness, inadequate schools, lack of public services, and lack of political representation contribute to the problem. The reporters also commented, "These suburbs are not poor by accident. Greater St. Louis is one of the most racially and economically segregated areas in the country, a result of long standing discriminatory practices by banks, homebuilders and landlords, as well as local governments."

The article was disgraceful and built on falsehoods. Unfortunately, they are not the only journalists across the country reporting this type of nonsense. Did these news reporters not take the time to discover the facts of the incidents and research The Community Reinvestment Act of 1977, the Dodd-Frank Act, and the current laws on discrimination impacting banks and housing lenders? Did they do so and the facts, federal Acts, and discrimination laws not fit their narrative so they were conveniently dismissed? How about just simply providing an accurate unbiased story?

Let's look at reality versus this politically correct nonsense. I obtained the following information from an op-ed by Cal Thomas. He said Baltimore, where the rioting was similar to Ferguson, has received over $1.8 billion in stimulus money from the Obama administration. Over $461 million was to invest in education and $26.5 million was for crime prevention. They have also raised taxes to generate revenue.

I could not find the same information for St. Louis and Ferguson but I did receive an email from a friend that contained the ten poorest cities in the United States with populations over 250,000 and included their poverty levels by percent. They are in rank order: Detroit, 32.5%; Buffalo, 29.9%; Cincinnati, 27.8%; Cleveland, 27.0%; Miami, 26.9%; St. Louis, 26.8%; El Paso, 26.4%; Milwaukee, 26.2%; Philadelphia, 25.1%; and Newark, 24.2%. Do you know what they all have in common? They have had democratic mayors for at least the past 26 years. The average number of years these cities have had democratic mayors is 65 years and two have never had a republican mayor. I assume all or most of these mayors are progressives.

My friend's email commented the poor habitually elect democrats and they are still poor. It also contained my favorite quote by Einstein, "The definition of insanity is doing the same thing over and over again and expecting different results." I don't blame the poor for their plight. I blame the progressive politicians who use the poor to get elected. The poor are sucked into an endless trap of poverty because of their politicians' ineptness, their politicians' personal benefit, or both.

I really liked what the email said at the end. It said:

- You cannot help the poor by destroying the rich.
- You cannot strengthen the weak by weakening the strong.
- You cannot help little men by tearing down big men.
- You cannot bring about prosperity by encouraging thrift.
- You cannot establish sound security on borrowed money.
- You cannot keep out of trouble by spending more than you own.
- You cannot lift the wage earner up by pulling down the wage payer.
- You cannot further the brotherhood of man by inciting class hatred.
- You cannot build character and courage by taking away people's initiative and independence.
- You cannot help people permanently by doing for them, what they could and should do for themselves.

These are The Ten Cannots by Rev. William J. H. Boetcker who was an American religious leader, influential public speaker, and outspoken political conservative. It was originally published in 1916. We need politicians who think like Rev. Boetcker. The Republican Party should adopt his Ten Cannots as their platform. If they did, they would at least have a platform! Rev. Boetker was born in Hamburg, Germany in 1873 and moved to the United States as a young adult. He died in 1962. The email also contained a quote by Henry Ford that would be good food for thought for those voting for these progressive politicians to get a free ride. Ford said, "Any man who thinks he can be happy and prosperous by letting the government take care of him had better take a look at the American Indian." I have already expressed my own opinion regarding what has unfortunately happened to the American Indians.

Let's go back to Cal Thomas' op-ed. Thomas said, "When self-sufficiency is encouraged, you get more of it and when it is ignored or discouraged, you get less. Attacks on the rich have done nothing to improve the lives of the poor." He said, if politicians were sincere about helping people escape their bad circumstances, they would flood the poor neighborhoods with people who have successfully escaped similar circumstances and have them tell their success stories and be role models. Thomas questioned why these success stories aren't the focus of attention instead of racism and increased spending on failed government programs. He answered his own question by saying his answer was a cynical one. He commented, "Liberal democrats might loose a core constituency if more people became independent, or not as dependent, on government." I find it interesting that I have used Cal Thomas' op-eds so many times in the book and there is good reason for doing so. Cal Thomas is a man after my own heart.

Remember the Harvard University professor who was uncooperative with the police when the police responded to a telephone call that someone was suspiciously trying to enter a house? The professor refused to show them identification to prove it was his house and accused the police of racial profiling. Without having the facts, Obama also accused the police of racial profiling. When Obama discovered the truth, he invited the arresting policeman and the house owner to the White House garden to have a beer. That is not very presidential in my book. Now the White House has a "Beer Garden" in addition to the Rose Garden. Shouldn't Obama have found out the truth before he made a public accusation? Absolutely! Should he have not commented publicly at all regardless of what he found? Absolutely! Unless it is a significant racial event, the president should stay out of it. He is the president of all Americans, not a single race. What would he have done if the professor was white and the police were all black? You are correct—absolutely nothing!

Obama publicly expressed his racial bias again during the George Zimmerman and Trayvon Martin incident. My wife and I watched the entire George Zimmerman trial. No matter what anyone thinks about Zimmerman as a person, he was innocent of murder under the law in the death of Trayvon Martin. Florida's stand-your-ground law did not create an injustice as was widely reported and there was no evidence that Zimmerman racially profiled Trayvon. So what does Obama do? He shows up at his press secretary's daily press briefing unannounced and said Trayvon could have been his son or himself when he was young. If Obama had done his homework on Trayvon, I doubt he would have said that. Evidently, Trayvon was known to take and maybe even sell drugs and to have an attitude that got him into fights on a regular basis. It was also reported that items had been found in his locker at school that appeared to be stolen but it could not be proven.

Obama said at the press briefing that before he was a senator he saw women clutching their purses on elevators when they saw him and other blacks, people locking car doors when he and other blacks crossed the street, and people followed him around when he and other blacks went into department stores. Really? Was he telling the truth? I guess when he became a senator people stopped being afraid of him. What changed? Did he start wearing a shirt with U.S. Senator printed on it in big easy to read letters? How about when he became president? Now, people actually are afraid of him. He should have remained a senator. No one would care if he were still a senator. His stint in the Senate was like he wasn't even there.

Why is the President of the United States who represents all people from all races making such an issue of the Trayvon Martin case at an impromptu press conference, especially when he didn't have the facts just as in the Boston case? Obama didn't stop with these two situations. He continued fanning the racial flames with the unfortunate racial unrest in Ferguson and Baltimore. He has also publicly voiced racial comments regarding other situations the politically correct have turned into negative racial events. There have been so many; I can't keep up with them. His behavior in pushing racial political correctness is incredibly inappropriate for a president—especially when it is based on untruths. Obama has been noticeably absent when the situation is reversed and black person victimizes a white person or Hispanic.

Let's throw the DOJ and ex-Attorney General Eric Holder into the mix. When Al Sharpton and Jessie Jackson began to make a federal case (figuratively and literally) out of the Zimmerman incident before Zimmerman was charged, the DOJ interviewed about 30 or 40 people in Florida to determine if it was a federal civil rights case. They found nothing. Apparently Zimmerman wasn't even going to be charged with murder until all the pressure was put on the state by the race-baiters and the federal government. I also heard that Trayvon's family had already hired attorneys and a public relations firm before Zimmerman was charged. I can understand hiring attorneys but a public relations firm? For what?

It would be interesting to see what individuals or organizations footed all or part of the bills for the lawyers and the publicity. It was probably all the usual suspects. Did the family pay any of those bills or did they get to keep the entire $1 million they reportedly got from the homeowners association's insurance company?

What did the DOJ do after Zimmerman was found not guilty? They decided to do the same thing they did before the trial and investigated Zimmerman a second time. That was a long time ago and I have heard nothing since. I assume the issue is dead. They should spend more time trying to catch the real bad guys and quit playing ideological politics. Actually, do you know what happens when they catch bad guys involving racial affronts against whites? At least with the Black Panthers, they punted. Remember the two Black Panthers who were intimidating whites outside a voter polling station to keep them from voting? The DOJ let one of them go and "slapped the other on the wrist" and then let him go. When Holder was still attorney general, I heard a DOJ employee say on television that the department employees were basically told to let anything racial against blacks slide and only prosecute cases against whites. This employee eventually resigned over the issue. Did he resign on his own or was he forced to do so? Who knows!

Here is an interesting and very concerning follow-up to what I just said. When I was researching something else, I ran across articles on the Internet that associated Holder with radical groups in 1969 when he was at Columbia University. Those groups included SDS and the Black Panthers. I have found during my research that several progressive leaders of today including our president have had past association with radical anti-American organizations. Food for thought.

Here is another disturbing practice by the DOJ that reportedly began under Holder. It was widely reported in May of this year that a federal judge ordered DOJ attorneys to attend annual "ethics classes". This court order was in reference to DOJ attorneys intentionally being deceptive to the court to cover actions by the Obama administration. Our new attorney general immediately refused to do so and filled an appeal.

Let's take a close look at what happened in Ferguson. After the outrage regarding a white policeman killing an unarmed black kid was reported extensively and repeatedly on national news, we began to get a different picture. The kid had just stolen cigars at a convenience store and physically manhandled the owner who tried to stop him. The police released a video taken by a security camera showing the robbery and were severely criticized for disrespecting the kid. This video was released only after the news media had tried and convicted the police on national television and in the print media. I don't blame the police for releasing the video.

After the robbery, the kid and his companion were reported to be walking down the middle of the street and refused to move at the police's request. The police did not know the two were involved in a robbery at that time. The young black kid and the policemen who shot him had an altercation through the policemen's car window. The kid reportedly hit the policeman hard enough in the face to possibly fracture his eye socket. During the altercation the policemen's gun was discharged. It was reported that the kid attempted to take away the policeman's gun as the policeman was trying to defend himself. This kid was 6'4" tall and weighed almost 300 lbs. The young man then ran and the police officer got out of his car and chased after him. This is the point in time where witness accounts contradict each other. Most neighborhood witnesses said the kid surrendered, even dropping to his knees with his hands over his head. There were a few witness accounts that said the kid turned on the policeman and charged at him, which I believe is the truth and was supported by the autopsy.

There were many locally and national condemnations of the policeman who shot this unarmed kid six times. What if the kid did charge the policeman after he had already injured the policeman and had tried to shoot the policeman with the policeman's own gun? What if the policeman kept shooting to only wound the kid to stop him from charging? All but one bullet was in an extremity of the kid's body except for one to the head. Someone reported the kid lowered his head as he was charging. How many bullets does it take in a body's extremity to slow down or stop a 6'4" kid weighing 300lbs? It was also reported that the kid might have had drugs in his system. By all accounts, this was a tragic case of a policeman defending himself that resulted in the death of a young man who was making bad decisions and caused his own death.

Political correctness was in full force. In order to demonstrate displeasure with the police, hundreds of people demonstrated and rioted. The demonstrators were both black and white. Many, if not most, came from communities outside Ferguson and from other states. Even the New Black Panthers showed up to offer their support. I wonder if the New Black Panthers included the same individuals who the DOJ let off the hook for voter intimidation. They certainly had prior experience.

I read some interesting reports regarding the other groups involved. It was reported there were several "national" radical groups that became involved to spur the violent rioting. They included the two radical organizations that were credited with developing the "Black Lives Matter" slogan for the Trayvon Martin case and the "Hands Up, Don't Shoot" slogan for the situation in Ferguson. Guess who reportedly is a major funder to most if not all of these radical organizations? Our friend, George Soros, supposedly gave over $30 million in one year to radical groups like these who operate in the United States. A reconstituted ACORN organization reportedly paid protestors $5,000 per month to protest in Ferguson. Let's also throw in Louis Farrakhan and his radical Nation of Islam organization, the Revolutionary Communist Party, SEIU, and Al Sharpton's National Action Network. So much for the citizens of Ferguson demonstrating and rioting to protest against racial injustice by the Ferguson police department.

These outside demonstrators clearly showed they were there to support the residents of the predominately black community and demand racial justice. For example, they fired guns and harassed the police who were trying to maintain order and keep the residents safe. They robbed and vandalized several businesses to give those greedy local small business owners who provided needed jobs for local residents what they deserved. One young restaurant owner was very stubborn and greedy. During the violence, he kept his employees on the payroll and made them come to work even though his restaurant was closed.

Remember what I said earlier in the chapter regarding the potential for all these radical groups organizing with radical Muslim terrorists and the potential impact of that alliance? Scary as hell! There is an enormous sub-culture in this country predicated on hate that has the collective goal of destroying traditional American culture and values. It depends upon the specific organization or individual as to the genesis of their motivation.

Obama made his usual public racial comments. Eric Holder went to Ferguson and announced the DOJ would assure justice for the kid who was killed and for all the blacks in the community. Here is the chief lawman in the country rushing to judgment regarding racial equality. Why wouldn't he? His boss does it on a routine basis. While Holder was in Ferguson he even sounded like his boss. He was quoted as saying, "I understand that mistrust (referring to blacks mistrusting the police). I am the Attorney General of the United States. But I am also a black man." He went on to share with his black audience his memories when he was angry and humiliated after being stopped by police and assured the audience he would investigate the Ferguson police department.

There was no surprise when the DOJ investigated the Ferguson Police Department and found there was racial bias toward the black community. Part of their conclusion stemmed from written and verbal interchanges between a very small number of officers and staff that were racially biased. These interchanges were very improper but they were between very few people and not endemic in the department. The DOJ report also said arrests were disproportionate among whites and blacks in relation to the population and generating revenue, rather than public safety, drove police practices. I agree there was inappropriate behavior by some employees in the department but the other findings sounded like an indictment looking for justification. The DOJ determined the local police made the demonstrations and rioting worse by having police dogs, employing tear gas, wearing military style uniforms and body armor, using military style weapons, and driving armored vehicles. I'm sure this behavior by the police was very offensive to those national radical groups and caused them to violently overreact.

The white democratic Governor of Missouri held a national news conference and very emphatically said the "policeman would be brought to justice". Wait a minute! I thought in America a person was assumed innocent until proven guilty. Isn't it the responsibility of the grand jury to review the evidence in the case and determine if there is probable cause to try the policeman for murder? Not true in a society built on political correctness and Marxist's culture. A person deemed to be at odds with the progressive politically correct is guilty until "they decide" differently. When I heard the governor say what he did, I was mystified and appalled. He should have been kicked out of office for being so irresponsible. It won't surprise you that this news conference took place after the governor had a conversation with the White House. Yes, that big White House in Washington.

I read an article on The New American website regarding a letter sent to Eric Holder by an ex-FBI agent and copied to several congressional leaders. The letter was about Holder's response to Trayvon Martin, Ferguson, the killing of the two white New York police officers, and his relationship to Al Sharpton. In the letter, the FBI agent blasted Holder's responses to these situations and for Holder calling America a "nation of cowards" regarding race relations. The most interesting reporting in the article was a comment allegedly made by Holder in response to statements by a Harlem preacher on racism in America. The preacher was quoted as saying, "No matter how affluent, educated, and mobile a black person becomes, his race defines him more particularly than anything else. Black people have a common cause that requires attending to, and this cause does not allow for the ridged class separation that is the luxury of the American whites. There is a sense in which every black man is as far from liberation as the weakest one if his weaknesses is attributable to racial injustice."

When asked to explain the preacher's statement, Holder reportedly commented, "It really says that … I am not the tall U.S. Attorney, I am not the thin United States Attorney. I am the black United States Attorney. And he was saying that no matter how successful you are, there's a common cause that bonds the black United States Attorney with the black criminal or the black doctor with the homeless person."

The chief lawman in the country bonds with criminals? I can understand "empathizes with" but "bonds with"? Wow! Maybe that answers a lot of questions regarding Holder deciding between what laws he enforced and those he didn't. I heard Michelle Malkin, one of my favorite political commentators, say on television that the Department of Justice does not enforce the law and is not the Department of Justice but rather the Department of Social Justice. Well-said Michelle!

What a missed opportunity for a very successful black man like the Attorney General of the United States to promote and encourage other blacks to strive for their dreams in a multiracial America. Instead, he encouraged blacks to put race before personal achievement and create a racially divided America. Holder is no longer in the national spotlight but there are many others out there today who are in a position to influence and encourage blacks to seek their dreams that are preaching the same negative rhetoric as Holder. That list includes our president and our First Lady. When I read The New American article, it gave me additional insight into the behaviors we observe by some regarding race relations. I said earlier that power and votes were reasons for promoting racial injustice. I can now add bigotry.

Let's go back to Ferguson. The Missouri governor wasn't the only one in contact with the White House. Our friend, Mr. Political Justice himself, Al Sharpton, was also in contact with the White House. It was reported he was communicating with Valerie Jarrett. I wonder which one instigated that discussion? Obama called in on Sharpton's radio show afterwards. While Obama was on the show, I wonder if he talked to Sharpton about paying the estimated $4.5 million he reportedly owes in state and federal taxes? How can Sharpton get away with that? Could you or I? We both know the answer to that one. You probably saw Sharpton several times on national television talking about Ferguson and speaking at the young man's funeral. Each time he spewed nothing but racism and political correctness. Jessie Jackson, Jr. came to town too but kept a low profile compared to Sharpton.

There was considerable talk about the governor taking the county prosecutor off the case because the prosecutor's father was a white policeman killed on duty by a black man. How ironic. The governor left that one alone, which I think was wise. It should be noted this white prosecutor has been re-elected several times by the citizens of Ferguson who are predominately black. The mayor was also white and there was significant politically correct criticism that these two men and all the policemen were white. The blacks can speak with their vote if they don't like it. That's the American way. Looks like the majority of the law-abiding black citizens of Ferguson did speak in the past. It will be interesting in future elections.

In August 2015, an article in my local newspaper reported there were 50 police officers in Ferguson and five are black. The article also said that the city council has two new black council members out of a total of six. Ferguson just recently hired a black police chief. There was a photo of a black female police sergeant in the article who rejected the media perception that the Ferguson police were "racist, mean, and targeted black people". She was quoted as saying, "Well, I'm black, so you mean to tell me because we have a disagreement I'm racist? That's not true."

The grand jury determined the evidence supported the actions of the white policeman and there was no trial. The policeman's life continued to be problematic and I am sure it will never be the same just because he was doing his job to protect the Ferguson community and risked his life doing it.

Since this unfortunate tragedy, there have been several altercations involving blacks and whites reported in the national news. When a white person attacks or murders a black person, the race of the perpetrator and victim is always reported as it was in Ferguson. A good example is a shooting resulting from an argument over loud music at a Jacksonville, Florida convenience store. Mainstream media reported that a white man in Jacksonville was convicted of shooting and killing a young black man. The evidence in that case supported the white man's guilt without question but I'm not sure that race was the issue as much as the shooter having a severe anger problem. The mantra in this case should have been that a man fatally shot a teenager over loud music at a convenience store and was brought to justice.

What is reported about race when the perpetrator is black and the victim is white, Asian, Hispanic, or even black? Nothing! Where are the politically correct in these situations? Nowhere! A black man shot two police officers in the head and killed them while they were sitting in their police car in Brooklyn, New York. His race was not widely reported. He killed them supposedly because he was upset over the incident in Ferguson and the recent chokehold death of a black man during an arrest by New York police. Mayor de Blasio, who is one of the staunchest progressives in America, supported demonstrations in New York City protesting the chokehold death. The New York police and others blamed Blasio for contributing to the death of these two policemen by encouraging anti-police protests that incited the black man to shoot the officers.

Where was the outrage and protests by the mainstream news media and the public for two slain police officers in Mississippi who were killed during the line of duty by four black individuals? One officer was white and one was black. How about the black man that walked up behind a white deputy sheriff in Houston at a gas station and shot the policeman in the back "execution style" several times. How about the black man arrested for the disappearance of and probably the rape and murder of a white University of Virginia college student? He was also connected to the rape and murder of other young white women in the area as well as one black woman. The race of the suspected murderer and the victims was not reported by the mainstream news media. They used the term "a man" rather than "a black man". No outrage here either.

Here is an example of politically correct reporting involving race that has a different twist. A black man who converted to the Islamic religion beheaded a fellow white female employee and was attempting to behead another white female employee. The chief operating officer of the company, who was also a volunteer policeman, stopped the second attack by shooting him. Fox News reported that the man was a Muslim who had tried unsuccessfully to recruit women at work to Islam. Fox also reported there was considerable reference to beheadings on his personal media site as well as radical Islamic rhetoric.

On the day of the attack, he had been suspended because he was confronting fellow employees saying he hated white people. Fox showed pictures of the man heavily bearded in Muslim garb in front of a Mosque. I did not see the reports of the attack on other television news shows; however, I understand they exercised political correctness and avoided the man's race and religion. It was eventually called workplace violence by local and national authorities. Does that sound familiar? Like in Fort Hood?

My local newspaper reported the following, "A man suspected of beheading a fellow female employee was a convicted felon who had been released from probation earlier this year, Oklahoma correction officials confirmed Thursday." There was no reference to the man being black and the woman being white. What is really scary about this story is the total lack of reference to radical Islam. The photograph used in my newspaper was that of a nice looking clean-shaven black man. In addition to political correctness involving race, this is an example of political correctness misinforming the public of potential danger and personal harm from home based terrorists.

I am only aware of one example where the mainstream news media reported the race of those involved when there was an attack by blacks on whites. The media reported that six "black" men attacked and seriously injured a "white" man and his "white" girlfriend outside a bar in Springfield, Missouri. The Springfield paper reported the police said they had no reason to believe race had anything to do with the attack. Maybe it did, maybe it didn't. Since the police could not find and interrogate the perpetrators, how do they know?

Unless there is a legitimate reason to do so, race should never be differentiated when reporting the news. It doesn't matter except for identification of at-large criminals or missing persons. On second thought, I need to correct myself regarding that statement. Race should be reported in one other situation. We should honor black achievement to help encourage and motivate young blacks to attain their potential rather than consistently portraying young blacks as victims with no future as our progressive friends do now.

As this book is being readied to go to press, there have been a recent series of fatal attacks on police officers. Two of the attacks resulted in mass casualties. Five police officers were killed and nine were wounded in Dallas by a black shooter that was reportedly seeking revenge for police killing a black man in St. Paul, Minnesota and another black man in Baton Rouge, Louisiana. Three police officers were killed and three were wounded in Baton Rouge by another black shooter for the same reason. The mainstream news media was irresponsible as usual in their reporting. Before any of the facts were known, the news media immediately accused the police officers who were involved in shooting the two black men of police brutality.

The mainstream news media was not by itself in being complicit in sending a false message to the American people. There were the usual suspects including our president. While Obama's comments regarding these tragedies were somewhat better than in the past, he still couldn't resist promoting gun control and criticizing America for racism. The following was taken from my local newspaper and CNN. At the memorial service for the Dallas officers, Obama commented that guns were easier for youths to obtain than computers. He also was quoted as saying, "I believe our sorrow can make us a better country. I believe our righteous anger can be transformed into more justice and more peace. ... If we cannot talk honestly and openly ... then we will never break this dangerous cycle." We all know that race relations have deteriorated significantly under Obama's presidency. He continuously tells us how bad race relations are without knowing or caring about the facts, just like the news media. I heard two police officials on television place the blame for attacks on police officers directly on Obama's shoulders.

George Bush also spoke and was truly presidential and healing in his remarks. He said, "Too often we judge other groups by their worst examples, while judging ourselves by our best intentions. This has strained the bonds of understanding and common purpose. ... We want the unity of hope, affection, and higher purpose." We miss you George!

As bad as the situation was in Ferguson, I think the Baltimore demonstrations and rioting were worse because of the continuing aftermath. What a travesty. Everybody lost and the fallout continues as we are now in the trial phase of the six police officers that were cited for wrongdoing. I assume everyone reading this is familiar with the death of Freddy Gray. He was arrested and while being transported to jail in the back of a police van, he incurred significant trauma to his neck and spine and died one week later in the hospital. There are conflicting stories regarding how the injury might have occurred and the Baltimore mayor and the Baltimore State's Attorney grossly mishandled the situation. I have seen hours of reporting on television and read many newspaper reports. Here is a summary of this tragic event.

Lets start with the demonstrations and rioting that took place after Freddy's funeral. Remember the DOJ determined and publicly reported that police made the demonstrations and rioting worse in Ferguson by having police dogs, employing tear gas, wearing military style uniforms and body armor, using military style weapons, and driving armored vehicles? The mayor of Baltimore is a 45-year-old black female and was reported to be involved in those task force findings. During the demonstrating and rioting after Freddy's funeral, the police were told to stand down and not intervene. I heard the mayor say on television that the protesters were "allowed space to destroy". What a nice gesture on her part, especially since the majority of the rioters were our "radical friends" from outside of Baltimore that we identified in the Ferguson riots and local Baltimore street gangs that found rare common ground to riot together. The riots resulted in the typical destruction and looting of businesses and several police were seriously injured.

The mayor received significant criticism after the riots for her comment regarding giving the rioters space to destroy and for ordering the police to stand down. After being criticized, she backtracked on her comment. She said she was misunderstood and restated her comment in a different way. She also avoided responsibility for telling the police to stand down. The police were clearly told to stand down and the mayor is the "big boss". The police commissioner, who was also black, obviously took the fall for the mayor's actions and inactions when she fired him.

The real tragedy, in addition to the death of Freddy Gray, was the indictment of the six police officers. The state's attorney is a young 36-year-old black woman. Just one day after the police concluded their investigation, she announced charges against them. The police officers include three white men, two black men, and one black woman. The black male policeman who was driving the van was charged with second-degree murder, involuntary manslaughter, second-degree assault, and misconduct in office. Three of the others were charged with involuntary manslaughter and all four of the others were charged with second-degree assault and misconduct in office. I watched the news conferences conducted by the state's attorney and read articles in which she was quoted. I was appalled at her unprofessional demeanor during this process as I was the mayor's conduct.

The mayor has announced she will not seek re-election in 2016. I found it unbelievable that she was asked to call the Democratic National Convention to order after Debbie Wasserman Schultz was fired because of the leaked emails showing the Democratic Party's bias against Bernie Sanders. That says a lot to me about the Democratic Party. The mayor goofed up and forgot to bang the gavel. After the way she handled the riots in Baltimore, that was not surprising.

Here are the reasons for my opinion regarding the conduct of the state's attorney. She commented before and during her announcement of charges against the police officers that, "We will pursue justice by any and all means necessary." She forgot to add the word "legal". Coincidence or slip of the tongue? When she announced charges she said, "To the people of Baltimore and the demonstrators across America, I heard your call for 'no justice, no peace'. Your peace is seriously needed as I seek to deliver justice to this young man." I learned the phrase "no justice, no peace" is an old phrase that has been around since the 1970s. No one knows where it actually came from but it certainly sounds like it is from the Critical Theory playbook. The state's attorney continued, "As young people, our time is now." What does that mean? Our time is now? How about the six police officers that you threw under the bus?

Let's look at the conflict of interest problems she has in this case? Her husband is the city councilman who represents the area where Freddy was arrested. She received $5,000 in campaign contributions from the attorney representing Freddy's family and appointed him to her transition team after she was elected. She actually represented Freddy in a 2012 criminal case and she lamented in a homecoming speech at her college alma mater in October 2014 that officer Wilson had not been indicted in Ferguson for killing the 18-year-old Brown "who was a boy". Where is the respect for the law here by an official that is sworn to uphold the law and support justice? In response to comments that those who were rioting and looting in Baltimore were "thugs", she said, "Those are young people crying out. There is a sense of hopelessness in this city." I have news for the state's attorney. Rioters and looters are "thugs" with self-serving and nefarious motives and not young people crying out.

This is classic progressivism. Ignore the laws I do not agree with and I will interpret and carry out the law in the manner that fits my ideological narrative. She also appeared on stage at a concert with Prince where he performed a protest song about Freddy's death, the riots, and social unrest in Baltimore. She is the person who filed charges against six policemen based upon evidence that is inconclusive at best. How inappropriate for her to appear with Prince! I know the grand jury supported the majority of her charges but I bet that is another story in itself. The police officers' attorneys have alleged that she "judge shopped" to obtain search warrants for the policemen's cell phones and has suppressed evidence from them they were entitled to. It was reported the evidence withheld includes the fact that Freddy has tried to injure himself in police custody on several occasions in order to collect money as a result of those injuries.

I plan to follow this story as an interested American who cares about justice and the outcome for six other Americans whom I believe were doing their jobs and took the hit for inept progressive politicians. Here are two personal observations to support my belief that they were just doing their job. The police were very familiar with Freddy and his antics. He had been arrested many times and had become a regular police informant to avoid jail time. This could justify why they ignored his pleas for medical attention and his physical antics as he was being taken to jail because they know him and his behavior. Secondly, a prisoner in the other side of the van said he heard loud noises that sounded like Freddy was banging his head against the wall. I honestly do not know what actually transpired but neither does the state's attorney.

I had hoped the trials could be moved to a non-biased venue so the officers could get a fair trial but that did not happen. I assume that outcome was politically driven. The officer that had the most serious charges against him was tried first. I read that is standard procure in situations like this one. That trial ended in a hung jury on all counts. A decision has been announced to re-try the police officer in September of this year and proceed with the other officers' trials before then. To show my personal bias, I hope they are all found innocent based upon what I know. It is not just these officers on trial. It is all the police officers across the country who are on trial.

Here is a very pleasing update. The second police officer who went to trial was found not guilty of all charges in May. He chose a bench trial by a judge over a jury trial. The judge was black and had prior experience with police officers. The AP reported the judge said, "The state's theory has been one of recklessness and negligence." Many news pundits said the judge's decision and comments were a significant affront to the state's attorney and showed she reacted to politics rather than doing her job and carrying out true justice. It gets better. The second officer who was tried was found not guilty by the same judge on all counts. There was considerable discussion after the trial that the state's attorney might be in legal trouble and/or disbarred because of her inappropriate handling of the case. As this book is going to press the same judge has acquitted a third officer. It appears all six will eventually be acquitted. Doesn't true justice make you feel good!!! The probable is that we should have never been here in the first place.

Let's take a look at the very troubling aftermath in Baltimore due to the lack of support for the police by the city administration, city council, and community in general—especially the black community. Gun violence went up 60% and homicides went up 40% after the police were told to stand down during the riots and the indictment of the police officers. Most of the homicides have taken place in the neighborhood where Freddy was arrested. There were 32 shootings alone during Memorial Day last year. The number of murders had been cut in half from the previous year before the Freddy Grey incident. Every article I read credited aggressive policing for the decrease in crime and murders prior to the demonstrating and rioting. Now, the police are not going to risk their lives or future when they are not supported or appreciated. How about the threat of imprisonment for doing their job? What do the politicians running the city do to address this serious problem? They fire the police commissioner and make some strong worthless comments about not tolerating the increase in crime. The problem is the politicians are the problem.

What has happened nationwide regarding crime since the onslaught began against our nation's police officers by radical groups, progressive leaning citizens, and progressive politicians like our president and previous attorney general? I read a May 2015 op-ed in The Wall Street Journal that was written by Heather Mac Donald who is a fellow at the Manhattan Institute and has also written a book titled *Are Cops Racists?* The articles I read and the reports I see on television support her op-ed. She said May 2015 was the most violent month Baltimore had seen in 15 years and gave the following statistics on the increase in murders from the previous year for other cities: St. Louis, 25%; Atlanta, 32%;

Chicago 17%; New York, 13%; and Milwaukee, 180%. No, that is not a typo for Milwaukee.

She also quoted the following statistics on the percentage increase in shootings: St. Louis, 39%; Chicago, 24%; Los Angeles, 25%; and New York, 7%. Those numbers become more telling when they are looked at on a neighborhood-by-neighborhood basis. For example, the 7% increase in New York looks good in comparison to the others. Crime had been substantially reduced in New York until mayor de Blasio caused the police to stand down on their aggressive policing. When that happened, police encounters with suspicious people in the East Harlem neighborhood dropped 95% and shootings went up 500%, not 7%. Los Angeles is another example. A specific south central neighborhood increased shootings by 100%, not 25%.

I saw another set of murder statistics on Fox News supporting Mac Donald's editorial that is even more dramatic. I assume the statistical variation results from using different time periods. The statistics on Fox showed the following increase in murders for six major cities: St. Louis, 58.6%; Houston, 53.0%; Baltimore, 48.4%; New Orleans, 39.1%; Chicago, 22.9%; and New York, 9.8%. The 58.6% statistic was dramatically different for St. Louis so I verified it on the Internet through a St. Louis Post Dispatch news article. As a footnote to these statistics, I read an email from a friend who said the United States is 3rd in murders throughout the world but if you delete the cities of Chicago, Detroit, New Orleans, and Washington, D.C. from U.S. murder statistics, the U.S. drops to 4th from the bottom. These four cities are said to have the toughest gun laws in the U.S. and democrats control all four. I did not verify the information contained in the email but I believe it to be true based upon other research I have done.

Here is an update on Baltimore homicide statistics reported in a syndicated news article by The Washington Post in April of this year. The article said Baltimore, Chicago, and Washington accounted for more than half of the increase in homicides in our 25 largest cities in 2015. Baltimore's homicides increased from 211 in 2014 to 344 in 2015. Chicago reported an increase from 411 to 465 and Washington's homicides increased from 105 to 162. Baltimore's homicides in 2015 were the most since 1993. This is a sad story for Baltimore. The city deserved more than their elected officials playing progressive politics rather than providing the strong management the citizens deserved.

Mac Donald said in her op-ed, "The most plausible explanation of the current surge in lawlessness is the intense agitation against American police departments over the past nine months." She is absolutely correct. Our police work hard and risk their lives to protect us. Our progressive politically correct politicians and non-politicians are tearing down the accomplishments the police have made in controlling crime and are putting them and Americans in increased danger.

Here is a June 2016 op-ed I read in The Wall Street Journal by Mac Donald that I found unbelievable. Chicago is consistently referred to as one of the most violent cities in America even though the city has some of the toughest gun laws. They signed an agreement in 2015 with the ACLU (yes, the ACLU) to provide oversight of the city's "stop activity" by the police. This was done to address the false narrative that the police were racial profiling. The police are now required to fill out a two-page card with 70 fields of information when they stop someone for any reason. It takes about 30 minutes to complete. The ACLU then reviews the cards.

Not surprisingly, police stops have decreased by almost 90% in the first quarter of 2016. Now, many more gang members are carrying guns who would not have carried them when the police were making routine stops before the ACLU got involved. As a result, the city is more dangerous and especially so in the black neighborhoods. Remember, the same thing happened in New York City when de Blasio curtailed stop and frisk. I cannot imagine in my wildest imagination any police department allowing the ACLU to look over the shoulder of their police officers.

Here is the tragic irony of these irresponsible progressive decisions. As bad as it is for the police, it is worse for the black inner-city communities where the vast majority of crime and murders take place. Mac Donald provided these statistics in her op-ed. In 2014, blacks made up 79% of all known nonfatal shooting suspects, 85% of all known robbery suspects, and 77% of all known murder suspects. Whites made up 1% of all known fatal shooting suspects, 2.5% of known robbery suspects, and 5% of known murder suspects. Whites are almost absent as violent street criminals. The op-ed said the percent of Chicago's population that is black versus white is the same at 32%. The number of police stops was 72% for blacks and 9% for whites. This last statistic was the basis of bringing in the ACLU, which in reality is no basis.

I read an article on the Internet written by Mac Donald, in addition to her op-eds, which is spot on. She ended the article by saying, "When prominent figures such as Barack Obama make sweeping claims about racial unfairness in the criminal justice system, they play with fire. Black prison rates result from crime, not racism. The dramatic drop in crime in the 1990s, to which sentencing policies unquestionably contributed, has freed thousands of law-abiding inner-city residents from the bondage of fear. The continuing search for the chimera of criminal-justice bigotry is a useless distraction that diverts energy and attention from the critical imperative of helping more inner-city boys stay in school—and out of trouble."

The Daily Signal published an article in July of this year that stated, "Blacks of all ages are killed at six times the rate of whites and Hispanics combined." This was in reference to crime in cities with large black populations. The cities referenced as the most dangerous were Chicago, St. Louis, Baltimore, Memphis, Milwaukee, Birmingham, Newark, Cleveland, and Philadelphia. It was also noted that all these cities have democratic governance and the blacks in those cities have significant political power. The article also noted that these cities have poor performing and unsafe schools, poor quality city services, and declining populations. The article commented, "The primary victims of lawlessness are black people."

The article quoted an excerpt from Mac Donald's latest book, *The War on Cops*. The excerpt says, "Blacks were charged with 62 percent of all robberies, 57 percent of all murders, and 45 percent of all assaults in the 75 largest U.S. counties in 2009, while constituting roughly 15 percent of the population in those counties. From 2005 to 2014, 40 percent of cop-killers were black. Given the racially lopsided nature of gun violence, a 26 percent rate of black victimization by the police is not evidence of bias."

The progressive politically correct masses out there are hypocritical on a colossal scale. Their goal is not to help black population. Their goal is to use the black population for their own self-serving purposes. All progressive politicians like votes. Some progressives use race-baiting to gain significant monetary gain. Some use it to feed their own personal issues relating to race. They all use racial issues to support their political ideology and often their actions contradict their stated goals. And, who pays the price? The black population they are purporting to save. It is a travesty of major proportions.

Let's take a specific look at Obama, Holder, Sharpton, and Jackson's motivations for their behavior. If they are so concerned about race relations and the black community, why are they only involved if a case can be made for white atrocities against blacks, regardless if it is true or not. They do not get involved in black atrocities against whites and other non-black races because these situations do not fit their narrative. How about the biggest racial atrocity of all—black on black crime in poor neighborhoods? I keep finding example after example where reality is not relevant for these four men when a politically correct point regarding racism against blacks is made.

During my research, I ran across a YouTube video of Obama giving a speech at the Cambridge (Massachusetts) Library in 1995 on his book *Dreams from my Father: A Story of Race and Inheritance*. I found it very telling. As he spoke, he appeared to be significantly struggling with his black identity. He said his book was not so much a memoir but a journey of discovery trying to make sense of his family. He said his father was a black African and his mother was a white American and he had spent most of his life trying to reconcile the terms of his birth with the reality of race and nationality.

As I said in chapter 7, he wants to make America a country where there is no distinction between blacks and whites. He does not like being considered a black minority in a white dominated world. That is why he acts out when a case can be made for racism in America, accurate or not, and lashes out at whites. Maybe he just resents being black and takes it out on whites. Who knows? There has to be some logical reason for his actions in these situations, because it is not normal behavior for a president—even for a black president.

A Bloomberg poll taken in December of 2014 showed the following feelings of those polled regarding race relations under Obama's presidency: a lot better, 3%; a little better, 6%; about the same, 36%; and worse, 53%. Rasmussen did a poll in January 2016 that said 50% of American adults think race relations are getting worse. That number was 44% in January 2015 and 30% in January 2014. As this book is going to press, a new poll done by Rasmussen in July of this year said 60% of likely voters believed that race relations have gotten worse under Obama. That is a 10% increase in 6 months. That is certainly not surprising but is extremely troubling.

I read an interesting syndicated news article by The Washington Post. A New York Times/CBS News poll taken during Obama's first year in office showed that 66 % of Americans said race relations were generally good. A recent New York Times/CBS News poll showed that only 37% of Americans believed that race relations were generally good. All of these polls are saying the same thing. Race relations in America have significantly deteriorated under Obama's presidency.

The Washington Post article also said the Pew Research Center produced a report in 2013 analyzing racial disparities in social and economic matters since Obama has been in office. The report showed there has been improvement in high school graduation rates and life expectancy for blacks and Hispanics from 2007 to 2013 but during the same period their wealth, home ownership, infant mortality rates, quality of education, and discipline in schools has suffered. Larry Elder, a conservative black lawyer and media personality, said in the 1960s 25% of black babies were born out of wedlock. He said now, under Obama, that number has risen to 75%.

You know Thomas Sowell is a black economist who I greatly admire. He published an op-ed in November 2015 that supports what Elder said. Sowell commented that we often hear the problems of the black race are a "legacy of slavery". He said they are a product of government welfare policies that began in the 1960s. Those welfare policies are a product of the Great Society we discussed in the last chapter. Sowell said the number of black children being raised in single-parent families in 1960 was 22% and increased to 67% by 1990. Homicide rates in 1960 among non-white males had decreased by 22% during the preceding decade but increased by 76% during the decade following 1960. He also said few people today know that marriage rates and rates of labor force participation were higher among blacks than among whites during the first century after slavery.

If Sharpton, Jackson, and others like them didn't focus on political correctness by race-baiting and stirring up racial trouble, they would be irrelevant in society. So, what do they do? They are constantly looking for issues, if not creating issues, to become relevant. For example, it was reported that Jackson was in Dallas because he believed the first patient in the U.S. to be diagnosed with Ebola during the 2014 outbreak was not being treated fairly because he was black. How did Jackson come up with that? Doesn't matter. He just does. I wonder if it was because it was reported by the national news that he played a minor role in the Ferguson case and he wanted more attention?

Don't forget these people need to be relevant to raise money as well as to feed their psychological needs. They certainly don't have a real paying job. For some reason that I do not understand, Jackson has publicly taken a back seat to Sharpton in promoting racial unrest. I wonder if it is because Jackson can't compete with Sharpton because of his aggressive tactics, political connections, and his National Action Network?

Our First Lady has also made herself relevant in race relations. She has on many occasions put down America in that regard. I want to share a story with you where she expressed enormous disrespect for our country. Remember when Obama was elected and she said she was proud of her country for the first time in her adult life? I thought that was odd and disrespectful for a new First Lady but I did not know that was a hint of things to come. Last year, she gave a commencement speech at Tuskegee University—a storied black university. Although she did offer encouragement to the graduates, she also painted a continuing racist picture of white America against black America.

I obtained the following quotes from The (New York) Daily News: (1) "so there will be times when you feel like folks look right past you, or they just see a fraction of who you really are"; (2) "we've both (referring to the president and herself) felt the sting of those daily slights throughout our lives—the folks who cross the street in fear of their safety, the clerks who kept a close eye on us in all those department stores, the people at formal events who assumed we were the help—and those who have questioned our intelligence, our honesty, even our love of this country"; (3) "I know that these little indignities are obviously nothing compared to what folks across the country are dealing with every single day—like those nagging worries that you are going to get stopped or pulled over for absolutely no reason"; (4) "the fear that your job application will be overlooked because of the way your name sounds"; (5) "the agony of sending your kids to schools that may no longer be separate, but far from equal"; and (6) "the realization that no matter how far you rise in life, how hard you work to be a good person, a good parent, a good citizen—for some folks it will never be enough".

These are unbelievable comments from a First Lady. My being "stunned" in reading them is an understatement. In fact, I was so stunned that I went to whitehouse.gov and read her speech in its entirety to see if the quotes were accurate. They were accurate word for word. The fact that she is the First Lady and her husband is president is in itself a contradiction to the points she was making. Why did she not use the accomplishments in life that she and her husband have achieved as positive motivation for these students to accomplish their dreams rather than talk so negatively about our country? This was another great opportunity lost to promote racial harmony versus promoting racial discord. I haven't studied our First Lady's background sufficiently to offer an opinion why she is so racist.

I enjoy watching Charles Barkley who is a very colorful basketball television commentator. For the politically correct, please calm down. I do not mean his "skin color". I found a quote that was attributed to him and is applicable regarding certain blacks being self-serving racists. He was quoted as saying, "When you are black, you have to deal with so much crap from black people."

The current progressive politicians in Washington depend heavily on the black vote. These politicians do not care about the well-being of blacks or the development of good race relations in our country as they proclaim. It is extremely dishonest, hypocritical, and self-serving. They have to keep the black vote relevant for themselves by portraying their support for blacks through political correctness even if the issues are fabricated. A Rasmussen poll taken in November of last year indicated that only 9% of likely voters believe most politicians raise racial issues to solve real problems, 78% believe politicians bring up race just to get elected, and the rest were unsure. Why does that 78% let the politicians who represent them get away with it without letting them know how they feel by speaking out and then voting for someone different next time?

The self-serving Washington politicians who do this are a political disgrace and harmful to the future of the black race. If they cared even a smidgen about what they claim to care about, they would be celebrating and supporting black successes instead of putting the black race down with all this racial suppression and inequality rhetoric. They would be looking for "real" ways to solve black poverty and black crime instead of making policies and giving entitlements that push poor blacks even more into economic dependence and into more crime, especially black on black crime.

I'm not naive enough to think that suppression and inequality of blacks don't exist. It happens. It also happens to every race including whites. Does it happen to blacks more proportionately when socioeconomic factors are taken into account? I really do not know the answer to that. Our progressive friends constantly make the case that it does because they want us to think so to support their progressive narrative. I do know that before Obama, Holder, and the progressives came into power; there was significant improvement in racial relations that was continually taking place in our country and the poverty rate and crime rate for blacks was much lower than it is today.

Why don't Obama and Holder tout to young black people their achievements as President and Attorney General of the United Sates and tell them they too have the opportunity to achieve lofty goals if they want them and work hard enough to attain them? Why don't Sharpton and Jackson promote successful blacks as role models for young black men and women? We know the answer to those two questions. It doesn't fit their narrative for their own self-serving needs. American culture has historically had and currently has countless successful blacks who refuse to be victims as promoted by those who attempt to create racial divide. Here are a few black success stories to make the point that highlight some of my favorite people.

I see blacks on the Fox News channel every day who have become very successful and through that success debunk this victim mentality by the politically correct. One of my favorites is Charles Payne. He is incredibly bright and appears to be a very nice guy. Besides having his own show on the Fox Business channel, he is a guest host on other Fox shows. He also has his own Wall Street stock market research firm. I heard him tell a story about how poor his family was when he was growing up in Harlem in New York City. He said he wanted a briefcase to take to school when he was a kid but his mother could not afford one. She found a way to buy him one for Christmas. When he took it to school, bullies attacked him and destroyed the briefcase he was so proud of.

Charles is a big guy. I can't imagine anyone attacking him today. He got the last laugh on those bullies who attacked him. He knew what he wanted, worked hard to get it, and got it. He is one of the most popular hosts on Fox Business and Fox News. His reported net worth is approximately $10 million. There are several other black news anchors on Fox who are very successful and who I really admire and enjoy, i.e., Harris Faulkner, Arthel Neville, Kelly Wright, and Juan Williams. It is also very common for Fox News to have black guest contributors on their news channel who are very sharp and successful.

Jason Riley, who I quoted in chapter 8, is a black person who is a member of The Wall Street Journal editorial board and wrote the book titled *Please Stop Helping Us*. It is a book that details how entitlement programs pushed by the federal government are depressing black opportunity rather than promoting it. He also wrote an editorial that is basically a summary of our discussion on race relations in America. He talked about how polls show a significant decline in race relations since Obama has been in office. He also talked about how Obama's actions involving the police, college admission policies, voter ID laws, zoning laws, minority housing, school discipline policies, and the criminal justice system have not supported the president's comment regarding the "United States of America" and have negatively impacted race relations.

Remember when Obama said, "There is not a liberal America and a conservative America—there is the United States of America. There is not a black America and a white America and a Latino America and Asian America—there is the United States of America." What happened? We learned the truth about Obama and his progressive cohorts.

Jason commented that Obama has Al Sharpton on speed dial and Sharpton is a regular visitor to the White House. He said Sharpton is the president's "point man" on civil rights issues. Jason concluded, "Given that the president is keeping company with someone who monetizes racial conflict for a living, it is any wonder that so many people believe race relations have regressed." Jason also commented, "The Black Lives Matter movement may be built on a falsehood—that cops shooting blacks is somehow a bigger problem than blacks shooting each other— but the falsehood will be indulged by politicians like Mr. Obama because the last thing Democrats want is for black people to stop seeing themselves as helpless victims of systematic racism." Jason ended his editorial by saying, "Community organizers specialize in creating social divisions, not bridging them. So do presidents who profit politically from racial anxiety. America has learned these lessons the hard way." Well said, Mr. Riley!

Here is further support for Jason's comment regarding the Black Lives Matter Movement being a falsehood. The activist group refused any endorsement and support from the Democratic National Committee. In fact, they inappropriately disrupted all of the democratic candidates at their political rallies. I found a statement released by the group in The Daily Caller that says it best. The group said, "While the Black Lives Matter Network applauds political change towards making the world safer for Black life, our only endorsement goes to the protest movement we've built together with Black people nationwide—not the self-interested candidates, parties, or political machine seeking our vote." The critical phrase here is "our only endorsement goes to the protest movement". This is the case with all of these radical protest groups. Their purpose is to protest—period, not to solve an issue or problem.

Do you know who is reported to be the first female millionaire in America? It was Sarah Breedlove who is known as Madam C.J. Walker. She lived from 1867 to 1919 and founded a company that developed and sold a line of beauty and hair products to black women. Oh, and she was black herself and quite a character. The first self-made female millionaire in America was black? What a great story we never hear about! I have already quoted Thomas Sowell and stated my great admiration for him. Anyone who would like to honestly understand the black race in America would do well by reading his op-eds published nationally on a regular basis.

How about Colin Powell, Thurgood Marshall, Clarence Thomas, and Condolezza Rice? I remember studying Booker T. Washington and George Washington Carver during my school days as being black heroes who left their mark on society in the late 1800s through the early 1900s. Booker T. was the founder of Tuskegee University. If he were alive today, I wonder how he would feel about our First Lady's commencement speech. I also wonder how he would feel about the whole issue of what progressives are doing to the black race in America since he supported education and economic advancement for the black community versus confrontation?

The majority of the black people I specifically referenced above are: politically conservative; use common sense, pragmatism, and facts; and live in reality. These characteristics are traits that apply to conservatives whether they are red, brown, yellow, black, or white. I borrowed this reference to skin color from a little song we used to sing in Sunday school when I was a kid. Remember the song? It goes like this: Jesus loves the little children; red, yellow, black, or white (the song now adds brown); they are precious in his sight; Jesus loves the little children of the world. It was much simpler then, when political correctness did not exist. We also got along much better with each other.

My wife and I were in the Texas State Capitol a few years ago and looked at several pictures on the wall of former state legislators. We were surprised at the number of blacks in the pictures as far back as the late 1800s. I bet one could find similar pictures in government buildings across the country. I don't bring these pictures up to minimize the atrocities that occurred toward blacks during and after slavery but to honor the accomplishments of blacks during this time period even in light of these atrocities.

There are numerous successful business leaders, political leaders, athletes, musicians, entertainers, singers, and actors who are black. There is a problem; however, within this list of occupations I want to point out. There are too many outspoken politically correct black progressives. You would think they would not practice such hypocrisy considering their own success. Unfortunately, there are many blacks within this list who I would not tout as black role models.

Here are some closing thoughts on political correctness and discrimination. Have you ever been discriminated against? I have—many times. I told you in the first chapter that I grew up in the hills of Eastern Kentucky—a hillbilly. I have on multiple occasions during my life been teased in a very negative way because of where I grew up. I was even teased by fellow Kentuckians when I moved from Eastern Kentucky to Central Kentucky during high school. It still happens today. I have heard things such as: did you wear shoes to school, did you date your cousin, do you have rotten teeth, etc. These people act like they are teasing but are they? These comments are personal criticism based upon where I grew up—discrimination. Although I always act like these comments don't bother me, they do. It is hurtful to hear critical comments toward yourself for any reason, teasing or not. Discrimination toward others is not limited to the black race. I am living proof.

I am not racially biased but I have to admit that I do have discriminatory biases toward people who portray certain characteristics. I am not going to share them with you because I am embarrassed to do so. I am proud of the fact that I realize my fallacy in having discriminatory thoughts and do not overtly act upon them verbally or otherwise. I tell myself to stuff it, leave it alone, and move on. I sometimes share my biases with my wife or close personal friends but that is as far as it goes.

Is race discrimination worse than other discriminatory practices? I do not think so. I am not referring to the denial of one's human rights. That is a very different story and should not be tolerated. I'm talking about discrimination that hurts the feelings of another person or group. Do you have discriminatory biases toward certain people? Absolutely—we all do. How about discrimination regarding occupation, residence, socio-economic status, religion, personal hobbies, weight, IQ, etc.? These are all areas of potential discrimination and have nothing to do with race. When someone emails you those awful pictures of people in Wal-Mart, do you laugh at the people in the pictures? Did you ever notice that they are always white and never black, Hispanic, or Asian.

My point is that all human beings have a built-in psychological penchant to discriminate against other human beings who are different from them. I have never met anyone who is not discriminatory toward certain characteristics of other people. Some people in society are much more prone to be discriminatory than others. In a perfect world, people would never discriminate toward anyone else for any reason but this is not a perfect world. It never has been and it never will be. Political correctness will never solve the problem of discrimination or any other ailment of society that it is proclaimed to do. Political correctness only exacerbates the problem by pitting us against each other rather than bringing us together. Hypocritically, the progressives who push political correctness are the worst of the worst in discrimination.

As I write this, I am reminded of the power of Judeo-Christian religion in defusing discrimination. That would be in line with why the Frankfort School wanted to get rid of religion in order to tear down society (Critical Theory) to implement their Marxist ideology. We have been flawed humans since the beginning of time and we will be to the end of time but we can improve ourselves to be better. This is done by self-introspection and personal effort through our personal values and beliefs. Judeo-Christian religion provides a powerful road map to take that journey.

I want to end this discussion on race relations with two intellectual thoughts from my hero, Thomas Sowell. He wrote an op-ed in response to the ridiculous debacle at this year's Academy Awards where our movie star friends acted like spoiled children needing a disciplinary hand. They were acting out because there were no black academy award winners. Sowell said, "The assumption seems to be that different groups would be proportionately represented if somebody were not doing somebody else wrong." He gave examples of differences between the black and white races that went both ways. He concluded, "But we can stop looking for villains every time we see differences. That is not likely to happen, however, when grievances can be cashed in for goodies—and polarize a whole society in the process."

Sowell's second op-ed was titled "The Progressive movement and the history of racism". He said, "The biggest difference between the left and right today, when it comes to racial issues, is that liberals tend to take the side of those blacks who are doing the wrong things—hoodlums the left depicts as martyrs, while the right defends those blacks more likely to be the victims of those hoodlums." The state's attorney from Baltimore needs a therapy session with Sowell.

We have come a very long way since the days of Martin Luther King and thank God for that literally and figuratively. Our country back then was full of discrimination practices against blacks that were very wrong, vulgar, and restricted their rights as Americans. My kids are color blind as are their friends. I wish the politically correct and race-baiters were as color blind. After all, we are one nation under God, indivisible, with liberty and justice for all.

We have analyzed Obama and his progressive politically correct behavior regarding race. Let's now take a quick look at some of his political correct behavior involving gay rights, women's rights, immigration, and homegrown terrorism. Obama found time to call some of the black families who lost loved one's in the racial events we discussed. He also has found time to call football players who announced they were gay. He even found time to call our friend Sandra Fluke and make sure she was OK after she was "attacked" by Rush Limbaugh.

He could not find time to call the family of the young girl who was murdered in front of her father in the sanctuary city of San Francisco by an illegal immigrant. The immigrant who had been deported five times for previous crimes and had just been released by the San Francisco police. He couldn't find time to call the families of the military personnel who were killed by a homegrown terrorist in Chattanooga, Tennessee. He couldn't even find time to lower the flag on the White House to honor them but found time to spend our money to light up the White House with rainbow colors when the Supreme Court made their decision on gay marriage. He found time to visit with victims and victims' families in San Bernardino only on his way to Hawaii for his Christmas vacation.

Most recently, Obama chose not to attend Justice Scalia's funeral even though Scalia was arguably the most respected Supreme Court Justice on the court when it comes to legal minds. He even had earned that respect from his liberal peers. He was also the longest serving. He didn't attend Nancy Reagan's funeral either. He did say he would have attended Muhammad Ali's funeral if it had not conflicted with his daughter's graduation. That's OK. Valarie Jarrett went.

Obama continuously acts in ways that divides the country rather than demonstrating true humanitarian presidential leadership. It never stops. How about the 14-year-old Muslim boy in Irving, Texas who took what he and his family called a homemade clock to school to show his teacher? The school thought it could be a bomb and called the police. He was handcuffed, arrested, and taken to police headquarters to be interrogated. The kid and his family accused the police of profiling him because he was a Muslim. Obama sent the boy a tweet inviting him to the White House that said, "Cool clock. Want to bring it to the White House? We should inspire more kids like you to like science. It's what makes America great."

I researched this story including listening to Glen Beck interview the mayor of Irving. Here is a summary of what I found. The apparatus was in a briefcase and was an old Radio Shack clock with some modifications made by the kid. It looked exactly like a bomb to me. Why would he put it in a briefcase? How does a clock by a "boy genus" look like a bomb? I heard that he showed the clock in the briefcase to one teacher who did not react to it so he showed it to another teacher who did react. The police were called and he was arrested. The police talked with him, did not charge him with a crime, and he was released. He was suspended from school for three days and his parents pulled him out of that school.

I read his father has links to CAIR. We talked about CAIR's connections with the Muslim Brotherhood and terrorist groups. Hamas is the most mentioned terrorist connection. We also talked about CAIR's connections to Obama and the White House. Is there any connection between CAIR and Obama asking the kid to visit the White House as if he is some kind of "Muslim" hero? I know what I think.

Supposedly, one could hear the boy's sister in the background telling him what to say when the press called to talk about the incident. I also read that the sister told MSNBC that she was suspended by the same school district a few years ago for making a bomb threat. This has all the appearance of an incident contrived by the family to create a national controversy to obtain a sympathetic news story toward Muslims and/or a legal settlement. Obama was knowingly or unknowingly complicit. As this story began to unfold in a direction different from a Muslim boy being discriminated against at school, the White House went quiet on the issue and to my knowledge the boy never visited with the president. I guess it became "old news" with a few other embarrassing stories we discussed in chapter 6.

After the story became old news at the White House, new news began to surface. The boy traveled around the world to speak out against racism. Fox News reported that he met the President of Turkey in New York City and visited several Middle Eastern countries including the Islamic countries of Qatar, Saudi Arabia, and Sudan. In Sudan he was photographed with al-Bashir who is the Sudanese leader wanted by the International Criminal Court for war crimes in Darfur. The boy's dad is an immigrant from Sudan and once ran for president against al-Bashir. The Daily Caller reported the attorneys for the family have sent a letter to the City of Irving and the Irving School District demanding $10 million and $5 million respectively and a written apology from the mayor and police chief. Wow! This kid must have really been offended.

Do these actions by the boy and his father leave any doubt in your mind as to what the family's intent was from the beginning? The boy apparently was a pawn to accomplish the real intent—promote American atrocities against Muslims and hopefully receive a monetary windfall. As I have pointed out several times in the book, this isn't the first time the White House has reacted inappropriately to promote their political correctness agenda before they had the facts.

Obama used a recent tragedy to help him push his politically correct gun control agenda. After the shooting at the community college in Roseburg, Oregon that killed 9 people, Obama immediately went on television to denounce violence and push gun control measures. He then announced that he was going to go to Roseburg and visit with the families of the victims. There was outrage in the community and around the country from those who do not support gun control. They were upset that Obama would use the tragedy to push his gun control agenda on national television and then travel to Roseburg to meet with the families as if he personally cared about them.

One victim's father publicly said he would not meet with Obama. Another victim's fiancé said the same thing. The meeting took place and the outcome was not reported. Oh, Obama was on his way to the west coast anyway to attend Democratic National Committee fundraisers in Seattle, San Francisco, and Los Angeles. Obama has been very efficient in combining fundraising and vacation trips to visit victims and victims' families in Roseburg and San Bernardino.

The Washington Post syndicated a news article the day after he met with the families and expressed an opinion about Obama's appropriateness in handling the situation in Oregon. The article said, "At an unassuming brick high school here, President Obama on Friday took part in what has become one of the grimmest rituals of his presidency: He met privately with the families of the nine victims of the country's latest mass shooting at Umpqua Community College." Obama was characterized in the article as "speaking softly" and "deeply frustrated" when he was talking to the press after the meeting. He was reported to use phrases such as "I've obviously got strong feelings", "today is about the families", and "somehow this has become routine".

The article was a sickening "love fest" toward Obama by our mainstream news media. The article sounded more like Obama was a grieving family member rather than the president. There was nothing in the newspaper report about the significant protest in Roseburg because Obama combined the tragedy with gun control and the family of at least two victims not attending his meeting because of that. WND reported hundreds of residents protested against the president because he "so quickly and callously politicized a tragedy". One resident was quoted as saying, "He made it very plain, 15 minutes after the shooting happened he politicized it. The bodies were not even cold."

Speaking of the president's behavior involving victims, here is an interesting observation by Glen Beck. Obama held a news conference in January of this year regarding his new executive actions aimed at curbing gun violence. During that news conference he appeared to be crying over the 2012 shooting of first graders at Sandy Hook Elementary in Newtown, Connecticut. Glen questioned why Obama would cry now and not when the shootings occurred. Good question. Glen said he had been taught how to put Vick's or some similar substance on his finger to make him cry when he touched his eye as is done in the theater. He questioned if Obama had done that for effect. I went back and watched

Obama's speech to see what I thought. Obama wiped his finger just under and next to his eyes multiple times. Interesting.

We have touched on the progressives push to indoctrinate our young people to their way of thinking. Let's now delve deeper into that topic and in terms of political correctness. My research did not find education being specifically recognized in Critical Theory as a topic of focus but many educators and educational systems in America are now employing all or most of the elements of Marxist Theory and Critical Thinking in the education of our children. It makes sense for them to do so to accomplish their mission.

In researching education and Critical Theory, I found a website called STUDY.com that sells elementary, high school, college, and other courses that are taken on the Internet. Here is an excerpt from the introduction to their course on Critical Theory and education:

> Just because things have always been viewed a certain way, doesn't mean that way is correct. In this lesson, we'll explore critical theory and how teachers can open their classrooms up to offer everyone a chance at success. Gina is in the sixth grade, and she's very excited to move to middle school. She wants to learn more about science and math, and maybe invent some cool technology when she's a grown-up. But there's an issue: Gina isn't from the best neighborhood. She's not white. And she's a woman. All three of those things can impact her education and, as an extension, her future. Critical theory is a philosophy that involves being critical of the prevailing view of society. In many cases, that means looking closer at beliefs that might favor privileged people, like rich, white men, over other people, like Gina. Critical theory in education is about questioning how our educational system can best offer education to all people. It offers opportunities and understanding of the different perspective of disadvantaged members of society. For example, poor children, like Gina, often go to more poorly funded schools than their middle and

upper class counterparts. And less funding can mean
issues like availability of technology or good teachers.
Let's look at how Critical Theory plays out in education
and what schools and teachers can do to be inclusive of
all types of students.

OK, let's explore how Critical Theory plays out in education and
how it works "to be inclusive of all types of students". In large part,
"education" in our schools today could be more appropriately called
"indoctrination". I guess Horkheimer, Marcuse, and their friends left a
few things for our modern society to come up with.

Some progressives push free college education for all Americans.
We should label it as free indoctrination or free progressive campaign
financing. For some reason, Obama has stopped talking about his plan
for free tuition at community colleges. Hillary has proposed a plan, if
she is elected president, to prevent college kids from having to obtain
loans for tuition at public collages and universities. What a deal! It's
supposed to cost society only $350 billion. Yes, that is with a "b" but
calm down. The $350 billion is over 10 years so that is only $35 billion
per year. You can afford that and have money left over for one of my
"smart" bridges! If Bernie is elected, he wants to give college education
away as a freebie. If that were to happen, forget the bridge. You wont
be able to afford it with your new tax bill.

Isn't it interesting that every cost or cost savings stated by the
government is always over a 10-year period and before the 10 years
are up they have added more costs or the savings do not materialize
so the original numbers are always worthless? The details of Hillary's
plan were not worked out when I wrote this. Bernie says the states will
pay 33% of the cost and the federal government will pay 67%. How is
he going to get the money? He says through a "Robyn Hood Tax" on
Wall Street. Good luck on that one. Do these progressives ever think
anything through? Remember what I said in chapters 2 and 4.

Speaking of billions, The Washington Post reported a recent study that
showed school teachers are in training an average of 19 schooldays per year,
which annually costs the largest 50 school districts $8 billion. The study
said the training is a waste of time. It is also a waste of taxpayer money.

It's OK, if someone doesn't want to go to college or isn't suited to do so. Remember Thomas Sowell's comments regarding inherent differences between the black and white races? The same applies to individuals of all races and to individuals within each race. People achieve success all the time without going to college. The individual in question decides what success is—not the government or the politically correct. According to progressives, everyone should have an affordable (which means you and I pay for their education through taxes) college education for the future of America or is it for the future of Marxist ideology?

Our local university just received a $2.3 million grant from the U.S. Department of Education. The news report said it was to "help insure academic success for students who are the first in their family to attend college, who come from low-income households, or who have a disability". Why? I borrowed money, obtained student loans, and sold my first house to pay for my degrees. Why are these students different? People who really want to go to college can find a way without handouts and have pride in doing so. It doesn't matter what their obstacles or physical handicaps are.

Here is a story a friend recently told me. Her son's best friend is black and her son is white. They both are exceptional students. Both parents of the white kid work so their family income is higher than the black kid's family income because only one parent works. The black kid was offered scholarships to attend prestigious universities. The white kid was not accepted to any prestigious colleges nor was he offered similar scholarships at less prestigious universities. My friend was happy for her son's best friend but felt her kid was being treated unfairly. Discrimination against the white kid? You bet!

A white female filed a lawsuit in 2009 after she was denied admission to the University of Texas at Austin because of the schools' affirmative action policies and the school's quota system that only guaranteed in-state high school students admission who were in the top 10 percent of their class. The student lost the case and, after several appeals, the Supreme Court heard the case in 2013 and remanded it to back to a lower court. After the young woman again lost her case, the Supreme Court decided to rehear the case and recently cited with the university in a 4 to 3 split. Justice Kagan recused herself. Supreme Court Justice Antonin Scalia was heavily criticized by the progressives when the Court previously heard the case for saying less qualified black students would be better off at less selective colleges. He cited research showing the placement of students at elite universities who don't have the credentials to be there struggle academically. As I said, we are really going to miss Scalia.

An op-ed by my friend Thomas Sowell supports Scalia. He said when he was teaching at Cornell University an "average" white student was unlikely to be admitted to Cornell but black students with the same credentials would. These black students who would be successful at most other colleges and universities received a "favor" of being admitted to Cornell and became "failures". Sowell referenced a book by Richard Sander and Stuart Taylor titled *Mismatch* that he said showed the hard facts. He gave an example from the book showing academic performances of black and Hispanic students rose substantially after affirmative-action admission policies were banned at the University of California system. Sowell said, "Instead of failing at Berkeley or UCLA, these minority students were now graduating from other campuses in the University of California system. They were graduating at a higher rate, with higher grades, and now more often in challenging fields like math, science, and technology." The principle of appropriate academic placement applies to students of all races including whites.

The topic of religion in schools is one of those topics that if you think it can't get worse, it always does. Christianity is basically banned by our public school systems but it is not the Supreme Court that banned religion in schools as some have claimed. It is the schools themselves banning religion for a multitude of reasons—all of them tied to political correctness. The Supreme Court banned "state sanctioned" and "mandatory" religion in schools to assure the separation of church and state. Progressives equate separation of church and state with God and the Constitution and say God should be separated from our country's founding principles. That is incorrect as well. Separation of church and state means "the state should not establish a religion, prefer one religion over another, or prevent the free exercise of religion" as was commonplace during and prior to medieval times and is still the practice today in other countries. We must always remember that Western religion is one of the barriers to Marxist evolution.

Here is a story concerning schools and religion that was on the front page of our local newspaper for several days. The story involves the cancellation of a local high school choir concert because it was to be held at a local Presbyterian church. This high school choir is very accomplished and has traveled around the United States performing in places like Carnegie Hall in New York City. Churches have been the venue for these concerts for 15 years and the church in question is the church of choice because of the exceptional quality of the acoustics and its low cost to rent. The proceeds from the concerts are used to offset the costs of the choir's travels. The news articles indicated that a parent and student complained to the ACLU about the choir singing at a church. The ACLU complained to the high school and the high school punted fearing a lawsuit even though it was reported that a lawsuit regarding this specific case had no merit. I might add that although students are required to participate in official concerts to obtain a grade, the choir is an elective course.

The concert was cancelled with less than 24 hours notice. The school officials were somewhat evasive in supplying information to the newspaper regarding details. The timing as to when the choir director asked permission to hold the concert and when the school canceled the concert is unclear. Who suffers in these incidences? The school kids and the parents of those kids who were denied their rights because of one student are the ones who suffer, not the one student and parent. I was glad to see approximately 50 parents get together to discuss the situation. I had sincerely hoped they would aggressively push back and correct this lunacy but apparently they didn't and the single student and parent along with the ACLU won.

The students themselves did push back and I am very proud of them. After the concert's cancellation, the choir members came to school one morning at 6:30 A.M. and sang the song *Unity* at the front door of the school to express their frustration. Later that day, the principal called a meeting with the choir members in the auditorium and told them the church could be one venue but not the only venue for their concerts. The newspaper said that the students walked out in masse after they asked the principal pointed questions and did not like the answers. Good for them. I would normally not condone this type of behavior but in this case the school deserved it. When the concert eventually took place at another high school, only 60 of the 175 choir members showed up to sing. One of the senior choir members who showed up said, "It was kind of like, take one for the team. This is really a sad start to my final year of choir."

The 115 students who did not show up were given an F for one-sixth of their final class grade. One of the parents said it best when he said, "I think its BS. It's political correctness gone amok, tyranny by the few." If schools and those pushing political correctness got significant push back from the majority, it would stop or at least significantly diminish this ridiculous nonsense. It will be interesting to see what happens in the choir's future. The choir did sing their Christmas concert at the Presbyterian church and it was reported that the choir members were ecstatic about the way they sounded. I'm sure their enthusiasm went beyond their sound. Unfortunately, I assume they will have to rotate performance venues in the future.

I have pointed out several times that our Constitution is founded upon God and Judeo-Christian principles. Here is an example in Florida where a school district acquiesced to anti- Christian groups upon the threat of being sued. The New York based Satanic Temple, The Freedom from Religion Foundation, and an un-named atheist group will more than likely be allowed to hand out their materials in Orlando schools this year. My local newspaper said The Satanic Temple is a relatively new group supporting social justice causes and believes that Satin is the "eternal rebel against the ultimate tyrant". They want to give out materials to school kids such as The Satanic Children's Big Book of Activities. I bet that book makes The Story of Stuff video look good.

The article didn't say who the ultimate tyrant is but I can only assume it is those of us who are not supporters of social justice. One of the justifications to allow this insanity is the school system permitting a group called the World Changers of Florida to distribute Bibles on two occasions. After I wrote this, I learned the Orange County (Orlando) School Board adopted a policy against distributing any material in the school system that is religious, political, or sectarian.

Here is another Florida story on anti-religious actions in our schools. A Florida Atlantic University professor teaching a class on intercultural communications instructed students to stomp on sheets of paper after they wrote the word Jesus on them. The school defended the exercise as encouraging students to look at issues from many perspectives. Stomping on Jesus is certainly a different perspective. A student complained and refused to do so. He was kicked out of class but was reinstated after the ensuing firestorm. I wonder if the professor would have instructed them to write Muhammad on a piece of paper and stomp on it?

I guess banning religion in schools does not apply to Islam. Did you know at least four states have reportedly set aside time and space for Muslim students to pray since they are supposed to pray five times per day. I found news reports saying Arizona, Michigan, Maryland, and California have supported this practice. There are probably more that have not made the news. We can thank our friends at CAIR for bringing Michigan schools to their knees on the matter—literally and figuratively. Christian kids have been sent home for such innocuous things as wearing t-shirts that reflect Christianity.

Our state legislature in Florida has a solution for that problem. They passed a bill titled the "Students Attired for Education Act (SAFE)". The act encourages school districts to create a uniform policy through at least the eighth grade by providing additional funding to those schools that do. George (Orwell), here we come.

Here is an update. Out of 24 elementary schools and 10 middle schools in our county, only seven elementary schools voted down the state proposal. An advisory committee parent at one of the seven schools said uniforms could lead to "students losing individuality". I agree with that parent. The state government is paying schools to enact a policy that takes away a student's individual rights? What's next? Sounds like a first step toward *1984* to me. Wouldn't Marx like that? In reality, this Act by itself is not a big deal but remember, "Stuff always starts somewhere."

Speaking of stuff always starts somewhere, how about this next one? Parents at a Boston public middle school became upset when their children had to read the Islamic conversion prayer called the Shahada in history class. The Shahada states Allah is the only god. The school defended itself by saying it is only requiring the students to learn about

Islam. The same thing happened at a Tennessee middle school this year and at the end of three weeks of study the class had to write the Shahada stating, "There is no God but Allah and Muhammad is the Messenger of Allah".

I wonder if these schools said the Lord's Prayer in these same classes to learn about Christianity? One of the Tennessee parents asked if one could imagine the outcry from the progressives if the children had been asked to write Jesus is Lord. How many schools out there are teaching Islam? My guess is the number would be startling, if we knew. I saved the worst until last. Three years ago a Boston school recited a Muslim poem over the intercom instead of the Pledge of Allegiance—on 9/11! This is unconscionable and shocking!

There are many examples across the country where schools have supported Islam but banned Christianity. I honestly do not know why these teachers are doing this. Do they hate the religious foundation of their country that much? Maybe they hate their country that much. Maybe they are just psychologically maladjusted or unhappy with life in general. No matter the reason, they are putting political correctness and Critical Theory over the best interest of their country and the young people they are responsible to teach. Muslims tried to build a Mosque at Ground Zero in New York City, which in my and others' opinion was a monument to "symbolize conquest". I wonder what kind of monument they will try to build for conquest in our schools? Like I consistently say, "When you think things can't get worse…"

American schools should teach the American values and principals upon which our country was founded that provide for individual freedom, individual thought, individual accomplishment, and equal rights and opportunity throughout life. The key here is "educating the individual" for success and happiness in life. They should not be allowed to teach progressive political ideology that is contrary to those values. The politically correct are indoctrinating our young people to their progressive ideology throughout all levels of education and pushing them away from what America stands for and the principles that gave our country its amazing success.

For example, they want to suppress rewards for achievement in high school and grade school so that everyone is regarded as equal. This philosophy is paramount in Marxist ideology. One of the most glaring examples took place in Massachusetts. A school principal cancelled the school's honor program so that the students who did not get an award would not feel self-conscious and disappointed in themselves. The principal said it could be "devastating" for students who worked hard but did not earn good enough grades to receive an award.

How devastating is it for the students who worked hard, achieved an award, and were denied? If it were possible, it would be interesting to do an experiment to see how many kids in this school who "honestly" worked hard did not achieve grades good enough to be rewarded. If there were any kids in that category, their personal issues need to be dealt with for their own future good. There is also a more sinister purpose here whether those practicing political correctness in our schools know it or not. The more our kids are dumbed down and robbed of their motivation and spunk, the easier they are to be controlled by progressive authoritarians.

I saw a report on Fox News concerning indoctrination in the Lincoln, Nebraska public school system that I would find reprehensible if it weren't so ridiculous. I researched the story online and found a news article that had been published in the Lincoln newspaper. The news article was particularly irritating since the junior high school and senior high school specifically referenced are the schools my own kids attended. According to the article, the teachers were given a handout that suggested they create names for their student classes and used "purple penguins" as the example. Neither my kids nor their classmates were purple penguins. They were young boys and girls.

Here's what happened. The Lincoln School System gave teachers a handout as part of an effort to educate them and administrators about transgender issues. The coordinator of social workers and counselors for the school system told the Lincoln newspaper they were doing this to help "all" the kids succeed. She said the school system has kids with a variety of circumstances and they need to equitably serve all kids. The handout was full of advice for teachers on how to help transgender students. One of the suggestions besides using "purple penguins" was to not use phrases such as "boys and girls", "ladies and gentlemen", and "you guys" to get their kids' attention. A Fox News commentator said the handout was full of advice for teachers as they deconstruct and reconstruct what constitutes a boy and what constitutes a girl and he sarcastically suggested, "To avoid offense, those terms will henceforth be known as the "b-word" and the "g-word."

I listened to an Internet video of the school system superintendent addressing the issue to the news media. He appeared to be defensive and dismissive of its importance. I do not know him but I do personally know the two superintendents before him and I cannot imagine that type of response from either of them. Actually, I cannot imagine this issue even occurring during their leadership. Lincoln is one of the most conservative communities in the country. I strongly believe that transgendered kids should be treated with the same sensitivity and respect as any other kid but not at the expense of the other kids. This is another example of the politically correct penalizing and discriminating against the majority to achieve what they (and I emphasize "they") hypocritically deem as fairness and equality.

Progressive indoctrination stories involving our schools never stop. They are like the Energizer Bunny. They just keep going, going, and going. This next story is almost as bad as the one about the Boston school and the Muslim poem on 9/11. A Michigan high school was involved in this debacle. A father was trying to help his daughter find her way at her new school. He was refused admission to the school by security because the way he was dressed might offend other students at the school. How was he dressed? He was wearing his military uniform. I find this story totally repugnant. The school principal took care of it and apologized but how can that happen?

Here is one that took place right here in my own community of Naples. Our local newspaper reported a story regarding a video shown at one of our local high schools on climate change. The video said the continued use of fossil fuels would bring an end to civilization, as we know it. That's scary! Maybe I should review my position on climate change again. Or, maybe not! The Keystone XL Pipeline or any other pipeline should not be built. I guess Obama is right. A primary mission of the U.S. military is to protect the profits of oil companies. No wonder Obama is cutting the size and budget of our military. Climate change is a matter of good versus evil. Looks like they would support God and

Christianity rather than always tearing it down. The video advocated a rapid phase out of fossil fuels and equated this movement with the civil rights and anti-nuclear movements of the 1960s and 1970s. A parent, who is a local attorney, bitterly complained and I would characterize the response of the school board and superintendent confusing and evasive at best.

I can certainly guess what their position was. Here is why I say that. My local newspaper published a guest editorial I had written in opposition to a controversial project in our community called the Blue Zones initiative. It is a Marxist based farce that proclaims to make our community healthier by "nudging" our community to better health. Does nudging sound familiar? One of the school board members called me and asked if I would speak at the next school board meeting regarding my views on the Blue Zones issue. She and one other school board member (both conservatives) believed the Blue Zones project proposed for the school system negatively impacted the school kids because of its restriction of free choice. Of course, I said yes. That is where I saw the video on the brownies. Three of the five school board members and the school superintendent were obviously in the "progressive tank" as evidenced by the 3 to 2 vote to approve the project.

About 25 people, mostly parents, spoke in opposition of the project and only 2 or 3 spoke in favor. The Blue Zones leaders were there but sat quietly. I had corresponded with the school board chairman prior to the meeting and it was obvious by her response the decision had already been made to support the ideologically progressive program. The actions regarding the project at the official school board meeting were a ruse. That is the progressive way. I wonder what they would have done if hundreds of parents had attended the meeting to push back? We had better start finding out!

Here are a couple of examples demonstrating less traditional ways progressive educators are attempting to indoctrinate our children into progressive thinking. A schoolteacher in Albany, New York gave her English class an assignment to practice the "art of persuasive argument" by writing a letter to a Nazi government official making the case that "Jews are evil". I read where another teacher gave her class a crossword puzzle that defined conservatives as those who want to "restrict all personal freedom" and encourage "prosperity through economic freedom". Liberals were defined as those who are "for equality" and "personal freedom for everyone". She needs a remedial course on Marxist theory. She has it backwards. Conservatives believe in "personal freedom" and "economic freedom", whereas progressive liberals believe in "everyone being equal" which results in "everyone's personal and economic freedom being limited".

We can thank Michelle Obama and her "healthy eating initiative" we discussed in chapter 4 for this next one. Our school system banned bake sales and candy sales to provide a healthier environment for our kids. What is the PTA going to do? They have also banned "sweets" from birthday celebrations at school. They could title that school policy, "From Cupcakes to Carrots." Remember, they serve brownies and frosted cookies to influence the kids' behavior in order to get more federal money. Pure progressive hypocrisy!

Here is a story with a different twist. It is a story of a failed attempt to obtain an affirmation toward American values from a group of teachers. We go back to Nebraska. This time, it is where my wife went to school in Hastings. Two Nebraska citizens advocated that the state schools comply with a 1951 state law requiring teachers to sign a pledge stating, "I believe in the United States of America as a government of the people, by the people, for the people; whose just powers are derived from the consent of the governed." The superintendent of the county school system on the advise of the system's attorney was going to enforce the law to avoid a potential law suit and asked the teachers to sign. Some unhappy teachers, who stayed anonymous, notified the ACLU and you can imagine the rest.

The ACLU said requiring the teachers to sign was contrary to a U.S. Supreme Court Decision that took place after the state law came into being and it was unconstitutional. Really? Signing a pledge to support your country is unconstitutional? The ACLU further said the Supreme Court has confirmed several times that public employees may not be required to sign such a pledge because such pledges are "vague" and "subject to wide interpretation". A written explanation of what makes America a democratic republic is vague and subject to wide interpretation? Only, if you are a progressive Marxist! My research indicated the ACLU's positions were a stretch.

The ACLU included in their letter that the employees who complained loved their jobs but "they have deeply held beliefs that do not permit them to sign an outdated McCarthy era pledge". I find that last comment disgusting. The school superintendent backed down 100%. The winning percentage for the America we know and love is decreasing at an increasing rate in these politically correct Marxist conflicts.

I want to share one positive outcome that took place in a New York City public school just before Christmas last year. Yes, Mayor de Blasio's city. A school principle in Brooklyn changed Thanksgiving to a "harvest festival" and banned Santa Clause and the Pledge of Allegiance. After significant pushback by parents, city officials got involved and the principal rescinded the policy. This is what happens when Americans push back hard enough.

Let's move away from this elementary and high school politically correct lunacy and look at some recent events involving progressive thinking at our nation's colleges and universities. At the University of California, deans and department heads were invited but not mandated to attend a seminar regarding a new faculty-training guide. The guide was developed to train professors to "enhance department and campus climate toward inclusive excellence". What does that mean? The university system believes phrases such as "America is the land of opportunity" and America is a melting pot" are what they call "micro-aggressions" and could leave some students feeling discriminated against.

Here is another doozy. The Columbia Law School allowed their students to postpone taking their final exam if the student felt their performance on the test would be hindered by the grand jury decision to not indict the police officers involved in the Michael Brown case in Ferguson and the Eric Garner chokehold case in New York. The interim dean of the law school wrote in an email the students could postpone their exams because they might be experiencing "trauma during the exam period". He said, "The grand juries' determinations to return non-indictments in the Michael Brown and Eric Garner cases have shaken the faith of some in the integrity of the grand jury system and in the law more generally. For some law students, particularly, though not only, students of color, this chain of events is all more profound as it threatens to undermine a sense that the law is a fundamental pillar of society designed to protect fairness, due process and equality."

How about this nonsense "shaking the integrity" of the Columbia Law School? This action is so preposterous, I cannot even think of any sarcastic comment to say that fits the situation. Maybe a law professor at New York University said it for me. He said, "It shows a remarkable degree of empathy. Students cannot expect that from their boss in practice, nor I imagine would they ask for it. And they certainly can't expect it from a judge when papers are due. But you know, academia institutions are a world of their own." You certainly got that right Mr. law professor.

After I wrote the above, micro-aggression has increasingly gotten out of control in higher education as well as primary and secondary education. I can give you multiple examples that are so bizarre you can't make the stuff up. It appears the push is coming from the federal government, our Millennial population, and progressive leaning school faculty and non-faculty.

Here is a recent example from the University of North Carolina that I learned about on Fox News' *Outnumbered*. The Employee Forum is a group of 50 elected non-faculty employees who develop and publish recommendations and post them online. They published what they referred to as micro-aggression guidelines and cautioned employees to adhere to these guidelines in order to not display biases against others.

The published guidelines included actions such as the following as being offensive and should not be used: "I love your shoes to a women in leadership after a speech" because it recognizes a person's dress more than their intellect; "Please stand and be recognized" because not everyone can stand; "Where are you from" because it denotes they are not American and do not belong to the community; "I think we should have our staff retreat at the country club and plan a round of golf" because it suggests employees have the financial resources and exposure to a fairly expensive and inaccessible sport; and "unit celebrations, academic calendars, and encouraged vacations are organized around major religious observances" because it centers around the Christian faith and minimizes non-Christian spiritual rituals and observances". The last one would ban having a Christmas vacation. The university removed the recommendations immediately after significant outcry. This is another example demonstrating the effectiveness of conservative push back. Unfortunately, many campuses are getting away with this nonsense.

Conservatives on the North Carolina campus said this micro-aggression was liberal progressives policing free speech and gave other examples such as conservative messages on campus being treated as offensive by progressive students, progressive students staging a walkout on conservative speaker Ben Shapiro, and conservative groups not being invited to a diversity dinner. We have two dynamics going on here. One is the politically correct movement in steroids by naive Millennials and second is a concerted movement by students, faculty, and university employees who adhere to progressive ideology restricting free speech in order to promote their progressive ideology.

Some colleges and universities now have "safe spaces" on campus where students can go and escape these awful micro-aggressions. Wow, things have changed since I was in school! I wrote in my last book that one of the most important functions of college was to act as a "maturation incubator" in preparing students to transition from an adolescent into a mature adult. We didn't have any safe spaces. Are these young people going to live in "flower garden cocoons" when they leave college? I guess the progressives will fix their world for them with political correctness. Unfortunately, that world is our world too.

I read an article in The Atlantic on the topic titled "The Coddling of the American Mind". The title couldn't say it better. As I said earlier, the more our young people are dumbed down and robbed of their motivation and spunk, the easier they are to be controlled by progressive authoritarians. The more I write this book the more *1984* becomes real to me. Also, how does that "coddling" impact our future generations' mental being in a tough world full of bad guys and opportunists?

How about the debacle at the University of Missouri? After a segment of the student population claimed chronic racism on campus, the president and chancellor of the university resigned. I assume they were forced to do so by the university's trustees. What part might the federal government have played? What do you think about the football team refusing to play unless the president resigned and the football coach supporting that position? Doesn't the coach work for the president? Sounds like the coach should have been the one to leave the university. He did resign later but it was because he unfortunately has cancer.

There was no proof regarding the claims by individual students of racism on campus and no follow-up investigation was done but it cost the two leaders of the university their jobs. What kind of message does that send to other faculty and students around the country? How much does that embolden progressives and radical wackos?

The president was a conservative and tried to run the university under conservative principles. In doing that, he not only angered the students but the faculty as well. The faculty said he was inept at his job as was the chancellor. I honestly do not know the details of what actually happened but I do know the situation was grossly mishandled. It made the university look bad and sent the wrong message to the students as to "who is" or I should say "who is not" in charge.

I saw a video on Fox News showing a visiting professor in the University of Missouri journalism department demanding that a young freelance journalist covering the resignation story leave an area on campus where a number of students who supported the resignations were congregating. When the young reporter refused and claimed his First Amendment rights she yelled to the students, "I need some muscle over here." This was a person teaching in the journalism department attacking a journalist doing their job! After the incident, she was reassigned. How about getting rid of her? This situation was totally out of control. The whole University of Missouri event gives one a hint of what anarchy would be like. Progressives love anarchy until the existing established authority is destroyed. Then, they take over and establish their own autocratic authority.

Here is a different story of a university out of control. The university is Yale. A filmmaker and satirist named Ami Horowitz made a video of himself asking Yale students to sign a petition to repeal the First Amendment. The First Amendment provides Americans freedom of religion and the right of free speech, press, and assembly. Out of approximately 100 students interviewed, 60 students signed the petition (some very enthusiastically) and only 15 refused to sign because they did not agree. This is shocking to me.

Horowitz showed his film on Fox News and commented on his findings. He said he did this to gauge the true level of anti-free speech sentiment on college campuses. He said Yale is among several colleges around the country where students and faculty members have lobbied for safe spaces where ideas, statements, and persons deemed disagreeable or offensive are not welcome. Horowitz concluded, "Why would Yale students, or university students anywhere in this country, feel a fidelity to our fundamental beliefs, when their professors try to shoehorn sentiment at every opportunity?"

Without well-defined lines of acceptable behavior and strong discipline, our colleges and universities are turning out young adults with unrealistic expectations in their fairytale world. This is a formula for disaster for those young adults as well as the rest of us. They are reflecting the progressive politically correct movement that is increasingly taking over our country and will only assist in getting us to that progressive Marxist world faster.

Progressives are also attempting to change history in our elementary and high school textbooks and in college and university admission tests. If this progressive onslaught is successful, it could be the biggest indoctrination threat to our American way of life by brainwashing our children and adolescents, beginning at an early age.

You might remember the huge 2010 controversy in Texas over the content of their schools' textbooks. Educational standards were adopted by a state education panel and approved by the State Board of Education that were successful in stopping textbooks proposed for their elementary and high school geography, history, and U.S. government classes containing progressive propaganda. This issue was especially important because the Texas school system is so large it significantly influences textbooks used in other states. The membership of the State Board of Education has now changed and there was a renewed effort to instill progressive propaganda in the schoolbooks again. Fortunately, the board voted 10 to 5 in November 2014 to approve the books that complied with the 2010 guidelines.

Among the topics the progressives want out of the textbooks is any reference to creationism, Judeo-Christian influence on our Constitution, any challenge to human responsibility for climate change, and negativity toward Muslims. The progressives also say the guidelines previously approved by the state education panel downplay slavery's roll as the cause of the Civil War. I will agree that creationism is controversial but their position on our Constitution and on climate change is progressive BS. I do not have sufficient information regarding Muslim textbook content to comment on that topic but, from what we have already discussed, one can easily guess what the issues are.

Slavery is a big issue in our U.S. culture even today because the progressives will not turn it loose. Don't forget the importance of the black race in Critical Theory. Progressives continuously want to paint America as a mean, awful, and inhumane country that embraced black slavery until the Civil War. They also contend America has continued to deny blacks their civil rights after the Civil War and are now enslaving the black race in poverty. We have previously addressed civil rights and the issue of poverty. Let's take a pragmatic historical look at black slavery in America and the Civil War. I have commented in the book that slavery has been going on all over the world at least since recorded history and involves men, women, and children of all races. I found one source that said slavery has existed since 3000 B.C. It is still rampant around the world today including the United States as we discussed earlier in the chapter. In researching slavery timelines, I discovered that slavery began in the U.S. in 1619.

One can argue that slavery was and was not the cause of the Civil War and many historians do. Here is a brief history and you can make up your own mind. Abraham Lincoln and the republicans (yes, the republicans) supported the banning of slavery in all U.S. territories during the 1860 presidential election but not in the southern states where slavery existed. The southern democrats (yes, democrats) supported slavery because slaves were the labor force for their very lucrative cotton industry that depended upon the exportation of cotton to Europe.

Before Lincoln's inauguration, seven southern states seceded from the Union and formed the Confederacy. The first states that seceded thought the British would join them in the Civil War. Lincoln told the Southern States during his inauguration address, "I have no purpose, directly or indirectly to interfere with the institution of slavery in the United States where it exists. I believe I have no lawful right to do so, and I have no inclination to do so." Lincoln was inaugurated on March 4, 1861 and Confederate forces fired on Fort Sumter the following April 12th. Four more Southern States joined the Confederacy after that attack occurred and so begin the Civil War. Four slave states did not secede from the Union and were called Border States.

The strategy of the anti-slavery republicans was containment. They wanted to stop the expansion of slavery and put slavery on a path to extinction. It was not to abolish slavery as widely proclaimed today. The South; however, felt even this action was an infringement on their Constitutional rights and would eventually destroy their economy. Remember, this was during a time when slavery was commonplace throughout the world.

Wikipedia summarizes the reasons for the Civil War into four categories. First, Many Union and Confederate leaders and soldiers believed slavery caused the Civil War. Union soldiers primarily believed they were fighting to emancipate the slaves even though president Lincoln had expressed otherwise. The Confederates fought to protect southern society and slavery was part of that society. The second reason given was "sectionalism" which includes the differences in the economies, social structure, customs, and political values between the North and the South. The third reason was "protectionism". The northern republicans in Congress supported their manufacturing interests by fostering high tariffs (protectionism). The southern democrats in Congress supported low tariffs to promote free trade because of their very lucrative cotton trade with Europe. Europe sold products to the United States and Southerners were afraid raising tariffs on European products would destroy that trade and their ability to sell cotton to Europe. The fourth reason was "states rights". The South believed that each state had the right to leave the Union at any time they wished because the Constitution was a "compact" between the states. Northerners rejected that position as being opposed to the intent of the founding fathers whose objective was to set up a "perpetual union". Most historians agree with the northerners on that one and so do I.

The Civil War is still used today by progressives to create controversy even though it was abolished 151 years ago. I doubt there are very few Americans who have the knowledge I have shared with you about slavery and the Civil War. We need to keep the facts straight regarding our history and progressive propaganda out.

The College Board is the national organization that administers the Advanced Placement (AP) exams taken by high school students when they apply to colleges. The College Board made a recent attempt to alter accurate historical information in their exams to reflect progressive ideological propaganda. I first discovered this issue regarding the AP exams in a March 2015 syndicated op-ed by a Los Angeles Times reporter. The op-ed said lawmakers in Oklahoma, Colorado, Texas, Georgia, Nebraska, Tennessee, and elsewhere were trying to prohibit high schools in their states from adopting the new American History AP exams. Although the College Board does not have any control over the literature that is used to teach history, they do publish a guide for the teachers to prepare the students for their exam. It is a back door way to influence the curriculum taught to students.

The op-ed quoted critics who said the proposed guide teaches a "revisionist view" of the American past in that every trace of American exceptionalism has been scrubbed. The following example was given. The College Board proposed the transcontinental railroad brought more settlers west leading to conflict with American Indians. This conflict resulted in their diminished existence, threatened their native culture and identity, and led to the near extinction of the buffalo. The Board also said the emphasis on Manifest Destiny was built upon a belief of white racial superiority and a sense of American cultural superiority.

The College Board did not include the technological achievement the railroad represented or its contributions to American society. They also left out that American Indians were fighting among themselves and breaking treaties with the U.S. government, which contributed to their diminished existence. The College Board did not mention the positive aspects of Manifest Destiny in expanding opportunity for Americans and providing geographic expansion of the United States to allow and promote democracy for those who wanted to migrate here from other countries and achieve economic opportunity and freedom of self-governance. I have also read arguments that Manifest Destiny contributed significantly to women's rights including the right to vote and, as we discussed, the end of slavery. It is a fascinating topic of U.S. history and how our country developed.

The op-ed also delved into the history of the term "American Exceptionalism" which I found very interesting. I did research on my own and here is a composite of that research. Alexis de Tocqueville was a French political thinker who wrote *Democracy in America* in the early 1800s. The book has been said by many historians to be one of the most influential books ever written about America. Tocqueville said what set the United States apart from his native France was our absence of feudal traditions and our government structure was the model for the future regarding equality and liberty. Historian Frederick Jackson Turner wrote a seminal essay in 1893 titled *The Significance of the Frontier in American History* saying the distinctive character of the United States could be attributed to its "frontier experience".

Turner is absolutely correct and his comment points out a great progressive fallacy we discussed in chapter 9. We hear the progressives say "we are are a country of immigrants" and we should allow illegal immigrants from Latin countries and immigrant refugees from war-torn countries to come to America. I said in chapter 9 our immigrant ancestors came here for freedom and opportunity to succeed in life. They were hard working opportunists who took risks and made many sacrifices. I believe the majority of the illegal immigrants from Latin America who the Obama administration is encouraging to come here and all or most of the immigrants from war-torn countries the administration wants to relocate here would live indefinitely on government support. Americans would support them rather than they support America to keep our country strong. Their strongest contribution to America will be to increase the progressive voter base. That's a detriment, not a contribution.

Neither Tocqueville nor Turner coined the term "American exceptionalism". So, who did? Would you believe Stalin did or at least caused it to be coined? There are other versions of how the term came into being but I like the one about Stalin the best. Supposedly, Stalin criticized the American Communist Party for their belief that America was independent of Marxist theory because of our natural resources, industrial capacity, and absence of ridged class distinctions. Stalin supposedly referred to it as American exceptionalism. This is one time the American Communist Party was right.

The College Board's revision of American history focused on racial and cultural division and left out unifying figures such as Benjamin Franklin and Martin Luther King. The new corrected version now includes those two historical figures, more focus on America's founders, and a unified American identity. The Board also scrubbed their obnoxious expressions of bias against America, free market capitalism, and whites. For example, the College Board originally noted free market capitalism widened the income gap between the rich and poor without pointing out how every American's income and economic well-being has been pulled up by our economic system.

Looks like the federal government decided to help the College Board out with their attempt to alter racial and cultural history after the College Board got their wings clipped. As I am editing, Treasury Secretary Jacob Lew announced that Harriet Tubman would replace Andrew Jackson on the front of the $20 bill and relegate Jackson to the back. Sounds very symbolic to me. All the usual progressive suspects trashed Jackson. He was referred to in the news as "a slave owner president who forced Cherokees and many other Indian nations on deadly marches out of their southern homelands". I have absolutely nothing against Harriet Tubman. She has her place in history. She should be honored but not at the expense of a president who is inappropriately maligned to promote the continuation of racial divide in our country.

There was a political cartoon in my local newspaper that depicted Tubman's head, raised arm, and fist jutting out from a $20 bill. The caption said "Harriet Tubman—Abolitionist". The raised arm and fist is commonly referred to as the Black Power salute and denotes "communism and socialism". It is also symbolic of the Black Lives Matter movement. Take your pick of symbolism to explain the political cartoon; however, they are basically one in the same.

One of the newspaper articles I read on the topic said, "Change is also coming to other bills: The history making appearances of Martin Luther King, Jr. and opera singer Marian Anderson at the Lincoln

Memorial will be displayed on the back of the $5 bill, and suffragettes marching for the right of women to vote will appear on the steps of the U.S. Treasury, on the back of the $10 bill." Lew said the changes would take place in 2020. I have no problem making changes to our currency to honor the black race or women's rights but this approach is a very "chicken s _ _ _" way to diminish major public resistance and make the changes after the dust settles. It is extremely underhanded but clever if the motivation is to sneak historical change into our society. This is the progressive way.

Back to the College Board and their efforts to change history. They picked on WW II and made America look bad regarding the treatment of Japanese Americans and the dropping of the atomic bomb on Hiroshima and Nagasaki. The new corrected version talks about how we won a war that was a fight for freedom and democracy against fascist and militarist ideologies. As I said before, we saved Europe and who knows where else if we hadn't intervened. I read comments by several conservatives who said the changes made by the College Board could have been better. At least changes were made but only because the College Board is the only "show in town" and was threatened with competition by the states that stood up to them. Again, this shows the impact of standing up to these progressives. Ben Carson said, "Most people when they finish that course, they'd be ready to sign up for ISIS." Andrea Tantaros, one of my favorite Fox News personalities, said the material contained "meaningless liberal crap" that's "trickling down to our kids level". Stay tuned on this one. It is not over.

Classic Marxist indoctrination is taking place at all levels in our schools through political correctness (Critical Theory). Tear down traditional American values and religion, no one is permitted to achieve, everyone is on the same level, and a radical few control the majority because they know better than the rest of us what is best. I have said over, over, and over that it flies in the face of everything America stands for. The Theory of Critical Thinking is not just working in our schools but throughout America. It is erasing and restating history. It is brainwashing our children and our adult citizens. It is taking away the traditional American values that have made us what we are. It is planting new mores in our society supporting Marxist ideology. Mr. Horkheimer and Mr. Marcuse, you had your theory right. It's just taking longer than you thought. You didn't know it would take this much time for our society to become spoiled and lethargic enough to latch on to your utopian fallacies.

Here is a summary of an op-ed by Thomas Sowell. It was titled "America can't waste time on irresponsible education". In reference to Goddard College having a convicted cop killer address their students from prison, he said, "Such 'educators' teach minorities born with an incredibly valuable windfall gain—American citizenship—that they are victims who have a grievance against people today who have done nothing to them, because of what other people did in other times." He continued, "Nothing is easier than to prove that America, or any other society of human beings, is far from being the perfect gem that any of us can conjure up in our imagination." Sowell concluded that the points progressives make are always only one side of the story and are made in isolation of reality in order to support their ideology. We talked about this personality trait in chapters 2 and 4.

Sowell made his point regarding human beings being far from perfect using the Middle East, North Korea, the Ottoman Empire, Stalin, Mao, the Nazi Holocaust, Pol Pot, and slavery. As you know, Sowell is black. He pointed out slavery was not unique to the American south. He said, "Slavery was a worldwide curse for thousands of years, as far back as recorded history goes." He said there were black slave owners as well as white slave owners and slavery was common in Asia and Polynesia. He also said the indigenous people of the Western hemisphere enslaved other indigenous people before anyone on this side of the Atlantic had ever seen a European.

He commented that more whites were brought as slaves to North Africa than blacks brought as slaves to the United States. He also commented that white slaves were still being bought and sold in the Ottoman Empire, decades after blacks were freed in the United States. Sowell concluded his comments on human failings around the world by saying, "What does this all mean? In addition to the chilling picture that it paints of human nature, it means that Americans today—all Americans—are among the luckiest people to have ever inhabited this planet."

He ended his op-ed by pointing out most Americans living in officially defined poverty have central air-conditioning, cable television, microwaves, ovens, and a motor vehicle. He said, as a person who studied Latin America, poverty as defined in the United States today is upper middle class in Mexico. Sowell rhetorically asked, "Do we still need to do better?" He answered, "Yes, human beings all over the world are not even close to running out of room for improvement."

I raised the question earlier whether or not classic liberals knowingly support Marxist political correctness or just fall in the trap of doing so? Here's a related question. Is the psychological make-up of liberal thinking such that Marxist ideology is inherent in all liberal ideology? In other words, Marxist ideology is not the foreign anti-American political ideology we have always opposed in American society but rather is naturally inherent in our liberal leaning American population. We know progressive liberals are Marxists. Are all liberals closet Marxists to a degree and the majority of them don't realize it? Yes, they are.

Let me add more complexity. Does that also apply to conservatives? I have given considerable thought to this and it does. No, I am not going "loony tunes" on you! The ideology we derive from our mental being is not totally black and white. There are varying shades of grey. In writing this book, I have learned there are some elements of Marxist ideology in all of our thinking no matter what our political identity. All Marxist values are not contrary to traditional American values. How about the fair and equal treatment of all members of society? How about everyone having equal economic opportunity? I think that is how classic liberals get "sucked into" political correctness. Marxist values come into conflict with traditional American values when the "methods" in achieving those common philosophical values come into conflict.

Here is an example using the common value that all individuals have the right to "equal economic opportunity". Traditional American values dictate that all individuals have the "equal right to achieve" economic opportunity. Marxism dictates that every individual lives in a classless society and all individuals "share equally" in economic opportunity. The means to accomplish that value are in direct conflict. If classic liberals who get sucked into progressive political correctness "pragmatically" thought through their actions and looked at the total picture, they wouldn't necessarily support the Marxist approach. I refer you back to liberal core personal traits in chapter 2 where perhaps the most distinct difference in classic liberals and conservatives is idealism versus pragmatism. For conservatives, the concept of an economy where everyone shares equally is so blatantly contrary to traditional American values and conservative ideology; it is a black and white decision not to support Marxist ideology and political correctness in achieving a Marxist society.

An individual is identified as a liberal, conservative, or progressive by the degree to which certain ideological traits drive his or her thinking. How can a staunch conservative like myself support women's choice on abortion or support gay rights? I strongly believe in American traditional values and the Constitution. I also believe in doing what I consider to be the right thing to do based upon my personal core personality traits and personal beliefs. Variation in behaviors among members of an ideological grouping like conservatism is normal and healthy as long as those behaviors adhere to that group's core beliefs.

We human beings are not robots, as the progressives would like us to become under their rule. Can a liberal's behavior adhere to a specific conservative belief and the individual still be a liberal? Absolutely! Can a conservative's behavior adhere to a specific liberal belief and the individual still be a conservative? Absolutely! Ideological balance between liberals and conservatives has kept America strong for over 240 years until the progressive movement began to dominate our society and destroy that balance. How about progressives? Does the same theory apply to them? Progressives do not think in terms of behaviors that support traditional American values or the Constitution. That is why the progressives are true Marxists and are inflexible to any compromise. Their core personality traits, mental being, and beliefs and behaviors are totally devoted to their anti-American Marxist ideology. It is their way or the highway.

Here is a message for conservatives, liberals, and progressives. Political correctness is destructive to our American society. It is based on Marxist philosophy that has an abysmal record in accomplishing what Marx intended it to do because his philosophy is built on utopian fantasy. In fact, Marxist philosophy and principles result in the opposite of

R. Lynn Wilson

intentions 100% of the time. For example, instead of liberating society; Marxism suppresses society. Marxist ideology is totally contrary to the founding philosophy and resulting founding principles of American society, which provide: the most personal opportunity; the most personal freedom; the best standard of living; and the best personal safety in the world. Here is my counter to political correctness: use common sense; be pragmatic; employ facts; live in reality; honor your fellow man; and abide by the principles of the Declaration of Independence, the Constitution, and laws of our country. Conservatives, don't give up. Liberals, think about it. Progressives? Forget it! It is your way or the highway. It reminds me of the socialists coining the term "political correctness" to describe the ideological inflexibility of the communists in the early 1900s. I doubt those socialists were very flexible either since they were Marxists just like you progressives and the communists they dissed.

I want to close this chapter with another quote by Ben Carson who said, "Is there a French dream, a British dream, a Nigerian dream? No, there is the American dream." Why would any American allow the progressive movement to destroy our incredible way of life? That is what the remainder of this book is about.

564

CHAPTER 11

Why US?

The movement in the United States to bring about radical change to our traditional American values is pressing forward at an increasing speed. After I wrote the last chapter, "why us" or "why (the) U.S." became a nagging question for me. So, why are radical progressives so hell bent on changing our traditional American culture when we are now the most successful civilization in the history of mankind with our standard of living, freedom from oppression, personal safety, individual rights, and individual opportunity?

The answer to that question is multi-dimensional. Different people have different motivations to bring about radical change in our country. I am going to categorize them into five groups. The first group is made up of intellectual elites who want to impose their utopian ideas on us. The second group consists of narcissists "drunk" with ego and desire for power. The third group involves liberal individuals who have honorable intentions but are manipulated by the intellectual elite and the narcissists. The fourth group includes those who are troubled, misguided, and angry individuals who basically don't know what they want. And, I would be remiss without including Muslims as a fifth group.

Intellectual elites are progressives who are way too smart for their own good and our good as they aggressively work to drag us into their naive utopian world of intellectual fantasy. Individuals like philosophers Karl Marx and Friedrich Engels; Max Horkheimer and Herbert Marcuse who started The School of Critical Theory; and college professors like Cass Sunstein, Bill Ayers, and Ward

Churchill who teach our young people progressive nonsense and write nonsensical progressive books have certain traits in common. I have already commented on Sunstein and Ayers and will comment on Ayers and Churchill in the next chapter. Intellectual elites are not able to function like normal people in the real world because of their utopian mental being. They are incredibly warped about the true meaning of society, do not grasp how a successful society operates, and do not have an accurate understanding of human behavior. They are extremely intelligent and believe they are smarter than the rest of us and must protect us from ourselves.

These people never hold a position of true responsibility in the real world? They are not capable of doing so and migrate to jobs that allow them their elitists thinking. Climate research is a classic example. They also migrate to our educational system from the elementary level through the college level and are protected by tenure. Tenure protects them so they can hide and survive in their utopian cocoon under the guise of free speech and academic freedom. Unfortunately, this also provides them the ability to indoctrinate our young people with their destructive ideology. I often wonder how difficult it is for the teachers and professors who do not share their elitist and utopian mental being to cope working with them as colleagues.

The world is full of progressives who are narcissists. Narcissism comes in varying degrees from mild to severe. Any of us who have obtained a level of success in our professions have some degree of narcissism. The vast majority of us would be classified as mildly neurotic narcissists. Unfortunately, there are narcissists who are excessively neurotic narcissists and those who are psychotic narcissist. Excessive neurotic narcissism is problematic but those who are psychotic are dangerous in two significant aspects. First, they have no feeling of remorse and they either rationalize their failures as successes or compartmentalize their failures out of their conscious mind. They never feel any responsibility for their failed actions. Second, they have no empathy for people who are harmed by their actions. It is all about them and their desires. Traditional American values, our Constitution, and the laws of our country are obstacles to these narcissistic progressives and they must eradicate them to achieve their objectives.

I said in the last chapter that all of us have certain elements of Marxist ideology in our thinking. The progressive intellectual elite and progressives who are excessive narcissists manipulate liberal individuals who have honorable intentions toward the "dark side" of Marxist thinking. A classic liberal is one who supports our traditional American values, our Constitution, and our country's laws through liberal ideology based upon his or her personal beliefs and values. A progressive liberal differs from a classic liberal in that she or he interprets and supports liberal ideology in a radical way with total disregard to traditional American values, the Constitution, or the laws of our country.

How do progressives manipulate classic liberals to join them considering these significant differences? They utilize the classic liberal's core personality traits. The most significant liberal core trait used by progressives is idealism versus pragmatism. Remember from chapter 2 that any unintended outcomes of classic liberal actions are overshadowed and obliterated by the unwavering intensity and commitment to achieve liberal ideological goals. Classic liberals focus on the desired benefit of a liberal ideological effort rather than the actual outcome or any resulting negative implications that might occur.

Other personal core traits contributing to the manipulation of classic liberals include rationalization of behavior, ideological bias, and the belief that the end justifies the means. I do not know how many classic liberals fall into this progressive trap. As I watch classic liberals on television and interact with them on a personal basis, they are all over the map regarding the progressive movement. The number involved is very significant, dangerous for our country, and increasing.

The United States and the world are full of troubled, misguided, and angry individuals who basically don't know what they want in life. The underlying motivations for those who join radical anti-American progressive groups are not different than the underlying motivations we discussed for radical Muslims in chapter 9. They have become disenfranchised in our society because of one or more of the following reasons: deep-rooted mental dysfunction resulting from their family's gene pool; dysfunctional behavior resulting from family and/or environmental influence; or a feeling of hopelessness resulting from poverty and/or lack of education. The main dissimilarity between radical

Muslims and anti-American radicals is the disenfranchised Muslims routinely channel their anger through their Islamic religion and join radical Muslim groups in search of a feeling of belonging and purpose and to express their dysfunctional mental being. Troubled, misguided, and angry anti-Americans channel their dysfunctional mental being through radical anti-American progressive organizations in their search of belonging and purpose and to express their dysfunctional mental being. Examples would be communist, socialist, or other racial oriented organizations. They may also go in and out of these organized movements or simply isolate themselves from mainstream society.

It appears these radical anti-American organizations are growing in size and number. This is a very troubling trend. The vast majority, if not all, of the people who are demonstrating and rioting are doing so to act out their dysfunction; not to protest some legitimate issue in earnest. Unfortunately, the mainstream news media doesn't understand or appear to care about the true reasons for these increasing demonstrations and riots. They use them as fodder to support their progressive biased reporting.

I said I would be remiss without including Muslims as a fifth group. Here's why. We have repeatedly talked about the tight religious grip that Islam has on the Muslim population. Islam is a religion that does not allow the separation of church and state or protect individual rights as required by our Judeo-Christian based Constitution and ingrained in our traditional American values. The Bible teaches us how to live from our hearts—from the inside. The Quran teaches how to live through sharia Law—from the outside. An op-ed by Cal Thomas commented that two years ago the U.S. Commission on International Freedom said "10 of the 15 worst violators of religious freedom in the world" are nations where Islam is the dominant religion.

Western culture is much more permissive regarding social norms like sexuality and is much more tolerant of people's behavior in general. Western culture also comes into conflict with the Muslim culture when it comes to the rights of all individuals including women and gays. As the Muslim population grows in the U.S., it will increasingly come into conflict with our American culture. We have discussed throughout the book the conflict these differences cause between traditional Muslims and our traditional American society.

Muslim organizations like the Muslim Brotherhood and CAIR do not support our American culture as they claim and routinely undermine our culture in covert ways. Behind the scenes they are continuously fighting our American way of life on our own soil. There are also a multitude of mosques and other Muslim organizations in America that do not support our American culture as we discussed in chapter 9. There are Muslims and Muslim organizations that are more moderate and do assimilate into American culture but they are a small minority.

Progressive intellectual elitists, progressive political narcissists, troubled-misguided-angry-radicals, and the Muslim culture have one big common enemy—us!

CHAPTER 12

Effective Conservative Strategy!

———

There is no question by now that I adhere to strong conservative values. In this chapter, I am going to channel those values into my personal political opinions. After all, the book is titled *One American's Opinion.* I have commented elsewhere that a balance between conservatism and liberalism is healthy. I honestly believe that but I also believe it is conservative political ideology that is most supportive of traditional American values and the Constitution and should be the driver of our country's politics. If you are a classic liberal, I understand, appreciate, and respect your right to disagree. If you are a progressive, we are not in the same galaxy.

I want to begin by looking at conservatism and the Republican Party. I said in chapter 2 the terms republican and conservative are commonly used interchangeably except for one caveat. The caveat is most republican politicians today fall into the political trap of making decisions based on their political future rather than making decisions based on their best conservative judgment. Many times I question whether or not the Republican Party is even conservative at all. The party seems to be centrist at best.

The majority of republican politicians show little or no passion for true conservative ideology and they are seemingly afraid of their own shadow (maybe I should say the democrats' shadow) in standing up for any conservative principles. They appear so afraid of receiving criticism and potentially losing votes that they get as close to the middle as possible to make themselves nondescript and be in a position to defend their position either way. It's our fault as voters that these politicians get re-elected but what choice do we have? They are seemingly all alike and getting worse.

The Democratic Party is not without their identity problems either. During a *Hardball with Chris Mathews* show, Mathews asked Debby Wasserman Schultz, when she was still the Democratic Committee Chairwoman, what the difference was between a democrat and a socialist. This was after asking her if Senator Bernie Sanders should be given a primetime speaking opportunity at their national convention if he was not their nominee. I saw a clip of the interchange. Wassermann was speechless during this exchange and, if you are familiar with Wasserman, that is hard to believe. Mathews repeated the question a couple of different ways and still did not get a straight answer. He only got nervous laughs and efforts by Wasserman to change the subject. Out of frustration, Mathews finally said, "I think there's a big difference. I think there is a huge difference." Can you believe Chris Mathews said emphatically that there is a big difference between a democrat and a socialist? Wonders never cease to amaze!

This observation is important for several reasons. First, it shows the Democratic Party doesn't want to admit it is supporting political candidates who are openly Marxist sympathizers like Bernie Sanders. The party fears it will turn off much of its classic liberal base and independents. Second, to deny support for a Marxist candidate like Sanders poses a risk of losing progressive democrats, Millennials, and splitting the party. Third, it exposes the party for what it has morphed into. It is a Marxist political party in liberal clothing. This line of thinking was supported by a Rasmussen poll taken in October of last year. The democrats polled said they now have a positive view of socialism because of the Bernie Sanders campaign and they were evenly split as to whether they liked socialism or capitalism more. They sure as hell need to read this book. That is unbelievable! These people are living in their naive ideological caves we discussed in chapter 2.

I have repeatedly said it doesn't take much research or intellect to compare the personal success all Americans have achieved in our capitalistic, free market, and individual freedom inspired America as compared to any other country in the world. That success also includes Americans considered to be at or below the poverty level.

When the few republican politicians in Congress who are willing to buck the establishment do so, they are crucified as "radical out of touch right-wing idiots" by the opposition, the news media, and their own party. Ted Cruz immediately comes to mind. This is not an endorsement of Ted Cruz but it is an endorsement of Ted Cruz's moxie to buck the establishment and stand up for what he believes. Senator Ben Sasse from Nebraska is another politician who is causing fellow republicans to be uncomfortable because he is standing up for conservative principals. According to pundits, that is the reason Trump has gotten the support he has. People do not necessarily like what Trump says but they like his moxie in saying it.

Has congressional decision-making improved since the republicans obtained control of both the House and the Senate? The answer is a resounding no! Here is a great example. We heard from republican politicians how the republican controlled Congress was going to use the 2015 budget bill to "wreck havoc" with Obamacare and to defund Planned Parenthood. John Boehner was replaced with Paul Ryan last October and we conservatives had high hopes something good was going to happen. What happened? It appeared that same old same old happened. Nothing happened to Obamacare or Planned Parenthood in the budget bill and we wound up with a two-year bill that did nothing to address our national debt problem. The only thing our republican Congress appeared to do was to fund all of Obama's programs and make him smile when he signed the bill.

I saw Paul Ryan on television after the bill passed. He was very enthusiastic. He said there were a lot of good things in the bill that were not as obvious as Obamacare and Planned Parenthood and Congress was going to tackle those two issues this year. Well, they passed a bill repealing Obamacare and defunding Planned Parenthood. It is no surprise Obama vetoed it. At least they did it. Ryan says to stay tuned to this year's Congress and we will see a much more aggressive effort on the part of congressional republicans to represent conservative values. I have a lot of respect for Ryan so I am hopeful. We'll see.

Here is an example of inappropriate messaging by our past republican House leadership toward democratic leadership. There is nothing wrong with a civil, respectful, and productive relationship but there is a limit.

I saw a big picture in our local newspaper of John Boehner hugging and planting a big "smooch" on Nancy Pelosi's cheek as she handed the gavel to him when he took over as Speaker of the House in 2011. She had a soft "warm fuzzy" look on her face and Boehner was grinning like a Cheshire cat. I was honestly shocked that Boehner appeared so lovey-dovey after the disgusting and dishonest way Pelosi has treated conservative Americans and our country in general. Boehner should have been respectful but he went way over the top and gave the wrong message. When Ryan took over as Speaker, Pelosi also handed him the gavel. It was a much different picture. They shook hands and gave each other a respectful smile. That's the way it should be.

Here is a side bar on Pelosi. Judicial Watch uncovered in 2010 that she took 85 trips between March 2009 and June 2010 on military jets at a cost of $2,100,744. On two occasions there were family members involved. A total of $101,429 of that cost was spent on inflight services for food and drink. On one of her congressional delegation flights from Washington to Israel and Iraq, the "drink" included: Makers Mark; Courvoisier; Johnny Walker Red; Grey Goose; Bailey's; Bacardi; Jim Beam; Beefeater; Dewar's; Bombay Sapphire; Jack Daniel's; Corona; and several bottles of wine. I wish our members of Congress were as specific and committed in their political positions as they are to what they drink. Judicial Watch also discovered that Pelosi had a history of scheduling flights and then canceling or changing them at the last minute. Judicial Watch President, Tom Fitton, said, "Pelosi's abusive use of military aircraft demonstrates a shocking lack of regard for the American taxpayer and the men and women who serve in the U.S. Air Force. Speaker Pelosi may have a frequent flyer record for taxpayer-financed luxury jet travel."

I am not the only one who is disappointed by our republican controlled Congress. A Rasmussen poll was conducted in December 2015 after the budget bill was passed and signed into law. The purpose of the survey was to evaluate the public's opinion of Congress now that the House and Senate are both controlled by republicans. Only 10% of eligible voters thought things were better, 47% thought things were worse, and 37% rated Congress the same as before the republicans took over both branches. It looks worse when the results are broken down by political party. It is not surprising that 70% of democrats believe Congress is doing a worse job but 22% of republicans and 46% of independents believe they are. Only 19% of republicans believe things are better.

We do have an option that has merit in addressing this issue. As I said in chapter 3, I have always been opposed to term limits but I am now enamored with it. It wouldn't be perfect and it has some downside but it could have a positive effect in stopping or at least curtailing the mentality that says, "I will do whatever is necessary to insure my perpetual political future." If a politician knew he or she could not be re-elected by law then perhaps they might make tougher unpopular decisions that are the right decisions for the country, especially toward the end of their terms.

This may be naive on my part. They might just find another political office to run for and continue the same behavior from one office to the next. I hate to be so cynical but it doesn't take much intellect to observe and understand what is happening in the Republican and Democratic Parties. The republicans are afraid of their own shadows and do not make any difficult decisions. The democrats consistently support their party's position even when that position is purely ideological in nature and not in the best interest of their constituents or their country. A friend sent me the following quote that was attributed to Ronald Reagan but I could not confirm it was by him. The quote is, "Both politicians and diapers need to be changed often and for the same reason." No matter where it came from the quote is well said!

Maybe another option in the future could be electing robots. I have been reading recently that robots are getting closer and closer to achieving artificial intelligence. Just think! We could vote in elections for the robot of our choice depending upon its stated ideology. The robots would have conservative or liberal software depending upon which ideology they represent. The independent politicians always caucus with the liberals so the independent robot would have a watered-down liberal version. There would be no progressive software.

Think of the advantages. We could save millions, if not billions, of dollars in salaries, benefits, personal expenses, and office expenses. We would not have the personal scandals we do today. All the voting outcomes would be predictable and honest depending upon the robot's electoral mandate. Our congressional representatives would have a 100% attendance at their committee meetings and a 100% voting record as opposed to their spotty records of today. Do you ever observe on television the empty seats at important committee meetings or the number of absentees when votes on bills are counted? It's amazing. Where are they? Certainly not doing their jobs we hired them to do. The robots would also be programed to actually read the bills before they voted on them.

Decision-making would improve and we would get a lot more done. In reality, I'm afraid my idea is only a pipe dream. How do the democratic and republican programs for the robots get written in order to reflect the true wishes of the voters? And, eventually, self-serving humans would find ways to corrupt the robots and we would be back to square one. Oh well, it wouldn't be near as much fun anyway. On second thought, I don't know about you but we are having way too much fun for me and it's getting very old.

Since I have hacked off all the politicians in Washington, I want to sincerely apologize to those of you who are doing a good job regardless of which party you are in. I challenge the rest of you to step back, take a deep breath, and ponder what I have said. Can you be honest with yourself regarding your behavior in representing the constituency that hired you to represent them and change that behavior? If you can't, you don't belong in your position and there are more than a few of you.

Now that I have that diatribe off my chest, let's get down to business. I want to begin by asking you to articulate the political platform of the Republican Party. You can't, because there isn't one. How can a political party ever expect success if no one knows what it stands for. The party says it stands for conservative values. What conservative values are they referring to? No one knows because they never clearly articulate an ideological platform! I call the Republican Party the Ambiguity Party.

I always enjoy reading Peggy Noonan's editorials in The Wall Street Journal. There was a great one in September 2014 regarding the ineptness of the Republican Party. She said the republicans have done a good job of assuring their candidates were not nutty persons who said nutty things. Noonan then quoted Kellyanne Conway of The Polling

Company who said, "It's not enough for voters to have a candidate who doesn't say something controversial. They need something compelling." This was before Trump's success, which proves Conway correct even with all of Trump's crudeness, arrogance, and rudeness.

The editorial said the Republican Party's consultants blamed republican problems on the fact that the Democratic Party raises more money and the republicans need more money to win. How naive, stupid, or both. Take your pick. Noonan commented, "Shouldn't the Republican Party make it clear right now exactly what it is for and what it intends to do?" She gave the following example to support her comment. She said the republican leadership in Washington takes the position that, "If you are explicit in terms of larger policy ideas, you just give Democrats something to shoot at. Don't give them a target." She gave Obamacare, foreign policy, and the IRS as examples of issues the public find so unpopular that they are more than enough reason to vote republican. She concluded, "Don't give the voters a reason not to!"

A November 2015 Rasmussen poll supports Noonan's and my position on the Republican Party and its lack of political direction. Only 38% of republicans polled said that the Republican Party has a plan for where it wants to take the nation. Surprisingly, only 41% of democrats feel the Democratic Party has a plan. I think the democratic number is a reflection of the current state of affairs in Washington that we have discussed throughout the book concerning the progressive movement.

As this book is being readied for press, the Republican National Convention just concluded. I thought Trump hit some good points such as Obamacare and national security in his acceptance speech but did not articulate an overall specific republican platform as I had hoped. Even though Trump mentioned Obamacare and national security, I think Noonan's editorial reflects the continuing attitude of the Republican Party in not articulating a firm stance on issues.

Let's take a minute to talk about the Tea Party. First of all, it is not a political party. It is a conceptual means to allow people to express their conservative political feelings. Tea Partiers basically believe in low taxes, small government, free market capitalism, individual freedom, and the Constitution. Libertarians believe in low taxes, small government, free market capitalism, individual freedom, and the Constitution as well.

That's strange? Isn't that what the Republican Party says it believes in? You couldn't prove it by listening to and watching the Republican Party's leadership. So what does the Republican Party believe in? Who knows! Like I said at the beginning of the chapter, they are all over the place and take no position on specific issues. They criticize Tea Partiers as radicals and I guess they feel that Libertarians are even wackier.

I want to share my personal Tea Party experience with you. My wife and I went to three Tea Party rallies on a major street corner here in Naples. The rallies were in conjunction with the 2010 midterm elections. It was estimated there were 3,000 people at each rally. The opposition claimed there were only a few hundred. It was closer to 3,000. What an incredible experience, which I will never forget. There were men, women, and children demonstrating peacefully and patriotically waving American flags and carrying homemade signs supporting traditional American values and our Constitutional rights.

The vast majority of people in the cars and trucks going by honked their horns and waved in support. That support included people of different races and different economic backgrounds. It was American pride and support in steroids for what America stands for. We had a few negative responses from the passing traffic but they were insignificant in comparison to the overwhelming positive response. I can still vividly remember the enormous emotional pride we felt as Americans at those events. I wish that same pride was consciously and overtly permeating throughout our American society today. Most of the progressive political bums would be voted out of office and this politically correct nonsense would be under control.

What would a conservative Washington look like in a perfect world? I'm going express my opinion by playing "What would I do, if I were president". The first thing I would do is to surround myself with the smartest and most experienced people I could find in their field of expertise who strongly supported traditional American values and the Constitution. That would include conservatives and non-conservatives as long as the non-conservatives are pragmatic enough to do what is best for the country rather than what is best for their ideology. I would then develop a culture of open communication, teamwork, and compromise between members of my administrative staff and the republican and democratic members of Congress. We could then begin to address and implement effective policy and laws throughout the federal government that support what is best for the country. The key here is to accomplish "what is best for our country", not "what is best for me". That is called leadership, which is totally lacking in Washington today.

Now that we have the infrastructure in place, I would implement the following practices and policies. First and foremost, I would implement a strong culture of employee accountability that would result in effective decision-making and outcomes. This in return would establish an internal culture that would allow the government to operate efficiently. The next thing I would do is to have each and every one of my cabinet members come up with a plan to get rid of waste and downsize her or his departments. The government employee unions will love me for that one and stop donating money to my political coffers, which would be an additional good thing. Campaign financing is out of control in buying political favors and promoting waste and inefficiency. It desperately needs reform. I would push legislation to do that.

Speaking of unions, I would push congress to pass a law that federal employees could no longer be unionized. I would need to make sure the Secret Service had my back on that one. We have repeatedly seen what angry unions and their supporters do when they do not like something or they want something. Maybe I could get a concealed gun permit and carry a gun (Reagan supposedly did after he was shot). Better yet, I could obtain an open carry permit and have the gun in a cowboy style holster or two guns in a double holster like in the Wild West. Now that would be an interesting situation for my progressive "anti-gun" friends. They would have to deal with a two-fisted gun-toting president. I wonder what history would "call me" if I did that. I could get a horse and mimic President Teddy Roosevelt who was president from1901until1909.

On second thought, being compared to Teddy Roosevelt is going too far but at least he was a republican president. Or was he? He formed the Progressive Party in 1912 also known as the Bull Moose Party. Roosevelt referred to himself as a bull moose after he formed the new party. What? Roosevelt started the formal progressive movement in national politics? Yes, he did! Unless you are a U.S. history buff, I was as surprised as you are when I discovered this. It is a fascinating story. To avoid another book in a book, here is the Cliff Notes version.

The progressive era in the United States took place from 1890 to 1920 according to the sources I used to research this topic. Those sources included a paper from Georgetown University written by Eleanor Roosevelt; Wikipedia sites for the Progressive Party, Teddy Roosevelt, and Woodrow Wilson; and a report on American Progressivism by Glenn Beck. The 1890 to 1920 time frame refers to the formal progressive period in America but progressive ideology probably was in our country before then.

According to Eleanor Roosevelt, progressivism began as a social movement and morphed into a political movement. The early progressives rejected Social Darwinism and believed that providing a good education, a safe environment, and an efficient work place would solve our society's problems of poverty, violence, greed, racism, and class warfare. Just to be clear, Social Darwinism and my analogy to Darwin theory are not the same. Progressives lived primarily in the cities, were college educated, and believed that government could be the tool for change.

Teddy Roosevelt formed the Progressive Party after a split with the Republican Party and his hand picked presidential successor William Howard Taft. The split occurred because Roosevelt increasingly became disappointed with Taft's conservative policies and decided to again run for president against Taft and Woodrow Wilson. That is certainly interesting; a republican president becoming upset because his successor was too conservative? Actually, even though Roosevelt was a "republican in name", he was a "progressive at heart". His platform was titled New Nationalism and called for a strong government to regulate industry, protect the middle and working classes, and carry on "great national projects".

His New Nationalism platform was very paternalistic and in direct opposition to Wilson's individualistic philosophy in his "New Freedom" platform. Wilson; however, strayed from the individualistic philosophy after he became president and was credited with overseeing the passage of progressive legislative policies that were unparalleled until FDR's New Deal in 1933. Roosevelt ran a robust campaign but in the end lost to Wilson due to his lack of campaign funds and lack of support from business and fellow republicans who had supported him in the past but chose to stay with the Republican Party.

Many historians said it was the split in the Republican Party that allowed Wilson to win. Wilson got 42% of the vote while Roosevelt got 27% and Taft got 23%. The Progressive party existed on the federal and state level until it finally split up in 1918 with almost all of the party members re-joining the conservative dominated Republican Party. Those that still had loyalty to the progressive movement joined the "New Deal" Democratic Party coalition of FDR in the 1930s.

My discovery raised a question in my mind. Were the progressive movement and the Marxist movement in our country connected? I found my answer in the report written by Glenn Beck. Karl Marx and Friedrich Engels wrote their book in 1848 promoting Marxism. The progressive movement started in the 18th century in Europe in a period known as the Age of Enlightenment. The principle goals of the Age of Enlightenment were liberty, progress, reason, tolerance, fraternity, and ending the abuses of church and state. During the Progressive Era when Roosevelt and Wilson were presidents there was a socialist movement taking place in America. Roosevelt and Wilson were critical of the socialist movement in 1912 because they ran against a socialist candidate named Eugene Debs. Bernie Sanders is not the first.

The progressives were ambivalent toward the socialists not because there was a disagreement in philosophy but because socialism was a movement by the lower classes and the progressives were elitist. The progressives looked down upon the socialists as being beneath them. The progressive concept of government closely coincided with the socialists' concept and, as we all know, was in significant conflict with our Constitution. Wilson wrote an essay in 1887 called Socialism and Democracy. He said socialism stands for "unfettered state power, which trumps any notion of individual rights". He also wrote, "(Socialism) proposes that all idea of limitation of public authority by individual rights be put out of view. No line can be drawn between private and public affairs which the state may not cross at will." Wilson said that he found nothing wrong with this in principle, since it was the logical extension of "genuine democratic theory". He concluded:

> In fundamental theory socialism and democracy are almost if not quite one and the same. They both rest at bottom upon the absolute right of the community to determine its own destiny and that of its members. Limits of wisdom and convenience to the public control there may be: limits of principle there are, upon analyses, none.

Wilson and the progressives had very negative feelings about another principle of our Constitution. They were strongly against separation of powers. They said it made government inefficient and made it difficult, if not impossible, to expand the power of government to accomplish progressive goals. Wasn't it the intent of our founding fathers to prevent one branch of government from gaining too much power and control? As I say that and as I write this book, I am astonished at how genius our founding fathers were in establishing such an incredible government structure as our Constitution. The progressives felt the presidency was a way of circumventing the obstacle of separation of powers. It will be interesting to see how history will treat Obama in this matter. As aggressive as Obama is in using the presidency to circumvent separation of powers, can you imagine what it would be like with Clinton or Sanders as president? Let's hope we only have to imagine.

Roosevelt's New Nationalism platform also argued for a new concept of government where individual rights would no longer serve as the "principled boundary" the state was prohibited from crossing. Roosevelt wrote:

> We grudge no man a fortune in civil life if it is honorably obtained and well used. It is not even enough that it should have been gained without doing damage to the community. We should permit it to be gained only so long as the gaining represents benefit to the community. This, I know, implies a policy of far more active government interference with social and economic conditions in this country than we have yet had, but I think we have got to face the fact that such an increase in government control is now necessary.

Now you know. The progressive movement has been active in our government since at least 1901 when Roosevelt became president, if not before. To research back further would be another book in a book. I also could not find any formal connection between this progressive movement and the Marxist Critical Theory movement. I was more than surprised to discover what I have just told you. It is amazing how time forgets and distorts history. Sometimes it is unintentional as is the case with this story but unfortunately sometimes it is intentional for deceitful reasons like supporting political correctness falsehoods.

A good example of unintentional historical misunderstanding is our founding fathers, the Declaration of Independence, and the ensuing Revolutionary War. Until I saw the series special on PBS about Samuel Adams and Bill O'Reilly's series titled *Legends and Lies: The Patriots*, I assumed all of our founding fathers were enthusiastically 100% in lock step to declare our independence from the British and our battle with them was swift and decisive. After all, the Declaration of Independence was signed by each of our founding fathers and the only event I remembered was the Boston Tea Party.

These specials pointed out that it was very difficult to get everyone to sign the document because many of them had reasons not to do so. It took a lot of hard work and convincing to get all the signatures. The biggest surprise was John Hancock. In the beginning, he refused to sign because his trade business was very lucrative and he did not want to lose it. He signed only after the British created a situation that ruined his business and sign he did, in bold fashion. He did not sign his name so big because he loved his country. He signed his name big because he was mad at the British and wanted to get back at them.

Many colonists did not support succession from Great Britain. I was surprised at how difficult, bloody, and messy it was during the ensuing battles to gain our independence. It took eight years of battle and there were awful atrocities committed by the British against the colonists. I always find history to be fascinating, especially when you learn the actual events and not the version that is summarized into short sound bites for brevity or sanitized to reflect bias.

I know I strayed but I hope you find this history of our country as fascinating as I do. Let's get back to if I were president. Now that we have the infrastructure in place, we can build a strong nation. Until the last two years, I would have said the number one issue in the country was the economy. The rise of Islamic terrorism and aggression by Russia, China, Iran, and North Korea has changed my opinion. Recent polls show Americans agree with me. A poll taken by The Wall Street Journal and NBC in December 2014 showed 40% of Americans said national security and terrorism is our top issue and job creation and economic growth is number two at 23%.

That is a change from April 2014 when 29% said job creation and economic growth was number one and 21% said national security was number two. The other issues voiced in the April and December polls remained in the same rank order. They are as follows showing the December 2014 poll percentages of importance: the deficit and government spending, 11%; healthcare, 9%; climate change, 9%; immigration, 7%; and religious and moral values, 3%. Before the Orlando terrorist attack, recent polls had indicated the top two issues may have been reversing again. Which one is first or second depends upon the news of the day as evidenced by the Fox News poll in chapter 8 that was done just after the Orlando attack.

I found an additional polling question connected to the December 2014 poll to be very interesting. Those polled were asked if they were looking for a different style of presidential leadership by our next president as compared to Obama? Twenty-five percent said they wanted the next president to take a similar approach but 73% said they wanted a change. I would have liked it to be 100% but the 73% is not bad and is higher than I thought it would be. Very surprisingly, 46% of democratic voters said they wanted change. Now we're getting somewhere.

Our foreign policy and national security has gone to hell. I would get the best military minds in our country together including those who were instrumental in the wars in Iraq and Afghanistan who have retired, were forced to retire, or fired. Together, we would develop a comprehensive plan to put ISIS and other Islamic terrorists on their proverbial rear ends and restore reasonable stability to the Middle East. I would then coordinate that plan with our Middle East and NATO allies who would be willing to join us in the fight and assure them we are in it for victory no matter what it takes. And yes, that would definitely include so called "boots on the ground" and those boots would belong to soldiers from all members of the coalition including us. That coalition led by the United States would then kick the Islamic terrorists' butts with those boots and accomplish our mission to support peace in the Middle East and protect U.S. and coalition citizens at home and abroad. The terrorists would not know what hit them!

I would at the same time have my own apology tour and apologize to all of our allies and friends regarding our blatant absence as the leader of the free world and pledge to them our future leadership, friendship, and support. I would also apologize to them for letting them down during the past seven years. I would especially apologize to Israel for throwing them under the bus more than once. Lastly, after I have proven we are back militarily, I would get in front of Russia, China, Iran, and North Korea and tell them to "bring it on—the party is over".

Now that we have addressed our foreign policy and our country's safety, it's time to trigger a robust economy. The first thing I would do is to get rid of Obamacare. I would organize a think tank (not one of those so-called blue-ribbon commissions that do nothing but create a report and nothing happens) composed of the smartest and most pragmatic people I could find that clearly understand the different components of the healthcare system. I would have them work with me to develop recommendations to my staff and Congress on how the federal government can work with the healthcare and health insurance industry to get us out of the Obamacare mess we are in now. Access to care, as pushed by the progressives, is not the issue. The real issue is cost and its relationship to maintaining quality of care.

Here is a summary of the approach I included in chapter 8 from my previous book? I would incentivize cost savings through patients having financial "skin in the game" when they make their decisions in accessing healthcare services. This approach has proven to be successful. I would also find ways to encourage patients to develop and utilize living wills. Tort reform would be a top priority. I would work with Congress to implement tort reform legislation to stop these insane frivolous lawsuits and limit damages paid to plaintiffs. One effective approach would be to pass legislation to institute financial risk for attorneys who lose liability cases. The impact of frivolous lawsuits on healthcare costs is enormous in creating excessive defensive medical practices and exorbitant malpractice insurance costs. Tort reform would also curtail inappropriate and unnecessary costs to other industries and individuals. We need to stop lawyers from routinely filing multiple lawsuits and throwing them at the courtroom wall to see what sticks.

At the same time we were working to reduce the cost of healthcare, I would rescind the Obama administration's countless progressive regulations that are very onerous and create unnecessary expense. This would remove uncertainty from the marketplace, reduce cost to businesses, and spur economic growth. The membership of the National Labor Relations Board would be reconstituted to rescind the Board's pro-union actions that put unfair regulations on business.

I would develop a corporate tax structure decreasing taxes on domestic small business as well as our larger domestic and global businesses to make us tax competitive throughout the world. At the same time, I would revise the tax code for all U.S. citizens to make it more simple and fair. Included in that revision would be a requirement for "every citizen" to pay taxes, no matter how little it might be, to give all Americans "skin in the game". At the same time, I would review all hidden and regressive taxes to ascertain their validity and necessity. Finally, I would require the federal bureaucrats in my administration to re-commit their support for our Constitution, free market capitalism, and individualism; which are the basic principles that made America the greatest country in the world. If they don't re-commit, they would be looking for a new job.

A longer-term issue related to the economy is the national debt. In addition to instilling accountability in employee decision making, improving employee performance, and reducing the size of government; I would develop a plan to drastically cut back entitlement programs and provide assistance to only those with true proven need. This would be difficult and complicated but it can be done. Lastly, I would develop annual conservative based budgets for the federal government that are honestly designed to effectively and significantly reduce the deficit. I can promise you the savings would not be spread over a 10-year-period. Federal law mandates an annual budget but last year was the first time one has been passed since Obama was elected.

Immigration is one of our country's most controversial issues. I would make it very simple. The first thing I would do is to tightly (and I do mean tightly) secure the border. I would involve the border patrol agents in developing the plan and provide strong support to them as they carry out the plan. I would then provide a path to amnesty for all current illegals who have not committed a serious crime by developing a reasonable and responsible system for them to become legitimate U.S. citizens. I would send any illegal that has committed a serious crime back to their "home sweet home" after they have served appropriate time in prison. If they were caught sneaking into the United States again, I would put them back in prison long enough to get their attention and deport them again. If they come back a third time they would really wish they had stayed home.

We need to be serious and very tough and they need to know it. Any illegal alien that is eligible for citizenship under amnesty who does not follow the established procedure to become a citizen would also be sent home when they are caught and I would increase our ability to do so. I would also revise the current law regarding so-called "refugees" from other countries who claim to be escaping abuse, persecution, and violence. These refugees would be thoroughly scrutinized for legitimacy and they would be few and far between. Lastly I would aggressively go after those from other countries who overstay their visas.

I can't leave this topic regarding my presidency until I address the biggest socioeconomic issue in our country and that is poverty and crime in inner city black ghettos. I would put together a group of people who truly understand black ghetto issues and have them work with me, my administration, and Congress to develop a plan of action to address problems in these ghettos head on. I can assure you the plan would not be based around entitlements. It would be based upon hard decisions, tough love, and long-term results. It would involve economic progress in those areas, strengthening the family unit, tough policing, and would be based on a multigenerational time frame for total success.

Finally and very importantly, our country needs healing from all the divisiveness the Obama administration has created regarding race relations, political correctness, and ideological political division. We need to get back to the principles that have made America the greatest country in the history of the world. As president, I would demonstrate love, caring, respect, and equality for all citizens who show respect for their fellow Americans, traditional American values, the Constitution, and the rule of law. Others would have a problem with me because I would have a problem with them and they would know it.

There you have it! President Wilson's plan of action in a perfect world. I certainly would be a far cry from my namesake Woodrow Wilson. We all know the world is far from perfect. The real question is how close can we come? The closer we set our goals to perfection the better chance we have to achieve it. So, what is an effective platform for the Republican Party? The top priority would be to bolster national security by repairing foreign relations with our allies, forming a military coalition composed of the U.S., NATO, and Middle Eastern countries, and use all of that militarily might to decimate ISIS and radical Islam as quickly as reasonably possible. This would send a message to the entire world that U.S. world leadership and exceptionalism is back.

The second priority would be to improve the economy and unemployment through less government regulation, providing more certainty in the marketplace, the repeal of Obamacare, and tax reform. The third priority would be to secure our borders, tighten immigration laws, and give amnesty to all current illegal aliens who do not have serious criminal records. The fourth priority would be to reduce the size of government and government programs including welfare to get spending under control and reduce the national debt. This would also include putting more accountability into government operations. The fifth priority would be to relinquish power on the federal level to state and local governments to affect more local regulatory decision-making and less federal control. The sixth priority is to focus on the well-being of those less fortunate and bring them out of poverty. The seventh and final priority would be to heal the country. That would be my 7-step republican platform.

The Republican Party would be met by a progressive onslaught to aggressively discredit that 7-step platform and republican politicians would need to be prepared. Republican politicians have been rather docile in the past to attacks by their adversaries. They should not; however, get into a "pissing-contest" in defending their positions. When you are "wallowing in the mud with a skunk" you both wind up stinking. Let your adversaries "sink in their own stink" so to speak. That doesn't mean republicans shouldn't point out the progressive's shortcomings and pragmatically attack them. The Republican Party needs to take the high ground and exhibit pride and confidence in their platform by convincingly concentrating on its positive benefits to Americans and how that is better for Americans than their opponent's platform.

Polls show the majority of likely voters are fed up with the direction our country is headed under progressive rule. A McClatchy-Marist poll done in April of this year said that 68% of those polled felt the country was going in the wrong direction and only 27% felt we are going in the right direction. A more recent poll in July by Rasmussen was similar with only 24% of those polled saying the country was headed in the right direction. The majority of Americans want new leadership in the White House to bring forth positive results for our country.

Let's take a look at the presidential candidates Americans have chosen to be our new president and get us out of this mess. Let's start with the democrats. Bernie Sanders lost to Hillary Clinton in the democratic primary, which was "rigged" in Clinton's favor. Sanders is a self-proclaimed socialist, which is against everything America stands for. His promise of free education, free healthcare, and other "socialist goodies" is not free and will go a long way in increasing taxes on everyone and not just the rich. He would increase our national debt toward the point of bankruptcy. I might add that he appears to be a pacifist in this dangerous world. We have already talked about the standard of living and serious immigration issues in the countries he says America should emulate versus the standard of living and personal security we now enjoy. He would have made everything people are riling against worse. He had significant support from Millennials and many other democrats.

I found an October 2015 Rasmussen poll on this issue to be shocking and very disappointing. The poll said that most democrats have a positive view of socialism and are about evenly divided as to whether they like socialism or capitalism best. The democrats who were polled by Rasmussen were clueless and that is the biggest problem we have in America today. If they did have a clue, there would be great pushback on our current progressive Obama administration. This poll demonstrates the naivety and lack of understanding regarding what has made our country the great country it is. Republicans are not innocent regarding this issue either.

How about Clinton? She is a staunch progressive. One can decide where she is on the Marxist spectrum. She is careful not to specifically identify herself ideologically like Sanders. At least he is honest. She touted less expensive education and healthcare rather than free education and free healthcare but is now supporting Sander's platform on these issues in an effort to get his followers' votes. She is good at one-liners regarding issues such as improving the middle class and women's rights but there is no substance. It is just empty rhetoric to stir the emotions of those who are listening in hopes of obtaining their votes.

She had no noteworthy accomplishments as a U.S. Senator or as Secretary of State. The Benghazi debacle was a tragic disaster and by all accounts could have been prevented if she had done her job. And, we have to question her integrity after what we have heard about her email scandal and the money that her and Bill's foundation received because of questionable behavior while she was in office. What if she is indicted? That is certainly a possibility. Knowing what I know about the law and knowing what I read and hear about her actions in this matter, I do not know how she cannot be indicted. I would not hold my breath; however, with this administration in charge. I do hear great things about the character of James Comey and that he would not give in to White House pressure and will do the right thing. Unfortunately, he might be overridden.

Well, here is an update that I assume you already know about regarding Hillary being indicted. During a 15-minute news conference, Comey said Clinton was "extremely careless" and "reckless" but her actions were not criminal. He concluded that no "reasonable" prosecutor would take the case to court and no further action is necessary. Attorney General Loretta Lynch confirmed those findings. Here is a curious series of events. On a Monday, Bill Clinton met with Loretta Lynch privately in her airplane in Phoenix for 30 minutes. She said it was a chance meeting and they mostly discussed golf and grandkids. The following weekend, which was the Fourth of July weekend, the FBI interviewed

Hillary Clinton for 31/2 hours. The following Tuesday morning Comey announces that Clinton will not be indicted. Within two hours of the announcement, Clinton and Obama board Air Force One to go to North Carolina for a campaign rally where Obama announces she will be the greatest president in history.

Optics could not be worse. I and most of the political pundits see progressive political corruption at its finest. It is a sign of what is to come if progressive Hillary Clinton is elected president. Take what I have written about Obama's presidency and kick it up a notch. I think Comey; however, might be smarter and more calculating to do the right thing for the long run than the pundits give him credit for. Time will tell. I saw Comey during his hearing before Congress on the matter. He gave an impressive performance to justify his decision and appeared very sincere. It is noteworthy that when Comey was asked at the hearing if the Clinton Foundation was under investigation, he refused to comment one way or the other. What does the general public think about Comey's decision not to indict Clinton? A Rasmussen poll showed 79% of republicans, 63% of independents, and 25% of democrats surveyed disagreed with Comey's decision.

How about Donald Trump. His campaign is one of antagonism toward anyone who opposes him and, unless he is scripted, expounds unrealistic rhetoric toward solving major issues. Many political pundits have said those characteristics are his attraction to his supporters. He shows considerable arrogance and is sensitive to any criticism. I heard him say once he did have advisors he listened to but he mostly listened to himself. After he became the presumptive republican nominee, he has toned down to a degree. He needs the money and the votes the republican establishment can provide and I doubt he can win without both.

There is a big question regarding Trump's true ideology. He is not a true conservative, liberal, or progressive. He seems to support whatever is to his advantage at the time. I am encouraged that he and the Republican Party leadership are communicating to establish common ground they can both support during the general election. That was reflected in his acceptance speech at the Republican National Convention. I heard someone say this was a shotgun wedding. I think that is true. The only question is which one will have the shotgun, if Trump wins the election and becomes president?

Our country is in desperate need of leadership and healing. Trump, at times, seems to realize his shortcomings and changes his demeanor. He sounds especially good when he is reading from a script. I find that encouraging but we are who we are. Unfortunately, we do not know who writes the speeches or how much Trump believes in and supports them. I have great concern that he would be the leader America needs to solve the issues we have discussed in this book and provide the healing our society needs after what Obama and his progressive friends have done to split our country apart. Right now, he is the only hope we conservatives have and I will support that. It will be extremely important with whom he surrounds himself and if he listens to them and is willing to take risks to do the right thing. His vice presidential pick was a good start.

I went through this exercise to make a significant point. Society has chosen Clinton and Trump to be our top candidates for president. I will be the first to admit that we humans are flawed creatures and no one is perfect but I do not understand how our society can pick these two individuals when society is fully aware of what I have described about each of them? They both have extremely high unfavorable ratings in the polls. This paradigm is very important to think about for the next chapter.

Thomas Sowell made the same point recently in a great op-ed on this topic. He said, "We must face the fact that the front-runners in both political parties represent a new low, at a time of domestic polarization and unprecedented nuclear dangers internationally. This year's general election will offer a choice between a thoroughly corrupt liar and an utterly irresponsible egomaniac." He concluded, "More than two centuries ago, Thomas Jefferson said, 'Eternal vigilance is the price of liberty.' If so, can people who cannot be bothered to look up from their electronic devices expect to remain a free people?"

A wining formula for the future of the Republican Party would be: a strong, positive, confident, and convincing approach; having an effective conservative plan; and demonstrating the party is listening to the electorate. Can the Republican Party successfully stand up and be counted as the party for America's future? Here is my friend Thomas Sowell again who said, "The presidential election prospects for the democrats are so bad this year that only the republicans can save them— as republicans have saved them before." I'm with Sowell on that one.

How about the upcoming House and Senate elections? The few congressional men and women who are proven Tea Partiers are the only ones I see in Washington standing up and fighting for traditional American values and the sovereignty of our Constitution. Both the Republican Party and our progressive adversaries label these Tea Partiers as radical troublemakers. I have observed a few other republican women and men in Congress stand up for traditional American values and our Constitution but how far they are willing to go and how hard they will fight is unknown.

The election on November 8, 2016 will be a pivotal date in America's history just like the date 4 months, 4 days, and 240 years before. Are you superstitious? I am not but I was struck by the fact that the months and days are the number 4 and the number of years contains the number 4, so I was compelled to research what I could find about the number 4. I found an interesting website called mysticalnumbers.com. The site said the meaning of the number 4 was in part: the number of stability, order, and completion of justice; the number of Earth and mankind; and the number that symbolizes building a strong foundation. That whet my appetite even more so I looked further. Did you know that James Madison was our 4th president and was the principal author of our Constitution? In 1941, FDR gave his Four Freedoms speech. He said that people "everywhere in the world" should enjoy: 1) Freedom of speech; 2) Freedom of worship; 3) Freedom from want; 4) and Freedom from fear. Make out of the number 4 what you want but in this political climate, I will take what I can get. The next chapter will put this entire book together and I will give my opinion of the future of America.

CHAPTER 13

Do We Win or Lose the Battle?

Do we patriotic Americans who believe in the principles set forth in the Declaration of Independence and the Constitution win or lose the battle to save our country? As I begin to write this chapter, I honestly do not know. It's not that I haven't thought about the answer multiple times. I am conflicted between the reality of what I wrote in the first twelve chapters and my ingrained positive attitude. Therefore, let's journey through this chapter together and see if we come to the same conclusion. If you're superstitious, chapter 13 is not symbolic. It just worked out that way.

Let's start with a quick recap of the historical beginning of the United States. The first humans came to what is now the United States sometime between 13,000 and 40,000 years ago depending upon which theory is accurate. If that time frame sounds very broad, scientists believe with reasonable accuracy that the Earth is around 4.5 billion years old, humans appeared between 2.5 and 3.2 million years ago, and civilized societies are believed to have begun about 11,000 years ago. That makes 13,000 to 40,000 years a very narrow time period for me. The first colonists migrated to the United States in the 1600s. We discussed in chapter 9 that the United States was officially founded 240 years ago and, in comparison, the Roman Empire lasted 1,500 years and Ancient Egypt survived 3,100 years. No civilized society has lasted forever. Do we think we will be the first? What happens to the United States of America if we do not stand up for and preserve our traditional American values and our Constitution? What is the time frame for events in our country's future? Let's try to answer those questions.

Why did the colonists who began settling here in the 1600s and the immigrants who migrated here afterwards come to the United States? If you look back at our history, they came here for three main reasons: to escape religious persecution, escape repression, and for better economic opportunity. It is not a coincidence the Declaration of Independence and the Constitution of the United States were written to provide us with: the unalienable rights of life, liberty, and the pursuit of happiness; religious freedom; and equal opportunity. Why on God's green earth would progressives want to take that away? We have learned throughout the book that progressive Marxist leaders will not lose their freedom and opportunity. They will gain more freedom and opportunity through the power they achieve by taking away freedom and opportunity from the rest of us.

Why would our society allow that to happen? Let's revisit some of the things we have discussed regarding the frailty of our society. I want to point out that I am not suggesting our society is anything less than what have I stated over and over throughout the book and that is our society is the greatest society on Earth. What I am pointing out is that any society, including ours, has its shortcomings. The vital question for this chapter is, "How will our society deal with our shortcomings and what will be the outcome?"

I want to go back to chapter 1 and my childhood. Please bear with me on my references and comparisons if you are too young to remember them. They will still make their point. Let's start with entertainment and its influence on society or is it the other way around and society's influence on entertainment. I can't answer that one. It really doesn't matter. What matters is what it represents about the progression or maybe I should say the regression of morality in our society. I grew up with family television shows like *All in the Family, Father Knows Best, My Little Margie, Ozzie and Harriet, The Donna Reid Show, Leave It To Beaver, and The Brady Bunch* that promoted strong family values. The Bob Hope, Red Skeleton, Andy Griffith, and Dick Van Dyke shows along with shows like *I Love Lucy, Gilligan's Island, Gomer Pile, Beverly Hillbillies, Green Acres, Bewitched,* and *Mr. Ed* provided family humor. The late night crowd watched the more "adult type" shows of Steve Allen, Jack Paar, and Johnny Carson. How about the variety shows of Ed Sullivan and Dinah Shore?

In addition to humor and variety, western and mystery/detective shows dominated prime time television. My favorites were *Gunsmoke, Bonanza, Have Gun Will Travel, The Rifleman, Rawhide, Wagon Train, Dragnet, Perry Mason, Hawaiian Eye, Hawaii Five-O, Route 66, 77 Sunset Strip,* and the *Rockford Files.* Who could forget *Alfred Hitchcock Presents* and *The Twilight Zone?* My Saturday mornings began with watching old movie reruns staring Roy and Dale Rogers, Hopalong Cassidy, and Flash Gordon. I followed that up with *Lassie* and *Sky King.* In the afternoons after school, I watched reruns of Our Gang/ The Little Rascals, The Bowery Boys, and the Three Stooges. When I was real young I watched Howdy Doody, Buffalo Bob and Clarabell in the afternoons. I even ordered one of Howdy Doody's green magnetic plastic applications for my television screen so I could use a crayon to play games with them on the plastic during the show. Extremely crude compared to today.

These television shows and movies all have something in common. They entertained in a nonviolent and nonsexual way, taught strong moral values, and promoted strong family unity. How does that compare to today? I don't have to tell you. My wife and I are certainly not prudes but we find what is happening today in television and film to be repulsive and troubling. There is increasingly more graphic sex, increasingly more graphic violence, and increasingly more so-called reality shows that promote the worst side of human behavior. I watch as little of these shows on television as I can which is getting harder and harder because of their proliferation on cable and satellite television.

My wife and I were channel surfing to find something enjoyable to watch the other night. *National Geographic, The History Channel, The Learning Channel, The Travel Channel, The Food Channel,* and who knows how many other channels all had these so-called reality shows on them. What happened to the programing that these shows were originally developed to show? Reality shows demonstrate our society's fascination with watching fellow humans exhibit anger, act out sexually, demonstrate ignorance, and make fools of themselves. At the sports club gym where I live, most of the exercise machines have televisions built into them. One day, when I was working out on a bike, I was surfing the television channels and came across a survival reality show where the participants were in the nude. Was that a surprise! Their private parts were blurred out on the screen but not for long. I saw it again as I was channel surfing a few weeks later and the show took the blur off of their butts. What's next? There isn't much left. Unbelievable!

How about the evolution of television shows based on the music industry? Is that a drastic evolution! I used to watch *The Mickey Mouse Club, American Bandstand*, and *Soul Train*. They were juvenile compared to *MTV* when *MTV* began telecasting their risqué music videos. I do remember *VH1* being tamer than *MTV*. *MTV* and *VH1* have evolved significantly during the past several years. I thought that *MTV* and *VH1* were still music video television channels. When I researched their websites, I found much more than I expected. *MTV* and *VH1* are now basically vulgar and over the top reality program channels featuring guess what—sex, violence, and troubled relationships. They still have music videos but that is not the main programing they push on their websites. I was very surprised at the programing I found and wondered what impact it has on young people who watch their shows. I knew I was out of the loop on current programing for young people since my children are grown and now have kids of their own but I had no idea how much until I researched *MTV* and *VH1*. I'll sum up my comments on the current state of television by saying that Mr. Rogers went to Heaven and television has gone to hell.

Movies are even worse. When I was growing up, violence in movies consisted of cowboys falling off horses when they were shot, police and crooks grabbing their chest when they were shot, and actors taking swings at each other during fights that were so fake that you could see the swings miss. One time I saw the person that was supposedly hit by a fist fall the wrong way. When it was time for sex, the camera always moved slowly toward the ceiling or the sky. Real early on, television shows even made husbands and wives sleep in twin beds.

Today our movies increasingly have lots of violence with lots of blood and gore and lots of nudity with lots of sex. Who needs to go to Barnes & Noble and spend money to purchase a book on how to improve your sex life? Just go to the movies with all the graphic how-to scenes that are included with the movie. I'm not a prude and

I understand and agree that society's culture and mores should mature over time but there is a point when that maturity crosses the line.

The permissiveness of violence and sex on television and in the movies is growing at an exponential rate. As violence and sex in movies increase, acceptance increases. A Rasmussen poll taken in January of last year said only 39% of those polled now think movies and the movie industry have a negative impact on American society. That is down from 50% in 2013 and 51% in 2011. It was bad enough in 2011 and 2013 and the trend is disturbing. How about the violence and sex contained in video games for children, adolescents, and young adults. I wonder what the polls would show on that?

My wife and I must be "babes in the woods". We were both stunned to learn from the news that a website named Ashley Madison catered to married people who were searching for affairs. It was a news story because the site was hacked and the names of those signed up on the site were released. I don't know how you feel but I say good for whoever hacked the site. It was reported that millions of people were signed up. The reports did say some people had signed up more than once to present different images to attract more people but millions? I Googled the website to see what came up (I sure as heck did not click on the site.) and I was even more shocked to see another website under that one titled Affair Hub that advertised the top 10 dating sites for extramarital affairs. It certainly is dark in my cave but I like it that way. Oh, by the way. One news report said the top city for those who sign up on the site is Washington, D.C. I will let you put your own punch line on that one.

Fox news showed a t-shirt company's video advertisement that used three young girls dressed in "little princess" garb who were reported to be between six and thirteen years old. The girls used the F-bomb over and over in demonstrating anger to advocate feminism and women's equality. They also made several references to their breast and butts in making their points. Where was the total outrage from society on that one? What does it say about their parents? What gave the advertiser confidence they could do that and get away with it, let alone actually sell their t-shirts? Whatever did give them confidence was correct. They got away with it. I do not know about their sales.

What does this discussion on sex and violence have to do with those of us patriots that love traditional American values winning or losing the battle? I'll answer that question with another question. What do the above observations say about the moral evolution of our society during the last fifty years? Think polymorphous perversity. Marcuse and Horkheimer are really grinning in their graves as they see our society slip into this Marxist trap and polymorphous perversity is just the "tip of the iceberg".

I want to share with you a story that I read in our local newspaper that involves the promotion of drugs rather than sex and violence. Toys "R" Us was selling action figures from the television show titled *Breaking Bad*. I had never heard of the show until I read the article. When I looked it up on the Internet, I discovered that it was the highest rated television show of all time by Guinness World Records. That tells you even more about my wife and me and what we watch on television for entertainment.

In case you are like us, the show is about a high school chemistry teacher who started selling drugs with a former student to secure the future financial security of his family after he learned he had terminal lung cancer. The action figures include a sack of cash and a bag of meth. In outrage, after learning Toys "R" Us was selling these toys to kids, a mother who actually lives in our county in Florida began a national campaign to petition Toys "R" Us to stop. She got 8,500 signatures online and Toys "R" Us announced an "indefinite sabbatical". Notice they didn't say they would stop selling them permanently.

The actor who has received several best supporting actor awards for his role in the show launched a counter-petition and got 30,000 signatures in an attempt to pressure Toys "R" Us to resume selling the action figures. The news article said that after he initially contacted Toys "R" Us he got 10,000 more signatures and was trying to get 50,000. He also compared the action figures with Barbie Dolls by asking which is worse? There is something very wrong with this picture when thinking in terms of family values.

We should all be proud of the mother for taking aggressive action to stand up for her traditional American values and doing the right thing for her kids and the kids of others who feel the same. Toys "R"

Us defended their company after they pulled the toys off the shelves. They said the toys had been on shelves in an area for older children that were clearly labeled for children over 15 years of age. Well, good for them! They only glorified illegal drugs to children 15 years of age and older. The star of *Breaking Bad* tweeted, "I'm so mad, I'm burning my Florida Mom action figure in protest." He is the star of the highest rated television show ever and demonstrates that much lack of maturity and disrespect for other's opinions.

Let's talk about electronic communication like Twitter. My green plastic screen application for the *Howdy Doody Show* is laughable today as is the game of *Pong* we talked about in chapter 1. The electronics our kids and we adults have access to today is amazing. It is mind boggling what will be available in the future. Our electronic evolution has provided many positive benefits to society in areas such as medicine, entertainment, education, business applications, home applications, automobile safety, and making life easier.

There is also a downside and it is a big one. We discussed in chapter 7 how electronic innovations in interpersonal communication and entertainment are creating significant problems with the relational fabric that holds society together. The Wall Street Journal has a regular cartoon titled Pepper and Salt. The other day the cartoon depicted two young women sitting on a step talking to each other. One of them said, "He was well-dressed, charming, and witty. And then I heard his ringtone." Another cartoon in my local newspaper is titled Moderately Confused. A young man and a young woman are walking past each other with their heads looking down at their phones. The caption said, "I remember looking up from my phone once…It was horrifying!" A few days later, there was another Moderately Confused cartoon showing two young guys sitting at a table drinking coffee and looking at their phones. One says to the other, "She's just playing hard to retweet". These cartoons make the point and I find it very telling there are so many of these type cartoons today.

I read a troubling newspaper article syndicated by The San Diego Union-Tribune also supporting this point. The headline said, "Bye, cable! Bye, TV?" The article was about kids who were in the 6 to 12-year-old-range who were moving away from television. The article commented that the vast majority of American teens have access to a mobile or smart phone and called them the future "cord cutters" of America because television sets are becoming obsolete to them. A market study by a kids research firm named Smarty Pants said 81% of the kids ages 6 to 8 use YouTube and 71% use Netflix. Seventy-six percent of 9 to12-year-olds use YouTube and Netflix. These kids are using YouTube to replace traditional television and as their go-to search engine.

An executive from another kids marketing research firm named KidSay said in the article that kids using YouTube should be at least 13 years old but 8-year-olds use it all the time. The article pointed out two family video blogs (vblogs) titled *Bratayleys* and *Shaytards* were very popular with pre-teen girls because they are like reality shows on YouTube but are created by real families with their own kids featured prominently in the vblogs. The appeal for young girls was said to be an intimacy and a connection to the families that feels more real to them than what is on television. How about these girls' own families? What family values are these kids learning from these reality shows? Do the kids' real families agree with the two shows' values or do they even care? Does that make a statement about the kids' families if these reality shows are so appealing in intimacy and connection? Do these kids even spend time with their families?

It is hard to get an entire family around a smart phone or (computer) tablet to connect as a family and spend time together like we can with television. These shows on YouTube and Netflix are in addition to all the electronic games and other apps on the phones and tablets to which the kids are so addicted. You can buy very sophisticated interactive electronic games to play with family and friends but these are not the games to which kids are addicted. I found it interesting there are at least two companies dedicated to this kind of market research for young kids. That gives a hint as to where this is all going.

I shared this article with one of my daughters who has an 11-year-old girl and 12-year-old boy. I learned my grandkids watch YouTube and Netflix but the shows they watch are monitored and the time they spend on their smart phones and tablets is restricted. Think about how you communicate with your family, friends, and others now as opposed to only a few years ago. What has emails, texting, Facebook, and tweeting done to your interpersonal face-to-face interactions or real-time voice-to-voice communication? How has it affected your relationship with family and friends? Are the benefits worth the down side?

I am in no way suggesting we put the kibosh on electronic technology and its incredible potential for society. I am saying; however, there are unintended consequences that are realistically impossible to avoid and have significant bearing on this chapter's conclusion. As this technology grows, it puts increasing strain on our interpersonal relationships with our families and our friends. In my leadership book, I made a case for my strong belief that interpersonal relationships are the most important aspect of one's life. Positive interpersonal relationships promote good mental health, personal happiness, and personal prosperity. Important relationships for me in rank order are my family, my friends, and my fellow humans.

Being a native Kentuckian, I love horse racing. You may or may not know who Bob Baffert is. He is a famous horse trainer and was the trainer of American Pharoah, the horse that won the Triple Crown last year. It was the first time a horse has won the Triple Crown in 37 years. I watched his television interview after the race. He was asked what he was thinking about. He said, "It's very emotional. I'm thinking about my parents. I wish they were alive to see this. They were with me today. I was talking to them the whole time." Baffert is in front of millions of people around the world and could have given a multitude of answers but he is thinking of his parents who are deceased. What a testimonial to family relations and their importance. I found another quote by Bruce Springsteen regarding his parents. He said, "There is not a note that I play on stage that can't be traced back to my mother and father." Both of these quotes support my On Golden Pond Syndrome theory.

Many people would add pets to their list of relationships. My wife and I would too but our pet went to "doggie heaven" a few years ago. Actually, we still miss him and think about him often after almost ten years. Without these relationships, life would be rather boring and meaningless unless your life is all about you and what a waste of a life, if yours is only about you.

I am also compelled to add one additional factor to my list of what is most important in our lives. It is the vast natural habitat on our incredibly beautiful planet God has given us to sustain us and enjoy. After all, if you believe in evolution and natural selection as I do, that is where we humans came from. It would make sense that we would be innately bonded to it. Some people would say that you couldn't believe in both God and evolution. Why not? Just because I don't believe in the "literal interpretation" of the Bible, it doesn't mean that I don't believe the Bible is the Book of God and reasonably reflects biblical history and Judeo-Christian theology. Believing the Bible is the book of God also doesn't mean that I believe God is a physical entity who lives in a physical place called Heaven rather than being the spirit of Judeo-Christian Theology that lives in our hearts. The Bible does what it does in a less than perfect way. After all, we imperfect humans wrote it. But that does not mean the Bible isn't the most perfect standard we have on Earth by which to live our lives.

My wife and I have friends who send us numerous emails that float around on the Internet. Many of these emails emphasize the importance of and graphically show the power of human relationships, our fascination with and love of animals, and the natural beauty of the Earth. Not only are these relationships always connected in these emails, they are often cloaked in Christianity. These emails demonstrate the power of positive human association and bonding and our connection to nature. We don't need a progressive Marxist vision of human interaction to provide its version of justice, fairness, and opportunity. We need each other bonded by positive interpersonal relationships, a set of workable societal mores (traditional American values and laws) that provide justice and fairness, and the personal opportunity provided by our wonderful Constitution and articulated by our Declaration of Independence. As a matter of clarification, I said we don't need a progressive Marxist vision rhetorically as it is the antithesis of justice, fairness, and opportunity.

Our progressive friends with their Marxist vision for society would like nothing better than to break the bonds of those interpersonal relationships and replace our traditional American values and our Constitution with their self-serving Marxist propaganda and principles. The more we decrease our interpersonal relationships, the easier we are to control and manipulate. Imagine changing our current laws to new laws based upon the Marxist political correctness (Critical Theory) movement we are currently being inundated with. Couple those new laws with elitist progressive Marxist leaders who quietly and often secretly changing laws and regulations to take total control of governing our country. Then, envision what our society would be like.

The book, *Animal Farm*, I mentioned in chapter 5 is a great analogy to read on this topic. It extols the ideal that everyone being equal is a farce and does not work. Orwell actually supported socialism when he wrote the book and wrote it to expound on the failure of communism in Russia. The story goes like this. The farm animals chase the farm owner off the farm at the encouragement of one of the pigs based upon a philosophical doctrine of Animalism (an allegoric reference to communism) developed by the pigs. That doctrine supposedly rids them of tyranny and sets them free. They name the farm Animal Farm. The animals are now all equal (Marxist theory) and everyone is happy and prosperous until one of the pigs nefariously rises up to lead the farm in a very devious and dishonest way. The pig becomes a dictator and all of his fellow pigs get special privileges. As the pigs take total control of the farm and increasingly become more oppressive, the rest of the animals are controlled in the same manor or worse than they were before the farmer was chased away.

In the beginning, when the animals took over, the Animalism doctrine provided Seven Commandments that were written on the wall in a big barn. They were as follows:

1. Whatever goes upon two legs is an enemy.
2. Whatever goes upon four legs, or has wings, is a friend.
3. No animal shall wear clothes.
4. No animal shall sleep in a bed.
5. No animal shall drink alcohol.
6. No animal shall kill any other animal.
7. All animals are equal.

The animals added the adage "Four legs good, two legs bad" to the Commandments. After the pigs took control of the farm they secretly changed some of the Commandments to circumvent accusations by the other animals that the pigs were breaking them. The pigs changed the following Commandments:

4. No animal shall sleep in a bed "with sheets".
5. No animal shall drink alcohol "to excess".
6. No animal shall kill any other animal "without cause".

Eventually, all the Commandments were replaced with the adages "All animals are equal, but some are more equal than others" and "Four legs are good, two legs better". The latter adage was changed as the pigs became more human in their actions.

Does this sound familiar? *Animal Farm* was published the year I was born in 1945 but articulates very well what is happening in America today. It is taking place right before our very eyes as the progressive movement unfolds. Progressives tout all the great changes and improvements they have made and are going to make to greatly benefit society and then we wake up and find out we are America in Marxland. Why? The progressives say people in general need public and private organizations (like the federal government) to help us make decisions since we are prone to make poor choices and look back in bafflement. One thing we can always count on is anything the progressives do "for us" is actually "for them" to gain power and control and live the life they wish to live at our expense. Just like the pigs in Animal Farm.

While I was researching this chapter, I ran across a term that is very appropriate to describe the kind of leadership our founding fathers envisioned for America. That term is "moral leadership". Although it is a widely used term, I found a great definition on the website of the Global Ethics Network. Andrew Carnegie founded the Global Ethics Network approximately 100 years ago. The definition I found was in a 2013 blog written by a young female high school teacher in Bhutan. Yes, Bhutan. Her definition parallels the definition of organizational leadership that I developed for my last book. She said:

> Moral leadership is based upon: leading by example and persuading others; developing the capabilities of others; having personal integrity and being trusted; being driven by core ideas such as justice; and having a deep sense of ethics. Moral leaders are motivated by a higher purpose. They are visionary and effect positive change. They have a highly developed sense of emotional intelligence and strong social skills to overcome obstacles, successfully negotiate, navigate diversity, and establish unity. Moral leaders are the conscious and moral compass of those they lead and the glue that holds a moral society together.

This is an incredible definition of leadership. The teacher ended her blog by saying, "We are living through tough times, both socially and economically. The world around us is rapidly evolving and transforming. We need many more leaders who will guide us through the maze of change into the world of tomorrow that is better than today. And the leader we love to have is of course a Moral Leader." Sounds like she is referring to America. Does the paradigm I discussed in the last chapter regarding the top two presidential candidates who have been picked by our society fit the paradigm of moral leadership? What does that say about our future?

Now, I'll be the first to admit that no human on Earth, including a moral leader, is a perfect creature but some humans are closer to being perfect than others. What happens to our society if we began to loose our moral leadership? Society begins to break apart. What happens, if at the same time, Judeo-Christian based interpersonal relationships and bonding with our physical environment is severely diminished? Life, as we now know it, becomes increasingly less meaningful and we become less motivated to make society work for us and for those around us. We become more inwardly focused in our thoughts and emotions and become self-indulging, which increasingly gives the progressives opportunity for control and manipulation.

When we humans no longer have our intrinsic relational connections we are susceptible to a new paradigm to fill that void. We are susceptible to being manipulated and brainwashed and can become controlled as in Orwell's *1984*. I expressed in chapter 5 that when we lose personal values that are important to us, a significant emotional void results in our lives and we eventually accept a replacement to fill that void even though it may be less than or in conflict with what we originally had. I will say again, we are "very fragile creatures" when it comes to our emotions and mental well-being.

Since progressive Obama has been president, we have experienced significant erosion of moral leadership within our society. If another progressive such as Hillary Clinton succeeds Obama as president, it is going to get much worse at a faster pace as the progressives eliminate more and more obstacles to that moral erosion.

I want to clarify what I said regarding our bonding with the environment being diminished or taken away. How can that be? Our progressive friends portray to care so much about environmental preservation. That is a ruse. The radical environmental groups portray to care because it gives them a forum to act out their radical mental being. If it weren't the environment, they would find some other cause. The progressive politicians express their support for the environment because it gives them an ideological platform and a means to increase their control over us through significant regulation and environmental control. It also is very financially lucrative for some politicians and others as we discussed in chapter 8. Diabolical, isn't it? I have never heard a progressive relate the power of the environment in relation to Christianity and humanity.

Our traditional American culture is under siege by radical progressives and their Marxist based political correctness. Critical Theory works. As a result, our traditional American society is breaking apart and a Marxist based society is creeping in to fill the void with increasing speed. Actually, it would be more correct to say Marxism is being rammed in. This is in spite of Constitutional mandates and current laws contrary to what is happening. Progressive politicians in control pick and chose the laws they ignore and the ones they enforce to speed the way. They would make Alinsky proud. We know that Horkheimer and Marcuse are grinning big.

This new Marxist cultural paradigm is greatly enhanced by the unintended consequences of an electronic age out of control and the diminishing of interpersonal relationships including the family unit. These two forces are working in tandem today and will become stronger in the future as the electronic age increases in dominance over our lives.

As society becomes more technologically advanced, another unintended consequence involves medical science. We read on a regular basis about new ways of non-traditional conception and the increasing ability to do human genetic engineering. This new technology runs the gambit from promising to the absurd. Here is an example of the absurd. I read a syndicated newspaper article by the Los Angeles Times in August 2014 that reported findings in a journal titled Nature. The journal proposed that bad memories in mice could be modified into positive memories. They supposedly did this by breaking the memories of mice into components and "rewiring the connections" through manipulation of the mice's neurons. They used a blue light during positive experiences for the mice and then returned the mice to their previous bad situations and used the blue light again. The blue light manipulated them to experience good feelings, which overrode their bad memories. This gives new meaning to the "blue light special".

I guess humans are next. Actually, it sounds like we're already there. There was an interview in the article regarding this topic with a professor at the Massachusetts Institute of Technology. The professor said one might think of memory as being something that is fixed but that is far from reality. He said it is a creative process that sometimes leads to an entirely false memory. He gave the example that a family vacation in the Bahamas would be a very positive memory unless there was a swimming accident, which could suddenly make that happy time seem like a very negative one. He said our memory is malleable and feelings associated with a positive or negative memory isn't just stored in one place in our brain. He went on to explain in very medical terms where our memories are stored.

The professor didn't elaborate on his analogy but I assume he was suggesting that we humans could have our memories changed to our liking. I thought we humans were an amalgamation of the sum total of our past life. How about having our memories changed to someone else's liking? Sounds like new-fashioned-old-fashioned brain washing to me. It reminds me of those robotic-like humans marching expressionless in unison in Orwell's *1984*.

Who knows where all the new technology and science will take our society but I can assure you as the progressive movement continues to take hold, it will have a significant negative effect on traditional family values and our current way of life. We have discussed throughout the book that Marxist based societies become apathetic to values like the ones that have made our country great and the result is domination by self-serving autocratic leaders. It's like these autocratic leaders are the professors and scientists; the rest of us are their experimental laboratory. All progressive leaders may not be as evil as Stalin, Lenin, Mao, Pol Pot, Castro, and Chávez but the end result is always some degree of evil. A Marxist society is anything but a "just and prosperous society for all". It is a self-serving progressive leader's "dream come true".

The evolution of society is unavoidable. It is the way humanity evolves as society matures intellectually, emotionally, and technologically. If society did not evolve, we would still be living in caves. The evolution of society becomes a problem when it crosses the boundaries necessary to maintain justice, fairness, and equal opportunity for all of its members. It takes principled cultural norms, just laws, objective political ideology, and moral leadership to create and maintain these desired boundaries to prevent self-destruction. I have said my favorite story in this regard is the story of Moses being away for forty days and forty nights from the Israelites he was leading to the Promised Land. When he came down from the mountain with the Ten Commandments, he found the people he freed from tyrannical Egyptian rule and unimaginable hardships worshiping a golden idol and engaging in sin and gluttony.

The human memory is very short when it comes to remembering how we got to where we are and how to prevent "backsliding" as in the Baptist church. Human nature is an interesting phenomenon. It seems all of humanity has the innate desire to practice the sin and gluttony (polymorphous perversity) demonstrated by the Israelites and to forget how we obtained our successes in life. I found a great quote on this topic from Milton Freedman. He said, "I want people to take thought about their condition and to recognize that the maintenance of a free society is a very difficult and complicated thing and it requires a self-denying ordnance of the most extreme kind." Freedman has always been one of my favorite economists and now even more so since he appears to be an astute philosopher as well. Is it possible for any society to avoid self-destruction over time? That is the question for this final chapter.

In doing my research on the topic of societal evolution, I routinely ran into Alexis de Tocqueville and his book *Democracy in America*. Tocqueville felt American democracy had actually evolved over a period of 700 years as the way of the future for society and resulted from people searching for equality and liberty to replace feudal traditions. Frederick Jackson Turner attributed America's success in achieving American exceptionalism to our society's "pioneer spirit". Was Tocqueville wrong about American democracy and have we lost that pioneer spirit? Let's take a look.

I found an interesting article on Tocqueville's book written by Arthur Milikh for The Daily Signal in July 2015. Here is a synopsis with my personal iteration. Tocqueville felt the power of the majority could be the downfall of American society, although he believed America could overcome such obstacles for long-term success. His concern regarding the power of the majority was based upon our government being a democratic republic and the majority could use their voting power to tyrannize unpopular minorities and marginal individuals including ethnic, religious, political, and racial groups. He said this could be done through "soft despotism", which is an illusion that the minority is in control when they actually have very little influence over the government and are controlled in an oppressive way that is not obvious to the people.

Despots (those who have absolute power in a cruel and oppressive way) tyrannized in the past through "blood and iron" but modern democratic despotism does not act in that manner. Tocqueville said, "It leaves the body and goes straight for the soul". The majority reaches into citizens' minds and hearts, which break the citizens' will to resist, to question authority, and to think for themselves. The majority's moral power makes citizens internally ashamed to contradict it and, in effect, silences them. This silencing culminates in a secession of thinking. Tocqueville feared the majority's tastes and opinions could occupy all sentiment and thought of society and this would weaken and isolate individuals.

The author of the article said something very profound. He said, "Equality can go along with freedom, but it can even more easily go along with despotism. In fact, much of the world did go in the direction of democratic despotism—wherein the great mass of citizens is indeed equal, save for a ruling elite, which governs them." He gave the example of North Korea. That is a very profound and disturbing thought. Tocqueville believed this type of majority influence on the mind weakens and isolates individuals and in turn would create fertile ground for a new type of oppression that "will resemble nothing that has preceded it in the world".

Tocqueville foresaw an "immense tutelary (protector or guardian) power" which would degrade citizens rather than destroy their bodies and over time the government would take away the citizens' free will and their capacity to think and act. This would reduce society to "a herd of timid and industrious animals of which the government is the shepherd". He posed a solution in that he said those who read his book would come to understand that the defects of modern democracy require great attention and careful management. I would call it moral leadership. Tocqueville specifically hoped American society would strive "to preserve for the individuals the little independence, force, and originality" that remains to the individual as the majority takes hold of the power. He also said our lawmakers need to focus on policies that make individuals stronger, more independent, more able to resist tyranny of the majority, and more able to resist the tyranny of a constantly growing government. Tocqueville wanted us to, "... remember constantly that a nation cannot remain strong when each man in it is individually weak, and that neither social forms nor political schemes have yet been found that can make a people energetic by composing it of pusillanimous (showing a lack of courage or determination) and soft citizens."

Tocqueville's predictions and my own analysis of what is happening today in our country are running parallel except for two differences, albeit significant differences. Tocqueville predicted it would be the majority dominating society when in reality it is the minority progressives who are doing so. The second difference is that he predicted it would be the moral power of the majority that would "shame" the minority to be subservient to the majority when in reality it is the unceasing pounding of the majority by the progressive minority that is beating the majority into submission through government control and political correctness using intimidation, legal action, and shame. Tocqueville wrote his book in 1835 and died in 1859, so he never knew about Critical Theory.

Here is an outlandish example of progressive ideology tyrannizing society. A couple of years ago, a popular television host on MSNBC, Melissa Harris-Perry, did a commercial for the networks' new slogan "Lean Forward". She said, "We have never invested as much in public education as we should have because we've always had a private notion of children. Your kid is yours and totally your responsibility. We haven't had a very collective notion of these are our children. So part of it is we have to break through our kind of private idea that kids belong to their parents, or kids belong to their families, and recognize that kids belong to whole communities." You may remember the firestorm from conservatives when this happened. Not so much from the progressives. In fact, the host received a lot of support from progressives and I seriously doubt she said this on her own without the endorsement of the MSNBC network.

This progressive concept of kids belonging to the community reminds me of the actions by the states of Washington and Oregon usurping parental authority we discussed in chapter 10. This progressive concept is also supported by the increasing intrusion on traditional family prerogatives we discussed regarding political correctness. The recent federal guidelines and accompanying threats by the federal government regarding transgender identity and bathroom rules is another example.

Remember from chapter 7 the word "Forward" has long ties to Marxism and radicalization? It means to "move forward" past capitalism toward socialism, communism, and other radical political ideology. Does this phrase look familiar? We used to see it regularly on podiums when our own president Obama was speaking. That is shocking to me but not really. Interestingly, I heard Clinton use the term at the end of one of her campaign speeches recently.

I debated whether or not to put the next text in the book because I could not confirm its authenticity. There were several authors given credit including Tocqueville. Alexander Frasier Tytler (1747-1883) is the one most often given credit. He was a Scottish advocate, judge, writer, and a professor of universal history and Greek and Roman antiquities at the University of Edinburgh. With his background, he is the most likely person to have written it. That is, if it was written by only one person. I was so compelled by what it says; the author didn't matter to me. It articulated my feelings and beliefs succinctly and completely. It was supposedly written in 1887 and is about the fall of the Athenian Republic some 2,000 years earlier. The Athenian Republic was the first known democracy in the world.

The text is as follows:

> A democracy is always temporary in nature; it simply cannot exist as a permanent form of government. A democracy will continue to exist up until the time that voters discover that they can vote themselves generous gifts from the public treasury. From that moment on, the majority always votes for the candidates who promise the most benefits from the public treasury, with the result that every democracy will finally collapse over loose fiscal policy always followed by a dictatorship. The average age of the world's greatest civilizations from the beginning of history has been about 200 years. During those 200 years, those nations always progressed through the following sequence: from bondage to spiritual faith; from spiritual faith to great courage; from courage to liberty; from liberty to abundance; from abundance to apathy; from apathy to dependence; and from dependence to bondage.

I hope that text grabbed you as hard as it did me. It is so powerful. Remember the quote by H. L. Mencken in chapter 7? His quote concluded by saying, "On some great and glorious day, the plain folks of the land will reach their hearts desire at last and the White House will be occupied by a downright fool and complete narcissistic moron." I would add "progressive Marxist" to Mencken's list of personal adjectives.

I want to go back to Tocqueville and discuss the importance of Christianity. The Daily Signal published a story in April 2016 regarding Tocqueville and Christianity written by Carson Holloway. Holloway commented that Tocqueville said: 1) American democracy owes its origin and preservation to Christianity; 2) religion should be considered the first of America's political institutions; 3) the spirit of Christianity helped American democracy continue to flourish after it had been established; and 4) political freedom requires unshakable moral foundation that only religion can supply. Holloway said democracy could also succumb to despotism of the government when the people are so committed to the pursuit of their own private interests that they neglect the active participation necessary to the preservation of their liberty. Holloway remarked that Tocqueville argued Christianity also supports American democracy by "countering these dangerous tendencies".

Cal Thomas wrote an op-ed in April on this topic as well. He said the Berna (research) Group reported the percentage of Americans who are "post Christian" increased from 37% in 2013 to 44% in 2015. Thomas also quoted a May 2015 Pew Research Center study that said the percentage of Americans who are religiously unaffiliated (atheist, agnostic, or nothing in particular) has jumped from 16.1% to 22.8%. Pew Research commented this group was "comparatively young and getting younger". Thomas said, "Before secularists start rejoicing they should consider what happens to nations that abandon faith, or transfer faith to political leaders whose unwillingness to solve problems is behind much of the anger and frustration of both parties." Boy, does this hit home?

I am a firm supporter regarding separation of church and state as articulated in chapter 10, which says the government should not establish a religion, prefer one religion over another, or prevent the free exercise of religion. I also firmly believe that Christianity should not be erased from our country's founding principles and should define the moral foundation of our society. We are in dire danger of losing that Judeo-Christian influence which is critical in fending off Critical Theory and Marxist rule.

Let's review again who are making the Marxist movement a reality in America. They are socialists, communists, and other Marxist theory advocates. They are fascists, anarchists, and other troubled wackos who are full of hate and America is a convenient object. They are fellow citizens, friends, neighbors, teachers, and even family members who have been indoctrinated into a Marxist based philosophy without even knowing it. They are well-meaning and not so well-meaning politicians that govern our daily life and our future as well as the life and future of our children, grandchildren, and subsequent generations. They are organizations portraying to do good things for society that are actually progressive organizations with hidden agendas to implement their Marxist ideology as the dominant ideology in our society. And finally, they are us when we do not stand up to this onslaught and fight for what we believe in. The more I do research and the more I personally observe what is happening, the more I realize how pervasive the progressive movement is and continually gaining strength. It is very subtle in many cases and not so subtle in other cases but it is there moving very methodically throughout our society on a consistent and persistent basis.

Go on websites such as The Center for American Progress or Media Matters for America and read their progressive anti-American propaganda. These are only two of a multitude of progressive organizations and progressive news sites that can be found on the Internet. It is also easy to find websites on the Internet that are U.S. based socialist and communist organizations. I find it interesting how interconnected many of these organizations are with common progressive undertakings and common board members as we learned in chapter 5.

It is often the case that demonstrators are not really demonstrating for the cause they say they are. The vast majority of demonstrations are a vehicle for troubled radicals to push their anti-American philosophy and act out their personal issues. For example, protesters at Occupy Wall Street were brandishing signs and posters that had communistic symbols and the name of a communist organization on them. Ferguson and Baltimore are also examples. Progressive organizations and progressive individuals support many of these groups in various ways.

Often there are many well-meaning people who get caught up in radical progressive organizations and radical demonstrations and are taken advantage of by progressive radicals for their nefarious purposes. I recently saw a Haggar The Horrible cartoon that makes this point. In the first picture, there were six people going down a path carrying signs. Three signs read "Save the Dragons". The other three signs said "Dragons Forever", "I Love Dragons", and "Dragons are Good". Lucky Eddie (Haggar's friend) said, "Yesss!" Hagar responded, "Do you really think the demonstration will save the dragons?" Lucky Eddie responds, "If they save one dragon, then it's worth it!" The last picture in the cartoon shows all six signs lying on the ground and all the people are missing. The dragon is walking away and goes "Urp!" Haggar says, "Looks like they saved one dragon from hunger!" I am sure the dragon was a progressive Marxist and the people carrying the signs were well-meaning classic liberals and others being led down the path to destruction.

I asked in chapter 4, "Where is the House Un-American Activities Committee?" It disbanded in 1975 because some in Washington thought the committee was "un-American". What??? It wasn't; however, the only congressional committee to investigate political activities against our country. There were several during earlier years. Where are they today? Good question but a better question is "why is there not one"? There are too many progressives in Washington who do not believe in what the Declaration of Independence and the Constitution stand for and do not believe in our traditional American values. Classic liberal politicians are in the category of believers but are becoming smaller in number. Republican politicians are in absentia except for a few.

There is no effective national movement today in or out of government to protect and save our American way of life. The only effective national movement is to change it and it is shockingly pervasive and successful. I see progressives in positions of power and influence in government and private sectors increasingly shutting down those who disagree with them by using the legal and regulatory system and public scorn. Non-conservative news sources are increasingly distorting the news to support the progressive movement.

Well, Obama will be gone after 2016 and we can take our country back. We won't have to worry about this radical progressive "Forward" ideology in Washington next term—right? If Hillary is elected president, it would be like Obama gone underground. Remember, they both subscribe heavily to Alinsky's radical teachings and Clinton wrote her college thesis on Alinsky. She reportedly conversed with Alinsky on several occasions. The Forward signs would not be visible on Clinton's podiums but I guarantee you they would be there. According to the research I have done involving Clinton, she embraces a Marxist based ideology and is very similar in ideology as Obama. She is just much more subtle with it. Any future democratic president would continue to take us down the progressive Marxist road. The only variable is the speed and depth it will occur and that depends upon the individual.

How could a progressive democrat possibly have a chance at becoming president against a republican conservative candidate? Americans are fed-up with the government's approach to national security, the economy, and the country's mood in general under current democratic leadership. Americans are fed-up with being fed-up. How can a republican lose? Remember what Sowell said, "The presidential election prospects for the democrats are so bad this year that only the republicans can save them—as republicans have saved them before."

Trump is the presumptive republican nominee and he has been non-committal in his ideology. Even though there are efforts to bring Trump and the republican establishment together ideologically, there is a likelihood he would not strongly adhere to the conservative principles that we need to reignite our traditional American values, the Constitution, and American exceptionalism. Any republican president would have a monumental task to undo the damage the progressives have done to our country and we have already discussed the weakness of republican politicians and the Republican Party to provide the leadership and grit needed to accomplish that task

What are the chances to get a republican elected president in 2016 and keep the majority in the House and Senate? First, let's take a look at what Sowell is talking about. There was no way Obama could get re-elected in the last presidential election. No incumbent in our history had ever been re-elected with the economy as stagnant and the national debt as high as it was. Well, he did get elected. How? The Democrats "changed the game". They took the narrative away from the economy and the national debt by creating bogus and ridiculous issues like the republican's war on women campaign. Hard to believe but it worked. It was genius.

The republicans have no formal political platform. Maybe they will forge one in their discussions with Trump. If no one knows what republicans stand for, how can anyone get excited about voting for a republican unless he or she is a dyed in the wool republican that will vote only for republicans and go vote no matter what? Another important issue is the republicans' inability to stand up to progressive aggression. This is reflected by Mitt Romney's lackluster personal performance in light of the onslaught against him by the progressives. Romney said the right things and would have made a great president in my opinion but he could not sell himself or effectively defend himself from progressive political attacks. Because of these factors, many conservatives stayed home. Liberals and moderates were more motivated to go to the polls and the fabricated democratic messaging appealed to moderates more than the republican messaging or I should say the republican "lack of messaging".

According to The Wall Street Journal, the following are the statistical differences in voter turnout between the 2010 midterm election when republicans won back the House and the 2012 presidential election: white voters down 5%, black voters up 2%, and Hispanic voters up 2%; young voters 18 to 29 years old up 7% and voters 65 and older down 5%; liberal voters up 5%, moderate voters up 3%, and conservative voters down a whopping 7%. The progressives got their base out to vote much more effectively than republicans. They had a "well oiled machine" and more aggressive enthusiasm to win. I keep hearing that Trump does not have a strong political machine to get out the votes. I believe there was significant democratic voter fraud as well in 2012, which is unethical and illegal. But, those votes count the same as legal votes in the final count if you don't get caught.

The Brookings Institute analyzed the 2012 election in conjunction with the demographic changes taking place in America and came up with the following conclusion. They said voter turnout will be less important for democratic victories in the future as long as they maintain their strong voting margins among minorities because American demographics are changing in their favor. I have made this point over and over in the book. They said republicans cannot count on the white vote to win presidential elections in the future and must begin to attract the minority vote. The Institute concluded that "demography is becoming destiny" in national elections. Their conclusion supports why the progressives are so aggressive in entitlement programs and in legal and illegal immigration.

Democrats are again promoting a republican war on women for the 2016 election. They are also saying republicans do not support the middle class and income equality, which is Marxist based BS. Job growth and the economy are paramount among Americans and vacillates with national security as the number one issue depending up what is going on in the world and at home at a specific time. Democrats are not talking about these three top issues with voters because they have not responsibly addressed them during the last 7 years. Amazingly, republicans are not holding the democrats accountable nor offering any meaningful resolution. The democrats were smart enough to change the game in 2012 while the republicans stood by and let them do it and it looks like the same thing is happening again for 2016.

Let's look at voter data from a different standpoint. Research by Gallup and the Pew Research Center indicates that moderate democrats are becoming more liberal and many republicans are becoming conservative independents. Those that still claim to be republican are more conservative than conservative independents. The bottom line is that the number of conservatives is roughly the same as in recent years while the number of liberals moving left of center in the Democratic Party is increasing and creating less diversity within the party. This phenomenon is the central factor in the political polarization between democrats and republicans and is solidifying the Democratic Party as the Progressive Party. The moderates on both sides are becoming fewer and fewer. Surprisingly, Gallup said that conservatives still outnumber liberals by 38% to 23% among voters.

If the majority of voters still claim to be conservative, where were they during the last election? Conservatives showed up better in the 2014 election than in past elections but still only about 40% of eligible conservatives voted. I need someone to explain this to me. Our country is politically "going to hell in a hand basket" which has an enormous direct negative impact on all conservatives but only 40% show up to vote to stop it. I also need to ask about classic liberals. Where are you? It seems that people in our society are more interested and involved in voting for contestants on television talent shows than voting for people in political elections to secure their own future. The voting apathy in our society is astounding but fits the narrative I presented earlier in the chapter. It's too late to wake up after you get hit in the head with a baseball bat or I should say a progressive Marxist bat.

Now, back to the earlier question regarding the possibility of a progressive democrat having a chance at becoming president against a republican conservative candidate? If the Democratic Party did it in the last presidential election, they can do it again unless the Republican Party can learn to how to win elections. The last chapter was devoted to effective conservative strategy. Can the Republican Party pull it off? I don't know, but from what I have seen so far for 2016, it is more of the same old loosing strategy. You would think republicans would have learned from the last presidential election and the 2014 mid-term election. The only unknown is the effect that Trump's non-traditional campaign style will affect the election but that is a double-edged sword. Many conservatives are turned off by Trump's style and say they will not vote. At least the Republican Party is trying to resolve this issue. The question remains as to how successful the party will be in doing that and what else they do to build a winning ticket.

Based upon the mood of the country, the republicans should have walked away with the 2014 mid-term congressional election. They didn't. They won but it was close. Again, they did not have a platform or enthusiastically counter the democratic agenda. Charles Krauthhammer said in an op-ed, "Memo to the GOP. You had a great night on Tuesday. But remember. You didn't win it. The Democrats lost it." He and Sowell are right about both elections. The republicans ran on Obama's very low standing with voters and tied their political opponents to Obama. That was it. That is no way to win an election unless you get lucky and fortunately the republicans did. You have to let people know what you stand for and than stand up and fight for what you believe. Negative campaigns are successful but they can only go so far. The republicans were lucky that Obama's record was so bad and people were upset about it. You can't always count on your competition handing it to you on a silver platter.

In order to win, a candidate usually has to promote a compelling message like "we are five days away from fundamentally transforming the United States of America". The majority of voting Americans voted for Obama in his first presidential election and had no real idea of what he meant. If they had, he would have lost big time. They just knew he had a vision and the conviction to carry out that vision and "assumed" it would be a change for their own good. They blindly followed him because they read into what he said what they wanted to hear. I see the same phenomenon during this election with Trump but Trump is appealing to a much smaller group of voters because his demeanor and rhetoric has also turned off many voters. Even with the great majority of Americans not happy with the current progressive democratic presidency, it is anything but assured to put a republican in the White House in 2016.

Cal Thomas nailed it recently. He said, "Two forces are at work undermining our foundations. One is apathy and the other is a determined assault on the beliefs, traditions, practices, and faith that once characterized America. Either one causes harm enough but when both are in play, we become like a boxer who is pummeled unconscious by a relentless opponent." Thomas continued, "The most effective response to people operating this cultural and political wrecking ball is to turn the tables. ... Traditionalists don't have to play defense. They have only to remind Americans of the mess the secular progressives have made. Having been handed by the 'greatest generation' a nation with numerous opportunities and a bright future, the Baby Boomers and their progeny set about destroying it on the alter of self-indulgence. ... 'We the people' remain the most powerful force among us. ... Fear of losing what we have should motivate traditionalists to begin fighting back against an anti-American tide that is undermining truths once considered self-evident. But they must first win the argument before wining the next election."

Maybe there is hope for our country if we can wait four more years. At last year's MTV Video Music Awards (Remember my comments regarding MTV.), entertainer Kanye West announced on stage after an 8-minute diatribe that he was going to run for president in 2020. The young crowd cheered loudly! He said he had been smoking pot, so maybe he was just kidding. The MTV Video Music Awards Show highlighted sex and drugs so maybe a president West could make our country "feel good" again. Actually, maybe not! I found what I saw to be vulgar. No, I did not watch the show. I saw video clips on television and Internet news. Watching those clips reminded me of how the office of the President of the United States has lost such esteem and respect under Obama. Where is the respect, awe, and the high esteem that the job commanded in the past? More importantly, what were those young people thinking? The problem is they're not.

If republicans win the presidency and keep the House and Senate in 2016, we can take back our country and save America from the progressive Marxist movement that is changing the way we live—right? Let's answer that question by summarizing what I have written about the current state of our country.

We have discussed the general attitudes and socio-economic practices of Gen Xers and Millennials who are the "future of America". The majority of them are knowingly or unknowingly in the progressive camp. There has been a major issue recently regarding the news sources Millennials and GenXers use for their political and government news. Pew Research determined 61% of Millennials and 51% of Gen Xers obtain political and government news from Facebook. Many participants in the study use multiple sources rather than a single source. Forty-four percent of Millennials also obtain political and government news from CNN, 37% from local television, 33% from Google news, and 30% from Fox News. In addition to Facebook, 46% of Gen Xers obtain political and government news from local television, 45% from CNN, and 36% from Fox News. For comparison, only 39% of Baby Boomers use Facebook, 60% use local television, 47% use Fox, and 47% use NBC. The survey showed that young people trust liberal news sources more than they do conservative news sources. I think that is reflective of their liberal bias.

Facebook was heavily criticized because some ex-employees said news was purposefully heavily skewed to liberal thought. Obviously,

Facebook denied it. I saw Elliot Zuckerberg, founder of Facebook, talking on television before this news broke and his comments were very liberal. I will give Zuckerberg credit for meeting with conservative news pundits to discuss the issue after his company was criticized. There are two important facts to be taken from this topic. First, the amount of news young people are obtaining from the Internet is significant and increasing. Second, the amount of progressive liberal ideology our young people are being inundated with is also significant and increasing.

Merriam-Webster defines a patriot as, "A person who loves and strongly supports or fights for his or her country." The majority of our young people have not developed into American patriots. I don't see the attitudes of these young people changing in the future, even as they mature, unless some dramatic attitude-altering event occurs. That is highly improbable. The event would need to be painful enough to generate an appreciation of what has made America great and also the appreciation of the materialistic and non-materialistic facets of life they now they take for granted.

A 2014 op-ed by Cal Thomas chastised our society for allowing this disconnect to happen and also used the same argument to give insight into why some of our young people have abandoned our country to fight for ISIS. Thomas said, "Since the turbulent '60s, some Americans have chosen to ignore, even oppose, values taught to their forbearers. These tenants began with personal responsibility, hard work, capitalism, self-reliance, faith in God, and patriotism." I find it very interesting and perhaps very telling that he refers back to the "turbulent '60s" as the beginning of the deterioration of American value system. I agree with him. That is when Critical Theory began to take hold in our country.

Thomas continued in his op-ed, "Even conservatives who still cling to those values in theory are doing less in practice to affirm them. Too many have their children in public schools that challenge their beliefs. Too many conservative families are breaking up, instilling conditional love in their children (Note that he said conditional versus unconditional love.)." Thomas quoted a well known journalist to bolster his comments, "As Peter Beinart wrote in last February's National Journal, 'The very attributes conservatives say make America special—religiosity, patriotism, and mobility—are ones they've inadvertently undermined.

It is any wonder millennials are less impressed with their country?" Thomas concluded his op-ed with the following, "Meanwhile, we had better get back to teaching the current and future generations what we used to teach, or risk losing not only them but our entire nation."

Polls show the majority of our young adults claim to be politically independent. Although they claim to be independent, they are more liberal than conservative and it puts the majority of them under the manipulative practices of progressives. You know by now that Ronald Reagan is one of my heroes of American politics as he is with the majority of conservatives. He is such a conservative hero that I have recently heard progressives refer to him as the standard for republican political policy when they are blurting out some of their political propaganda. I hear them say "Reagan did it too" just like they used Bush in the past. I guess they felt they finally used up Bush and it's more powerful to use Reagan. Reagan did have an incredible understanding of what makes America America and how to maintain it. I found a quote by him that fits this discussion regarding our country's youth. He said, "Freedom is never more than one generation away from extinction. We didn't pass it to our children in the bloodstream, it must be fought for, protected, and handed on for them to do the same."

Jesse Watters and his *Watters' World* interviews demonstrate in a dramatic way the lack of interest and knowledge by Millennials and Gen Xers regarding what is happening within our country and externally to our country. That lack of interest and lack of knowledge has significant bearing on American's future. One could argue that Watters, for effect, only interviews people who are "over the top" in their appearance, lack of knowledge, and attitudes toward society. As I said in chapter 7, he does often go after young people who are "disenfranchised" and who "beat to a different drummer" but the interviewees also include people who are not odd in appearance or thought and college students who are working toward their college degrees.

The insight from his interviews into the mindset of young Americans is profound. Their lack of knowledge regarding our country's history and founding principles, our country's political and non-political current events, and what is happening throughout the world is stunning. I recently saw Watters interview a nice looking and nicely dressed young woman who was going to see the new play titled *Hamilton*. The play just won eleven Tony Awards and is currently the hottest play on the planet. He asked her if she knew who Alexander Hamilton was and she had no clue. She was just interested in seeing the new award winning play.

It is amazing but not surprising how politically progressive these young people are and totally clueless as to the consequences of their progressive ideas. Most of them actually act as if they don't care. Watters' interviews are very entertaining but they are also discouraging when one hears the young people answer his questions the way they do. Actually, adults aren't any better. A Rasmussen poll taken in September of last year indicated that only 63% of Americans know which party controls the House or Senate. A poll by the Annenberg Public Policy Center found that only one-third of Americans could name all three branches of government. If that is not bad enough, one-third could not name any branch of government.

Watters' interviews aren't the only examples that provide discouragement regarding our young people. I saw a video by Campus Reform, which claims to be the number one source for college news. The video was very telling. Several students were interviewed at Harvard University. The interviewer asked which was a bigger threat to world peace—America or ISIS? They all said America was the bigger threat. They also blamed America for the creation of ISIS. Critics of the interview said the interviewer was picking and choosing responses for the video to make his point. True or not, I am disturbed that even one student at one of the most prestigious universities in America would blame their own country for such a travesty in the world when it is so blatantly false. How did they get so misguided? I heard someone on television say, "That's just liberal Harvard." Really???

That last story reminds me of two interviews I saw on Fox News by Megyn Kelly. These interviews gave insight into how our young people are influenced at our universities by radical progressive professors. One interview was with Bill Ayers. The other was with Ward Churchill who was a long-term professor at the University of Colorado before he was finally terminated for supposedly faulty research. It is suspected that he was actually fired after a long and strengthening groundswell against him and the university because of his radicalism such as referring in one of his books to those killed in the World Trade Center terror attack as "little Eichmanns". How in the world could a major university employ someone as radical as Churchill as a "teacher" of our young adults? It totally mystifies me. Although there was some hedging by each of them, both Ayers and Churchill said a future attack on the United States could be justified under the right circumstances. Ayers was referring to an internal attack like those made by his Weather Underground group and Churchill was referring to an outside attack from groups like al-Qaeda or ISIS.

These two guys truly are radical anti-Americans. There is a fine line between treason and free speech but I wonder what would happen if we started trying people like those two for treason. We haven't had a trial for treason since 1952. That might get the attention of some of these radical college professors. If these people don't like America, let them go find their own utopian paradise. What hypocrites! They put down the very country that allows them to spew their vitriol. Most countries would put them in jail or worse. They do not deserve to have the benefit of what America offers to them like the free speech they use as hate speech against American values and principals.

My extensive watching and reading news reports and researching this book convinces me that patriotic Americans in general are unaware of the extent that our young people have been and are being indoctrinated with anti-American propaganda from a very early age into adulthood. It is extensive and consistently getting worse. I have given many examples in the book. It's that old adage to "get them while they're young". I see no end in sight and "they are the future American society" after we're gone.

Can those of us who are the patriotic older Gen Xers, Baby Boomers, and senior Americans who love our country defeat the progressives, turn the Millennials and younger Gen Xers around ideologically, and get our beloved America back on track? Let's take a look. We have discussed the increasing decline of morality in our country through polymorphous perversity. We talked about the effects of political correctness and electronic innovations in breaking apart the interpersonal bonding and traditional moral fabric of our society. That includes the lessening of close relationships between parent and child.

Entitlements are increasingly becoming more prevalent and the ethnic and cultural makeup of our country is being intentionally changed to secure progressive votes. This evolution opens the door for progressives to insert their radical Marxist ideology in our society and to destroy the justice, fairness, and opportunity afforded to us through traditional American values and our existing Constitution. This phenomenon is in full swing, and increasingly becoming more pervasive.

The majority of Gen Xers and Millennials are drawn more toward Marxist based ideology than American traditionalism and society is ineffective in doing anything about it. Schools are indoctrinating our young people to Marxist based philosophy starting in primary education and continuing through college, and again, society is ineffective in doing anything about it. It is stunning how progressives have infiltrated America with shadow organizations and radical groups that oppose and fight our traditional American values. It is also stunning how engrained progressives are in federal, state, and local governments and taking down our traditional American values through legislation and executive fiat, which is often without legal basis.

In addition to the president and his White House staff, there are progressives in Congress and progressive federal employees who have demonstrated a willingness and eagerness to punish citizens who take steps to preserve our traditional American ideology and to uphold our country's laws. The progressives in government have deceptively attempted to adopt legislation, policies, and mechanisms to monitor and coerce broadcast and print media that oppose them. I have seen congressional conservatives ask all the right questions to government officials involved in these improper and illegal progressive tactics and raucously debate their progressive colleagues during hearings on these matters and what happens? Nothing. Absolutely, nothing! It's just on to the next hearing. Our best and most effective government watchdog, the mainstream news media, are knowingly and unknowingly complicit in aiding the progressives in their dastardly deeds. Those in the mainstream news media who aren't complicit are threatened by the progressives to back down.

If the progressive democratic candidate wins the presidency in this upcoming election, America will continue its current progressive path at an increasing rate. Our country will swiftly slide far into the progressive abyss. Too many progressive regulations and laws will be passed and Marxist based ideology will become too ingrained in our society during that presidency for any future recovery. Look how far progressivism has come and how far traditional American values and the tenets of our Constitution have declined under Obama. He has created a powerful Marxist base upon which progressives can build their Marxist empire. Conservatives and classic liberals will find it impossible to tear that base apart.

Progressive behavior will escalate to make as many voters as possible dependent on the government for their livelihood and put all citizens under increasing government control. It gives progressives dominant political power in perpetuity. Unfortunately, there has been greater federal government control over our lives since our country began regardless of which party was in office. It is ironic that government tyranny is the very reason the United States of America was formed in the first place. I have decided it is an unintended consequence of any government model including our American Constitution model. Tocqueville was right.

Is putting a republican president in the White House and republicans keeping the House and Senate in 2016 going to save America from this egregious progressive movement? It will obviously slow the progressives down but is it enough to restore and preserve our traditional American values into the future? In other words, "Do American patriots who believe in traditional American values and the Constitution win or lose the battle to save our country?" My answer to that question is very troubling for me to say and it makes me very sad to say it but we are on the road to lose the battle. I am by nature a very positive person and my glass is always half full but I am also a very pragmatic and realistic person. What I have articulated in this book regarding the direction in which our society is naturally progressing and the fervor and success of the progressives in our country is too overwhelming to overcome in the long term.

The real question is not do we win or lose the battle but how fast do we lose the battle. Is it during the next presidency after Obama? Is it during the next decade or next two decades? How about three, four, or five decades? Now, I think we are starting to go beyond the time frame. It depends who is in the White House during this time. This situation has been building for many decades, even during times when we have had conservative presidents and conservative majorities in Congress. Having conservatives and classic liberals in political office has slowed it down but has not stopped it. Radical Marxist based ideology has continued to grow in our country exponentially in spite of what non-progressive Americans do to preserve our traditional values. As time goes on, government is becoming increasingly bigger, more powerful, and more intrusive in our lives. This gives progressives greater capacity to control us.

The only thing that will save us from this radical ideology is an overwhelming patriotic American pushback against it and I do not see that happening. Even with the current massive and aggressive onslaught by progressive Washington to "fundamentally change America", there is no significant effort by non-progressive Americans to stop it. I know there are conservative organizations, conservative pundits, and conservative politicians working hard to counter this progressive movement but they have basically had no impact.

We haven't had a patriotic rally in Naples since 2010 or anything in Washington like Glen Beck's Restoring Honor rally on the Lincoln Mall that had hundreds of thousands in attendance. I will always remember, when Beck's rally was over, the attendees left the mall totally clean and in perfect condition. This is in contrast to rallies such as the Occupy Wall Street rally by our progressive friends that left the area in disgusting condition. There was civility at Beck's rally and violence including rape at The Wall Street debacle. Stay tuned America. These comparisons are more symbolic of the future than you might think.

We need to all become Howard Beale and declare, "I'm mad as hell and I'm not going to take this any more!" Imagine the power and impact of pushing back against the progressive movement with the following: multiple large peaceful rallies in cities across America like the ones we had in Naples; multiple peaceful rallies in Washington like Glen Beck's on the Lincoln Mall; countless telephone calls and letters to our political representatives; overpowering attendance at politicians' town hall meetings; innumerable hits on social networking sites; overwhelming calls, emails, and tweets to television and radio shows when they ask for opinions and sometimes when they don't; limitless letters to the editor and multiple opinion editorials in local newspapers; and informed voting each and every election by all registered voters. I would settle for the vast majority of registered voters actually voting.

I can go on but you understand my message. These pushbacks are happening to some degree but nowhere the magnitude needed to make a difference. The problem is a movement like I described must have central leadership leading the charge. Could it be the Republican Party? Could it be a private conservative based organization? Could it be an individual that would become our messiah for America? How about our next republican president? That would be our most logical answer because of the power entrusted upon the president. That person would need to be passionate about traditional American values and the Constitution and have the courage and resolve to make America America again. If we could find that central leadership, we would have millions of people speaking out against the progressives and their Marxist movement on a consistent basis over a long period of time. We would eventually shut the progressives up as we overpowered them. Then, they would go back underground and lay low until they get their mojo back again. Unfortunately, they will. They always do. This is a battle forever to save our country and, right now, we are losing with no victory in sight.

Plato said, "If you do not take an interest in the affairs of your government, then you are doomed to live under the rule of fools." I would add "progressive Marxists fools who are dictatorial and self-indulging at the expense of those they rule". How are they are fools? They are fools because they fight and destroy everything that would bring them and their fellow man true happiness and prosperity in life. They are forever trapped in a world of selfishness, deceit, and manipulation of others to attain their warped sense of being. Remember from chapter 11, they are the intellectually elite, narcissists, and misguided angry people. Plato died almost 2,400 years ago. I wonder what he would say about our plight in America if he were alive today? What would Tocqueville say?

Like it or not, the theories and principals of Alinsky, Cloward and Piven, and Critical Theory work and are working big time in the America we love. Progressives have always been around before Obama including at least two past U.S. presidents—FDR and Woodrow Wilson. Our country has had closet Marxists for decades, if not from our beginning, who are now comfortable in coming out of the woodwork to push and achieve their ideology during Obama's progressive presidency. They are recruiting knowing and unknowing classic liberals to join their cause.

Let's look at a quick summary of the reasons for the current success by progressive Marxists. Our country's vast population growth during the last 240 years has resulted in a more complex society and an increased percentage of individuals who are disenfranchised from society for a multiplicity of reasons. The following exacerbates the problem: the mobility and changing mores of our society; the breakdown of the family unit; the denigration of religion; and a spoiled society based upon entitlement versus achievement. The original colonists came to America to escape religious persecution, escape repression, and to find better economic opportunity. The good life our founding fathers gave to us has spoiled our society resulting in unrealistic expectations, gluttony, polymorphous perversity, other perversities, and fanciful utopian Marxist ideology. We have a lack of memory, understanding, and appreciation of how America became America and the sacrifices made for our personal good. We are just like the Israelites. America can only remain America through the pioneering spirit that got us here by virtue of personal struggle, hard work, sacrifice, and the love and respect of our fellow man. That pioneer spirit has to be combined with strong adherence to the principles and laws set forth in the Declaration of Independence and the Constitution, which provides our society's foundational structure.

I read an op-ed by Cal Thomas in March of this year that supports my point. He said, "We have an education system that doesn't educate. Students get diplomas and degrees, but can't find jobs. Television spews out 'reality shows' that have nothing to do with reality. Kids seem to know more about sex than they do about schoolwork. Judges issue ruling that conform more to opinion polls than the Constitution. The strangest behavior is trotted out as the next civil rights movement and anyone who says 'no' is branded a bigot." He concluded, "Many fallen nations collapsed not from war but from moral rot."

When I started writing this book, I did not fully understand the depth and history of what was happening to America. I now understand what is happening and why. I have also learned that there are only two approaches to society throughout the world. There is the Marxist way and there is the American way. There are societies like those in many European countries that are primarily Marxist based but have also adapted characteristics of traditional American governance as Tocqueville hoped they would. They are now losing the battle to progressive Marxist ideology for the same reasons we are. They are also facing the additional societal problem of being overrun by the Muslim culture. How long before the Muslim culture issue arises to a problematic state in America and compounds the problems of our progressive Marxist evolution?

Maybe it was too idealistic on my part to assume our American way of life could last forever but I did believe that until I wrote this book. The history of the United States in comparison to the beginning of Earth and our planet's first human habitation is not even a speck in time. The history of the United States in comparison to the existence of a civilized world is miniscule. Our country's existence of 240 years occupies only 2% of that time frame.

My wife and I have studied the Roman and Ancient Egyptian cultures and visited the geographical areas where they existed. The Roman culture lasted 1,500 years and the Ancient Egyptians managed to make it 3,100 years until they succumbed to Roman rule. Both societies were victims of their own success. They became lazy and glutinous and then self-destructed. The demise of these two powerful and dominant societies is a lesson for America. What happened when the Roman culture collapsed? The Western world went into the Dark Ages for almost 350 years. I said in chapter 8 that if America falls permanently to progressive ideology, America and the rest of world can look forward to the darkness of the Progressive Ages. I have always heard that the Dark Ages weren't as dark as history portrays. I would not say the same about the Progressive Ages.

Historically, throughout civilization on Earth, it has not been a question of whether or not a successful culture can last forever but how long it can last. There is no culture that has outlasted the test of time. What makes us think we will be different? Now you know my analysis and my painful prediction for the future of America. Do you agree? If not, nothing would please me more than for you to be right and prove me wrong.

I want to end this book with quotes from three people whom I greatly admire. Margaret Thatcher said, "We shall have to learn to be one nation again or one day we will be no nation." Abraham Lincoln said, "America will never be destroyed from the outside. If we falter and lose our freedoms, it will be because we destroyed ourselves." It was kind of eerie that I found these next two quotes from Ronald Reagan after I had written the content for this chapter including my comments regarding the dark ages. He said, "If we lose this way of freedom, history will record with the greatest astonishment that those who had the most to lose did the least to prevent its happening. You and I have a rendezvous with destiny. We'll preserve for our children this, the best hope for man on Earth, or we'll sentence them to take the last step into a thousand years of darkness."

EPILOGUE

It has been three months since this book was first published. I am sitting here after the presidential election pondering what I should write in this Epilogue regarding the impact Donald Trump's win will have on my prediction in chapter 13 for the future of America. Had the winner been Hillary Clinton, I know exactly what I would write. To paraphrase a comment by Eric Bolling on Fox News' *The Five*, "Behind Hillary's door, we know there is certain death (for America) but behind Trump's door, we have a 50/50 chance." Let's look at that in more detail. Edward Klein wrote in his book titled *Guilty As Sin* that a Hillary Clinton presidency would result in:

- More taxpayer-financed "free stuff" for favored Democratic groups
- More national debt
- More business regulations
- More government-directed crony capitalism
- More layoffs
- More unconstitutional executive orders
- More politics of envy
- More illegal immigrants
- More Islamic terrorism
- More Clinton scandals
- More favors for big-bucks contributions
- More gridlock in Washington
- More division between blacks and whites
- More criticism of the police and more crime and disorder
- More Obamacare and higher premiums
- More downsizing of the armed forces

- More late-term abortions
- More out-of-wedlock children supported by welfare
- More gun control
- More federal control of public schools
- More "multi-gender" bathrooms
- More liberal Supreme Court Justices
- More political correctness
- More assaults on free speech on college campuses
- More chaos in the Middle East
- More humiliation from China, Russia, and Iran
- More, in other words, of the last eight years under president Obama

As I read the list, it sounded like a summary of the topics in this book. A Hillary Clinton presidency would have been a continuation of the Obama administration on steroids with unbridled personal corruption thrown in. Speaking of unbridled personal corruption, I decided to research Hillary's personality traits like I did Obama's. I concluded that she exhibits personality traits associated with antisocial personality disorder. The Mayo Clinic provides the following definition:

- Disregard for right or wrong
- Persistent lying or deceit
- Being callous, cynical, and disrespectful of others
- Using charm or wit to manipulate others for personal gain or personal pleasure
- Arrogance, a sense of superiority and being extremely opinioned
- Recurring problems with the law, including criminal behavior
- Repeatedly violating the rights of others through intimidation and dishonesty
- Impulsiveness or failure to plan ahead
- Hostility, significant irritability, agitation, aggression or violence
- Lack of empathy for others and lack of remorse about harming others
- Unnecessary risk-taking or dangerous behavior with no regard for the safety of self or others

- Poor or abusive relationships
- Failure to consider the negative consequences of behavior or learn from them
- Being consistently irresponsible and repeatedly failing to fulfill work or financial obligations

The Mayo Clinic website went on to say that inherited genes could make someone vulnerable to this disorder and being subjected to abuse, neglect, and an unstable life during childhood are risk factors. I have read Edward Klein's books regarding Hillary Clinton titled *Blood Feud*, *Unlikeable*, and *Guilty As Sin*. Klein's writings about Hillary fit these traits and risk factors to a T. This provides an explanation as to how she could lie to the families of those who were killed in Benghazi and then lie that she didn't lie. As I did with Obama, I went to the Internet to see if anyone else shared my opinion. The Internet was full of opinions that Hillary suffered from antisocial personality disorder.

Anyone who runs for president has to be a little crazy, right? Well, I wouldn't go that far but I would say that it takes someone with a strong ego and a good dose of narcissism to have the motivation to run for president, go through what it takes to win the presidency, and then do the job. How about president-elect Donald Trump? He also has a major dose of ego and narcissism like Hillary but there is a major difference between Trump, Hillary, and Obama. I surmised in chapter 7 and in this Epilogue that the ego and narcissism exhibited by Hillary and Obama result from psychotic based behavior. If you remember from chapter 7, psychotic behavior results in the inability to accept that you are wrong and in a lack of empathy for others.

I believe Trump's ego and narcissism is neurotic based behavior; therefore, he can accept that he can be wrong and does have empathy for others. This conclusion is very significant when judging Trump's ability to be an effective president. Trump showed his outrageous ego and narcissistic side in spades during his campaign until the last few weeks before the election. Although that behavior probably got him the republican nomination, it was not presidential and almost cost him the general election by giving the Clinton campaign organization and the mainstream news media great fodder to discredit him as presidential material. Which Donald Trump will show up as president? Trump's ego and narcissism could actually be the catalyst to make him a strong and effective president. It will motivate him to want to go down in history as being admired and successful and he is smart enough to know that his past outrageous behavior will not get him there.

Here is the path I believe he will take to accomplish his legacy. First I want to acknowledge that Trump is neither a republican nor a democrat. He is an opportunist that used the republican ticket to win the presidency but does; however, exhibit strong conservative beliefs and behaviors. Even though the republican ticket won the presidency and kept the House and the Senate, the Republican Party is still in shambles as I discussed in chapter 12. The Republican Party won only because Americans voted against the status quo. There seems to be a renewed energy for the party to get its act together but only time will tell.

Can Trump be a president who will bring America back to its traditional roots and save us from the progressive Marxist destruction that I predicted in chapter 13? With that question in mind, let's look into the future of a Trump presidency. He will nominate a conservative for Senate confirmation to replace Supreme Court Justice Antonin Scalia and any other Justices that will be replaced during his presidency. This is crucial in upholding the Constitution and traditional American values. Justice Ginsburg is 83, Justice Kennedy is 80, and Justice Breyer is 78. Who knows how many replacements will occur during Trump's presidency.

Trump will not condone the enormous deceit, corruption, political retribution, and other scandals practiced by the Obama administration as spelled out in Chapter 6 and throughout this book. He will make a good faith effort to run the government more like a business and minimize the "close enough for government work" mentality we looked at in chapter 7 regarding government operations.

The economy and job growth were major thrusts of his campaign. I'm uncertain about the potential success of his stated approach to trade agreements. He will have to address regulation strangulation on business and industry, tax reform for business and individuals, and entitlements to those who deserve and don't deserve them. He will also have to abolish Obamacare and curtail government spending and growth. I believe he will make a good faith effort in these areas but will need the help of knowledgeable advisors, a strong Cabinet, and a supportive Congress to be successful; which will be interesting but doable.

We discussed Obama's disastrous and dangerous foreign policy in chapter 9. Trump will have to embrace our old friends and allies around the world and convince them "we are back" and we "have their backs". He needs to revisit his comments on NATO and think that issue through with his foreign policy and military advisors. He may change his mind on that one. He needs to be presidential but at the same time show our enemies and the bad guys around the world "their party is over". I think he can do that but it will be interesting how he does it. He will have to support American exceptionalism and be much more aggressive in foreign policy than Obama. I have no doubt he will revive our decimated military and shake up its current "yes man" leadership.

Trump's hardest job will involve some of the most controversial issues during his campaign. He said he would build a wall across the entire Mexican border and send all illegal immigrants back home. I have already stated my opinion on that one in chapters 8 and 12. I think he will seek advice from the Border Patrol and secure the border through physical means and electronic surveillance. He will have to revise his position on sending all illegals home. It's just not possible to do so and has significant implications for our society. He has already softened his stance on mass deportation but has correctly announced that those who are convicted felons will be deported. I think he will, with his advisors, come up with a plan for a path to citizenship for illegal immigrants who have not committed a serious crime. I also think he will address immigration with an "eye on national security" as well as the issue of "Americanism" for those seeking U.S. citizenship. I hope he stands up to progressive mayors like de Blasio in New York, Emanuel in Chicago, and others to address the illegality and danger of sanctuary cities. Obama's messianic and globalist "no borders" policy has been disastrous and dangerous for the country and was also supported by and proposed by Hillary.

One of Trump's most important undertakings as president is to reverse the impact of Obama's, Holder's, Sharpton's, and others' assault on race relations discussed in chapter 10. This will require a lot of maturity, patience, and collegial work with minority communities as well as society as a whole. I think he will move in that direction. Along with that issue is the issue of poverty and crime in our inner cities. He has said he will address it. I hope he gets the right council to advise him and has the perseverance to follow through. This will be a very arduous and difficult task over more than one generation.

I believe he is capable of being a strong, successful, and conservative president. I base that on what I observed during the weeks before Election Day and during the three weeks after he won the election prior to this Epilogue being written and published. I actually saw humility on his part when he met with Obama and congressional leaders and during his interview with Lesley Stahl on *60 Minutes*. I also base my opinion on the fact that he is unorthodox in the political world and not part of the political establishment—at least not yet. He has the potential to significantly shake things up in a positive way for the benefit of the country. Only time will tell! He is off to a very good start. He is reaching out to his adversaries. The people who have been picked thus far to fill top posts, along with those being considered for others, are strong conservatives and people whom I admire and respect. He is receiving criticism from the political establishment and the mainstream news media for his picks, which is a positive sign that he is making the right choices.

The paramount question is, "Will he and Congress prove my prediction wrong for the long-term future of America?" Let's start with the mainstream news media. On Election Day, my local newspaper reported an AP syndicated news article that carried the headline "Trump campaign faces voter fraud charges". After both my wife and I read the article, we found no mention of anything remotely connected to Trump and voter fraud. The article was about an organization hired by the Republican National Committee that was accused of voter fraud in 2012 (yes, 2012) and was cleared of any wrongdoing. A USA TODAY headline the day after the election said, "Rise in racist acts follows elections." A New York Times headline stated, "Democrats, Students and Foreign Allies Face The Reality Of A Trump Presidency."

The mainstream news media truly wants Trump and the republicans to fail, which means America fails. How sad is that for our country? It is hypocrisy at its worst! Merriam Webster says that soul-searching is the examination of one's conscience, especially with regard to motives and values. Even if these politically biased journalists read chapter 6 and searched their ethical souls after reading what I quoted from John Adams, James Madison, Benjamin Franklin, Thomas Jefferson, George Washington, the Sedona Observer's Code of Ethics, and the Society of Professional Journalists' Code of Ethics; they would still find a way to rationalize their progressive influenced behavior. The news media will only get worse in biased and inaccurate reporting to support and defend their anti-conservative ideology as the new Trump administration and republican Congress take actions to reinstate traditional American values and honor the Constitution.

How about the Marxist based income redistribution policies and the Marxist based politically correct beliefs and behaviors articulated in this book that are promoted and implemented by the progressive movement and now supported and expected by a significant percentage of the American population? How about the Marxist based moral decay taking place in our country? Even Halloween is not exempt. A major haunted house attraction in my community advertised that no one under 18 would be admitted after 8:30 P.M. because of "graphic sexual content" and "explicit language". One of my favorite local newspaper columnists said, "It's almost Halloween and you know what that means. Kids in costumes, candy and graphic sexual content . . . what is concerning is the societal movement toward sexualizing everything that can be sexualized." This is Marcuse's polymorphous perversity we discussed in chapter 10 at its finest or, more appropriately, at its worst. Misguided Americans searching for Marxist utopia.

Our new conservative government in Washington can slow the progressive movement down by reversing progressive based laws, overturning progressive legislation, deleting progressive regulations, and omitting progressive rhetoric but cannot stop the Marxist influence on our society. This is an issue for society itself. I said in chapter 13 that it would take a Howard Beale declaration (I'm mad as hell and I'm not going to take this any more!) by our society to save America from the progressive movement and restore the values as set forth in the Declaration of Independence, the Constitution, and Judeo-Christian religion. Was this presidential election a Howard Beale moment? Let's take a look.

According to the United States Election Project, there are roughly 231.5 million people eligible to vote in America. Only 131.7 million voted. That's just 57%. Where are the other 43%? Even though Trump won the electoral vote, Hillary won the popular vote (the 5th time this has happened in the history of our country) by over 1 million votes. This presidential election was hardly a Howard Beale moment.

We talked about Gen Xers and Millennials being the future of America in chapters 7, 8, and 13. What was their reaction to Trump's election? There has been open anger, disbelief, and grief by a preponderance of young people because of Trump's victory. There were demonstrations from coast to coast. I am sure many were by radical groups who protest anything they can find to protest about. I would not be surprised if some were not paid protesters like those who were allegedly paid by the Democratic Party and/or the Clinton campaign to physically attack Trump supporters at Trump rallies. But, how about the rest?

One of the most immature actions was by the millennial who plays Aaron Burr in *Hamilton*. I am not sure the play's writer and creator, who apparently is a progressive activist, didn't orchestrate his actions. The millennial verbally attacked Mike Pence after the play was over as the vice president-elect was leaving the theater. As the *Hamilton* cast held hands across the stage, the actor preached to Pence, "We, sir, we are the diverse America who are alarmed and anxious that your new administration will not protect us, our planet, our children, our parents, or defend us and uphold our inalienable rights. We truly hope that this show has inspired you to uphold our American values and to work on behalf of us."

A significant number of young people in the audience booed Pence and cheered the actor on. We talked in chapter 13 about the millennial interviewed by Jesse Watters who was going to see *Hamilton* because it was a popular play and had no clue who Hamilton was. I said it was amazing but not surprising how politically progressive these young people are and how totally clueless they are regarding the inappropriateness and consequences of their progressive ideology in the real world. Who are the true bigots in this scenario? Especially, considering that the play's posted casting call said, "NON-WHITE [*sic*] men and women, ages 20s to 30s." This was one of the most egregious acts of bigotry, hypocrisy, rudeness, and disrespect I have ever seen.

Colleges, universities, and even high schools across the country coddled students to help them get over their "grief". Professors at many colleges and universities cancelled classes and exams to help students deal with their "Trump trauma". Thousands of high school students in several cities walked out of their schools to protest the election without any consequence. In my day, we would have been suspended from school for that behavior. How are our young people ever going to grow up to responsible adulthood? They're not! I worry about what is going to happen when these young people become the bulk of American society and are forced to face reality. They have no clue regarding the struggles endured and sacrifices made by individual Americans and America as a country in order to give them what they have today. This cluelessness gives elitist Marxist progressives the ability to exercise control over them with historical misinformation and utopian promises.

The Victims of Communism Memorial Foundation released a report this year titled "U.S. Attitudes Towards Socialism". The report showed that only 42% of Millennials viewed capitalism "favorably" while only 37 % had a "very unfavorable" view of communism. One-third of Millennials believed that more people were killed under Bush's presidency than under Stalin's reign. We learned in chapter 10 that an estimated 62 million people were killed under Stalin. I'm still searching to find out who Bush killed. Forty-five percent of young people between 16 and 20 years old said they would vote for a socialist and twenty-one percent said they would vote for a communist. As I said, a preponderance of young people are clueless to the real world.

We discussed in chapters 7, 8, 10, and 13 the following adverse influences on young people: the breakdown of the family unit; geographic mobility; an attitude of "want and get" versus "want, strive, and get"; the diminished role of religion; moral decay; the electronic age; and the progressive takeover of our educational system. This is not an optimistic picture for eradicating progressive Marxist based ideology from dominance in our society in the long term, as these young people become America's leaders and the country's dominant voting block. The traditional American values that provide Americans the most personal opportunity, the most personal freedom, the best standard of living, and the best personal safety in the entire world are fading from our young society.

Back to the paramount question. Will Trump and Congress prove my prediction wrong for the long-term future of America by restoring and preserving our traditional American values and honoring the Constitution; therefore, saving us from progressive Marxist destruction? Trump's campaign motto was "Make America Great Again". Trump and Congress cannot do it by themselves. This issue is bigger than them alone. The final outcome belongs to American society. The politicians are only able to kick the can down the road. How long is that road? I said in chapter 13 it would be one to five decades depending upon who won this presidential election. We will have a better understanding of that time frame as the Trump presidency unfolds. Dinesh D'Souza said, "They can't take America from us without our consent." It will take a Howard Beale declaration by the vast majority of Americans—not just the 28% who did so in this presidential election—to withhold that consent in perpetuity. There is always hope and I am encouraged by what I have seen thus far regarding the Trump administration but based upon what we know about our future leaders and voters, I just don't see it.

SOURCES

Because of the vast number and variety of sources I used to support and enhance my opinions, I forewent a standard bibliography and standard reference footnotes. I did identify references in the text when I used specific sources to make or support a point in order to give the reference credit, to provide validation for my supporting information, and to allow the reader to research the reference and learn more if they wish. Last year refers to 2015 and this year refers to 2016. Recent refers to the months just previous to and including July 2016. The primary sources for my reference material were: Fox News; The Naples Daily News; The Wall Street Journal; The Heritage Foundation; The Daily Signal, which is the multimedia news organization of The Heritage Foundation; Judicial Watch; conservative and liberal Internet websites; Internet websites for national newspapers; and Wikipedia.

INDEX